Rick Steves'

GREAT
BRITAIN
2006

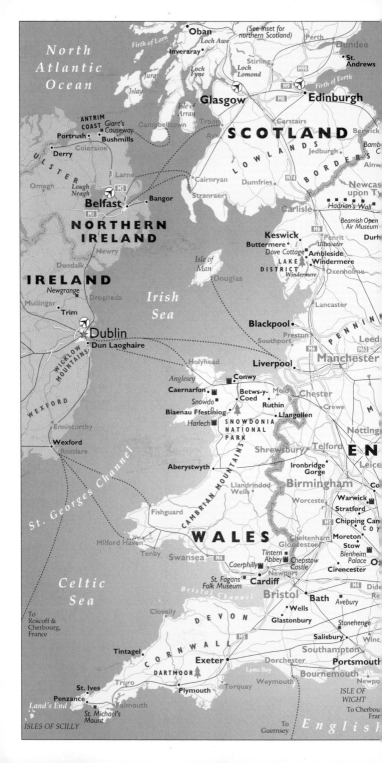

To Orkney Islands
Scrabster
Thurso
John o'Groats
Wick

Isle of Lewis
Stornoway

OUTER HEBRIDES

The Minch

North
Uist

Ullapool

Colbost
Glendale
South
Uist
Isle of
Skye
Portree

Kyle

*Sea of
the
Hebrides*

Mallaig

To
Bergen,
Norway

Isle of Mull
Iona

Kerrera
Seil

Oban

Firth of Lorn

Jura

Islay

Loch Awe

Inveraray

Loch
Fyne

Inverness
Culloden
Battlefield

HIGHLANDS
Caledonian Canal
Loch Ness
Aviemore

Moray Firth

Aberdeen

SCOTLAND

Fort
William
Ben
Nevi
Glencoe
Loch Linnhe

Criantarich

Perth

Pitlochry

Dundee
St. Andrews

Stirling

Loch
Lomond

M90
M9
Firth of Forth

Glasgow

M8

Edinburgh

dlesbrough
Staithes
Whitby
Pickering
Scarborough

York

Bridlington

Kingston

Lincoln

NDS

AND

*North
Sea*

King's
Lynn

Norwich

Peter-
borough

Ely

Northampton

EAST

Cambridge

ANGLIA

Ipswich

Harwich

Luton

Hertford

Stansted

Colchester

Windsor

London

City

Heathrow

Greenwich

Southend-on-Sea

atwick

SOUTH
DOWNS

M23

Ramsgate

M2

M20

Canterbury

Folkestone

Dover

righton

Hastings

Rye

Eastbourne

Beachy
Head

istreham
-Havre,
e

Channel

Channel
Tunnel

Calais

Boulogne

A16

FRANCE

To Esbjerg,
Denmark

To Hoek Van
Holland, Denmark

Ostende

Dunkerque

Lille

A26

Bruges

Ghent

Waterloo

Brussels

BELGIUM

NETH.

Antwerp

E313

E17

E40

E42

Namur

E42

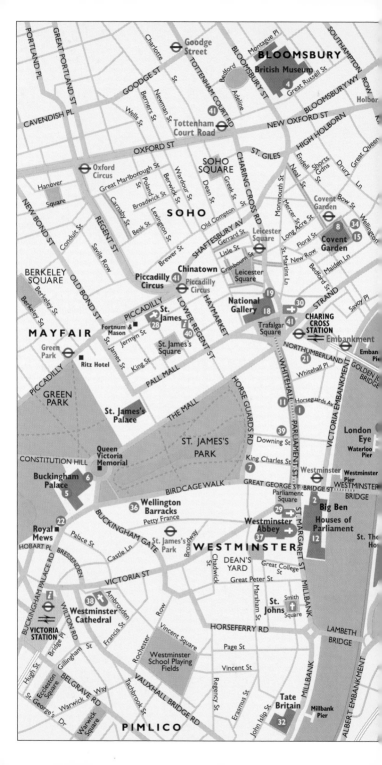

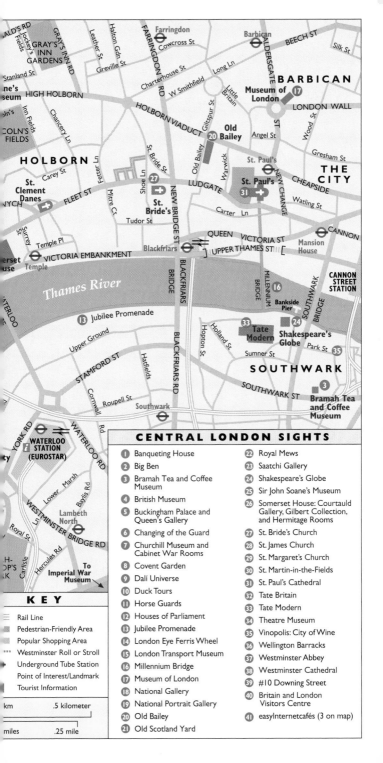

CENTRAL LONDON SIGHTS

1. Banqueting House
2. Big Ben
3. Bramah Tea and Coffee Museum
4. British Museum
5. Buckingham Palace and Queen's Gallery
6. Changing of the Guard
7. Churchill Museum and Cabinet War Rooms
8. Covent Garden
9. Dalí Universe
10. Duck Tours
11. Horse Guards
12. Houses of Parliament
13. Jubilee Promenade
14. London Eye Ferris Wheel
15. London Transport Museum
16. Millennium Bridge
17. Museum of London
18. National Gallery
19. National Portrait Gallery
20. Old Bailey
21. Old Scotland Yard
22. Royal Mews
23. Saatchi Gallery
24. Shakespeare's Globe
25. Sir John Soane's Museum
26. Somerset House: Courtauld Gallery, Gilbert Collection, and Hermitage Rooms
27. St. Bride's Church
28. St. James Church
29. St. Margaret's Church
30. St. Martin-in-the-Fields
31. St. Paul's Cathedral
32. Tate Britain
33. Tate Modern
34. Theatre Museum
35. Vinopolis: City of Wine
36. Wellington Barracks
37. Westminster Abbey
38. Westminster Cathedral
39. #10 Downing Street
40. Britain and London Visitors Centre
41. easyInternetcafés (3 on map)

KEY

- ≡ Rail Line
- Pedestrian-Friendly Area
- Popular Shopping Area
- •••• Westminster Roll or Stroll
- ● Underground Tube Station
- Point of Interest/Landmark
- Tourist Information

| km | .5 kilometer |
| miles | .25 mile |

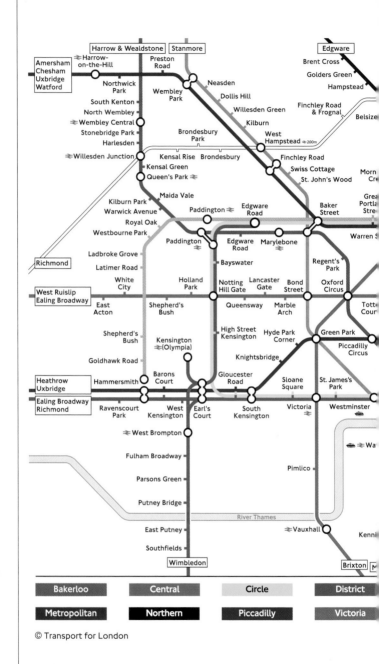

Rick Steves'
GREAT
BRITAIN
2006

AVALON
TRAVEL

CONTENTS

Top Destinations in Great Britain

INTRODUCTION

This book breaks Britain into its top big-city, small-town, and rural destinations. It gives you all the information and opinions necessary to wring the maximum value out of your limited time and money in each of these destinations. If you plan a month or less for Britain and have a normal appetite for information, this book is all you need. If you're a travel-info fiend, this book sorts through all the superlatives and provides a handy rack upon which to hang your supplemental information.

Experiencing British culture, people, and natural wonders economically and hassle-free has been my goal for more than 25 years of traveling, tour guiding, and travel writing. With this new edition I pass on to you the lessons I've learned, updated for your trip in 2006. Note that Northern Ireland—part of the United Kingdom—is covered in my book *Rick Steves' Ireland.*

Rick Steves' Great Britain is a personal tour guide in your pocket. The places I cover are balanced to include a comfortable mix of exciting big cities and great-to-be-alive-in small towns. While including the predictable biggies (such as Big Ben, Stratford-upon-Avon, and Stonehenge), the book also mixes in a healthy dose of Back Door intimacy (windswept Roman lookouts, angelic boys' choirs, and nearly edible Cotswold villages). I've been selective. On a short trip, visiting both Oxford and Cambridge is redundant; I cover just the best (Cambridge). There are plenty of great countryside palaces; again, I recommend just the best (Blenheim).

The best is, of course, only my opinion. But after spending half my adult life researching Europe, I've developed a sixth sense for what travelers enjoy. The places featured in this book will knock your spots off.

This Information Is Accurate and Up-to-Date

This book is updated every year. Most publishers of guidebooks that cover a country from top to bottom can afford an update only every two or three years (and even then, it's often by e-mail or fax). Since this book is selective, covering only the sights that make the top month of sightseeing in Britain, I can update it in person each summer. The telephone numbers, hours, and prices of the places listed in this book are accurate as of mid-2005. Even with annual updates, things change. Still, if you're traveling with the current edition of this book, I guarantee you're using the most up-to-date information available in print. For the latest, visit www.ricksteves .com/update. Also at my Web site, you'll find a valuable list of reports and experiences—good and bad—from fellow travelers who have used this book (www.ricksteves.com/feedback).

Use this year's edition. People who try to save a few bucks by traveling with an old book are not smart. They learn the seriousness of their mistake...in Britain. Your trip costs about $10 per waking hour. Your time is valuable. This guidebook saves lots of time.

About This Book

This book is organized by destinations, each one a mini-vacation on its own, filled with exciting sights and homey, affordable places to stay. In the following chapters, you'll find:

Planning Your Time, a suggested schedule with thoughts on how to best use your limited time.

Orientation, including tourist information, city transportation, and an easy-to-read map designed to make the text clear and your arrival smooth.

Self-Guided Walks, taking you through interesting neighborhoods, with a personal tour guide in hand.

Sights, a succinct overview of Britain's most important sights, arranged by neighborhood, with ratings: ▲▲▲—Don't miss; ▲▲—Try hard to see; ▲—Worthwhile if you can make it; No rating—Worth knowing about.

Sleeping and Eating, with addresses and phone numbers of my favorite good-value hotels and restaurants.

Transportation Connections to nearby destinations by train or bus, and route tips for drivers.

The **appendix** is a traveler's tool kit, with helpful information on telephoning, festivals and holidays, climate and temperature, converting to metric, and a British–Yankee vocabulary list.

Browse through this book, choose your favorite destinations, and link them up. Then have a great trip! Traveling like a temporary local, you'll get the absolute most out of every mile, minute, and dollar. And as you travel the route I know and love, I'm happy you'll be meeting some of my favorite British people.

PLANNING

Trip Costs

Five components make up your trip costs: airfare, surface transportation, room and board, sightseeing/entertainment, and shopping/miscellany.

Airfare: Don't try to sort through the mess. Find and use a good travel agent. A round-trip, U.S.–London flight costs $400–1,000 (even cheaper in winter), depending on where you fly from and when. Consider saving time and money by flying "open-jaw" (into one city and out of another; for instance, into London and out of Edinburgh).

Surface Transportation: For a three-week whirlwind trip of all my recommended British destinations, allow $500 per person for public transportation (train pass and key buses) or $850 per person for car rental (based on 2 people sharing a 3-week rental), including gas and insurance. Car rental is cheapest if arranged from the U.S. Train passes are normally available only outside of Europe (although you can buy a bus pass in Britain). You may save money by simply buying tickets as you go (see "Transportation," page 18).

Room and Board: You can manage just fine in Britain on an average of $100 per day per person for room and board (allow less for villages and more for London and other cities). A $100-per-day budget allows $10 for lunch, $15 for dinner, $5 for snacks and ale, and $70 for lodging (based on 2 people splitting a $140 double room that includes breakfast). That's doable outside of London (allow $120 per day in London). Students and tightwads can do it on $40 ($25 for hostel bed, $15 for groceries).

Sightseeing and Entertainment: Fortunately, many of the best sights in London are free, including the British Museum, National Gallery, Tate Britain, Tate Modern, and the British Library. Figure on paying $6–30 for the major sights that charge admission (Westminster Abbey-$14, Tower of London-$26), $4 for minor ones (climbing church towers), $12 for guided walks, and $30 for bus tours and splurge experiences (Welsh and Scottish folk evenings). An overall average of $20 a day works for most. Don't skimp here. After all, this category is the driving force behind your trip—you came to sightsee, enjoy, and experience Britain.

You may be tempted to buy the Great British Heritage Pass, which gets you into about 600 historic sights throughout Great Britain (£28/$50 for 4 days, £39/$75 for 7 days, £52/$95 for 15 days, £70/$130 for 30 days, valid for a calendar year, sold at Heathrow Airport TI and the Britain and London Visitors Centre on Lower Regent Street in London; for more information, see www.visitbritain.com). If you're bringing children, don't buy passes for them, since

Britain's Best Three-Week Trip (By Car)

Day	Plan	Sleep in
1	Arrive in London, bus to Bath	Bath
2	Bath	Bath
3	Pick up car, Avebury, Wells, Glastonbury	Bath
4	South Wales, St. Fagans, Tintern	Chipping Campden
5	Explore the Cotswolds, Blenheim	Chipping Campden
6	Stratford, Warwick, Coventry	Ironbridge Gorge
7	Ironbridge Gorge, Ruthin banquet	Ruthin (if banquet) or Conwy
8	Highlights of North Wales	Ruthin or Conwy
9	Liverpool, Blackpool	Blackpool
10	South Lake District	Keswick area
11	North Lake District	Keswick area
12	Drive up west coast of Scotland	Oban
13	Highlands, Loch Ness, Scenic Highlands Drive	Edinburgh
14	Edinburgh	Edinburgh
15	Edinburgh, possible side-trip to Glasgow	Edinburgh
16	Hadrian's Wall, Beamish, Durham's Cathedral and evensong	Durham
17	North York Moors, York, turn in car	York
18	York	York
19	Early train to London	London
20	London	London
21	London	London
22	Whew!	

While this three-week itinerary is designed to be done by car, it can be done by train and bus or, better yet, with a rail-'n'-drive pass (best car days: Cotswolds, North Wales, Lake District, Scottish Highlands, Hadrian's Wall). For three weeks without a car, I'd probably cut back on the recommended sights with the most frustrating public transportation (South and North Wales, Ironbridge Gorge, the Highlands). Lacing together the cities by train is very slick. With more time, everything is workable without a car.

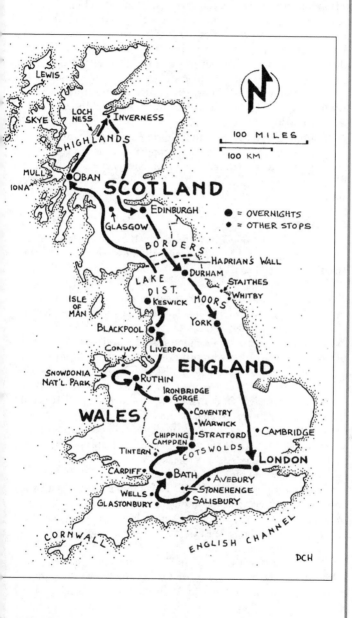

kids get in free or cheap at most sights. People traveling by car—easily able to get to the more remote sights—are more likely to get their money's worth out of the pass if traveling in peak season (Easter–Oct). The pass is a lesser value off-season (Nov–Easter) when many of the smaller, out-of-the-way sights are closed.

Garden-and-estate enthusiasts might consider a one-year National Trust membership, which gains you access to more than 300 historic houses and gardens throughout Britain (£38/year, www.nationaltrust.org.uk).

Shopping and Miscellany: Figure $2 per postcard, tea, or ice-cream cone and $5 per beer. Shopping can vary in cost from nearly nothing to a small fortune. Good budget travelers find that this category has little to do with assembling a trip full of lifelong and wonderful memories.

When to Go

For England and Wales, July and August are peak season—my favorite time—with very long days, the best weather, and the busiest schedule of tourist fun. For Scotland, the weather is best in May and June.

Prices and crowds don't go up during peak times as dramatically in Britain as they do in much of Europe. Still, travel during "shoulder season" (May, early June, Sept, and early Oct) is easier and a bit less expensive. Shoulder-season travelers get minimal crowds, decent weather, the full range of sights and tourist fun spots, and the joy of being able to just grab a room almost whenever and wherever they like—often at a flexible price.

Winter travelers find absolutely no crowds and soft room prices, but shorter sightseeing hours and fewer activities. Some attractions are open only on weekends or are closed entirely in the winter (Nov–Feb). Confirm your sightseeing plans locally, especially when traveling outside of peak season. The weather can be cold and dreary, and nightfall draws the shades on sightseeing well before dinnertime. While England's rural charm falls with the leaves, city sightseeing is fine in the winter.

Plan for rain no matter when you go. Just keep going and take full advantage of bright spells. Conditions can change several times in a day, but rarely is the weather extreme. Daily averages throughout the year range between 42° and 70° Fahrenheit. Temperatures below 32° or above 80° are cause for headlines (see the climate chart in the appendix). July and August are not much better than shoulder months. May and June can be lovely anywhere in Britain. While sunshine may be rare, summer days are very long. The summer sun is up from 6:30 until 22:30. It's not uncommon to have a gray day, eat dinner, and enjoy hours of sunshine afterward.

Sightseeing Priorities

Depending on the length of your trip, here are my recommended priorities:

3 days:	London
5 days, add:	Bath, Cotswolds, Blenheim
7 days, add:	York
9 days, add:	Edinburgh
11 days, add:	Stratford, Warwick, Blenheim
14 days, add:	North Wales, Wells/Glastonbury/Avebury
17 days, add:	Lake District, Hadrian's Wall, Durham
21 days, add:	Ironbridge Gorge, Blackpool, Scottish Highlands
24 days, add:	Choose two: Glasgow, Cambridge, South Wales

(This includes virtually everything on the "Britain's Best Three-Week Trip" itinerary and map on pages 4 and 5, respectively.)

Itinerary Specifics

Most people fly into London and remain there for a few days. Instead, consider a gentler small-town start in Bath, and let London be the finale at the end of your trip. You'll be more rested and ready to tackle Britain's greatest city. Heathrow Airport has direct bus connections to Bath and other cities.

To give yourself a little rootedness, minimize one-night stands. It's worth a long drive after dinner to be settled into a town for two nights. B&Bs are also more likely to give a better price to someone staying more than one night.

Many people save a couple of days and a lot of miles by going directly from the Lake District to Edinburgh and skipping the long joyride through Scotland. If it's Celtic Britain you're after, visit Wales rather than Scotland.

Before You Go

- Reserve rooms (or at least a room for your first night).
- If you'll be traveling in late June, July, or August and want to sleep in my most highly recommended B&Bs and hotels, book your accommodations as soon as you're ready to commit to a date.
- If you'll be attending the Edinburgh Festival (Aug 13–Sept 3 in 2006), you can book tickets in advance (from mid-April on) by calling the festival office at tel. 0131/473-2000 or ordering online at www.eif.co.uk (see page 421). And while you're at it, book your Edinburgh room.
- Confirm car rental and pick-up plans with your rental agency (picking up a car on Sat afternoon or Sun may be difficult).
- If you want to attend the pageantry-filled Ceremony of the Keys at the Tower of London, write for tickets (for specifics, see page 97).

Within a Day or Two of Arrival

- If you'll be in London the last night of your trip, reserve a room and book tickets for a London play or concert. You can book a play from home (see details on page 111), but to keep it simple and to leave my options open, I book plays while in London.
- If the Royal Shakespeare Company will be performing at the Stratford theater when you're in or near Stratford, consider reserving a ticket (tel. 0870-609-1110, www.rsc.org.uk).

Travel Smart

Your trip is like a complex play—easier to follow and to really appreciate on a second viewing. While no one does the same trip twice to gain that advantage, reading this book in its entirety before your trip accomplishes much the same thing.

Reread entire chapters as you travel, and visit local tourist information offices. Upon arrival in a new town, lay the groundwork for a smooth departure. Buy a phone card and use it for reservations and confirmations. You speak the language—use it! Enjoy the friendliness of the local people. Ask questions. Most locals are eager to point you in their idea of the right direction. Those who expect to travel smart, do. Bring along a pocket-size notebook to organize your thoughts. Plan ahead for laundry, Internet stops, and picnics. Mix intense and relaxed periods. Every trip (and every traveler) needs at least a few slack days. Pace yourself. Assume you will return.

Design an itinerary that enables you to hit the various sights at the best possible times. As you read this book, make note of festivals, colorful market days, and days when sights are closed. Sundays have pros and cons, as they do for travelers in the U.S. (special events, limited hours, closed shops and banks, limited public transportation, no rush hours). Saturdays are virtually weekdays. Popular places are even more popular on weekends—especially sunny weekends, which are sufficient cause for an impromptu holiday in this soggy corner of Europe. Be aware of upcoming holidays that could affect your trip (see page 14) and book your rooms in advance.

RESOURCES

Tourist Information Offices

In the U.S.

The **Visit Britain** office is a wealth of knowledge. You can contact them at: tel. 800/462-2748, fax 212/986-1188, 551 Fifth Ave. #701, New York, NY 10176, www.visitbritain.com, travelinfo@visitbritain .org. Ask for free maps of Britain and London and any specific information you may want (such as regional information, a garden-tour map, urban cultural activities brochures, and so on).

London-Specific Web Sites: To study ahead, also visit www.timeout.com/london, www.thisislondon.com, and www .londontown.com.

In Great Britain

Virtually every town in Britain has a tourist information center (abbreviated as **TI** in this book). Take full advantage of this service. Arrive (or telephone) with a list of questions and a proposed sightseeing plan. Pick up maps, brochures, and walking-tour information. In London, you can pick up everything you'll need for Britain in one stop at the Britain and London Visitors Centre (see page 3).

While TIs can be good resources, remember that they are money-making enterprises. Getting a room through the TI can be handy in a jam, but it comes with bloated prices and fees—and the TI takes a cut from your host. Skip the TI's room-finding services and call direct.

Rick Steves' Guidebooks, Public Television Show, and Radio Show

Rick Steves' Europe Through the Back Door gives you budget-travel skills, such as minimizing jet lag, packing light, planning your itinerary, traveling by car or train, finding rooms, changing money, avoiding rip-offs, buying a mobile phone, hurdling the language barrier, staying healthy, taking great photographs, using a bidet, and much more. The book also includes chapters on 38 of my favorite "Back Doors," six of which are in Great Britain.

Country Guides: These annually updated books offer you the latest on the top sights and destinations, with tips on how to make your trip efficient and fun. Here are the titles:

Rick Steves' Best of Europe
Rick Steves' Best of
  Eastern Europe
Rick Steves' England
  (new in 2006)
Rick Steves' France
Rick Steves' Germany
  & Austria

Rick Steves' Great Britain
Rick Steves' Ireland
Rick Steves' Italy
Rick Steves' Portugal
Rick Steves' Scandinavia
Rick Steves' Spain
Rick Steves' Switzerland

City and Regional Guides: Updated every year, these focus on Europe's most compelling destinations. Along with specifics on sights, restaurants, hotels, and nightlife, you'll get self-guided, illustrated tours of the outstanding museums and most characteristic neighborhoods.

Rick Steves' Amsterdam,
    Bruges & Brussels
Rick Steves' Florence
    & Tuscany
Rick Steves' London
Rick Steves' Paris

Rick Steves' Prague
    & the Czech Republic
Rick Steves' Provence
    & the French Riviera
Rick Steves' Rome
Rick Steves' Venice

Rick Steves' Phrase Books: In much of Europe, a phrase book is as fun as it is necessary. This practical and budget-oriented series covers French, German, Italian, Spanish, Portuguese, and French/Italian/German. You'll be able to make hotel reservations over the phone, chat with your cabbie, and bargain at street markets.

And More Books: *Rick Steves' Europe 101: History and Art for the Traveler* (with Gene Openshaw) gives you the story of Europe's people, history, and art. Written for smart people who were sleeping in their history and art classes before they knew they were going to Europe, *101* helps Europe's sights come alive. However, this book has far more coverage of the European continent than of Britain.

Rick Steves' Easy Access Europe, geared for travelers with limited mobility, covers London, Paris, Bruges, Amsterdam, and the Rhine River Valley.

Rick Steves' Postcards from Europe, my autobiographical book, packs 25 years of travel anecdotes and insights into the ultimate 2,000-mile European adventure.

My latest book, *Rick Steves' European Christmas*, covers the joys, history, and quirky traditions of the holiday season in seven European countries, including England.

Public Television Show: My series, *Rick Steves' Europe,* keeps churning out shows (60 at last count), including several featuring the sights in this book.

Radio Show: My new weekly radio show, which combines call-in questions (à la *Car Talk*) and interviews with travel experts, airs on public radio stations. For a schedule of upcoming topics and an archive of past programs (just click on a topic of your choice to listen), see www.ricksteves.com/radio.

Other Guidebooks

You may want some supplemental travel guidebooks, especially if you're traveling beyond my recommended destinations. I know it can hurt to spend $30 on extra books and maps, but when you consider the money they'll save you and the improvements they'll make in your $3,000 vacation, not buying them would be penny-wise and pound-foolish.

While this book offers everything you'll need for the structure of your trip, each place you will visit has plenty of great little

---

Begin Your Trip at www.ricksteves.com

At www.ricksteves.com you'll find a wealth of **free information** on destinations covered in this book, including fresh European travel and tour news every month and helpful "Graffiti Wall" tips from thousands of fellow travelers.

While you're there, the **online Travel Store** is a great place to save money on travel bags and accessories designed by Rick Steves to help you travel smarter and lighter, plus a wide selection of guidebooks, planning maps, and DVDs.

Traveling through Europe by rail is a breeze, but choosing the right railpass for your trip—amidst hundreds of options—can drive you nutty. At www.ricksteves.com, you'll find **Rick Steves' Annual Guide to European Railpasses**—your best way to convert chaos into pure travel energy. Buy your railpass from Rick, and you'll get a bunch of free extras to boot.

Travel agents will tell you about mainstream tours of Europe, but they won't tell you about **Rick Steves' tours.** Rick Steves' Europe Through the Back Door travel company offers more than two dozen itineraries and 300 departures reaching the best destinations in this book...and beyond. You'll enjoy the services of a great guide, a fun bunch of travel partners (with small groups of about 25), and plenty of room to spread out in a big, comfy bus. You'll find trips to fit every vacation size, from weeklong city getaways to longer cross-country adventures. For details, visit www.ricksteves.com or call 425/771-8303 ext 217.

---

guidebooks to fill you in on local history. For cultural and sightseeing background in bigger chunks, Michelin and Cadogan guides to London, England, and Britain are good. The best budget travel guides to Britain are the *Lonely Planet* and *Let's Go* guidebooks. *Lonely Planet*'s guidebook is more thorough and informative, but it's not annually updated. *Let's Go* is annually updated and youth-oriented, with good coverage of nightlife, hostels, and cheap transportation deals.

Recommended Books and Movies

To get the feel of Great Britain past and present, consider reading some of these books or seeing these films:

Non-Fiction: For a better understanding of the British, check out *A History of Britain, Volumes I & II* (by Simon Schama; a companion series is also available on DVD). *A Traveller's History of England* (Christopher Daniell), *A Traveller's History of Scotland* (Andrew Fisher), and *A History of Wales* (John Davies) provide good, succinct summaries of British history. Other possibilities include

Britain Almanac

Official Name: The United Kingdom of Great Britain and Northern Ireland (locals say U.K. or Britain).

Population: Britain's 60 million people (nearly that of California) are a mix of Celtic DNA, plus about 3 percent recent immigrants, largely from India and Pakistan. Seven in 10 British call themselves Christian (half of those are Anglican), but in any given week, more Brits attend mosque than an Anglican service.

Latitude and Longitude: 54ºN and 2ºW. The latitude is similar to Alberta, Canada. Britain sits a mere 21 miles northwest of France.

Area: From "Britannia's" 19th-century peak of power, when it dominated much of the globe, the British Empire lost colonies and fought two world wars, shrinking to a quarter of its former size. Today, this nation of one large island, a chunk of another large island, and many small ones is 95,000 square miles, about the size of Oregon or Michigan.

Geography: Most of the isles consist of low hills and rolling plains. The climate is moderate; about every other day, the TV weather channel shows clouds blowing in from the southwest. The country's highest point is 4,400-foot Ben Nevis in Western Scotland. Britain's longest river, the Severn, loops 220 miles from the mountains of Wales east into England, then south to the Bristol Channel. The Thames River runs 215 miles east–west through the heart of southern England (including London).

Biggest Cities: London is the capital, with nine million people. Industrious Birmingham has 2.6 million, Glasgow has 2.1 million, and the port of Liverpool has 500,000.

Economy: The Gross Domestic Product is $1.7 trillion (slightly more than California), and the GDP per capita is $28,000 (25 percent less than California). Money-makers include banking and insurance, meat-and-potatoes farming, shipping, trade with the

the humorous *Notes From A Small Island* (Bill Bryson), *The Matter of Wales* (Jan Morris), and Susan Allen Toth's *My Love Affair with England; England As You Like It;* and *England For All Seasons*.

Fiction: Much British fiction is already familiar to North American readers, but here are a few you might have missed.

Classics: *Mapp & Lucia* (E.F. Benson), *The Warden* (Anthony Trollope), *Brideshead Revisited* (Evelyn Waugh), anything by Charles Dickens, Jane Austen, the Brontë sisters, Thomas Hardy, Agatha Christie, or P.G. Wodehouse.

Historical: *The Pillars of the Earth* (Ken Follett), *London, Sarum,* and *The Forest* (Edward Rutherford), *A Morbid Taste for Bones: The First Chronicle of Brother Cadfael* (Ellis Peters), *Restoration* (Rose

U.S. and Germany, and energy production. Heavy industry—the engine that once drove the Industrial Revolution—is now in decline. The economy and pound sterling are strong, and most Brits oppose joining the euro monetary system. The Blair government's military commitment in Iraq has pinched government spending on social services, while one in six Brits lives in poverty.

Government: Queen Elizabeth II officially heads the country, but in practice it's Prime Minister Tony Blair who leads the majority party in parliament. The House of Commons has 659 seats, apportioned by elections in May of 2006. (The upper-house House of Lords is now a mere advisory body.) Britain's traditional two-party system—Labour and Conservatives ("Tories")—now has a smaller third player, the Liberal Democrats. Britain is a member of the European Union (but not the euro system) and is one of the five permanent members (with veto power) of the UN Security Council. In 1999, Scotland, Wales, and Northern Ireland were granted their own parliament.

Flag: The "Union Jack" combines two red crosses on a field of blue: the English cross of St. George and the x-like Scottish cross of St. Andrew.

The Average Brit: Eats 35 pounds of pizza and 35 pounds of chocolate a year, and weighs 12 stone (170 pounds). He or she is 39 years old, has 1.66 children, and will live to age 78. He/she drinks 2.5 cups of tea a day and 2.5 glasses of wine a week (Americans drink less than half that). He/she works a month more each year than the average German, has free healthcare, and gets 23 vacation days a year (versus 12 in the U.S. and 39 in France). He/she sleeps 7.5 hours a night, and throws out 1,500 pounds of trash a year. The average Brit speaks one language and, when quizzed, can name three of the seven continents.

Tremain), *Here Be Dragons* (Sharon Kay Penman), and *The Other Boleyn Girl* (Philippa Gregory).

Lighter Reads: *Outlander* (Diana Gabaldon), *Bridget Jones's Diary* (Helen Fielding), *The Sunday Philosophy Club* (Alexander McCall Smith), *Harry Potter* series (J.K. Rowling), and anything by Nick Hornby, Jane Green, and Tony Parsons.

Films: *Harry Potter* movies, *Ladies in Lavender* (2004), *Bridget Jones's Diary* (2001), *Gosford Park* (2001), *Shakespeare in Love* (1998), *Billy Elliott* (2000), *Elizabeth* (1998), *Braveheart* (1995), *Rob Roy* (1995), *Howard's End* (1992), *The Full Monty* (1997), *Brassed Off* (1996), *Hope and Glory* (1987), *Chariots of Fire* (1981), *The Wicker Man* (1973), *Local Hero* (1983), *Monty Python and the Holy Grail*

(1975), *Remains of the Day* (1993), *Shadowlands* (1993), *The Madness of King George* (1994), *Anne of a Thousand Days* (1969), *A Man for All Seasons* (1966), *Mrs. Miniver* (1942), *Mary Poppins* (1964), *Goodbye Mr. Chips* (1939), *Secrets & Lies* (1996), *Sliding Doors* (1998), *Tom Jones* (1963), *Topsy-Turvy* (1999), *The End of the Affair* (1999), *An Ideal Husband* (1999), *My Fair Lady* (1964), *84 Charing Cross Road* (1987), and *I Know Where I'm Going!* (1945, filmed on Island of Mull in Scotland).

Maps

The black-and-white maps in this book, drawn by Dave Hoerlein, are concise and simple. Dave, who is well traveled in Britain, has designed the maps to help you locate recommended places and get to the TI, where you'll find more in-depth, cheap (or free) maps. The color maps at the front of the book will help you navigate from town to town. Before you buy a map, look at it to make sure it has the level of detail you want.

Train travelers can do fine with a simple rail map and city maps from TIs. (Get a free map of London and Britain from Visit Britain before you go; see "Tourist Information Offices," page 8.) If you're driving, get a road atlas (1 inch equals 3 miles) covering all of Britain. Ordnance Survey, AA, and Bartholomew editions are all available for about £7 at tourist information offices, gas stations, and bookstores. Drivers, hikers, and bikers may want more detailed maps for the Cotswolds, North Wales, and Lake District.

PRACTICALITIES

Red Tape: You need a passport, but no visa or shots.

Time: In Britain—and in this book—you'll be using the 24-hour clock. After 12:00 noon, keep going—13:00, 14:00, and so on. For anything above 12, subtract 12 and add p.m. (14:00 is 2 p.m.).

Britain is five/eight hours ahead of the East/West Coasts of the U.S. and one hour behind the rest of Europe.

Business Hours: Most shops are open Monday through Saturday from roughly 10:00–18:00, with a late night on Wednesday or Thursday (until 19:00 or 20:00), depending on the neighborhood. On Sunday, when some stores are closed, street markets are lively with shoppers. All stores close on Christmas; smaller shops close on December 26 as well.

Holidays: Bank holidays bring most businesses to a grinding halt on New Year's Day, Good Friday (April 14 in 2006), Easter Monday (April 17), the first and last Mondays in May (May 1 and 29), the last Monday in August (Aug 28), Christmas, and December 26. Most museums are closed on Good Friday, December 24 and 25, and January 1. For a list of events and festivals, which can also enhance or complicate your sightseeing plans, see page 505.

Discounts: While discounts (called "concessions" in Britain) are not listed in this book, nearly all British sights are discounted for seniors (loosely defined as anyone retired or willing to call themselves a "senior"), youths (ages 8–18), students, groups of 10 or more, and families (2 full-price parents take kids in for about half price). For transportation discounts, see "Senior, Youth, and Family Deals," page 24.

Watt's Up? If you're bringing electrical gear, you'll need an adapter plug. Britain's plugs have three square-shaped prongs (not the 2 round prongs used by continental Europe). You may also need a converter to deal with the increased voltage. Travel appliances often have convenient, built-in converters; look for a voltage switch marked 120V (U.S.) and 240V (Europe).

News: Americans keep in touch in Europe with the *International Herald Tribune* (published almost daily via satellite). Every Tuesday, the European editions of *Time* and *Newsweek* hit the stands with articles of particular interest to travelers in Europe. Sports addicts can get their fix from *USA Today*. Good Web sites include www.europeantimes.com and http://news.bbc.co.uk.

MONEY

Banking

Bring plastic (ATM, credit, or debit cards) along with several hundred dollars in hard cash as an emergency backup. Traveler's checks are a waste of time and money.

Before you go, verify with your bank that your card will work, inquire about fees (can be up to $5 per transaction), and alert them that you'll be making withdrawals in Europe; otherwise, the bank may not approve transactions if it perceives unusual spending patterns. Bring an extra card in case one gets demagnetized or gobbled up by a machine. Since fees are charged per exchange, and most ATM screens top out at £200, save money by pushing the "other amount" button and asking for a higher amount. If you end up with lots of large bills, break them (for free) at a bank, especially if you like shopping at mom-and-pop places; they rarely have huge amounts of change.

Credit (or debit) cards are handy for booking rooms and theater and transportation tickets over the phone, and necessary for renting a car. In general, Visa and MasterCard are far more widely accepted than American Express.

Even in jolly olde England, you should use a money belt (a pouch with a strap that you buckle around your waist like a belt and wear under your clothes). Thieves target tourists. You can

Exchange Rate

I list prices in pounds (£) throughout this book.

One British pound (£1) = about $1.80

While the euro is now the currency of most of Europe, Britain is sticking with its pound sterling. The British pound (£), also called a "quid," is broken into 100 pence (p). Pence means "cents." You'll find coins ranging from 1p to £2 and bills from £5 to £50. Some travelers try to kid themselves that pounds are dollars. But when they get home, that £1,000-pound Visa bill isn't asking for $1,000...it wants $1,800. To avoid this shock, double British prices to estimate dollars. By overshooting it, you'll spend less...maybe even less than you budgeted (good luck).

Scotland and Northern Ireland issue their own currency in pounds, worth the same as an English pound. English, Scottish, and Northern Ireland's Ulster pounds are technically interchangeable in each region, although Scottish and Ulster pounds are "undesirable" in England. Banks in any of the three regions will convert your Scottish or Ulster pounds into English pounds for no charge. Don't worry about the coins, which are accepted throughout Britain.

carry lots of cash safely in a money belt, and given bank and ATM fees, you should.

Don't be petty about changing money; it's inefficient and expensive to visit ATMs and banks frequently to withdraw a minimum amount of cash each time. Change a week's worth of money, stuff the bills in your money belt, and travel!

Tips on Tipping

Tipping in Britain isn't as automatic and generous as it is in the U.S., but for special service, tips are appreciated, if not expected. As in the U.S., the proper amount depends on your resources, tipping philosophy, and the circumstance, but some general guidelines apply.

Restaurants: At pubs where you order at the counter, don't tip. At a pub or restaurant with wait staff, check the menu or your bill to see if the service is included; if not, tip around 10 percent (for details, see page 41).

Taxis: To tip the cabbie, round up. For a typical ride, round up to a maximum of about 10 percent (to pay a £4.50 fare, give £5; or for a £28 fare, give £30). If the cabbie hauls your bags and zips you to the airport to help you catch your flight, you might want

Damage Control for Lost or Stolen Cards

If you lose your credit, debit, or ATM card, you can stop people from using your card by reporting the loss immediately to the respective global customer-assistance centers. Call these 24-hour U.S. numbers collect: Visa (tel. 410/581-9994), MasterCard (tel. 636/722-7111), and American Express (tel. 336/393-1111).

Have, at a minimum, the following information ready: the name of the financial institution that issued you the card, along with the type of card (classic, platinum, or whatever). Ideally, plan ahead and pack photocopies of your cards—front and back—to expedite their replacement. Providing the following information will allow for a quicker cancellation of your missing card: full card number, whether you are the primary or secondary cardholder, the cardholder's name exactly as printed on the card, billing address, home phone number, circumstances of the loss or theft, and identification verification (your birthdate, your mother's maiden name, or your Social Security number—memorize this, don't carry a copy). If you are the secondary cardholder, you'll also need to provide the primary cardholder's identification verification details. You can generally receive a temporary card within two or three business days in Europe.

If you promptly report your card lost or stolen, you typically won't be responsible for any unauthorized transactions on your account, although many banks charge a liability fee of $50.

to toss in a little more. But if you feel like you're being driven in circles or otherwise ripped off, skip the tip.

Special Services: Tour guides at public sites often hold out their hands for tips after they give their spiel. If I've already paid for the tour, I don't tip extra, though some tourists do give a pound, particularly for a job well-done. I don't tip at hotels, but if you do, give the porter about 50 pence for carrying bags and leave a pound in your room at the end of your stay for the maid if the room was kept clean. In general, if someone in the service industry does a super job for you, a tip of a pound or two is appropriate...but not required.

When in doubt, ask. If you're not sure whether (or how much) to tip for a service, ask your hotelier or the tourist information office; they'll fill you in on how it's done on their turf.

VAT Refunds for Shoppers

Wrapped into the purchase price of your British souvenirs is a Value Added Tax (VAT) that's generally about 17.5 percent. If you make a purchase of more than £20 at a store that participates in the VAT refund scheme, you're entitled to get most of that tax back. Personally, I've never felt that VAT refunds are worth the hassle, but if you do, here's the scoop.

If you're lucky, the merchant will subtract the tax when you make your purchase (this is more likely to occur if the store ships the goods to your home). Otherwise, here's what you'll need to do:

Get the paperwork. Have the merchant completely fill out the necessary refund document, called a "Tax-Free Shopping Cheque." You'll have to present your passport at the store.

Get your stamp at the border or airport. Have your cheque(s) stamped at your last stop in the European Union (e.g., the airport) by the customs agent who deals with VAT refunds. It's best to keep your purchases in your carry-on for viewing, but if they're too large or dangerous to carry on, then track down the proper customs agent to inspect them before you check your bag. You're not supposed to use your purchased goods before you leave. If you show up at customs wearing your new Wellingtons, officials might look the other way—or deny you a refund.

Collect your refund. You'll need to return your stamped documents to the retailer or its representative. Many merchants work with a service, such as Global Refund or Premier Tax Free, which have offices at major airports, ports, or border crossings. These services, which extract a 4 percent fee, can refund your money immediately in your currency of choice or credit your card (within 2 billing cycles). If you have to deal directly with the retailer, mail the store your stamped documents and then wait. It could take months.

Customs Regulations

You can take home $800 in souvenirs per person duty-free. The next $1,000 is taxed at a flat 3 percent. After that, you pay the individual item's duty rate. You can also bring in duty-free a liter of alcohol (slightly more than a standard-size bottle of wine), a carton of cigarettes, and up to 100 cigars. As for food, anything in cans or sealed jars is acceptable. Skip dried meats, cheeses, and fresh fruits and veggies. To check customs rules and duty rates, visit www.customs.gov.

TRANSPORTATION

By Car or Train?

Cars are best for three or more traveling together (especially families with small kids), those packing heavy, and those scouring the countryside. Trains and buses are best for solo travelers, blitz tourists, and city-to-city travelers.

Britain has a great train-and-bus system, and travelers who don't want (or can't afford) to drive a rental car can enjoy an excellent tour using public transportation. Britain's 100-mph train system is one of Europe's best. Buses pick you up when the trains let you down.

In Britain, my choice is to connect big cities by train and to explore rural areas (the Cotswolds, North Wales, Lake District, and the Highlands) footloose and fancy-free by rental car. The mix works quite efficiently (e.g., London, Bath, Edinburgh, and York by train with a rental car for the rest). You might consider a BritRail Pass 'n' Drive, which gives you various combinations of rail days and car days to use within two months' time.

Deals on Rails, Wheels, and Wings in Britain

Regular tickets on Britain's great train system (15,000 departures from 2,400 stations daily) are the most expensive per mile in all of Europe. Those who save the biggest are those who book in advance, leave after rush hour (after 9:30), or ride the bus.

As with airline tickets, there can be many different prices for the same train journey. A clerk at any station (or the helpful folks at tel. 0845-748-4950, 24 hours daily) can figure out the cheapest fare for your trip. Savings can be significant. For a London–Edinburgh round-trip (standard class), the full fare, with no date stipulated for the return trip, is £206; if you book the day of departure for travel after 9:30, it's £90; and the cheapest fare, booked several weeks in advance as two one-way tickets, is £25.

For schedules, visit http://bahn.hafas.de/bin/query.exe/en (Germany's excellent all-Europe timetable), www.nationalrail.co.uk, or www.thetrainline.com. While not required on British trains, reservations are free, and a good idea for long journeys or any train on Sunday. Make them at any train station before 18:00 on the day before you travel.

Buying Train Tickets in Advance: The best fares go to those who book their trips well in advance of their journey. (While only a 7-day minimum advance booking is officially required for the cheapest fares, these go fast—especially in summer—so a 6–8 week advance booking is often necessary.) Keep in mind that return (round-trip) fares are not always cheaper than buying two single (one-way) tickets when booking in advance. Also note that cheap advance tickets often come with the toughest refund restrictions, so be sure to nail down your travel plans before you reserve. To book ahead, go direct to any station, book online at www.nationalrail.co.uk, or call 0845-748-4950 (from the U.S., call 011-44-845-748-4950, phone answered 24 hours) to find out the schedule and best fare for your journey; then you'll be referred to

Sample Train Journey

Here is a typical example of a personalized train sched-ule printed out by Britain's train stations. At the Llandudno Junction station in North Wales, I told the clerk I wanted to leave after 16:30 for Moreton-in-Marsh in the Cotswolds.

Stations	Arrive	Depart	Class
Llandudno Junction	—	16:41	Standard
Crewe	17:56	18:11	Standard
Smethwick	19:20	19:33	Standard
Worcester	20:20	20:58	1st/Standard
Moreton-in-Marsh	21:37	—	

Even though the trip involved three transfers, this schedule allowed me to easily navigate the rails. It's helpful to ask at the information desk (or any conductor) for the final destination of your next train so you'll be able to figure out quickly which platform it's departing from (e.g., upon arrival at Worcester, I looked for "Oxford" on the station's overhead train schedule to determine where to catch my train to Moreton-in-Marsh; often the conductor on your previous train can even tell you the platform your next train will depart from, but it's wise to confirm). Note that on the smaller runs, only standard (sec-ond) class is available. If you're exploring Britain's backcountry with a BritRail pass, rather than invest the extra money in first class, buy standard class—because that's how you'll travel.

Lately Britain's train system has experienced a lot of delays, causing more and more travelers to miss their connec-tions. Don't schedule your connections too tightly if you have to be at your destination at a specific time.

the appropriate number to call—depending on the particular rail company—to book your ticket. If you order online, be sure you know what you want; it's tough to reach a person who can change your online reservation. You'll pick up your ticket at the station (unless your order was lost—this service still has some glitches). If you want your ticket mailed to you in the U.S., you need to allow a couple of weeks and cover the shipping costs. Note that BritRail passholders cannot use the Web to make reservations.

Buying Train Tickets en Route: If you'd rather have the flexibility of booking tickets as you go, you can save a few pounds by buying return (round-trip) tickets, buying before 18:00 the day before you depart, and traveling after the morning rush hour (this usually means after 9:30 Mon–Fri). Preview your options at www.nationalrail.co.uk or www.thetrainline.com.

BritRail Routes

* MAP NOT TO SCALE

London Train Stations

— RAIL
--- BUS
(6H) FERRY w/ CROSSING TIME
✈ AIRPORT

❶ Victoria – S. & S.E. England; conn. to Paris & Brussels

❷ Charing Cross – S.E. England

❸ Waterloo – S. England; Eurostar to Paris & Brussels via Chunnel

❹ Liverpool Street – E. England; conn. to Amsterdam

❺ King's Cross – E. England, N.E. England, E. Scotland

❻ St. Pancras – Central England

❼ Euston – N. & N.W. England, N. Wales, W. Scotland

❽ Paddington – W. England, S. Wales

London Airports

Ⓐ Heathrow
Ⓑ Gatwick
Ⓒ Luton
Ⓓ Stansted
Ⓔ London City

Railpasses

Prices listed are for 2005. My free Rick Steves' Guide to European Railpasses has the latest prices and details (and easy online ordering) at www.ricksteves.com/rail.

BRITRAIL CONSECUTIVE PASS

Type of Pass	Adult 1st Class	Adult Standard	Senior 1st Class	Youth 1st Class	Youth Standard
4 consec. days	$315	$209	$268	$237	$157
8 consec. days	455	299	387	342	225
15 consec. days	679	449	578	510	337
22 consec. days	859	575	731	645	432
1 month	1019	679	867	765	510

BRITRAIL FLEXIPASS

Type of Pass	Adult 1st Class	Adult Standard	Senior 1st Class	Youth 1st Class	Youth Standard
4 days in 2 months	$395	$265	$336	$297	$199
8 days in 2 months	579	385	493	435	289
15 days in 2 months	869	585	739	652	439

"Standard" is the polite British term for "second" class. No senior discounts for standard class. For each adult pass you buy, one child (5-15) can travel free with you (ask for the "Family Pass"). Additional kids pay the normal half-adult rate. Kids under 5: free.

Note: Overnight journeys begun on your BritRail pass or Flexipass' final night can be completed the day after your pass expires—only BritRail allows this trick. A bunk in a twin sleeper costs $60.

BRITRAIL PASS 'N DRIVE

Any 3 rail days and 2 car days in 2 months.

	1st Class	2nd Class	Extra Car Day
Mini car	$385	$275	$49
Compact car	400	290	61
Intermediate car	410	300	73

Prices are approximate per person for 2 traveling together. Third and fourth person sharing car pay $340 in 1st or $230 in 2nd class. Senior, child, and single adult rates also available. To order Britrail Pass 'N Drive, call your travel agent or Rail Europe at 800/438-7245.

Britain:

The map shows approximate point-to-point one-way 2nd-class fares in $US by rail (solid line) and bus (dashed line). First class costs 50% more. Add up fares for your itinerary to see whether a railpass will save you money.

BRITRAIL LONDON PLUS PASS

Type of Pass	Adult 1st Class	Adult Standard	Senior 1st Class	Youth 1st Class	Youth Standard
2 out of 8 days	$99	$69	$85	$75	$52
4 out of 8 days	$169	$129	$144	$127	$97
7 out of 15 days	$225	$169	$192	$169	$127

Covers trips to much of southeast England including London, Oxford, Cambridge, and Salisbury. Not valid for Bath, Exeter, or Heathrow Express. The pass is valid on the Gatwick and Stansted Express. See coverage map online at www.ricksteves.com/rail/greatbritain.htm. Kids 5-15 pay $31 (1st class) or $21 (2nd class) flat fare per pass.

BRITRAIL ENGLAND CONSECUTIVE PASS

Type of Pass	Adult 1st Class	Adult Standard	Senior 1st Class	Youth 1st Class	Youth Standard
4 consec. days	$249	$169	$212	$187	$127
8 consec. days	365	239	311	274	180
15 consec. days	545	365	464	409	274
22 consec. days	689	459	586	517	345
1 month	815	539	693	612	405

Covers travel only in England, not Scotland, Wales, or Ireland. No senior 2nd class pass discount.

BRITRAIL ENGLAND FLEXIPASS

Type of Pass	Adult 1st Class	Adult Standard	Senior 1st Class	Youth 1st Class	Youth Standard
4 days in 2 months	$315	$209	$268	$237	$157
8 days in 2 months	465	309	396	349	232
15 days in 2 months	699	469	595	525	352

Covers travel only in England, not Scotland, Wales, or Ireland. No senior 2nd class pass discount.

BRITRAIL SCOTTISH FREEDOM PASS

4 days out of 8 flexipass	$214
8 days out of 15 flexipass	279

Good on trains in Scotland, standard class, and not before 9:15 a.m. Monday-Friday, and covers Caledonian MacBrayne and Strathclyde ferry service to Scotland's most popular islands, some Citylink buses & more. Kids 5-15 half fare. Children under 5 free. Also sold in Scotland.

BRITRAIL PASS PLUS IRELAND

	First Class	Standard Class
5 days out of 1 month	$579	$419
10 days out of 1 month	959	669

This pass covers the entire British Isles (England, Wales, Scotland, Northern Ireland, and the Republic of Ireland) including a round-trip Stena Line ferry crossing between Wales or Scotland and the Emerald Isle during the pass' validity (okay to leave via one port and return via another). Reserve boat crossings a day or so in advance—sooner for holidays. One child (5-15) travels along free with each pass. Extra kiddies pay half fare; under 5 free.

Senior, Youth, and Family Deals: To get a third off the price of most point-to-point rail tickets, seniors can buy a Senior Railcard (for age 60 and above, www.senior-railcard.co.uk), and young people can buy a Young Persons Railcard (for ages 16–25, or full-time students 26 and above with a valid ISIC card, www.youngpersons-railcard.co.uk). Each card costs £20. A Family Railcard allows adults to travel cheaper (about 33 percent) while their kids age 5 to 15 receive a 60 percent discount for most trips (£20, maximum of 4 adults and 4 kids, www.family-railcard.co.uk). Any of these cards are valid for a year on virtually all trains except special runs like the Heathrow Express and Eurostar (fill out application at station, brochures on racks in info center, need to show passport). Youth also need to submit a passport-type photo for the Young Persons Card.

Railpasses: Consider getting a railpass. The BritRail pass comes in "consecutive day" and "flexi" versions, with price breaks for youths, seniors, off-season travelers, and groups of three of more. Standard class is a good choice since many of the smaller train lines don't even offer first-class cars. BritRail passes cover England, Scotland, and Wales.

There are now England-only or Scotland-only passes, England/Ireland passes, "London Plus" passes (good for travel in most of southeast England but not in London itself), and BritRail Pass 'n' Drive passes (which offer you some rail days and some car-rental days). All BritRail passes (except the Scotland-only pass), as well as Eurailpasses, get you a discount on the Eurostar train that zips you to continental Europe under the English Channel. These passes are sold outside of Europe only. For specifics, contact your travel agent or see www.ricksteves.com/rail.

Buses: Although buses are about a third slower than trains, they're also a lot cheaper. Round-trip bus tickets usually cost less than two one-way fares (e.g., London–York one-way costs £23; round-trip costs £30). And buses go many places that trains don't. Budget travelers can save a wad with a bus pass. The National Express sells Brit Xplorer bus passes for unlimited travel on consecutive days (£80/7 days, £140/14 days, £219/28 days, sold over the counter, non-UK passport required, tel. 0870-580-8080, www.nationalexpress.com). If you want to take a bus from your last destination to Heathrow or Gatwick airports, ask about the many National Express Flight Link and Jet Link buses. Bus stations are normally at or near train stations (in London, the bus station is a block southwest of Victoria Station). The British distinguish between "buses" (for local runs with lots of stops) and "coaches" (long-distance express runs).

A couple of companies offer **backpacker's bus circuits.** These hop-on, hop-off bus circuits take mostly youth hostellers around the country super-cheap and easy with the assumption that they'll be sleeping in the hostels along the way. For instance, **Haggis Backpacker** offers three- to eight-day tours of Scotland, England, or Wales (from £85/3 days, £150/6 days, ticket good for 3 months, hostels are reserved for you but not included in the tour price, tel. 0131/557-9393, www.radicaltravel.com, haggis@radicaltravel .com).

Flights: Before buying a ticket for a long train trip, consider a flight offered by one of the discount airlines such as Ryanair (British tel. 0871-246-0000, www.ryanair.com), Virgin Express (British tel. 020/7744-0004, www.virgin-express.com), easyJet (British tel. 0870-600-0000, www.easyjet.com), or bmi british midland (British tel. 0870-607-0555 or U.S. tel. 800/788-0555, U.S. office sells "Discover Europe Air Pass," www.flybmi.com; also check subsidiary, bmi baby, at www.bmibaby.com). For more info, see "Discounted Flights from London" (page 144) and visit www.cheapflights.co.uk. Use the search engine www.skyscanner.net to search fares on all of these airlines, plus some you haven't even heard of.

Round-trip can be cheaper than one-way. To get the best prices, book in advance, as soon as you have a date set. Each flight has an allotment of cheap seats; these sell fast, leaving the higher-priced seats for latecomers.

Car Rental and Leasing

To save money, arrange your car rental from the States (either on your own or through your travel agent) rather than in Britain. The best rates are weekly with unlimited mileage or leasing (possible for rentals of more than 17 days—see below). Expect to pay about $570 per week, including gas and insurance, for a basic rental. As long as you're age 75 or younger, you can pick up and drop off just about anywhere, anytime. For a trip covering both Britain and Ireland, you're better off with two separate car rentals. If you pick up the car in a smaller city, such as Bath, you'll more likely survive your first day on the British roads. If you drop the car off early or keep it longer, you'll be credited or charged at a fair, prorated price. Big companies have offices in most cities. (Ask to be picked up at your hotel.) Small local rental companies can be cheaper but aren't as flexible.

The 1.3-liter Ford Escort–category car costs about $50 more per week than the smallest cars but feels better on motorways and safer on small roads. Remember, minibuses are a great budget way to go for five to nine people. An automatic transmission is going to add at least 25 percent to the car rental cost over a manual trans-mission. Weigh this against the fact that in Britain you'll be sitting on the right side of the car, and shifting with your left hand...while driving on the left side of the road.

For peace of mind, I spring for the Collision Damage Waiver insurance (CDW, about $15–25 per day), which limits my financial responsibility in case of an accident. Unfortunately, CDW now has a high deductible hovering at about $1,200. When you pick up your car, many car-rental companies will try to sell you "super CDW" at an additional cost of $7–15 per day to lower the deductible to zero.

Some credit cards offer CDW-type coverage for no charge to their customers. Quiz your credit-card company on the worst-case scenario. You have to choose either the coverage offered by your car-rental company or by your credit-card company. This means that if you go with the credit-card coverage, you'll have to decline the CDW offered by the car-rental company. In this situation, some car-rental companies put a hold on your credit card for the amount of the full deductible (which can equal the value of the car). This is bad news if your credit limit is low—particularly if you plan on using that card for other purchases during your trip.

STOP AND LEARN THESE ROAD SIGNS

Speed Limit (km/hr) — Yield — No Passing — End of No Passing Zone

One Way — Intersection — Main Road — Freeway

Danger — No Entry — No Entry for cars — All Vehicles Prohibited

Parking — No Parking — Customs — Peace

Another alternative is buying CDW insurance from Travel Guard for $9 a day (U.S. tel. 800/826-4919, www.travelguard.com). It's valid throughout Europe, but some car-rental companies refuse to honor it, especially in Italy and the Republic of Ireland. Oddly, residents of some states (including Washington) are not allowed to buy this coverage.

In sum, buying CDW—and the supplemental insurance to buy down the deductible, if you choose—is the easiest but priciest option. Using the coverage that comes with your credit card is cheaper, but can involve more hassle. If you're taking a short trip, an easy solution is to buy Travel Guard's very affordable CDW. For longer trips, look into leasing.

Leasing: For trips of two and a half weeks or more, leasing (which automatically includes CDW insurance with no deductible) is the best way to go. By technically buying and then selling back the car, you save lots of money on tax and insurance. Leasing provides you a brand-new car with unlimited mileage and a 24-hour emergency assistance program. You can lease for little as 17 days to as long as six months. Car leases must be arranged from the U.S. A reliable company offering 17-day lease packages for about $700 is Europe by Car (U.S. tel. 800/223-1516, www.europebycar.com).

Driving

Your U.S. license is all you need to drive in Britain. Driving in Britain is basically wonderful—once you remember to stay on the left and after you've mastered the roundabouts. Traffic in roundabouts has the right-of-way; entering traffic yields (look to your right as you merge). It helps to remember that the driver is always in the center of the road. But be warned: Every year I get a few cards from traveling readers advising me that, for them, trying to drive Britain was a nerve-racking and regrettable mistake. If you want to get a little slack on the roads, drop by a gas station or auto shop and buy a green "L" (new driver with license) sign to put in your window (don't get the red "L" sign, which means you're a student driver without a license and thus prohibited from driving on motorways).

A British Automobile Association membership comes with most rentals. Understand its towing and emergency-road-service benefits. Gas (petrol) costs almost $7 per gallon and is self-serve. Green pumps are unleaded. Seat belts are required by law. Speed limits are 30 mph in town, 70 mph on the motorways, and 50 or 60 mph elsewhere. The national sign for 60 mph is a white circle with a black slash. Note that road-surveillance cameras strictly enforce speed limits. Any driver (including foreigners renting cars) photographed speeding will get a nasty bill in the mail. (Cameras—you'll see the foreboding gray boxes—flash on your rear license plate in order not to invade the privacy of anyone sharing the front seat with someone they shouldn't be with.) Avoid driving in big cities whenever possible. Most have modern ring roads to skirt the congestion. The shortest distance between any two points is usually the motorway. Road signs can be confusing, too few, and too late. Study your map before taking off. Know the cities you'll be lacing together, since road numbers are inconsistent. Miss a motorway exit and you can lose 30 minutes. A Britain road atlas, easily purchased in Britain, is money well spent (see "Maps," page 14).

Parking is confusing. One yellow line marked on the pavement means no parking Monday through Saturday during work hours. Double yellow lines mean no parking at any time. Broken yellow lines mean short stops are OK, but you should always look for explicit signs or ask a passerby. White lines mean you're free to park.

Even in small towns, rather than fight it, I just pull into the most central and handy "pay and display" car park I can find. Rates

Britain by Car: Mileage and Time

m = miles
h = hours

Note: Your times may vary based on traffic, construction, and road conditions.

SCOTLAND

Inverness
85m • 3h
90m • 1.75h
Glencoe
90m • 2.75h
Pitlochry
35m • 1h →
Oban
120m • 3h
70m • 1.5h
125m • 3.25h
100m • 2.5h
50m • 1h
Glasgow
Edinburgh
75m • 2h
Holy Island
80m • 1.75h
90m • 2.25h
135m • 2.5h
130m • 3h
100m • 2.5h
125m • 2.75h
Stranraer
145m • 3h
Hadrian's Wall (Housesteads Fort)
65m • 1.5h
50m • 1h
Keswick
(N. Lake Dist.)
Durham
20m • .5h →
120m • 3h
Windermere
(S. Lake Dist.)
75m • 1.5h
60m • 1.25h →
90m • 1.75h
Blackpool
120m • 2.5h
York
55m
1.25h →
40m • .75h
60m • 1.25h
Liverpool
130m • 3.5h
160m • 3h
Holyhead
25m • .5h →
Conwy
30m • 1.25h
220m • 4h
15m • .5h →
30m •
Caernarfon
1h
Ruthin
75m • 2h
145m • 2.75h
25m • .75h →
Snowdonia
30m
(Betws-y-Coed)
1h
60m • 1.5h
Iron-
bridge
Gorge
ENGLAND
170m • 4h
70m • 1.75h
Warwick
10m • .25h
150m • 3.5h
Stratford
↓ 2h
110m
2h
Cambridge
10m • .5h
WALES
Cotswolds
(Chipping Campden)
100m • 2h
90m • 2h
60m • 1.25h
Cardiff
65m • 1.75h
55m • 1.25h →
20m • .75h
Bath
115m • 2.5h
London
Wells
40m • 1h
100m • 2h
75m • 1.5h
10m • .25h →
Glastonbury
50m • 1.25h
Salisbury (Stonehenge)
Dover

are reasonable by U.S. standards. Locals love to share "pay and display" stickers. If you stand by the machine, invariably someone on their way out with time left on their sticker will give it to you. Keep a bag of coins in the ashtray for parking meters.

Set your car up for a fun road trip. Establish a cardboard-box munchies pantry. Buy a rack of liter boxes of juice for the trunk. Buy some Windex and a roll of paper towels for cleaner sightseeing.

COMMUNICATING

Telephones

Smart travelers learn the phone system and use it daily for making hotel/restaurant reservations, verifying hours at sights, and phoning home. Phoning is especially important when you're in London—always use the telephone to confirm tour times, book theater tickets, or make reservations at fancy restaurants. If you call before heading out, you'll travel more smoothly.

Types of Phones

You'll encounter various kinds of phones in Britain.

• British **public pay phones** are great, easy-to-use, and everywhere. Phones clearly list which coins they'll take (usually from 10p to £1, with a minimum toll of 30p; some new phones even accept euro coins), and a display shows how your money supply's doing. Only completely unused coins will be returned, so put in biggies with caution. (If money's left over, rather than hanging up, push the "make another call" button.) You can also pay for calls on these phones with a major credit card (see "Paying for Calls," below).

The only tricky public payphones you'll use are the expensive, coin-op ones in bars and B&Bs. Some require money before you dial, while others wait until after you're connected. Many have a button you must push before you begin talking. But all have clear instructions.

• **Hotel room phones** are fairly cheap for local calls, but pricey for international calls, unless you use an international phone card (see below).

• **American mobile phones** work in Europe if they're GSM-enabled, tri-band (or quad-band), and on a calling plan that includes international calls. With a T-Mobile phone, you can roam using your home number, and pay $1–2 per minute for making or receiving calls.

• Some travelers buy a **European mobile phone** in Europe. For about $125, you can get a phone that will work in most countries once you pick up the necessary chip (about $30) per country.

Or you can buy a cheaper, "locked" phone that only works in the country where you purchased it (about $100, includes $20 worth of calls). If you're interested, stop by any European shop that sells mobile phones (such as Vodafone, O2, and Orange); you'll see prominent store window displays. You aren't required to (and shouldn't) buy a monthly contract—buy prepaid calling time instead (as you use it up, buy additional minutes at newsstands or mobile-phone shops). If you're on a budget, skip mobile phones and use phone cards instead.

In London, some hotels will lend you mobile phones (but you pay the 50-cents-a-minute usage fee). Ask your hotel about this if you'd like to be connected.

Paying for Calls

You can spend a fortune making phone calls in Britain...but why would you? Here's the skinny on different ways to pay, including the best deals.

• You can use a **major credit card** to pay for both domestic and international calls from a public pay phone. Just insert the card into the phone and dial away (minimum charge for a credit-card call is 50p). This is a handy way to make quick calls, but the rates are high, so avoid long chats.

• Prepaid **international calling cards** are the cheapest way to make international calls from Britain (usually about a nickel per minute to the U.S.). These and are sold at most newsstands, mini-marts, post offices, and exchange bureaus in denominations of £5, £10, and £20.

There are many different brands, so ask the clerk which one has the best rates to wherever you're calling (Unity and Post Office brands have a reputation for having the cheapest per-minute rates). Because cards (and card companies) are occasionally duds, avoid the high denominations.

Since you don't insert these cards into the phone, you can use them from anywhere, including your hotel room, avoiding pricey hotel rates. You'll actually get more minutes per card if you call from your hotel rather than phone booths, which come with a hefty surcharge. Make sure, however, that your hotel isn't overcharging you to dial the access number (it's free to dial from phone booths).

To use a card, scratch off the back to reveal your code. After you dial the access phone number, the message tells you to enter your code and then dial the phone number you want to call. (If you have several access numbers listed on your card, you'll save money overall if you choose the one starting with 0800 rather than 0845 or 0870.) To call the U.S., see "How to Dial," below. To make calls within Britain, dial the area code plus the local number; when using an international calling card, the area code must be dialed even if you're calling across the street. These cards work only within the country of purchase (e.g., one bought in Britain won't work in France).

To make numerous, successive calls with an international calling card without having to redial the long access number each time, press the keys (see instructions on card, usually ##) that allow you to launch directly into your next call. Remember that you don't need the actual card to use a card account, so it's sharable. You can write down the access number and PIN in your notebook and share it with friends.

• **Dialing direct from your hotel room** without using an international calling card is usually quite expensive for international calls. I always ask first how much I'll be charged. Keep in mind that you might have to pay for local and occasionally even toll-free calls.

• **Receiving calls in your hotel room** is often the cheapest way to keep in touch with the folks back home—especially if your family has an inexpensive way to call you (either a good deal on their long-distance plan, a prepaid calling card with good rates to Europe, or access to an internet phone service such as Skype— www.skype.com). Give them a list of your hotels' phone numbers before you go. As you travel, send your family an e-mail or make a quick payphone call to set up a time for them to call you, and then wait for the ring.

• **U.S. calling cards** (such as the ones offered by AT&T, MCI, or Sprint) are the worst option. You'll nearly always save a lot of money by paying with a British phone card.

How to Dial

Calling from the U.S. to Britain, or vice versa, is simple—once you break the code. The European calling chart on page 502 will walk you through it. Remember that British time is five/eight hours ahead of the East/West Coasts of the U.S. and one hour behind the rest of Europe.

Dialing within Britain: Britain, like much of the U.S., uses an area-code dialing system. If you're dialing within an area code, you just dial the local number to be connected; but if you're calling outside your area code, you have to dial both the area code (which starts with a 0) and the local number.

Area codes are listed by city on phone-booth walls or are available from directory assistance (dial 192, free from phone booths). It's most expensive to call within Britain from 8:00–13:00 and cheapest from 17:00–8:00. Still, a short call across the country is inexpensive; don't hesitate to call long distance.

Dialing International Calls: For a listing of country codes, see the appendix. When making an international call to Britain, first dial the international access code of the country you're in (011 from the U.S. or Canada, 00 if you're calling from Europe), then Britain's country code (44), then the area code (without its initial 0) and the local number. For example, London's area code is 020. To call one of my recommended London B&Bs from the U.S., dial 011 (U.S. international access code), 44 (Britain's country code), 20 (London's area code without its initial 0), then 7730-8191 (the B&B's number).

To dial out of Britain, start your call with its international code (00), then dial the country code of the country you're calling, then the number you're calling. To call my office from Britain, I dial 00 (Britain's international access code), 1 (U.S. country code), 425 (Edmonds' area code), then 771-8303.

E-mail and Mail

E-mail: Internet cafés are easy to find in big cities like Edinburgh and London (the huge easyInternetcafé company has branches at popular spots such as Victoria Station; for more information, see page 51). Many libraries offer free access, but they also tend to have limited opening hours and may require reservations. Look for the places listed in this book, or ask the local TI, computer store, or your B&B host. Some hotels have a dedicated computer for guests' e-mail needs. Small places are accustomed to letting clients sit at their desk for a few minutes just to check their e-mail, if you ask politely.

Mail: Get stamps at the neighborhood post office, newsstands within fancy hotels, and some mini-marts and card shops. To arrange for mail delivery, reserve a few hotels along your route in advance and give their addresses to friends. Allow 10 days for a letter to arrive. Phoning and e-mailing is so easy that I've dispensed with mail stops altogether.

SLEEPING

In the interest of smart use of your time, I favor accommodations (and restaurants) handy to your sightseeing activities. Rather than list hotels scattered throughout a city, I choose two or three favorite neighborhoods and recommend the best accommodations values in each, from $20 bunk beds to fancy-for-my-book $270 doubles. Outside of London you can expect to find good doubles for $70–120, including cooked breakfasts and tax.

I've described my recommended hotels and B&Bs with a

standard code. Prices listed are for one-night stays in peak season, include a hearty breakfast (unless otherwise noted), and assume you're booking direct and not through a TI. Prices can soften off-season, for stays of two nights or longer, or for payment in cash (rather than credit card). Particularly at nicer hotels, ask about deals (usually offered for 2-night stays, sometimes mid-week or weekends, often called Leisure Breaks); the room price doesn't drop dramatically, but the pricey breakfasts are usually included. Booking a big hotel in advance usually gets you the highest-priced "rack rate." Calling the same day can get you a deeply discounted rate.

When establishing prices with a hotelier or B&B owner, confirm if the charge is per person or per room (if a price is too good to be true, it's probably per person).  Because many places in Britain charge per person, small groups often pay the same for a single and a double as they would for a triple. Note: In this book, room prices are listed per room, not per person.

Most places I list have three floors of rooms, steep stairs, and no elevator. If you're concerned about stairs, call and ask about ground-floor rooms. Remember that in Europe, the "first floor" is one floor above street level (what we would call the "second floor" back home).

Virtually all rooms have sinks. Rooms with a bathroom in your room (toilet plus shower and/or tub) are called "en suite"; rooms that lack private plumbing are "standard." As more rooms go en suite, the hallway bathroom is shared with fewer standard rooms. If money's tight, ask for standard rooms.

Britain has a rating system for hotels and B&Bs. These diamonds and stars are supposed to imply quality, but I find that they mean only that the place sporting these symbols is paying dues to the tourist board. Rating systems often have little to do with value.

For listings of more accommodations, particularly if you travel beyond my recommended destinations, visit www.smoothhound .co.uk, which offers a range of accommodations for towns throughout Britain and Northern Ireland (searchable by town, airport, hotel name, or price range).

Bed-and-Breakfasts

Compared to hotels, bed-and-breakfasts (B&Bs) give you double the cultural intimacy for half the price. In 2006, you'll pay £25–50 (about $45–90) per person for a B&B. Prices include a big cooked breakfast. The amounts of coziness, tea, and biscuits that are tossed in varies tremendously.

If you have a reasonable but limited budget, skip hotels. Go the B&B way. If you can use a telephone and speak English, you'll enjoy homey, friendly, clean rooms at a great price by sticking to my listings. Always call first. If you're traveling beyond my recommended destinations, you'll find B&Bs where you need them. Any town with tourists has a TI that books rooms or can give you a list and point you in the right direction. In the absence of a TI, ask people on the street for help.

"Twin" means two single beds, and "double" means one double bed. If you'll take either one, let them know or you might be needlessly turned away. "Standard" rooms come with just a sink (many better places have standard rooms that they don't even advertise). If you want a room that contains a private bathroom, specify "en suite"; B&B owners sometimes use the term "private bathroom" for a bathroom down the hall that only your room has the key for.

B&Bs range from large guest houses with 15–20 rooms to small homes renting out a spare bedroom. The philosophy of the management determines the character of a place more than its size and facilities offered. Avoid places run as a business by absentee owners. My top listings are run by people who enjoy welcoming the world to their breakfast table.

The B&Bs I've recommended are nearly all stocking-feet comfortable and "homely," as they say in England. I look for a place that has friendly hosts (i.e., they enjoy Americans); a location in a central, safe, quiet neighborhood; clean rooms with firm beds; a good value; and no mention in other guidebooks (and therefore it's filled mostly by English travelers). In certain cases, my recommendations don't meet all of these prerequisites. I'm more impressed by a handy location and a fun-loving philosophy than hair driers and shoe-shine machines.

A few tips: B&B proprietors are selective as to whom they invite in for the night. At some B&Bs, children are not welcome. Risky-looking people (2 or more single men are often assumed to be troublemakers) find many places suddenly full. If you'll be staying for more than one night you are a "desirable." Sometimes staying several nights earns you a better price—ask about it. If you book through a TI, it takes a 10 percent commission and may charge you an extra pound or two. If you book direct, the B&B gets it all (and you'll have a better chance of getting a discount). I have negotiated special prices with this book (often for cash). You should find prices quoted here to be good through 2006 (except for major holidays and festivals). In popular weekend-getaway spots, you're unlikely to find a place to take you for Saturday night only.

If my listings are full, ask for guidance. (Mentioning this book can help.) Owners usually work together and can call up an ally to land you a bed.

B&Bs are not hotels: If you want to ruin your relationship with your hostess, treat her like a hotel clerk. Americans often assume they'll get new towels each day. The British don't, and neither will you. Hang them up to dry and reuse.

B&Bs have plenty of stairs. Expect good exercise and be happy you packed light. Some B&Bs stock rooms with a hot-water pot, cups, tea bags, and coffee packets (if you prefer decaf, buy a jar at a grocery, and dump into a baggie for easy packing). Electrical outlets sometimes come with switches on the outlet to turn the current on or off; if your electrical appliance isn't working, flip the switch.

In B&Bs, no two showers are alike. Sometimes you'll encounter "telephone" showers—a handheld nozzle in a bathtub. Many B&Bs have been retrofitted with plumbing, and water is heated individually for each shower rather than by one central heating system. While the switch is generally left on, in some rooms you'll have a hot-water switch to consider. Any cord hanging from the ceiling is for lights or fans (not emergencies). Once in the shower, you'll find a multitude of overly clever mechanisms designed to somehow get the right amount and temperature of water. Good luck.

Cheap, Modern Hotels

Hotel chains, offering predictably comfortable accommodations at reasonable prices, are popping up in the center of big cities in Britain.

These hotels are ideal for families, offering simple, clean, and modern rooms for up to four people (2 adults/2 children) for £50–90, depending on the location. Note that couples or families (up to 4) pay the same price for a room. Most rooms have a double bed, single bed, five-foot trundle bed, private shower, WC, and TV. Hotels usually have an attached restaurant, good security, and a 24-hour staffed reception desk. Of course, they're as cozy as a Motel 6, but many travelers love them. You can book over the phone (or online) with a credit card, then pay when you check in. When you check out, just drop off the key, Lee.

If you choose to stay in these, book through their Web sites, as the room rates are often dramatically less for online bookings. The biggies are Travelodge (reservations tel. 0870-085-0950, www .travelodge.co.uk) and Premier Travel Inn (the very recent merger of Travel Inn and Premier Lodge: Travel Inn reservations tel. 0870-242-8000, Premier Lodge reservations tel. 0870-201-0203, www.travelinn.co.uk). The Irish chain Jurys Inn also has some hotels in Britain (you can reserve at Irish tel. 01/607-0000 or U.S. tel. 800/423-6953, call their hotels directly, or book online at www .jurys.com).

Couples could also consider Holiday Inn Express, spreading throughout Britain. These are like a Holiday Inn Lite, with cheaper prices and no restaurant. Many of their hotels allow only two per room, but some take up to four (doubles cost about £60–100, make sure Express is part of the name or you'll pay more for a regular Holiday Inn, reservations tel. 0870-400-9670, www.hiexpress .co.uk).

Making Reservations

It's possible to travel at any time of year without reservations, but given the high stakes, erratic accommodations values, number of people traveling with this book, and the quality of the gems I've listed, I highly recommend calling ahead for rooms at least a few days in advance as you travel.

When tourist crowds are down and you're traveling without reservations, you might make a habit of calling your hotel between 9:00 and 10:00 on the day you plan to arrive, when the hotel knows who'll be checking out and just which rooms will be available. I've taken great pains to list telephone numbers with long-distance instructions (see "Communicating," page 29; also see the appendix). Get a phone card and use it to confirm and reconfirm as you travel. A hotel receptionist will trust you and hold a room until 16:00 without a deposit, though some will ask for a credit-card number.

Honor your reservations or cancel by phone: Trusting travelers to show up is a huge, stressful issue and a financial risk for small B&B owners. I promised the owners of the places I list that you will be reliable when you make a telephone reservation; please don't let them (or me) down. If you'll be delayed or won't make it, simply call in. Americans are notorious for reserving B&Bs long in advance and never showing up (causing B&B owners to lose money—and respect for Americans). Being a little late is no problem if you are in telephone contact. Long-distance calls are cheap and easy from public phone booths.

Note that B&B owners will likely ask you the approximate time you'll arrive. Unlike hotels, most B&Bs don't have staff available to receive guests when they're out, so it helps them plan their days if they know when you're likely to show up.

While it's generally easy to find a room, a few national holidays jam things up (especially bank holiday Mondays) and merit your making reservations long in advance (see "Holidays," page 505). Mark these dates in red on your travel calendar. Monday bank holidays are preceded by busy weekends; book the entire weekend in advance.

Sleep Code

To help you easily sort through the accommodations listed, I've divided the rooms into three categories based on the price for a standard double room with bath.

$$$ **Higher Priced**
$$ **Moderately Priced**
$ **Lower Priced**

To give maximum information with a minimum of space, I use this code to describe accommodations listed in this book. Prices are listed per room, not per person. Breakfast is included.

S = Single room, or price for one person in a double.

D = Double or twin room. (I specify double- and twin-bed rooms only if they are priced differently, or if a place has only one or the other. When reserving, you should specify.)

T = Three-person room (often a double bed with a single).

Q = Four-person room (adding an extra child's bed to a triple is usually cheaper).

b = Private bathroom with toilet and shower or tub.

s = Private shower or tub only. (The toilet is down the hall.)

Non-smoking—With this edition, about 80 percent of my recommended B&Bs prohibit smoking. While some places allow smoking in the sleeping rooms, breakfast rooms are nearly always smoke-free.

Family deal—Indicates that parents with young children can easily get a room with an extra child's bed or a discount for larger rooms. Call to negotiate the price. Teenage kids are generally charged as adults. Little kids sleep almost free.

According to the above code, a couple staying at a "Db-£60" hotel would pay a total of £60 (about $110) per night for a room with a private toilet and shower (or tub). The hotel accepts credit cards or cash. You can assume credit cards are accepted unless otherwise noted.

If you know exactly which dates you need and really want a particular place, reserve a room before you leave. To reserve from home, contact the hotel by e-mail, phone, or fax. To e-mail or fax, use the form in the appendix (online at www.ricksteves.com /reservation). A two-night stay in August would be "two nights, 16/8/06 to 18/8/06"—Europeans write the date day/month/year, and hotel jargon uses your day of departure. You'll often be asked for one night's deposit. Your credit-card number and expiration date will usually be accepted as a deposit, though you may need to send a signed traveler's check or a bank draft in the local currency. Faxing your card number (rather than e-mailing it) keeps it private, safer, and out of cyberspace. If your credit card is the deposit, you can pay with your card or cash when you settle up the bill. Call to confirm your stay a day or two before you arrive. If you don't show up (or if you cancel with short notice), you'll be billed for one night.

Hotels in larger cities sometimes have strict cancellation policies (you might lose, say, a deposit if you cancel within 2 weeks of your reserved stay, or you might be billed for the entire visit if you leave early); ask about cancellation policies before you book.

On the road, reconfirm your reservations a day or two in advance for safety (or you may be bumped—really). Also, don't just assume you can extend. Take the time to consider in advance how long you'll stay.

Hostels

If you're traveling alone, hosteling is the best way to conquer hotel loneliness. Hostels are also a tremendous source of local and budget travel information. You'll pay an average of £12 for a bed and £3 for breakfast. Anyone of any age can hostel in Britain. While there are no membership concerns for private hostels, IYHF hostels require membership. Those without cards simply buy one-night guest memberships for £1.50.

Britain has hundreds of hostels of all shapes and sizes. Choose your hostel selectively. Hostels can be historic castles or depressing huts, serene and comfy or overrun by noisy children. Unfortunately, many of the international youth hostels have become overpriced and, in general, I no longer recommend them. The only time I do recommend them is if you're on a very tight budget, want to cook your own meals, or are traveling with a group that likes to sleep on bunk beds in big rooms. The informal private hostels are often more fun, easygoing, and cheaper. These alternatives to the International Youth Hostel Federation (IYHF) hostels are more common than ever. Hostels of Europe (www.hostelseurope.com) and Hostels.com have good listings. You can book online for many hostels (for London: www.hostellondon.com; for England and Wales: www.yha.org.uk; and for Scotland: www.hostel-scotland.co.uk).

EATING

England's reputation for miserable food is now dated, and the British cuisine scene is lively, trendy, and pleasantly surprising. (Unfortunately, it can also be expensive.) Even the basic, traditional pub grub has gone "upmarket," and you'll generally find fresh vegetables rather than soggy fries and mushy peas.

Your £7 budget choices are "early bird" restaurant specials, bakeries, ethnic eateries, cafeterias, fast food, picnics, fish-and-chips, pizza, pubs, or greasy spoon cafés. Here are a few tips on budget eating.

The hearty British **breakfast** can tide many travelers over until dinner. This traditional "fry," also known as a "heart attack on a plate," is especially feast-like if you've just come from the land of the skimpy continental breakfast across the Channel.

Your standard fry gets off to a healthy start with juice and cereal or porridge. (Try Weetabix, a soggy English cousin of shredded wheat.) Next, with tea or coffee, you get a heated plate with a fried egg, lean Canadian-style bacon, a bad sausage, a grilled tomato, and often a slice of delightfully greasy pan toast and sautéed mushrooms. Toast comes on a rack (to cool quickly and crisply) with butter and marmalade. Try kippers (herring fillets smoked in an oak fire). Order only what you'll eat. Hoteliers and B&B hostesses don't like to see food wasted. And there's nothing wrong with skipping the "fry"—few locals actually start their day with this heavy traditional breakfast.

These days, the best coffee is served in a *cafetière* (also called a "French press"). When your coffee has steeped as long as you like, plunge down the filter and pour. To revitalize your brew, pump the plunger again.

Many B&Bs don't serve breakfast until 8:00. If you need an early start, ask politely if it's possible. While they may not make you a cooked breakfast, they can usually put out cereal, toast, juice, and coffee.

Picnicking saves time and money. Fine park benches and polite pigeons abound in most neighborhoods. You can easily get prepared food to go. Bakeries sell yogurt, cartons of "semi-skimmed" milk, pastries, and pasties (PAST-eez). Pasties are "savory" (not sweet) meat pies that originated in the mining country; they had big crust handles so miners with filthy hands could eat them and toss the crust. Modern mini-markets have long hours, convenient locations, and sell healthy fruit, vegetable, and meat plates in picnic-friendly portions.

Good sandwich shops and corner grocery stores are a hit with local workers eating on the run. Decent packaged sandwiches (£2–3) are sold everywhere. Try boxes of orange juice (pure, by the liter), fresh bread, tasty English cheese, meat, a tube of Colman's English mustard, local eatin' apples, bananas, small tomatoes, a small tub of yogurt (they're drinkable), trail mix or nuts, plain or chocolate-covered "digestive biscuits," and any local specialties. At open-air markets and supermarkets, you can get produce in small

---

English Chocolate

My chocoholic readers are enthusiastic about English chocolates. Their favorites include Cadbury Wispa Gold bars (filled with liquid caramel), Cadbury Crunchie bars, Nestle's Lion bars, Cadbury's Boost bars (a shortcake biscuit with caramel in milk chocolate), and Galaxy chocolate bars (especially the ones with hazelnuts). Thornton shops (in larger train stations) sell a box of sweets called the Continental Assortment, which comes with a tasting guide. The highlight is the mocha white-chocolate truffle. Many like British M&Ms (Smarties) better than American ones. For a few extra pence, adorn your ice-cream cone with a "flake"—a chocolate bar stuck right into the middle.

---

quantities (3 tomatoes and 2 bananas cost me 50p). Supermarkets often have good deli sections, even offering Indian dishes, and sometimes salad bars. I often munch a relaxed "meal on wheels" in a car or train, or on an open-top bus tour or river cruise, to save 30 precious minutes for sightseeing. If you're planning a picnic dinner in a smaller town, buy ahead, because grocery stores can close as early as 17:00.

At classier restaurants, look for **"early bird specials,"** allowing you to eat well and affordably, but early (about 17:30–19:00, last order by 19:00). A top-end, £25-for-dinner–type restaurant often serves the same quality two-course lunch deals for £10.

Ethnic restaurants from all over the world add spice to England's cuisine scene. Eating Indian or Chinese is cheap (even cheaper if you take it out). Sampling Indian food is "going local" in cosmopolitan, multiethnic Britain.

Afternoon Tea

People of leisure punctuate their afternoon with a "cream tea" at a tearoom. You'll get a pot of tea, small finger foods (like cucumber sandwiches), homemade scones, jam, and thick clotted cream. For maximum pinkie-waving taste per calorie, slice your scone thin like a miniature loaf of bread. Tearooms, which often serve appealing light meals, are usually open for lunch and close at about 17:00, just before dinner.

While teatime is still going strong, the new phenomenon is coffee shops: Starbucks and its competitors have sprouted up all over, providing cushy and social watering holes with comfy chairs, easy WCs, £2 lattes, and a nice break between sights.

Pub Grub and Beer

Pubs are a basic part of the British social scene, and, whether you are a teetotaler or a beer guzzler, they should be a part of your travel here. Pub is short for "public house." It's an extended living room where, if you don't mind the stickiness, you can feel the pulse of Britain. Most traditional atmospheric pubs are in the country-side and smaller towns. Unfortunately, many city pubs have been afflicted with an excess of brass, ferns, and video games. Many other pubs have found that selling beer is more profitable than selling meals and only cook at lunchtime. In any case, smart travelers use the pubs to eat, drink, get out of the rain, watch the latest sporting event, and make new friends.

Pub grub gets better each year. For £6–8, you'll get a basic budget hot lunch or dinner in friendly surroundings. The *Good Pub Guide,* published annually by the British Consumers Association, is excellent. Pubs attached to restaurants often have fresher food and a chef who knows how to cook.

Pubs generally serve traditional dishes, like fish-and-chips, vegetables, "bangers and mash" (sausages and mashed potatoes), roast beef with Yorkshire pudding (batter baked in the oven), and assorted meat pies, such as steak-and-kidney pie or shepherd's pie (stewed lamb topped with mashed potatoes). Side dishes include salads (sometimes even a nice self-serve salad bar), vegetables (especially mushy peas), and—invariably—"chips" (French fries). "Crisps" are potato chips. A "jacket potato" (baked potato stuffed with fillings of your choice) can almost be a meal in itself. A "ploughman's  lunch" is a modern "traditional English meal" of bread, cheese, and sweet pickles that nearly every tourist tries...once. These days, you'll likely find more Italian pasta, curried dishes, and quiche on the menu than "traditional" fare.

Meals are usually served from 12:00 to 14:00 and from 18:00 to 20:00—not throughout the day. Typically, there's no table service. Order at the bar, then take a seat and they'll bring the food when it's ready (or sometimes you pick it up at the bar). Pay at the bar (sometimes when you order, sometimes after you eat). In general, don't tip at pubs. Tip (up to 10 percent) only if you're in the pub's restaurant section and you order off a menu from a waiter who takes your order at your table (but look at the bill first; if it lists a service charge, there's no need to tip beyond that).

Servings are hearty, service is quick, and you'll rarely spend more than £8. Your beer or cider adds another couple of pounds.

(Free tap water is always available.) Pubs that advertise their food and are crowded with locals are less likely to be the kind that serve only lousy microwaved snacks.

The British take great pride in their beer. Many Brits think that drinking beer cold and carbonated, as Americans do, ruins the taste. Most pubs will have **lagers** (cold, refreshing, American-style beer), **ales** (amber-colored, cellar-temperature beer), **bitters** (hop-flavored ale, perhaps the most typical British beer), and **stouts** (dark and somewhat bitter, such as Guinness). At pubs, long hand pulls are used to pull the traditional, rich-flavored "real ales" up from the cellar. These are the connoisseur's favorites: fermented naturally, varying from sweet to bitter, often with a hoppy or nutty flavor. Notice the fun names. Short hand pulls at the bar mean colder, fizzier, mass-produced, and less interesting keg beers. Mild beers are sweeter, with a creamy malt flavoring. Irish cream ale is a smooth, sweet experience. Try the draft cider (sweet or dry).

Order your beer at the bar and pay as you go. An average beer costs £3. Part of the experience is standing before a line of "hand pulls," or taps, and wondering which beer to choose.

Drinks are served by the pint (20-ounce imperial size) or the half-pint. Proper English ladies like a half-beer and half-lemonade **shandy.**

Besides beer, many pubs actually have a good selection of wines by the glass, a fully stocked bar for the gentleman's "G and T" (gin and tonic), and the increasingly popular bottles of alcohol-plus-sugar (e.g. Bacardi Breezers) for the younger, working-class set. Teetotalers can order from a wide variety of soft drinks. Children are served food and soft drinks in pubs (sometimes in a courtyard or the restaurant section), but you must be 18 to order a beer.

Pub hours vary. The strict wartime hours (designed to keep the wartime working force sober and productive) ended in 1988, and now pubs generally serve beer Mon–Sat from 11:00–23:00 and Sun 12:00–22:30 (though pubs can be open later, particularly on Fri–Sat). As it nears closing time, you'll hear shouts of "Last orders." Then comes the 10-minute warning bell. Finally, they'll call "Time!" to pick up your glass, finished or not, when the pub closes.

A cup of darts is free for the asking. Sitting or standing at the bar indicates you're interested in a conversation (while sitting at a table, you're likely to be left alone). People go to a "public house" to be social. They want to talk. Get vocal with a local. The pub is the next best thing to having relatives in town. Cheers!

TRAVELING AS A TEMPORARY LOCAL

We travel all the way to Europe to enjoy differences—to become temporary locals. You'll experience frustrations. There are certain truths that we find God-given and self-evident, such as cold beer, ice in drinks, bottomless cups of coffee, "the customer's always right," easy shower faucets, and driving on the right-hand side of the road. One of the benefits of travel is the eye-opening realization that there are logical, civil, and even better alternatives. A willingness to go local ensures that you'll enjoy a full dose of British hospitality.

If there is a negative aspect to the image the British have of Americans, it is that we are big, aggressive, impolite, rich, loud, superficially friendly, and a bit naive. Americans tend to be noisy in public places, such as restaurants and trains. Our raised voices can demolish Britain's reserved and elegant ambience. Talk softly. While the British look bemusedly at some of our Yankee excesses—and worriedly at others—they nearly always afford us individual travelers all the warmth we deserve.

Judging from all the happy postcards I receive from travelers who have used this book, it's safe to assume you'll enjoy a great, affordable vacation—with the finesse of an independent, experienced traveler. Thanks, and have a brilliant holiday!

BACK DOOR TRAVEL PHILOSOPHY
From *Rick Steves' Europe Through the Back Door*

Travel is intensified living—maximum thrills per minute and one of the last great sources of legal adventure. Travel is freedom. It's recess, and we need it.

Experiencing the real Europe requires catching it by surprise, going casual..."Through the Back Door."

Affording travel is a matter of priorities. (Make do with the old car.) You can travel—simply, safely, and comfortably—anywhere in Europe for $100 a day plus transportation costs (allow more for London). In many ways, spending more money only builds a thicker wall between you and what you came to see. Europe is a cultural carnival, and, time after time, you'll find that its best acts are free and the best seats are the cheap ones.

A tight budget forces you to travel close to the ground, meeting and communicating with the people, not relying on service with a purchased smile. Never sacrifice sleep, nutrition, safety, or cleanliness in the name of budget. Simply enjoy the local-style alternatives to expensive hotels and restaurants.

Extroverts have more fun. If your trip is low on magic moments, kick yourself and make things happen. If you don't enjoy a place, maybe you don't know enough about it. Seek the truth. Recognize tourist traps. Give a culture the benefit of your open mind. See things as different but not better or worse. Any culture has much to share.

Of course, travel, like the world, is a series of hills and valleys. Be fanatically positive and militantly optimistic. If something's not to your liking, change your liking. Travel is addictive. It can make you a happier American as well as a citizen of the world. Our Earth is home to six billion equally important people. It's humbling to travel and find that people don't envy Americans. They like us, but, with all due respect, they wouldn't trade passports.

Globe-trotting destroys ethnocentricity. It helps you understand and appreciate different cultures. Regrettably, there are forces in our society that want you dumbed down for their convenience. Don't let it happen. Thoughtful travel engages you with the world—more important than ever these days. Travel changes people. It broadens perspectives and teaches new ways to measure quality of life. Many travelers toss aside their hometown blinders. Their prized souvenirs are the strands of different cultures they decide to knit into their own character. The world is a cultural yarn shop. And Back Door travelers are weaving the ultimate tapestry. Come on, join in!

LONDON

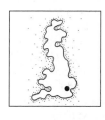

London is more than 600 square miles of urban jungle. With nine million people—who don't all speak English—it's a world in itself and a barrage on all the senses. On my first visit I felt very, very small.

London is more than its museums and landmarks. It's a living, breathing, thriving organism...a coral reef of humanity. The city has changed dramatically in recent years, and many visitors are surprised to find how "un-English" it is. Whites are now a minority in major parts of the city that once symbolized white imperialism. Arabs have nearly bought out the area north of Hyde Park. Chinese take-outs outnumber fish-and-chips shops. Many hotels are run by people with foreign accents (who hire English chambermaids), while outlying suburbs are home to huge communities of Indians and Pakistanis. With the English Channel Tunnel in place and union with Europe inevitable, many locals see even more holes in their bastion of Britishness. London is learning—sometimes fitfully—to live as a microcosm of its formerly vast empire.

With just a few days here, you'll get no more than a quick splash in this teeming human tidal pool. But with a good orientation, you'll find London manageable and fun. You'll get a sampling of the city's top sights, history, and cultural entertainment, and a good look at its ever-changing human face.

Blow through the city on the open deck of a double-decker orientation tour bus and take a pinch-me-I'm-in-London walk through the West End. Ogle the crown jewels at the Tower of London, hear the chimes of Big Ben, and see the Houses of Parliament in action. Cruise the Thames River and take a spin on the London Eye Ferris Wheel. Hobnob with the tombstones in

Westminster Abbey, enjoy Shakespeare in a replica of the Globe Theatre, and stand in awe over the original Magna Carta at the British Library. Visit with Leonardo, Botticelli, and Rembrandt in the National Gallery. Whisper across the dome of St. Paul's Cathedral and rummage through our civilization's attic at the British Museum. And sip your tea with pinky raised and clotted cream dribbling down your scone. Spend one evening at a theater and the others catching your breath.

Planning Your Time

The sights of London alone could easily fill a trip to Britain. It's a great one-week getaway. On a three-week tour of Britain I'd give it three busy days. If you're flying in, consider starting your trip in Bath and making London your British finale. Especially if you hope to enjoy a play or concert, a night or two of jet lag is bad news.

Here's a suggested schedule:

Day 1: 9:00–Tower of London (Beefeater tour, crown jewels); 12:00–Munch a sandwich on the Thames while cruising from the Tower to Westminster Bridge; 13:00–Follow the self-guided Westminster Walk (see page 67) with a quick visit to the Churchill Museum and Cabinet War Rooms; 15:30–Trafalgar Square and National Gallery; 17:30–Visit the Britain and London Visitors Centre near Piccadilly, planning ahead for your trip; 18:30–Dinner in Soho. Take in a play or 19:30 concert at St. Martin-in-the-Fields.

Day 2: 8:30–If traveling around Britain, spend 30 minutes in a phone booth getting all essential elements of your trip nailed down. If you know where you'll be and when, call those B&Bs now. 9:00–Take a hop-on, hop-off bus tour (consider hopping off near the end for the 11:30 Changing of the Guard at Buckingham Palace); 12:30–Covent Garden for lunch and people-watching; 14:00–Tour the British Museum. Have a pub dinner before a play, concert, or evening walking tour.

Days 3 and 4: Choose among these remaining London highlights: Tour Westminster Abbey, British Library, Imperial War Museum, the two Tates (Tate Modern on the south bank for modern art, Tate Britain on the north bank for British art), St. Paul's Cathedral, or the Museum of London; take a spin on the London Eye Ferris Wheel or a cruise to Kew or Greenwich; do some serious shopping at one of London's elegant department stores or open-air markets; or take another historic walking tour.

After considering nearly all of London's tourist sights, I have pruned them down to just the most important (or fun) for a first visit of up to seven days. You won't be able to see all of these, so don't try. You'll keep coming back to London. After 25 visits myself, I still enjoy a healthy list of excuses to return.

London's Neighborhoods

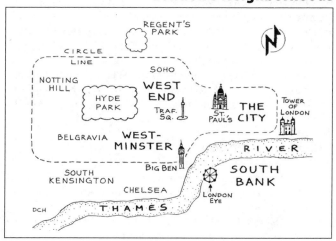

ORIENTATION

(area code: 020)

To grasp London comfortably, see it as the old town in the city center without the modern, congested sprawl. The Thames River runs roughly west to east through the city, with most of the visitor's sights on the north bank. Mentally, maybe even physically, trim down your map to include only the area between the Tower of London (to the east), Hyde Park (west), Regent's Park (north), and the Thames (south). (This is roughly the area bordered by the Tube's Circle Line.) This three-mile stretch between the Tower and Hyde Park (about a 90-min walk)—looking like a milk bottle on its side (see above)—holds 80 percent of the sights mentioned in this book.

London is a collection of neighborhoods:

The City: Shakespeare's London was a walled town clustered around St. Paul's Cathedral. Today, it's the modern financial district.

Westminster: This neighborhood includes Big Ben, Parliament, Westminster Abbey, and Buckingham Palace, the grand government buildings from which Britain is ruled.

The West End: Lying between Westminster and the City (that is, at the "west end" of the original walled town), this is the center of London's cultural life. Trafalgar Square has major museums. Piccadilly Circus and Leicester Square host tourist traps, cinemas, and nighttime glitz. Soho and Covent Garden are thriving people-zones housing theaters, restaurants, pubs, and boutiques.

The South Bank: Until recently, the entire south bank of the Thames River was a run-down, generally ignored area, but now it's the hottest real estate in town, with upscale restaurants, major new sightseeing attractions, and pedestrian bridges allowing easy access from the rest of London.

Residential Neighborhoods to the West: Though they lack major tourist sights, Mayfair, South Kensington, Notting Hill, Chelsea, and Belgravia are home to London's wealthy and trendy, as well as many shopping streets and enticing restaurants.

Tourist Information

The Britain and London Visitors Centre, just a block off Piccadilly Circus, is the best tourist information service in town (Mon–Fri 9:00–18:30, Sat–Sun 10:00–16:00, phone not answered after 17:00 Mon–Fri and not at all Sat–Sun, booking service, 1 Lower Regent Street, tel. 020/8846-9000, www.visitbritain.com, www.visitlondon.com). If you're traveling beyond London, take advantage of the Centre's well-equipped England desk. Bring your itinerary and a checklist of questions. At the London desk, pick up these free publications: *London Map and Guide*, *London Planner* (a great free monthly that lists all the sights, events, and hours), walking-tour schedule fliers, a theater guide, *Central London Bus Guide*, and the Thames River Services brochure. After you've grazed through the great leaflet racks, head upstairs for the inviting tables and Internet access (with disk-burning service).

The Britain and London Visitors Centre ("pink desk") sells long-distance bus tickets and passes, train tickets (convenient for reservations), British Heritage Passes, and tickets to plays (20 percent booking fee). They also sell **Fast Track tickets** to some of London's attractions (at no extra cost), allowing you to skip the queue at the sights. These can be worthwhile for places that sometimes have long ticket lines, such as the Tower of London, London Eye Ferris Wheel, and Madame Tussaud's Waxworks. While the Visitors Centre books rooms, you can avoid their £5 booking fee by calling hotels direct (see "Sleeping").

The **London Pass** provides free entrance to most of the city's sights, but since many museums are free, it's hard to justify the purchase. Still, fervent sightseers can check the list of covered sights and do the arithmetic (£27/1 day, £42/2 days, £52/3 days, £72/6 days, includes 160-page guidebook, tel. 0870-242-9988 for purchase instructions, www.londonpass.com).

Nearby you'll find the **Scottish Tourist Centre** (Mon–Fri 8:00–20:00, Sat 9:00–17:30, Sun 10:00–16:00, Cockspur Street, tel. 0845-225-5121, www.visitscotland.com) and the slick **French National Tourist Office** (Mon–Fri 10:00–18:00, Sat until 17:00, closed Sun, 178 Piccadilly Street, tel. 0906/824-4123).

Unfortunately, **London's Tourist Information Centres** (which present themselves as TIs at major train and bus stations and airports) are now simply businesses selling advertising space to companies with fliers to distribute. For solid information, visit the Britain and London Visitors Centre, mentioned above.

Local bookstores sell London guides and maps; *Bensons Map Guide* is the best (£3, also sold at newsstands).

Arrival in London

By Train: London has eight train stations, all connected by the Tube (subway) and all with ATMs, exchange offices, and luggage storage. From any station, ride the Tube or taxi to your hotel.

By Bus: The bus ("coach") station is one block southwest of Victoria Station, which has a TI and Tube entrance.

By Plane: For detailed information on getting from London's airports to downtown London, see "Transportation Connections" (page 141).

Helpful Hints

Pedestrian Safety: Cars drive on the left side of the road, so before crossing a street, I always look right, look left, then look right again just to be sure.

Medical Problems: Local hospitals have 24-hour-a-day emergency care centers where any tourist who needs help can drop in and, after a wait, be seen by a doctor. The quality is good and the price is right (free). Your hotel has details. St. Thomas' Hospital, immediately across the river from Big Ben, has a fine reputation.

Theft Alert: The Artful Dodger is alive and well in London. Be on guard, particularly on public transportation and in places crowded with tourists. Tourists, considered naive and rich, are targeted. More than 7,500 handbags are stolen annually at Covent Garden alone.

U.S. Embassy: It's at 24 Grosvenor Square (for passport concerns, open Mon–Fri 8:30–17:30, closed Sat–Sun, Tube: Bond Street, tel. 020/7499-9000).

Changing Money: ATMs are the way to go. While regular banks charge several pounds to change traveler's checks, American Express offices offer a fair rate and will change any brand of traveler's checks for no fee. Handy AmEx offices are at Heathrow's Terminal 4 Tube station (daily 7:00–19:00) and near Piccadilly (Mon–Sat 9:00–18:00, Sun 10:00–17:00, 30 Haymarket, tel. 020/7484-9610; refund office 24-hr tel. 0800/521-313). Marks & Spencer department stores also give good rates with no fees.

London

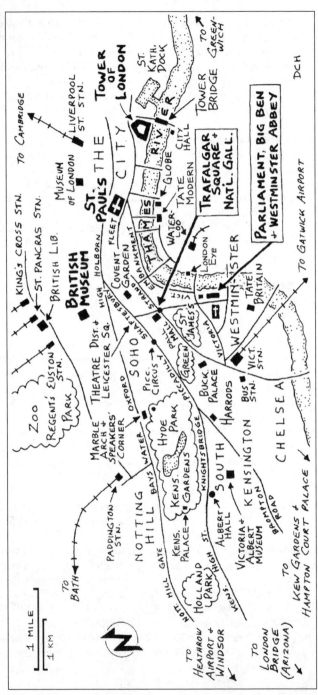

Avoid changing money at exchange bureaus. Their latest scam: They advertise very good rates with a same-as-the-banks fee of 2 percent. But the fine print explains that the fee of 2 percent is for buying pounds. The fee for selling pounds is 9.5 percent. Ouch!

Internet Access: The **easyInternetcafé** chain offers up to 500 computers per store and is open long hours daily. Depending on the time of day, a £2 ticket buys anywhere from 80 minutes to six hours of computer time. The ticket is valid for four weeks and multiple visits at any of their branches: Trafalgar Square (456 Strand), Tottenham Court Road (#9–16), Oxford Street (#358, opposite Bond Street Tube station), and Kensington High Street (#160–166). They also sell 24-hour, seven-day, and 30-day passes (www.easyinternetcafe.com). **Access Printers**, across the street from Victoria Station (next to the Apollo Victoria Theatre), has plenty of terminals (£1/30 min, open long hours daily).

Travel Bookstores: Stanfords Travel Bookstore, in Covent Garden, is good and stocks current editions of my books (Mon–Fri 9:00–19:30, Sat 10:00–19:00, Sun 12:00–18:00, 12 Long Acre, tel. 020/7836-1321). Two impressive Waterstone's bookstores have the biggest collection of travel guides in town: on Piccadilly (Mon–Sat 10:00–22:00, Sun 12:00–18:00, 203 Piccadilly, tel. 020/7851-2400) and on Trafalgar Square (Mon–Sat 9:30–21:00, Sun 12:00–18:00, next to Costa Café, tel. 020/7839-4411).

Left Luggage: As security concerns heighten, train stations have replaced their lockers with left-luggage counters. Each bag must go through a scanner (just like at the airport), so lines can be long. Expect a wait to pick up your bags, too (each item-£6/24 hrs, daily 7:00–24:00). You can also check bags at the airports (£5/day). If leaving London and returning later, you may be able to leave a box or bag at your hotel for free—assuming you'll be staying there again.

Getting Around London

To travel smart in a city this size, you must get comfortable with public transportation. London's excellent taxis, buses, and subway system make a private car unnecessary. In fact, the "congestion charge" of £8 levied on any private car entering the city center has been effective in cutting down traffic jam delays and bolstering London's public transit. The revenue raised subsidizes the buses, which are now cheaper, more frequent, and even more user-friendly than before. Today, the vast majority of vehicles in the city center are buses, taxis, and service trucks. (Drivers, for all the details on the congestion charge, see www.cclondon.com.)

Affording London's Sights

London is, in many ways, Europe's most expensive city, with lots of pricey sights but—fortunately—lots of freebies, too.

Many of the city's biggest and best museums won't cost you a dime. Free sights include the British Museum, British Library, National Gallery, National Portrait Gallery, Tate Britain, Tate Modern, Wallace Collection, Imperial War Museum, Victoria and Albert Museum, Natural History Museum, Science Museum, National Army Museum, Sir John Soane's Museum, Theatre Museum, the Museum of London, and on the outskirts of town, the Royal Air Force Museum London.

Some museums, such as the British Museum, request a £2–3 donation, but whether you contribute or not is up to you. Many offer essential audioguides for about £3. If I spend the money on an audioguide, I don't feel bad about not donating otherwise.

Other freebies to consider: You can get into the Tower of London by attending the Ceremony of the Keys (which requires a reservation made long in advance—see page 97). You can view the legal action at Old Bailey and the legislature at work in the Houses of Parliament. There are plenty of free concerts, such as the lunch concerts at St. Martin-in-the-Fields. You can also enjoy the pageantry of Changing of the Guard and the wild people-watching scene at Covent Garden.

Smaller churches let worshippers in free (even tourist worshippers), having given up on asking for donations. The big sightseeing churches—Westminster Abbey and St. Paul's—charge £8 for admission, but offer free evensong services virtually daily and a free organ recital on Sunday.

When budgeting your sightseeing money, consider the £5.50 city walking tours as one of the best deals going. The hop-on, hop-off big-bus tours (£16–20), while expensive, provide a great overview, and include boat tours as well as city walks, depending on the company you choose (see page 61). A one-hour Thames ride costs about £7, but generally comes with an entertaining commentary (see page 65).

By Taxi: London is the best taxi town in Europe. Big, black, carefully regulated cabs are everywhere. I've never met a crabby cabbie in London. They love to talk, and they know every nook and cranny in town. I ride in one each day just to get my London questions answered. Rides start at £2.20. Connecting downtown sights is quick and easy and will cost you about £5 (for example, St. Paul's to the Tower of London). For a short ride, three people in a cab travel at Tube prices. Groups of four or five should taxi everywhere. While telephoning a cab will get you one in a few minutes, it's generally not necessary; hailing a cab is easy and costs less. If a

The queen charges big time to open her palace to the public: Buckingham Palace (£14, open Aug–Sept only) and her art gallery and carriage museum (adjacent to the palace, about £7 each) are interesting but expensive. While Kensington Palace (£11) and Hampton Court Palace (£12) are pricey, they are well-presented and a reasonable value if you have a real interest in royal history. Anyone visiting both the Tower of London and Hampton Court Palace saves £6.50 by getting the £20 combo-ticket.

Gimmicky private enterprises can charge sky-high prices, such as the London Dungeon (£14) and the fun, popular, and overpriced Madame Tussaud's Waxworks (£23, but £14 after 17:00). The two privately run £9 museums (Dalí Universe and Saatchi Gallery), which capitalize on their location next to the popular London Eye Ferris Wheel, are both bad values.

Big-ticket sights worth their admission fees are Kew Gardens (£8.50), Shakespeare's Globe Theatre (£9, includes a tour), and the Cabinet War Rooms, with its fine new Churchill Exhibit (£10). The London Eye Ferris Wheel is an unforgettable experience (£12.50), and Vinopolis wine museum provides a classy way to get a buzz and call it museum-going (£12.50 entry includes 5 small glasses of wine).

Many smaller museums cost about £5. My favorites include the three Somerset House museums (Courtauld Gallery, Heritage Rooms, and the Gilbert Collection) and the Wellington Museum at Apsley House.

Seek out the freestanding "tkts" booth at Leicester Square to get discounted tickets to London's famous shows. Theater tickets are sold for that day only, and the booth tacks on a £2.50 service charge. But it's still a good deal, offering discounts from 25 to 50 percent (see page 111).

These days, London doesn't come cheap. But with its many free museums and affordable plays, this cosmopolitan, cultured city offers days of sightseeing thrills without requiring you to pinch your pennies (or your pounds).

cab's top light is on, just wave it down. (Drivers flash lights when they see you.) They have a tiny turning radius, so you can wave at cabs going in either direction. If waving doesn't work, ask someone where you can find a taxi stand.

Don't worry about meter cheating. British cab meters come with a sealed computer chip and clock that ensures you'll get the regular tariff #1 most of the time, tariff #2 during "unsociable hours" (18:00–6:00 in the morning, plus Sat–Sun), and tariff #3 only on holidays. (Rates only go up about 10 percent with each higher tariff.) All extra charges are explained in writing on the

Handy Buses

Since the institution of London's "congestion charge" for cars, the bus system is faster, easier, and cheaper than ever. Tube-oriented travelers need to make a point to get over their tunnel vision, learn the bus system, and get around fast and easy.

Here are some of the most useful routes:

Route #9: High Street Kensington to Harrods to Hyde Park Corner to Piccadilly Circus to Trafalgar Square.

Routes #11 and #24: Victoria Station to Westminster Abbey to Trafalgar Square (#11 continues to St. Paul's).

Route #RV1: Tower of London to Tower Bridge to Tate Modern/Shakespeare's Globe to London Eye/Waterloo Station/County Hall Travel Inn accommodations to Trafalgar Square to Covent Garden (a scenic joyride).

Route #15: Paddington Station to Oxford Circus to Regent Street/TI to Piccadilly Circus to Trafalgar Square to Fleet Street to St. Paul's to Tower of London.

Route #188: Waterloo Station/London Eye to Trafalgar Square to Covent Garden to British Museum to British Library.

In addition, several buses (including #6, #12, #13, #15, #23, #139, and #159) make the corridor run from Trafalgar, Piccadilly Circus, and Oxford Circus to Marble Arch.

---

cab wall. The only way a cabbie can cheat you is to take a needlessly long route. Another pitfall is taking a cab when traffic is bad to a destination efficiently served by the Tube. On my last trip to London, I hopped in a taxi at South Kensington for Waterloo Station and hit bad traffic. Rather than spending 20 minutes and £2 on the tube, I spent 40 minutes and £16 in a taxi.

Tip a cabbie by rounding up (maximum 10 percent). If you over-drink and ride in a taxi, be warned: Taxis charge £40 for "soiling" (a.k.a. pub puke).

By Bus: Riding city buses doesn't come naturally to many travelers, but if you make a point to figure out the system, you'll swing like Tarzan through the urban jungle of London. Pick up the free *Central London Bus Guide* at a transport office or TI for a fine map listing all the bus routes best for sightseeing.

If you learn how to decipher bus stop signs, you can figure out on your own where to catch the bus to get to your destination.

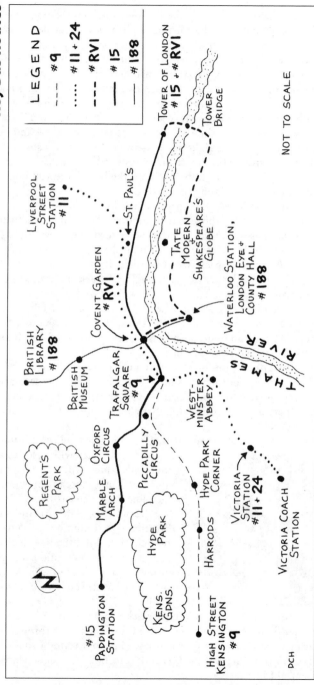

Key Bus Routes

LEGEND

- – – #9
- ⋯⋯ #11 + 24
- – – #RVI
- —— #15
- —— #188

NOT TO SCALE

Find a bus stop and study the signs mounted on the pole next to the stop. You'll see a chart listing (alphabetically) the destinations served by buses that pick up at this spot or nearby; the names of the buses; and alphabet letters that identify exactly where the buses pick up. After locating your destination, remember or write down the bus name and bus stop letter. Next, refer to the neighborhood map (also on the pole) to find your bus stop. Just match your letter with a stop on the map. Make your way to that stop—you'll know it's yours because it will have the same letter on its pole—and wait for the bus with the right name to arrive. Some fancy stops have electric boards indicating the minutes until the next bus arrives; but remember to check the name on the bus before you hop on. Crack the code and you're good to go.

On most buses, you'll pay at a machine at the bus stop (exact change only), then show your ticket (or Tube pass) as you board. On other buses, you can pay the conductor (take a seat, and he'll come and collect £1.20). Any ride in downtown London costs £1.20. A ticket six-pack costs £6 and an all-day bus pass costs £3. If you're staying longer, consider the £8 all-week bus pass. The best views are upstairs.

If you have a Travelcard (see below), get in the habit of hopping buses for quick little straight shots, even just to get to a Tube stop. During bump-and-grind rush hours (8:00–10:00 and 16:00–19:00), you'll go faster by Tube.

By Tube: London's subway system (called the Tube or Underground, but never "subway") is one of this planet's great people-movers and the fastest—and cheapest—long-distance transport in town (runs Mon–Sat about 5:00–24:00, Sun about 7:00–23:00).

Survey a Tube map. At the front of this book, you'll find a

complete Tube map with color-coded lines and names. You can also pick up a free Tube map at any station. Each line has a name (such as Circle, Northern, or Bakerloo) and two directions (indicated by the end-of-the-line stop). Find the line that will take you to your destination, and figure out roughly what direction (north, south, east, west) you'll need to go to get there.

In the Tube station, feed your ticket into the turnstile, reclaim it, and hang onto the ticket—you'll need it to get through the turnstile at the end of your journey. Find your train by following signs to your line and the (general) direction it's headed (such as Central Line: east).

Since some tracks are shared by several lines, you'll need to double-check before boarding a train: First, make sure your destination is one of the stops listed on the sign at the platform. Also, check the electronic signboards that announce which train is next, and make sure the destination (the end-of-the-line stop) is the one you want. Some trains, particularly on the Circle and District lines, split off for other directions, but each train has its final destination marked above its windshield. When in doubt, ask a local or a blue-vested staff person for help.

Trains run roughly every three to 10 minutes. If one train is absolutely packed and you notice another to the same destination is coming in three minutes, you can wait to avoid the sardine experience. The system can be fraught with construction delays and breakdowns, so pay attention to signs and announcements explaining necessary detours. The Circle Line is notorious for problems. Rush hours (8:00–10:00 and 16:00–19:00) can be packed and sweaty. Bring something to do to make your waiting time productive. If you get confused, ask for advice at the information window located before the turnstile entry.

You can't leave the system without feeding your ticket to the turnstile. Hang on to your ticket. (The turnstile will either eat your now-expired single-trip ticket, or spit your still-valid pass back out.) Save walking time by choosing the best street exit—check the maps on the walls or ask any station personnel. "Subway" means "pedestrian underpass" in "English." For Tube and bus information, visit www.tfl.gov.uk (and check out the journey planner). And always...mind the gap.

Cost: Any ride in Zone 1 (on or within the Circle Line, including virtually all my recommended sights and hotels) costs £2. Tube tickets are also valid on city buses.

You can avoid ticket-window lines in Tube stations by buying tickets from coin-op or credit-card machines; practice on the punchboard to see how the system works (hit "Adult Single" and your destination). These tickets are valid only on the day of purchase.

The fare for most rides in the center is £2. Go farther, and you owe more. Beware: Overshooting your zone nets you a £10 fine.

If you want to travel a little each day or if you're part of a group, a £17 **Carnet** (CAR-nay) saves £3: You get 10 separate tickets for Tube travel in Zone 1, paying £1.70 per ride rather than £2. Wait for the machine to lay all 10 tickets.

London Tube and Bus Passes: Consider using the following passes, valid on both the Tube and buses. Note that all passes can be purchased as easily as a normal ticket at any Tube station, can get you a 30 percent discount on most Thames cruises (details online at www.tfl.gov.uk, look under "Tickets and Oyster"), and

London at a Glance

▲▲▲British Museum The world's greatest collection of artifacts of Western civilization, including the Rosetta Stone and the Parthenon's Elgin Marbles. **Hours:** Daily 10:00–17:30, Thu–Fri until 20:30 but only a few galleries open after 17:30.

▲▲▲National Gallery Remarkable collection of European paintings (1250–1900), including Leonardo, Botticelli, Velázquez, Rembrandt, Turner, van Gogh, and the Impressionists. **Hours:** Daily 10:00–18:00, Wed until 21:00.

▲▲▲British Library Impressive collection of the most important literary treasures of the Western world, from the Magna Carta to Handel's *Messiah*. **Hours:** Mon–Fri 9:30–18:00, Tue until 20:00, Sat 9:30–17:00, Sun 11:00–17:00.

▲▲▲Westminster Abbey Britain's finest church and the site of royal coronations and burials since 1066. **Hours:** Mon–Fri 9:30–15:45, Wed also until 19:00, Sat 9:30–13:45, closed Sun to sightseers but open for services.

▲▲▲St. Paul's Cathedral The main cathedral of the Anglican Church, designed by Christopher Wren, with a climbable dome and daily evensong services. **Hours:** Mon–Sat 8:30–16:30, closed Sun except for worship.

▲▲▲Tower of London Historic castle, palace, and prison, today housing the crown jewels and a witty band of Beefeaters. **Hours:** March–Oct Tue–Sat 9:00–18:00, Sun–Mon 10:00–18:00; Nov–Feb Tue–Sat 9:00–17:00, Sun–Mon 10:00–17:00.

▲▲▲London Eye Ferris Wheel Enormous observation wheel, dominating—and offering commanding views over—London's skyline. **Hours:** April–mid-Sept daily 9:30–21:00, until 22:00 in July–Aug, mid-Sept–March daily 9:30–20:00, closed Jan.

▲▲▲Tate Modern Works by Monet, Matisse, Dalí, Picasso, and Warhol displayed in a converted powerhouse. **Hours:** Daily 10:00–18:00, Fri–Sat until 22:00.

▲▲▲Churchill Museum and Cabinet War Rooms Underground WWII headquarters of Churchill's war effort. **Hours:** Daily April–Sept 9:30–18:00, Oct–March 10:00–18:00.

▲▲Tate Britain Collection of British painting from the 16th century through modern times, including works by William

Blake, the Pre-Raphaelites, and J. M. W. Turner. **Hours:** Daily 10:00–17:50.

▲▲**Houses of Parliament** London's famous neo-Gothic landmark, topped by Big Ben and occupied by the Houses of Lords and Commons. **Hours** (both Houses): Generally Mon 14:30–22:30, Tue–Thu 11:30–19:30, Fri 9:30–15:00, closed Sat–Sun.

▲▲**Imperial War Museum** Examines the military history of the bloody 20th century. **Hours:** Daily 10:00–18:00.

▲▲**National Portrait Gallery** *Who's Who* of British history, featuring portraits of this nation's most important historical figures. **Hours:** Daily 10:00–18:00, Thu–Fri until 21:00.

▲▲**Buckingham Palace** Britain's royal residence with the famous Changing of the Guard. **Hours:** Palace—Aug–Sept only, daily 9:30–17:00; Guard—almost daily in summer at 11:30, every other day all year long.

▲▲**Shakespeare's Globe** Timbered, thatched-roofed reconstruction of the Bard's original wooden "O." **Hours:** Mid-May–Sept exhibition open daily 9:00–18:00, 30-minute tours go on the half-hour from 9:30 generally until 12:30, until 11:30 on Sun, 17:30 on Mon; Oct–mid-May exhibition open daily 10:00–17:00 with 30-min tours on the half-hour. Plays are also held here; see page 113.

▲▲**Victoria and Albert Museum** The best collection of decorative arts anywhere. **Hours:** Daily 10:00–17:45, Wed and last Fri of the month until 22:00 except mid-Dec–mid-Jan.

▲▲**Somerset House** Grand 18th-century civic palace housing three fine-art museums: Courtauld Gallery (decent painting collection), Hermitage Rooms (rotating exhibits from famous St. Petersburg museum), and the Gilbert Collection (decorative arts). **Hours:** Daily 10:00–18:00.

▲▲**Old Operating Theatre Museum** 19th-century hall where surgeons performed amputations for an audience of aspiring med students. **Hours:** Daily 10:30–17:00.

▲▲**Vinopolis: City of Wine** Offers a breezy history of wine with plenty of tasting opportunities. **Hours:** Daily 12:00–18:00, Fri–Sat and Mon until 21:00.

London for Early Birds and Night Owls

Most sightseeing in London is restricted to between 10:00 and 18:00. Here are a few exceptions:

Sights Open Early

British Library: Mon–Sat at 9:30.

Buckingham Palace: Aug–Sept daily at 9:30.

Churchill Museum and Cabinet War Rooms: April–Sept daily at 9:30.

Hampton Court Palace: Tue–Sun at 9:30.

Houses of Parliament: Fri at 9:30.

Kew Gardens: Daily at 9:30.

London Eye Ferris Wheel: Daily at 9:30.

Madame Tussaud's Waxworks: Sat–Sun at 9:30.

Shakespeare's Globe: Mid-May–Sept exhibition opens at 9:00, tours start at 9:30.

Southwark Cathedral: Mon–Fri at 8:00, Sat–Sun at 9:00.

St. Paul's Cathedral: Mon–Sat at 8:30.

Tower of London: Mon–Sat at 9:00 (Tue–Sat in winter).

Westminster Abbey: Mon–Sat at 9:30.

Westminster Cathedral: Daily at 9:30.

Sights Open Late

British Library: Tue until 20:00.

British Museum (some galleries): Thu–Fri until 20:30.

Houses of Parliament (when in session): Mon until 22:30, Tue–Thu until 19:30.

London Eye Ferris Wheel: Daily until 21:00 (22:00 in July–Aug, 20:00 in winter).

National Gallery: Wed until 21:00.

National Portrait Gallery: Thu–Fri until 21:00.

Saatchi Gallery: Mon–Thu until 20:00, Fri–Sat until 22:00.

Sir John Soane's Museum: First Tue of month until 21:00.

Tate Modern: Fri–Sat until 22:00.

Victoria and Albert Museum: Wed and last Fri of month until 22:00.

Vinopolis: Mon and Fri–Sat until 21:00.

come in a pricier all-zone version.

If you figure you'll take three rides in a day—and many travelers do—a day pass is a good deal. The **One-Day Travelcard,** covering Zones 1 and 2, gives you unlimited travel for a day. The regular price is £6, but an "Off-Peak" version is only £4.70; it's good for travel starting after 9:30 on weekdays and anytime on weekends. A One-Day Travelcard for Zones 1 through 6, which includes Heathrow Airport, costs £12; the restricted "Off-Peak" version (good for travel after 9:30 on weekdays and all day on weekends and holidays) costs £6. Families save with the One-Day Family Travelcard (good for 1–2 adults and 1–4 children, price varies depending on number in family and number of zones).

The **Three-Day Travelcard,** covering Zones 1 and 2 for £15, costs 20 percent less than three One-Day Travelcards and is good any time of day. Most travelers staying three days will easily take enough Tube and bus rides to make this worthwhile.

The **7-Day Travelcard** costs £21.40 and covers Zones 1 and 2.

Groups of 10 or more can travel all day on the Tube for £3.70 each (but not on buses).

You'll likely see signs advertising the **Oyster Card,** designed for commuters (or tourists staying a week or more). The prepaid, rechargeable pass is good for Tube and/or bus trips, depending on what version you buy. You'll pay a £3 deposit to use the card (refundable at any Tube station ticket office). For specifics, visit www.oystercard.com.

TOURS

▲▲▲**Hop-on, Hop-off Double-Decker Bus Tours**—Two competitive companies (Original and Big Bus) offer essentially the same tours with buses that have either live guides or a tape-recorded, dial-a-language narration. This two-hour, once-over-lightly bus tour drives by all the famous sights, providing a stress-free way to get your bearings and at least see the biggies. You can sit back and enjoy the entire two-hour orientation tour (a good idea if you like the guide and the weather), or hop on and hop off at any of the

nearly 30 stops and catch a later bus. Buses run about every 10–15 minutes in summer, every 20 minutes in winter. It's an inexpensive form of transport as well as an informative tour. Buses operate daily (from about 9:00 until early evening in summer, until late afternoon in winter) and stop at Victoria Station, Marble Arch, Piccadilly Circus,

Daily Reminder

Sunday: Some sights don't open until noon. The Tower of London and British Museum are both especially crowded today. Hyde Park Speakers' Corner rants from early afternoon until early evening. These places are closed: Banqueting House, Sir John Soane's Museum, and legal sights (Houses of Parliament, City Hall, and Old Bailey; the neighborhood called The City is dead). Evensong is at 15:00 at Westminster Abbey (plus free organ recital at 17:45) and 15:15 at St. Paul's (plus free organ recital at 17:00); both churches are open during the day for worship but closed to sightseers. Many stores are closed. There are no plays on Sunday as actors take a day off. Street markets flourish: Camden Lock, Spitalfields, Greenwich, and Petticoat Lane.

Monday: Virtually all sights are open except for Apsley House, the Theatre Museum, Sir John Soane's Museum, and a few others. The St. Martin-in-the-Fields church offers a free 13:00 concert. At Somerset House, the Courtauld Gallery is free until 14:00. Vinopolis is open until 21:00. Houses of Parliament are usually open until 22:30.

Tuesday: All sights are open; the British Library is open until 20:00. St. Martin-in-the-Fields has a free 13:00 concert. On the first Tuesday of the month, St. John Soane's Museum is also open 18:00–21:00.

Wednesday: All sights are open, plus evening hours at Westminster Abbey (until 19:00, but no evensong), the

Trafalgar Square, and elsewhere.

Both Original and Big Bus offer a core two-hour overview tour, two other routes, and a narrated Thames boat tour covered by the same ticket (buy ticket from driver, credit cards accepted at major stops such as Victoria Station, ticket good for 24 hours, bring a sweater and a camera). Big Bus tours are a little better but more expensive (£20), while Original tours are cheaper (£13.50 with this book) and nearly as good. Pick up a map from any flier rack or from one of the countless salespeople and study the complex system. Note: If you start at Victoria Station at 9:00, you'll finish near Buckingham Palace in time to see the Changing of the Guard at 11:30; ask your driver for the best place to hop off. Sunday morning—when the traffic is light and many museums are closed—is a fine time for a tour. The last full loop leaves Victoria at 17:00. Both companies have entertaining as well as boring guides. The narration is important. If you don't like your guide, jump off and find another. If you like your guide, settle in for the entire loop. Unless you're using the bus tour mainly for hop-on, hop-off transportation,

National Gallery (until 21:00), and Victoria and Albert Museum (until 22:00).

Thursday: All sights are open, British Museum until 20:30 (selected galleries), National Portrait Gallery until 21:00. St. Martin-in-the-Fields hosts a 19:30 evening concert (for a fee).

Friday: All sights are open, British Museum until 20:30 (selected galleries only), National Portrait Gallery until 21:00, Vinopolis until 21:00, Tate Modern and Saatchi Gallery until 22:00. Best street market: Spitalfields. St. Martin-in-the-Fields offers two concerts (13:00-free, 19:30-fee).

Saturday: Most sights are open except legal ones (Old Bailey, City Hall, Houses of Parliament—open summer Sat for tours only; skip The City). Vinopolis is open until 21:00, Tate Modern and Saatchi Gallery until 22:00. Best street markets: Portobello, Camden Lock, Greenwich. Evensong is at 15:00 at Westminster Abbey, 17:00 at St. Paul's. St. Martin-in-the-Fields hosts a concert at 19:30 (fee).

Notes: Evensong occurs daily at St. Paul's (Mon–Sat at 17:00 and Sun at 15:15) and daily except Wednesday at Westminster Abbey (Mon–Tue and Thu–Fri at 17:00, Sat–Sun at 15:00). London by Night Sightseeing Tour buses leave from Victoria Station every evening at 19:30 and 21:30. The London Eye Ferris Wheel spins nightly until 21:00, until 22:00 in summer, until 20:00 in winter (closed Jan).

consider saving money with a night tour (described below).

Original London Sightseeing Bus Tour: Live-guided buses have a Union Jack flag and a yellow triangle on the front of the bus. If the front has many flags or a green or red triangle, it's a tape-recorded multilingual tour—avoid it, unless you have kids who'd enjoy the entertaining recorded kids' tour (£16, £2.50 discount with this book, limit 2 discounts per book, they'll rip off the corner of this page—raise bloody hell if they don't honor this discount, ticket good for 24 hours, tel. 020/8877-1722, www.theoriginaltour.com). Your ticket includes a 50-minute round-trip boat tour from Westminster Pier (departs hourly, tape-recorded narration) or a point-to-point boat trip from Embankment Pier to Greenwich, with stops in between (14 departures per day).

Big Bus Hop-on, Hop-off London Tours: For £20 (£18 if you book online), you get the same basic tour plus coupons for several silly one-hour London walks and the scenic and usually entertainingly guided Thames boat ride (normally £5.60) between Westminster Pier and the Tower of London. The pass and extras are valid for 24 hours. Buses with live guides are marked in front with a picture of a red bus; buses with tape-recorded spiels display a picture of a blue bus and headphones. These pricier tours tend to have better, more dynamic guides than Original (daily 8:30–18:00, winter until 16:30, from Victoria Station, tel. 020/7233-9533, www .bigbus.co.uk).

At Night: The London by Night Sightseeing Tour runs basically the same circuit as the other companies, but after hours, with none of the extras (e.g., walks, boat tours), and for half the price. While the narration can be pretty lame, the views at twilight are grand (£9, pay driver or buy tickets at Victoria Station or Paddington Station TI, April–Sept only, 2-hour tour with live guide, normally departs 19:30–21:30 every half hour from Victoria Station, live guides at 19:30, 20:30, and 21:30, Taxi Road, at front of station near end of Wilton Road, tel. 020/8646-1747, www .london-by-night.net). Munch a scenic picnic dinner from the top deck for a memorable and economical evening.

▲▲**Walking Tours**—Several times a day, top-notch local guides lead (often big) groups through specific slices of London's past. Schedule fliers litter the desks of TIs, hotels, and pubs. *Time Out* lists many, but not all, scheduled walks. Simply show up at the announced location, pay £5.50, and enjoy two chatty hours of Dickens, the Plague, Shakespeare, Legal London, the Beatles, Jack the Ripper, or whatever is on the agenda. Original London Walks, the dominant company, lists its extensive daily schedule in a beefy, plain, black-and-white *The Original London Walks* brochure (walks offered year-round—even Christmas, private tours for £95, tel. 020/7624-3978, for a recorded listing of today's walks call 020/7624-9255, www.walks.com). They also run **Explorer day trips,** a good option for those with limited time and transportation (different trip daily: Stonehenge/Salisbury, Oxford/Cotswolds, York, Bath, and so on).

The Beatles: Fans of the still–Fab Four can take one of the Beatles walks (Original London Walks, above, has 5/week; Big Bus, above, has a daily walk included with their bus tour), visit the Beatles Shop (daily, 231 Baker Street, next to Sherlock Holmes Museum, Tube: Baker Street, tel. 020/7935-4464), or go to Abbey Road and walk the famous crosswalk (at intersection with Grove End, Tube: St. John's Wood).

Private Guides—Standard rates for London's registered guides are £100 for four hours, £159 for eight hours (tel. 020/7403-2962, www.touristguides.org.uk, www.blue-badge.org.uk). Robina Brown leads tours of small groups in her Toyota Previa (£220/half-day, £320–400/day, tel. 020/7228-2238, www.driverguidetours .com, robina@driverguidetours.com). Janine Barton provides a similar driver-and-guide tour and similar prices (tel. 020/7402-4600, jbsiis@aol.com) and offers a 15 percent discount to readers of this book. Robina and Janine's services are particularly helpful for wheelchair-bound travelers who want to see more of London. Brit Lonsdale, an energetic mother of twins, is another registered London guide (£100/half-day, £159/day, tel. 020/7386-9907, brittl @ntlworld.com).

London Duck Tours—A bright-yellow amphibious WWII-vintage vehicle (the model that landed troops on Normandy's beaches on D-Day) takes a gang of 30 tourists past some famous sights on land—Big Ben, Trafalgar Square, Piccadilly Circus—then splashes into the Thames for a cruise (£18, 2/hr, daily 10:00–17:30, 75 min—45 min on land and 30 min in the river, these book up in advance, departs from Chicheley Street—you'll see the big ugly vehicle parked 100 yards behind London Eye Ferris Wheel, Tube: Waterloo or Westminster, tel. 020/7928-3132, www.londonducktours .co.uk). All-in-all, it's good fun at a rather steep price; the live guide works hard and it's kid-friendly to the point of goofiness.

▲▲Cruises—Boat tours with entertaining commentaries sail regularly from many points along the Thames. It's confusing, since there are several companies offering essentially the same thing. Your basic options are downstream (to the Tower and Greenwich), upstream (to Kew Gardens and Hampton Court), and round-trip scenic tour cruises. Most people depart from the Westminster Pier (at the base of Westminster Bridge under Big Ben). You can catch most of the same boats (with less waiting) from Waterloo Pier at the London Eye Ferris Wheel across the river. For pleasure and efficiency, consider combining a one-way cruise (to Kew, Greenwich, or wherever) with a Tube ride back. While Tube and bus tickets don't work on the boats, a Travelcard can snare you a 33 percent discount on most cruises (just show the card when you pay for the cruise). Children and seniors get discounts. You can purchase drinks and scant, pricey snacks on board. Buy boat tickets at the small ticket offices on the docks. Clever budget travelers pack a small picnic and munch while they cruise.

Here are some of the most popular cruise options:

To the Tower of London: City Cruises boats sail 30 minutes to the Tower from Westminster Pier (£5.60 one-way, £6.80 round-trip, one-way included with Big Bus London tour; covered by £9 "River Red Rover" ticket that includes Greenwich—see next paragraph; 3/hr during June–Aug daily 9:40–20:40, 2/hr and shorter hours rest of year).

To Greenwich: Two companies head to Greenwich from Westminster Pier. Choose between **City Cruises** (£6.80 one-way, £8.60 round-trip; or get their £9 all-day, hop-on, hop-off "River Red Rover" ticket to have option of getting off at London Eye and Tower of London; June–Aug daily 10:00–17:00, less off-season, every 40

Thames Boat Piers

While Westminster Pier is the most popular, it's not the only dock in town. Consider all the options:

Westminster Pier, at the base of Big Ben, offers round-trip sightseeing cruises and lots of departures in both directions.

Waterloo Pier, at the base of London Eye Ferris Wheel, is a good, less-crowded alternative to Westminster, with many of the same cruise options.

Embankment Pier is near Covent Garden, Trafalgar Square, and Cleopatra's Needle (the obelisk on the Thames). You can take a round-trip cruise from here, or catch a boat to the Tower of London and Greenwich.

Tower Millennium Pier is at the Tower of London. Boats sail west to Westminster Pier or east to Greenwich.

Bankside Pier (near Tate Modern and Shakespeare's Globe) and **Millbank Pier** (near Tate Britain) are connected to each other by the "Tate to Tate" ferry service.

min, 70 min to Greenwich, usually narrated only downstream—to Greenwich, tel. 020/7740-0400, www.citycruises.com) and **Thames River Services** (£6.80 one-way, £8.60 round-trip, April–Oct daily 10:00–16:00, July–Aug until 17:00, has shorter hours and runs every 40 min off-season, 2/hr, 50 min, usually narrated only to Greenwich, tel. 020/7930-4097, www.westminsterpier.co.uk).

To Kew Gardens: Westminster Passenger Services Association leaves for Kew Gardens from Westminster Pier (£11 one-way, £17 round-trip, 4/day, generally departing 10:30–14:00, 90 min, narrated for 45 min, tel. 020/7930-2062, www.wpsa .co.uk). Some boats continue on to **Hampton Court Palace** for an additional £3 (and 90 min). Because of the river current, you'll save 30 minutes cruising from Hampton Court back into town.

Round-Trip Cruises: Fifty-minute round-trip cruises of the Thames go hourly from Westminster Pier to the Tower of London (£8, included with Original London Bus tour—listed above, tape-recorded narration, Catamaran Circular Cruises, tel. 020/7987-1185). The London Eye Ferris Wheel operates its own "River Cruise Experience," offering a similar 40-minute live-guided circular tour from Waterloo Pier (£10, £21 with Ferris Wheel, reservations recommended, departures generally :45 past hour, tel. 0870-443-9185, www.ba-londoneye.com).

From Tate to Tate: This boat service for art-lovers connects the Tate Modern and Tate Britain in 18 scenic minutes, stopping at the London Eye Ferris Wheel en route (£4 one-way or £7 for a day ticket; with a Travelcard it's £2.70-one-way/£4.50-day ticket; buy ticket at gallery desk or on board, departing every 40 min from 10:00–17:00, tel. 020/7887-8008).

On Regent's Canal: Consider exploring London's canals by taking a cruise on historic Regent's Canal in north London. The good ship *Jenny Wren* offers 90-minute guided canal boat cruises from Walker's Quay in Camden Town through scenic Regent's Park to Little Venice (£7, March–Oct daily 12:30 and 14:30, Sat–Sun also at 16:30, Walker's Quay, 250 Camden High Street, 3-min walk from Tube: Camden Town, tel. 020/7485-6210, www.walkersquay .com). While in Camden Town, stop by the popular, punky Camden Lock Market to browse through trendy arts and crafts (daily 10:00–18:00, busiest on weekends, a block from Walker's Quay).

SELF-GUIDED WALK

Westminster Walk

Just about every visitor to London strolls the historic Whitehall boulevard from Big Ben to Trafalgar Square. Beneath London's modern traffic and big-city bustle lies 2,000 fascinating years of history. This three-quarter-mile, self-guided orientation walk (see map on page 68) gives you a whirlwind tour and connects the sights listed in this section.

Start halfway across **Westminster Bridge** (❶) for that "Wow, I'm really in London!" feeling. Get a close-up view of the **Houses of Parliament** and **Big Ben** (floodlit at night). Downstream you'll see the **London Eye Ferris Wheel.** Down the stairs to Westminster Pier are boats to the Tower of London and Greenwich.

En route to Parliament Square, you'll pass a **statue of Boadicea** (❷), the Celtic queen defeated by Roman invaders in A.D. 60.

To thrill your loved ones (or bug the envious), call home from a pay phone near Big Ben at about three minutes before the hour. You'll find a phone on Great George Street, across from **Parliament Square.** As Big Ben chimes, stick the receiver outside the booth and prove you're in London: Ding dong ding dong... dong ding ding dong.

Wave hello to Churchill in Parliament Square (❸). To his right is **Westminster Abbey** with its two stubby, elegant towers.

Walk north up Parliament Street (which turns into Whitehall) toward Trafalgar Square. You'll see the thought-provoking **Cenotaph** (❹) in the middle of the street, reminding passersby

Westminster Walk

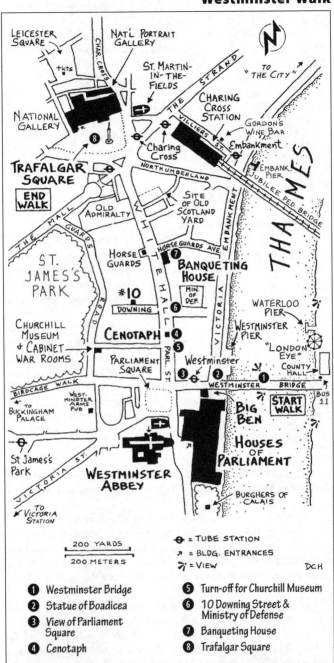

200 YARDS

200 METERS

⊕ = TUBE STATION

↗ = BLDG. ENTRANCES

⤗ = VIEW

DCH

❶ Westminster Bridge

❷ Statue of Boadicea

❸ View of Parliament Square

❹ Cenotaph

❺ Turn-off for Churchill Museum

❻ 10 Downing Street & Ministry of Defense

❼ Banqueting House

❽ Trafalgar Square

of Britain's many war dead. To visit the Churchill Museum and Cabinet War Rooms (see below), take a left before the Cenotaph, on King Charles Street (**❺**).

Continuing on Whitehall, stop at the barricaded and guarded **#10 Downing Street** to see the British "White House" (**❻**), home of the prime minister. Break the bobby's boredom and ask him a question.

Nearing Trafalgar Square, look for the **Horse Guards** behind the gated fence (Changing of the Horse Guards Mon–Sat 11:00, Sun at 10:00, dismounting ceremony daily at 16:00) and the 17th-century **Banqueting House** across the street (**❼**; described below).

The column topped by Lord Nelson marks **Trafalgar Square** (**❽**). The stately domed building on the far side of the square is the **National Gallery** (free) which has a classy café upstairs in the Sainsbury wing. To the right of the National Gallery is **St. Martin-in-the-Fields Church** and its Café in the Crypt.

To get to Piccadilly from Trafalgar Square, walk up Cockspur Street to Haymarket, then take a short left on Coventry Street to colorful **Piccadilly Circus.**

Near Piccadilly you'll find the **Britain and London Visitors Centre** (on Lower Regent Street) and piles of theaters. **Leicester Square** (with its half-price "tkts" booth for plays, see page 111) thrives just a few blocks away. Walk through seedy **Soho** (north of Shaftesbury Avenue) for its fun pubs (see "Eating," page 137, for "Food is Fun" Dinner Crawl). From Piccadilly or Oxford Circus, you can take a taxi, bus, or the Tube home.

SIGHTS

Westminster Abbey

As the greatest church in the English-speaking world (worth ▲▲▲), Westminster Abbey has been the place where England's kings and queens have been crowned and buried since 1066. A thousand years of English history—3,000 tombs, the remains of 29 kings and queens, and hundreds of memorials—lie within its walls and under its stone slabs. Like a stony refugee camp huddled outside St. Peter's Pearly Gates, this place has a story to tell and the best way to

enjoy it is with a **tour** (audioguide-£3, live guide-£4; many prefer the audioguide because it's self-paced).

Three tiny **museums** ring the cloisters: the Chapter House (where the monks held their daily meetings, notable for its fine architecture and well-described but faded medieval art), the Pyx Chamber (containing an exhibit on the king's treasury), and the Abbey Museum (which tells of the abbey's history, royal coronations, and burials). Look into the impressively realistic eyes of Henry VII's funeral effigy (one of a fascinating series of wax-and-wood statues that, for 3 centuries, graced royal coffins during funeral processions).

Experience an **evensong** service—awesome in a nearly empty church (weekdays except Wed at 17:00, Sat–Sun at 15:00). The 40-minute **free organ recital** on Sunday at 17:45 is another highlight. Organ concerts (different from the Sunday recital) held here are great and inexpensive; look for signs with schedule details (or visit www.westminster-abbey.org).

Cost, Hours, Information: £8, includes cloisters and Abbey Museum; abbey open Mon–Fri 9:30–15:45, Wed until 19:00, Sat 9:30–13:45, last entry 60 min before closing, closed Sun to sightseers but open for services; cloisters open daily 8:00–18:00; Abbey Museum daily 10:30–16:00. Photography is prohibited. (Tube: Westminster or St. James's Park, call for tour schedule, tel. 020/7222-7110.)

The main entrance, on the Parliament Square side, often has a sizable line; visit early or late to avoid tourist hordes. Midmornings are most crowded. On weekdays after 15:00 it's less crowded; come then and stay for the 17:00 evensong (except Wed). Since the church is often closed to the public for special services, it's wise to call first.

For a free peek inside and a quiet sit in the nave, you can tell a marshal at the west end (where the tourists exit) that you'd like to pay your respects to Britain's Unknown Soldier. If the marshal is nice, he might let you slip in.

Between the Abbey and Trafalgar Square

▲▲**Houses of Parliament (Palace of Westminster)**—This neo-Gothic icon of London, the royal residence from 1042 to 1547, is now the meeting place of the legislative branch of government. Tourists are welcome to view debates in either the bickering House of Commons or the genteel House of Lords (in session when a flag flies atop the Victoria Tower). While the actual debates are generally extremely dull, it is a thrill to be inside and see the British government inaction (both Houses usually open Mon 14:30–22:30, Tue–Thu 11:30–19:30, Fri 9:30–15:00, closed Sat–Sun, generally less action and no lines after 18:00, use St. Stephen's entrance, Tube:

Westminster, tel. 020/7219-4272 for schedule, www.parliament .uk). The House of Lords has more pageantry, shorter lines, and less interesting debates (tel. 020/7219-3107 for schedule, and visit www.parliamentlive.tv for a preview). If there's only one line outside, it's for the House of Commons. Go to the gate and tell the guard you want the Lords (that's the 2nd "line" with no people in it; it just takes a few minutes and both are worth seeing). You may pop right in—that is, after you've cleared the security gauntlet. Once you've seen the Lords (hide your HOL flier), you can often slip directly over to the House of Commons and join the gang waiting in the lobby. Inside the lobby, you'll find an announcement board with the day's lineup for both houses.

Just past security to the left, study the big dark **Westminster Hall,** which survived the 1834 fire. The hall was built in the 11th century and its famous self-supporting hammer-beam roof was added in 1397. The Houses of Parliament are located in what was once the Palace of Westminster, long the palace of England's medieval kings, until it was largely destroyed by fire in 1834. The palace was rebuilt in the Victorian Gothic style (a move away from neoclassicism back to England's Christian and medieval heritage, true to the Romantic age). It was completed in 1860.

Houses of Parliament tours are offered in August and September (£7, 75 min; roughly Mon, Tue, Fri, and Sat 9:15–16:30; Wed and Thu 13:15–16:30; to avoid waits, book in advance through First Call, tel. 0870-906-3773, www.firstcalltickets.com, no booking fee). Meet your Blue Badge guide (at the Sovereign's Entrance—far south end) for a behind-the-scenes peek at the royal chambers and both Houses.

The **Jewel Tower** is the only other part of the old Palace of Westminster to survive (besides Westminster Hall). It contains a fine little exhibit on Parliament (1st floor—history; 2nd floor—Parliament today) with a 25-minute video and lonely, picnic-friendly benches (£2, April–Sept daily 10:00–17:00, across street from St. Stephen's Gate, tel. 020/7222-2219).

Big Ben, the clock tower (315 feet high), is named for its 13-ton bell, Ben. The light above the clock is lit when the House of Commons is sitting. The face of the clock is huge—you can actually see the minute hand moving. For a good view of it, walk halfway over Westminster Bridge.

▲▲▲**Churchill Museum and Cabinet War Rooms**—This is a fascinating walk through the underground headquarters of the British government's fight against the Nazis in the darkest days of the Battle for Britain. The 27-room nerve center of the British war effort was used from 1939 to 1945. Churchill's room, the map room, and other rooms are just as they were in 1945. For details on all the blood, sweat, toil, and tears, pick up the excellent and included audioguide

at the entry and punch in codes as you go to hear about each display. Don't bypass the new Churchill Museum (entrance is a half-dozen rooms into the exhibit), giving a human look at the man behind the famous cigar, bowler hat, and V-for-victory sign. It shows his wit, irascibility, work ethic, American ties, writing talents, and drinking habits. A long touch-the-screen timeline lets you zero in on events in his life from birth (Nov 30, 1874) to his election as prime minister in 1940. It's all the more amazing considering that, in the 1930s, the man who became my vote for greatest statesman of the 20th century was considered a washed-up loony ranting about the growing threat of fascism (£10, daily 9:30–18:00, last entry 60 min before closing, on King Charles Street, 200 yards off Whitehall, follow the signs, Tube: Westminster, tel. 020/7930-6961, www.iwm.org.uk). The shop is great for anyone nostalgic for the 1940s.

If you're hungry, get your rations at the Switch Room café (in the museum) or, for a nearby pub lunch, try the Westminster Arms (food served downstairs, on Storeys Gate, a couple of blocks south of War Rooms).

Horse Guards—The Horse Guards change daily at 11:00 (10:00 on Sun), and there's a colorful dismounting ceremony daily at 16:00. The rest of the day, they just stand there—terrible for camcorders (on Whitehall, between Trafalgar Square and #10 Downing Street, Tube: Westminster). While Buckingham Palace pageantry is canceled when it rains, the horse guards change regardless of the weather.

▲**Banqueting House**—England's first Renaissance building was designed by Inigo Jones in about 1620. It's one of the few London landmarks spared by the 1698 fire and the only surviving part of the original Palace of Whitehall. Don't miss its Rubens ceiling, which, at

Charles I's request, drove home the doctrine of the legitimacy of the divine right of kings. In 1649—divine right ignored—Charles I was beheaded on the balcony of this building by a Cromwellian Parliament. Admission includes a restful 20-minute audiovisual history, which shows the place in banqueting action; a 30-minute audio tour—interesting only to history buffs; and a look at the exquisite banqueting hall (£4, Mon–Sat 10:00–17:00, closed Sun, last entry at 16:30, subject to closure for government functions, aristocratic WC, immediately across Whitehall from the Horse Guards, Tube: Westminster, tel. 020/7930-4179). Just up the street is Trafalgar Square.

Trafalgar Square

Trafalgar Square

▲▲**Trafalgar Square**—London's recently renovated central square, the climax of most marches and demonstrations, is a thrilling place to simply hang out. Lord Nelson stands atop his 185-foot-tall fluted granite column, gazing out to Trafalgar, where he lost his life but defeated the French fleet. Part of this 1842 memorial is made from his victims' melted-down cannons. He's surrounded by giant lions, hordes of people, and—until recently—even more pigeons. London's mayor, Ken Livingstone, nicknamed "Red Ken" for his passion for an activist government, decided that London's "flying rats" were a public nuisance and evicted the venerable seed salesmen (Tube: Charing Cross).

▲▲▲**National Gallery**—Displaying Britain's top collection of European paintings from 1250 to 1900—including works by

National Gallery Highlights

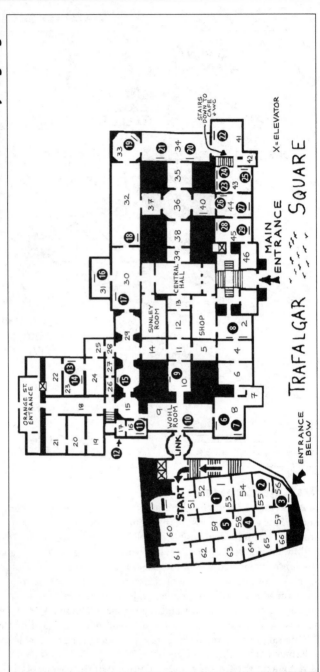

MEDIEVAL & EARLY RENAISSANCE

1 Wilton Diptych
2 UCCELLO – Battle of San Romano
3 VAN EYCK – The Arnolfini Marriage

ITALIAN RENAISSANCE

4 BOTTICELLI – Venus and Mars
5 CRIVELLI – The Annunciation with St. Emidius

HIGH RENAISSANCE

6 MICHELANGELO – Entombment
7 RAPHAEL – Pope Julius II
8 LEONARDO DA VINCI – The Virgin of the Rocks; Virgin and Child with St. John the Baptist and St. Anne

VENETIAN RENAISSANCE

9 TITIAN – Bacchus and Ariadne
10 TINTORETTO – The Origin of the Milky Way

NORTHERN PROTESTANT ART

11 VERMEER – A Young Woman
12 "A PEEPSHOW"
13 REMBRANDT – Belshazzar's Feast
14 REMBRANDT – Self-Portrait

BAROQUE & ROCOCO

15 RUBENS – The Judgment of Paris
16 VAN DYCK – Charles I on Horseback
17 VELÁZQUEZ – The Rokeby Venus
18 CARAVAGGIO – The Supper at Emmaus
19 BOUCHER – Pan and Syrinx

BRITISH

20 CONSTABLE – The Hay Wain
21 TURNER – The Fighting Téméraire
22 DELAROCHE – The Execution of Lady Jane Grey

IMPRESSIONISM & BEYOND

23 MONET – Gare St. Lazare
24 MONET – The Water-Lily Pond
25 MANET – The Waitress (Corner of a Café-Concert)
26 RENOIR – Boating on the Seine
27 SEURAT – Bathers at Asnières
28 VAN GOGH – Sunflowers
29 CEZANNE – Bathers

Leonardo, Botticelli, Velázquez, Rembrandt, Turner, van Gogh, and the Impressionists—this is one of Europe's great galleries. While the collection is huge, following the route suggested on the map on page 74 will give you my best quick visit. The audioguide tours (suggested £4 donation) are the best I've used in Europe. On the first floor, the "Art Start" computer room lets you study any artist, style, or topic in the museum, and print out a tailor-made tour map.

In 2006, the new main entrance will open, offering visitors a grand first impression of Britain's greatest collection of paintings.

Cost, Hours, Information: Free, daily 10:00–18:00, Wed until 21:00, free one-hour overview tours daily at 11:30 and 14:30 plus Wed at 18:00 and 18:30. Photography is prohibited. It's on Trafalgar Square (Tube: Charing Cross or Leicester Square, tel. 020/7839-3321, www.nationalgallery.org.uk).

▲▲**National Portrait Gallery**—Put off by halls of 19th-century characters who meant nothing to me, I used to call this "as interesting as someone else's yearbook." But a selective walk through this 500-year-long *Who's Who* of British history is quick and free and puts faces on the story of England. A bonus is the chance to admire some great art by painters such as Holbein, Van Dyck, Hogarth, Reynolds, and Gainsborough. The collection is well-described, not huge, and in historical sequence, from the 16th century on the second floor to today's royal family on the ground floor.

Some highlights: Henry VIII and wives; several fascinating portraits of the "Virgin Queen" Elizabeth I, Sir Francis Drake, and Sir Walter Raleigh; the only real-life portrait of William Shakespeare; Oliver Cromwell and Charles I with his head on; self-portraits and other portraits by Gainsborough and Reynolds; the Romantics (Blake, Byron, Wordsworth, and company); Queen Victoria and her era; and the present royal family, including the late Princess Diana.

The excellent audioguide tours (free, but £2 donation requested) describe each room (or era in British history) and more than 300 paintings. You'll learn more about British history than art and actually hear interviews with 20th-century subjects as you stare at their faces.

Cost, Hours, Information: Free, daily 10:00–18:00, Thu–Fri until 21:00. It's 100 yards off Trafalgar Square (around corner from National Gallery, opposite Church of St. Martin-in-the-Fields, Tube: Charing Cross or Leicester Square, tel. 020/7306-0055, www.npg.org.uk). The elegant Portrait Restaurant on the top floor comes with views and high prices; the cheaper Portrait Café is in the basement.

▲**St. Martin-in-the-Fields**—This church, built in the 1720s with a Gothic spire atop a Greek-type temple, is an oasis of peace on the wild and noisy Trafalgar Square (free, donations welcome, open daily, Tube: Charing Cross, www.smitf.com). St. Martin cared for the poor. "In the fields" was where the first church stood on this spot (in the 13th century), between Westminster and the City. Stepping inside, you still feel a compassion for the needs of the people in this community. A free flier provides a brief yet worthwhile self-guided tour. The church is famous for its concerts. Consider a free lunchtime concert (Mon, Tue, and Fri at 13:00) or an evening concert (£8–18, at 19:30 Thu–Sat and on some Tue and Wed, box office tel. 020/7839-8362, church tel. 020/7766-1100). Downstairs, you'll find a ticket office for concerts, a gift shop, a brass-rubbing center, and a fine support-the-church cafeteria (see page 130).

More Top Squares: Piccadilly, Soho, and Covent Garden

For a "Food is Fun" dinner crawl from Covent Garden to Soho, see "Eating," page 137.

▲▲**Piccadilly Circus**—London's most touristy square got its name from the fancy ruffled shirts—*picadils*—made in the neighborhood long ago. Today, the square, while pretty grotty, is surrounded by fascinating streets swimming with youth on the rampage. For over-stimulation, drop by the extremely trashy **Pepsi Trocadero Center's** "theme park of the future" for its Segaworld virtual-reality games, nine-screen cinema, and thundering IMAX theater (admission to Trocadero is free; individual attractions cost £2–8; before paying full price for IMAX, look for a discount ticket at brochure racks at the TI or hotels; located between Coventry and Shaftesbury, just off Piccadilly, Tube: Piccadilly Circus). Chinatown, to the east, has swollen since the British colony of Hong Kong was returned to China in 1997. Nearby Shaftesbury Avenue and Leicester Square teem with fun-seekers, theaters, Chinese restaurants, and street singers.

Soho—North of Piccadilly, seedy Soho is becoming trendy and is well worth a gawk. But Soho is also London's red light district, where "friendly models" wait in tiny rooms up dreary stairways and voluptuous con artists sell strip shows. While venturing up a stairway to check out a model is interesting, anyone who goes into any one of the shows will be ripped off. Every time. Even a £5 show in a "licensed bar" comes with a £100 cover or minimum (as it's printed on the drink menu) and a "security man." You may

London's Top Squares

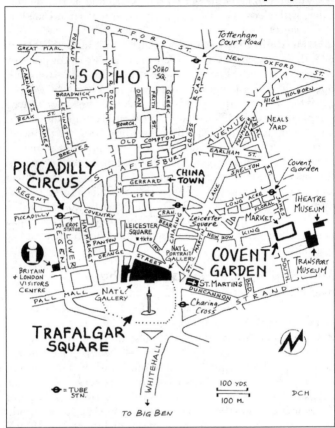

accidentally buy a £200 bottle of bubbly. And suddenly, the door has no handle.

Telephone sex is hard to avoid these days in London. Phone booths are littered with racy fliers of busty ladies "new in town." Some travelers gather six or eight phone booths' worth of fliers and take them home for kinky wallpaper.

▲▲Covent Garden—This boutique-ish shopping district is a people-watcher's delight, with cigarette eaters, Punch-and-Judy acts, food that's good for you (but not your wallet), trendy crafts, sweet whiffs of marijuana, two-tone hair (neither natural), and faces that could set off a metal detector (Tube: Covent Garden). For better Covent Garden lunch deals, walk a block or two away from the eye of this touristic hurricane (check out the places north of the Tube station along Endell and Neal Streets).

Museums near Covent Garden

▲▲**Somerset House**—This grand 18th-century civic palace offers a marvelous public space, three fine art collections, and a river-

side terrace (between the Strand and the Thames). The palace once housed the national registry that records Britain's births, marriages, and deaths, "...where they hatch 'em, match 'em, and dispatch 'em." Step into the courtyard to enjoy the fountain. Go ahead...walk through it. The 55 jets get playful twice an hour. (In the winter, this becomes a popular ice-skating rink with a toasty café for viewing.)

Surrounding you are three small and sumptuous sights: the Courtauld Gallery (paintings), the Gilbert Collection (fine arts), and the Hermitage Rooms (the art of czarist Russia). All three are open the same hours (daily 10:00–18:00, last entry 17:15, £5 per sight, £8 for any 2 sights, £12 for all 3, easy bus #6, #9, #11, #13, #15, or #23 from Trafalgar Square, Tube: Temple or Covent Garden, tel. 020/7848-2526 or 020/7845-4600, www.somerset-house .org.uk). The Web site lists a busy schedule of tours, kids' events, and concerts. The riverside terrace is picnic-friendly (deli inside lobby).

The **Courtauld Gallery** is less impressive than the National Gallery, but its wonderful collection of paintings is still a joy. The gallery is part of the Courtauld Institute of Art, and the thought-ful description of each piece of art reminds visitors that the gallery is still used for teaching. You'll see medieval European paintings and works by Rubens, the Impressionists (Manet, Monet, Degas), Post-Impressionists (such as Cézanne), and more (£5, free Mon until 14:00, downstairs cafeteria, lockers, and WC).

The **Hermitage Rooms** offer a taste of Romanov imperial splendor. As Russia struggles and tourists are staying away, some-one had the bright idea of sending the best of its art to London to raise some hard cash. These five rooms host a different collection every six months, with a standard intro to the czar's winter palace in St. Petersburg (£5, tel. 020/7420-9410). To see what's on, visit www.somerset-house.org.uk/attractions/hermitage.

The **Gilbert Collection** displays 800 pieces of the finest in European decorative arts, from diamond-studded gold snuffboxes to intricate Italian mosaics. Maybe you've seen Raphael paintings and Botticelli frescoes...but this lush collection is refreshingly dif-ferent (£5, includes free audioguide with a highlights tour and a helpful loaner magnifying glass).

Central London

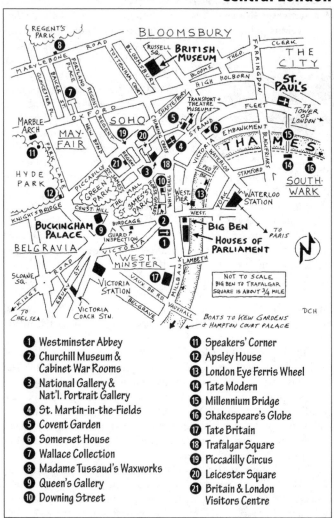

1 Westminster Abbey
2 Churchill Museum & Cabinet War Rooms
3 National Gallery & Nat'l. Portrait Gallery
4 St. Martin-in-the-Fields
5 Covent Garden
6 Somerset House
7 Wallace Collection
8 Madame Tussaud's Waxworks
9 Queen's Gallery
10 Downing Street
11 Speakers' Corner
12 Apsley House
13 London Eye Ferris Wheel
14 Tate Modern
15 Millennium Bridge
16 Shakespeare's Globe
17 Tate Britain
18 Trafalgar Square
19 Piccadilly Circus
20 Leicester Square
21 Britain & London Visitors Centre

▲London Transport Museum—This wonderful museum is a delight for kids. Whether you're cursing or marveling at the buses and Tube, the growth of Europe's biggest city has been made possible by its public transit system. Watch the growth of the Tube, then sit in the simulator to "drive" a train (£6, kids under 16 free, Sat–Thu 10:00-18:00, Fri 11:00–18:00, in southeast corner of Covent Garden courtyard, Tube: Covent Garden, tel. 020/7379-6344 or recorded info 020/7565-7299).

North London

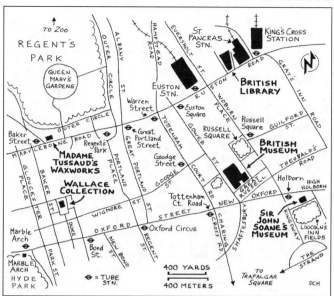

Theatre Museum—This earnest museum traces British theater from Shakespeare to today (free, Tue–Sun 10:00–18:00, closed Mon, free guided tours at 12:00 and 14:00, a block east of Covent Garden's marketplace down Russell Street, Tube: Covent Garden, tel. 020/7943-4700, www.theatremuseum.org.uk).

North London
▲▲▲British Museum, Great Court, and Reading Room—
Simply put, this is the greatest chronicle of civilization...anywhere. A visit here is like taking a long hike through Encyclopedia Britannica National Park. Entering on Great Russell Street, you'll step into the Great Court, the glass-domed hub of a two-acre cultural complex, containing restaurants, shops, and lecture halls plus the Round Reading Room.

The most popular sections of the museum fill the ground floor: Egyptian, Mesopotamian, and ancient Greek—with the famous Elgin Marbles from the Athenian Parthenon. Huge winged lions (which guarded Assyrian palaces 800 years before Christ) guard these great ancient galleries. For a brief tour, connect these ancient dots:

Start with the **Egyptian.** Wander from the Rosetta Stone past the many statues. At the end of the hall, climb the stairs to mummy land.

British Museum Overview

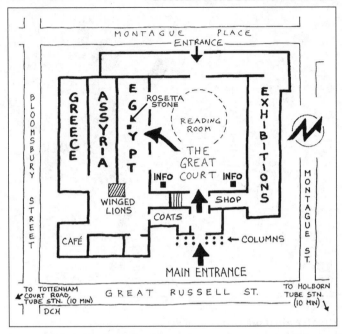

Back at the winged lions, explore the dark, violent, and mysterious **Assyrian** rooms. The Nimrud Gallery is lined with royal propaganda reliefs and wounded lions.

The most modern of the ancient art fills the **Greek** section. Find Room 11 behind the winged lions and start your walk through Greek art history with the simple and primitive Cycladic fertility figures. Later, painted vases show a culture really into partying. The finale is the Elgin Marbles. The much-wrangled-over bits of the Athenian Parthenon (from 450 B.C.) are even more impressive than they look. To best appreciate these ancient carvings, take the audioguide tour (available in this gallery).

Be sure to venture upstairs to see artifacts from **Roman Britain** (Room 50) that surpass anything you'll see at Hadrian's Wall or elsewhere in Britain. Nearby, the Dark Age Britain exhibits offer a worthwhile peek at that bleak era; look for the Sutton Hoo Burial Ship artifacts from a seventh-century royal burial on the east coast of England (Room 41). A rare Michelangelo cartoon is in Room 90.

The **Great Court** is Europe's largest covered square—bigger than a football field. This people-friendly court—delightfully out of the London rain—was for 150 years one of London's great lost spaces...closed off and gathering dust. While the vast

British Museum wraps around the court, its centerpiece is the stately **Reading Room**—famous as the place Karl Marx hung out while formulating his ideas on communism and writing *Das Kapital*. The Reading Room—one of the fine cast-iron buildings of the 19th century—is open to the public, but there's little to see that you can't see from the doorway.

Hours and Location: The British Museum is free (£3 donation requested, daily 10:00–17:30, plus Thu–Fri until 20:30—but from 17:30 only selected galleries and the Reading Room are open, least crowded weekday late afternoons, Great Russell Street, Tube: Tottenham Court Road, tel. 020/7323-8000, recorded info tel. 020/7388-2227, www.thebritishmuseum.ac.uk). The Reading Room is free and open daily 10:00–17:30 (Thu–Fri until 20:30). Computer terminals within the Reading Room offer COMPASS, a database of information about selected museum items (also available on their Web site, listed above). The Great Court has longer opening hours than the museum (daily 9:00–18:00, Thu–Sat until 23:00).

Tours: The various Eye-Opener tours are free (nearly hourly 11:00–15:30, 50 min); each one is different, focusing on one particular subject within the museum. The Highlights tours are expensive but meaty (£8, 90 min, at 10:30, 13:00, and 15:00). There are also several different audioguide tours (£3.50, requires leaving photo ID), including Top 50 Highlights (90 min), the Parthenon Sculptures (60 min), and Family Tours (length varies).

▲▲▲**British Library**—The British Empire built its greatest monuments out of paper. And it's in literature that England made her lasting contribution to civilization and the arts. Britain's

national archives has more than 12 million books, 180 miles of shelving, and the deepest basement in London. But everything that matters for your visit is in one delightful room labeled "The Treasures." This room is filled with literary and historical documents that changed the course of history. You'll trace the evolution of European maps over 800 years. Follow the course of the Bible—from the earliest known gospels (written on scraps of papyrus) to the first complete Bible to the original King James version and the Gutenberg Bible. You'll see Leonardo's doodles, the Magna Carta, Shakespeare's First

British Library Highlights

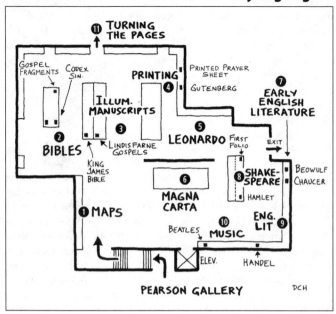

Folio, the original *Alice in Wonderland* in Lewis Carroll's handwriting, and manuscripts by Beethoven, Mozart, and Lennon and McCartney. Finish in the fascinating *Turning the Pages* exhibit, which lets you actually browse through virtual manuscripts of a few of these treasures on a computer (free, Mon–Fri 9:30–18:00, Tue until 20:00, Sat 9:30–17:00, Sun 11:00–17:00; 60-min tours for £6 usually offered Mon, Wed, and Fri–Sun at 15:00, Sat 10:30, and Sun 11:30; call 020/7412-7332 to confirm schedule and reserve; for £3.50 audioguide, leave photo ID or 20 deposit; Tube: King's Cross, turn right out of station and walk a block to 96 Euston Road, library tel. 020/7412-7000, www.bl.uk). The ground-floor café is next to a vast and fun pull-out stamp collection, and the cafeteria upstairs serves good hot meals.

▲**Wallace Collection**—Sir Richard Wallace's fine collection of 17th-century Dutch Masters, 18th-century French Rococo, medieval armor, and assorted aristocratic fancies fills the sumptuously furnished Hertford House on Manchester Square. From the rough and intimate Dutch life-scapes of Jan Steen to the pink-cheeked Rococo fantasies of Boucher, a wander through this little-visited mansion makes you nostalgic for the days of empire (free, Mon–Sat 10:00–17:00, Sun 12:00–17:00, audioguide-£3, just north of Oxford Street on Manchester Square, Tube: Bond Street, tel. 020/7563-9500, www.wallacecollection.org).

▲**Madame Tussaud's Waxworks**—This is gimmicky and expensive but dang good. The original Madame Tussaud did wax casts of heads lopped off during the French Revolution (such as Marie-Antoinette's). She took her show on the road and ended up in London. And now it's much easier to be featured. The gallery is one big *Who's Who* photo-op—a huge hit with the kind of travelers who skip the British Museum. After looking a hundred famous people in their glassy eyes and surviving a silly hall of horror, you'll board a Disney-type ride and cruise through a kid-pleasing "Spirit of London" time trip. Your last stop is the auditorium for a 15-minute stage show. They've dumped anything really historical (except for what they claim is the blade that beheaded Marie-Antoinette) because "there's no money in it and we're a business."

Now, it's all about squeezing Brad Pitt's bum, wining and dining with George Clooney, and partying with Beyoncé, Kylie, Britney, and Posh (admission varies with time but about £23, kids-£19, after 17:00 it's £14, kids-£9; children under 5 always free; Mon–Fri 10:00–18:30, Sat–Sun 9:30–18:30, last entry 60 min before closing, Marylebone Road, Tube: Baker Street). The waxworks are popular. Avoid a wait by either booking ahead to get a ticket with an entry time (tel. 0870-400-3000, online at www.madame-tussauds.com for a £2 fee, or at no extra cost at the Britain and London Visitors Centre or the TIs at Victoria and Waterloo train stations) or arriving at 17:00 (avoiding any lines and saving £9 on admission—90 min is plenty of time for the exhibit).

Sir John Soane's Museum—Architects and fans of eclectic knickknacks love this quirky place, as do Martha Stewarts and lovers of Back Door sights. Tour this furnished home on a bird-chirping square and see 19th-century chairs, lamps, and carpets, wood-paneled nooks and crannies, and stained-glass skylights. The townhouse is cluttered with Soane's (and his wife's) collection of ancient relics, curios, and famous paintings, including Hogarth's series on *The Rake's Progress* (read the fun plot) and several excellent Canalettos. In 1833, just before his death, Soane established his house as a museum, stipulating that it be kept as nearly as

possible in the state he left it. If he visited today, he'd be entirely satisfied. You'll leave wishing you'd known the man (free, Tue–Sat 10:00–17:00, first Tue of the month also 18:00–21:00, closed Sun–Mon, good £1 brochure, £3 guided tours Sat at 14:30, quarter-mile southeast of British Museum, Tube: Holborn, 13 Lincoln's Inn Fields, tel. 020/7405-2107).

Buckingham Palace

▲**Buckingham Palace**—This lavish home has been Britain's royal residence since 1837. When the queen's at home, the royal standard flies (a red, yellow, and blue flag); otherwise the Union Jack flaps in the wind. Recently, the queen has opened her palace to the public—but only in August and September when she's out of town (£14 for state apartments and throne room, Aug–Sept daily 9:30–18:50, only 8,000 visitors a day—to get an entry time, come early or for £1 extra you can book ahead by phone or online, Tube: Victoria, tel. 020/7766-7300, www.royalcollection.org.uk).

▲**Queen's Gallery at Buckingham Palace**—Queen Elizabeth's 7,000 paintings make up the finest private art collection in the world. It's actually a collection of collections, built on by each successive monarch since the 16th century, and rivaling Europe's biggest national art galleries. She rotates her paintings, enjoying some privately in her many palatial residences while sharing others with her subjects in public galleries in Edinburgh and London. Small, thoughtfully presented, and always exquisite displays fill the handful of rooms open to the public in a wing of Buckingham Palace. As you're in "the most important building in London," security is tight. You'll see a temporary exhibit and the permanent "treasures"—which come with a room full of "antique and personal jewelry." Compared to the crown jewels at the Tower, it may be Her Majesty's bottom drawer—but it's still a dazzling pile of diamonds. Temporary exhibits change about twice a year and are always lovingly described with the included audioguides. While the admissions come with an entry time, this is only enforced during rare days when crowds are a problem (£7.50, £11.50 with Royal Mews, daily 10:00–17:30, last entry 60 min before closing, Tube: Victoria, tel. 020-7766-7301 but Her Majesty rarely answers). Men shouldn't miss the mahogany-trimmed urinals.

Royal Mews—The queen's working stables, the "mews," are open to visitors. The visit is likely to be disappointing (you'll see 2 horses out of the queen's 30, a fancy car, and a bunch of old carriages) unless you follow the included guided tour, in which case it's thoroughly entertaining—especially if you're interested in horses and/or royalty. The 45-minute tours go twice an hour and finish with the Gold State Coach (c. 1760, 4 tons, 4 mpg). Queen Victoria said absolutely no cars. When she died, in 1901, the mews got its first Daimler. Today,

Buckingham Palace Area

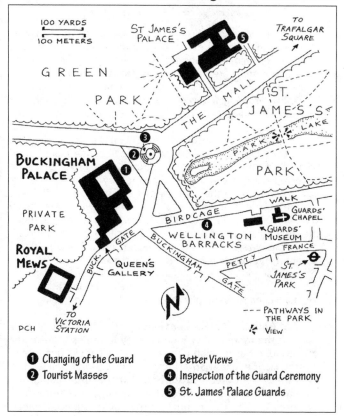

100 YARDS
100 METERS

ST JAMES'S PALACE

TO TRAFALGAR SQUARE

GREEN PARK

THE MALL

ST. JAMES'S PARK LAKE

BUCKINGHAM PALACE

❶ ❷ ❸

PARK

PRIVATE PARK

WALK

BIRDCAGE

GUARDS' CHAPEL

❹ GUARDS' MUSEUM

WELLINGTON BARRACKS

FRANCE

ROYAL MEWS

BUCK. GATE

BUCKINGHAM GATE

PETTY

ST. JAMES'S PARK

QUEEN'S GALLERY

TO VICTORIA STATION

PCH

--- PATHWAYS IN THE PARK

VIEW

❶ Changing of the Guard
❷ Tourist Masses
❸ Better Views
❹ Inspection of the Guard Ceremony
❺ St. James' Palace Guards

along with the hay-eating transport, the stable is home to five Rolls-Royce Phantoms (£6, £11.50 with Queen's Gallery, Aug–Sept Sat–Thu 10:00–17:00, March–July and Oct Sat–Thu 11:00–16:00, closed Fri, closed Nov–Feb, Buckingham Palace Road, Tube: Victoria, tel. 020/7766-7302).

▲▲**Changing of the Guard at Buckingham Palace**—The guards change with much fanfare at about 11:30 almost daily in the summer and, at a minimum, every other day all year long (no band when wet). Each month it's either daily or on odd or even days. Call 020/7321-2233 for the day's plan or check www.royalresidences .com. Then hop into a big black taxi and say, "Buck House, please" (a.k.a. Buckingham Palace).

Harry Potter's London

Harry Potter's story is set in a magical Britain, and all of the places mentioned in the books except London are fictional, but you can visit many real film locations. Many of the locations are closed to visitors, though, or are an un-magical disappointment in person, unless you're a huge fan. For those diehard fans, here's a list.

Spoiler Warning: Information in this sidebar will ruin surprises for those who haven't yet read the Harry Potter *series or seen the movies.*

Harry's story begins in suburban London, in the fictional town of Little Whinging. In the first film, the gentle-giant Hagrid on his flying motorcycle touches down at #4 Privet Drive. He leaves baby Harry—who was orphaned by the murder of his wizard parents—on the doorstep to be raised by an anti-magic aunt and uncle. The scene was shot in the town of **Bracknell** (pop. 50,000, 10 miles west of Heathrow) on a street of generic brick rowhouses called Picket Close. Later, 10-year-old Harry first realizes his wizard powers when talking with a boa constrictor, filmed at the **London Zoo's Reptile House** in Regent's Park (Tube: Great Portland Street). Harry soon gets invited to Hogwarts School of Witchcraft and Wizardry, where he'll learn the magical skills he'll need to eventually confront his parents' murderer, Lord Voldemort.

Big Ben and **Parliament,** along the Thames, welcome Harry to the modern city inhabited by Muggles (non-magic folk). London bustles along oblivious to the parallel universe of wizards. Hagrid takes Harry shopping for school supplies. They enter the glass-roofed **Leadenhall Market** (Tube: Bank), and approach a **storefront** in Bull's Head Passage—the entrance to the Leaky Cauldron pub (which, in the books, is placed among the bookshops of Charing Cross Road). The pub's back wall parts, opening onto the magical Diagon Alley (filmed on a set at Leavesden Studios, north of London), where Harry shops for wands, cauldrons, and wizard textbooks. He pays for it with gold

Most tourists just mob the palace gates for a peek at the Changing of the Guard, but those who know the drill will enjoy the event more. Here's the lowdown on what goes down: It's just after 11:00 and the on-duty guards, actually working at nearby St. James's Palace, are ready to finish their shift. At 11:15, these tired guards, along with the band, head out to the Mall, and then take a right turn for Buckingham Palace. Meanwhile, their replacement guards—fresh for the day—gather at 11:00 at their Wellington Barracks, 500 yards east of the palace (on Birdcage Walk), for a review and inspection. At 11:30, they also head for Buckingham Palace. As both the tired and fresh guards converge on the palace,

Galleons from goblin-run Gringotts Bank, filmed in the marble-floored and chandeliered Exhibition Hall of **Australia House** (Tube: Temple), home of the Australian Embassy.

Harry catches the train to Hogwarts at **King's Cross Station**. (The fanciful exterior shot from film #2 is actually nearby **St. Pancras Station**.) Inside the glass-roofed train station, on a **pedestrian sky bridge** over the tracks, Hagrid gives Harry a train ticket. Harry heads to platform 9 3/4, actually filmed at **platform 4**. Harry and his new buddy Ron magically push their luggage carts through a brick pillar between the platforms, emerging onto a hidden platform. (For a fun photo op, find the *Platform 9 3/4* sign and the luggage card that appears to be disappearing into the wall.)

A red steam train—the Hogwarts Express—speeds them through the (Scottish) countryside to Hogwarts, where Harry will spend the next seven years. Harry is taught how to wave his wand by tiny Professor Flitwick in a wood-paneled classroom filmed at **Harrow School** in Harrow on the Hill, eight miles northwest of London (Tube: Harrow on the Hill).

In film #3, Harry careens through London's lamplit streets on a purple three-decker bus that dumps him at the Leaky Cauldron. In this film, the pub's exterior was shot on rough-looking Stoney Street at the southeast edge of **Borough Street Market**, by the Market Porter Pub, with trains rumbling overhead (Tube: London Bridge).

Other scenes from the books are set in London—Sirius Black and the Order reside at "Twelve Grimmauld Place" and Harry plumbs the depths of the "Ministry of Magic"—but these places are fictional.

Finally, cinema buffs can visit Leicester Square (Tube: Leicester Square), where Daniel Radcliffe and other stars strolled past paparazzi and down red carpets to the Odeon Theater to watch the movies' premieres.

the Horse Guard enters the fray, marching down the Mall from the Horse Guard Barracks on Whitehall. At 11:45, it's a perfect storm of Red Coat pageantry, as all three groups converge. Everyone parades around, the guard changes (passing the regimental flag, or "color") with much shouting, the band plays a happy little concert, and then they march out. A few minutes later, fresh guards set up at St. James's Palace, the tired ones dress down at the barracks, and the tourists disperse.

Stake out the high ground on the circular Victoria Monument for the best overall view. Or start early either at St. James' Palace or the Wellington Barracks (the inspection is in full view of the street) and stride in with the band. The marching troops and bands are colorful and even stirring, but the actual Changing of the Guard is a nonevent. It is interesting, however, to see nearly every tourist in London gathered in one place at the same time. Afterwards, stroll through nearby St. James's Park (Tube: Victoria, St. James's Park, or Green Park).

West London

▲**Hyde Park and Speakers' Corner**—London's "Central Park," originally Henry VIII's hunting grounds, has more than 600 acres of lush greenery, a huge man-made lake, the royal Kensington Palace, and the ornate neo-Gothic Albert Memorial across

from the Royal Albert Hall. Early afternoons on Sunday (until early evening), Speakers' Corner offers soapbox oratory at its best (Tube: Marble Arch). "The grass roots of democracy" is actually a holdover from when the gallows stood here and the criminal was allowed to say just about anything he wanted to before he swung. I dare you to raise your voice and gather a crowd—it's easy to do.

The Princess Diana Memorial Fountain opened in 2004 in honor of the "People's Princess" who once lived in nearby Kensington Palace. The low-key circular stream is in the eastern part of the park, near the Serpentine Gallery. (Don't be confused by signs to the Diana Princess of Wales Children's Playground, also found within the park.)

▲**Apsley House (Wellington Museum)**—Having beaten Napoleon at Waterloo, the Duke of Wellington was once the most famous man in Europe. He was given London's ultimate address, #1 London. His newly refurbished mansion offers one of London's best palace experiences. An 11-foot-tall marble statue (by Canova) of Napoleon, clad only in a fig leaf, greets you. Downstairs is a small gallery of Wellington memorabilia (including a pair of Wellington boots). The lavish upstairs shows off the duke's fine collection of paintings, including works by Velázquez and Steen (£4.50, Tue–Sun 10:00–17:00, until 16:00 in winter, closed Mon, well-described by included audioguide, 20 yards from Hyde Park Corner Tube station, tel. 020/7499-5676, www.english-heritage .org.uk). Hyde Park's pleasant and picnic-wonderful rose garden is nearby.

▲▲**Victoria and Albert Museum**—The world's top collection of decorative arts (vases, stained glass, fine furniture, clothing, jewelry, carpets, and more) is a surprisingly interesting assortment of

West London

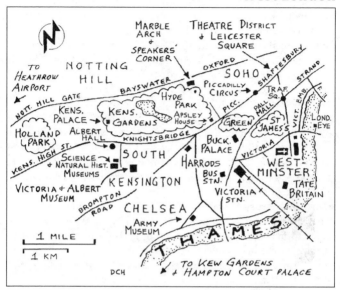

crafts from the West as well as Asian and Islamic cultures.

The V&A grew out of the Great Exhibition of 1851—that ultimate festival celebrating the greatness of Britain. After much support from Queen Victoria and Prince Albert, it was renamed after the royal couple.

Many visitors start with the **British Galleries** (upstairs)—a one-way tour stretching through 400 years of British lifestyles, almost a museum in itself.

In Room 46 are the plaster casts of **Trajan's Column,** a copy

of Rome's 140-foot spiral relief telling the story of the conquest of Romania. (The V&A's casts are copies made for the benefit of 19th-century art students who couldn't afford a railpass.) Plaster casts of **Renaissance sculptures** (Room 46B) let you compare Michelangelo's monumental *David* with Donatello's girlish

David; see also Ghiberti's bronze Baptistery doors that inspired the Florentine Renaissance.

In Room 48A are **Raphael's "cartoons,"** seven huge water-color designs by the Renaissance master for tapestries meant for the Sistine Chapel. The cartoons were sent to Brussels, cut into strips (see the lines), and placed on the looms. Notice that the scenes, the

Acts of Peter and Paul, are the reverse of the final product (lots of left-handed saints).

Cost, Hours, Location: Free, £3 donation requested, possible fee for special exhibits, daily 10:00–17:45, open every Wed and last Fri of month until 22:00 except mid-Dec–mid-Jan. (Tube: South Kensington, a long tunnel leads directly from the Tube station to the museum, tel. 020/7942-2000, www.vam.ac.uk).

The museum has 150 rooms and more than 12 miles of corridors. While just wandering works well here, consider catching one of the free 60-minute orientation **tours** (daily, on the half-hour from 10:30–15:30, also daily at 13:00, Wed at 16:30, and a half-hour version at 18:30) or buying the fine £5 *Hundred Highlights* guidebook, or the handy £1 *What to See at the V&A* brochure (outlines 5 self-guided, speedy tours).

▲**Natural History Museum**—Across the street from Victoria and Albert, this mammoth museum is housed in a giant and wonderful Victorian, neo-Romanesque building. Built in the 1870s specifically for the huge collection (50 million specimens), it has two halves: the Life Galleries (creepy-crawlies, human biology, the origin of species, "our place in evolution," and awesome dinosaurs) and the Earth Galleries (meteors, volcanoes, earthquakes, and so on). Exhibits are wonderfully explained, with lots of creative interactive displays. Pop in, if only for the wild collection of dinosaurs and the roaring *Tyrannosaurus rex*. Free 45-minute highlights tours occur daily about every hour from 11:00 to 16:00 (free, possible fee for special exhibits, Mon–Sat 10:00–18:00, Sun 11:00–18:00, last entrance 17:30, a long tunnel leads directly from South Kensington Tube station to museum, tel. 020/7942-5000, exhibit info and reservations tel. 020/7942-5011, www.nhm.ac.uk).

▲**Science Museum**—Next door to the Natural History Museum, this sprawling wonderland for curious minds is kid-perfect. It offers hands-on fun, from moon walks to deep-sea exploration, with trendy technology exhibits, an IMAX theater (£7–10 tickets for grownups, kids less), cool rotating themed exhibits, and a kids' zone in the basement (free, daily 10:00–18:00, Exhibition Road, Tube: South Kensington, tel. 0870-870-4868, www.sciencemuseum .org.uk).

▲▲**Kensington Palace**—In 1689, King William and Queen Mary moved their primary residence from Whitehall in central London to the more pristine and peaceful village of Kensington (now engulfed by London). With a little renovation help from Sir Christopher Wren, they turned the existing house into Kensington Palace, which was the center of English court life until 1760, when the royal family moved into Buckingham Palace. Since then, lesser royals have bedded down in Kensington Palace (as Prince Charles and Princess Diana did from their 1981 marriage until her death in 1997). The palace, while still functioning as a royal residence, also welcomes visitors with an impressive string of historic royal apartments and a killer wardrobe of queens' dresses and ceremonial clothing (late 19th and 20th centuries). For the time being, Lady Diana's fashion-statement dresses are also on display. Enjoy a re-created royal tailor and dressmaker's workshop, the 17th-century splendor of the apartments of William and Mary, and the bed where Queen Victoria was born (fully clothed). The displays are wonderfully described by the included audioguide (£11, daily 10:00–18:00, until 17:00 in winter, a 10-min hike through Hyde Park from either Queensway or High Street Kensington Tube station, tel. 0870-751-5170). Garden enthusiasts enjoy popping into the secluded Sunken Garden, 50 yards from the exit. And ladies with fancy hats sip tea at the nearby Orangery, built as a greenhouse for Queen Anne in 1704 (daily 10:00–18:00, à la carte lunch 12:00–15:00, afternoon tea 15:00–18:00, sit indoors or outside overlooking the garden).

Victoria Station—From underneath this station's iron-and-glass canopy, trains depart for the south of England and Gatwick Airport. While Victoria Station is famous and a major Tube stop, few tourists actually take trains from here—most just come to take in the exciting bustle. It's a fun place to just be a "rock in a river" teeming with commuters and services. The station is surrounded by big red buses and taxis, travel agencies, and lousy eateries. It's next to the main bus station (National Express) and the best inexpensive B&Bs in town.

Westminster Cathedral—This largest Catholic church in England, just a block from Victoria Station, is striking but not very historic or important to visit. It opened in 1903 and has a brick neo-Byzantine flavor (surrounded by glassy office blocks). While it's definitely not Westminster Abbey, half the tourists wandering around inside seem to think it is. The highlight is the lift to the viewing gallery atop its bell tower (fine view, £3 for the lift, daily 9:30–17:00, just off Victoria Street, Tube: Victoria).

National Army Museum—This museum is not as awe-inspiring as the Imperial War Museum, but it's still fun, especially for kids into soldiers, armor, and guns. And while the Imperial War Museum is limited to wars of the 20th century, this tells the story of the British Army from 1415 through the Gulf War and Bosnia with lots of Redcoat lore and a good look at Waterloo. Kids enjoy trying on a Cromwellian helmet, seeing the skeleton of Napoleon's horse, and peering out from a WWI trench through a working periscope (free, daily 10:00–17:30, follow arrows in carpet to stay on track, bus #239 from Victoria Station stops at museum's door, Royal Hospital Road, Chelsea, Tube: Sloane Square, tel. 020/7730-0717).

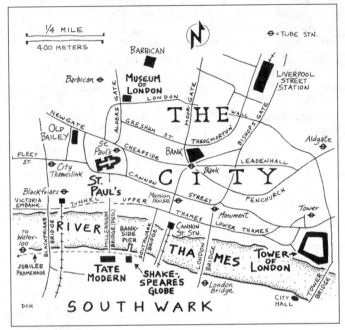

East London: The City

▲▲**The City of London**—When Londoners say "The City," they mean the one-square-mile business, banking, and journalism center that 2,000 years ago was Roman Londinium. The outline of the Roman city walls can still be seen in the arc of roads from Blackfriars Bridge to Tower Bridge. Within the City are 23 churches designed by Sir Christopher Wren, mostly just ornamentation around St. Paul's Cathedral. Today, while home to only 5,000 residents, the City thrives with more than 500,000 office workers coming and going daily. It's a fascinating district to wander on weekdays, but since almost nobody actually lives there, it's dull in the evenings and on Saturday and Sunday.

▲**Old Bailey**—To view the British legal system in action—lawyers in little blond wigs speaking legalese with a British accent—spend a few minutes in the visitors' gallery at the Old Bailey, called the "Central Criminal Court." Don't enter under the dome; signs point you to the two visitors' entrances (free, Mon–Fri about 10:30–16:30 depending on caseload, closed Sat–Sun, reduced hours in Aug; no kids under 14; no bags, mobile phones, or cameras, but small purses OK; you can check your bag at Bailey's Sandwich Bar across the street for £2 or at any other entrepreneurial place nearby; Tube: St. Paul's, 2 blocks northwest of St. Paul's on Old

St. Paul's Cathedral

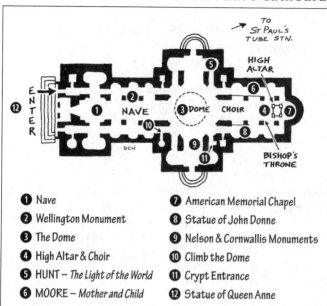

1 Nave
2 Wellington Monument
3 The Dome
4 High Altar & Choir
5 HUNT – *The Light of the World*
6 MOORE – *Mother and Child*
7 American Memorial Chapel
8 Statue of John Donne
9 Nelson & Cornwallis Monuments
10 Climb the Dome
11 Crypt Entrance
12 Statue of Queen Anne

Bailey Street, follow signs to public entrance, tel. 020/7248-3277).
▲▲▲**St. Paul's Cathedral**—Wren's most famous church is the great St. Paul's, its elaborate interior capped by a 365-foot dome.

The crypt (included with admission) is a world of historic bones and memorials, including Admiral Nelson's tomb and interesting cathedral models. The great West Door is opened only for great occasions, such as the wedding of Prince Charles and the late Princess Diana in 1981. Stand in the back of the church and imagine how Diana felt before making the hike to the altar with the world watching. Sit under the second-largest dome in the world and eavesdrop on guided tours.

Since World War II, St. Paul's has been Britain's symbol of resistance. Despite 57 nights of bombing, the Nazis failed to destroy the cathedral, thanks to the St. Paul's volunteer fire watch, who stayed on the dome. Climb the dome for a great city view and some fun in the Whispering Gallery—where the precisely designed barrel of the dome lets sweet nothings circle audibly around to the opposite side.

The **evensong** services are free, but nonpaying visitors are not allowed to linger afterward (Mon–Sat at 17:00, Sun at 15:15, 40 min). Sunday services are at 8:00, 10:15, 11:30 (sung Eucharist), 15:15 (evensong), and 18:00, with a **free organ recital** at 17:00.

Cost, Hours, Information: £8, includes church entry and dome climb, Mon–Sat 8:30–16:30, last entry 16:00, last dome entry 16:15, closed Sun except for worship. No photography is allowed. Ninety-minute "Super Tours" of the cathedral and crypt cost £2.50 (Mon–Sat at 11:00, 11:30, 13:30, and 14:00—confirm schedule at church or call tel. 020/7236-4128; £3.50 for 1-hour audioguide which covers 17 stops, available Mon–Sat 9:15–15:30). There's a cheery café in the crypt of the cathedral (Tube: St. Paul's, tel. 020/7236-4128, www.stpauls.co.uk).

▲**Museum of London**—London, a 2,000-year-old city, is so littered with Roman ruins that when a London builder finds Roman antiquities, he doesn't stop work. He simply documents the finds, moves the artifacts to a museum, and builds on. If you're asking, "Why did the Romans build their cities underground?" a trip to the creative and entertaining London Museum is a must. Stroll through London history from pre-Roman times through the 1920s. This regular stop for the local school kids gives the best overview of London history in town (free, Mon–Sat 10:00–18:00, Sun 12:00–18:00, Tube: Barbican or St. Paul's, tel. 0870-444-3852).

Geffrye Decorative Arts Museum—Walk through a dozen English front rooms dating from 1600 to 1990 (free, Tue–Sat 10:00–17:00, Sun 12:00–17:00, closed Mon, Tube: Liverpool Street, then bus #149 or #242 north, tel. 020/7739-9893).

▲▲▲**Tower of London**—The Tower has served as a castle in wartime, a king's residence in peace time, and, most notoriously, as the prison and execution site of rebels. You can see the crown jewels,

take a witty Beefeater tour, and ponder the executioner's block that dispensed with troublesome heirs to the throne and a couple of Henry VIII's wives. The crown jewels, dating from the Restoration, are the best on Earth— and come with hour-long lines for most of the day. To avoid the crowds, arrive when the Tower opens and go straight for the jewels, doing the Beefeater tour and White Tower later—or do the jewels after 16:30.

Cost, Hours, Information: £14.50, family-£42, £20 for one-day combo-ticket with Hampton Court Palace, March–Oct Tue–Sat 9:00–18:00, Sun–Mon 10:00–18:00; Nov–Feb Tue–Sat 9:00–17:00, Sun–Mon 10:00–17:00; last entry 60 min before closing. The long but fast-moving ticket line is worst on Sunday. No photography is allowed of the jewels or in chapels. (Tube: Tower

Tower of London

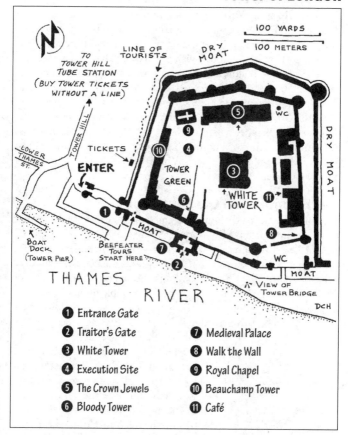

100 YARDS
100 METERS

N

TO
TOWER HILL
TUBE STATION
(BUY TOWER TICKETS
WITHOUT A LINE)

LINE OF
TOURISTS

DRY
MOAT

DRY
MOAT

TOWER HILL

LOWER
THAMES
ST.

TICKETS

ENTER

TOWER
GREEN

WC

⑤

⑨

⑩

④

⑥

③

*WHITE
TOWER

⑪

⑧

BOAT
DOCK
(TOWER PIER)

BEEFEATER
TOURS
START HERE

MOAT

①

⑦

②

WC

MOAT

THAMES

RIVER

VIEW OF
TOWER BRIDGE

DCH

❶ Entrance Gate

❷ Traitor's Gate

❸ White Tower

❹ Execution Site

❺ The Crown Jewels

❻ Bloody Tower

❼ Medieval Palace

❽ Walk the Wall

❾ Royal Chapel

❿ Beauchamp Tower

⓫ Café

Hill, tel. 0870-751-5177, recorded info tel. 0870-756-6060, booking tel. 0870-756-7070.) You can avoid the long lines by picking up your ticket at any London TI or the Tower Hill Tube station ticket office.

Ceremony of the Keys: Every night at precisely 21:30, with pageantry-filled ceremony, the Tower of London is locked up (as it has been for the last 700 years). To attend this free 30-minute event, you need to request an invitation at least two months before your visit. Write to Ceremony of the Keys, H.M. Tower of London, London EC3N 4AB. Include your name; the addresses, names, and ages of all people attending (up to 6 people, nontransferable, no kids under age 8 allowed); requested date; alternative dates; and two international reply coupons (buy at U.S. post office—if your post office doesn't have the $1.75 coupons in stock, they can order them; the turnaround time is a few days).

More Sights Next to the Tower—The best remaining bit of London's **Roman Wall** is just north of the tower (at the Tower Hill Tube station). The impressive Tower Bridge is freshly painted and restored; for more information on this neo-Gothic maritime gateway to London, you can visit the **Tower Bridge Experience** for its 1894–1994 history exhibit and a peek at its Victorian engine room (£5.50, family-£10 and up, daily 10:00–1830, last entry at 17:30, good view, poor value, enter at the northwest tower, tel. 020/7403-3761). The chic **St. Katharine Yacht Harbor,** just east of the Tower Bridge, has mod shops and the classic old Dickens Inn, fun for a drink or pub lunch. Across the bridge is the South Bank, with the upscale Butlers Wharf area, City Hall, museums, and promenade.

South London, on the South Bank
The South Bank is a thriving arts and cultural center tied together by a riverside path. This popular, pub-crawling walk—called the Jubilee Promenade—stretches from Tower Bridge past Westminster Bridge, where it offers grand views of the Houses of Parliament. (The promenade hugs the river except just east of London Bridge, where it cuts inland for a couple of blocks.)

City Hall—Opened in 2002, the glassy, egg-shaped building near the south end of Tower Bridge is London's City Hall, designed by

Sir Norman Foster, the architect who worked on London's Millennium Bridge and Berlin's Reichstag. An interior spiral ramp allows visitors to watch and hear the action below in the Assembly Chamber; ride the lift to the second floor (the highest visitors can go) and spiral down. The Visitors Centre on the lower ground floor has a handy cafeteria. A top-floor observation deck known as "London's Living Room" is open for tours, usually on Monday morning (phone-in reservation required), and on occasional weekends from 10:00–16:30 (Visitors Centre open Mon–Fri 8:00–20:00, closed Sat–Sun, Tube: London Bridge station plus 10-min walk, or Tower Hill station plus 15-min walk; the Hall occasionally opens up for public tours—call or check Web site to confirm tour times and opening hours, tel. 020/7983-4100, www.london.gov.uk).

▲▲▲**London Eye Ferris Wheel**—Built by British Airways, the wheel towers above London opposite Big Ben. This is the world's highest observational wheel, giving you a chance to fly British Airways without leaving London. Designed like a giant bicycle

The South Bank

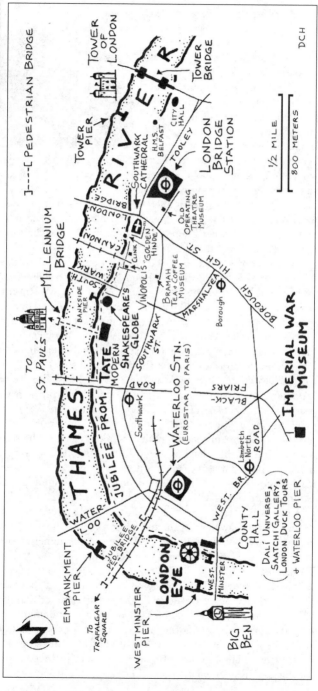

wheel, it's a pan-European under-
taking: British steel and Dutch
engineering, with Czech, German,
French, and Italian mechanical
parts. It's also very "green," running extremely efficiently and
virtually silently. Twenty-five
people ride in each of its 32 air-
conditioned capsules for the 30-
minute rotation (each capsule has a

bench, but most people stand). From the top of this 450-foot-high
wheel—the highest public viewpoint in the city—Big Ben looks
small. You go around only once; save a shot on top for the glass
capsule next to yours. Its original five-year lease has been extended
to 25 years, and it looks like this will become a permanent fixture
on the London skyline. Thames boats come and go from here using
the Waterloo Pier at the foot of the wheel.

Cost, Hours, Location: £12.50, April–mid-Sept daily 9:30–
21:00, until 22:00 in July–Aug, mid-Sept–March 9:30–20:00,
often closed Jan for maintenance, Tube: Waterloo or Westminster,
www.ba-londoneye.com (10 percent discount for booking online).

Visitors face two lines: one to get your ticket, and the other to
board. You can generally just buy your ticket at the wheel (never
more than a 30-min wait, worst on weekends and school holidays).
If you want to book a ticket (with an assigned time) in advance,
call 0870-500-0600 or book online at www.ba-londoneye.com
(and save 10 percent). Upon arrival, you either pick up your
pre-booked ticket (if you've reserved ahead; use the ATM-type
machines to save time—just type in your confirmation number)
or wait in the line inside to buy tickets. Then you join the ticket-
holders' line at the wheel (starting 10 min before your assigned
half-hour time slot).

Dalí Universe—Cleverly located next to the hugely popular
London Eye Ferris Wheel, this exhibit features 500 works of
mind-bending art by Salvador Dalí. While pricey, it's entertaining if you like Surrealism and want to learn about Dalí (£9,
audioguide-£2.50, daily 10:00–18:30, generally summer evenings
until 20:00, last entry 1 hour before closing, Tube: Waterloo or
Westminster, tel. 020/7620-2720).

▲Saatchi Gallery—The contemporary-art gallery at the base of
the London Eye features young British artists. Rather than halls
of staid canvases, the collection displays many installations, each
in their own room, giving the place a kind of funhouse, macabre
atmosphere. Exhibits are changed routinely. Here are several I've
seen: Damien Hirst's vision of mortality (live insects feeding on a
rotting cow's head, then dying on a bug zapper); Ron Mueck's *Dead*

Dad, an ultra-realistic (half-size) corpse in silicon and acrylic; and Tracey Emin's installation of her messy bedroom.

Visitors may be put off or simply grossed out. It's "just conceptual art," but the concepts are realized on a large scale, with big money and ultra-modern technical know-how, and displayed in a wood-paneled Edwardian-era setting. You may not like it, you may be offended, you may find it passé—but it's something to e-mail home about (£8.75, daily 10:00–20:00, Fri–Sat until 22:00, last entry 45 min before closing, located next to London Eye, Tube: Waterloo or Westminster).

▲▲**Imperial War Museum**—This impressive museum covers the wars of the last century, from heavy weaponry to love notes and Vargas Girls, from Monty's Africa campaign tank to Schwartzkopf's Desert Storm uniform. You can trace the development of the machine gun, watch footage of the first tank battles, see one of more than a thousand V2 rockets Hitler rained on Britain in 1944 (each with more than a ton of explosives), hold your breath through the gruesome WWI trench experience, and buy WWII-era toys in the fun museum shop. The "Secret War" section gives a fascinating peek into the intrigues of espionage in World Wars I and II. The section on the Holocaust is one of the best on the subject anywhere. Rather than glorify war, the museum does its best to shine a light on the powerful human side of one of mankind's most persistent traits (free, daily 10:00–18:00, 2 hours is enough time for most visitors, Tube: Lambeth North or bus #12 from Westminster, tel. 020/7416-5000).

The museum is housed in what was the Royal Bethlam Hospital. Also known as "the Bedlam asylum," the place was so wild it gave the world a new word for chaos: "bedlam." Back in Victorian times, locals—without trash-talk shows and cable TV—came here for their entertainment. The asylum was actually open to the paying public on weekends.

▲▲▲**Tate Modern**—Dedicated in the spring of 2000, the striking museum across the river from St. Paul's opened the new century with art from the old one. Its powerhouse collection of Monet, Matisse, Dalí, Picasso, Warhol, and much more is displayed in a converted powerhouse. Each year, the main hall features a different monumental installation by a prominent artist (free, fee for special exhibitions, Sun–Thu 10:00–18:00, Fri–Sat 10:00–22:00, Fri–Sat evenings a good time to visit, audioguide-£2, multimedia handheld device-£3.50, call to confirm schedule, view café on top floor; cross the Millennium Bridge from St. Paul's, or Tube: Southwark plus a 10-min walk; or connect by Tate Boat ferry from Tate Britain for £4—see specifics on page 66; tel. 020/7887-8008, www.tate.org.uk).

▲**Millennium Bridge**—The pedestrian bridge links St. Paul's Cathedral and the Tate Modern across the Thames. This is

London's first new bridge in a century. When it first opened, the $25 million bridge wiggled when people walked on it, so it promptly closed for a $7 million stabilization; now it's stable and open again (free). Nicknamed "a blade of light" for its sleek minimalist design—370 yards long, four yards wide, stainless steel with teak planks—it includes clever aerodynamic handrails to deflect wind over the heads of pedestrians.

▲▲**Shakespeare's Globe**—The original Globe Theater has been rebuilt, half-timbered and thatched, as it was in Shakespeare's time. (This is the first thatched roof in London since they were out-

lawed after the Great Fire of 1666.) The Globe originally accommodated 2,000 seated and another 1,000 standing. (Today, slightly smaller and leaving space for reasonable aisles, the theater holds 900 seated and 600 groundlings.) Its promoters brag that the theater melds "the three A's"—actors, audience, and architecture—with each contributing to the

play. Open as a museum and a working theater, it hosts authentic old-time performances of Shakespeare's plays. The Globe's exhibition on Shakespeare is the world's largest, with interactive displays and film presentations, a sound lab, a script factory, and costumes. The theater can be toured when there are no plays going on—it's worth planning ahead for these excellent tours.

Cost, Hours, Information: £9 includes exhibition and actor-led guided tour; mid-May–Sept exhibition open daily 9:00–18:00, tours go on the half hour from 9:30, generally until 12:30, until 11:30 on Sun, 17:30 on Mon; Oct–mid-May exhibition open daily 10:00–17:00 with 30-min tours on the half hour as above (on the South Bank directly across Thames over Southwark Bridge from St. Paul's, Tube: London Bridge plus a 10-min walk, tel. 020/7902-1500, www.shakespeares-globe.org). For details on seeing a play, see page 113. The Globe Café is open daily (10:00–18:00, tel. 020/7902-1433).

Bramah Tea and Coffee Museum—Aficionados of tea or coffee will find this small museum fascinating. It tells the story of each drink almost passionately. The owner, Mr. Bramah, comes from a big tea family and wants the world to know how the advent of

Crossing the Thames on Foot

You can cross the Thames on any of the bridges that carry car traffic over the river, but London's two pedestrian bridges are more fun. The Millennium Bridge connects the sedate St. Paul's Cathedral with the great Tate Modern. The Golden Jubilee Bridge (consisting of 2 walkways that flank a railway trestle) links bustling Trafalgar Square on the North Bank with the London Eye Ferris Wheel and Waterloo Station on the South Bank. Replacing the old, run-down Hungerford Bridge, the Golden Jubilee Bridge—well-lit with a sleek, futuristic look—makes this busy route safer and more popular.

commercial television, with breaks not long enough to brew a proper pot of tea, required a faster hot drink. In came the horrible English instant coffee. Tea countered with finely chopped leaves in tea bags, and it's gone downhill ever since (£4, daily 10:00–18:00, 40 Southwark Street, Tube: London Bridge plus 3-min walk, tel. 020/7403-5650, www.bramahmuseum.co.uk). Its café, which serves more kinds of coffees and teas than cakes, is open to the public (same hours as museum). The #RV1 bus zips you to the museum easily and scenically from Covent Garden.

▲▲**Old Operating Theatre Museum and Herb Garret**—Climb a tight and creaky wooden spiral staircase to a church attic where you'll find a garret used to dry medicinal herbs, a fascinating exhibit on Victorian surgery, cases of well-described 19th-century medical paraphernalia, and a special look at "anesthesia, the defeat of pain." Then you stumble upon Britain's oldest operating theater, where limbs were sawed off way back in 1821 (£4.75, daily 10:30–17:00, 9a St. Thomas Street, Tube: London Bridge, tel. 020/7955-4791, www.thegarret.org.uk).

▲▲**Vinopolis: City of Wine**—While it seems illogical to have a huge wine museum in London, Vinopolis makes a good case. Built over a Roman wine store and filling the massive vaults of an old wine warehouse, the museum offers an excellent audioguide with a light yet earnest history of wine. Sipping various reds and whites, ports, and champagnes—immersed in your headset as you stroll— you learn about the libation from its Georgian origins to Chile, including a Vespa ride through Chianti country in Tuscany. Allow some time, as the included audioguide takes 90 minutes—the sipping can slow things down wonderfully (£12.50 with 5 tastes, only £11 Tue–Thu; don't worry...for £3 you can buy 5 more tastes inside; £15 gets you a premium service with a couple of especially fine wines and tasting lesson, daily 12:00–18:00, Mon and Fri–Sat until 21:00, last entry 2 hours before closing, between the Globe and Southwark Cathedral at 1 Bank End, Tube: London Bridge, tel. 0870-241-4040 or 020/7940-8322, www.vinopolis.co.uk).

Lesser Sights in Southwark, on the South Bank

These sights, while mediocre, are worth knowing about. The area stretching from the Tate Modern to London Bridge, known as Southwark (SUTH-uck), was for centuries the place Londoners would go to escape the rules and decency of the city and let their hair down. Bear-baiting, brothels, rollicking pubs, and the-ater—you name the dream, and it could be fulfilled just across the Thames. A run-down warehouse district through the 20th century, it's been gentrified with classy restaurants, office parks, pedestrian promenades, major sights (such as the Tate Modern and Shakespeare's Globe—described above), and this colorful collec-tion of lesser sights. The area is easy on foot and a scenic—though circuitous—way to connect the Tower of London with St. Paul's.

Southwark Cathedral—While made a cathedral only in 1905, it's been the neighborhood church since the 13th century and comes with some interesting history (Mon–Fri 8:00–18:00, Sat–Sun 9:00–18:00, last entry 30 min before close, evensong services weekdays at 17:30, Sun at 15:00, audioguide-£2.50, Tube: London Bridge, tel. 020/7367-6700).

The Clink Prison Museum—Proudly the "original clink," this was where law-abiding citizens threw Southwark troublemakers until 1780. Today, it's a low-tech torture museum filling grotty old rooms with papier-mâché gore. Unfortunately, there's little to seriously deal with the fascinating problem of law and order in Southwark, where 18th-century Londoners went for a good time (overpriced at £5, daily 10:00–18:00, July–Sept until 21:00, 1 Clink Street, Tube: London Bridge, tel. 020/7403-0900, www.clink.co.uk).

***Golden Hinde* Replica**—This is a full-size replica of the 16th-century warship in which Sir Francis Drake circumnavigated the globe from 1577 to 1580. Commanding this ship, Drake earned the reputation as history's most successful pirate. The original is long gone, but this boat has logged more than 100,000 miles, including its own voyage around the world. While the ship is fun to see, its interior is not worth touring (£3.50, daily 10:00–17:30, may be closed if rented out for birthday parties, school groups, or weddings, Tube: London Bridge, tel. 0870-011-8700, www.goldenhinde.co.uk).

HMS *Belfast*—"The last big-gun armored warship of World War II" clogs the Thames just upstream from the Tower Bridge. This huge vessel—now manned with wax sailors—thrills kids who always dreamed of sitting in a turret shooting off their imaginary guns. If you're into WWII warships, this is the ultimate...otherwise, it's just lots of exercise with a nice view of Tower Bridge (£8, daily March–Oct 10:00–18:00, Nov–Feb 10:00–17:00, last entry 45 min before closing, Tube: London Bridge, tel. 020/7940-6300).

South London, on the North Bank

▲▲**Tate Britain**—One of Europe's great art houses, Tate Britain specializes in British painting from the 16th century through modern times. The museum has a good representation of William Blake's religious sketches, the Pre-Raphaelites' realistic art, and J. M. W. Turner's swirling works (free, £2 donation requested, daily 10:00–17:50, last entry at 17:00).

The museum offers a fine, free, and necessary **audioguide** plus free **tours** (normally Mon–Fri at 11:00—16th, 17th, and 18th centuries; at noon—19th century; at 14:00—Turner; at 15:00—20th century; Sat–Sun at noon and 15:00—highlights; call to confirm schedule, tel. 020/7887-8000, recorded info tel. 020/7887-8008, www.tate.org.uk). No photography is allowed. (Tube: Pimlico, then 7-min walk; or arrive directly at museum by taking bus #88 from Oxford Circus or #77A from National Gallery, or more fun, the £4 Tate Boat ferry from Tate Modern—see specifics on page 66.)

Greater London

▲**Kew Gardens**—For a fine riverside park and a palatial greenhouse jungle to swing through, take the Tube or the boat to every botanist's favorite escape, Kew Gardens. While to most visitors the Royal Botanic Gardens of Kew are simply a delightful opportunity to wander among 33,000 different types of plants, to the hardworking organization that runs the gardens, it's a way to pro-

mote understanding and preservation of the botanical diversity of our planet. The Kew Tube station drops you in an herbal little business community, a two-block walk from Victoria Gate (the main garden entrance). Pick up a map brochure and check at the gate for a monthly listing of best blooms.

Garden-lovers could spend days exploring Kew's 300 acres. For a quick visit, spend a fragrant hour wandering through three buildings: the Palm House, a humid Victorian world of iron,

Greater London

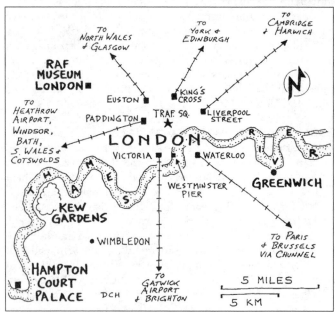

glass, and tropical plants built in 1844; a Waterlily House that Monet would swim for; and the Princess of Wales Conservatory, a modern greenhouse with many different climate zones growing countless cacti, bug-munching carnivorous plants, and more (£8.50, £6 at 15:00 or later, Mon–Fri 9:30–18:30, Sat–Sun 9:30–19:30, until 16:30 or sunset off-season, galleries and conservatories close at 17:30, a £3.50 narrated floral 35-minute joyride on little train departs on the hour until 16:00 from Victoria Gate, Tube: Kew Gardens, boats run between Kew Gardens and Westminster Pier—see page 66, tel. 020/8332-5000, www.rbgkew.org.uk). For a sun-dappled lunch, walk 10 minutes from the Palm House to the Orangery (£6 hot meals, daily 10:00–17:30).

▲**Hampton Court Palace**—Fifteen miles up the Thames from downtown (£15 taxi ride from Kew Gardens) is the 500-year-old palace of Henry VIII. Actually, it was the palace of his minister, Cardinal Wolsey. When Wolsey, a clever man, realized Henry VIII was experiencing a little palace envy, he gave the mansion to his king. The Tudor palace was also home to Elizabeth I and

Charles I. Sections were updated by Christopher Wren for William and Mary. The stately palace stands overlooking the Thames and includes some impressive Tudor rooms, including a Great Hall with a magnificent hammer-beam ceiling. The industrial-strength Tudor kitchen was capable of keeping 600 schmoozing courtesans thoroughly—if not well—fed. The sculpted garden features a rare Tudor tennis court and a popular maze.

The palace, fully restored after a 1986 fire, tries hard to please, but it doesn't quite sparkle. From the information center in the main courtyard, visitors book times for tours with tired costumed guides or pick up audioguides for self-guided tours of various wings of the palace (all free). The Tudor Kitchens, Henry VIII's Apartments, and the King's Apartments are most interesting. The Georgian Rooms are pretty dull. The maze in the nearby garden is a curiosity some find fun (maze free with palace ticket, otherwise £3.50). The palace costs £12 (1-day combo-ticket with Tower of London-£20, kids-£12.50, April–Oct Mon 10:15–18:00, Tue–Sun 9:30–18:00, Nov–March until 16:30, tel. 0870-751-5175, recorded info tel. 0870-752-7777). Note that there are often discounts available for people riding the train from London to the palace. When you buy your ticket at Waterloo Station, ask for the voucher that gives a second adult 50 percent off and free admission for kids.

The train (2/hr, 30 min) from London's Waterloo station drops you just across the river from the palace. Consider arriving at or departing from the palace by boat (connections with London's Westminster Pier, see page 65); it's a relaxing and scenic three-hour cruise past two locks and a fun new/old riverside mix.

Royal Air Force Museum London—A hit with aviation enthusiasts, this huge aerodrome and airfield contain planes from World War II's Battle of Britain up through the Gulf War. You can climb inside some of the planes, try your luck in a cockpit, and fly with the Red Arrows in a flight simulator (free, daily 10:00–18:00, café, shop, parking, Tube: Colindale—top of Northern Line Edgware branch, Grahame Park Way, tel. 020/8205-2266, www.rafmuseum .org.uk).

Disappointments of London

On the South Bank, the London Dungeon, a much-visited but amateurish attraction, is just a highly advertised, overpriced haunted house—certainly not worth the £20 admission, much less your valuable London time. It comes with long and rude lines. Wait for Halloween and see one in your hometown to support a better cause. "Winston Churchill's Britain at War Experience" (next to the London Dungeon) also wastes your time and money (especially considering the wonderful new Churchill Museum in the Cabinet War Rooms; see page 71). The Jack the Ripper walking tours (by any of several companies) are big sellers, but don't offer much. Anything actually relating to the notorious serial killer was torn down a century ago, and all that's left are a few small sights and lots of bloody stories.

SHOPPING

Harrods—Harrods is London's most famous and touristy department store. With a million square feet of retail space on seven floors, it's a place where some shoppers could spend all day. (To me, it's a department store.) Big yet classy, Harrods has everything from elephants to toothbrushes (Mon–Sat 10:00–19:00, closed Sun, mandatory storage for big backpacks-£2.50, on Brompton Road, Tube: Knightsbridge, tel. 020/7730-1234, www.harrods .com).

Sightseers should pick up the free *Store Guide* at any info post. Here's what I enjoyed: On the Ground and Lower Ground Floors, find the Food Halls, with their Edwardian tiled walls, creative and exuberant displays, and staff in period costumes—not quite like your local supermarket back home.

Descend to the Lower Ground Floor and follow signs to the Egyptian Escalator, where you'll find a memorial to Dodi Fayed and Princess Diana. The huge (and slightly creepy) bronze statue was commissioned by Dodi Fayed's father, Mohamed al-Fayed, who owns Harrods. Photos and flowers honor the late Princess and her lover, who both died in a car crash in Paris in 1997. See the wineglass still dirty from their last dinner, and the  engagement ring that Dodi purchased the day before they died.

Ride the Egyptian Escalator—lined with pharaoh-headed sconces, papyrus-plant lamps, and hieroglyphic balconies (Harrods' owner is from Egypt)—to the Fourth Floor. From the escalator, make a U-turn left and head to the far corner of the store (toys) to find child-size luxury cars that actually work. A junior Jaguar or Mercedes will set you back about $13,000. The child's Hummer ($30,000) is as big as my car.

Also on the Fourth Floor is The Georgian Restaurant. Enjoy a fancy tea under a skylight as a pianist tickles the keys of a Bösendorfer, the world's most expensive piano (tea-£19, includes finger sandwiches and pastries, served after 15:45).

Many of my readers report that Harrods is overpriced, snooty, and teeming with American and Japanese tourists. Still, it's the palace of department stores. The nearby Beauchamp Place is lined with classy and fascinating shops.

Harvey Nichols—Once Princess Diana's favorite, "Harvey Nick's" remains the department store *du jour* (Mon–Tue and Sat 10:00–19:00, Wed–Fri until 20:00, Sun 12:00–18:00, near Harrods, Tube: Knightsbridge, 109 Knightsbridge, www.harveynichols.com). Want to pick up a little £20 scarf for the wife? You won't do it here, where they're more like £200. The store's fifth floor is a veritable food fest, with a gourmet grocery store, a fancy (smoky) restaurant, a Yo! Sushi bar, and a lively café. Consider a take-away tray of sushi to eat on a bench in the Hyde Park rose garden two blocks away.

Toys—The biggest toy store in Britain is **Hamleys,** with seven floors buzzing with 28,000 toys, managed by a staff of 200. At the "Bear Factory," kids can get a made-to-order teddy bear by picking out a "bear skin," and watch while it's stuffed and sewn (Mon–Sat 9:00–20:00, Thu until 21:00, Sun 12:00–18:00, 188 Regent Street, tel. 0870-333-2455, www.hamleys.com).

Street Markets—Antique buffs, people-watchers, and folks who brake for garage sales love to haggle at London's street markets. There's good early-morning market activity somewhere any day of the week. The best are **Portobello Road** (Mon–Wed and Fri–Sat 8:00–18:30, closes at 13:00 on Thu, closed Sun, Tube: Notting Hill Gate, near recommended B&Bs, tel. 020/7229-8354) and **Camden Lock Market** (daily 10:00–18:00, Tube: Camden Town, tel. 020/7284-2084, www.camdenlock.net). The TI has a complete, up-to-date list. Warning: Markets attract two kinds of people—tourists and pickpockets.

Famous Auctions—London's famous auctioneers welcome serious bidders. You can preview estate catalogs or browse auction calendars online. For questions—or to set up a private appointment—contact **Sotheby's** (Mon–Fri 9:00–16:30, closed Sat–Sun, 34–35 New Bond Street, Tube: Oxford Circus, tel. 020/7293-5000, www.sothebys.com) or **Christie's** (Mon–Fri 9:00–16:30, Sun 14:00–17:00, closed Sat, 8 King Street, Tube: Green Park, tel. 020/7839-9060, www.christies.com).

ENTERTAINMENT

Theater (a.k.a. "Theatre")

London's theater rivals Broadway's in quality and beats it in price. Choose from Shakespeare, musicals, comedy, thrillers, sex farces, cutting-edge fringe, revivals starring movie celebs, and more. London does it all well. I prefer big, glitzy—even bombastic—musicals over serious chamber dramas, simply because London can deliver the lights, sound, dancers, and multimedia spectacle I rarely get back home.

London's Major Theaters

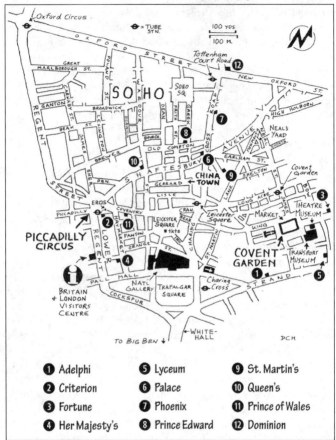

1. Adelphi
2. Criterion
3. Fortune
4. Her Majesty's
5. Lyceum
6. Palace
7. Phoenix
8. Prince Edward
9. St. Martin's
10. Queen's
11. Prince of Wales
12. Dominion

Most theaters, marked on tourist maps (also see map above), are found in the West End between Piccadilly and Covent Garden. Box offices, hotels, and TIs offer a handy free *Theatre Guide* (also at www.londontheatre.co.uk). Performances are nightly except Sunday, usually with one or two matinees a week (Shakespeare's Globe is the rare theater that does offer performances on Sunday, mid-May–Sept). Tickets range from about £8 to £40. Matinees are generally cheaper and rarely sell out.

To book a seat, simply call the theater box office directly, ask about seats and available dates, and buy a ticket with your credit card. You can call from the U.S. as easily as from England (check www.officiallondontheatre.co.uk, the American magazine *Variety*, or photocopy your hometown library's London newspaper theater section). Arrive about 30 minutes before the show starts to pick up your ticket and to avoid lines.

For a booking fee, you can reserve online (www.ticketmaster
.co.uk or www.firstcalltickets.com) or call Keith Prowse Ticketing,
formerly Global Tickets (U.S. tel. 800/223-6108). While booking through an agency is quick and easy, prices are inflated by a
standard 25 percent fee. Ticket agencies (whether in the U.S., at
London's TIs, or scattered throughout the city) are scalpers with
an address. If you're buying from an agency, look at the ticket
carefully (your price should be no more than 30 percent over the
printed face value; the 17.5 percent VAT is already included in the
face value) and understand where you're sitting according to the
floor plan (if your view is restricted, it will state this on the ticket;
for floor plans of the various theaters, see www.theatremonkey
.com). Agencies are worthwhile only if a show you've just got to
see is sold out at the box office. They scarf up hot tickets, planning
to make a killing after the show is sold out. U.S. booking agencies
get their tickets from another agency, adding even more to your
expense by involving yet another middleman. Many tickets sold
on the street are forgeries. Although some theaters have booking
agencies handle their advance sales, you'll stand a good chance of
saving money and avoiding the middleman by simply calling the
box office directly to book your tickets (international phone calls
are cheap and credit cards make booking a snap).

Theater Lingo: Stalls (ground floor), dress circle (first balcony), upper circle (second balcony), balcony (sky-high third balcony), slips (cheap seats on the fringes). Many cheap seats have a
restricted view (behind a pillar).

Cheap Theater Tricks: Most theaters offer cheap returned
tickets, standing-room, matinee, and senior or student standby
deals. These "concessions" are indicated with a "conc" or "s" in
the listings. Picking up a late return can get you a great seat at a
cheap-seat price. If a show is "sold out," there's usually a way to get
a seat. Call the theater box office and ask how.

Many theaters are so small that there's hardly a bad seat.
After the lights go down, scooting up is less than a capital offense.
Shakespeare did it.

Half-Price "tkts" Booth: This famous ticket booth at
Leicester Square sells discounted tickets for top-price seats to
shows on the push list the day of the show only (£2.50 service
charge per ticket, Mon–Sat 10:00–19:00, Sun 12:00–15:30, matinee tickets from noon, lines often form early, list of shows available
online, www.tkts.co.uk). Most tickets are half-price; other shows
are discounted 25 percent.

Here are some sample prices: A top-notch seat to *Chicago* costs
£40 bought directly from the theater, but only £22.50 at Leicester
(LESS-ter) Square. The cheapest balcony seat (bought from the

What's On in the West End

Here are some of the perennial favorites that you're likely to find among the West End's evening offerings. If spending the time and money for a London play, I like a full-fledged high-energy musical.

Generally you can book tickets for free at the box office or for a £2 fee by telephone or online.

Musicals

Chicago—A chorus-girl-gone-bad forms a nightclub act with another murderess to bring in the bucks (£15–42.50, Mon–Thu and Sat 20:00, Fri 20:30, matinees Fri 17:00 and Sat 15:00, Adelphi Theatre, Strand, Tube: Covent Garden or Charing Cross, booking tel. 020/7344-0055, www.chicagothemusical.com).

Mamma Mia!—This high-energy spandex-and-platform-boots musical weaves together 20 or 30 ABBA hits to tell the story of a bride in search of her real dad as her promiscuous mom plans her Greek Isle wedding. The production has the audience dancing by its happy ending (£25–49, Mon–Thu and Sat 19:30, Fri 20:30, matinees Fri 17:00 and Sat 15:00, Prince of Wales Theatre, Coventry Street, Tube: Piccadilly Circus, booking tel. 0870-850-0393).

Les Misérables—Claude-Michel Schönberg's musical adaptation of Victor Hugo's epic follows the life of Jean Valjean as he struggles with the social and political realities of 19th-century France. This inspiring mega-hit takes you back to the days of France's struggle for a just and modern society (£10–45, Mon–Sat 19:30, matinees Wed and Sat 14:30, Queen's Theatre, Shaftesbury Avenue, Tube: Piccadilly Circus, box office tel. 020/7494-5040, www.lesmis.com).

Phantom of the Opera—A mysterious masked man falls in love with a singer in this haunting Andrew Lloyd Webber musical about

theater) is £15. Half-price tickets can be a good deal, unless you want the cheapest seats or the hottest shows. But check the board; occasionally they sell cheap tickets to good shows. For example, a first-class seat to the long-running *Les Misérables* (which rarely sells out) costs £45 when bought from the theater ticket office, but you'll save 25 percent and pay £36.50 at the tkts booth. Note that the real half-price booth (with its new "tkts" name) is a freestanding kiosk at the edge of the garden in Leicester Square. Several dishonest outfits nearby advertise "official half-price tickets"; avoid these.

A second tkts booth has opened at the Canary Wharf Docklands Light Railway (DLR) Station. The freestanding kiosk is located near platforms #4 and #5 above the DLR concourse life beneath the stage of the Paris Opera (£15–45, Mon–Sat 19:30, matinees Tue and Sat 14:30, Her Majesty's Theatre, Haymarket, Tube: Piccadilly Circus, booking tel. 0870-890-1106, www .thephantomoftheopera.com).

The Lion King—In this Disney extravaganza featuring music by Elton John, Simba the lion learns about the delicately balanced circle of life on the savanna (£17.50–40, Tue–Sat 19:30, matinees Wed and Sat 14:00 and Sun 15:00, Lyceum Theatre, Wellington Street, Tube: Charing Cross or Covent Garden, booking tel. 0870-243-9000 or 020/7344-4444, theater info tel. 020/7420-8112, www.thelionking.co.uk).

We Will Rock You—If you're a Queen fan or not, this musical tribute more to the band than to Freddie Mercury, is an understandably popular celebration of their work (£23.50–55, Mon–Fri at 19:30, matinees Wed and Sat at 14:30, Dominion Theatre, Tottenham Court Road, Tube: Tottenham Court Road, Ticketmaster tel. 0870-169-0116, www.queenonline.com /wewillrockyou).

Thrillers
The Mousetrap—Agatha Christie's whodunit about a murder in a country house continues to stump audiences after 50 years (£11.50–30, Mon–Sat 20:00, matinees Tue 14:45 and Sat 17:00, St. Martin's Theatre, West Street, Tube: Leicester Square, box office tel. 0870-162-8787).

The Woman in Black—The chilling tale of a solicitor who is haunted by what he learns when he closes a reclusive woman's affairs (£12.50–32.50, Mon–Sat 20:00, matinees Tue 15:00 and Sat 16:00, Fortune Theatre, Russell Street, Tube: Covent Garden, box office tel. 020/7369-1737, www.thewomaninblack.com).

(Mon–Sat 11:30–18:00, closed Sun, Tube: Canary Wharf).

West End Theaters: The commercial (non-subsidized) theaters cluster around Soho (especially along Shaftesbury Avenue) and Covent Garden. With a centuries-old tradition of pleasing the masses, these present London theater at its glitziest. See the "What's On in the West End" sidebar.

Royal Shakespeare Company: If you'll ever enjoy Shakespeare, it'll be in Britain. The RSC performs at various theaters around London and in Stratford year-round. To get a schedule, contact the RSC (Royal Shakespeare Theatre, Stratford-upon-Avon, tel. 01789/403-444, www.rsc.org.uk).

Shakespeare's Globe: To see Shakespeare in a replica of the theater for which he wrote his plays, attend a play at the Globe. This round, thatch-roofed, open-air theater performs the plays much as Shakespeare intended (with no amplification). The play's the thing from mid-May through September (usually Tue–Sat 14:00 and 19:30, Sun at either 13:00 and 18:30 or 16:00 only, Mon at 19:30, tickets can be sold out months in advance). You'll pay £5 to stand and £13–29 to sit (usually on a backless bench; only a few rows and the pricier Gentlemen's Rooms have seats with backs; £2 cushions are considered a good investment by many). The £5 "groundling" tickets—while the only ones open to rain—are most fun. Scurry in early to stake out a spot on the stage's edge leaning rail, where the most interaction with the actors occurs. You're a crude peasant. You can lean your elbows on the stage, munch a picnic dinner, or walk around. I've never enjoyed Shakespeare as much as here, performed as it was meant to be in the "wooden O." Plays can be long. Many groundlings leave before the end. If you like, hang out an hour before the finish and beg or buy a ticket from someone leaving early (groundlings are allowed to come and go).

For information on plays or £9 tours (see page 102), contact the theater at tel. 020/7902-1500 (or see www.shakespeares-globe.org). To reserve tickets for plays, call or drop by the box office (Mon–Sat 10:00–18:00, until 20:00 on day of show, at Shakespeare's Globe at New Globe Walk entrance, tel. 020/7401-9919). If you reserve online (www.wayahead.com/shakespeares-globe), be warned: Your ticket price will have an added booking fee.

The theater is on the South Bank, directly across the Thames over the Millennium Bridge from St. Paul's Cathedral (Tube: Mansion House or London Bridge). The Globe is inconvenient for public transport, but the courtesy phone in the lobby gets a minicab in minutes. (These minicabs have set fees—e.g., £8 to South Kensington—but generally cost less than a metered cab and provide fine and honest service.) During theater season, there's a regular supply of black cabs outside the main foyer on New Globe Walk.

Fringe Theatre: London's rougher evening-entertainment scene is thriving, filling pages in *Time Out*. Choose from a wide range of fringe theater and comedy acts (generally £5).

Classical Music

For easy, cheap, or free concerts in historic churches, check the TIs' listings for **lunch concerts,** especially:

- Wren's St. Bride's Church, with free lunch concerts Mon–Fri at 13:15 (church tel. 020/7427-0133, www.stbrides.com).
- St. James at Piccadilly, with concerts on Mon, Wed, and Fri at 13:10 (suggested donation £3, info tel. 020/7381-0441, www.st-james-piccadilly.org).

- St. Martin-in-the-Fields, offering free concerts on Mon, Tue, and Fri at 13:00, church tel. 020/7766-1100, www.smitf.com).

St. Martin-in-the-Fields also hosts fine **evening concerts** by candlelight (£8–18, Thu–Sat at 19:30, sometimes also on Tue or Wed, box office tel. 020/7839-8362).

At St. Paul's Cathedral, **evensong** is held Monday through Saturday at 17:00 and on Sunday at 15:15. At Westminster Abbey, it's sung weekdays at 17:00 (but not on Wed) and Saturday and Sunday at 15:00. Free **organ recitals** are held on Sunday at Westminster Abbey (17:45, 30 min, tel. 020/7222-7110) and at St. Paul's (17:00, 30 min, tel. 020/7236-4128).

For a fun **classical event** (mid-July–early Sept), attend a "Prom Concert" (shortened from "Promenade Concert") during the annual festival at the Royal Albert Hall. Nightly concerts are offered at give-a-peasant-some-culture prices to "Promenaders"— those willing to stand throughout the performance (£4 standing-room spots sold at the door, £7 restricted-view seats, most £22 but depends on performance, Tube: South Kensington, tel. 020/7589-8212, www.royalalberthall.com).

Some of the world's best **opera** is belted out at the prestigious Royal Opera House, near Covent Garden (box office tel. 020/7304-4000, www.royalopera.org), and at the less-formal Sadler's Wells Theatre (Rosebery Avenue, Islington, Tube: Angel, info tel. 020/7863-8198, box office tel. 0870-737-7737, www.sadlerswells.com).

Walks, Bus Tour, and Cruises

Guided **walks** are offered several times a day. Original London Walks is the most established company (tel. 020/7624-3978, www.walks.com). Daytime walks vary: ancient London, museums, legal London, Dickens, Beatles, Jewish quarter, Christopher Wren, and so on. In the evening, expect a more limited choice: ghosts, Jack the Ripper, pubs, or a literary theme. Get the latest from a TI, fliers, or *Time Out*. Show up at the listed time and place, pay £5.50, and enjoy the two-hour tour.

To see the city illuminated at night, consider a **bus** tour. A two-hour London by Night Sightseeing Tour leaves every evening from Victoria Station (see page 64).

SLEEPING

London is expensive. Cheaper rooms are relatively dumpy. Don't expect £90 cheeriness in a £60 room. For £70 ($125), you'll get a double with breakfast in a safe, cramped, and dreary place with minimal service and the bathroom down the hall. For £90 ($160), you'll get a basic, clean, reasonably cheery double in a usually

London's Hotel Neighborhoods

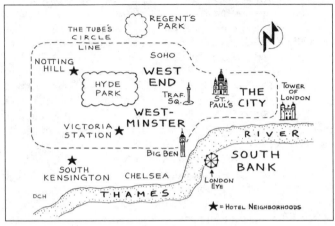

cramped, cracked-plaster building with a private bath, or a soulless but comfortable room without breakfast in a huge Motel 6–type place. My London splurges, at £100–150 ($180–270), are spacious, thoughtfully appointed places good for entertaining or romancing. Off-season, it's possible to save money by arriving late without a reservation and looking around. Competition softens prices, especially for multi-night stays. Hearty English or generous buffet breakfasts are included unless otherwise noted, and TVs are standard in rooms.

Reserve your London room with a phone call or e-mail as soon as you can commit to a date. To call a London hotel from the United States or Canada, dial 011-44-20 (London's area code without the initial zero), then the local eight-digit number. Some hotels will hold a room until 16:00 without a deposit, although most places will ask you for a credit-card number. The pricier ones have expensive cancellation policies (such as no refund if you cancel with less than 2 weeks' notice). Some fancy £120 rooms rent for a third off if you arrive late on a slow day and ask for a deal.

Looking for Hotel Deals Online

Given the high hotel prices and relatively weak dollar, consider turning to the Internet to help score a hotel deal. Various Web sites list rooms in high-rise, three- and four-star business hotels. You'll give up the charm and warmth of a family-run establishment, and breakfast will probably not be included, but you might find the price is right.

Start by checking the Web sites of several big hotel chains to get an idea of typical rates and to check for online-only deals. Big London hotel chains include: Millennium/Copthorne

Sleep Code

(£1 = about $1.80, country code: 44, area code: 020)
S = Single, **D** = Double/Twin, **T** = Triple, **Q** = Quad, **b** = bathroom, **s** = shower only. Unless otherwise noted, credit cards are accepted and prices include a generous breakfast and all taxes.

To help you sort easily through these listings, I've divided the rooms into three categories based on the price for a double room with bath:

$$$ Higher Priced—Most rooms £100 or more.
$$ Moderately Priced—Most rooms between £70–100.
$ Lower Priced—Most rooms £70 or less.

(www.millenniumhotels.com), Thistle (www.thistlehotels.com), Intercontinental/Holiday Inn (www.ichotelsgroup.com), Radisson (www.radisson.com), and Red Carnation (www.redcarnationhotels .com). For information on the no-frills, more Motel 6-type chains, see "Big, Cheap, Modern Hotels," below.

Auction-type sites (such as www.priceline.com) can be great for matching flexible travelers with empty hotel rooms, often at prices well below the hotel's own rates. Don't feel you have to start as high as the site's suggested opening bid. (For more about the complicated world of online bidding strategies and success stories from other travelers, see biddingfortravel.com or betterbidding .com.) Warning: Scoring a deal this way may require more patience and flexibility than you have, but if you enjoy shopping for cars, you'll probably like this, too.

Other favorite hotel discount sites mentioned by my readers include londontown.com, lastminute.com, visitlondon.com, findlondonrooms.com, and eurocheapo.com. Check the "Graffiti Wall" at ricksteves.com for the latest tips and discoveries.

For a good overview on finding London hotel deals, go to smartertravel.com and click on "Hotels," then "City Guides," and finally "Find the best hotel value in London."

Big, Cheap, Modern Hotels

These places—popular with budget tour groups—are well-run and offer elevators and all the modern comforts in a no-frills, practical package. With the notable exception of my second listing, they are often located on busy streets in dreary train-station neighborhoods, so use common sense after dark and wear your money belt. The doubles for £75–100 are a great value for London. Midweek prices are generally higher than weekend rates. Online bookings are often the easiest way to make reservations, and will get you a discount if you're staying at a Jurys or a Travelodge.

$$$ Jurys Inn Islington rents 200 compact, comfy rooms near King's Cross station (Db/Tb-£100, some discounted rooms available online, 2 adults and 2 kids—under age 12—can share 1 room, breakfast extra, non-smoking floors, 60 Pentonville Road, Tube: Angel, tel. 020/7282-5500, fax 020/7282-5511, www.jurysdoyle.com).

$$ Premier Travel Inn London County Hall, literally down the hall from a $400-a-night Marriott Hotel, fills one end of London's massive former County Hall building. This place is wonderfully located near the base of the London Eye Ferris Wheel and across the Thames from Big Ben. Its 300 slick rooms come with all the necessary comforts (Db-£87–90 for 2 adults and up to 2 kids under age 15, couples can request a bigger family room—same price, breakfast extra, book in advance, no-show rooms are released at 15:00, elevator, some smoke-free and easy-access rooms, 500 yards from Westminster Tube stop and Waterloo Station, Belvedere Road, you can call central reservations at 0870-242-8000 or 0870-238-3300, you can fax 020/7902-1619 but you might not get a response, it's easiest to book online at www.premiertravelinn.com).

$$ Premier Travel Inn London Southwark, with 55 rooms, is near Shakespeare's Globe on the South Bank (Db for up to 2 adults and 2 kids-£83–85, Bankside, 34 Park Street, tel. 0870-990-6402, www.premiertravelinn.com).

$$ Premier Travel Inn King's Cross, with 276 rooms, is just east of King's Cross station (Db-£75–85, non-smoking rooms available, breakfast extra, 24-hour reception, elevator, 26–30 York Way, tel. 0870-990-6414, fax 0870-990-6415, www.premiertravelinn.com).

Other **$$ Premier Travel Inns** charging £75–85 per room include **London Euston** (big, blue, Lego-type building packed with families on vacation on handy but noisy street, 141 Euston Road, Tube: Euston, tel. 0870-238-3301), **London Kensington** (11 Knaresboro Place, Tube: Earl's Court or Gloucester Road, tel. 0870-238-3304), and **London Putney Bridge** (farther out, 3 Putney Bridge Approach, Tube: Putney Bridge, tel. 0870-238-3302). Avoid the **Tower Bridge** location, which is an inconvenient, 15-minute walk from the nearest Tube stop. For any of these, call 0870-242-8000, fax 0870-241-9000, or best, book online at www.premiertravelinn.com.

$$ Hotel Ibis London Euston, which feels a bit classier than a Premier Travel Inn, is located on a quiet street a block behind and west of Euston Station (380 rooms, Db-£70–80, breakfast extra, no family rooms, non-smoking floor, 3 Cardington Street, tel. 020/7388-7777, fax 020/7388-0001, www.ibishotel.com, h0921@accor-hotels.com).

$ Travelodge London Islington is another typical chain hotel with lots of cookie-cutter rooms just south of King's Cross Station (Db-£60–80, some £26 rooms available online only for scattered dates, breakfast extra, family rooms, non-smoking rooms, 100 Kings Cross Road, tel. 0870-191-1773, fax 020/7833-8261, www .travelodge.co.uk). Other Travelodge London locations are at **King's Cross, Covent Garden, Liverpool Street,** and **Farringdon.** For all the details on each, see www.travelodge.co.uk.

Victoria Station Neighborhood (Belgravia)

The streets behind Victoria Station teem with budget B&Bs. It's a

safe, surprisingly tidy, and decent area without a hint of the trashy, touristy glitz of the streets in front of the station. West of the tracks is Belgravia, where the prices are a bit higher and your neighbors include Andrew Lloyd Webber and Margaret Thatcher (her policeman stands outside 73 Chester Square). East of the tracks is Pimlico—cheaper and just as handy, but the rooms can be a bit dowdier. Decent eateries abound (see "Eating," page 137).

All the recommended hotels are within a five-minute walk of the Victoria Tube, bus, and train stations. On hot summer nights, request a quiet back room. Nearby is the 400-space Semley Place NCP **garage** (£30/day, possible discounts with hotel voucher, just west of the Victoria Coach Station at Buckingham Palace Road and Semley Place, tel. 0870-242-7144, www.ncp.co.uk). The handy **Pimlico Launderette** is about five blocks southwest of Warwick Square (daily 8:00–20:00, self-service or full service, south of Sutherland Street at 3 Westmoreland Terrace, tel. 020/7821-8692). **Launderette Centre** is a block north of Warwick Square (Mon–Fri 8:00–22:00, until 19:30 on Sat and Sun, £7 wash and dry, £9 with service, 31 Churton Street, tel. 020/7828-6039).

$$$ Lime Tree Hotel, enthusiastically run by David Davies and his daughter Charlotte, comes with 30 spacious and thoughtfully decorated rooms and a fun-loving breakfast room (Sb-£75–80, Db-£105–130 depending on room size, Tb-£140–160, family room-£150–175, £10 discount per night with cash, all rooms nonsmoking, quiet garden, David deals in slow times and is creative at helping travelers in a bind, 135 Ebury Street, tel. 020/7730-8191, fax 020/7730-7865, www.limetreehotel.co.uk, info@limetreehotel .co.uk, trusty Alan covers the night shift).

Victoria Station Neighborhood

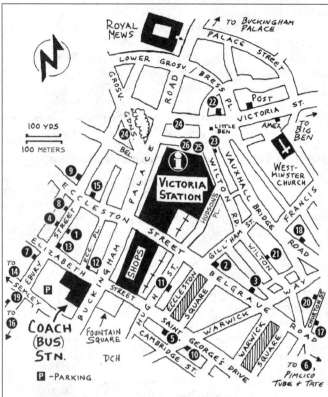

1. Lime Tree Hotel
2. Quality Hotel Westminster
3. Winchester Hotel
4. James House & Cartref House Hotels
5. Elizabeth Hotel & Jubilee Hotel
6. To Holiday Inn Express
7. Morgan House
8. Collin House Hotel
9. Harcourt House
10. Elizabeth House & Bakers Hotel
11. Cherry Court Hotel
12. Goya Spanish Rest. & Tapas Bar
13. Ebury Wine Bar
14. To Duke of Wellington Pub
15. Jenny Lo's Tea House
16. To La Poule au Pot Rest.
17. Grumbles Restaurant
18. The Jugged Hare Pub
19. The Belgravia Pub
20. Chimes English Rest. & Cider Bar
21. Seafresh Fish Restaurant
22. Sainsbury's Local Grocery
23. Internet Café
24. Bus Tours (Day)
25. Bus Tours (Night)
26. TI, Tube, Taxis, City Buses

$$$ Quality Hotel Westminster is big, modern (but with tired carpets), well-located, and a good bet for no-nonsense comfort (Db-£130, check for various Web specials, drop-ins can ask for "saver prices" on slow days, breakfast extra or bargained in, non-smoking floor, elevator, 82 Eccleston Square, tel. 020/7834-8042, fax 020/7630-8942, www.hotels-westminster.com, winchesterhotel17 @hotmail.com).

$$$ Holiday Inn Express fills an old building with 52 fresh, modern, and efficient rooms (Db-£114 rack rate, often £80—especially Sun or if booked online; family rooms, up to 2 kids free, non-smoking floor, elevator, Tube: Pimlico, 106 Belgrave Road, tel. 020/7630-8888, fax 020/7828-0441, www.hiexpressvictoria .co.uk, info@hiexpressvictoria.co.uk).

$$ Winchester Hotel is family-run and perhaps the best value, with 18 fine rooms and a caring management (Db-£85, Tb-£110, Qb-£140, cash only, no groups, no infants, 17 Belgrave Road, tel. 020/7828-2972, fax 020/7828-5191, www.winchester-hotel .net, enquiry@winchester-hotel.net, commanded with panache by irrepressible Jimmy and his crew: Juanita, Andrew, and Frank). The Winchester also rents apartments—with kitchenettes, sitting rooms, and beds on the quiet back side—around the corner (£125–230).

$$ James House and **Cartref House** are two nearly identical, well-run, smoke-free, 10-room places on either side of Ebury Street (S-£52, Sb-£62, D-£70, Db-£85, T-£95, Tb-£110, family bunk-bed Qb-£135, 5 percent discount with cash, all rooms with fans, strictly no smoking, James House at 108 Ebury Street, tel. 020/7730-7338; Cartref House at 129 Ebury Street, tel. 020/7730-6176, www.jamesandcartref.co.uk, info@jamesandcartref.co.uk, run by Derek and Sharon).

$$ Elizabeth Hotel is a stately old place overlooking Eccleston Square, with fine public spaces and 40 well-worn, slightly overpriced, but spacious and decent rooms (S-£55, Sb-£77, D-£77, small Db-£93, big Db-£105, Tb-£118, Qb-£130, Quint/b-£135, 37 Eccleston Square, tel. 020/7828-6812, fax 020/7828-6814, www.elizabethhotel.com, info@elizabethhotel.com). Be careful not to confuse this hotel with the nearby (cheaper but also recommended) Elizabeth House. Elizabeth Hotel also rents apartments that sleep up to six (£195/night, includes breakfast).

$$ Harcourt House rents 10 newly-refurbished, neo-Victorian, smoke-free rooms (Sb-£60, Db-£80, 50 Ebury Street, tel. 020/7730-2722, www.harcourthousehotel.co.uk, harcourthouse@talk21.com, run by helpful David and Glesni Wood and cute dog Suki).

$$ Morgan House rents 11 good rooms and is entertainingly run, with lots of travel tips and friendly chat—especially about the local rich and famous—by owner Rachel Joplin and manager Davinia (S-£46, D-£66, Db-£86, T-£86, family suites-£110–122 for 3–4 people, 120 Ebury Street, tel. 020/7730-2384, fax 020/7730-8442, www.morganhouse.co.uk, morganhouse@connect.com).

$$ Collin House Hotel, clean, simple, and efficiently run, offers 12 relatively spacious rooms with woody, modern furnishings (Sb-£55, D-£68, Db-£82, T-£95, non-smoking rooms, 104 Ebury St, tel. & fax 020/7730-8031, www.collinhouse.co.uk, booking@collinhouse.co.uk, absentee owner).

$ Cherry Court Hotel, run by the friendly and industrious Patel family, rents 12 small, basic, air-conditioned rooms in a central location (Sb-£45, Db-£55, Tb-£75, Qb-£90, Quint/b-£105, prices promised with this book through 2006, paying with credit card costs 5 percent extra, fruit-basket breakfast in room, entirely non-smoking, free Internet access with free disk burning, peaceful garden patio, 23 Hugh Street, tel. 020/7828-2840, fax 020/7828-0393, www.cherrycourthotel.co.uk, bookings@cherrycourthotel.co.uk).

$ Jubilee Hotel is a well-run slumber-mill with 26 tiny rooms and many tiny beds—but good prices for London (S-£35, Db-£50, tiny D-£50, tiny Db-£60, Db-£65, Tb-£75, Qb-£95, 5 percent discount with this book through 2006, 31 Eccleston Square, tel. 020/7834-0845, www.jubileehotel.co.uk, reservations@jubileehotel.co.uk). The Jubilee is run by Bob Patel, whose family runs the Cherry Court, listed above.

$ Elizabeth House offers 40 of some of the best cheap—albeit spartan—rooms in town, with a professional reception and a guests' kitchen where you can do your own cooking (S-£35, D-£50, Db-£60, Tb-£70, Q-£80, Qb-£85, Quint/b-£90, includes continental breakfast, avoid some street noise by requesting quiet room in the back, 118 Warwick Way, tel. 020/7630-0741, fax 020/7630-0740, www.elizabethhouse.co.uk, elizabethhouselondon@yahoo.co.uk).

$ Bakers Hotel is a cheapie, with 10 small, tight, and very simple rooms, but it's well-located and offers youth hostel prices and a full breakfast (S-£30, D-£46, T-£55, 126 Warwick Way, tel. 020/7834-0729, www.bakershotel.co.uk, reservations@bakershotel.co.uk, Amin Jamani).

"South Kensington," She Said, Loosening His Cummerbund

To live on a quiet street so classy it doesn't allow hotel signs, surrounded by trendy shops and colorful restaurants, call "South Ken" your London home. Shoppers like being a short walk from Harrods and the designer shops of King's Road and Chelsea. When I splurge, I splurge here. Sumner Place is just off Old Brompton Road, 200 yards from the handy South Kensington

South Kensington Neighborhood

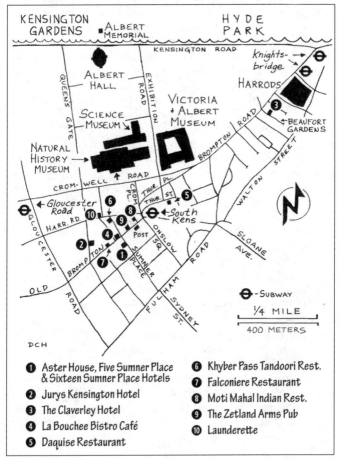

KENSINGTON GARDENS

■ ALBERT MEMORIAL

HYDE PARK

KENSINGTON ROAD

Knights-→ bridge

QUEENS GATE

ALBERT HALL

EXHIBITION ROAD

HARRODS

SCIENCE MUSEUM

VICTORIA & ALBERT MUSEUM

BROMPTON ROAD

BEAUFORT GARDENS

NATURAL HISTORY MUSEUM

CROM-WELL ROAD

WALTON STREET

❸

←Gloucester Road

❻

THUR. PL.
THUR. ST.

❺

GLOUCESTER

HARR. RD.

❿

❽

❾

←South Kens

❹

Post

ONSLOW SQ.

SLOANE AVE.

❷

BROMPTON

SUMNER PLACE

❶

ROAD

❼

OLD

ROAD

FULHAM ROAD

SYDNEY ST.

N

⊖ - SUBWAY

¼ MILE

400 METERS

DCH

❶ Aster House, Five Sumner Place & Sixteen Sumner Place Hotels
❷ Jurys Kensington Hotel
❸ The Claverley Hotel
❹ La Bouchee Bistro Café
❺ Daquise Restaurant

❻ Khyber Pass Tandoori Rest.
❼ Falconiere Restaurant
❽ Moti Mahal Indian Rest.
❾ The Zetland Arms Pub
❿ Launderette

Tube station (on Circle Line, 2 stops from Victoria Station, direct Heathrow connection). There's a taxi rank in the median strip at the end of Harrington Road. The handy **Wash & Dry launderette** is on the corner of Queensberry Place and Harrington Road (daily 8:00–21:00, bring 20p and £1 coins).

$$$ Aster House, run by friendly and accommodating Simon and Leonie Tan, has won the "Best B&B in London" award three times in the last five years. It has a sumptuous lobby, lounge, and breakfast room. Its rooms are comfy and quiet, with TV, phone, and air-conditioning. Enjoy breakfast or just lounging in the whisper-elegant Orangery, a Victorian greenhouse (Sb-£90, Db-£130, bigger Db-£160, deluxe 4-poster Db-£175, these prices with this book through 2006, entirely non-smoking, 3 Sumner Place, tel. 020/7581-5888, fax 020/7584-4925, www.asterhouse.com, asterhouse@btinternet.com). Simon and Leonie also offer free Internet access, Wi-Fi, and loaner mobile phones to their guests.

$$$ **Five Sumner Place Hotel** has received several "Best Small Hotel in London" awards in the last decade. The 13 rooms in this 150-year-old building are tastefully decorated, and the breakfast room is a conservatory/greenhouse (Sb-£100, Db-£155, third bed-£25, ask for 20 percent Rick Steves discount in 2006; TV, phone, and fridge in room by request; non-smoking rooms, elevator, 5 Sumner Place, tel. 020/7584-7586, fax 020/7823-9962, www.sumnerplace.com, reservations@sumnerplace.com).

$$$ **Sixteen Sumner Place,** for well-heeled travelers, has over-the-top formality and class packed into its 42 rooms, plush lounges, and tranquil garden. It's in a labyrinthine building, with modern decor throughout (Db-£170–250—but soft, breakfast in the garden, elevator, 16 Sumner Place, tel. 020/7589-5232, fax 020/7584-8615, U.S. tel. 800/553-6674, www.firmdale.com, sixteen@firmdale.com).

$$$ **The Claverley,** two blocks from Harrods, is on a quiet street similar to Sumner Place. The 30 fancy, dark-wood-and-marble rooms come with all the comforts (S-£80, Sb-£100–110, Db-£150, sofa-bed Tb-£190–215, ask for Rick Steves discount, plush lounge, non-smoking rooms, elevator, 13–14 Beaufort Gardens, Tube: Knightsbridge, tel. 020/7589-8541, fax 020/7584-3410, U.S. tel. 800/747-0398, www.claverleyhotel.co.uk, reservations @claverleyhotel.co.uk).

$$$ **Jurys Kensington Hotel** is big, stately, and impersonal, with a greedy pricing scheme (Db-£100–140 depending on "availability," ask for a deal, breakfast extra, piano lounge, non-smoking floors, elevator, 109–113 Queen's Gate, tel. 020/7589-6300, fax 020/7581-1492, www.jurysdoyle.com, kensington@jurysdoyle .com).

Notting Hill and Bayswater Neighborhoods

Residential Notting Hill has quick bus and Tube access to downtown, and, for London, is very "homely" (a.k.a. homey) It's also peppered with trendy bars and restaurants, and is home to the historic Coronet movie theater, as well as the famous Portobello Road Market (see page 109).

Popular with young international travelers, Bayswater's Queensway street is a multicultural festival of commerce and eateries (see "Eating," page 139). The neighborhood does its dirty clothes at **Galaxy Launderette** (£4 self-serve, £8 full-serve, daily 8:00–20:00, corner of St. Petersburgh Place and Moscow Road at 65 Moscow Road, tel. 020/7229-7771). For **Internet access,** you'll find several stops along busy Queensway and a self-serve bank

Notting Hill and Bayswater Neighborhoods

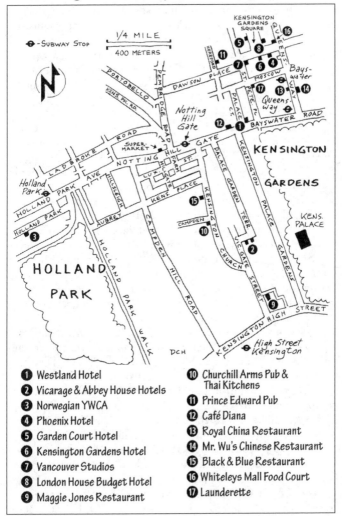

1. Westland Hotel
2. Vicarage & Abbey House Hotels
3. Norwegian YWCA
4. Phoenix Hotel
5. Garden Court Hotel
6. Kensington Gardens Hotel
7. Vancouver Studios
8. London House Budget Hotel
9. Maggie Jones Restaurant
10. Churchill Arms Pub & Thai Kitchens
11. Prince Edward Pub
12. Café Diana
13. Royal China Restaurant
14. Mr. Wu's Chinese Restaurant
15. Black & Blue Restaurant
16. Whiteleys Mall Food Court
17. Launderette

of easyInternetcafé computer terminals at the food circus level of the Whiteleys Shopping Centre (daily 8:30–24:00, corner of Queensway and Porchester Gardens).

Near Kensington Gardens Square

Several big old hotels line the quiet Kensington Gardens Square (not to be confused with the much bigger Kensington Gardens), a block west of bustling Queensway, north of Bayswater Tube station. These hotels are quiet for central London.

$$$ Phoenix Hotel, a Best Western modernization of a 125-room hotel, offers American business-class comforts; spacious, plush public spaces; and big, fresh, modern-feeling rooms. Its prices—which range from fine value to rip-off—are determined by a greedy computer program, with huge variations according to expected demand. See their Web site and book online to save money (Db-£90–150, elevator, 1–8 Kensington Gardens Square, tel. 020/7229-2494, fax 020/7727-1419, U.S. tel. 800/528-1234, www.phoenixhotel.co.uk, info@phoenixhotel.co.uk).

$$ Garden Court Hotel rents 34 comfortable, smoke-free rooms. It's newly refurbished and has a garden (S-£40, Sb-£62, D-£64, Db-£92, T-£84, Tb-£114, Q-£94, Qb-£135, 10 percent discount with this book through 2006, elevator, 30 Kensington Gardens Square, tel. 020/7229-2553, fax 020/7727-2749, www.gardencourthotel.co.uk, info@gardencourthotel.co.uk, well-run by Edward and his trusty first mate Paul).

$$ Kensington Gardens Hotel laces 16 decent rooms together in a tall, skinny place with lots of stairs and no elevator (Ss-£45–50, Sb-£50–55, Db-£75, Tb-£95, book by phone or e-mail rather than through the pricier Web site, 9 Kensington Gardens Square, tel. 020/7221-7790, fax 020/7792-8612, www.kensingtongardenshotel.co.uk, info@kensingtongardenshotel.co.uk, charming Rowshanak).

$$ Vancouver Studios offers 45 modern rooms with fully-equipped kitchenettes (utensils, stove, microwave, and fridge) rather than breakfast (small Sb-£60, small Db-£85, big Db-£100, Tb-£120, extra bed-£18, 10 percent discount with weeklong stay or more, call to confirm reservation a night or two before, welcoming lounge and garden, near Kensington Gardens Square at 30 Prince's Square, tel. 020/7243-1270, fax 020/7221-8678, www.vancouverstudios.co.uk, info@vancouverstudios.co.uk).

$ London House Budget Hotel is a threadbare, nose-ringed slumber mill renting more than 200 beds in about 80 stark rooms. While their rack rates are high (to hide Web booking commissions for those who don't go direct), their own Web site offers much better prices such as Db-£46 (S-£50, Sb-£56, twin-£54, Db-£60, dorm bed-£16, prices flex downward with demand, includes continental breakfast, lots of school groups, free Internet access, 81 Kensington Gardens Square, tel. 020/7243-1810, fax 020/7243-1723, www.londonhousehotel.co.uk, londonhousehotel@yahoo.co.uk).

Near Kensington Gardens

$$$ Westland Hotel is comfortable, convenient, and hotelesque, with a fine lounge and spacious rooms. Rooms are recently refurbished and quite plush. Their £105 doubles (less your 10 percent discount—see below) are the best value (Sb-£88–99, Db-£105, deluxe Db-£121, cavernous deluxe Db-£138, sprawling Tb-£132–154, gargantuan Qb-£150–175, Quint/b-£165–187, 10 percent discount with this book if claimed upon arrival; elevator, free garage with 6 spaces; between Notting Hill Gate and Queensway Tube stations; 154 Bayswater Road, tel. 020/7229-9191, fax 020/7727-1054, www.westlandhotel.co.uk, reservations@westlandhotel .co.uk).

$$$ Vicarage Private Hotel, understandably popular, is family-run and elegantly British in a quiet, classy neighborhood. It has 17 rooms furnished with taste and quality, a TV lounge, and facilities on each floor. Mandy, Richard, and Krassi maintain a homey and caring atmosphere (S-£46, Sb-£75, D-£78, Db-£102, T-£95, Tb-£130, Q-£102, Qb-£140, cash only, 6-min walk from Notting Hill Gate and High Street Kensington Tube stations, near Kensington Palace at 10 Vicarage Gate, tel. 020/7229-4030, fax 020/7792-5989, www.londonvicaragehotel.com, reception @londonvicaragehotel.com).

$$ Abbey House Hotel, next door, is basic but its 16 rooms are bright, friendly, and sleepable (S-£45, D-£74, T-£90, Q-£100, Quint-£110, cash only, 11 Vicarage Gate, tel. 020/7727-2594, fax 020/7727-1873, www.abbeyhousekensington.com, abbeyhousedesk@btconnect.com, Rodrigo).

Near Holland Park

$ Norwegian YWCA (Norsk K.F.U.K.) is for women under 30 only (and men under 30 with Norwegian passports). Located on a quiet, stately street, it offers non-smoking rooms, a study, TV room, piano lounge, and an open-face Norwegian ambience (goat cheese on Sundays!). They have mostly quads, so those willing to share with strangers are most likely to get a bed (July–Aug: Ss-£33, shared double-£31/bed, shared triple-£26/bed, shared quad-£23/bed, includes breakfast and sack lunch; Sept–June: same prices also include dinner; 52 Holland Park, tel. 020/7727-9346, fax 020/7727-8718, www.kfuk.dial.pipex.com, kfuk.hjemmet@kfuk -kfum.no). With each visit, I wonder which is easier to get—a sex change or a Norwegian passport?

Other Neighborhoods

Near Covent Garden: **$$$ Fielding Hotel,** located on a charming, quiet pedestrian street just two blocks east of Covent Garden, offers 24 no-nonsense rooms, bright orange hallways, and lots of stairs. You're paying about £20 extra for rather small, basic rooms in a very fine location (Db-£100–115, Db with sitting room-£130, no breakfast, no smoking, no kids under 13, 4 Broad Court, Bow Street, tel. 020/7836-8305, fax 020/7497-0064, www.the-fielding -hotel.co.uk).

Downtown near Baker Street: $$$ **The 22 York Street B&B** offers a less hotelesque alternative in the center, renting 18 stark, hardwood, comfortable rooms (Db-£100, Tb-£141, 2-night minimum, strictly smoke-free, social breakfast, inviting lounge; from Baker Street Tube station, walk 2 blocks down Baker Street and take a right, 22 York Street; tel. 020/7224-3990, fax 020/7224-1990, www.22yorkstreet.co.uk, mc@22yorkstreet.co.uk, energetically run by Liz and Michael Callis).

Near Buckingham Palace: $$ **Vandon House Hotel,** run by the Central College in Iowa, is packed with students most of the year, but its 33 rooms are rented to travelers from late May through August at great prices. The rooms, while institutional, are comfy, and the location is excellent (S-£43, D-£68, Db-£84, Tb-£99, Qb-£118, only single beds, non-smoking, elevator, on a tiny road 3-min walk west of St. James's Park Tube station and 7-min walk from Victoria Station, near east end of Petty France Street at 1 Vandon Street, tel. 020/7799-6780, fax 020/7799-1464, www.vandonhouse.com, info@vandonhouse.com).

Euston Station: The $$ **Methodist International Centre,** a modern, youthful, Christian residence, fills its lower floors with international students and its top floor with travelers. Rooms are modern and simple yet comfortable, with fine bathrooms, phones, and desks. The atmosphere is friendly, safe, clean, and controlled; it also has a spacious lounge and game room (Db-£85, 2-course buffet dinner-£13, non-smoking rooms, elevator, on a quiet street a block west of Euston Station, 81–103 Euston Street—not Euston Road, Tube: Euston Station, tel. 020/7380-0001, fax 020/7387-5300, www.micentre.com, acc@micentre.com). In June, July, and August, when the students are gone, they also rent simpler rooms (S-£45, D-£68).

Hostels and Dorms

$ A cluster of three **St. Christopher's Inn** hostels, south of the Thames near London Bridge, rent £16–20 beds (Tube: Borough or London Bridge, 161–165 Borough High Street, tel. 020/7407-1856, www.st-christophers.co.uk).

$ The **City of London Youth Hostel,** near St. Paul's, is clean, modern, friendly, and well-run. You'll pay £17 per bed in an 11-bed dorm, about £25 for a bed in their three- to eight-bed rooms, or £32 for a single room (£2 extra if you have no hostel card, 193 beds, cheap meals, open 24 hours, Tube: St. Paul's, 36 Carter Lane, tel. 020/7236-4965, fax 020/7236-7681, www.yha.org.uk, city@yha.org.uk).

$ The **University of Westminster** opens up its dorm rooms to travelers during summer break, from mid-June through mid-September. Located in several high-rise buildings scattered around central London, the rooms—some with private bathrooms, others with shared bathrooms nearby—come with access to well-stocked kitchens and big lounges (S-£27–35, D-£47–56, tel. 020/7834-1169, www.wmin.ac.uk/comserv, comserv@wmin.ac.uk). University College London also has rooms for travelers from mid-June until mid-September; for details see www.ucl.ac.uk/residences.

Near Gatwick and Heathrow Airports

Near Gatwick Airport: **$ London Gatwick Airport Premier Travel Inn** rents cheap rooms at the airport (Db-£58, £2.50 shuttle bus from airport, tel. 0870-238-3305, www.premiertravelinn .com). **$ Gatwick Travelodge** has budget rooms two miles from the airport (Db-£50, £3 shuttle from airport, breakfast extra, Church Road, Lowfield Heath, Crawley, tel. 0870-191-1531, www .travelodge.co.uk).

$ Barn Cottage, a converted 16th-century barn, sits in the peaceful countryside, with a tennis court, small swimming pool, and a good pub within walking distance. It has two wood-beamed rooms, antique furniture, and a large garden that makes you forget Gatwick is 10 minutes away (S-£50, D-£60, cash only, can drive you to airport or train station for £8, Church Road, Leigh, Reigate, Surrey, tel. 01306/611-347, warmly run by Pat and Mike Comer). Do not confuse this place with others of the same name; this Barn Cottage has no Web site.

$ Wayside Manor Farm is another rural alternative to a bland airport hotel. This four-bedroom countryside place is a 10-minute drive from Gatwick (Db-£65, Tb-£80, Norwood Hill, near Charlwood, tel. 01293/862-692, www.wayside-manor.com, info@wayside-manor.com).

Near Heathrow Airport: It's so easy to get to Heathrow from central London, I see no reason to sleep there. But for budget beds near the airport, consider **$ Heathrow Ibis** (Db-£68, Db-£45 on Fri–Sun nights, breakfast extra, £3 shuttle bus to/from terminals except T-4, look for "Hopabus" run by National Express, 112 Bath Road, tel. 020/8759-4888, fax 020/8564-7894, www.ibishotel.com, h0794@accor-hotels.com).

EATING

If you want to dine (as opposed to eat), check out the extensive listings in the weekly entertainment guides sold at London newsstands (or catch a train for Paris). The thought of a £40 meal in Britain generally ruins my appetite, so my London dining is limited mostly to easygoing, fun, but inexpensive alternatives. I've listed places by neighborhood—handy to your sightseeing or hotel.

Pub grub is the most atmospheric budget option. Many of

London's 7,000 pubs serve fresh, tasty buffets under ancient timbers, with hearty lunches and dinners for £6–8.

Ethnic restaurants—especially Indian and Chinese—are popular, plentiful, and cheap. Most large museums (and many churches) have inexpensive, cheery cafeterias. Of course, picnicking is the fastest and cheapest way to go. Good grocery stores and sandwich shops, fine park benches, and polite pigeons abound in Britain's most expensive city.

Near Trafalgar Square

Each of these places is within about 100 yards of Trafalgar Square. To locate the following restaurants, see the map on page 131.

St. Martin-in-the-Fields Café in the Crypt is just right for a tasty meal on a monk's budget, sitting on somebody's tomb in an ancient crypt. While their enticing buffet line is kept stocked all day, their cheap sandwich bar is generally sold out by 11:30 (£6–8 cafeteria plates, Mon–Wed 10:00–20:00, Thu–Sat 10:00–22:00, Sun 12:00–20:00, profits go to the church, underneath St. Martin-in-the-Fields Church on Trafalgar Square, tel. 020/7839-4342). While here, check out the concert schedule for the busy church upstairs.

The Chandos Pub's Opera Room floats amazingly apart from the tacky crush of tourism around Trafalgar Square. Look for it opposite the National Portrait Gallery (corner of William Street and St. Martin's Lane) and climb the stairs to the Opera Room. This is a fine Trafalgar rendezvous point—smoky, but wonderfully local. They serve traditional, plain-tasting £6–7 pub meals (kitchen open Mon–Wed 11:00–19:00, Thu–Sun until 18:00, order and pay at the bar, tel. 020/7836-1401). The ground-floor pub is a "spit and sawdust" type of pub, with serious beer and some toasted sandwiches.

Gordon's Wine Bar, with a simple, steep staircase leading into a candlelit 15th-century wine cellar, is filled with dusty old bottles, faded British memorabilia, and local nine-to-fivers. At the buffet, choose a hot meal or a fine plate of cheeses and various cold cuts. (One £7 cold plate, which comes with a salad bar and a couple of glasses of wine, provides a light, economical meal for two.) Then step up to the wine bar and consider the many varieties of wine and port available by the glass. This place is passionate about port. The low, carbon-crusted vaulting deeper in the back seems to intensify the Hogarth-painting atmosphere. While it's crowded, you can normally corral two chairs and grab the corner of a table (arrive before 17:30 to get a seat, Mon–Sat 11:00–23:00, Sun 12:00–22:00, 2 blocks from Trafalgar Square, bottom of Villiars Street at #47, Tube: Embankment, tel. 020/7930-1408). On hot days, the crowd spills out into a leafy back patio.

Central London Eateries

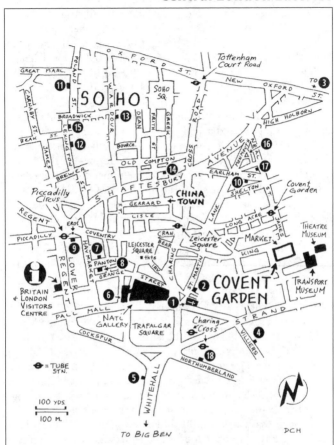

1. St. Martin-in-the-Fields Café in the Crypt
2. The Chandos Pub's Opera Room
3. To The Princess Louise Pub
4. Gordon's Wine Bar
5. The Lord Moon of the Mall Pub
6. Crivelli's Garden Restaurant
7. Pizza Express, Stockpot & West End Kitchen
8. Woodland South Indian Vegetarian Rest.
9. Criterion Brasserie
10. Belgo Centraal
11. Yo! Sushi
12. Wagamama Noodle Bar
13. Soho Spice Indian & Busaba Eathai Thai Rest.
14. Y Ming Chinese Rest.
15. Andrew Edmunds & Mildred's Vegetarian Rest.
16. Neal's Yard Eateries
17. Food for Thought Café
18. Sherlock Holmes Pub

The Lord Moon of the Mall Pub fills a great old former Barclays Bank building a block down Whitehall from Trafalgar Square. They have real ales on tap and good, cheap pub grub, including a two-meals-for-the-price-of-one deal (£7.50, offer valid Mon–Fri 14:00–21:30, all day Sat–Sun). The pub is kid-friendly and smoke-free throughout (daily 10:00–23:00, 18 Whitehall, tel. 020/7839-7701). Nearby are several cheap cafeterias and pizza joints.

Sherlock Holmes Pub has a casual ground-floor section serving cheap grub and a stodgier upstairs restaurant with a spy-theme menu (£10 main courses). Fans of the fictional detective will appreciate the wonderful replica of Holmes' 221-B Baker Street home and the pub's location in the former Northumberland Hotel (featured in Holmes stories). The former Old Scotland Yard was just across the street (daily 11:00–23:00, 10 Northumberland Street, Tube: Charing Cross/Embankment, tel. 020/7930-2644).

Crivelli's Garden Restaurant, serving a classy lunch in the National Gallery, is a good place to treat your palate to pricey, light Mediterranean cuisine (£15 lunches, daily 10:00–17:00, first floor of Sainsbury Wing).

Cheap Eating near Piccadilly

Hungry and broke in the theater district? Head for Panton Street (off Haymarket, 2 blocks southeast of Piccadilly Circus) where several hard-working little places compete, all seeming to offer a three-course meal for about £7. Peruse the entire block (vegetarian, Japanese, Pizza Express, Moroccan, Thai, Chinese, and 2 famous London eateries) before making your choice. **Stockpot** is a mushy-peas kind of place, famous and rightly popular for its edible, cheap meals (daily 7:00–22:00, 38 Panton Street). The **West End Kitchen** (across the street at #5, same hours and menu) is a direct competitor that's just as good. Vegetarians prefer the **Woodland South Indian Vegetarian Restaurant**.

The palatial **Criterion Brasserie** serves a special £15 two-course "Anglo-French" menu (or £18 for 3 courses) under gilded tiles and chandeliers in a dreamy Byzantine church setting from 1880. It's right on Piccadilly Circus but a world away from the punk junk. The house wine is great and so is the food (specials available Mon–Sat 12:00–14:30 & 17:30–19:00, closed Sun, tel. 020/7930-0488). After 19:00, the menu becomes really expensive. Anyone can drop in for coffee or a drink.

Hip Eating from Covent Garden to Soho

London has a trendy, Generation-X scene that most Beefeater-seekers miss entirely. These restaurants are scattered throughout the hipster, gay, and girlie-bar district, teeming each evening with fun-seekers and theatergoers. Even if you plan to have dinner elsewhere, it's a treat to just wander around this lively area. Beware of the extremely welcoming girls that stand outside the strip bars. But if you're curious, head down Great Windmill Street and stop by the door at each of the three bars. Enjoy the sales pitch, but only fools enter—like a fish attracted to a fancy, well-polished lure, you hardly see the hook. Naive guys bite for the "£5 drink and show" and step in...and then can't get out without emptying their wallets.

Belgo Centraal serves hearty Belgian specialties. It's a seafood, chips, and beer emporium dressed up as a mod-monastic refectory—with noisy acoustics and waiters garbed as Trappist monks. The classy restaurant section is more comfortable and less rowdy, but usually requires reservations. It's often more fun to just grab a spot in the boisterous beer hall, with its tight, communal benches (no reservations accepted). The same menu and specials work on both sides. Belgians claim they eat as well as the French and as heartily as the Germans. Specialties include mussels, great fries, and a stunning array of dark, blond, and fruity Belgian beers. Belgo actually makes Belgian things trendy—a formidable feat (£10–14 meals; open daily until 23:00; Mon–Fri 17:00–18:30—or 5 p.m.–6:30 p.m.—"beat the clock" meal specials for £5–6.30—the time you order is the price you pay—and you get mussels, fries, and beer; no meal-splitting after 18:30, and you must buy food with beer; daily £6 lunch special 12:00–17:00; 2 kids eat free for each parent ordering a regular entree; 1 block north of Covent Garden Tube station at intersection of Neal and Shelton streets, 50 Earlham Street, tel. 020/7813-2233).

Yo! Sushi is a futuristic Japanese-food-extravaganza experience. It's not cheap, but it's sure to be a memorable experience, complete with thumping rock, Japanese cable TV, a 195-foot-long conveyor belt—the world's longest sushi bar—and automated sushi machines. For £1 each you get unlimited tea and water (from spigot at bar, with or without gas). Snag a bar stool and grab dishes as they rattle by (priced by color of dish; check the chart: £1.50–5 per dish, £1.50 for miso soup, daily 12:00–24:00, 2 blocks south of Oxford Street, where Lexington Street becomes Poland Street, 52 Poland Street, tel. 020/7287-0443). (If you like Yo!, there are several locations around town, including a handy branch a block from the London Eye on Belvedere Road, as well as outlets within Selfridges, Harvey Nichols department stores, and Whiteleys Mall on Queensway—see page 140.)

Wagamama Noodle Bar is a noisy, pan-Asian, organic slurpathon. As you enter, check out the kitchen and listen to the roar of the basement, where benches rock with happy eaters. Everybody

Pub Appreciation

The pub is the heart of the people's England, where all manner of folks have, for generations, found their respite from work and a home-away-from-home. England's classic pubs are national treasures, with great cultural value, rich history, and—not to mention—good beer and grub.

The Golden Age for pub-building was in the late Victorian era (c. 1880–1905), when pubs were independently owned and land prices were high enough to make it worthwhile to invest in fixing up pubs. The politics were pro-pub as well: Conservatives, backed by Big Beer, were in, and temperance-minded liberals were out.

Especially in class-conscious Victorian times, traditional pubs were divided into sections by elaborate screens (now mostly gone), allowing the wealthy to drink in a more refined setting, while commoners congregated on the pub's rougher side. These were really "public houses," featuring nooks (snugs) for groups and clubs to meet, friends and lovers to rendezvous, and so on. Since many pub-goers were illiterate, pubs were simply named for the picture hung outside (e.g., The Crooked Stick, The Queen's Arms—meaning her coat of arms).

Historic pubs dot the London cityscape. The only place to see the very oldest-style tavern in the "domestic tradition" is at **Ye Olde Cheshire Cheese**, which was rebuilt in 1667 from a 16th-century tavern (open daily, 145 Fleet Street, located on map on page 135, Tube: Blackfriars, tel. 020/7353-6170). Imagine this place in the pre-Victorian era: With no bar, drinkers gathered around the fireplaces, while tap boys shuttled tankards up from the cellar. (This was long before bar-room taps were connected to casks in the cellar. Oh, and don't say "keg"—that's a gassy modern thing.)

Late Victorian pubs, such as the 1897 **Princess Louise** (open daily, 208 High Holborn, see map on page 131, Tube: Holborn, tel. 020/7405-8816) are more common. These places are fancy, often coming with heavy embossed wallpaper ceilings, decorative tile work, fine-etched glass, ornate carved stillions (the big central hutch for storing bottles and glass), and even urinals equipped with a place to set your glass. London's best Art Nouveau pub is **The Black Friar** (c. 1900–1915), with fine carved capitals, lamp holders, and quirky phrases worked into the decor (open daily, across from Tube: Blackfriars at 174 Queen Victoria Street, tel. 020/7236-5474).

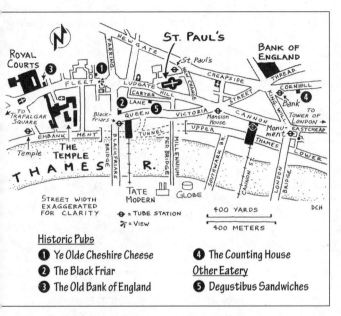

Historic Pubs

❶ Ye Olde Cheshire Cheese

❷ The Black Friar

❸ The Old Bank of England

❹ The Counting House

Other Eatery

❺ Degustibus Sandwiches

The "former-bank pubs" represent a more modern trend in pub building. As banks increasingly go electronic, they're moving out of lavish, high-rent old buildings. Many former banks are being refit as pubs with elegant bars and free-standing stillions, providing a fine centerpiece. Three such pubs are **The Old Bank of England** (closed Sat–Sun, 194 Fleet Street, Tube: Temple, tel. 020/7430-2255), **The Jugged Hare** (open daily, 172 Vauxhall Bridge Road, see map on page 120, Tube: Victoria, tel. 020/7828-1543; see longer listing on page 138) and **The Counting House** (closed Sat–Sun, 50 Cornhill, Tube: Bank, tel. 020/7283-7123; described more fully on page 140).

Go pubbing in the evening for a lively time, or drop by during the quiet late morning (from 11:00), when the pub is empty and filled with memories. For more information, see Bob Steel's Web site, www.aletrails.com. Bob also offers an historic pubs tour (about £50 for a leisurely half-day walk).

sucks. Stand against the wall to feel the energy of all this "positive eating" (£12 meals, daily 12:00—23:00, crowded after 20:00, non-smoking, 10-A Lexington Street, tel. 020/7292-0990 but no reservations taken). If you like this place, there are now handy branches all over town, including one near the British Museum (Streatham Street), High Street Kensington (#26), in Harvey Nichols (109 Knightsbridge), Covent Garden (Tavistock Street), Leicester Square (Irving Street), Piccadilly Circus (Norris Street), Fleet Street (#109), and between St. Paul's and the Tower of London (22 Old Broad Street).

Soho Spice Indian is where modern Britain meets Indian tradition—fine cuisine in a trendy, jewel-tone ambience. Unlike many Indian restaurants, when you order an entrée here (£10), it comes with side dishes—nan, dal, rice, and vegetables (£7 lunch special, daily 12:00–22:30, non-smoking, 5 blocks north of Piccadilly Circus at 124 Wardour Street, tel. 020/7434-0808).

Busaba Eathai Thai Restaurant is a hit with locals for its snappy service, casual-yet-high-energy ambience and good, inexpensive Thai cuisine. You'll sit communally around big, square 16-person hardwood tables or in two-person tables by the window—with everyone in the queue staring at your noodles. They don't take reservations, so arrive by 19:00 or line up (£10–14 meals, daily 12:00–23:00, 106 Wardour Street, tel. 020/7255-8686).

Y Ming Chinese Restaurant—across Shaftesbury Avenue from the ornate gates, clatter, and dim sum of Chinatown—has clean European decor, serious but helpful service, and authentic Northern Chinese cooking (good £10 meal deal offered 12:00–18:00—last order at 18:00, Mon–Sat 12:00–23:30, closed Sun, 35 Greek Street, tel. 020/7734-2721).

Andrew Edmunds Restaurant is a tiny, candlelit place where you'll want to hide your camera and guidebook and act as local as possible. This great little place—with a jealous and loyal clientele—is the closest I've found to Parisian quality in a cozy restaurant in London. The modern European cooking with a creative seasonal menu is worth the splurge (£25 meals, daily 12:30–15:00 & 18:00–22:45, come early or call ahead, request ground floor rather than basement, 46 Lexington Street in Soho, tel. 020/7437-5708).

Mildred's Vegetarian Restaurant, across from Andrew Edmunds, has cheap prices, an enjoyable menu, and a plain-yet-pleasant interior filled with happy eaters (£7 meals, Mon–Sat 12:00–23:00, closed Sun, 45 Lexington Street, tel. 020/7494-1634).

Neal's Yard is *the* place for cheap, hip, and healthy eateries near Covent Garden. The neighborhood is a tabouli of fun, hippie-type cafés. One of the best is **Food for Thought,** packed with local health nuts (good £5 vegetarian meals, Mon–Sat 12:00–20:30, Sun 12:00–17:00, non-smoking, 2 blocks north of Covent Garden Tube station, 31 Neal Street, tel. 020/7836-0239).

The Soho "Food is Fun" Three-Course Dinner Crawl: For a multicultural, movable feast, consider eating (or splitting) one course and enjoying a drink at each of these places. Start at about 18:00 to avoid lines, get in on early specials, and find waiters willing to let you split a meal. Prices, while reasonable by London standards, add up. Servings are large enough to share. All are open nightly. Arrive before 18:00 at **Belgo Centraal** and split the early-bird dinner special: a kilo of mussels, fries, and dark Belgian beer. At **Yo! Sushi,** have beer or sake and a few dishes. Slurp your last course at **Wagamama Noodle Bar.** Then, for dessert, people-watch at Leicester Square, where the serf's always up.

Near Recommended Victoria Station Accommodations

Here are places a couple of blocks southwest of Victoria Station where I've enjoyed eating (see map on page 120).

Ebury Wine Bar, filled with young professionals, provides a classy atmosphere, delicious £15–18 meals, and a £14 two-course special from 18:00–19:30. In the delightful back room, the fancy menu features modern European cuisine with an accent on French; at the wine bar, find cheaper food that's still a cut above pub grub. This is emphatically a "traditional wine bar," without a single beer on tap (Mon–Sat 11:00–23:00, Sun 18:00–22:00, reserve for after 20:00, 139 Ebury Street, at intersection with Elizabeth Street, near bus station, tel. 020/7730-5447).

Goya Spanish Restaurant and Tapas Bar is popular for its classy, old-church-library ambience and tasty, reasonably priced food (£15 meals, good Spanish wine by the glass, daily 11:30–23:0, 2 Eccleston Place, tel. 020/7730-4299). Several cheap places are around the corner on Elizabeth Street (#23 for take-out or eat-in, super-absorbent fish-and-chips).

The Duke of Wellington pub is good, if somewhat smoky, and dominated by local drinkers. It's the neighborhood place for dinner, with woody sidewalk seating and an inviting interior (£6–7 meals, daily specials, Mon–Sat 11:00–15:00 & 18:00–21:00, closed Sun, 63 Eaton Terrace, at intersection with Chester Row, tel. 020/7730-1782).

The Belgravia Pub is new and more family-friendly than The Duke of Wellington, earning a good reputation for its salads and English and Italian fare (£4–6 meals, beer garden seating or plush interior, open daily, corner of Ebury Street and South Eaton Place).

Jenny Lo's Tea House is a simple, budget place serving up reliably tasty £5–8 eclectic Chinese-style meals to locals in the know. While the menu is small, everything is high quality. Jenny clearly learned from her father, Ken Lo, one of the most famous Cantonese chefs in Britain, whose fancy place is just around the corner (Mon–Fri 11:30–15:00 & 18:00–22:00, Sat 18:00–22:00, closed Sun, cash only, 14 Eccleston Street, tel. 020/7259-0399).

La Poule au Pot, ideal for a romantic splurge, offers a classy, candlelit ambience with well-dressed patrons and expensive but fine country-style French cuisine (£15 lunch, £25 dinners, daily 12:30–14:30 & 18:45–23:00, Sun until 22:00, leafy patio dining, reservations smart, end of Ebury at intersection with Pimlico, 231 Ebury Street, tel. 020/7730-7763).

Grumbles brags it's been serving "good food and wine at non-scary prices since 1964." Offering a delicious mix of "modern eclectic French and traditional English," this hip and cozy little place is *the* spot to eat well in this otherwise workaday neighborhood (£12–22 meals, £10 lunch specials, reservations wise, self-serve launderette across the street open evenings, 2 nice sidewalk tables, daily 12:00–14:30 & 18:00–22:30, half a block north of Belgrave Road at 35 Churton Street, tel. 020/7834-0149). While they have seating downstairs, I'd avoid it; call ahead to reserve a spot outside or on the appealing and cozy ground floor.

Chimes English Restaurant and Cider Bar comes with a fresh country farm ambience, serious ciders (rare in London), and very good, traditional English food (2-course meals £13, hearty salads, daily 12:00–14:30 & 17:30–22:15, 26 Churton Street, tel. 020/7821-7456). Experiment with the cider—it's legal here...just barely.

The Jugged Hare Pub is in a lavish old bank building, its vaults replaced by kegs of beer and a fine kitchen. They have a fun, traditional menu with more fresh veggies than fries, and a plush and vivid pub scene good for a meal or just a drink (£7 meals, daily 12:00–21:00, 172 Vauxhall Bridge Road, tel. 020/7828-1543).

Seafresh Fish Restaurant is the neighborhood place for plaice—either take-out on the cheap or eat-in, enjoying a chrome-and-wood mod ambience with classic and creative fish-and-chips cuisine. It feels like the chippie of the 21st century (meals £5 to go, £8–10 to sit, daily 12:00–15:00 & 17:00–22:30, closed Sun, 80 Wilton Road, tel. 020/7828-0747).

If you miss America, there's a mall-type **food court** at Victoria Place, upstairs in Victoria Station; **Café Rouge** seems to be the most popular here (£8–11 dinners, daily 9:30–22:30).

Groceries in and near Victoria Station: A large grocery, **Sainsbury's Local,** is on Victoria Street in front of the station, just past the buses (daily 6:00–24:00). In the station you'll find another, smaller Sainsbury's (at rear entrance, on Eccleston Street) and a couple other late-hours mini-markets.

Near Recommended Notting Hill B&Bs and Bayswater Hotels

Queensway is a multi-ethnic food circus, lined with lively and inexpensive eateries. See the map on page 125.

Maggie Jones, exuberantly rustic and very English, serves my favorite £30 London dinner. You'll get fun-loving if brash service, and solid English cuisine, including huge plates of crunchy vegetables—by candlelight. Avoid the stuffy basement on hot summer nights, and request upstairs seating for the noisy but less cramped section. If you eat well once in London, eat here—and do it quick, before it burns down (daily 12:30–14:30 & 18:30–23:00, less expensive lunch menu, reservations recommended, friendly staff, 6 Old Court Place, just east of Kensington Church Street, near High Street Kensington Tube stop, tel. 020/7937-6462).

The **Churchill Arms** pub and **Thai Kitchens** is a local hangout, with good beer and old-English ambience in front and hearty £6 Thai plates in an enclosed patio in the back. You can eat the Thai food in this tropical hideaway or in the smoky but wonderfully atmospheric pub section. Arrive by 18:00 to avoid a line. During busy times, diners are limited to an hour at the table (daily 12:00–21:30, 119 Kensington Church Street, tel. 020/7792-1246).

Prince Edward Pub serves good pub grub in a quintessential pub setting (£8–10 meals, daily 12:00–15:00 & 18:00–22:00, closed Sun evenings, plush-pubby indoor seating or sidewalk tables, 2 blocks north of Bayswater Road at the corner of Dawson Place and Hereford Road, 73 Prince's Square, tel. 020/7727-2221).

Café Diana is a healthy little eatery serving sandwiches, salads, and Middle Eastern food. It's decorated—almost shrine-like—with photos of Princess Diana, who used to drop by for pita sandwiches (daily 8:00–22:30, 5 Wellington Terrace, on Bayswater Road, opposite Kensington Palace Garden Gates—where Di once lived, tel. 020/7792-9606).

Black and Blue is a trendy bistro serving steaks and burgers to local hipsters. Follow the crowds to the gas torches and patio seating (£10–12 meals, daily 12:00–23:00, 215 Kensington Church Street, tel. 020/7727-0004).

Royal China Restaurant is filled with London's Chinese, who consider this one of the city's best eateries. It's dressy in black, white, and chrome, with candles, brisk waiters, and fine food (£7–10 dishes, dim sum until 17:00, Mon–Sat 12:00–23:00, Sun 11:00–22:00, 13 Queensway, tel. 020/7221-2535).

Mr. Wu's Chinese Restaurant serves a 10-course buffet in a cramped little cafeteria. Just grab a plate and help yourself (£5, daily 12:00–23:00, check quality of buffet—right inside entrance—before committing as pickings can get slim, across from Bayswater

Tube station, 54 Queensway, tel. 020/7243-1017).

Whiteleys Mall Food Court offers a fun selection of ethnic and fast-food eateries among Corinthian columns in a delightful mall (open daily long hours; options include Yo! Sushi, good salads at Café Rouge, pizza, Starbucks, and an Internet café; second floor, corner of Porchester Gardens and Queensway).

Supermarket: **Europa** is a half-block from the Notting Hill Gate Tube stop (Mon–Sat 8:00–23:00, Sun 12:00–18:00, 112 Notting Hill Gate, near intersection with Pembridge Road).

Near Recommended Accommodations in South Kensington

Popular eateries line Old Brompton Road and Thurloe Street (Tube: South Kensington). For locations, see the map on page 123. The **Tesco Express** grocery store is handy for picnics (daily 7:00–24:00, 54 Old Brompton Road).

La Bouchee Bistro Café is a classy, hole-in-the-wall touch of France—candlelit and woody—serving early-bird, two-course £10 meals daily until 19:00 and £15 *plats du jour* all *jour* (daily 12:00–15:00 & 17:30–23:00, 56 Old Brompton Road, tel. 020/7589-1929). For Italian cuisine, **Falconiere Restaurant,** just down the street, is also popular (£8 pastas, £10 plates, £19 3-course dinner special, closed Sun, 84 Old Brompton Road, tel. 020/7589-2401).

Daquise, an authentic-feeling 1930s Polish time-warp, is ideal if you're in the mood for kielbasa and kraut. It's likeably dreary—fast, cheap, family-run, and a much-appreciated part of the neighborhood (£10 meals, £8 lunch special includes wine, daily 11:30–23:00, non-smoking, 20 Thurloe Street, tel. 020/7589-6117).

The Khyber Pass Tandoori Restaurant is nondescript but handy, serving tasty Indian cuisine. Locals in the know travel to eat here (£12 dinners, daily 12:00–14:30 & 18:00–23:30, 21 Bute Street, tel. 020/7589-7311).

Moti Mahal Indian Restaurant is a new favorite for value, offering Khyber Pass some competition. Find minimalist-yet-classy mod ambience and attentive service (daily 12:00–23:00, 3 Glendower Place, tel. 020/7584-8428).

The Zetland Arms serves good pub meals with a classic pub ambience on the ground floor and a fancier olde English restaurant atmosphere upstairs (same menu throughout, £6–10 meals, hearty £9 specials, table service, Mon–Fri 12:00–22:00, Sat–Sun 13:00–22:30, 2 Bute Street, tel. 020/7589-3813).

Elsewhere in London

Between St. Paul's and the Tower: The **Counting House,** formerly an elegant old bank, offers great £7 meals, nice homemade meat pies, fish, and fresh vegetables (Mon–Fri 12:00–21:00, closed

Sat–Sun, gets really busy with the buttoned-down 9-to-5 crowd after 12:15, near Mansion House in the City, 50 Cornhill, tel. 020/7283-7123).

Near St. Paul's: **Degustibus Sandwiches** is where a top-notch artisan bakery meets the public, offering fresh, you-design-it sandwiches, salads, and soups with simple seating or take-out picnic sacks (great parks nearby), just a block below St. Paul's (Mon–Fri 7:00–17:00, closed Sat–Sun, from church steps follow signs to youth hostel a block downhill, 53 Carter Lane, tel. 020/723-60056).

Near the British Library: Drummond Street (running just west of Euston Station) is famous in London for very cheap and good Indian and vegetarian food. Consider **Chutneys** and **Ravi Shankar** for a good *thali*.

TRANSPORTATION CONNECTIONS

Heathrow Airport

Heathrow Airport is the world's fourth busiest. Think about it: 63 million passengers a year on 425,000 flights from 170 destinations riding 90 airlines, like some kind of global maypole dance. While many complain about Heathrow, I think it's a great and user-friendly airport. Read signs, ask questions. For Heathrow's airport, flight, and transfers information, call the switchboard at 0870-000-0123 (www.baa.com). It has four terminals: T-1 (mostly domestic flights, with some European), T-2 (mainly European flights), T-3 (mostly flights from the United States), and T-4 (British Air transatlantic flights and BA flights to Paris, Amsterdam, and Athens). Taxis know which terminal you'll need.

Each terminal has an airport information desk, car-rental agencies, exchange bureaus, ATMs, a pharmacy, a **VAT refund desk** (tel. 020/8910-3682; you must present the VAT claim form from the retailer here to get your tax rebate on items purchased in Britain, see page 17 for details), and a **baggage-check desk** (£6/day, daily 6:00–23:00 at each terminal). Get online 24 hours a day at Heathrow's **Internet cafés** (T-4, mezzanine level) and at wireless "hotspots" in its departure lounges (T-1, T-3, and T-4). There are **post offices** in T-2 and T-4. Each terminal has cheap **eateries** (such as the cheery Food Village self-service cafeteria in T-3). The **American Express** desk, in the Tube station at Terminal 4 (daily 7:00–19:00), has rates similar to the exchange bureaus upstairs, but doesn't charge a commission (typically 1.5 percent) for cashing any type of traveler's check.

Heathrow's small **TI**, even though it's a for-profit business, is worth a visit to pick up free information: a simple map, the *London Planner*, and brochures (daily 8:30–18:00, 5-min walk from T-3 in Tube station, follow signs to Underground; bypass queue for transit info to reach window for London questions). Have your partner stay with the bags at the terminal while you head over to the TI.

If you're taking the Tube into London, buy a one-day Travelcard pass to cover the ride (see below).

Getting to London from Heathrow Airport

By Tube (Subway): For £3.80, the Tube takes you the 14 miles to downtown London in 50 minutes on the Piccadilly Line, with stops (among others) at South Kensington, Leicester Square, and King's Cross station (6/hr; depending on your destination, may require a change). Even better, buy a One-Day Travelcard that covers your trip into London and all your Tube travel for the day (£12 covers peak times, £6 "off-peak" card starts at 9:30, less-expensive Travelcards cover the city center only—see page 57 for details).  Buy it at the Tube station ticket window. You can generally hop on the Tube at any terminal, but for most of 2006, Terminal 4's Tube station will be closed for renovation. You can still catch the Tube by taking a shuttle bus (from stop D) to the nearest station (allow 15 extra min).

If taking the Tube to the airport, note that Piccadilly Line cars post which airlines are served by which terminals.

By Airport Shuttle Bus: The famous Airbus (which shuttled a generation of travelers between the airport and downtown) has finally bit the dust—replaced by the train link and mini-bus shuttles. Hotelink offers door-to-door service (Heathrow-£17 per person, Gatwick-£22 per person, book the day before departure, buy online and save £1–2, tel. 01293/532-244, www.hotelink.co.uk, reservations@hotelink.co.uk).

By Taxi: Taxis from the airport cost about £45 to west and central London (one hour). For four people traveling together, this can be a deal. Hotels can often line up a cab back to the airport for about £30. For the cheapest taxi to the airport, don't order one from your hotel. Simply flag down a few and ask them for their best "off-meter" rate.

By Heathrow Express Train: This slick train service zips you between Heathrow Airport and London's Paddington Station. At Paddington Station, you're in the thick of the Tube system, with easy access to any of my recommended neighborhoods—Notting Hill Gate is just two stops away. It's only 15 minutes to downtown from Terminals 1, 2, and 3, and 20 minutes from Terminal 4 (at the airport, you can use the Express as a free transfer between terminals). Buy your ticket to London before you board, or pay a £2 surcharge to buy it on the train (£14, but ask about discount promos at Heathrow ticket desk, kids under 16 ride half-price, under 5 ride free, covered by BritRail pass, 4/hr, daily 5:10–23:30, tel. 0845-600-1515, www.heathrowexpress.co.uk). For one person on a budget, combining the Heathrow Express with either a Tube or taxi ride (between your hotel and Paddington Station) is nearly as fast and half the cost of taking a cab directly to (or from) the airport. For groups of three or more, a taxi is faster and easier, as well as cheaper.

Getting to Bath from Heathrow Airport

By Bus: Direct buses run daily from Heathrow to Bath (11/day, 2.5 hrs, £15, tel. 0870-575-7747, www.nationalexpress.com). BritRail passholders may prefer the 2.5-hour Heathrow-Bath bus/train connection via Reading (£10 for bus, rail portion free with pass, otherwise £33 total, payable at desk in terminal): First catch the twice-hourly RailAir Link shuttle bus to Reading (RED-ding), then hop on the hourly express train to Bath.

Most Heathrow buses depart from the common area serving Terminals 1, 2, and 3 (a 5-min walk from any of these terminals), although some depart from T-4 (bus tel. 0870-574-7777).

Gatwick Airport

More and more flights, especially charters, land at Gatwick Airport, halfway between London and the southern coast (recorded airport info tel. 0870-000-2468).

Getting to London: Express trains—clearly the best way into London from here—shuttle conveniently between Gatwick and London's Victoria Station (£13, £24 round-trip, 4/hr during day, 1–2/hr at night, 30 min, runs daily 5:00–24:00, can purchase tickets on train at no extra charge, tel. 0845-850-1530, www.gatwickexpress.co.uk). If you're traveling with three others, buy your tickets at the station before boarding and you'll travel for the price of two. The only restriction on this impressive deal is that you have to travel together. So if you see another couple in line, get organized and save 50 percent.

You can save a few pounds by taking South Central rail line's slower and less frequent shuttle between Victoria Station and Gatwick (£9, 3/hr, 1/hr midnight–4:00 in the morning, 45 min, tel. 0845-748-4950, www.southcentraltrains.co.uk).

Getting to Bath: To get to Bath from Gatwick, you can catch a bus to Heathrow and the bus to Bath from there. By train, the best Gatwick–Bath connection involves a transfer in Reading (2.5 hrs, irregular schedule; avoid transfer in London, where you'll have to change stations).

London's Other Airports

If you're flying into or out of **Stansted** (airport tel. 0870-000-0303), you can take the National Express bus between the airport and downtown London's Victoria Coach Station (£10, 2/hr, 1.5 hrs, runs 4:00–24:00, picks up and stops throughout London, tel. 0870-575-7747, www.nxairport.com), or take the Stansted Express train (£15, connects to London's Liverpool Station, 40 min, 2–4/hr, 5:00–23:00, tel. 0845-850-0150, www.stanstedexpress.com). Stansted is expensive by cab; figure £80 one-way from central London.

For **Luton** (airport tel. 01582/405-100, www.london-luton.com), here are three choices. You can take the easyJet bus, which runs between the airport and the Baker Street Tube stop (£1, open to non-easyJet passengers as well, 40 min, every 45 min, runs 7:15–20:00, www.easybus.co.uk). Or hop on Green Line's bus #757, which links the airport and London's Victoria Station at Buckingham Palace Road—stop 6 (£10, £9 for easyJet passengers, 2/hr, 1–1.25 hrs depending on time of day, runs 4:30–24:00, tel. 0870-608-7261, www.greenline.co.uk). Or you can connect by rail to London's Kings Cross station (£12, runs 5:00–23:00, 25 min, tel. 0845-748-4950); catch the free five-minute shuttle from outside the terminal to the Luton Parkway train station.

There's a slim chance you might use **London City Airport** (tel. 020/7646-0088, www.londoncityairport.com). Blue shuttle buses connect the airport to the Liverpool Street Station (£7 one-way, 30 min), a hub for the Tube.

Connecting London's Airports

The **National Express Central Bus Station** offers direct Jetlink bus connections from **Heathrow** to **Gatwick Airport** (2/hr, 70 min or more, depending on traffic), departing just outside arrivals at all terminals (£17 one-way, £22 round-trip). To make a flight connection between Heathrow and Gatwick, allow three hours between flights.

More and more travelers are taking advantage of cheap flights out of London's smaller airports. A handy National Express bus runs between Heathrow, Gatwick, Stansted, and Luton airports—easier than having to cut through the center of London. Buses are frequent (less so between Stansted and Luton) and cheap: Heathrow–Luton is 1.5 hours direct and costs £16. Check schedules at www.nxairport.com.

Discounted Flights from London

Although bmi british midland has been around the longest, the other small airlines generally offer cheaper flights. A visit to www.skyscanner.net sorts the many options offered by the myriad discount airlines, enabling you to see the best schedules for your trip and come up with the best deal.

With **bmi british midland,** you can fly inexpensively to destinations in the U.K. and beyond (fares start at about £30 one-way to Edinburgh, Paris, Brussels, or Amsterdam; or about £50 one-way to Dublin; prices can be higher, but there can also be much cheaper Internet specials—check online). For the latest, call British tel. 0870-607-0555 or U.S. tel. 800/788-0555 (check www.flybmi.com and their subsidiary, bmi baby, at www.bmibaby.com). Book in advance. Although you can book right up until the flight departs, the cheap seats will have sold out long before, leaving the most expensive seats for latecomers.

With no frills and cheap fares, **easyJet** flies from Luton, Stansted, and Gatwick. Prices are based on demand, so the least popular routes make for the cheapest fares, especially if you book early (tel. 0905-821-0905 to book by phone, 65p per minute, or do it free online at www.easyjet.com).

Ryanair is a creative Irish airline that prides itself on offering the lowest fares. It flies from London (mostly Stansted airport) to often obscure airports in Dublin, Glasgow, Frankfurt, Stockholm, Oslo, Venice, Turin, and many others. Sample fares: London–Dublin—£60 round-trip (sometimes as low as £15), London–Frankfurt—£67 round-trip (Irish tel. 0818-303-030, British tel. 0871-246-0000, www.ryanair.com). Because they offer promotional deals any time of year, you can get great prices on short notice. Be aware of their stiff fees for extra baggage. You can carry on only a small daybag and check 15 kilograms—about 33 pounds—of baggage for free. You'll pay €7 per extra kilo. If you're packing an extra 10 kilos, a cheap €30 flight skyrockets to €100.

Virgin Express is a British-owned company with good rates (book by phone and pick up ticket at airport an hour before your flight, www.virgin-express.com). Virgin Express flies from London Heathrow and Brussels. From its hub in Brussels, you can connect cheaply to Barcelona, Madrid, Nice, Málaga, Copenhagen, Rome, or Milan (round-trip from Brussels to Rome for as little as £105). Their prices stay the same whether or not you book in advance.

Trains and Buses

London, Britain's major transportation hub, has a different train station for each region. Waterloo handles the Eurostar to Paris. King's Cross covers northeast England and Scotland. Paddington covers west and southwest England (Bath) and South Wales. For information call 0845-748-4950 (or visit www.nationalrail.co.uk or www.eurostar.com; £5 booking fee for telephone reservations). Also see the BritRail Routes map on page 21. Note that for security reasons, stations offer a left-luggage service (£6/day) rather than lockers.

National Express' excellent bus service is considerably cheaper than trains (call 0870-575-7747, or visit www.nationalexpress.com or the bus station a block southwest of Victoria Station.)

To Bath: Trains leave London's Paddington Station twice every hour between 7:00 and 19:00 (at :15 and :45 after each hour) for the 90-minute ride to Bath (costs £34 if you leave after 9:30 any day but Fri, when it's £40).

To get to Bath via Stonehenge, consider taking a guided bus tour from London to Stonehenge and Bath and abandoning the tour in Bath. Evan Evans' tour for £56 (includes admissions). The tour leaves from the Victoria Coach station every morning at 8:45 (you can stow your bag under the bus), stops in Stonehenge (45 min), and then stops in Bath for lunch and a city tour before returning to London (offered year-round). You can book the tour at the Victoria Coach station, the Evan Evans' office (258 Vauxhall Bridge Road, near Victoria Coach station, tel. 020/7950-1777, U.S. tel. 866/382-6868, www.evanevans.co.uk, reservations@evanevanstours.co.uk), or at the Green Line Travel Office (4a Fountain Square, across from Victoria Coach station, tel. 0870-608-7261, www.greenline .co.uk). Golden Tours also runs a fully guided Stonehenge–Bath tour for a similar price (departs from Fountain Square, located across from Victoria Coach Station, tel. 020/7233-7036, U.S. tel. 800/548-7083, www.goldentours.co.uk, reservations@goldentours .co.uk). Another similarly priced day-trip hits Oxford, Stratford, and Warwick.

To Points North: Trains run hourly from London's King's Cross station, stopping in York (2 hrs), Durham (3 hrs), and Edinburgh (4.5 hrs).

To Dublin, Ireland: The boat/bus journey takes between 9 and 10 hours and goes all day or all night (£29–57, 2/day, tel. 0870-514-3219, www.nationalexpress.com or www.eurolines.co.uk). Consider a cheap 70-minute Ryanair flight instead (see above).

Crossing the Channel by Eurostar Train

The fastest and most convenient way to get from the Eiffel Tower to Big Ben is by rail. Eurostar, a joint service of the Belgian, British, and French railways, is the speedy passenger train that zips you (and up to 800 others in 18 sleek cars) from downtown London to downtown Paris (12–15/day, 3 hrs) faster and easier than flying. The actual tunnel crossing is a 20-minute, black, silent, 100-mile-per-hour non-event. Your ears won't even pop. Eurostar trains also run directly from London to Disneyland Paris (1/day direct, more often with transfer at Lille).

Eurostar

Eurostar Fares

Channel fares (essentially the same between London and Paris or Brussels) are reasonable but complicated. Prices vary depending on when you travel, whether you can live with restrictions, and whether you're eligible for any discounts (youth, seniors, and railpass holders all qualify). Rates are lower for round trips and off-peak travel (midday, midweek, low-season, and low-interest). For specifics, visit www.ricksteves.com/rail/eurostar.htm.

As with airfares, the most expensive and flexible option is a **full-fare ticket** with no restrictions on refundability (even refundable after the departure date; for a one-way trip, figure about $375 in first class, $255 second class). A first-class ticket comes with a meal (a dinner departure nets you more grub than breakfast)—but it's not worth the extra expense.

Also like the airlines, **cheaper tickets** come with more restrictions—and are limited in number (so they sell out more quickly; for second-class, one-way tickets, figure $90–200). Non-full-fare tickets have severe restrictions on refundability (best-case scenario: you'll get 25 percent back, but with the cheapest options you'll get nothing). But several do allow you to change the specifics of your trip once before departure.

Those traveling with a railpass for Britain, France, or Belgium should look first at the **passholder** fare, an especially good value for one-way Eurostar trips (about $75). In Britain, passholder tickets can be issued only at the Eurostar office in Waterloo Station or the American Express office in Victoria Station—not at any other stations. You can also order them by phone (see below), then pick them up at Waterloo Station (see below).

Buying Eurostar Tickets

Refund and exchange restrictions are serious, so don't reserve until you're sure of your plans. If you're confident about the time and date of your crossing, order ahead from the U.S. Only the most expensive ticket (full fare) is fully refundable, so if you want to have more flexibility, hold off—keeping in mind that the longer you wait, the more likely the cheapest tickets will sell out. (You might end up having to pay for first class.)

You can check and book fares by phone or online in the U.S. (order online at www.ricksteves.com/rail/eurostar.htm, prices listed in dollars; order by phone at U.S. tel. 800/EUROSTAR) or in Britain (British tel. 0870-518-6186, www.eurostar.com, prices listed in pounds). While tickets are usually cheaper if purchased in the U.S., fares offered in Europe follow different discount rules—so it can be worth it to check www.eurostar.com before buying. If you buy from a U.S. company, you'll pay for ticket delivery in the United States. In Europe, you can buy your Eurostar ticket at any major train station in any country or at any travel agency that handles train tickets (expect a booking fee).

Remember that Britain's time zone is one hour earlier than France's. Times listed on tickets are local times (departure from London is British time, arrival in Paris in French time).

Waterloo Station: Check in at least 30 minutes in advance for your Eurostar trip. It's very similar to an airport check-in: You pass through airport-like security, show your passport to customs officials, and find a TV monitor to locate your departure gate. There are a few airport-like shops, newsstands, horrible snack bars, and cafés (bring food for the trip from elsewhere), pay-Internet terminals, and a currency-exchange booth with rates about the same as you'll find on the other end.

Cheap Passage by Tour: A tour company called Britain Shrinkers sells one- or two-day "Eurostar Tours" to Paris or Brussels, enabling you to side-trip to these cities from London for less than most train tickets alone. For example, a one-day Paris (with Métro pass) tour costs £129—instead of £149 for a regular one-way fare or £249 round-trip (tel. 0800-587-7660 or www.britainshrinkers.com). This can be a particularly good option if you need to get to Paris from London on short notice, when only the costliest fares are available.

Crossing the Channel without Eurostar

The old-fashioned ways of crossing the Channel are cheaper than crossing by Eurostar. They're also twice as romantic, complicated, and time-consuming. You'll get better prices arranging your trip in London than you would in the U.S. Taking the bus is cheapest, and round-trips are a bargain.

By Train and Boat: You'll need to book your own train tickets to Dover; prices are for the ferry only. The **Hoverspeed ferry** runs between Dover, England, and Calais, France (tel. 0870-524-0241, www.hoverspeed.com). Hoverspeed sells London–Paris rail and ferry packages: £44 one-way; £56 round-trip with five-day return; and £67 round-trip over more than five days. You can buy this package deal in person at Waterloo and Charing Cross stations. If you book by phone (number listed above), you must book at least two weeks in advance, and the ticket will be mailed to you (no ticket pickup at station for bookings by phone).

By **P&O Stena Line ferry** runs from Dover to Calais (£18 one-way or round-trip with 5-day return, £36 round-trip over more than 5 days, tel. 0870-520-2020, www.poferries.com).

By Bus: You can take the bus direct to Paris (8 hrs, 5/day), Brussels (9 hrs, 5/day), or Amsterdam (12 hrs, 4/day) from Victoria Coach Station (via boat or Chunnel, day or overnight). Sample prices to Paris for economy fares booked at least two days in advance are: £45 one-way, £62 round-trip (tel. 0870-514-3219; visit www.eurolines.co.uk and look for "fun fares").

By Plane: Check with budget airlines for cheap round-trip fares to Paris (see "Discounted Flights from London," page 144).

GREENWICH, WINDSOR, AND CAMBRIDGE

Greenwich, Windsor, and Cambridge (listed from nearest to farthest) are three of the best day trip possibilities near London. Greenwich is England's maritime capital; Windsor has a very famous castle; and Cambridge is easily England's best university town.

Getting Around England

By Train: The British rail system uses London as a hub and normally offers round-trip fares (after 9:30) that cost virtually the same as one-way fares. For day trips, "day return" tickets are best (and cheapest). You can save a little money if you purchase Super Advance tickets before 18:00 on the day before your trip.

By Train Tour: Original London Walks offers a variety of Explorer day trips year-round via train for about £10 plus transportation costs (pick up their walking-tour brochures at the TI or hotels, tel. 020/7624-3978, www.walks.com; see listing on page 115).

Greenwich

Tudor kings favored the palace at Greenwich. Henry VIII was born here. Later kings commissioned Inigo Jones and Christopher Wren to beautify the town and palace. In spite of Greenwich's architectural and royal treats, this is England's maritime capital, and visitors go for all things salty. Greenwich hosts historic ships, nautical shops, and hordes of tourists.

London Day Trips

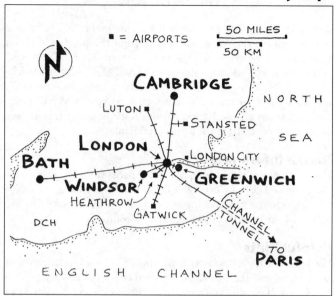

■ = AIRPORTS

50 MILES
50 KM

N

CAMBRIDGE

LUTON ■

■ ■ STANSTED

NORTH

LONDON

SEA

BATH

LONDON CITY

WINDSOR

GREENWICH

HEATHROW

GATWICK

CHANNEL TUNNEL

DCH

TO PARIS

ENGLISH CHANNEL

Planning Your Time

See the two ships—*Cutty Sark* and *Gipsy Moth IV*—upon arrival.
Then walk the shoreline promenade, with a possible lunch or
drink in the venerable Trafalgar Tavern, before heading up
to the National Maritime Museum and the Royal Observatory
Greenwich.

Getting to Greenwich

It's a joy by boat or a snap by Tube.

By Boat: From London (50–70 min, 2/hr), cruise down the
Thames from central London's piers at Westminster, Embankment,
or Tower of London (see "Cruises" on page 65).

By Tube: Take the Tube to Bank and change to the Dockways
Light Railway (DLR), which takes you right to the *Cutty Sark*
station in Greenwich (1 stop before the main Greenwich station,
20-min ride, all in Zone 2, included with Tube pass). Many DLR
trains terminate at Canary Wharf, so make sure you get on one
that continues to Lewisham or Greenwich.

By Train: Mainline trains also go from London (Charing
Cross, Waterloo East, and London Bridge stations) several times
an hour to the Greenwich station (10-min walk from the sights).

ORIENTATION

Covered markets and outdoor stalls make weekends lively. Save time to browse the town. Wander beyond the touristy Church Street and Greenwich High Road to where flower stands spill into the side streets and antique shops sell brass nautical knick-knacks. King William Walk, College Approach, Nelson Road, and Turnpin Lane are all worth a look. If you need pub grub, Greenwich has almost 100 pubs, with some boasting that they're mere milliseconds from the prime meridian.

Tourist Information

The TI faces the riverside square a few paces from the *Cutty Sark* (daily 10:00–17:00, 2 Cutty Sark Gardens, Pepys House, tel. 0870-608-2000, www.greenwich.gov.uk). Guided walks cover the big sights (£4, daily 12:15 and 14:15, departs from TI).

Helpful Hints

Markets: The town throbs with day-trippers on weekends because of its markets. The arts-and-crafts market is an entertaining mini–Covent Garden between College Approach and Nelson Road (Thu–Sun 10:00–17:00, biggest on Sun), and the antique market sells old odds and ends at high prices on Greenwich High Road, near the post office. To avoid the crowds, visit on a weekday.

Tram: A small tram runs from the National Maritime Museum to the Royal Observatory on top of the hill (free, daily 10:00–16:30, 2/hr, erratic in winter).

Supermarket: If you're picnicking, try the handy Marks & Spencer Simply Food on Church Street, across from the *Cutty Sark*. You can get everything from sandwiches to roast chicken to chocolate sundaes, and they throw in free plastic utensils.

SIGHTS

▲▲**Cutty Sark**—The Scottish-built *Cutty Sark* was the last of the great China tea clippers. Handsomely restored, she was the queen of the seas when first launched in 1869. With 32,000 square feet of sail, she could blow with the wind 300 miles in a day. Below deck, you'll see the best collection of merchant-ship figureheads in Britain and exhibits giving a vivid peek into the lives of Victorian sailors back when Britain ruled the waves. Stand at the big wheel and look up at the still-rigged

Greenwich

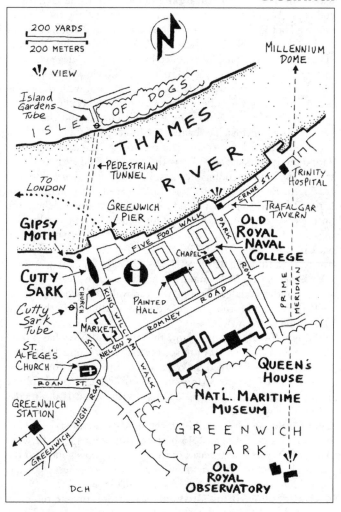

main mast towering 150 feet above. You may meet costumed storytellers spinning yarns of the high seas and local old salts giving knot-tying demonstrations (£4.50, daily 10:00–17:00, tel. 020/8858-3445, www.cuttysark.org.uk).

▲**Gipsy Moth IV**—Tiny next to the *Cutty Sark*, the 54-foot *Gipsy Moth IV* is the boat Sir Francis Chichester used for the first solo circumnavigation of the world in 1966 and 1967. Upon Chichester's return, Queen Elizabeth II knighted him in Greenwich, using the same sword Elizabeth I had used to knight Francis Drake in 1581 (free, viewable anytime, but interior not open to public).

Stroll the Thames to Trafalgar Tavern—From the *Cutty Sark* and *Gipsy Moth IV*, pass the pier and wander east along the Thames on Five Foot Walk (the width of the path) for grand views in front of the Old Royal Naval College (see below). Founded by William III as a naval hospital and designed by Wren, the college was split in two because Queen Mary didn't want the view from Queen's House blocked. The riverside view is good, too, with the twin-domed towers of the college (one giving the time, the other the direction of the wind) framing Queen's House, and the Royal Observatory Greenwich crowning the hill beyond.

Continuing downstream, just past the college, you'll see the **Trafalgar Tavern.** Dickens knew the pub well, and even used it as the setting for the wedding breakfast in *Our Mutual Friend.* Built in 1837 in the Regency style to attract Londoners downriver, the tavern is popular with Londoners (and tourists) for its fine lunches. The upstairs Nelson Room is still used for weddings. Its formal moldings and elegant windows with balconies over the Thames are a step back in time (daily 12:00–15:00 & 18:00–22:00, Sun lunch only, smoky, Park Row, tel. 020/8858-2909). From the pub, enjoy views of the white-elephant Millennium Dome a mile downstream.

From the Trafalgar Tavern, you can walk the two long blocks up Park Row and turn right onto the park leading up to the Royal Observatory Greenwich.

Old Royal Naval College—Now that the Royal Navy has moved out, the public is invited in to see the elaborate Painted Hall and Chapel, grandly designed by Wren and completed by other architects in the 1700s (free, Mon–Sun 10:00–17:00, in the 2 college buildings farthest from river, choral service Sun at 11:00 in chapel—all are welcome).

Queen's House—This building, the first Palladian-style villa in Britain, was designed in 1616 by Inigo Jones for James I's wife, Anne of Denmark. All traces of the queen are now gone, and the Great Hall and Royal Apartments serve as an art gallery for rotating exhibits (free, daily 10:00–17:00, tel. 020/8858-4422).

▲▲**National Maritime Museum**—Great for anyone remotely interested in the sea, this museum holds everything from *Titanic* tickets and Captain Scott's reindeer-hide sleeping bag (from his 1910 Antarctic expedition) to the uniform Admiral Nelson wore when he was killed at Trafalgar. Under a big glass roof—accompanied by the sound of creaking wooden ships and crashing waves—slick, modern displays depict lighthouse technology, a whaling cannon, and a Greenpeace "survival pod."

The Nelson Gallery, while taking up just a fraction of the floor space, deserves at least half your time here. It offers an intimate look at Nelson's life, the Napoleonic threat, Nelson's rise to power, and his victory and death at Trafalgar. Don't miss Turner's *Battle of*

Trafalgar—his largest painting and only royal commission.

Kids love the All Hands Gallery, where they can send secret messages by Morse code and operate a miniature dockside crane (free, daily 10:00–17:00, July–Aug 10:00–18:00; look for the events posted at entrance—singing, treasure hunts, storytelling—particularly on weekends; tel. 020/8858-4422, recorded info tel. 020/8312-6565, www.nmm.ac.uk).

▲▲**Royal Observatory Greenwich**—Located on the prime meridian (0° longitude), the observatory is the point from which all time is measured. However, the observatory's early work had nothing to do with coordinating the world's clocks to Greenwich Mean Time (GMT). The observatory was founded in 1675 by Charles II to find a way to determine longitude at sea. Today, the Greenwich time signal is linked with the BBC (which broadcasts the "pips" worldwide at the top of the hour).

Look above the observatory to see the orange Time Ball, also visible from the Thames, which drops daily at 13:00. (Nearby, outside the courtyard of the observatory, see how your foot measures up to the foot where the public standards of length are cast in bronze.)

In the courtyard, set your wristwatch to the digital clock showing GMT to a tenth of a second and straddle the prime meridian (called the "Times meridian" at the observatory, in deference to the *London Times,* which paid for the courtyard sculpture and the inset meridian line that runs banner headlines of today's *Times*—I wish I were kidding).

Inside, check out the historic astronomical instruments and camera obscura. Listen to costumed actors tell stories about astronomers and historical observatory events (shows may require small fee, daily July–Sept).

Cost and Hours: Free entry, daily 10:00–17:00, tel. 020/8858-4422, www.rog.nmm.ac.uk. The planetarium will be closed throughout 2007 for renovation.

Before you leave the observatory grounds, enjoy the view from the overlook: the symmetrical royal buildings; the Thames; the square-mile City of London, with its skyscrapers and the dome of St. Paul's Cathedral; the Docklands, with its busy cranes; and the huge Millennium Dome. At night (17:00–24:00), look for the green laser beam the observatory shines in the sky (best viewed in winter), extending along the prime meridian for 15 miles.

Windsor

Windsor, a compact and easy walking town of about 30,000 people, originally grew up around the royal residence. In 1070, William the Conqueror continued his habit of kicking Saxons out of their various settlements, taking over what the locals called "Windlesora" (meaning "riverbank with a hoisting crane"). It would eventually be called "Windsor." William built the first fortified castle on a chalk hill above the Thames; later kings added on to William's early designs, rebuilding and expanding the castle and surrounding gardens.

By setting up primary residence here, modern monarchs increased Windsor's popularity and prosperity—most notably, Queen Victoria, whose statue glares sternly at you as you approach the castle. After her death, Victoria rejoined her beloved husband Albert in the Royal Mausoleum at Frogmore House, a mile south of the castle in a private section of the Home Park (house and mausoleum rarely open; check www.royalcollection.org.uk). The current queen considers Windsor her primary residence, and the one where she feels most at home. You can tell if her majesty is in residence by checking to see which flag is flying above the round tower; if the royal standard (a red, yellow, and blue flag) is flying instead of the Union Jack, the Queen is at home.

While 99 percent of the visitors just come to see the castle and go, some enjoy spending the night. The town's charm is most evident when the tourists are gone. Consider overnighting here, since parking and access to Heathrow Airport are easy; day-tripping into London is feasible; and an evening at the horse races (on Mondays) is hoof-pounding, heart-thumping fun.

Getting to Windsor

By Train: Windsor has two train stations: Windsor Central (5-min walk to palace and TI) and Windsor & Eton Riverside (10-min walk to palace and TI). Thames Trains run between London's Paddington Station and Windsor Central (2/hr, 40 min, change at Slough, www.thamestrains.co.uk). South West Trains run between London's Waterloo Station and the Windsor & Eton Riverside station (2/hr, 50 min, info tel. 0845-748-4950, www.nationalrail .co.uk). If you're day-tripping into London from Windsor, you can save money by buying a One-Day Travelcard at the Windsor train station (£6, good after 9:30, covers rail transportation to and from London with an all-day Tube pass in town; see page 158).

By Bus: Green Line buses #700 and #702 run hourly between London's Victoria Colonnade (between the Victoria train and coach stations) and Windsor, where the bus stops in front of Legoland and near the castle; the castle stop is "Parish Church" (1.5 hrs). Bus info: tel. 0870-608-7261.

By Car: Windsor is 20 miles from London and just off Heathrow airport's landing path. The town (and then the castle and Legoland) is well-signposted from the M4 motorway. It's a convenient stop for anyone arriving at Heathrow, picking up a car,

Windsor

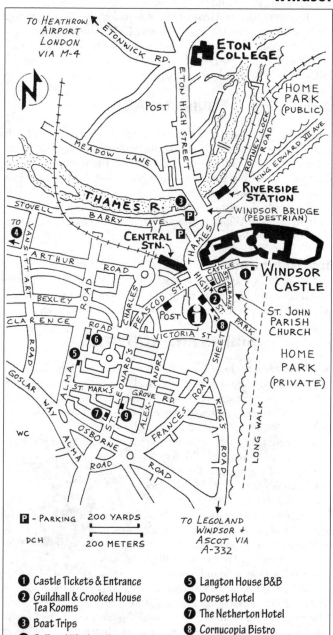

TO HEATHROW
AIRPORT
LONDON
VIA M-4

ETON COLLEGE

HOME PARK (PUBLIC)

ETONWICK RD.

POST

ETON HIGH STREET

MEADOW LANE

ROMNEY LOCK ROAD

KING EDWARD VII AVE.

RIVERSIDE STATION

THAMES R.

STOVELL

BARRY AVE.

WINDSOR BRIDGE (PEDESTRIAN)

TO ROYAL WINDSOR RACECOURSE

VANSITTART

CENTRAL STN.

THAMES

ARTHUR ROAD

CASTLE HILL

WINDSOR CASTLE

BEXLEY

CHARLES

ST. ALBAN'S ST.

ST. JOHN PARISH CHURCH

CLARENCE

ROAD

PEASCOD ST.

POST

VICTORIA ST.

ROAD

HOME PARK (PRIVATE)

GOSLAR WAY

ALMA

ST. MARK'S

LEONARD'S

GROVE RD.

ALEXANDRA

KING'S ROAD

ROAD

FRANCES ROAD

LONG WALK

WC

OSBORNE ROAD

ALMA ROAD

ROAD

P - PARKING

200 YARDS

200 METERS

DCH

TO LEGOLAND WINDSOR & ASCOT VIA A-332

❶ Castle Tickets & Entrance

❷ Guildhall & Crooked House Tea Rooms

❸ Boat Trips

❹ To Royal Windsor Racecourse

❺ Langton House B&B

❻ Dorset Hotel

❼ The Netherton Hotel

❽ Cornucopia Bistro

❾ Blondes Café & Tapas Bar

and not going into London.

From Heathrow Airport: Bus #50 makes the 30-minute trip between Windsor and the airport for £3 (2/hr), dropping you right below the castle near the TI. London black cabs can charge whatever they like from Heathrow to Windsor (and do); avoid them by calling a local Windsor cab (tel. 01753/677-677, £18 ride).

ORIENTATION

You'll find most shops and restaurants around the castle on High and Thames Streets, and down the pedestrian Peascod Street (which runs perpendicular to High Street). The train to Windsor Central station from Paddington (via Slough) will spit you out in a shady shopping pavilion only a few minutes' walk from the castle and TI (see "Getting to Windsor," above). The pleasant pedestrian shopping zone of Windsor litters the approach to its famous palace with fun temptations.

Tourist Information
The TI is on 24 High Street (April–Sept daily 10:00–17:00, Oct–March daily 10:00–16:00, tel. 01753/743-900, www.windsor.gov .uk). The TI sells half-price tickets to Legoland after 13:30.

SIGHTS AND ACTIVITIES

▲▲**Windsor Castle**—Windsor Castle, the official home of England's royal family for 900 years, claims to be the largest and oldest occupied castle in the world. Thankfully, touring it is simple: You'll see immense grounds, lavish staterooms, a crowd-pleasing dollhouse, an art gallery, and the chapel.

Immediately upon entering, you pass through a simple modern building housing a historical  overview of the castle. This excellent intro is worth a close look, since you're basically on your own after this. Inside, you'll find the motte (artificial mound) and bailey (fortified stockade around it) of William the Conqueror's castle still visible. Dating from 1080, this was his first castle in England.

Follow the signs to the staterooms/gallery/dollhouse. Queen Mary's Dollhouse—a palace in miniature (1:12 scale from 1923) and "the most famous dollhouse in the world"—comes with the longest wait. You can skip that line and go immediately into the lavish staterooms. Strewn with history and the art of a long line of kings and queens, it's the best I've seen in Britain—and well-restored after the devastating 1992 fire. Take advantage of the talkative docents in each room, who are happy to answer your questions. The adjacent gallery is a changing exhibit featuring the royal art collection (and some big names, such as Michelangelo and Leonardo). Signs direct you (downhill) to St. George's Chapel. Housing 10 royal tombs, it's a fine example of Perpendicular Gothic, with classic fan vaulting spreading out from each pillar (dating from about 1500). Next door is the sumptuous 13th-century Albert Memorial Chapel, redecorated after the death of Prince Albert in 1861 and dedicated to his memory.

Cost and Hours: £12.50, £32 for family (£3.50 audioguide is better than official guidebook for help throughout). March–Oct daily 9:45–17:15, last entry 16:00, Nov–Feb closes at 16:15 (Changing of the Guard most days at 11:00, nightly evensong in chapel at 17:15—free for worshippers, tel. 020/7321-2233, recorded info tel. 01753/831-118, www.royal.gov.uk). As you enter, ask about the warden's free 30-minute guided walks around the grounds (2/hr). They cover the grounds but not the castle, which is well described by the audioguide.

Legoland Windsor—Fun for Legomaniacs under 12, this huge, kid-pleasing park five miles from Windsor Castle has dozens of tame but fun rides (often with very long lines) scattered throughout its 150 acres. An impressive Mini-Land has 50 million Lego pieces glued together to create 800 tiny buildings and a mini-tour of Europe (£24, children-£22, under 3 free, £10 if you enter during last 2 hours; Windsor TI sells half-price tickets after 13:30; April–Oct daily 10:00–17:00, 18:00, or 19:00 depending upon season and day; closed most Tue–Wed in Sept–Oct, closed Nov–March except Dec 21–Jan 5 when it's open for the holidays, £2.50 round-trip shuttle bus runs from near Windsor's Parish Church, 2/hr, clearly signposted, easy free parking, tel. 0870-504-0404, www.legoland.co.uk—discount for online bookings).

Boat Trips on the Thames—Boat trips leave every 30 minutes, ferrying you up and down the river for relaxing views of the castle, the village of Eton, Eton College, and the Royal Windsor Racecourse. Relax onboard and munch a picnic (£4.50, £12 family ticket, 2/hr from 11:00–17:00, 40 min, longer trips available, tel. 01753/851-900, www.boat-trips.co.uk). There's also a longer 2-hour circular trip (£7, 1/day).

Horse Racing—Every Monday evening, the horses race near Windsor at the Royal Windsor Racecourse. The romantic way to get there is by a 10-minute shuttle boat (see "Boat Trips," above; £6 entry, off A308 between Windsor and Maidenhead, info tel. 0870-220-0024, www.windsor-racecourse.co.uk).

Eton College—Across the bridge, you'll find many post-castle tourists filing towards the college, a "public" (our "private") school

Sleep Code

(£1 = about $1.80, country code: 44, area code: 020)
S = Single, **D** = Double/Twin, **T** = Triple, **Q** = Quad, **b** = bathroom,
s = shower only. Unless otherwise noted, credit cards are accepted, and prices include a generous breakfast and all taxes.

To help you sort easily through these listings, I've divided the rooms into three categories based on the price for a double room with bath:

$$$ **Higher Priced**—Most rooms £100 or more.
$$ **Moderately Priced**—Most rooms between £70–100.
$ **Lower Priced**—Most rooms £70 or less.

that has educated quite a few prime ministers, as well as members of the royal family. The college is sparse on sights.

SLEEPING

$$ Langton House B&B is a stately Victorian home with three well-appointed rooms lovingly maintained by Paul and Sonja Fogg (Sb-£63, D-£75, T-£85, Q-£95, prices soft in winter, family-friendly, guest kitchen, Internet access, 5 percent extra to use credit card, 46 Alma Road, tel. & fax 01753/858-299, www.langtonhouse.co.uk, paul@langtonhouse.co.uk).

$$ Dorset Hotel rents four bright, spacious rooms in an elegant home on a quiet side street (Sb-£65, Db-£80, Tb-£95, parking, 4 Dorset Road, tel. 01753/852-669, Marie Cameron).

$$ The Netherton Hotel is a creaky and tired place with 12 no-personality rooms and lots of stairs (Db-£65, Tb-£85, family room-£95, 96 St. Leonard's Road, tel. 01753/855-508, fax 01753/621-267, netherton@btconnect.com).

EATING

Cornucopia Bistro, a favorite with locals, is a welcoming little place two minutes from the TI and castle, just beyond the tourist crush. They serve tasty international dishes with everything proudly made from scratch. The hardwood floors add a rustic elegance (£7.50 2-course lunches, £9 2-course dinners, Mon–Sat 12:00–14:30 & 18:00–22:00, Sun 12:00–14:30 only, 6 High Street, tel. 01753/833-009, Mark Simmons).

The Crooked House, across from the TI, is a touristy 17th-century, timber-framed teahouse that serves fresh, hearty £6–8 lunches and cream teas in a tipsy interior or outdoors on its cobbled lane (daily 9:30–18:00, 51 High Street, tel. 01753/857-534). The important-looking building next door is the Guildhall, where Charles finally married Camilla Parker Bowles in April 2005.

Blondes is a lively café and tapas bar that dishes up good food all day, including breakfast (until 15:00), fresh salads, and steaks (Mon–Fri 9:00–15:30 & 18:00–24:00, Sat 8:00–24:00, Sun 9:00–18:00, 45 St. Leonard's Road, tel. 01753/470-079). While nothing really special, this place is handy to the recommended Windsor accommodations.

Cambridge

Cambridge, 60 miles north of London, is world-famous for its prestigious university. Wordsworth, Isaac Newton, Tennyson, Darwin, and Prince Charles are a few of its illustrious alumni. This historic town of 100,000 people is more pleasant than its rival, Oxford. Cambridge is the epitome of a university town, with busy bikers, stately residence halls, plenty of bookshops, and proud locals who  can point out where DNA was modeled, the first atom was split, and electrons were discovered.

In medieval Europe, higher education was the domain of the Church, and was limited to ecclesiastical schools. Scholars lived in "halls" on campus. This academic community of residential halls, chapels, and lecture halls connected by peaceful garden courtyards survives today in the colleges that make up the universities at Cambridge and Oxford. By 1350 (Oxford is roughly 100 years older), Cambridge had eight colleges, each with a monastic-type courtyard and lodgings. Today, Cambridge has 31 colleges. While a student's life revolves around his or her independent college, the university organizes lectures, presents degrees, and promotes research.

The university dominates—and owns—most of Cambridge. The approximate term schedule is late January to late March (called Lent term), mid-April to mid-June (Easter term), and early October to early December (Michaelmas term). The colleges are closed to visitors during exams, in mid-April and late June, but King's College Chapel and the Trinity Library stay open, and the town is never sleepy.

Planning Your Time

Cambridge is worth most of a day but not an overnight. Arrive in time for the 11:30 walking tour—an essential part of any visit—and spend the afternoon touring King's College Chapel and Fitzwilliam Museum (closed Mon) or simply enjoying the ambience of this stately old college town.

Getting to Cambridge

By Train: It's an easy and economical trip from London, 50 minutes away. Catch the train from London's King's Cross Station (2/hr, fast trains leaving at :15 and :45 past each hour run in each direction, 50 min, one-way £16, cheap day-return for £16.50 if you depart London after 9:30 weekdays or anytime Sat–Sun).

ORIENTATION

Cambridge is congested but small. Everything is within a pleasant walk. There are two main streets, separated from the river by the most interesting colleges. The town center, brimming with tearooms, has a TI and a colorful open-air market (daily 9:30–16:00, on Market Hill Square; arts and crafts Sun 10:30–16:30, clothes and produce rest of week).

Tourist Information

At the station, a City Sightseeing office dispenses free city maps and sells fancier ones. The official TI is well signposted and just off Market Hill Square. They book rooms for £3 and sell a 30p mini-guide/map (Mon–Fri 10:00–17:30, Sat 10:00–17:00, Sun 11:00–16:00, closed Sun Nov–Easter, toll tel. 0906/586-2526 costs 60p/min, room-booking line: tel. 01223/457-581).

Arrival in Cambridge

To get to downtown Cambridge from the train station, take a 20-minute walk (the City Sightseeing map is fine for this), a £4 taxi ride, or bus #C1 or #C3 (£1, every 5–10 min). Drivers can follow signs to any of the handy and central Short Stay Parking Lots.

Helpful Hints

Supermarkets: A Marks & Spencer Simply Food grocery is at the train station; a larger Marks & Spencer is on the main square, Market Hill Square (Mon–Sat 8:30–19:00, Sun 11:00–17:00). The J. Sainsbury supermarket, with slightly longer hours, is three blocks north of the main square on Sidney Street. A good picnic spot is Laundress Green, a grassy park on the river, at the end of Mill Lane near the Silver Street punts.

Cambridge

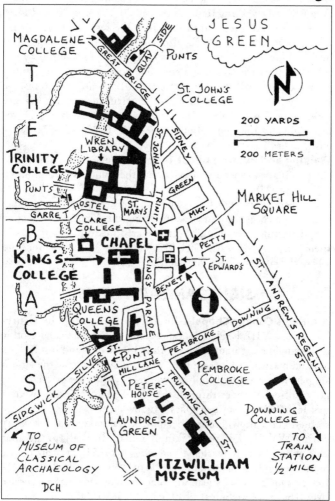

Bike Rental: Cambridge Station Cycles, located to your right as you exit the station, rents bikes (£6/half-day) and stores luggage (£2–3 per bag depending on size, Mon–Fri 7:00–20:00, Sat 9:00–17:00, Sun 10:00–16:00, tel. 01223/307-125).

TOURS

▲▲**Walking Tour of the Colleges**—A walking tour is the best way to understand Cambridge's mix of "town and gown." The walks give a good rundown of the historic and scenic highlights of the university, as well as some fun local gossip. From July through August, **daily walking tours** start at 10:30, 11:30, 13:30, and 14:30 (offered by and leaving from the TI). The rest of the year, they run daily at 13:30 (April–Oct also daily at 11:30). Tours cost £8.50 and include admission to King's College Chapel. Drop by the TI one hour early to snare a spot. Particularly if you're coming from London, call the day before (tel. 01223/457-574) to reserve a spot with your credit card and confirm departure. **Private guides** are also available (£45 per hour for the basic tour, £57 for a 2-hour city tour—excellent values, tel. 01223/457-574, www.visitcambridge.org).

Walking and Punting Ghost Tour—If you're in Cambridge in the evening, consider a spooky trip on the Cam (£14, 90 min, tel. 01223/457-574).

Bus Tours—City Sightseeing hop-on, hop-off bus tours are informative and cover the outskirts, including the American Cemetery (£8, departing every 15 min, can use credit card to buy tickets in their office in train station, tel. 01708/866-000). Walking tours go where the buses can't—right into the center.

SIGHTS AND ACTIVITIES

▲▲**King's College Chapel**—Built from 1446 to 1515 by Henrys VI through VIII, England's best example of Perpendicular Gothic is the single most impressive building in town. Stand inside, look up, and marvel, as Christopher Wren did, at what was the largest single span of vaulted roof anywhere—2,000 tons of incredible fan vaulting. Wander through the Old Testament, with twenty-five 16th-century stained-glass windows (the most Renaissance stained glass anywhere in one spot; it was taken out for safety during WWII, then painstakingly replaced). Walk to the altar and admire Rubens' masterful *Adoration of the Magi* (£4.50, erratic hours depending on school and events, but usually daily 9:30–16:00). During term, you're welcome to enjoy an evensong service (Mon–Sat at 17:30, Sun at 15:30, tel. 01223/331-447).

▲▲**Trinity College**—Half of Cambridge's 63 Nobel Prize winners have come from this richest and biggest of the town's colleges, founded in 1546 by Henry VIII. Don't miss the Wren-designed library, with its wonderful carving and fascinating original manuscripts (£2.20, 10p leaflet, Mon–Fri 12:00–14:00, also Sat 10:30–12:30 during term, always closed Sun and during exams; or visit the library for free during the same hours from the riverside entrance by the Garret Hostel Bridge, tel. 01223/338-400). Just outside the library entrance, Sir Isaac Newton, who spent 30 years at Trinity, clapped his hands and timed the echo to measure the speed of sound as it raced down the side of the cloister and back. In the library's display cases (covered with brown cloth that you flip back), you'll see handwritten works by Newton, Milton, Byron, Tennyson, and Housman, alongside Milne's original *Winnie the Pooh* (the real Christopher Robin attended Trinity College).

▲▲**Fitzwilliam Museum**—Britain's best museum of antiquities and art outside of London is the Fitzwilliam. Enjoy its wonderful paintings (Old Masters and a fine English section featuring Gainsborough, Reynolds, Hogarth, and others, plus works by all the famous Impressionists), old manuscripts, and Greek, Egyptian, and Mesopotamian collections (free, Tue–Sat 10:00–17:00, Sun 12:00–17:00, closed Mon, tel. 01223/332-900, www.fitzmuseum .cam.ac.uk).

Museum of Classical Archaeology—While this museum contains no originals, it offers a unique chance to see accurate copies (19th-century casts) of virtually every famous ancient Greek and Roman statue. More than 450 statues are on display (free, Mon–Fri 10:00–17:00, sometimes also Sat 10:00–13:00 during term, always closed Sun, Sidgwick Avenue, tel. 01223/335-153). The museum is a five-minute walk west of Silver Street Bridge; after crossing the bridge, continue straight until you reach a sign reading *Sidgwick Site* (museum is on your right; the entrance is away from the street).

▲**Punting on the Cam**—For a little levity and probably more exercise than you really want, try hiring one of the traditional (and inexpensive) flat-bottom punts at the river and pole yourself up and down (around and around, more likely) the lazy Cam. Once you get the hang of it, it's a fine way to enjoy the scenic side of Cambridge. After 17:00 it's less crowded and less embarrassing.

Three places, one at each bridge, rent punts (£60 deposit required, can use credit card) and offer £14 50-minute punt tours. Trinity Punt, at Garrett Hostel Bridge near Trinity College, has the best prices (£8–10/hr rental, ask for free short lesson, tel. 01223/338-483). Scudamore's runs two other locations: the central Silver Street Bridge (£12–14/hr rentals) and the less-convenient Quayside at Great Bridge, at the north end of town (£14–16/hr, tel. 01223/359-750, www.scudamores.com). Depending on the weather, punting season runs daily March through October, with Silver Street open weekends off-season.

TRANSPORTATION CONNECTIONS

From Cambridge by Train to: York (hrly, 2.5 hrs, transfer in Peterborough, about £50), **London** (2/hr, 50 min). Train info: tel. 0845-748-4950.

By Bus to: Heathrow (1/hr, 2.5 hrs). Bus info: tel. 0870-575-7747.

BATH

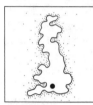

The best city to visit within easy striking distance of London is Bath—just a 90-minute train ride away. Two hundred years ago, this city of 85,000 was the trendsetting Hollywood of Britain. If ever a city enjoyed looking in the mirror, Bath's the one. It has more "government-listed" or protected historic buildings per capita than any other town in England. The entire city, built of the creamy warm-tone limestone called "Bath stone," beams in its cover-girl complexion. An architectural chorus line, it's a triumph of the Georgian style. Proud locals remind visitors that the town is routinely banned from the "Britain in Bloom" contest to give other towns a chance to win. Bath's narcissism is justified. Even with its mobs of tourists (2 million per year), Bath is a joy to visit.

Long before the Romans arrived in the first century, Bath was known for its mineral hot springs. The importance of Bath has always been shaped by the healing allure of its 116° hot springs. Romans called the popular spa town Aquae Sulis. The town's importance carried through Saxon times, when it had a huge church on the site of the present-day abbey and was considered the religious capital of Britain. Its influence peaked in 973 with King Edgar's sumptuous coronation in the abbey. Later Bath prospered as a wool town.

Bath then declined until the mid-1600s, when it was just a huddle of huts around the abbey, with hot, smelly mud and 3,000 residents, oblivious to the Roman ruins 18 feet below their dirt floors. Then, in 1687, Queen Mary, fighting infertility, bathed here. Within 10 months she gave birth to a son...and a new age of popularity for Bath.

The revitalized town boomed as a spa resort. Ninety percent

Bath

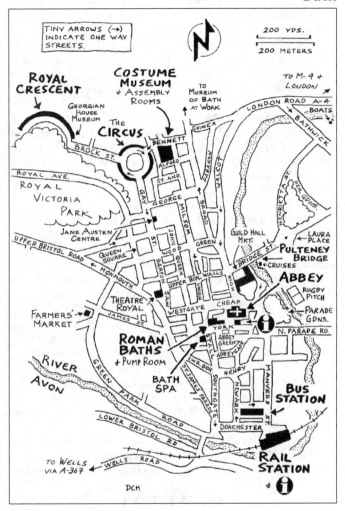

TINY ARROWS (→) INDICATE ONE WAY STREETS.

N

200 YDS.
200 METERS

ROYAL CRESCENT

COSTUME MUSEUM & Assembly Rooms

GEORGIAN HOUSE MUSEUM

TO MUSEUM OF BATH AT WORK

TO M-4 & LONDON

THE CIRCUS

BENNETT

GUINEA

LONDON ROAD A-4

BOATS

BATHWICK

BROCK ST.

ALFRED

ST. AND.

PARAGON

WALCOT

HEN. GDNS.

HENRIETTA ST.

ROYAL AVE.

GAY

GEORGE

MILSOM

BROAD

ROYAL VICTORIA PARK

JANE AUSTEN CENTRE

QUEEN SQUARE

MONMOUTH

ST.

JOHN

WOOD

QUEEN

BARTON

GREEN

UPPER BOR.

WALLS

BRIDGE ST.

GREEN

GUILD HALL MKT.

LAURA PLACE

PULTENEY BRIDGE

CRUISES

ABBEY

UPPER BRISTOL ROAD

THEATRE ROYAL

JAMES ST.

WESTGATE

UNION

CHEAP

HIGH

RUGBY PITCH

PARADE GDNS.

FARMERS' MARKET

YORK

ABBEY GREEN

ABBEY GATE

N. PARADE RD.

ROMAN BATHS & Pump Room

LWR. BOR. WALLS

ST. JAMES PARADE

BATH SPA

HENRY

SOUTHGATE

MANVERS

BUS STATION

NEWARK ST.

RIVER AVON

GREEN PARK

ROAD

LOWER BRISTOL RD.

DORCHESTER

TO WELLS VIA A-367

WELLS ROAD

RAIL STATION

DCH

of the buildings you'll see today are from the 18th century. Local architect John Wood was inspired by the Italian architect Andrea Palladio to build a "new Rome." The town bloomed in the neoclassical style, and streets were lined not with scrawny sidewalks but with wide "parades," upon which the women in their stylishly wide dresses could spread their fashionable tails.

Beau Nash (1673–1762) was Bath's "master of ceremonies." He organized both the daily regimen of the aristocratic visitors and the city, lighting and improving street security, banning swords, and opening the Pump Room. Under his fashionable baton, Bath became a city of balls, gaming, and concerts—the place to see and be seen in England. This most civilized place became even more so with the great neoclassical building spree that followed.

The buzz in the early 21st century is that the venerable baths will be in the spotlight again. When the new spa finally opens (after years of delays) and taps Bath's soothing hot springs, the town will once again attract visitors in need of a cure or a soak.

Planning Your Time

Bath deserves two nights even on a quick trip. On a three-week British trip, spend three nights in Bath, with one day for the city and one for a side trip to Wells, Glastonbury, and Avebury (see next chapter). Bath could easily fill another day. Ideally, use Bath as your jet-lag recovery pillow, and do London at the end of your trip.

Consider starting a three-week British vacation this way:

Day 1: Land at Heathrow. Connect to Bath (easy bus to Reading, then train to Bath—see "Getting to Bath from Heathrow Airport," page 143). While you don't need or want a car in Bath, and some rental companies have an office there, those who land early and pick up their cars at the airport can visit Windsor Castle (near Heathrow) and/or Stonehenge on their way to Bath.

Day 2: 9:00–Tour the Roman Baths; 10:30–Catch the free city walking tour; 12:30–Picnic on the open deck of a Bath tour bus; 14:00–Free time in the shopping center of old Bath; 15:30–Tour the Costume Museum; 20:00–Bizarre Bath comedy walk.

Day 3: Pick up your rental car and tour Avebury, Glastonbury (abbey and Tor), and Wells (17:15 evensong weekdays at the cathedral). Without a car, consider a one-day Avebury/Stonehenge/cute towns minibus tour from Bath (Mad Max tours are best; see "Tours," below).

Day 4: 9:00–Leave Bath for South Wales; 10:30–Tour Museum of Welsh Life; 15:00–Stop at Tintern Abbey, then drive to the Cotswolds; 18:00–Set up in your Cotswolds home base.

ORIENTATION

(area code: 01225)
Bath's town square, three blocks in front of the bus and train station, is a bouquet of tourist landmarks, including the abbey, Roman and medieval baths, and the royal Pump Room.

Tourist Information

The TI is in the abbey churchyard (Mon–Sat 9:30–17:00, Sun 10:00–16:00, tel. 0870-420-1278, www.visitbath.co.uk). Pick up the 50p Bath mini-guide (includes a map) and the free, info-packed *This Month in Bath*. Browse through scads of fliers, books, and maps. Skip their room-finding service (£5 fee and your host is nicked 10 percent) and book direct.

Arrival in Bath

The Bath **train station** has small-town charm, a national and international tickets desk, and a privately run tourism office masquerading as a TI. The **bus station** is immediately in front of the train station. To get to the TI from either station, walk two blocks up Manvers Street and turn left at the triangular "square," by following the small TI arrow on a signpost. My recommended B&Bs are all within a 10- to 15-minute walk or a £4 taxi ride from the station.

Helpful Hints

Festivals: The **Bath Literature Festival** is an open book from March 4 to 12 in 2006 (www.bathlitfest.org.uk). The **Bath International Music Festival** bursts into song from May 19 to June 4 in 2006 (classical, folk, jazz, contemporary; for the lineup, see www.bathmusicfest.org.uk), overlapped by the eclectic **Bath Fringe Festival** from May 26 to June 11 (theater, walks, talks, bus trips; www.bathfringe.co.uk). The **Jane Austen Festival** unfolds genteelly mid- to late-September (www.janeaustenfestival.co.uk). Bath's festival box office sells tickets for most events, and can tell you exactly what's on tonight (2 Church Street, tel. 01225/463-362, www.bathfestivals .org.uk). Bath's local paper, the *Bath Chronicle*, publishes a "What's On" event listing on Fridays (www.thisisbath.com).

Internet Access: Try the Internet place a block in front of the train station (daily 9:00–22:00, on Manvers Street, tel. 01225/443-181).

Laundry: The **Spruce Goose Launderette** is around the corner from the recommended Brock's Guest House on the pedestrian lane called Margaret's Buildings (daily 8:00–21:00, self-service or full-service on same day if dropped off at 8:00, tel. 01225/483-309). Anywhere in town, **Speedy Wash** can pick up your laundry for same-day service (£10/bag, Mon–Fri 7:30–17:30, most hotels work with them, tel. 01225/427-616). East of Pulteney Bridge, the humble **Lovely Wash** is on Daniel Street (daily 9:00–21:00, self-service only).

Car Rental: Hertz and **Enterprise** are each handy to central Bath, and have roughly the same rates: £40/day, £80/weekend, and £160/week. Enterprise provides a pickup service for customers to and from their hotels, but doesn't do one-way rentals (at Lower Bristol Road in Bath, tel. 01225/443-311). Hertz is just outside Bath train station (tel. 01225/442-911). **National/Alamo** is a £7 taxi ride from the train station, but often has better rates than Hertz, and will do one-way rentals (at Brass Mill Lane—go west on Upper Bristol Road, tel. 01225/481-898). **Europcar** advertises it's in Bath but is relatively far outside of town. **Avis** is a mile from the Bristol train station; you'd need to rent a car to get there. Most offices close Saturday afternoon and all day Sunday, which complicates weekend pickups. Ideally, take the train or bus from London to Bath and rent a car as you leave Bath, rather than from within London.

TOURS

Of Bath

▲▲▲Walking Tours—Free two-hour tours are offered by **The Mayor's Corps of Honorary Guides,** led by volunteers who want to share their love of Bath with its many visitors. Their chatty, historical, and gossip-filled walks are essential for your understanding of this town's amazing Georgian social scene. How else will you learn that the old "chair ho" call for your sedan chair evolved into today's "cheerio" farewell? Tours leave from in front of the Pump Room (free, no tips, year-round Sun–Fri at 10:30 and 14:00, Sun at 10:30 only; evening walks offered May–Sept at 19:00 on Tue, Fri, and Sat). Advice for theatergoers: Guides stop to talk outside the Theatre Royal. You can skip out a moment, pop into the box office, and snare a great deal on a play for tonight (see "Nightlife" on page 179 for details).

For a **private tour,** call the local guides' bureau (£52/2 hrs, tel. 01225/337-111). For **Ghost Walks, Pub Crawls,** and **Bizarre Bath** tours, see "Nightlife," page 179.

Taxi Tours—Local taxis, driven by good talkers, go where big buses can't. A group of up to four can rent a cab for an hour (about £20) and enjoy a fine, informative, and—with the right cabbie—entertaining private joyride. It's probably cheaper to let the meter run than to pay for an hourly rate, but ask the cabbie for advice.

▲▲City Bus Tours—Two companies run hop-on, hop-off bus tours through Bath. Jump on anytime, pay the driver, and climb upstairs. If you're on a Classic City Tour, enjoy the rapid-fire spiel of your live guide; City Sightseeing has taped commentary only (17 signposted pick-up points, generally 4/hr from 9:30–17:00, more frequent and with longer hours in summer). On a sunny day, this is a multitasking tourist's dream-come-true: You can munch a sandwich, work on a tan, snap great photos, and learn a lot all at the same time. Save money by doing the bus tour first—ticket stubs get you minor discounts at many sights. Choose between...

Classic City Tours (red with white stripe): These buses follow the same route as transit buses. (They're required to take passengers across town for the normal £1 fare.) They come with live guides, and are a better value than City Sightseeing (£6.50/2 days, tours run Mon–Sat).

City Sightseeing (red-orange buses): Tickets on this bus line are more expensive (£9, good for 24 hours on either route). But they have two advantages over Classic City Tours: They run on Sundays and they have a second "Skyline" route outside of town, handy for those wanting to visit the American Museum on the outskirts of town.

Of Stonehenge, Avebury, and the Cotswolds

Bath is a good launchpad for visiting Wells, Avebury, Stonehenge, and more.

Mad Max Minibus Tours—Operating daily from Bath, Maddy and Paul offer thoughtfully organized, informative tours that run with a maximum group size of 16 people. Their **Stone Circles and Villages** full-day tour (8:45–16:30) covers 110 miles and visits Stonehenge, the Avebury Stone Circle, and two cute villages—Lacock and Castle Combe. The southernmost Cotswold village, Castle Combe is as sweet as they come (£22.50, cash only, Stonehenge admission not included).

Mad Max also offers the **Cotswold Discovery** full-day tour, a picturesque romp through the countryside, with stops in the Cotswolds' quainter villages, including Stow-on-the-Wold, Bibury, Tetbury, the Coln Valley, and others. If you request this in advance, you can use the tour as transportation to get to Stow or Moreton, and bring your luggage along (£25, runs Sun, Tue, and Thu 8:45–17:15). Their short tour of **Stonehenge and Bradford-on-Avon**—a worthwhile extra stop, with a fascinating Saxon church—leaves daily at 13:30 and ends at 17:15 (£12.50, Stonehenge entry extra).

All tours depart from Bath at the Glass House shop on the corner of Orange Grove, a one-minute walk from the abbey. Arrive a few minutes before your departure time. Only cash is accepted as payment.

It's better to book ahead for these popular tours via e-mail (www.madmaxtours.co.uk, maddy@madmax.abel.co.uk) rather than by phone (Mon–Fri 8:00–18:00, tel. 01225/464-323). Please honor or cancel your seat reservation.

More Bus Tours—If Mad Max is booked up, don't fret. Plenty of companies in Bath offer tours of varying lengths, prices, and destinations. Note that the cost of admission to sites is usually not included with any tour. **Scarper Tours** runs a minibus tour to Stonehenge (£12.50, departs daily Easter–Sept 9:30 and 13:30, Oct–Easter 13:30 only, tel. 07739/644-155, www.scarpertours .com); they also run a Glastonbury and Wells trip (daily, ask at TI or check their Web site). *Heritage City Guided Tour* does a "Stonehenge Express" trip out to the rocks and back (£14, 3.25 hrs,

Bath at a Glance

▲▲▲**Roman and Medieval Baths** Ancient baths that gave the city its name, tourable with good audioguide. **Hours:** Daily April–Sept 9:00–18:00, July–Aug until 22:00, Oct–March 9:00–17:30.

▲▲▲**Costume Museum** 400 years of fashion under one roof, plus opulent Assembly Rooms. **Hours:** Daily March–Oct 11:00–18:00, Nov–March 11:00–17:00.

▲▲▲**Museum of Bath at Work** Gadget-ridden, circa-1900 engineer's shop, foundry, factory, and office, best enjoyed with a live tour. **Hours:** April–Oct daily 10:30–17:00, weekends only in winter.

▲▲**Royal Crescent and the Circus** Stately Georgian (neoclassical) buildings from Bath's late-18th-century glory days. **Hours:** Always viewable.

▲▲**Georgian House at No. 1 Royal Crescent** Best opportunity to explore the interior of one of Bath's high-rent Georgian beauties. **Hours:** Mid-Feb–Oct Tue–Sun 10:30–17:00, closes at 16:00 in Nov, closed Mon and Dec–mid-Feb.

▲**Pump Room** Swanky Georgian hall, ideal for a spot of tea or a taste of unforgettably "healthy" spa water. **Hours:** Daily 9:30–12:00 for coffee, 12:00–14:30 for lunch, 14:30–17:00 for high tea (open for dinner July–Aug only).

departs from Grand Parade circle behind abbey, daily at 10:00 and 14:00, tel. 01225/444-102).

Celtic Horizons, run by retired teacher Alan Price, offers tours from Bath to a variety of destinations, such as Stonehenge, Avebury, Wells, and South Wales. He can provide a convenient transfer service (to—or from—London, Heathrow, the Cotswolds, and so on) which can include a tour itinerary en route. He also does personalized genealogy tours. His comfortable minivan seats one to eight people; allow around £20/hr per person. It's best to make arrangements via e-mail at alan@celtichorizons.com (www.celtichorizons.com, tel. 01373/461-784).

SIGHTS

▲▲▲**Roman and Medieval Baths**—In ancient Roman times, high society enjoyed the mineral springs at Bath. From Londinium, Romans traveled so often to Aquae Sulis, as the city was called, to

▲**Abbey** 500-year-old Perpendicular Gothic church, graced with beautiful fan vaulting and stained glass. **Hours:** Mon–Sat 9:00–18:00, Sun usually 13:00–14:30 & 15:30–17:30, closes at 16:30 in winter.

▲**Pulteney Bridge and Parade Gardens** Shop-strewn bridge and relaxing riverside gardens. **Hours:** Bridge—always open; gardens—April–Sept daily 10:00–19:00, May–Aug until 20:00, shorter hours off-season.

▲**American Museum** An insightful look at colonial/early-American lifestyles, with 18 furnished rooms complete with guides eager to talk. **Hours:** April–Oct Tue–Sun 14:00–17:30, closed Mon and Nov–March.

Jane Austen Centre Exhibit on 19th-century Bath-based novelist, best for her fans. **Hours:** Mon–Sat 10:00–17:30, Sun 10:30–17:30.

Building of Bath Museum Architecture buff's guide to Bath. **Hours:** Tue–Sun 10:30–17:00, closed Mon.

Thermae Bath Spa Long-delayed, brand-new relaxation center, putting the bath back in Bath. **Hours:** Should possibly, maybe, finally open in 2006.

"take a bath" that finally it became known simply as Bath. Today, a fine museum surrounds the ancient bath. It's a one-way system leading you past well-documented displays, Roman artifacts,

mosaics, a temple pediment, and the actual mouth of the spring, piled high with Roman pennies. Enjoy some quality time looking into the eyes of Minerva, goddess of the hot springs. The included self-guided tour audioguide makes the visit easy and plenty informative. For those with a big appetite for Roman history, in-depth 40-minute tours leave from the end of the museum at the edge of the actual bath (included with ticket, on the hour, a poolside clock is set for the next departure time). The water is greenish because of the lead—don't drink it. You can revisit the museum after the tour

(£9.50, £12.50 combo-ticket includes Costume Museum—a £3.25 savings, family combo-£33.50, combo-tickets good for 1 week, April–Sept daily 9:00–18:00, July–Aug until 22:00, last entry an hour before closing, Oct–March until 17:30, tel. 01225/477-784, www.romanbaths.co.uk). The museum and baths are fun to visit in the evening—romantic, gas-lit, and all yours. After touring the Roman Baths, stop by the attached Pump Room for a spot of tea, or to gag on the water.

▲**Pump Room**—For centuries, Bath was forgotten as a spa. Then, in 1687, the previously barren Queen Mary bathed here, became pregnant, and bore a male heir to the throne. A few years later Queen Anne found the water eased her gout. Word of its wonder waters spread, and Bath was back on the aristocratic map. High society soon turned the place into one big pleasure palace. The Pump Room, an elegant Georgian hall just above the Roman Baths, offers the visitor's best chance to raise a pinky in this Chippendale grandeur. Drop by to sip coffee or tea or enjoy a light meal (daily 9:30–12:00 for morning coffee; 12:00–14:30 for lunch—£16 2-course menu; 14:30–17:00 for traditional high tea—£12; £7 tea/coffee and pastry available in the afternoons; open for dinner July–Aug only; live music daily—string trio 10:00–12:00, piano 12:00–14:30, string trio 15:00–17:00; tel. 01225/444-477). Above the newspaper table and sedan chairs, a statue of Beau Nash himself sniffles down at you.

The Spa Water: This is your chance to sip a famous (but forgettable) "Bath bun" and split (and spit) a 50p drink of the awful curative water. The water is served from the King's Spring by appropriately attired Martin, who's ready to minuet (but refuses to gavotte). He explains that the water is 10,000 years old, pumped from nearly 100 yards deep, and marinated in wonderful minerals.

Convenient public WCs are in the entry hallway that connects the Pump Room with the baths (but are not associated with the spa water).

Thermae Bath Spa—After simmering unused for a quarter-century, Bath's natural thermal springs will possibly once again offer R&R for the masses. The state-of-the-art leisure and curative spa, housed in a complex combining old buildings with controversial new, blocky architecture, is scheduled to open (after numerous delays) in 2006. The only natural thermal spa in the United Kingdom, it will include an open-air rooftop thermal pool and all the "pamper thyself" extras—aromatherapy steam rooms, mud wraps, and various healing-type treatments and classes. Swimwear will be required (if it ever opens, it'll be open daily 9:00–22:00, £17/2 hrs, £23/4 hrs, £35/full day; treatments, massage, and solarium cost extra—ranging from £26–68; 100 yards from Roman and medieval

baths on Beau Street, tel. 01225/331-234, www.thermaebathspa
.com for the latest).

▲**Abbey**—The town of Bath wasn't much in the Middle Ages,
but an important church has stood on this spot since Anglo-
Saxon times. In 973, Edgar was crowned here. Dominating the
town center, the present church—the last great medieval church

of England—is 500 years old and a
fine example of Late Perpendicular
Gothic, with breezy fan vaulting and
enough stained glass to earn it the
nickname "Lantern of the West." The
glass, red-iron gas-powered lamps,
and heating grates on the floor are
all remnants of the 19th century.
The window behind the altar shows
52 scenes from the life of Christ. A
window to the left of the altar shows
that coronation of Edgar in 973
(worth the £2.50 donation, Mon–Sat

9:00–18:00, Sun usually 13:00–14:30 & 15:30–17:30, closes at 16:30
in winter, handy flyer narrates a self-guided 19-stop tour, www
.bathabbey.org). Posted on the door is the schedule for concerts,
services, and **evensong** (Sun at 15:30 year-round, plus most Sat in
Aug at 17:00). The facade (c. 1500, but mostly restored) is interesting for some of its carvings. Look for the angels going down the
ladder. The statue of Peter (to the left of the door) lost his head to
mean iconoclasts; it was re-carved out of his once super-size beard.
Take a moment to appreciate the abbey's architecture from the
Abbey Green square.

A small but worthwhile exhibit, the abbey's **Heritage Vaults,**
tell the story of Christianity in Bath since Roman times (£1, Mon–
Sat 10:00–16:00, last entry 15:30, closed Sun, entrance just outside
church, south side).

▲**Pulteney Bridge, Parade Gardens, and Cruises**—Bath is
inclined to compare its shop-lined Pulteney Bridge to Florence's
Ponte Vecchio. That's pushing it. But to best enjoy a sunny day,
pay about £1 to enter the Parade Gardens below the bridge
(April–Sept daily 10:00–19:00, May–Aug until 20:00, shorter
hours off-season, includes deck chairs, ask about concerts held
some Sun at 15:00 in summer, tel. 01225/394-041). Taking a
siesta to relax peacefully at the riverside provides a wonderful
break (and memory).

Across the bridge at Pulteney Weir, tour boat companies run
cruises (£7, up to 7/day if the weather's good, 50 min to Bathampton
and back, WCs on board). Take whatever boat is running. Avon
Cruisers actually stop in Bathampton (allowing you to hop off and

walk back); Pulteney Cruisers have a sundeck ideal for picnics.

Guildhall Market—The little shopping mall, located across from Pulteney Bridge, is a frumpy time-warp in this affluent town, but it's fun for browsing and picnic shopping. Its cheap Market Café is recommended under "Eating," page 188.

Victoria Art Gallery—The one-room gallery, next to Guildhall Market, is filled with paintings from the 18th and 19th centuries (free, includes audioguide, daily 10:00–17:00, WC).

▲▲Royal Crescent and the Circus—If Bath is an architectural cancan, these are the knickers. These first Georgian "condos" by John Wood (the Elder and the Younger) are well-explained in the city walking tours. "Georgian" is British for "neoclassical," or dating from the 1770s. As you cruise the Crescent, pretend you're rich. Pretend you're poor. Notice the "ha ha fence," a drop-off in the front yard that acted as a barrier, invisible from the windows,  for keeping out sheep and peasants. The refined and stylish Royal Crescent Hotel sits unmarked in the center of the crescent. You're welcome to (politely) drop in to explore its fine ground floor public spaces. A gracious and traditional cream tea is served in the garden out back (£11, daily 12:00–17:30).

Picture the round Circus as a colosseum turned inside out. Its Doric, Ionic, and Corinthian capital decorations pay homage to its Greco-Roman origin, and are a reminder that Bath (with its 7 hills) aspired to be "the Rome of England." The frieze above the first row of columns has hundreds of different panels, each representing the arts, sciences, and crafts. The first floor was high off the ground, to accommodate aristocrats on sedan chairs and women with Cher-like hairdos. The tiny round windows on the top floors were the servants' quarters. While the building fronts are uniform, the backs are higgledy-piggledy, infamous for their "hanging loos." Stand in the middle of the Crescent among the grand plane trees, on the capped old well. Imagine the days when there was no indoor plumbing, and the servant girls gathered here to fetch water—this was gossip central. Standing on the well, your clap echoes three times around the circle (try it).

▲▲Georgian House at No. 1 Royal Crescent—This museum (corner of Brock Street and Royal Crescent) offers your best look into a period house. It's worth the £4 admission to get behind one of those classy exteriors. The volunteers in each room are determined to fill you in on all the fascinating details of Georgian life...like how high-class women shaved their eyebrows and pasted on carefully trimmed strips of furry mouse skin in their place. On the bedroom dresser sits a bowl of black beauty marks and a hair scratcher from those pre-shampoo days. Fido spent his days in the kitchen tread-mill powering the rotisserie (mid-Feb–Oct Tue–Sun 10:30–17:00, closes at 16:00 in Nov, closed Mon and Dec–mid-Feb, "no stiletto heels, please," tel. 01225/428-126, www.bath-preservation -trust.org.uk).

▲▲▲**Costume Museum**—One of Europe's great museums, it displays 400 years of fashion—one frilly decade at a time—and is housed within Bath's Assembly Rooms. Follow the excellent included audioguide tour and allow two hours (£6.25, £12.50 combo-ticket covers Roman Baths—saving you £3.25, family combo-£33.50, daily March–Oct 11:00–18:00, Nov–Feb 11:00–17:00, last entry 1 hour before closing, tel. 01225/477-789, www .museumofcostume.co.uk).

The **Assembly Rooms,** which you can see for free en route to the museum, are big, grand, empty rooms. Card games, con-certs, tea, and dances were held here in the 18th century, before the advent of fancy hotels with grand public spaces made them obsolete. Note the extreme symmetry (pleasing to the aristocratic eye) and the high windows (which assured their privacy). After the Allies bombed the historical and well-preserved German city of Lübeck, the Germans picked up a Baedeker guide and chose a similarly lovely city to bomb: Bath. The Assembly Rooms—gutted in this war time tit-for-tat by WWII bombs—have since been restored to their original splendor. (Only the chandeliers are original.)

Below the Costume Museum (left as you leave, 20 yards away) is one of the few surviving sets of iron house hardware. "Link boys" carried torches through the dark streets, lighting the way for big shots in their sedan chairs as they traveled from one affair to the next. The link boys extinguished their torches in the black conical "snuffers." The lamp above was once gas-lit. The crank on the left was used to hoist bulky things to various windows (see the hooks). Few of these sets survived the dark days of the WWII Blitz, when most were collected, melted down, and turned into weapons to power the British war machine. (Recent headlines have revealed to the Brits that all this patriotic extra commitment to the national struggle was for naught as the metal ended up on junk heaps.)

▲▲▲**Museum of Bath at Work**—This is the official title for Mr. Bowler's Business, a 1900s engineer's shop, brass foundry, and fizzy-drink factory with a Dickensian office. It's just a pile of mean-ingless old gadgets until a volunteer guide lovingly resurrects Mr. Bowler's creative genius. Also featured are various Bath creations through the years, including a 1914 car and the versatile plasticine (proto-Play-Doh, handy for clay-mation and more). Don't miss the fine "Story of Bath Stone" in the basement. While there are included audioguides, the live tours are the key (wonderful 45-min tours go regularly). If rushed, join one already in session (£4, April–Oct daily 10:30–17:00, last entry at 16:00, weekends only in winter, 2 steep blocks up Russell Street from Assembly Rooms, tel. 01225/318-348).

Jane Austen Centre—This exhibition focuses on Jane Austen's five years in Bath (around 1800), and the influence Bath had on her writing. While the exhibit is thoughtfully done and a hit with "Jane-ites," there is little of historic substance here. You'll walk through a Georgian town house that she didn't live in, and see mostly enlarged reproductions of things associated with her writing. The museum describes various places from two novels set in Bath (*Persuasion* and *Northanger Abbey*). After a live intro (15 min, 3/hr) explaining how this romantic but down-to-earth girl dealt with the silly, shallow, and arrogant aristocrats' world where "the doing of nothings all day prevents one from doing anything," you see a 15-minute video and wander through the rest of the exhibit (£4.65; March–Oct Mon–Sat 10:00–17:30, Sun 10:30–17:30; Nov–Feb 11:00–16:30, 40 Gay Street between Queen's Square and the Circus, tel. 01225/443-000, www.janeausten.co.uk). Avid fans gather in mid- to late-September for the annual Bath Jane Austen Festival (readings and lectures, www.janeaustenfestival.co.uk).

If you're male and feeling left out, head one door downhill from the museum and look through the window. You'll see a fine delftware-decorated powder bowl designed for men to touch up their wigs.

Building of Bath Museum—This offers an intriguing look behind the scenes at how the Georgian city was actually built. It's just a couple rooms of exhibits, but those interested in construction—inside and out—find it worth the £4 (Tue–Sun 10:30–17:00, closed Mon, above the Circus on a street called "The Paragon," tel. 01225/333-895).

▲American Museum—I know, you need this in Bath like you need a Big Mac. But this museum offers a compelling look at colonial and early-American lifestyles. Each of 18 completely furnished rooms (from the 1600s to the 1800s) is hosted by an eager guide waiting to fill you in on the candles, maps, bedpans, and various religious sects that make domestic Yankee history surprisingly interesting. One room is a quilter's nirvana (£6.50, April–Oct Tue–Sun 14:00–17:30, closed Mon and Nov–March, nice arboretum, at Claverton Manor, tel. 01225/460-503, www.americanmuseum .org). The museum is outside of town and a headache to reach if you don't have a car (10-min walk from bus #18).

ACTIVITIES

Walking—The Bath Skyline Walk is a six-mile wander around the hills surrounding Bath (leaflet at TI). Plenty of other scenic paths are described in the TI's literature. For additional options, get *Country Walks around Bath*, by Tim Mowls (£4.50 at TI).

Hiking the Canal to Bathampton—An idyllic towpath leads from the Bath train station along an old canal to the sleepy village of Bathampton. Immediately behind the station, cross the footbridge and see where the canal hits the river. Turn left, noticing the series of industrial-age locks, and walk along the towpath, giving thanks that you're not a horse pulling a barge. You'll be in Bathampton in less than an hour, where a classic pub awaits with a nice lunch and cellar-temp beer.

Boating—The Bath Boating Station, in an old Victorian boathouse, rents boats and punts (£5 per person/first hr, then £1.50/additional hour, April–Sept daily 10:00–18:00, closed off-season, Forester Road, 1 mile northeast of center, tel. 01225/312-900).

Swimming—The Bath Sports and Leisure Centre has a fine pool for laps as well as lots of water slides and entertaining gadgets for kids (£3, daily 8:00–22:00 but kids' hours are limited, call for open swim times, just across North Parade Bridge, tel. 01225/462-565).

Shopping—There's great browsing between the abbey and the Assembly Rooms (Costume Museum). Shops close at 17:30, some have longer hours on Thursday, and many are open on Sunday (11:00–17:00). Explore the antique shops lining Bartlett Street just below the Assembly Rooms.

NIGHTLIFE

Events are listed in *This Month in Bath* (free, available at TI) and "What's On," appearing Fridays in the local newspaper, the *Bath Chronicle* (www.thisisbath.com).

▲▲▲**Bizarre Bath Street Theater**—For an immensely entertaining walking-tour comedy act "with absolutely no history or culture," follow J. J. or Noel Britten on their creative and entertaining Bizarre Bath walk. This 90-minute "tour," which plays off local passersby as well as tour members, is a belly laugh a minute (£6, April–Sept nightly at 20:00, smaller groups Mon–Thu, heavy on magic, careful to insult all minorities and sensitivities, just racy enough but still good family fun, leave from Huntsman pub near the abbey, confirm at TI or call 01225/335-124, www.bizarrebath.co.uk).

▲**Plays**—The 18th-century Theatre Royal, newly restored and one of England's loveliest, offers a busy schedule of London West End–type plays, including many "pre-London" dress-rehearsal runs (£11–25, generally start at 19:30 or 20:00, box office open

Mon–Sat 10:00–20:00, closed Sun, tel. 01225/448-844, www
.theatreroyal.org.uk). Forty nosebleed spots on a bench (misnamed
"standby seats") go on sale at noon on the day of each performance
(£5, pay cash at box office or call and book with credit card, 2 tickets maximum). Or, you can snatch up any unsold seat in the house
for £10–15 a half hour before "curtain up."

A handy cheap-sightseers' tip: During the free Bath walking
tour, your guide stops here. Pop into the box office, ask what's playing tonight, and see if there are many seats left. If the play sounds
good and if plenty of seats remain unsold, you're fairly safe to come
back 30 minutes before curtain time to buy a ticket at that £10
price. Oh...and if you smell jasmine, it's the ghost of Lady Grey, a
mistress of Beau Nash.

Evening Walks—Take your choice: comedy (Bizarre Bath,
described above), history, ghost, or pub crawl. The free city history
walks (such a standard every day and described on page 170) are
now offered summer evenings (May–Sept 19:00 on Tue, Fri, and
Sat, 2 hrs, leave from Pump Room). Ghost Walks are a popular way
to pass the after-dark hours (£6, 20:00, 2 hrs, unreliably Mon–Sat
April–Oct; in winter Fri only; leave from Garrick's Head pub near
Theatre Royal, tel. 01225/350-512, www.ghostwalksofbath.co.uk).
York and Edinburgh—which have houses thought to be actually
haunted—are better for these walks.

The **Great Bath Pub Crawl,** a relaxed stroll through the
town, gives an insight into pubs: "the busy man's recreation,
the idle man's business, the melancholy man's sanctuary, and
the stranger's welcome" (£5, tours May–Sept nightly at 20:00,
depart from outside the centrally located Parade Park Hotel, 10
North Parade, tel. 01225/310-364, www.greatbathpubcrawl.com,
info@greatbathpubcrawl.com).

Pubs—Most pubs in the center are very noisy, catering to a rowdy
twenty-something crowd. But on the top end of town you can
still find some classic, old places with inviting ambience and live
music.

The **Bell** has a jazzy, pierced-and-tattooed, bohemian feel, but
with a mellow older crowd. They serve pizza in the garden out back
(live music Mon and Wed evenings and Sun lunch, 103 Walcot
Street, tel. 01225/460-426).

The **Farmhouse** fills its spacious and laid-back interior with
live jazz nightly from 21:00 (open mic on Tue, top of Landsdown
Road, tel. 01225/316-162).

The **Star Pub** is less inviting and more cramped, but it's much
appreciated by local beer lovers for its fine ale and "no machines
or music to distract from the chat." It's called a "spit 'n' sawdust"
place. And its long bench, nicknamed "death row," still comes
with a complimentary pinch of snuff from tins on the ledge (top of

Paragon Street, tel. 01225/425-072).

The **Old Green Tree Pub** is a rare, quiet traditional pub right in the town center (locally brewed real ales, non-smoking room, no children, Green Street, tel. 01225/448-259; also recommended under "Eating," page 188, for lunch).

Summer Nights at the Baths—In July and August, you can stretch your sightseeing day at the Roman Baths, open nightly until 22:00 (last admission 21:00), when they're far less crowded and more atmospheric, with their gas lamps flaming.

SLEEPING

Bath is a busy tourist town. To get a good B&B, make a telephone reservation in advance. Competition is stiff, and it's worth asking any of these places for a weekday, three-nights-in-a-row, or off-season deal. Friday and Saturday nights are tightest, especially if you're staying only one night, since B&Bs favor those staying longer. If staying only Saturday night, you're very bad news to a B&B hostess. At B&Bs (and cheaper hotels), expect lots of stairs and no elevators.

B&Bs near the Royal Crescent

These listings are all a 15-minute uphill walk or an easy £4 taxi ride from the train station. Or take any hop-on, hop-off bus tour from the station, and get off at the stop nearest your B&B (for Brock's, Assembly Rooms, and Marlborough Lane listings hop off at Royal Avenue; confirm with driver), check in, then finish the tour later in the day. All of these B&Bs are non-smoking. Marlborough Lane places have easier parking, but are less centrally located.

$$$ **The Town House,** overlooking the Assembly Rooms, is genteel and homey, with three fresh, mod rooms that have a

---

Sleep Code

(£1 = about $1.80, country code: 44, area code: 01225)
S = Single, **D** = Double/Twin, **T** = Triple, **Q** = Quad, **b** = bathroom, **s** = shower only. Unless otherwise noted, credit cards are accepted.

To help you sort easily through these listings, I've divided the rooms into three categories based on the price for a standard double room with bath:

$$$ **Higher Priced**—Most rooms £80 or more.
$$ **Moderately Priced**—Most rooms between £50–80.
$ **Lower Priced**—Most rooms £50 or less.

Bath Accommodations

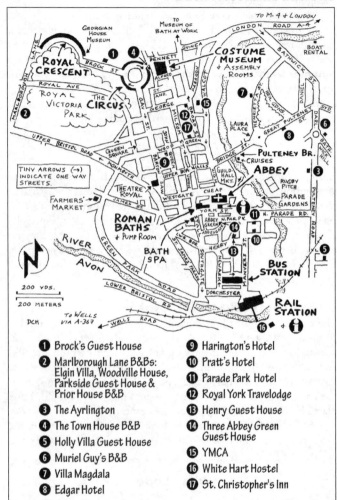

1. Brock's Guest House
2. Marlborough Lane B&Bs: Elgin Villa, Woodville House, Parkside Guest House & Prior House B&B
3. The Ayrlington
4. The Town House B&B
5. Holly Villa Guest House
6. Muriel Guy's B&B
7. Villa Magdala
8. Edgar Hotel
9. Harington's Hotel
10. Pratt's Hotel
11. Parade Park Hotel
12. Royal York Travelodge
13. Henry Guest House
14. Three Abbey Green Guest House
15. YMCA
16. White Hart Hostel
17. St. Christopher's Inn

hardwood stylishness. In true B&B style, you'll enjoy breakfast at a big family table with the other guests (Db-£80–85, Fri and Sat Db-£90–98, 2-night minimum, prices promised with this book through 2006, 7 Bennett Street, tel. & fax 01225/422-505, www.thetownhousebath.co.uk, stay@thetownhousebath.co.uk, Alan and Brenda Willey).

$$ Elgin Villa rents five comfy, well-maintained rooms (Ss-£38, Sb-£50, Ds-£50, Db-£75–80, Tb-£92, Qb-£112, more expensive for 1 night, discounted for 3 nights, Wi-Fi access, parking, 6 Marlborough Lane, tel. 01225/424-557, www.elginvilla.co.uk, stay@elginvilla.co.uk, friendly Anna Rutherford).

$$ Brock's Guest House puts the bubbles in your Bath experience. Marion Dodd has redone her Georgian town house (built by John Wood in 1765) in a way that would make the great architect proud. It's located between the prestigious Royal Crescent and the courtly Circus (6 rooms, Db-£70–80, deluxe Db-£90, Tb-£95, reserve with credit card far in advance, little library on top floor, 32 Brock Street, tel. 01225/338-374, fax 01225/334-245, www.brocksguesthouse.co.uk, marion@brocksguesthouse.co.uk).

$$ Parkside Guest House has five thoughtfully appointed Edwardian rooms and a spacious back garden (Db-£69, 11 Marlborough Lane, tel. & fax 01225/429-444, www.parksidebandb.co.uk, post@parksidebandb.co.uk, Erica and Inge Lynall).

$$ Prior House B&B, with four well-kept rooms, is run by hardworking Lynn Shearn (D-£50, Db-£55, serve-yourself breakfast at a common table, 3 Marlborough Lane, tel. 01225/313-587, www.greatplaces.co.uk/priorhouse, priorhouse@greatplaces.co.uk).

$ Woodville House, warmly run by Anne Toalster, is a grandmotherly little house with three tidy, charming rooms sharing two WCs and a TV lounge. Breakfast is served at a big, family-style table (D-£45, 2-night minimum, cash only, some parking, below the Royal Crescent at 4 Marlborough Lane, tel. 01225/319-335, matoalster@freenet.co.uk).

B&Bs East of the River

These smoke-free listings are a 10-minute walk from the city center and generally a better value (but are less conveniently located).

$$$ The Ayrlington, next door to a lawn-bowling green, has attractive rooms with Asian decor, and hints of a more genteel time. Though this well-maintained hotel fronts a busy street, it's quiet and tranquil. Rooms in the back have pleasant views of sports greens and Bath beyond. For the best value, request a standard double with a view of Bath (huge price range due to varying sizes of rooms and policy of charging 30 percent more on Fri–Sun, Db-£75–175—see Web site for specifics; fine garden, easy parking, 24–25 Pulteney Road, tel. 01225/425-495, fax 01225/469-029, www.ayrlington.com, mail@ayrlington.com).

$$ Holly Villa Guest House, with a cheery garden, six bright rooms, and a cozy TV lounge, is enthusiastically and thoughtfully run by Jill and Keith McGarrigle (Ds-£55, small Db-£55, big Db-£60–65, Tb-£85, cash only, easy parking; 8-min walk from station and city center—walk over North Parade Bridge, take the first right, and then take the second left; 14 Pulteney Gardens, tel. 01225/310-331, www.hollyvilla.com, jill@hollyvilla.com).

$$ Muriel Guy's B&B is another good value, mixing Georgian glamour with homey warmth and modern, artistic taste within its five rooms. Muriel is a fun and endearing live wire who serves organic food (S-£35, Db-£60, Tb-£70, cash only; go over bridge on North Parade Road, left on Pulteney Road, cross to church, Raby Place is first row of houses on hill; 14 Raby Place, tel. 01225/465-120).

B&Bs East of Pulteney Bridge

These B&Bs are a five-minute walk from the city center.

$$$ Villa Magdala rents 18 rooms in a freestanding Victorian town house opposite a park. It's hotelesque and sparkles with elegance (Db-£95–160, depending on size of room and type of bed, less off-season; in quiet residential area, inviting lounge, smoke-free, parking, Henrietta Street, tel. 01225/466-329, fax 01225/483-207, www.villamagdala.co.uk, enquiries@villamagdala .co.uk, Roy and Lois).

$$ Edgar Hotel, with 18 simple rooms and lots of stairs, gives you a budget-hotel option in this smart Georgian neighborhood (Sb-£40–50, Db-£60–85 depending on room, Tb-£100, Qb-£120, less in winter, smaller rooms on top, avoid #18 on ground level, pleasant sitting room with old organ and gramophones, 64 Great Pulteney Street, tel. 01225/420-619, fax 01225/466-916, www .edgar-hotel.co.uk, edgar-hotel@breathe.com).

In the City Center

$$$ Three Abbey Green Guest House is newly renovated, bright, fresh, and located in a quiet courtyard only 50 yards from the abbey and the Roman Baths. Its spacious rooms are a fine value (Sb-£65, Db-£75–85, Tb-£95–110, Qb-£125, families welcome, tel. 01225/428-558. www.threeabbeygreen.com, stay@threeabbeygreen.com). It's managed by Sue and Derek, who also run the Henry Guest House (see below).

$$$ Harington's Hotel rents 13 fresh and newly refurbished rooms on a quiet street in the town center (Sb-£68–114, Db-£88–124, high prices are for Fri–Sat; smoke-free, lots of stairs, attached restaurant-bar open all day, 10 Queen Street, tel. 01225/461-728, fax 01225/444-804, www.haringtonshotel.co.uk, post@haringtonshotel.co.uk). Melissa and Peter offer a 5 percent discount with this book for two-night stays except on Fridays, Saturdays, and holidays.

$$$ Pratt's Hotel is as proper and old English as you'll find in Bath. Its creaks and frays are aristocratic. Its public places make you want to sip a brandy, and its 46 rooms are bright and spacious (Sb-£85, Db-£130, advance reservations get highest rate, drop-ins after 16:00 often snare Db for £75, dogs-£7.50 but children free, attached restaurant-bar, elevator, 4 blocks from station on South

Parade, tel. 01225/460-441, fax 01225/448-807, www.forestdale
.com, pratts@forestdale.com).

$$ Parade Park Hotel rents 35 modern, basic rooms in a very
central location (S-£38, D-£55, small Db-£65, large Db-£90,
Tb-£95, Qb-£120, smoke-free, lots of stairs, lively bar down-
stairs and noisy seagulls, 10 North Parade, tel. 01225/463-384, fax
01225/442-322, www.paradepark.co.uk, info@paradepark.co.uk).

$$ Royal York Travelodge—which offers 66 American-
style, characterless yet comfortable rooms—worries B&Bs with
its reasonable prices (Db-£70, Tb-same price, up to 2 kids sleep
free, breakfast extra, non-smoking rooms available, as low as £26
if you book online in advance, 1 York Building, George Street,
tel. 01225/448-999, central reservation tel. 08700-850-950, www
.travelodge.co.uk). This is especially economic for families of four
(who enjoy the Db price).

$$ Henry Guest House is a plain, newly redecorated, clean,
vertical, eight-room place. It's two blocks in front of the train sta-
tion on a quiet side street, run by a couple who genuinely cares about
your travel experience (S-£35, D-£50–60, T-£75, family deals, lots
of narrow stairs, 3 showers and 2 WCs for everybody, 6 Henry
Street, tel. 01225/424-052, fax 01225/316-669, www.thehenry
.com, stay@thehenry.com, helpful Sue and Derek).

Dorms

$ The YMCA, central on a leafy square, has 200 beds in industrial-
strength rooms (S-£23.50, twin-£36, beds in big dorms-£12–13,
£2 more per person on Fri and Sat, includes continental break-
fast, cheap lunches, lockers, Internet access, dorms closed 10:00–
14:00, down a tiny alley off Broad Street on Broad Street Place,
tel. 01225/325-900, fax 01225/462-065, www.bathymca.co.uk,
reservations@bathymca.co.uk).

$ White Hart Hostel is a simple place offering adults and fam-
ilies good, cheap beds in two- to six-bed dorms (£14/bed, D-£40,
Db-£60, family rooms, smoke-free, kitchen, 5-min walk behind
train station at Widcombe—where Widcombe Hill hits Claverton
Street, tel. 01225/313-985, www.whitehartbath.co.uk, run by Jo).

$ St. Christopher's Inn, in a prime, central location, is part
of a chain of low-priced, high-energy hubs for backpackers look-
ing for beds and brews (60 beds in 4- to 12-bed rooms-£16–19.50,
deals available online; lively and affordable restaurant and bar
downstairs, Internet access in lobby, smoke-free bedrooms, laun-
dry, lounge with video, 9 Green Street, tel. 01225/481-444, www
.st-christophers.co.uk). Their beds are so cheap because they know
you'll spend money on their beer.

EATING

Bath is bursting with quaint and stylish eateries. There's something for every appetite and budget—just stroll around the center of town. A picnic dinner of deli food or take-out fish-and-chips in the Royal Crescent Park is ideal for aristocratic hoboes. Reserve a table on Friday and Saturday evenings. Save money by eating before 19:00.

Near the Abbey

Three fine and popular places share North Parade Passage, a block south of the abbey:

Tilley's Bistro, popular with locals, serves healthy French, English, and vegetarian meals with candlelit ambience. Their fun menu lets you build your meal, choosing from an interesting array of £7 starters (Mon–Sat 12:00–14:30 & 18:30–23:00, closed Sun, reservations smart, non-smoking, North Parade Passage, tel. 01225/484-200).

Sally Lunn's House is a cutesy, quasi-historic place for traditional English meals, tea, pink pillows, and lots of lace (£15–20 meals, £10 early-bird 2-course special 17:00–19:00, nightly, smoke-free, 4 North Parade Passage, tel. 01225/461-634). Their forte is a variety of cream teas and buns (£7, until 18:00). Lunch customers get a free peek at the basement Kitchen Museum (otherwise 30p).

Crystal Palace Pub, with typical pub grub under rustic timbers or in the sunny courtyard, is a handy standby (meals-£7, served Mon–Sat 11:00–21:00, Sun 12:00–20:00, smoke-free, children welcome on patio until 16:30 but not indoors, 11 Abbey Green, tel. 01225/482-666).

Near the Train Station

These two places are two blocks up from the train station on Pierrepont Street.

Mai Thai Restaurant is a favorite with locals. It's cheap and crowded, serves good curry, and also does take-away food (£5–7 meals, daily 12:00–14:00 & 18:00–22:30, 6 Pierrepont Street, tel. 01225/445-557).

The Wife of Bath serves hearty English and French cuisine in a creaky, wood-beamed restaurant. They have an extensive wine selection, good "banoffee" (very sweet banana/toffee) pie, and a friendly waitstaff (£12–15 meals, £10 lunch and early-bird dinner special, Tue–Sat 12:00–14:00 & 17:30–22:00, Sun–Mon 17:30–22:00 only, down the stairs across the street from the Mai Thai on Pierrepont Street, tel. 01225/461-745).

Bath Restaurants

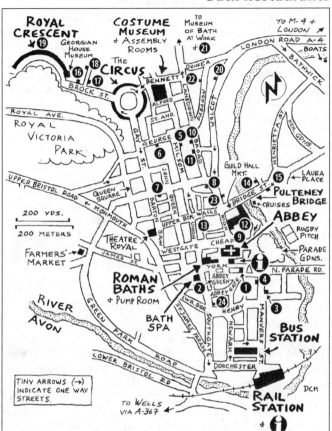

1. Tilley's Bistro & Sally Lunn's House
2. Crystal Palace Pub
3. Mai Thai Restaurant
4. The Wife of Bath
5. Loch Fyne Restaurant
6. Martini Restaurant
7. The Eastern Eye
8. Old Green Tree Pub
9. Browns Restaurant
10. Ask Restaurant
11. The Moon and Sixpence
12. Guildhall Market
13. Cornish Bakehouse
14. No. 5 Restaurant & Rajpoot Tandoori
15. Pastiche Bistro, Yak Yeti Yak & Boater Pub
16. Circus Restaurant
17. Papillon Bistro
18. Pinch of Salt Restaurant
19. Royal Crescent Hotel (Cream Teas)
20. The Bell Pub
21. To The Farmhouse Pub
22. Star Pub
23. Waitrose Supermarket
24. Marks & Spencer

Between the Abbey and the Circus

George Street is lined with cheery eateries: Thai, Italian, wine bars, and so on.

Loch Fyne Restaurant, a Scottish fish place with a bright, airy, and youthful atmosphere, fills a former bank. The fish is fresh, prices are reasonable (£10–14), the energy is high, and it doesn't feel like a chain (daily 12:00–22:00, 24 Milsom Street, tel. 01225/750-120).

Martini Restaurant, a hopping, purely Italian place, has class and jovial waiters (entrées-£12, pizzas-£7, plenty of veggie options, daily fish specials, extensive wine list, daily 12:00–14:30 & 18:00–22:30, reservations smart, smoke-free section, 9 George Street, tel. 01225/460-818, Nunzio, Franco, and Luigi).

The Eastern Eye is unique, serving decent Indian cuisine in an exquisite Georgian room under a triple-domed ceiling. The architecture almost overwhelms the food—and that's not a bad thing (£7 lunches, daily 12:00–14:30 & 18:00–23:00, 8 Quiet Street, tel. 01225/422-323).

Old Green Tree Pub, in the old town center, serves good lunches in a characteristic pub setting (real ales on tap, non-smoking room, lunch only 12:00–14:45, no children, Green Street, tel. 01225/448-259). As Bath is not a good pub-grub town, this is likely the best you'll do in the center.

Two big, noisy chain restaurants offer decent, inexpensive food to a loyal local following: **Browns** fills an old police station just across from the abbey, serving English food throughout the day (daily 12:00–23:00, kid-friendly, nice terrace, half-block east of the abbey, Orange Grove, tel. 01225/461-199). Family-friendly **Ask** is a similar place up the street (pizza and pasta for £7, noisy and cheap, good salads, George Street, tel. 01225/789-997).

The Moon and Sixpence, prized by locals for its quality international cuisine, is tucked away on a quiet lane. It's dressy and a bit smoky, with well-presented food (2-course lunch-£8.50, 3-course dinner-£27, daily 12:00–14:30 & 17:30–22:30, ground floor is preferable to upstairs, fine garden seating, 6a Broad Street, tel. 01225/460-962).

Guildhall Market, across from Pulteney Bridge, has produce stalls with food for picnickers. At its inexpensive Market Café, you can slurp a curry or sip a tea while surrounded by stacks of used books, bananas on the push list, and honest-to-goodness old-time locals (£4 meals, Mon–Sat 7:45–17:00, closed Sun, a block north of the abbey, on High Street).

The **Cornish Bakehouse,** near the Guildhall Market, has good take-away pasties (open until 17:30, 11a The Corridor, off High Street, tel. 01225/426-635).

Supermarkets: **Waitrose,** at the Podium shopping center, is great for picnics, with a good salad bar (Mon–Fri 8:30–20:00, Sat 8:30–19:00, Sun 11:00–17:00, just west of Pulteney Bridge and across from post office on High Street). **Marks & Spencer,** near the train station, has a grocery at the back of its department store (Mon–Sat 9:00–20:00, Sun 11:00–17:00, Stall Street).

East of Pulteney Bridge

No. 5 Restaurant serves classic French and Mediterranean cuisine in a stylish, intimate setting (main courses with vegetables-£16, daily 12:00–14:30 & 18:30–22:00, Mon–Tue are "bring your own bottle of wine" nights—no corkage fee, smart to reserve, smoke-free, just over Pulteney Bridge at 5 Argyle Street, tel. 01225/444-499).

Rajpoot Tandoori, next door to No. 5, serves—by all assessments—the best Indian food in Bath. You'll hike down deep into a cellar where the plush Indian atmosphere and award-winning cooking makes paying the extra pounds palatable. The seating is tight and the ceilings low, but it's smoke-free and air-conditioned (£8 3-course lunch special, £10 plates, daily 12:00–14:30 & 18:00–23:00, 4 Argyle Street, tel. 01225/466-833).

Yak Yeti Yak Restaurant, a fun Nepali place, is run by a cheerful, hardworking Nepali family that cooks up great traditional food at prices a Sherpa could handle (open daily, plenty of vegetarian plates, 12A Argyle Street, tel. 01225/442-299).

The Boater Pub offers a £5 lunch in its pleasant beer garden overlooking the river. It's popular with rowdy twenty-somethings for its good ales and riverside perch (lunch only 12:00–15:00, otherwise snacks, Mon–Sat 11:00–23:00, Sun 12:00–20:30, 9 Argyle Street, tel. 01225/464-211).

The feisty **Pastiche Bistro** offers inexpensive English food (2-course lunch-£6, 2-course dinner-£11, just east of Pulteney Bridge at 16 Argyle Street, tel. 01225/442-323).

Between the Circus and Royal Crescent

Circus Restaurant, a good value, gives modern English cuisine a Mediterranean twist. You'll get meat, fish, or veggies with an intimate, candlelit, Mozartean ambience. The three-course dinner special for £20 includes tasty vegetables and a selection of fine desserts (Wed–Sun 12:00–14:00 & 18:30–22:00, closed Tue lunch and all day Mon, reservations smart, 34 Brock Street, tel. 01225/318-918, Natasha serves while Adrian cooks).

Papillon Bistro is small, fun, and unpretentious, dishing up "modern-rustic cuisine from the south of France." It has cozy indoor and outdoor seating on a fine pedestrian lane (2-course meal-£8.50 from 12:00–18:30, 2-course dinners-£15–20, closed Sun–Mon, smart to reserve, 2 Margaret's Buildings, tel. 01225/310-064).

Pinch of Salt is a splurge, offering "world cuisine" in an uppity space—tight and trendy with mod decor—just off Brock Street (£14–17 main courses, Mon–Sat 12:00–14:00 and 19:00–22:00, closed Sun, 11 Margaret's Buildings, tel. 01225/421-251).

TRANSPORTATION CONNECTIONS

Bath's train station is called Bath Spa (train info: tel. 08457-484-950). The National Express bus office (Mon–Sat 8:00–17:30, closed Sun, bus info: tel. 08705-808-080) is one block in front of the train station.

From London to Bath: To get from London to Bath and see Stonehenge to boot, consider an all-day organized **bus tour** from London (and skip out of the return trip; see page 146 in the London chapter).

From Bath to London: You can catch a **train** to London's Paddington Station (2/hr, 90 min, £34 one-way after 9:30 but £40 on Fri), or save money—but not time—by taking the National Express **bus** to Victoria Station (nearly hourly, a little more than 3 hrs, one-way-£15, round trip-£22, www.nationalexpress.com).

From Heathrow to Bath: See page 143. Also consider taking a minibus with Alan Price; see "Celtic Horizons" on page 172.

From Bath to London's Airports: You can reach **Heathrow** by a train-and-bus combination (take train to Reading—runs hourly, catch airport shuttle bus from there—runs twice hourly, allow 2.5 hrs, £33, cheaper for BritRail passholders) or by National Express bus (11/day, 2.5 hrs, £15, tel. 08705-757-747). Or take the Celtic Horizons minibus to Heathrow; see page 172. You can get to **Gatwick** by bus (nearly twice hourly, 4.5 hrs, £24) or by train (hrly, 3 hrs, £30, transfer in Reading or Clapham Junction).

From Bath by Bus to: Cheltenham or **Gloucester** (1 direct bus/day, 2.5 hrs, more buses with transfer), **Stratford-upon-Avon** (1/day, 4 hrs, transfer in Bristol or Birmingham), and **Oxford** (1 direct bus/day, 2 hrs, more buses with transfer). Buses to **Wells** leave nearly hourly, but the last one back leaves before the even-song service is finished (75 min, last return 17:43).

From Bath by Train to: Moreton-in-Marsh (1/hr, 2 hrs, transfer in Didcot), **York** (hrly, change in Bristol, 5 hrs), **Oxford** (1/hr, 1.25 hrs, transfer in Didcot), **Birmingham** (1/hr, 2.5 hrs, transfer in Bristol), and **points north** (from Birmingham, a major transportation hub, trains depart for Blackpool, Scotland, and North Wales; use a train/bus combination to reach Ironbridge Gorge and the Lake District).

NEAR BATH

Glastonbury, Wells, Avebury, Stonehenge, and South Wales

Ooooh, mystery, history. Glastonbury is the ancient home of Avalon, King Arthur, and the Holy Grail. Nearby, medieval Wells gathers around its grand cathedral, where you can enjoy an evensong service. Then get neolithic at every Druid's favorite stone circles, Avebury and Stonehenge.

An hour west of Bath, at the Museum of Welsh Life, you'll find South Wales' story vividly told in a park full of restored houses. Relish the romantic ruins and poetic wax of Tintern Abbey, the lush Wye River Valley, and the quirky Forest of Dean.

Planning Your Time

Avebury, Glastonbury, and Wells make a wonderful day out from Bath. Splicing in Stonehenge is possible but stretching it. Everybody needs to see Stonehenge, but I'll tell you now, it looks just like it looks. You'll know what I mean when you pay to get in and rub up against the rope fence that keeps tourists at a distance. Avebury is the connoisseur's circle: more subtle and welcoming. Wells is simply a cute town, much smaller and more medieval than Bath, with a uniquely beautiful cathedral that's best experienced at the 17:15 evensong service. Glastonbury is normally done surgically, in two hours: See the abbey, climb the tor, ponder your hippie past (and where you are now), then scram.

Think of the South Wales sights as a different grouping. Ideally, they fill the day you leave Bath for the Cotswolds. Anyone interested in Welsh culture can spend four hours in the Museum of Welsh Life. Castle lovers and romantics will want to consider the Caerphilly Castle, Chepstow Castle, Tintern Abbey, and

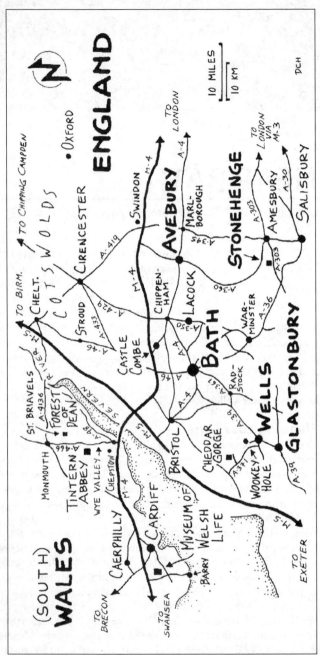

Forest of Dean. See the beginning of the Bath chapter for a day-by-day schedule (page 168).

Getting Around

Wells and Glastonbury are both easily accessible by bus from Bath. The **First bus company** offers a "First Day Southwest" ticket good for a day, that covers both journeys (£8, family-£16, Mon–Sat 8:00–17:30, closed Sun, office 1 block from Bath train station, tel. 0845-606-4446, www.firstgroup.com). Glastonbury and Wells are connected with each other by bus and by a 9.5-mile foot and bike path.

You can reach Avebury by taking the #X72 bus to Devizes (hrly, 1 hr), then picking up a frequent local bus to Avebury (15 min). Stonehenge is trickier. If you don't have a car, the most convenient and quickest way to see Avebury and Stonehenge is to take an all-day bus tour, or a half-day tour just to Stonehenge. Of those tours leaving from Bath, Mad Max is the liveliest (see page 171).

To get to South Wales from Bath, take a train to Cardiff (transfer in Bristol), then connect by bus (or train) to the sights.

Drivers can do a 107-mile loop, from Bath to Avebury (25 miles) to Glastonbury (56 miles) to Wells (6 miles) and back to Bath (20 miles). A loop from Bath to South Wales is 100 miles, mostly on the 70-mph motorway. Each of the Welsh sights is just off the motorway.

Glastonbury

Marked by its hill, or "tor," and located on England's most powerful line of prehistoric sites (called a "ley" line), the town of Glastonbury gurgles with history and mystery.

In A.D. 37, Joseph of Arimathea—one of Jesus' wealthy disciples—brought vessels containing the blood and sweat of Jesus to Glastonbury, and, with them, Christianity came to England. While this story is "proven" by fourth-century writings and accepted by the Church, the Holy Grail legend that came from it in the Middle Ages isn't. Many think the Grail trail ends at the bottom of the Chalice Well (described below), a natural spring at the base of the Glastonbury Tor.

In the 12th century, England needed a morale-boosting folk hero for inspiration during a war with France. The fifth-century

Celtic fort at Glastonbury was considered proof enough of the greatness of the fifth-century warlord Arthur. His supposed remains (along with those of Queen Guinevere) were dug up from the abbey floor, and Glastonbury became woven into the Arthurian legends. Reburied in the abbey choir, their gravesite is a shrine today.

In the 10th century, the Glastonbury Abbey was England's most powerful. By the year 1500, English monasteries owned one-sixth of all English land and had four times the income of the crown. Henry VIII dissolved the abbeys in 1536. He was particularly harsh on Glastonbury. He not only destroyed the abbey but also hung and quartered the abbot, sending the parts of his body on four different national tours...at the same time.

But Glastonbury rebounded. In an 18th-century tourism campaign, thousands signed affidavits stating that water from the Chalice Well healed them, and once again Glastonbury was on the tourist map. Today, Glastonbury and its tor are a center for searchers, too creepy for the mainstream church but just right for those looking for a place to recharge their crystals.

ORIENTATION

(area code: 01458)

Tourist Information: The TI is on High Street—as are many of the dreadlocked folks who walk it (Sun–Thu 10:00–17:00, Fri–Sat 10:00–17:30, until 16:00 in winter, tel. 01458/832-954, www .glastonbury.co.uk). The TI has several booklets about cycling and walking in the area. One 30p brochure outlines a good tor-to-town walk (a brisk 10 min). The TI's Millennium Trail pamphlet (60p) sends visitors on a historical scavenger hunt, following 20 numbered, marble plaques embedded in the pavement throughout the town.

Located in the TI, the Lake Village Museum—featuring tools made of stones, bones, and antlers—is nothing special. Tuesday is market day for crafts, knickknacks, and produce behind the TI (same hours as TI).

The **Tor Bus** shuttles visitors from the town center and abbey to the base of the tor. If you request it, the bus will stop at the Somerset Rural Life Museum and the Chalice Well (£1, 2/hr, daily 10:00–17:00 throughout the summer, bus does not run during lunchtime, catch bus at St. Dunstan's parking lot in the town center).

SIGHTS AND ACTIVITIES

▲▲**Glastonbury Abbey**—The evocative ruins of the first Christian sanctuary in the British Isles stand mysteriously alive in a lush, 36-acre park. Start your visit in the good little museum,

Glastonbury

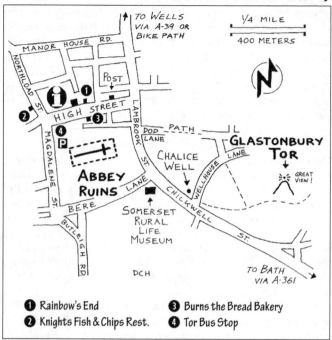

TO WELLS
VIA A-39 OR
BIKE PATH

¼ MILE

400 METERS

MANOR HOUSE RD.

NORTHLOAD ST.

POST

HIGH STREET

LAMBROOK ST.

DOD LANE

PATH

MAGDALENE ST.

P

BERE LANE

ABBEY RUINS

BUTLEIGH RD.

CHALICE WELL

WELLHOUSE LANE

GLASTONBURY TOR

GREAT VIEW !

CHILKWELL ST.

SOMERSET RURAL LIFE MUSEUM

DCH

TO BATH VIA A-361

❶ Rainbow's End
❷ Knights Fish & Chips Rest.
❸ Burns the Bread Bakery
❹ Tor Bus Stop

where a model shows the abbey in its pre–Henry VIII splendor, and exhibits tell the story of a place "grandly constructed to entice even the dullest minds to prayer." Today the abbey attracts people who find God within. Tie-dyed, starry-eyed pilgrims seem to float through the grounds naturally high. Others lie on the grave of King Arthur, whose burial site is marked off in the center of the abbey ruins. The only surviving building is the abbot's conical kitchen, which often comes with a cheery, singing monk demonstrating life in the abbey kitchen. If you'd like to see the demo, it's best to phone ahead for the schedule, especially off-season (£4, June–Aug daily 9:00–18:00, Sept–May 9:30 or 10:00 to dusk, closing times vary in the winter—call to check, last entry 30 min before closing, £1 audioguide is informative but can be long-winded, ask at entry for monk's "show" times, tel. 01458/832-267, www.glastonburyabbey .com).

Somerset Rural Life Museum—Exhibits include peat digging, cider making, and cheese making. The Abbey Farmhouse is now a collection of domestic and work mementos that illustrate the life of farmer John Hodges "from the cradle to the grave." The fine 14th-century barn, with its beautifully preserved wooden ceiling, is filled with Victorian farm tools and enthusiastic school children (free, Easter–Oct Tue–Fri 10:00–17:00, Sat–Sun 14:00–18:00, closed Mon; Nov–Easter Tue–Sat 10:00–17:00, closed Sun–Mon, last entry 30 min before closing, free parking, 8-min walk from abbey, at intersection of Bere Lane and Chilkwell Street, tel. 01458/831-197, county-museums@somerset.gov.uk).

Chalice Well—The well is surrounded by a peaceful garden. According to tradition, Joseph of Arimathea brought the chalice from the Last Supper to Glastonbury in A.D. 37. Even if the chalice is not in the bottom of the well and the water is red from rust and not Jesus' blood, the tranquil setting is one where nature's harmony is a joy to ponder. The stones of the well shaft date from the 12th century and are believed to have come from the church in Glastonbury Abbey (which was destroyed by fire). During the 18th century, pilgrims flocked to Glastonbury for the well's healing powers. Even today, there's a moment of silence at noon for world peace and healing. Have a drink or take some of the precious water home (£2.85, 60p–£1.20 bottles available, daily 10:00–18:00, less off-season, 4-min walk from Rural Life Museum, on Chilkwell Street—look for red sign, tel. 01458/831-154, www.chalicewell.org.uk).

Glastonbury Tor—Seen by many as a Mother Goddess symbol, the tor, a natural plug of sandstone on clay, has an undeniable geological charisma. The tower is the remnant of a 14th-century church of St. Michael. A fine Somerset view rewards those who hike to its 520-foot summit.

Back in the 1940s, Catherine Maltwood identified the signs of the zodiac in the ancient rock formations, hedgerows, and waterways surrounding Glastonbury. She saw the tor as the head of the phoenix, another symbol for Aquarius. If this sounds intriguing, you can buy her zodiac map at the TI (£2.50).

Path from Glastonbury Tor to Wells—A 9.5-mile cycling and foot path (a.k.a. Syrens Project) begins at the bottom of Glastonbury Tor and ends in Wells and is marked by nine large neolithic-looking sculptures along the way. Designed by local artists, these funky stones are carved with willow leaves, swans, and other images of the journey. You can rent a bike in Wells, but not Glastonbury.

Shopping—If you need spiritual guidance or just a rune reading, wander through the **Glastonbury Experience,** a New Age mall at the bottom of High Street.

EATING

Glastonbury, quickly becoming "the windy city," has no shortage of healthy eateries. The vegetarian **Rainbow's End** is one of several fine cafés for beans, salads, herbal teas, yummy homemade sweets, and New Age people-watching (£4–6 meals, daily 10:00–16:00, a few doors up from the TI, 17 High Street, tel. 01458/833-896). If you're looking for a midwife or a male-bonding tribal meeting, check their notice board.

Knights Fish and Chips Restaurant has been in business since 1909 because it serves good food (Mon 17:00–21:30, Tue–Sat 12:00–14:15 & 17:00–21:30, closed Sun, eat in or take away, 5 Northload Street, tel. 01458/831-882).

Burns the Bread makes hearty pasties (savory meat pies) as well as fresh pies and pastries. Ask about the Torsy Moorsy Cake. Grab a pasty and picnic with the ghosts of Arthur and Guinevere in the Abbey ruins (daily 7:00–17:00, 14 High Street, tel. 01458/831-532).

TRANSPORTATION CONNECTIONS

The nearest train station is in Bath.

From Glastonbury by Bus to: Wells (1/hr, 20 min, bus #173), **Bath** (5/day on Sun, 75 min; Mon–Sat no direct connections, transfer in Wells, allow 2 hrs).

Wells

Because this wonderfully preserved little town has a cathedral, it can be called a city. While it's the biggest town in Somerset, it's England's smallest cathedral city (pop. 9,400), with one of its most interesting cathedrals and a wonderful evensong service. Wells has more medieval buildings still doing what they were originally built to do than any town you'll visit. Market day fills the town square on Wednesday and Saturday.

Tourist Information: The TI, on the main square, has information about the town's sights and nearby cheese factories (April–Oct daily 9:30–17:30, Nov–March daily 10:00–16:00, tel. 01749/672-552, www.wells.gov.uk).

Local Guide: Edie Westmoreland is a good local guide who offers £3 town walks in the summer; her medieval dress makes her easy to spot (tours usually start at Penniless Porch on town square, book in advance with Edie, tel. 01934/832-350, or at TI).

SIGHTS AND ACTIVITIES

▲▲**Wells Cathedral**—England's first completely Gothic cathedral (dating from about 1200) is the highlight of the city. The newly restored west front displays nearly 300 original 13th-century carvings of kings and the **Last Judgment**. The bottom row of niches is empty, too easily reached by Cromwell's men, who were hell-bent on destroying "graven images." Stand back and imagine it as a grand Palm Sunday welcome with a cast of hundreds—all gaily painted back then, choristers singing boldly from holes above the doors and trumpets tooting through the holes up by the 12 apostles.

Inside, you're immediately struck by the general lightness and the unique "scissors" or hourglass-shaped **double arch** (added in 1338 to transfer weight from the west—where the foundations were sinking under the tower's weight—to the east, where they were firm). You'll be warmly greeted, reminded how expensive it is to maintain the cathedral, and given a map of its highlights.

Don't miss the fine 14th-century stained glass (the "Golden Window" on the east wall). The medieval **clock,** which depicts the earth at the center of the universe, does a silly but much-loved joust on the quarter hour (north transept, its face dates from 1390). The outer ring shows hours, the second ring shows minutes, and the inner ring shows the lunar dates.

In the **choir** (the central zone where the daily services are sung), the embroidery work on the cushions is worth a close look. The floral roof painting is based on the original medieval design, discovered under the 17th-century whitewash.

Head over to the south transept. Notice the carvings on the pillars. The figures depict medieval life—a man with a toothache, another man with a thorn in his foot, and, around the top, a ticked-off farmer chasing fruit stealers. Look at the tombstones set in the floor. Notice there is no brass. After the Reformation in the 1530s, the church was short on cash, so they sold the brass to pay for roof repairs.

Walk the well-worn steps up to the grand, fan-vaulted **chapter house**—an intimate place for the theological equivalent of a huddle among church officials. The cathedral **library** (50p, daily 14:30–16:30 only), with a few old manuscripts, offers a peek into a real 15th-century library.

The requested £5 donation for the cathedral is not intended to keep you out (daily 7:30–19:00 or dusk; 45-min tours Mon–Sat April–Oct at 10:00, 11:00, 13:00, 14:00, and 15:00; pay £2 photography fee at info desk, no flash in choir, good shop and the handy Cathedral Cloister Restaurant, tel. 01749/674-483, www.wellscathedral.org.uk). See "Cathedral Evensong Service," below.

Wells

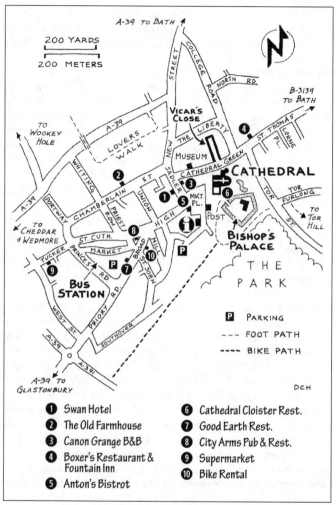

200 YARDS
200 METERS

A-39 TO BATH

STREET
COLLEGE ROAD
NORTH RD.

B-3139
TO BATH

VICAR'S CLOSE
THE LIBERTY
ST. THOMAS
PL.
LORNE

TO WOOKEY HOLE

A-39
LOVERS WALK

MUSEUM
CATHEDRAL GREEN

CATHEDRAL

4

WHITING
NEW ST
ST SADLER

TOR

TOR FURLONG
TO TOR HILL

PORTWAY
CHAMBERLAIN
PRIEST ROW
UNION
HIGH

2

3
1
MKT. PL.
5
6
7

TO CHEDDAR & WEDMORE

ST. CUTH.
MARKET
8

POST
BISHOP'S PALACE

A-39

TUCKER
PRINCES RD.
BROAD
JOHN
HILL
10

THE PARK

9

BUS STATION

WEST ST.
PRIORY RD.
SOUTHOVER

A-39
A-381

P PARKING
--- FOOT PATH
---- BIKE PATH

A-39 TO GLASTONBURY

DCH

1 Swan Hotel
2 The Old Farmhouse
3 Canon Grange B&B
4 Boxer's Restaurant & Fountain Inn
5 Anton's Bistrot
6 Cathedral Cloister Rest.
7 Good Earth Rest.
8 City Arms Pub & Rest.
9 Supermarket
10 Bike Rental

The mediocre city museum is next door to the cathedral. For a fine cathedral-and-town view from your own leafy hilltop bench, hike 10 minutes from here up Tor Hill.

▲▲Cathedral Evensong Service—Weekdays at 17:15 and Sunday at 15:00, the cathedral choir takes full advantage of heavenly acoustics with a 45-minute evensong service. You will sit right in the old "quire" as you listen to a great pipe organ and boys' and men's voices (generally not sung when school is out in July and Aug unless a visiting choir performs, tel. 01749/674-483 to check). At 17:05 the verger ushers visitors to their seats.

There's usually plenty of room.

On weekdays, if you need to catch the last bus to Bath at 17:43, request a seat on the north side of the presbytery, so you can slip out the side door without disturbing the service (10-min walk to station from cathedral).

Cathedral Green—In the Middle Ages, the cathedral was enclosed within the "Liberty," an area free from civil jurisdiction until the 1800s. The Liberty included the green on the west side of the cathedral, which, from the 13th to the 17th centuries, was a burial place for common folk, including 17th-century plague victims. During the Edwardian period, a local character known as Boney Foster used to dig up the human bones and sell them to tourists. The green later became a cricket pitch, then a field for grazing animals, and finally the perfect setting for an impressive cathedral.

Vicar's Close—Lined with perfectly pickled 14th-century houses, this is the oldest complete street in Europe (just a block north of the cathedral). It was built to house the vicar's choir, and it still houses church officials. Go into the chapel at the farthest end of the close and look out of the house on the left, which has been restored to its original state.

Bishop's Palace—Next to the cathedral stands the moated Bishop's Palace, built in the 13th century and still in use today as the residence of the Bishop of Bath and Wells. The interior offers a look at elegant furniture and clothing (£4, April–July and Sept–Oct Mon–Fri 10:30–18:00, Sun 12:00–18:00, closed Sat; Aug daily 10:30–18:00; closed Nov–March, tel. 01749/678-691).

The palace's spring-fed moat, built in the 14th century to protect the bishop during squabbles with the borough, now serves primarily as a pool for swans, which ring the bell to the left of the drawbridge for food. The bridge was last drawn in 1831. On the grounds (past the old-timers playing a proper game of croquet) is a fine garden with the idyllic springs that gave the city its name.

Path from Wells to Glastonbury Tor—The 9.5-mile bike/pedestrian path is ideal for cyclists and hikers. You can find the trailhead if you sneak behind the cathedral and look for the signs leading you to Glastonbury.

You can rent a bike in Wells at Bike City (£6.50/half-day, £8.50/day, Mon–Sat 9:00–17:30, closed Sun, helmets available, 31 Broad Street, tel. 01749/671-711; no bike rental in Glastonbury).

Near Wells

Cheddar Cheese—If you're in the mood for a picnic, drop by any local aromatic cheese shop for a great selection of tasty Somerset cheeses. Real farmhouse cheddar puts American cheddar to Velveeta shame.

The **Cheddar Gorge Cheese Company,** eight miles west of Wells, welcomes and educates guests (take A39, then A371 to Cheddar Gorge, tel. 01934/742-810). For all things cheddar in Somerset, check out www.cheddarsomerset.co.uk.

▲**Wookey Hole**—This lowbrow commercial venture, possibly worthwhile as family entertainment, is a real hodgepodge. It starts with a 35-minute wookey-guided tour of some big but mediocre caves, complete with history, geology lessons, and witch stories. Then you're free to wander through a traditional paper-making mill, with a demonstration, and into a 19th-century amusements room—a riot of color, funny mirrors, and old penny-arcade machines that visitors can actually play for as long as their pennies last (pennies on sale there). They even have old girlie shows (£9.90 at the gate, £9 tickets available at Wells or Bath TIs, daily 10:00–17:00, closed Dec 17–25, 2 miles east of Wells, tel. 01749/672-243, www.wookey.co.uk).

Scrumpy Farms—Scrumpy is the wonderfully dangerous hard cider brewed in this part of England. You don't find it served in many pubs because of the unruly crowd it attracts. Scrumpy, at 8 percent alcohol, will rot your socks. "Scrumpy Jack," carbonated mass-produced cider, is not real scrumpy. The real stuff is "rough farmhouse cider." This is potent stuff. It's said some farmers throw a side of beef into the vat, and when fermentation is done only the teeth remain.

TIs list local cider farms open to the public, such as **Mr. Wilkins' Land's End Cider Farm,** a great Back-Door travel experience (free, Mon–Sat 10:00–20:00, Sun 10:00–14:00, west of Wells in Mudgley, take B3139 from Wells to Wedmore, then B3151 south for 2 miles, farm is a quarter mile off B3151—tough to find, get close and ask locals, tel. 01934/712-385).

Glastonbury's **Somerset Rural Life Museum** has a cider exhibit (see page 196). Apples are pressed from August through December. Hard cider, while not quite scrumpy, is still typical of the West Country, but more fashionable, decent, and accessible. You can get a pint of hard cider at nearly any pub, drawn straight from the barrel—dry, medium, or sweet.

SLEEPING

Wells is a pleasant overnight stop with a handful of agreeable B&Bs and eateries. The Swan Hotel and the Canon Grange B&B (as well as the nearby Boxer's Restaurant at the Fountain Inn, below) are all within a block of each other, behind (east of) the cathedral. The Old Farmhouse is a short walk away. If you're coming in on B3139 from Bath, they're just before the cathedral.

Sleep Code

(£1 = about $1.80, country code: 44, area code: 01749)
S = Single, **D** = Double/Twin, **T** = Triple, **Q** = Quad, **b** = bathroom, **s** = shower only. Unless otherwise indicated, you can assume credit cards are accepted.

To help you sort easily through these listings, I've divided the rooms into three categories based on the price for a standard double room with bath:

$$$ **Higher Priced**—Most rooms £80 or more.
 $$ **Moderately Priced**—Most rooms between £40–80.
  $ **Lower Priced**—Most rooms £40 or less.

In Wells

$$$ Swan Hotel, facing the cathedral, is a big, overpriced hotel (Sb-£89–110, Db-£130–158, often cheaper if you just show up, ask about their weekend deals, breakfast-£9.50, non-smoking rooms, Sadler Street, tel. 01749/836-300, fax 01749/836-301, www.bhere .co.uk, swan@bhere.co.uk).

$$ The Old Farmhouse, a five-minute walk from the town center, welcomes you with a secluded front garden and tastefully decorated rooms. Upon request, owner Felicity Wilks—a Cordon Bleu chef—can cook up a four-course dinner for £28 per person (Db-£65, secured parking, 62 Chamberlain Street, tel. & fax 01749/675-058, www.plus44.com/oldfarmhouse).

$$ Canon Grange B&B is a 15th-century, watch-your-head beamed house directly in front of the cathedral. It has homey rooms and a cozy charm (Sb-£30–40, Db-£54–62, family room-£68, on the cathedral green, tel. 01749/671-800, www.canongrange.co.uk, canongrange@email.com).

Near Wells

$$ At Manor Farm B&B, two miles northwest of Wells, Fiona Fridd and her family will welcome you to their restored 14th-century manor house. Come here for a taste of English country life, complete with billiards and darts (Sb-£45–55, Db-£65–75, 2-night minimum for peak season weekends, Old Frome Road in East Horrington, tel. 01749/679-832, fax 01749/679-849, www .somersetbed.co.uk, info@somersetbed.co.uk).

EATING

Boxer's Restaurant, in the Fountain Inn, serves restaurant-quality food in a cheery pub atmosphere. Their award-winning cheese plate lets you sample cheddar and its local cousins. For a good, traditional local dish, try their founders beef pie (£8–15 meals, Mon–Sat 12:00–14:00 & 18:00–22:00, Sun 12:00–14:00 & 19:00–21:30, creative cooking, veggie options, real ales, draft cider, reservations wise on weekends, behind cathedral on St. Thomas Street, tel. 01749/672-317).

Anton's Bistrot on the main square is pleasant (£10–13 meals, daily 12:00–14:00 & 18:00–21:00, non-smoking section, veggie options, in Crown Hotel, tel. 01749/673-457).

For a heavenly lunch, consider the **Cathedral Cloister Restaurant** in the cathedral, along a lovely stone corridor with leaded windows (£3–5 lunches, Mon–Sat 10:00–17:00, Sun 13:00–17:00). The health-conscious **Good Earth** offers quiche, pasta, and salad; follow signs through the woody labyrinth to "counter service" (£5 meals, Mon–Sat 9:00–17:00, closed Sun, 4 Priory Road at bottom of Broad Street, tel. 01749/678-600).

The **City Arms Pub and Restaurant,** run by friendly owner Jim, is a favorite with locals. A city jail in Tudor times and still circled by medieval walls, the restaurant serves a variety of regional specialties, including veggie alternatives. The adjacent pub offers six ales on tap (£6–10 meals, Mon–Sat 9:00–22:00, Sun 9:00–21:00, 69 High Street, tel. 01749/673-916).

For picnickers, a Tesco **supermarket** is located west of the bus station on Tucker Street.

TRANSPORTATION CONNECTIONS

The nearest train station is in Bath. The bus station in Wells is actually a bus "lot," at the intersection of Priory and Princes roads.

From Wells by Bus to: Bath (hrly, 75 min, last bus leaves at 17:43), **Glastonbury** (hrly, 20 min), **London's Victoria Coach Station** (£17, hrly, 4 hrs, change in Bristol, buses run daily 6:20–17:45, National Express tel. 08705-808-080, www.nationalexpress.com).

Avebury

The stone circle at Avebury is bigger (16 times the size), less touristy, and, for many, more interesting than Stonehenge. You're free to wander among 100 stones, ditches, mounds, and curious patterns from the past, as well as the village of Avebury, which grew up in the middle of this fascinating, 1,400-foot-wide neolithic circle. The Avebury **TI** is helpful (hours vary, tel. 01672/539-425).

In the 14th century, in a kind of frenzy of religious paranoia, Avebury villagers buried many of these mysterious pagan stones. Their 18th-century descendants

broke up the remaining stones and used them for building material. In modern times, the buried stones were dug up and erected. Concrete markers show where the missing broken-up stones once stood.

Take the mile walk around the circle. Visit the **archaeology museum,** with its interactive exhibit in a 17th-century barn (£4.20, daily April–Oct 10:00–18:00, Nov–March until 16:00, tel. 01672/539-250).

Notice the pyramid-shaped **Silbury Hill,** a 130-foot-high, yet-to-be-explained mound of chalk just outside of Avebury. Nearly 5,000 years old, this mound is the largest man-made object in prehistoric Europe (with the surface area of London's Trafalgar Square and the height of the Nelson Column). It's a reminder that you've just scratched the surface of Britain's mysterious ancient and religious landscape.

In Avebury, the pleasant **Circle Restaurant** serves healthy vegetarian meals and unhealthy cream teas (daily April–Oct 10:00–17:00, Nov–March until 16:00, next to National Trust store, tel. 01672/539-514). The **Red Lion Pub** has inexpensive pub grub; a creaky, well-worn, dart-throwing ambience; and a medieval well in its dining room (£6–12 meals, daily 12:00–21:00, tel. 01672/539-266).

Sleeping in Avebury makes lots of sense, since the stones are lonely and wide open all night. **Mrs. Dixon's B&B,** directly across from Silbury Hill on the main road just beyond the Avebury tourist parking lot, rents three small, tidy rooms (S-£35, D-£45, includes breakfast, cash only, non-smoking, 6 Beckhampton Road, tel. 01672/539-588).

For transportation connections, see "Getting Around," page 193.

Stonehenge

Stonehenge, England's most famous stone circle, is an hour's drive from Glastonbury. Built sometime between 3000 and 1000 B.C. with huge stones brought all the way from Wales or Ireland, it

still functions as a remarkably accurate celestial calendar. A recent study of more than 300 similar circles in Britain found that each was designed to calculate the movement of the sun, moon, and stars, and even to predict eclipses in order to help these early societies know when to plant, harvest, and party. Today, as the summer solstice sun sets (on June 21) in just the right slot at Stonehenge, pagans boogie. Modern-day tourists are kept at a distance by a fence, but if you're driving, Stonehenge is just off the highway and worth a stop (£5.50). Even a free look from the road is impressive.

A new visitors center and shuttle bus to Stonehenge was slated to open in 2005, but it has been held up in planning and is unlikely to be finished in the next two years. When finished, the center will blend in with the landscape (essentially invisible from Stonehenge), traffic will be routed away from the stones through a tunnel, and visitors will take shuttle buses to the site.

Why didn't the builders of Stonehenge use what seem like perfectly adequate stones nearby? There's no doubt that the particular "blue stones" used in parts of Stonehenge were found only in (and therefore brought from) Wales or Ireland. Think about the ley lines. Ponder the fact that many experts accept none of the explanations of how these giant stones were transported. Then imagine congregations gathering here 4,000 years ago, raising thought levels, creating a powerful life force transmitted along the ley lines. Maybe a particular kind of stone was essential for maximum energy transmission. Maybe the stones were levitated here. Maybe psychics really do create powerful vibes. Maybe not. It's as unbelievable as electricity used to be (daily June–Aug 9:00–19:00, shorter hours off-season and June 20–22, closed Dec 24–26 & Jan 1, includes worthwhile hour-long audioguide—subject to availability, tel. 01980/625-368, lengthy recorded info tel. 01980/624-715, www.english-heritage.org.uk)

For transportation connections, see "Getting Around," page 193.

South Wales

▲**Cardiff**—The Welsh capital (pop. 300,000) has a newly renovated waterfront area, with shops, entertainment, and a pleasant modern center across from its castle (TI tel. 02920/227-281).

A visit to Cardiff's **castle** is interesting only if you catch one of the entertaining tours. With its ornate clock tower, the castle is the latest in a series of fortresses erected on the site by Romans, Normans, and assorted British lords. The interior is a Victorian fantasy (£6.90 with 50-min tour, tours every 30 min, £3.20 for grounds only without tour, daily 9:30–18:00, shorter hours off-season, last entry 1 hour before closing, tel. 02920/878-100, www.cardiffcastle.com).

▲▲**Museum of Welsh Life in St. Fagans**—This best look at traditional Welsh folk life displays more than 40 carefully reconstructed old houses from all corners of this little country in a 100-acre park under a castle. Each house is fully furnished and comes equipped with a local expert warming up beside a toasty fire, happy to tell you anything you want to know about life in this old cottage. Ask questions!

A highlight is the Rhyd-y-Car 1805 row house, which displays ironworker cottages as they might have looked in 1805, 1855, 1895, 1925, 1955, and 1985, offering a fascinating zip through Welsh domestic life from hearths to microwaves.

Step into an old schoolhouse, a chapel, or a blacksmith's shop to see traditional craft makers in action. Head over to the farm and wander among the livestock and funky old outbuildings. Then beam a few centuries forward to the House for the Future, an optimistic projection of domestic life in Wales 50 years from now. The timber house blends traditional building techniques with new technologies aimed at sustainability. The roof collects water and soaks up solar energy. The earth, which was removed to make way for the foundation, was made into bricks used in the structure.

In the main museum building, you'll see a great gallery displaying crude washing machines, the earliest matches, elaborately carved "love spoons," an impressive costume exhibit, and even a case of memorabilia from the local man who pioneered cremation. While everything is well explained, the £2 museum guidebook is a good investment.

The museum has three sections: houses, museum, and castle/garden. A small train trundles among the exhibits from Easter to October (5 stops, 50p per stop, whole circuit takes 45 min). If the sky's dry, see the scattering of houses first. Spend an hour in the large building's fascinating museum. The castle interior is royal enough and surrounded by a fine garden (free, daily 10:00–17:00, tel. 02920/573-500, www.nmgw.ac.uk). While the cafeteria near the entrance is handy, you'll eat light lunches better, cheaper, and with more atmosphere in the park at the Gwalia Tea Room. The Plymouth Arms pub just outside the museum serves the best food.

To get from the Cardiff train station to the museum in the village of St. Fagans, catch bus #32 (£1.50 one-way, £2.50 round-trip, exact change required; departs Cardiff station Mon–Sat at 10:20, 11:20, 13:20, 15:20, 18:20, and Sun hourly on the half hour between 9:30 and 18:00; tel. 0870-608-2608). Drivers leave M4 at Junction 33 and follow the signs. Leaving the museum, jog left on the freeway, take the first exit, and circle back, following signs to M4.

▲**Caerphilly Castle**—The impressive but gutted old castle, spread over 30 acres, is the second largest in Europe after Windsor. English Earl Gilbert de Clare erected this squat behemoth to try to establish a stronghold in Wales. With two concentric walls, it was considered to be a brilliant arrangement of defensive walls and moats. Attackers had to negotiate three drawbridges and four sets of doors and portcullises just to reach the main entrance. For the record, there were no known successful enemy forays beyond the current castle's inner walls.

The castle has its own leaning tower—the split and listing tower reportedly outleans Pisa's—and, some say, a resident ghost. Story has it that de Clare, after learning of his wife Alice's infidelity, exiled her back to France and had her lover killed. Upon learning of her paramour's fate, Alice died of a broken heart. Since then, the "Green Lady," named for her husband's jealousy, has reportedly roamed the ramparts.

Exhibits at the castle display clever catapults, castle-dwellers' tricks for harassing intruders, and a good dose of Welsh history (£3, June–Sept daily 9:30–18:00, May and Oct daily 9:30–17:00; Nov–April Mon–Sat 9:30–16:00, Sun 11:00–16:00; last entry 30 min before closing, 45-min audioguide-£1 with £5 deposit, 9 miles north of Cardiff, 30 min by car from Museum of Welsh Life in St. Fagans or take train from Cardiff to Caerphilly—3/hr, 20 min—and walk 5 min, tel. 02920/883-143, www.cadw.wales.gov.uk).

Chepstow Castle—Perched on a hill overlooking the pleasant village of Chepstow on one side and the Wye River on the other, this castle is worth a short stop for drivers heading for Tintern Abbey. The stone-built bastion dating to 1066 was among the first castles the British plunked down to secure their turf in Wales, and it remained in use through 1690. While many castles of the time were built first in wood, Chepstow, then a key foothold on the England–Wales border, was built from stone from the start for durability. As you clamber along the battlements, you'll find evidence of military architectural rehabs through the centuries, from Norman to Tudor right up through Cromwellian additions.

You can tell which parts date from Norman days—they're the ones made of yellow sandstone instead of the grayish limestone that makes up the rest of the castle (£3, daily June–Sept 9:30–18:00, Oct and April–May closes at 17:00, Nov–March closes at 16:00, last admission 30 min before closing, in Chepstow village a half mile from train station, tel. 01291/624-065, www.cadw.wales.gov .uk). At the castle gift shop, you can buy the inexpensive *Chepstow Town Trail* guidebooklet for a 21-stop, 1.5-hour stroll around the village that begins at the town gate. The gate is the spot where, in medieval times, folks arriving to sell goods or livestock were hit up for tolls.

▲▲**Tintern Abbey**—Inspiring monks to prayer, William Wordsworth to poetry, J. M. W. Turner to a famous painting, and rushed tourists to a thoughtful moment, this verse-worthy ruined-castle-of-an-abbey merits a five-mile detour off the motorway. Founded in 1131 on a site chosen by Norman monks for its tranquility, it functioned as an austere Cistercian abbey until its dissolution in 1536. The monks followed a strict schedule. They rose several hours after midnight for the first of eight daily prayer sessions and spent the rest of their time studying, working the surrounding farmlands, and meditating. Dissolved under Henry VIII's Act of Suppression in 1536, the magnificent church lingered in relative obscurity until tourists in the Romantic era (mid 18th century) discovered the wooded Wye valley and abbey ruins. J. M. W. Turner made his first sketches in 1792, and William Wordsworth penned "Lines Composed A Few Miles Above Tintern Abbey..." in 1798. Most of the external walls of the 250-foot-long, 150-foot-wide church still stand, along with the exquisite window tracery and outlines of the sacristy, chapter house, and dining hall. The daylight that floods through the roofless ruins highlights the Gothic decorated arches—in those days a bold departure from Cistercian simplicity (£3.20, June–Sept daily 9:30–18:00, April–May and Oct daily 9:30–17:00; Nov–March Mon–Sat 9:30–16:00, Sun 11:00–16:00; last entry 30 min before closing, 1-hr audioguide-£1 with £5 deposit, summertime concerts in the cloisters, tel. 01291/689-251, www.cadw.wales.gov.uk; from Cardiff catch a 1.5-hr bus or train to Chepstow, then 20-min bus or taxi from Chepstow to abbey). Visit early or late to miss crowds. The abbey's shop sells fine Celtic jewelry and other gifts. Take an easy 15-minute walk up to St. Mary's Church for a view of England just over the River Wye.

If seduced into spending the night, you'll find plenty of B&Bs near the abbey or in the charming castle-crowned town of Chepstow just down the road. The Tintern **TI** is helpful (April–Oct daily 10:30–17:30, closed Nov–March, tel. 01291/689-566).

▲**Wye River Valley and Forest of Dean**—This land is lush, mellow, and historic. Local tourist brochures explain the Forest of

Dean's special dialect, its strange political autonomy, and its oaken ties to Trafalgar and Admiral Nelson.

For a medieval night, check into the **St. Briavels' Castle Youth Hostel** (70 beds, £12.50 beds in 4- to 12-bed dorms, non-members-£3 extra, breakfast-£3.80, non-smoking, tel. 01594/530-272, stbriavels@yha.org.uk). The hostel hosts medieval banquets each week in August (£7.50, for hostel guests only, ask staff for schedule). An 800-year-old Norman castle used by King John in 1215 (the year he signed the Magna Carta), the hostel is comfortable (as castles go), friendly, and in the center of the quiet village of St. Briavels just north of Tintern Abbey. For dinner, eat at the hostel or walk "just down the path and up the snyket" to the **Crown Pub** (decent food and local pub atmosphere).

For tea and scones with a view, stop at the 17th-century **Florence Country House Hotel,** snuggled in the lower Wye Valley between Chepstow and Tintern. On a nice day, eat on the garden terrace and share river views with the cows lazing along the banks (Sb-£42, Db-£84, includes breakfast, tel. 01594/530-830, www.florencehotel.co.uk, enquiries@florencehotel.co.uk).

TRANSPORTATION CONNECTIONS

From Cardiff by Train to: Caerphilly (3/hr, 20 min), **Bath** (2/hr, 1 hr), **Birmingham** (2/hr, 2 hrs, change in Bristol, once an hour direct), **London** (2/hr, 2 hrs), **Chepstow** (10/day, 30 min, 6 miles to Tintern by bus). Train info: tel. 08457-484-950.

Route Tips for Drivers

Bath to South Wales: Leave Bath following signs for A4, then M4. It's 10 miles north (on A46 past a village called Pennsylvania) to the M4 freeway. Zip westward, crossing a huge suspension bridge into Wales (£4.80 toll westbound only). Stay on M4 (not M48) past Cardiff, take exit 33, and follow the brown signs south to the Museum of Welsh Life. To get to Tintern Abbey, take M4 to exit 21 and get on M48. The abbey is six miles (up A466, signs to Chepstow then Tintern) off M48 at exit 2, right where the northern bridge across the Severn hits Wales.

Cardiff to the Cotswolds via Forest of Dean: On the Welsh side of the big suspension bridge, take the Chepstow exit and follow signs up A466 to Tintern Abbey and the Wye River Valley. Carry on to Monmouth, and follow A40 and M50 to the Tewkesbury exit, where small roads lead to the Cotswolds.

THE COTSWOLDS

The Cotswold Hills, a 25-by-90-mile chunk of Gloucestershire, are dotted with villages and graced with England's greatest countryside palace, Blenheim.

As with many fairy-tale regions of Europe, the present-day beauty of the Cotswolds was the result of an economic disaster. Wool was a huge industry in medieval England, and Cotswold sheep grew the best wool. A 12th-century saying bragged, "In Europe the best wool is English. In England the best wool is Cotswold." The region prospered. Wool money built fine towns and houses. Local "wool" churches are called "cathedrals" for their scale and wealth. Stained-glass slogans say things like "I thank my God and ever shall, it is the sheep hath paid for all."

With the rise of cotton and the Industrial Revolution, the woolen industry collapsed. Ba-a-a-ad news. The wealthy Cotswold towns fell into a depressed time warp; the homes of impoverished nobility became gracefully dilapidated. Today, visitors enjoy a harmonious blend of man and nature—the most pristine of English countrysides decorated with time-passed villages, rich wool churches, tell-me-a-story stone fences, and "kissing gates" you wouldn't want to experience alone. Appreciated by throngs of 21st-century Romantics, the Cotswolds are enjoying new prosperity.

The north Cotswolds are best. Two of the region's coziest towns, Chipping Campden and Stow-on-the-Wold, are eight and four miles, respectively, from Moreton-in-Marsh, which has the best public transportation connections. Any of these three towns makes a fine home base for your exploration of the thatch-happiest of Cotswold villages and walks.

Planning Your Time

The Cotswolds are an absolute delight by car and, with patience, enjoyable even without a car. On a three-week British trip, I'd spend two nights and a day in the Cotswolds. The Cotswolds' charm has a softening effect on many uptight itineraries. You could enjoy days of walking from a home base here.

Chipping Campden and Stow-on-the-Wold are quaint without being overrun, and both have good accommodations. Stow has a bit more character for an overnight stay, and offers the widest range of choices. The plain town of Moreton is the only town of the three with a train station. With a car, consider really getting away from it all by staying in one of the smaller villages.

If you want to take in some Shakespeare, note that Stow, Chipping Campden, and Moreton are only a 30-minute drive from Stratford, which offers a great evening of world-class entertainment (see Stratford-upon-Avon chapter).

One-Day Driver's 100-mile Cotswold Blitz, Including Blenheim: Use a good map and reshuffle to fit your home base: 9:00–Browse through Chipping Campden, following the self-guided walk; 10:00–Joyride through Snowshill, Stanway, Stanton, the Slaughters, and Bourton-on-the-Water; 13:00–Have lunch at Stow-on-the-Wold, then follow the self-guided walk; 15:00–Drive 30 miles to Blenheim Palace and take the hour-long tour (last tour departs at 16:45); 18:00–Drive home for just the right pub dinner. (If planning on a gourmet countryside pub dinner, reserve in advance by phone.)

Getting Around the Cotswolds

By Bus: The Cotswolds are so well-preserved, in part, because public transportation to and within this area has long been miserable.

To explore the towns, use the two buses that hop through the region nearly hourly, lacing together main stops and ending at rail stations. In each case, there are about eight buses per day;

the entire trip takes about an hour; and you spend about £2 per hop (pay driver directly as you board). With the help of the TI, you can lace together a one-way or return trip by public transportation, making for a fine Cotswolds day. If you're traveling one-way between two train station, remember that the Cotswold villages—generally pretty clueless when it comes to the needs of travelers without a car—have no baggage-check services. You'll need to improvise. Remember

The Cotswolds

1 Cotswold Farm Park
2 Stanway House
3 Snowshill Lavender
4 Chastleton House

━━━ MAJOR ROAD
─── MINOR ROAD
···· COTSWOLD WAY
FOOTPATH

that service is poor on Saturday, and essentially non-existent on Sundays. For specifics, consult any TI or call the Cotswolds bus-travel info line at tel. 0870-608-2608, ext. 83.

While I've based this information on Moreton, you can derive Stow and Chipping Campden bus connections from this same write-up. Here are the bus lines that leave from Moreton:

Bus #M21/#22 runs from Moreton-in-Marsh to Bourton-on-the-Water (some to Broadway) to Chipping Campden to the Stratford-upon-Avon train station.

Bus #55 goes from Moreton-in-Marsh to Stow-on-the-Wold to Bourton-on-the-Water to Northleach to Cirencester to the Kemble train station.

By Bike: Despite narrow roads and high hedgerows (blocking some views), bikers enjoy the Cotswolds free from the constraints of bus schedules. For each area, TIs have fine route planners that indicate which peaceful, paved lanes are particularly scenic for biking.

There are no bikes for rent in Stow-on-the-Wold. At Moreton-in-Marsh's train station, **Country Lanes Cycle Centre** rents a good variety of bikes, throwing in expert advice and route maps for free (£15/day with lock and helmet, May–Sept generally daily 9:30–17:30, closed off-season, tel. 01608/650-0065, www.countrylanes.co.uk, Robert). Also in Moreton-in-Marsh, the **Toy Shop** rents mountain bikes (£14/day with route maps and bike locks, no helmets, Mon and Wed–Sat 9:00–17:00, closed Sun and Tue, High Street, tel. 01608/650-756). In Chipping Campden, try **Cotswold Country Cycles** (£12/day, tandems-£25/day, daily 9:30–dusk, includes helmets and route maps, delivery for a fee, tours available, 1.5 miles north of town at Longlands Farm Cottage, tel. 01386/438-706, mobile 077-1500-2972, www.cotswoldcountrycycles.com).

By Foot: Walking guidebooks abound, giving you a world of choices for each of my recommended stops (choose a book with clear maps). Villages are generally no more than three miles apart, and most have pubs that would love to feed and water you. For a list of guided walks, ask at any TI for the free AONB *(Area of Outstanding Natural Beauty)* brochure. The walks are free, range from two to 12 miles, and often involve a stop at a pub or tearoom (April–Sept).

By Car: Distances here are wonderfully short (but only if you invest in the Ordnance Survey map of the Cotswolds, sold locally at TIs and newsstands). Here are distances from Moreton: **Broadway** (10 miles), **Chipping Campden** (8 miles), **Stratford** (17 miles), **Warwick** (23 miles), **Stow** (4 miles).

Robinson's car-rental company, **Robinson Goss Self Drive,** is six miles north of Moreton-in-Marsh, and offers one-day rentals from £28, including everything but gas. They're in the middle of nowhere, but may pick you up for a charge of about £1/mile (Mon–Fri 8:30–17:00, Sat 8:30–12:30, closed Sun, tel. 01608/663-322, www.robgoss.co.uk).

Car hiking is great. In this chapter, I cover the postcard-perfect (but discovered) villages. With a car and the local Ordnance Survey map (£4.25), you can easily ramble about and find your own gems. The problem with having a car is that you are less likely to walk. Consider taking a taxi or bus somewhere, so that you can walk back to your car and enjoy the scenery.

By Taxi: Two or three town-to-town taxi trips can make more sense than renting a car. While taking a cab cross-country seems extravagant at about £2 per mile, the distances are short (Stow to Moreton is 4 miles, Stow to Chipping Campden is 10), and one-way walks are lovely. If you'll be taking a cab, consider hiring one at the hourly "touring rate" (£20–25), rather than the meter rate (e.g. £18 Stow to Chipping Campden). For a few more bucks, you can have a joyride peppered with commentary.

To scare up a taxi in Moreton, call Richard at **Four Shires** (mobile 077-4780-2555) or **Iain's Taxis** (mobile 07789-897-966, £20/hr); in Stow, call Iain (above), **Cotswold Safaris** (tel. 01451/832-422, £65/half-day car tour), or **Tony Knight** (mobile 078-8771-4047, £25/hr); and in Chipping Campden, try **Marnic Cars & Taxis** (tel. 01386/840-014, £30/hr) or **Cotswold Private Hire** (mobile 07980-857-833). If you call a cab, confirm that the meter will start only when you are actually picked up.

By Tour: Departing from Bath, **Mad Max Minibus Tours** offer a "Cotswold Discovery" full-day tour, and can drop you off in Stow with your luggage if you arrange it in advance (see specifics on page 171).

From Stratford, you can catch the **City Sightseeing** tour, which does a 15-village Cotswold blitz and makes several short stops (see page 246).

While none of the Cotswold towns offers regularly sched-uled walks, many have voluntary warden groups who love to meet visitors and give walks for just a small donation (£5 is plenty, £10 per group is great, specific contact information appears below for Chipping Campden and Stow).

Chipping Campden

Just touristy enough to be convenient, the north Cotswolds town of Chipping Campden (CAM-den) is a ▲▲ sight. This market town, once the home of the richest Cotswold wool merchants, has some incredibly beautiful thatched roofs. Both the great British historian G. M. Trevelyan and I call Chipping Campden's High Street the finest in England.

ORIENTATION

Walk the full length of High Street; its width is characteristic of market towns. Go around the block on both ends. On one end, you'll find impressively thatched homes (out Sheep Street, past the public WC and ugly gas station, and right on Westington Street). Walking north on High Street, you'll pass the Market Hall, the wavy roof of the first great wool mansion, a fine and free memorial garden, and, finally, the town's famous 15th-century Perpendicular Gothic "wool" church. (This route is the same as the self-guided town walk below.)

Tourist Information

Chipping Campden's TI is in the Old Police Station on High Street. Get the 20p town map (daily 10:00–17:30, tel. 01386/841-206, www.chippingcampden.co.uk and www.visitchippingcampden .com).

Helpful Hints:

Internet Access: Your best bet is to go back to London.

Bike Rental: Call Cotswold Country Cycles; see "Getting Around the Cotswolds—By Bike" (above).

Taxi: Try Marnic Cars & Taxis or Cotswold Private Hires; see "Getting Around the Cotswolds—By Taxi" (above).

Parking: Find a spot anywhere along High Street, and park for free with no time limit. There's also a pay-and-display lot (90-min maximum) next to the old market hall (across from TI).

Local Tours: The local members of the Cotswold Voluntary Wardens would be happy to show you around town for a small donation to their club (£10 for a 1-hour walk is more than enough, call Ann Colcomb—tel. 01386/832-131 or arrange through TI).

SELF-GUIDED WALK

Welcome to Chipping Campden

This 500-yard walk through "Campden" (as locals call their town) takes you from the TI to the church in about 30 minutes.

Begin at the **Magistrate's Court,** a meeting room in the old police station, located above the TI (free, same hours as TI, ask at TI to go up). Under the open-beamed courtroom, you'll find a casual little exhibit on the town's history.

Campden's most famous monument, the **Market Hall,** stands in front of the TI, marking the town center. It was built

in 1627 by the 17th-century Lord of the Manor, Sir Baptist Hicks. (Look for the Hicks family coat of arms in the building's facade.) Back then, it was an elegant—even over-the-top—shopping hall for the townsfolk who'd come here to buy their produce. In the 1940s, it was almost sold to an American, but the townspeople heroically raised

Cotswold Appreciation 101

Much history can be read into the names of the area. *Cotswold* could come from the Saxon phrase meaning "hills of sheep's coats." Or it could mean shelter ("cot" like cottage) on the open upland ("wold").

In the Cotswolds, a town's main street (called High Street) needed to be wide to accommodate the sheep and cattle being marched to market (and today, to park tour buses). Some of the most picturesque cottages were once humble row houses of weavers' cottages, usually located along a stream for their water-wheels (good examples in Bibury and Castle Combe). The towns run on slow clocks and yellowed calendars. An entire village might not have a phone booth that accepts a telephone card.

Fields of yellow (rapeseed) and pale blue (linseed) separate pastures dotted with black and white sheep. In just about any B&B, when you open your window in the morning you'll hear sheep baaing. The decorative "toadstool" stones dotting front yards throughout the region are medieval staddle stones, which buildings were set upon to keep the rodents out.

money to buy it first, then gave it to the National Trust for its preservation.

The timbers inside are true to the original. Study the classic Cotswold stone roof, still held together with wooden pegs nailed in from underneath. (Tiles were cut and sold with peg holes, and stacked like waterproof scales.) Buildings all over the region still use these stone shingles. Today, the hall hosts local fairs.

Chipping Campden's **High Street** has changed little architecturally since 1840. (The town's street plan survives from the 12th century.) Notice the harmony of the long rows of buildings. While the street comprises different styles through the centuries, everything you see was made of the same Cotswold stone—the only stone allowed today.

To be level, High Street arcs with the contour of the hillside. Because it's so wide, you know this was a market town. In past centuries, livestock and packhorses laden with piles of freshly shorn fleece would fill the streets. Campden was a sales and distribution center for the wool industry, and merchants from as far as Italy would come here for the prized raw wool.

High Street has no house numbers—people know the houses

Cotswold walls and roofs are made of the local limestone. The limestone roof tiles hang by pegs. To make the weight more bearable, smaller and lighter tiles are higher up. An extremely strict building code keeps towns looking what many locals call "overly quaint."

Towns are small, and everyone seems to know everyone. The area is provincial, gossipy, yet ever-so-polite, and people commonly catch themselves saying, "It's all very...mmm...yyya." Rich people open their gardens to support their favorite charities, while—until recently—the less couth enjoyed "badger baiting" (a gambling cousin of cockfighting in which a badger, with his teeth and claws taken out, is mangled by mean dogs).

This is walking country. The English love their walks and vigorously defend their age-old right to free passage. Once a year the Rambling Society organizes a "Mass Trespass," when each of the country's 50,000 miles of public footpaths is walked. By assuring each path is used at least once a year, they stop landlords from putting up fences. Any paths found blocked are unceremoniously unblocked.

Questions to ask locals: Does badger baiting survive? Do you think foxhunting should have been banned? Who are the Morris men? What's a kissing gate?

by their names. In the distance, you can see the town church (where this walk ends).

• *Hike up High Street to just before the first intersection.*

In 1367, William Grevel built what's considered Campden's first stone house: **Grevel House** (on the left). Sheep tycoons had big homes. Imagine back then, when this fine building was surrounded by humble wattle-and-daub huts. It had newfangled chimneys, rather than a crude hole in the roof. (No more rain inside!) Originally a "hall house" with just one big, tall room, it got its upper floor in the 16th century. The finely carved central bay window is a good early example of the Perpendicular Gothic style. The gargoyles scared away bad spirits—and served as rain spouts. The boot scrapers outside each door were a fixture in that muddy age—especially in market towns, where the streets were filled with animal dung.

• *Continue up High Street for about 100 yards. Go past Church Street (which we'll walk up later). Across the street, you'll find a small Gothic arch leading into a garden.*

The small and secluded **Ernest Wilson Memorial Garden,** once the church's vegetable patch, is a botanist's delight today. It's filled with well-labeled plants that the Victorian botanist Ernest Wilson brought back to England from his extensive travels in Asia. There's complete history of the garden on the board to the left of the entry (free, open daily until dusk).

• *Backtrack to Church Street. Turn left, walk past the Eight Bells Inn, and head around the corner.*

Sprawling adjacent the town church, the area known as **Baptist Hicks Land** holds Hicks' huge estate and manor house. This influential Lord of the Manor was from "a family of substance" who were merchants of silk and fine clothing as well as money lenders. Beyond the ornate gate, only a few outbuildings and the charred corner of his mansion survive. The mansion was burned by Royalists in 1645 during the Civil War—notice how Cotswold stone turns red when burned. Hicks housed the poor, making a show of his generosity, adding a long row of almshouses (with his family coat of arms) for neighbors to see as they walked to church. These almshouses (lining Church Street on the left) house pensioners today, as they have since the 17th century.

• *Walk between the almshouses and the wall that lines the Hicks estate to the church, where a scenic, tree-lined lane leads to the front door. On the way, notice the 12 lime trees, one for each of the apostles, that were planted in about 1760 (sorry, no limes).*

One of the finest churches in the Cotswolds, **St. James Church** graces one of its leading towns. Both the town and the church were built by wool wealth. The church is Perpendicular Gothic, with lots of light and strong verticality. Before you leave, notice the fine vestments and altar hangings behind protective blue curtains (near the back of the church). Tombstones pave the floor—memorializing great wool merchants through the ages.

At the altar is a brass relief of William Grevel, the first owner of the Grevel House (above), and his wife. In the way that Baptist Hicks dominated the town, Grevel dominates the church. His huge, canopied tomb is the ornate final resting place for Grevel and

his wife, Elizabeth. Study their faces, framed by fancy lace ruffs (trendy in the 1620s). Adjacent— as if in a closet—is a statue of their daughter, Lady Juliana, and her husband, Lutheran Yokels. Juliana commissioned the statue in 1642, when her husband died, but had it closed until *she* died in 1680. Then, the doors were opened, revealing these two people living happily ever after—at least in marble. The hinges were likely only ever used once.

SLEEPING

In Chipping Campden—as in any town in the Cotswolds—B&Bs offer a better value than hotels. Rooms are generally tight on Saturdays (when many charge a bit more and are reluctant to rent to 1-nighters) and in September, which is considered a peak month. Parking is never a problem. Always ask for a discount if staying longer than one or two nights.

$$$ Noel Arms Hotel, the characteristic old hotel on the main square, has welcomed guests for 600 years. Its lobby is decorated with armor, guns, and heraldry (insignias), and comes with a whiff of the medieval ages. Its 26 rooms are well-furnished with antiques (standard Db-£125, bigger Db-£150, fancier 4-post Db-£175, manager Loy promises a 10 percent discount with this 2006 book, some ground-floor doubles, attached restaurant/bar, High Street, tel. 01386/840-317, fax 01386/841-136, www.noelarmshotel .com, reception@noelarmshotel.com).

$$ Lygon Arms Hotel has small public areas and 10 cheery, open-beamed rooms (small older Db-£65, huge "superior" Db-£95, High Street, tel. 01386/840-318, www.lygonarms.co.uk, Sandra@lygonarms.co.uk, Sandra Davenport).

$$ Sandalwood House B&B is a big, comfy, modern home with a royal lounge and a sprawling back garden. Just a five-minute walk from the center of town, it's in a quiet, woodsy, pastoral setting. Its two cheery, pastel rooms are bright and spacious (D-£64, T-£85, cheaper if you order a light breakfast instead of full or stay 3 nights, cash only, no kids under age 7, non-smoking, friendly cat, tel. & fax 01386/840-091, Diana Bendall). To get to Sandalwood House, go west on High Street, and at the church and the Volunteer Inn, turn right and right again; look for a sign in the hedge on the left, and head up the long driveway.

Sleep Code

(£1 = about $1.80, country code: 44)
S = Single, **D** = Double/Twin, **T** = Triple, **Q** = Quad, **b** = bathroom, **s** = shower only. Unless noted otherwise, you can assume credit cards are accepted.

To help you sort easily through these listings, I've divided the rooms into three categories based on the price for a standard double room with bath:

$$$ **Higher Priced**—Most rooms £90 or more.
$$ **Moderately Priced**—Most rooms between £60–90.
$ **Lower Priced**—Most rooms £60 or less.

Chipping Campden

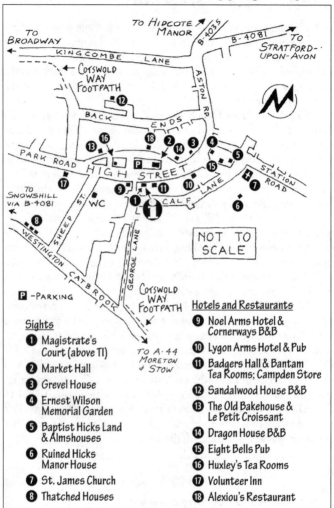

Sights

1 Magistrate's Court (above TI)
2 Market Hall
3 Grevel House
4 Ernest Wilson Memorial Garden
5 Baptist Hicks Land & Almshouses
6 Ruined Hicks Manor House
7 St. James Church
8 Thatched Houses

Hotels and Restaurants

9 Noel Arms Hotel & Cornerways B&B
10 Lygon Arms Hotel & Pub
11 Badgers Hall & Bantam Tea Rooms; Campden Store
12 Sandalwood House B&B
13 The Old Bakehouse & Le Petit Croissant
14 Dragon House B&B
15 Eight Bells Pub
16 Huxley's Tea Rooms
17 Volunteer Inn
18 Alexiou's Restaurant

$ **The Old Bakehouse** rents five small but pleasant rooms in a 600-year-old home with a plush fireplace lounge (Sb-£40, Db-£60, family deals, cash only, fun attic room that sleeps up to 5 has beams running through it, Lower High Street, tel. & fax 01386/840-979, oldbakehouse@chippingcampden-cotswolds.co.uk, Sarah Drinkwater).

$ **Dragon House B&B** rents tidy two-floor suites—with medieval beams—right on the center of High Street. They have laundry machines and a sumptuous, stay-awhile garden (Db-£58,

£5 off for 3 or more nights, cash only, near Market Hall, tel. & fax 01386/840-734, www.dragonhouse-chipping-campden.com, info@dragonhouse-chipping-campden.com, Valerie and Graeme the potter). They also have an apartment that sleeps up to six (Sat to Sat only, £250–500/week depending on month).

$ Cornerways B&B is a fresh, bright, and comfy modern home (not "oldie woldie") a block off High Street. It's run by the delightful Carole Proctor who can "look out the window and see the church where we were married." The huge, light, airy loft rooms are great for families (Db-£60, £5 off for 2 nights, Tb-£85, Qb-£105, children's discount, George Lane, just walk through the arch beside Noel Arms Hotel, tel. 01386/841-307, www.cornerways .info, carole@cornerways.info).

EATING

This town—so filled with wealthy residents and tourists—comes with lots of choices. Here are some local favorites:

Eight Bells Pub is a charming 14th-century inn on Leysbourne with a classy and woody restaurant and a more colorful pub (daily, £20 dinners, reservations recommended, tel. 01386/840-371).

For more character than at the Eight Bells, try the **Volunteer Inn,** which serves decent grub daily with a grassy courtyard out back (£5–8 meals, daily 12:00–14:00 & 19:00–21:00, Park Road). The **Lygon Arms Pub** is also good for food (daily).

To visit a cute tea room, try one of these places, located in the town center: **Badgers Hall Tea Room** is great for a wide selection of homemade cakes, crumbles, and scones. Along with light lunches, they serve an afternoon tea—a tall and ritualistic tray of dainty sandwiches, pastries, and scones with tea—for half the London price (£24 for 2 people, Wed–Mon 10:30–16:30, closed Tue, High Street). **Le Petit Croissant,** a cheery little French deli with a tearoom in the back, serves pastries, quiche, cheese, and wine (closed Sun–Mon and Tue–Sat 14:00–14:30, Lower High Street, tel. 01386/841-870). Two tea rooms on High Street, near the Market Hall, are both good values: **Huxley's** (closed Mon–Tue) and **Bantam Tea Rooms** (daily until 17:00, until 19:00 in summer).

Alexiou's, a fun Greek restaurant on High Street, serves hearty portions and breaks plates at closing every Saturday night (closed Sun to clean up, tel. 01386/840-826).

The small **Campden Store** is the town's main grocery; it's fine for picnics (daily 7:00–22:00, across from the market and next to TI on High Street). Munch lunch across the street, on the benches on the little green.

Near Chipping Campden

Located to the west of Chipping Campden, these are my nominations for the cutest Cotswold villages. Like marshmallows in hot chocolate, Stanway, Stanton, and Snowshill nestle side by side, awaiting your arrival. Other easy-to-access sights to the west and north of Chipping Campden are also included below.

Stanway

Stanway is notable for its manor house, **Stanway House**, worth ▲▲. Lord Neidpath, whose family tree charts relatives back to

1202, opens his melancholy home and grounds to visitors just two days a week in the summer (£6, July and Aug for sure, and either June or Sept, Tue and Thu 14:00–17:00, tel. 01386/584-469, www.stanwayfountain.co.uk). His lordship himself narrated the audioguides to his home (£2).

He recently restored "the tallest fountain in Britain" on the grounds—300 feet tall, gravity-powered, and quite impressive (fountain spurts for 30 min at 14:45 and 16:00 on opening days).

The bitchin' Tithe Barn (near where you enter the grounds) dates to the 14th century, and predates the manor. It was originally where monks—in the days before money—would accept one-tenth of whatever the peasants produced. Peek inside: This is a great hall for village hoedowns. While the Tithe Barn is no longer used to greet motley peasants and collect their feudal "rents," the lord still gets rent from his vast landholdings, and hosts community fêtes in his barn.

Stepping into the obviously very lived-in palace, you're free to wander around pretty much as you like. His lordship is often roaming about as well. The place feels like a time warp, even though the lord has recently remarried. Ask the ticket taker (inside) to demonstrate the spinning rent-collection table. In the great hall, marvel at the one-piece oak shuffleboard table and the 1780 Chippendale exercise chair (half an hour of bouncing on this was considered good for the liver).

The manor dogs have their own cutely painted "family tree," but Lord Neidpath admits that his last dog, C.J., was "all character and no breeding." Poke into the office. You can psychoanalyze the lord by the books that fill his library, the videos stacked in front of his bed (with the mink bedspread), and whatever's next to his toilet.

The place has a story to tell. And so do the docents stationed in each room—modern-day peasants who, even without family trees, probably have relatives going back just as far in this village. Really. Talk to these people. Probe. Learn what you can about this side of England.

Getting There: By car, leave B4077 at a statue of (the Christian) George slaying the dragon (of pagan superstition); you'll round the corner and see the manor's fine 17th-century Jacobean gatehouse. There's no real public transportation to Stanway.

From Stanway to Stanton: These towns are separated by a row of oak trees and grazing land, with parallel waves echoing the furrows plowed by medieval farmers. Centuries ago, farmers were allotted long strips of land called "furlongs." The idea was to dole out good and bad land equitably. (One square furlong equals an acre.) Over centuries of plowing these, furrows were formed. Let someone else drive, so you can hang out the window under a canopy of oaks, passing stone walls and sheep. Leaving Stanway on the road to Stanton, the first building you'll see (on the left, just outside Stanway) is a thatched cricket pavilion overlooking the village cricket green. Dating only from 1930, it's raised up (as medieval buildings were) on rodent-resistant staddle stones. Stanton's just ahead; follow the signs.

Stanton

Pristine Cotswold charm cheers you as you head the main street of the village of Stanton, worth ▲. Stanton's **Church of St. Michael** betrays a pagan past. It's safe to assume any church dedicated to St. Michael (the archangel who fought the devil) sits upon a sacred pagan site. Stanton is actually at the intersection of two ley lines (geographical lines along which many prehistoric sights are found). You'll see St. Michael's well-worn figure (with a sundial) above the door as you enter. Inside, above the capitals in the nave, find the pagan symbols for the sun and the moon. While the church probably dates back to the ninth century, today's building is mostly from the 15th century with 13th-century transepts. On the north transept, medieval frescoes show faintly through the 17th-century whitewash. (Once upon a time, medieval frescoes were considered too "papist.") Imagine the church interior colorfully decorated throughout. There is original medieval glass behind the altar. The list of rectors (left side wall) goes back to 1269. Finger the grooves in the back pews, worn away by sheepdog leashes. (A man's sheepdog accompanied him everywhere.)

Anyone can enjoy the Cotswolds from the saddle. **Jill Carenza's Riding Centre,** set just outside Stanton village, is in the most scenic corner of the region. The facility has 50 horses, and takes rank beginners on an hour-long scenic "hack" through the village and into the high country (£20/person for 1 hour; lessons, longer rides, rides for experts, and pub tours available; well-signposted in Stanton, tel. 01386/584-250, www.cotswoldsriding.co.uk). Jill rents four rooms at her **Vine B&B**, but it takes a backseat to the horses. There's no greeting or check-in, and guests wander around wondering which room is theirs. Still, it's convenient if you want to ride all day (Ds/Db-£60, most rooms with 4-poster beds, lots of stairs, tel. 01386/584-250, fax 01386/584-385, luicarenza@msn.com).

Snowshill

Another nearly edible little bundle of cuteness, Snowshill (SNOWS-hill) has a photogenic triangular square with a characteristic pub at its base. The **Snowshill Manor,** worth ▲, is a dark and mysterious old palace filled with the lifetime collection of Charles Paget Wade. It's one big, musty celebration of craftsmanship, from finely carved spinning wheels to frightening samurai armor to tiny elaborate figurines carved by prisoners from the bones of meat served at dinner. Taking seriously his family motto, "Let Nothing Perish," Wade dedicated his life and fortune to preserving things finely crafted. The house (whose management made me promise not to promote it as an eccentric collector's pile of curiosities) really shows off Mr. Wade's ability to recognize and

Snowshill Lavender

In the year 2000, farmer Charlie Byrd realized that tourists love lavender. He planted his farm with 250,000 plants, and now visitors are welcome to wander (free) among his 53 acres, which burst with gorgeous lavender blossoms from mid-June through late-August. His fragrant fantasy peaks late each July. Farmer Byrd makes his money producing lavender oil (a herbal product valued since ancient times for its  healing, calming, and fragrant qualities), running a fine little café (£5 lunches), and managing a delightful shop. Lavender—so famous in France's Provence—is not indigenous to this region, but it fits the climate and soil just fine. A free flier in the shop explains the variations of flowers blooming (farm free and open all the time, shop open Tue–Sun 10:00–17:00, closed Monday, tel. 01386/854-821, easy parking, a half-mile out of Snowshill on Chipping Campden Road).

acquire fine examples of craftsmanship. It's all very...mmm...yyya. The manor overlooks the town square, but there is no direct access from the town square. You park at the shop and walk 500 yards through the garden to get to the house (£7, house open April–Oct Wed–Sun 12:00–17:00, closed Mon–Tue and Nov–March, a golf-cart-type shuttle to the house is available if desired, tel. 01386/852-410, www.nationaltrust.org.uk/snowshillmanor). Note that this popular place allows only 20 people in every 10 minutes, and entry times are doled out at the ticket desk (reservations are not possible). Expect up to an hour delay on busy days, especially weekends.

Sleeping Near Snowshill: **$$ Sheepscombe B&B** is a pristine and modern home on a working sheep farm. It's immersed in the best of Cotswold scenery, 500 meters from the pretty, one-pub village of Snowshill. Jacki and Tim Harrison rent three modern, spacious, and thoughtfully appointed rooms (Db-£70–75, just south of Snowshill, look for signs, tel. 01386/853-769, www.broadway-cotswolds.co.uk, reservations@snowshill-broadway.co.uk).

More Sights near Chipping Campden

▲**Hidcote Manor**—If you like gardens, the grounds around this manor house, northeast of Chipping Campden, are worth a look. Garden designers here pioneered the notion of creating a series of outdoor "rooms," each with a unique theme (e.g. maple room, red room, and so on) and separated by a yew-tree hedge. Follow your nose through a clever series of small gardens that lead delightfully from one to the next. Among the best in England, Hidcote gardens are at their fragrant peak in May, June, and July (£6.60, April–Oct Sat–Wed 10:30–17:00, closed Thu–Fri and Nov–March, last entry 1 hour before closing, tearoom, 4 miles northeast of Chipping Campden on B4035, tel. 01386/438-333, www.nationaltrust.org.uk).

▲**Cotswold Farm Park**—Here's a delight for young and old alike. This park is the private venture of the Henson family, who are passionate about preserving rare and endangered breeds of local animals. While it feels like a kids' zone (with all the family-friendly facilities you can imagine), it's actually a fascinating chance for anyone to get up close and (very) personal with piles of mostly cute animals, including the sheep that made this region famous—the big and woolly Cotswold Lion. A busy schedule of demonstrations gives you a look at local farm life. Take full advantage of the excellent (and included) audioguide, narrated by founder Joe Henson

and filled with his passion for the farm's mission. Buy a bag of seed (40p) upon arrival, or have your map eaten by munchy goats as I did (£5.10, kids-£4, daily mid-March–early Sept 10:30–17:00, closed off-season, good £2 guidebook, decent cafeteria, tel. 01451/850-307, www.cotswoldfarmpark.co.uk, well signposted 5 minutes from Stow just off the Tewkesbury road—B4077). Check the events board as you enter (sheep show daily at 14:00). Tykes love the little tractor rides and zip line, but the "touch barn" is really where it's at for little kids.

Broadway—This postcard-pretty town, a couple of miles west of Chipping Campden, is filled with inviting shops and fancy teahouses. Because most big bus tours stop here, I give Broadway a miss. But with a new road that allows traffic to skirt the town, Broadway has gotten cuter than ever.

Stow-on-the-Wold

Ten miles south of Chipping Campden, Stow-on-the-Wold—with a name that means "meeting place on the uplands"—is the highest point of the Cotswolds. Despite its crowds, it retains its charm

and is worth ▲▲. Most of the tourists are day-trippers, so even summer nights are peaceful. Stow has no real sights other than the town itself, some good pubs, antique stores, and cute shops draped seductively around a big town square. Visit the church, with its evocative old door guarded by ancient yew trees and the tombs of wool tycoons. A visit to Stow is not complete until you've locked your partner in the stocks on the green.

Tourist Information

At the helpful TI on the main square, get the handy little 50p walking-tour brochure called *Town Trail* and the free *Cotswold Events* guide (March–Oct Mon–Sat 9:30–17:30, closed Sun, Nov–Feb closes at 16:30, tel. 01451/831-082). The TI also sells National Express Bus tickets, reserves tickets for events (Stratford plays, £2 fee), and books rooms for a £2 fee (save money and book direct).

Helpful Hints

Internet Access: Try the erratically open library across from the TI, or at the youth hostel (17:00–23:00 nightly).

Taxis: See "Getting Around the Cotswolds—By Taxi" (page 213).

Parking: Park anywhere on the Market Square free for two hours, or overnight between 16:00 and 11:00 (free from 18:00–9:00 plus any 2 hours—they note your license, so you can't just move to another spot, £40 tickets for offenders). Two "Long Stay" lots are 400 yards from the town square (free, follow the signs).

Local Tours: Jean Oxley heads the local Cotswold Voluntary Wardens, a group of guides who enjoy showing off their home-town to visitors. While no tours are regularly scheduled, they can be arranged usually at very short notice. They only ask for a small donation for their club—£10 per group for an hour-long walk is plenty (call 01451/830-200 or ask at the TI).

SELF-GUIDED WALK

Welcome to Stow-on-the-Wold

This little four-stop walk covers about 500 yards and takes about 45 minutes.

Start at the **Stocks on the Market Square**. Imagine this village during the time when people were publicly ridiculed here as a punishment. Stow was born in pre-Roman times; it's where three trade routes crossed at a high point in the region (altitude: 800 feet). This main square hosted an international fair starting

in 1107, and people came from as far away as Italy for the wool fleeces. This grand square was a vast, grassy expanse. Picture it in the Middle Ages (before the buildings in the center were added): a public commons and grazing ground, paths worn through the grass, and no well. Until 1867, Stow had no running water; women fetched water from the "Roman well" a quarter-mile away.

A thin skin of topsoil covers the Cotswold stones, from which these buildings were made. The **Stow Lodge** (next to the church) lies a little lower than the church; the lodge sits on the spot where locals quarried stones for the church. That building, originally the rectory, is now a hotel. The church (where we'll end this little walk) is made of Cotswold stone, and marks the summit of the hill upon which the town was built. The stocks are a great photo op (my kids locked me in for a photo our family used for a Christmas card).

• *Walk past the youth hostel to the market, and cross to the other side of the square. Notice how locals seem to be a part of a tight little community.*

For 500 years, the **Market Cross** stood in the market reminding all Christian merchants to "trade fairly under the sight of God." Notice the stubs of the iron fence in the concrete base—a reminder of how countless wrought-iron fences were cut down and given to the government to be melted down during World War II. (Recently, it's been disclosed that all that iron ended up in junk heaps—frantic patriotism just wasted.) The plaque on the cross honors the Lord of the Manor, who donated money back to his tenants, allowing the town to finally finance running water in 1878. Scan the square for a tipsy shop locals call the "wonky house." Because it lists (tilts) so severely, it's a listed building—the facade is protected (but the interior is modern and level). The Kings Arms pub, with its great gables and scary chimney, was once an inn where travelers could park their horses and spend the night. In the 1600s, this was considered the premium "posting house" between London and Birmingham. Today, the Kings Arms cooks up some of the best food in town.

During the English Civil War, which pitted Parliamentarians against Royalists, Stow-on-the-Wold remained staunchly loyal to the king. (Charles I is said to have eaten at the Kings Arms before a great battle.) Because of its allegiance, the town has an abundance of pubs with royal names (King's This and Queen's That).

• *Walk past the Kings Arms down Digbeth Street to the little triangular park located in front of the Methodist Church and across from the Royalist Hotel. This hotel—along with about 20 others—claims to be the oldest in England, dating from 947.*

The **Shrubbery Green** is where—twice a year, in late May and October—the Gypsie Horse Fair attracts Roma (Gypsies) and Travelers (Irish Tinkers) from far and wide. They congregate just down the street in Maugersbury. Locals paint a colorful picture of the Roma, Travelers, and horses inundating the town. The young women are dressed up because the fair also functions as a marriage market.

• *Hike up Sheep Street. You'll pass a boutique-filled former brewery yard, Fleece Alley (just wide enough for a single file of sheep to walk on—easier to count them on market days), and a fine antique bookstore. Turn right on Church Street, which leads past the best coffee shop in town (The Coffee House), and find the church.*

Before entering the **church,** circle it. On the back side, a door is flanked by two ancient yew trees. While to many it looks like the Christian "Behold, I stand at the door and knock" door, Tolkien fans see something quite different. J. R. R. Tolkien hiked the Cotswolds, and had a passion for sketching evocative trees such as this. *Fellowship of the Ring* enthusiasts are convinced this must be the inspiration for the door into Moria.

While the church (open daily—apart from services—9:00–18:00) dates from Saxon times, today's structure is from the 15th century. Its history is played up in leaflets and plaques just inside the door. The floor is paved with the tombs of big shots who made their money from wool, and are still boastful in death. (Find the tombs crowned with the bales of wool.)

During the Civil War (1615), more than 1,000 soldiers were imprisoned here. The tombstone in front of the altar remembers the Royalist Captain Keyt. His long hair, lace, and sash indicates he was a "cavalier," and true blue to the king (Cromwellians were called "round heads"—named for their short hair). Study the crude provincial art—child-like skulls and (in the upper corners) symbols of his service to the king (armor, weapons).

On the right wall, a monument remembers the many boys from this small town who were lost in World War I (50 out of a population of 2,000). There were far fewer in World War II. The biscuit-shaped plaque (to the left) remembers an admiral from Stow who lost four sons defending the realm. It's sliced from a ancient fluted column (which locals believe is from Ephesus, Turkey). While most of the windows are Victorian (19th-century), the two sets high up in the clerestory are from the dreamier Pre-Raphaelite school (c. 1920).

Finally, don't miss the kneelers, knitted by a committed band of women known as "the Kneeler Group." They meet every Tuesday morning at 10:30 in the Church Room to embroider, sip coffee, and enjoy a good chat. (The vicar assured me that any tourist wanting to join them would be more than welcome. The help would be appreciated and the company would be excellent.)

SLEEPING

(£1 = about $1.80, country code: 44, area code: 01451)

In Stow

$$$ Stow Lodge Hotel fills the historic church rectory with lots of old English charm. Facing the town square, with its own sprawling and peaceful garden, this lavish old place offers 21 large, thoughtfully appointed rooms, stately public spaces, and a cushy-chair lounge (Db-£90–125, closed Jan, smoke and you die—immediately, The Square, tel. 01451/830-485, fax 01451/831-671, www.stowlodge.com, enquiries@stowlodge.com, helpful Hartley family). The former stables out back have the cheaper rooms which, while not in the building proper, are at least as big and comfortable.

Stow-on-the-Wold

TO MORETON-IN-MARSH, STRATFORD-UPON-AVON, WARWICK & ⑫

TO BROADWAY & CHIPPING CAMPDEN

TESCO SUPERMKT

TO UPPER SWELL, FORD & STANWAY

PATH TO BROADWELL

BUS STOP

HIGH ST.

PARSON'S CORNER

STOCKS

WC

THE SQUARE

CHURCH

TO LOWER SWELL & GUITING POWER

POST

SHEEP ST.

DIGBETH

PARK ST.

TO ⑩ & UPPER & LOWER ODDINGTON

WC TO ⑪

DCH

BACK WALLS

TO BOURTON-ON-THE-WATER & THE SLAUGHTERS

🅿 —PARKING

① Stow Lodge Hotel
② The Old Stocks Hotel/Rest.
③ Crestow House
④ Chipping House B&B & Cross Keys Cottage
⑤ West Deyne B&B
⑥ The Pound B&B
⑦ Tall Trees B&B
⑧ Cotswold Garden Tea Room B&B
⑨ Stow Youth Hostel
⑩ To Fairview Farmhouse B&B
⑪ To Little Broom B&B
⑫ To Holmleigh B&B
⑬ Number Nine B&B, The Prince of India Rest., The Eagle & Child Pub & Greedy's Fish & Chips
⑭ The Kings Arms Pub
⑮ The Queen's Head Pub
⑯ The Coffee House
⑰ Long Stay Parking
⑱ Market Cross
⑲ Shrubbery Green

$$ The Old Stocks Hotel, facing the town square, is a good value, even though the building itself is classier than its 18 big, simply furnished rooms. It's friendly and family-run, yet professional as can be. Beware the man-killer beams (Sb-£40, Db-£80, Tb-£120, prices promised through 2006 with this book, family deals, attached bar and restaurant, garden patio, The Square, tel. 01451/830-666, fax 01451/870-014, www.oldstockshotel.co.uk, rs@oldstockshotel.co.uk, Jason and Helen Allen).

$$ Crestow House, a grand manor house, dates from the 16th century. It stands at the edge of town facing the wide open countryside, keeping its back to the main road. With a gracious spaciousness and its four rooms holding antique furniture, this creaky place oozes with charm and character (Db-£75, 2-night minimum, 10 percent off for 3 nights, no children under 12, non-smoking, sunny-even-in-the-rain conservatory, 2 blocks from The Square at intersection of A429 and B4068, tel. 01451/830-969, fax 01451/832-129, www.crestow.co.uk, fsimonetti@btinternet.com, Frank). Frank also rents a six-person cottage (£550/week in summer).

$$ Number Nine has three large, bright, recently refurbished rooms in a 200-year-old home with watch-your-head beamed ceilings and old wooden doors (Db-£60-70, 9 Park Street, tel. 01451/870-333, www.number-nine.info, enquires@number-nine .info, James and Carol Brown).

$ Cross Keys Cottage offers three attractive, smallish rooms in a well-maintained, 350-year-old beamed cottage (D-£60, Db-£65, Park Street, tel. & fax 01451/831-128, rogxmag@hotmail.com, Margaret and Roger Welton).

$ Chipping House B&B is a fine, warm, old place with three rooms and a welcoming lounge—it feels like a visit to auntie's house (Db-£55-65, cash only, non-smoking, Park Street, tel. 01451/831-756, chippinghouse@tesco.net, dog-lovers Merv and Carolyne Oliver).

$ West Deyne B&B, with two cozy rooms, a peaceful garden, a fountain, and a small conservatory overlooking the countryside, has a comforting, grandmotherly charm. It offers a plush privacy (D-£43-48, cash only, evening tea and biscuits, Lower Swell Road, tel. 01451/831-011, run by thoughtful Joan Cave).

$ The Pound is the quaint, 500-year-old-yet-fresh, heavy-beamed home of Patricia Whitehead. She offers two bright, inviting, twin-bedded rooms and a classic old fireplace lounge (D-£43-48, cash only, non-smoking, downtown on Sheep Street, tel. & fax 01451/830-229, brent.ford@zoom.co.uk).

$ Cotswold Garden Tea Room B&B rents two bright and comfy rooms in a charming if saggy 17th-century building. It has an inviting garden above a fun little tea room (D-£55, £5 less for 2 nights or in off-season, family deals, cash only, Digbeth Street, tel. 01451/870-999, www.cotswoldgardentearooms.co.uk, jackie@clarkson4946.fslife.co.uk, Jackie).

$ Tall Trees B&B, on the Oddington Road 100 yards outside of Stow, is a rough and real farm, renting six modern rooms in an old-style building (Db-£55-60, family room-£60-80, cash only, 2 ground-floor rooms, tel. 01451/831-296, fax 01451/870-049, talltreestow@aol.com, run by Jennifer). She also rents a lovely cottage that sleeps four (£80/night, £480/week, with a kitchenette, breakfast extra).

$ *Hostel:* The **Stow-on-the-Wold Youth Hostel,** on Stow's main square, is the only hostel in the Cotswolds, with 48 beds in nine rooms. It has a friendly atmosphere, good hot meals, and a members' kitchen (dorm bed-£14, non-members-£3 extra, includes sheets, some family rooms with private bathrooms, evening meals, reception closed 10:00–17:00, laundry, lockers, rental bikes, reserve long in advance, tel. 01451/830-497, fax 01451/870-102, www.yha .org.uk, stow@yha.org.uk, manager Rob). Anyone can eat here: breakfast is £3.80, and dinner is £7.50.

Near Stow

$ Fairview Farmhouse B&B feels more like a countryside mansion than a farmhouse. It's regally situated a mile outside Stow, and its six rooms come with all the thoughtful touches (Db-£60, deluxe Db-£65, 2-night minimum, cash only, non-smoking, just down Bledington Road, tel. & fax 01451/830-279, sdavis0145@aol .com, Susan and Andrew Davis may sell in 2006).

$ Little Broom B&B hides out in the neighboring hamlet of Maugersbury, which enjoys the peace Stow once had. It rents five cozy rooms that share a fine garden and a pool (S-£30, D-£45, Db-£50–55, apartment Db-£65 for 2 plus £10 for each extra person, cash only, non-smoking, tel. & fax 01451/830-510). Brenda keeps racehorses just beyond her pool, which hides in a low-lying greenhouse to keep it warm throughout the summer (guests welcome). It's an easy 10-minute walk from Stow: Head east on Park Street, taking the right fork to Maugersbury, then turn right on the road marked *No Through Road*.

$ Holmleigh B&B, in a rough and tumble working dairy farmhouse in the nearby hamlet of Donnington, rents a big, well-worn, grandmotherly room—the cheapest around (D-£40, cash only, open April–Oct, tel. 01451/830-792, Irene Garbett). Look for the sign (50 yards from the phone booth) in this picturesque hamlet—so small it has no shop, pub, or church.

EATING

In Stow

These places are all within a five-minute walk of each other, either on the main square or downhill on Queen and Park streets.

Stow Lodge is a formal but friendly bar serving fine £8 lunches and a popular £22 three-course dinner (daily 12:00–14:00 & 19:00–20:45, smoke-free, veggie options, good wines, also has pricier restaurant, just off main square). This is the choice of the town's proper ladies.

Old Stocks Hotel Restaurant, which might at first glance seem like a tired and big hotel dining room, is actually a classy place to dine. With attentive service and an interesting menu, they provide tasty and well-presented food. If they're not too busy, you can order more economically from the bar menu, and sit in the fancy dining room enjoying views of the square. In good weather, the garden out back is a hit (£8–15 meals, nightly 18:30–20:30, tel. 01451/830-666).

The Kings Arms, across the square, is the local food phenom. It has near-gourmet English and Mediterranean nightly specials on the blackboard, and serves them in a once-medieval, now-classy ambience (£20 2-course meals, daily 12:30–14:30 & 18:00–21:30, reserve for dinner, tel. 01451/830-364).

The Queen's Head faces the Market Square, next to the Stow Lodge. With a classic pub vibe, it's a great place to bring your dog, smoke a cigarette, eat pub grub, and drink the local Cotswold brew, Donnington Ale (£8 plates, daily 12:00–14:30 & 18:30–22:30).

The Prince of India offers good Indian food in a delightful setting, to take out or eat in (nightly 18:00–23:30, Park Street, tel. 01451/870-821).

The Eagle and Child Pub serves delicious food at good prices in a stripped-down pub (food daily 12:00–14:30 & 18:00–21:00, non-smoking section, Park Street, tel. 01451/830-670).

Greedy's Fish and Chips, on Park Street, is a favorite with locals for take-out (Mon–Sat 12:00–14:00 & 16:30–21:00, closed Sun).

Eating Cheaply: Head to the grassy triangle where Digbeth hits Sheep Street; there, you'll find take-out fish and chips, Indian food, and Chinese. You can picnic at the triangle, or on the benches by the stocks on Market Street. There are also small grocery stores that face the main square, and a big Tesco supermarket 200 yards north of town. The youth hostel (see above) welcomes non-hostelers for its evening family-style meal (£7.50, drop by early to confirm time and book a spot).

Pub Dinner Hike from Stow

From Stow, consider taking a half-hour scenic countryside walk past the old Roman Well to the village of Broadwell. There, the **Fox Inn** serves good pub dinners and draws traditional ales (daily 11:00–14:30 & 18:00–23:00, shorter hours Sun, on the village green, tel. 01451/870-909).

Great Country Pubs Near Stow

These three places—known for their great £10 meals and fine settings—are very popular. Arrive early or phone in a reservation. (If you show up at 20:00, it's unlikely that they'll be able to seat you for dinner if you haven't called first.) These pubs allow "well-behaved children," and are practical only for those with a car. The first two (in Oddington, 2 miles from Stow) are more trendy and fresh, yet still in a traditional pub setting. The Plough (in Ford, a few miles farther away) is your jolly olde dark pub.

The Horse and Groom Village Inn in Upper Oddington is a smart place with a sea-grass-green carpet in a 16th-century inn, serving modern English and Mediterranean food with a good wine list (plenty by the glass) and serious beer (daily 12:00–14:00 & 18:30–21:00, non-smoking section, tel. 01451/830-584).

The Fox Inn, a different Fox Inn than the one listed above, is old but fresh and famous among locals for its quality cooking (daily 12:00–14:00 & 18:30–22:00, in Lower Oddington, tel. 01451/870-555). They also rent out three rooms.

The Plough Inn fills a fascinating old building, once an old coaching inn and later a courthouse. Ask the bar staff for some fun history—like what "you're barred" means. Eat from the same traditional English menu in the restaurant, bar, or garden. They are serious about both their beer here and—judging by the extensive list of homemade temptations—their dessert (£10 meals, daily 12:00–21:00, 4 miles from Stow on Tewkesbury Road in hamlet of Ford, reservations smart, tel. 01386/584-215).

Near Stow-on-the-Wold

These sights are all south of Stow: Some are very close (Bourton-on-the-Water, the Slaughters, and Northleach) and some are up to 20 miles away (Blenheim Palace and Cirencester).

Bourton-on-the-Water

I can't figure out whether they call this "the Venice of the Cotswolds" because of its quaint canals or its miserable crowds. Either way, it's very pretty and worth ▲. This town—four miles south of Stow and a mile from the Slaughters (see below)—gets overrun by midday and weekend hordes. If you can avoid them, it's worth a drive-through, a few cynical comments, and maybe a short stop. While it's mobbed with Japanese tour groups during the day, it's pleasantly empty in the early evening and after dark.

Parking is predictably tough. Even during the busy business day, rather than park in the pay-and-display parking lot far from the center, drive right into town and wait for a spot on High Street just past the village green (there's a long row of free 2-hour spots in front of the Edinburgh Woolen Mills Shop). The **TI** is on Victoria Street (tel. is 01451/820-211, www.bourtoninfo.com).

Surrounding Bourton's green are sidewalks jammed with disoriented tourists wearing nametags. Bourton has three sights—each on High Street in the town center—worth considering. The **Model Railway Exhibition** has four impressive-only-to-train-buffs setups (£2.25, daily 11:00–17:00, located in the back of a hobby shop, tel. 01451/820-686, www.bourtonmodelrailway .co.uk). The light but fun **Model Village** recreates the town on a 1:9 scale in a tiny park, and has an attached room full of tiny models showing off various bits of British domestic life (£2.75 for the park, £1 more for the model room, daily 9:00–17:45, tel. 01451/820-467). The excellent **Motor Museum**, worth ▲, shows off a lifetime's accumulation of vintage cars, old lacquered signs, threadbare toys, and prewar memorabilia. Be sure to peek into the old-time vacation trailers, and talk to an elderly Brit touring the place for some personal memories (£3, March–Oct daily 10:00–18:00, closed Nov–Feb, in the mill facing the town center, tel. 01451/821-255). Families enjoy Bourton's new kid-perfect **leisure centre** (big pool and sauna).

Upper and Lower Slaughter

Lower Slaughter is a classic village, with ducks, a working water mill, and usually an artist busy at her easel somewhere. Just behind the skippable Old Mill Museum, two kissing gates lead to the path that goes to nearby Upper Slaughter. In Upper Slaughter, walk through the yew trees (sacred in pagan days) down a lane through the raised graveyard (a buildup of centuries of graves) to the peaceful church. In the back of the fine graveyard, the statue of a wistful woman looks over the tomb of an 18th-century rector (sculpted by his son). By the way, "Slaughter" has nothing to do with lamb chops. It comes from the sloe tree (the one used to make sloe gin). These towns are an easy two-hour round-trip walk from Bourton. You could also walk from Bourton through the Slaughters to Stow. The small roads from Upper Slaughter to Ford and Kineton are some of England's most scenic. Roll your window down and joy-ride slowly.

Blenheim Palace

Too many palaces can send you into a furniture-wax coma. But everyone should see Blenheim, worth ▲▲▲. Note: Americans who pronounce the place "blen-HEIM" are the butt of jokes. It's "BLEN-em."

The Duke of Marlborough's home—the largest in England—is still lived in, which is wonderfully obvious as you prowl through it.

John Churchill, first duke of Marlborough, beat the French at the Battle of Blenheim in 1704. So the king built him this nice home, perhaps the finest Baroque building in England. Ten dukes of Marlborough later, it's as impressive as ever. (The current 11th duke considers the 12th more of an error than an heir, and what to do about him is quite an issue.)

The 2,000-acre yard, well-designed by Lancelot "Capability" Brown, is as majestic to some as the palace itself. The view just past the outer gate as you enter is a classic.

The well-organized palace tour begins with a fine **Churchill exhibit** centered around the bed in which Sir Winston was born in 1874 (prematurely...begun while his mother was at a Blenheim Palace party). Take your time in the Churchill exhibit. Then catch the one-hour guided tours (6/hr, included with ticket, last tour at 16:45). When the palace is really busy, they dispense with guided tours and go "free flow," allowing those with an appetite for learning to strike up conversations with docents in each room.

For a more extensive visit, follow up the general tour with a 30-minute guided walk through the actual **private apartments** of the duke. Tours leave at the top and bottom of each hour (£4.50, May–Sept daily 12:00–16:30, tickets are limited, buy from table in library—last room of main tour, enter in corner of courtyard to left of grand palace entry).

Kids enjoy the **pleasure garden** (a tiny train takes you from the palace parking lot to the garden, but if you have a car, it's more efficient simply to drive there). A lush and humid greenhouse flutters with butterflies. A kid zone includes a few second-rate games and the "world's largest symbolic hedge maze." The maze is worth a look if you haven't seen one and could use some exercise. Churchill fans can visit his **tomb,** a short walk away, in the Bladon town churchyard.

Cost, Hours, Information: £13, family deals, mid-Feb–Dec daily 10:30–17:30, last tour departs at 16:45, palace closed but park open Jan–mid-Feb, tel. 01993/811-091, recorded info tel. 0870-060-2080, www.blenheimpalace.com).

Getting There: Blenheim Palace sits at the edge of the cute cobbled town of Woodstock. The train station nearest the palace (Hanborough, 1.5 miles away) has no taxi or bus service. Your easiest train connection is to Oxford; then take a bus to Blenheim (from the Oxford train station, it's a 5-min walk to Gloucester Green bus station, then catch bus #20a, #20b, or #20c to the palace gate, Mon–Sat 8:55–17:00, Sun 10:00–15:30, 2/hr, 30–40 min; bus tel. 01865/772-250). From Moreton-in-Marsh, you can either take the train to Oxford, or take a bus to Chipping Norton (20 min), then transfer to a bus to Woodstock Road (50 min; let bus driver know you are going to Blenheim).

Sleeping Near Blenheim Palace: Consider the charming 200-year-old **$$ Blenheim Guest House,** in the town center and literally next door to the palace (6 rooms, Db-£60–70 depending on size, 17 Park Street, tel. 01993/813-814, fax 01993/813-810, www.theblenheim.com, theblenheim@aol.com). **$$ The Townhouse** is a refurbished 18th-century stone house with five plush rooms (Sb-£55, Db-£80, Tb-£100; includes breakfast, afternoon tea, and snacks on weekends; in town center at 15 High Street, tel. & fax 01993/810-843). **$ Wishaw House B&B** is grandmotherly (1 D-£50, 2 Browns Lane, 5-min walk from palace, tel. 01993/811-343, Pat Hillier).

Northleach

One of the "untouched and untouristed" Cotswold villages (9 miles south from Stow, down A429), Northleach is worth ▲ and a short stop. The town's impressive main square and church attest to its position as a major wool center in the Middle Ages. Park on the square to check out the TI (which has walking brochures), the mechanical music museum (described below), and the church. The fine Perpendicular Gothic church of saints Peter and Paul has been called the "cathedral of the Cotswolds." It's one of the Cotswolds' finest two "wool" churches (along with Chipping Campden's), paid for by 15th-century wool tycoons. Find the oldest tombstone. The brass plaques on the floor memorialize big shots, showing sheep and sacks of wool at their long-dead feet and inscriptions mixing Latin and the old English. You're welcome to do some brass rubbing if you get a permit from the post office (£2.50).

▲**Keith Harding's World of Mechanical Music**—In 1962, Keith Harding, tired of giving ad-lib "living room tours" opened this delightful little one-room place. It offers a unique opportunity to listen to 300 years of amazing self-playing musical instruments. It's run by people who are passionate about the restoration work they do on these musical marvels. The curators delight in demonstrating about 20 of the museum's machines with each hour-long tour. You'll hear Victorian music boxes and the earliest polyphones (record players) playing cylinders and then discs—all from an age when music was made mechanically, without the help of electricity. The admission fee includes an essential hour-long tour (£5, daily 10:00–18:00, last entry 16:45, tours go constantly—join one in progress, guides usually take a break from 12:00–14:00, High Street, Northleach, tel. 01451/860-181, www.mechanicalmusic.co.uk).

Bibury

Six miles northeast of Cirencester, this village is a ▲ sight and a favorite with British picnickers fond of strolling and fishing. Bibury offers some relaxing sights, including a Cotswolds museum, a row of very old weavers' cottages, a trout farm, a stream teeming with fat fish and proud ducks, and a church surrounded by rosebushes, each tended by a volunteer of the parish. A protected wetlands area on the far side of the stream hosts newts and water voles—walk around to the old weavers' Arlington Row and back on the far side of the marsh, peeking into the rushes for wildlife.

Don't miss the scenic Coln Valley drive from A429 to Bibury through the enigmatic villages of Coln St. Dennis, Coln Rogers, Coln Powell, and Winson.

Cirencester

Nearly 2,000 years ago, Cirencester (SIGH-ren-ses-ter) was the ancient Roman city of Corinium. It's 20 miles from Stow down A429, which was called Fosse Way in Roman times. In Cirencester, a ▲▲ sight, stop by the Corinium Museum to find out why they say, "If you scratch Gloucestershire, you'll find Rome" (£4, Mon–Sat 10:00–17:00, Sun 14:00–17:00). Cirencester's church is the largest of the Cotswolds "wool" churches. The cutesy Brewery Art crafts center entertains visitors with traditional weaving and potting, workshops, an interesting gallery, and a good coffee shop. Monday and Friday are general-market days, Friday features an antique market, and Saturday hosts a crafts market. The **TI** is in the Cornhill Marketplace (Mon–Sat 9:30–17:30, closed Sun, tel. 01285/654-180).

Moreton-in-Marsh

This workaday town, worth ▲, is like Stow or Chipping Campden without the touristy sugar. Rather than gift and antique shops, you'll find streets lined with real shops: ironmongers selling cottage nameplates and carpet shops strewn with the remarkable patterns that decorate B&B floors. A shin-kickin' traditional market of 260 stalls fills High Street each Tuesday, as it has for the last 400 years (8:00–16:00, handicrafts, farm produce, clothing, great people-watching, best if you go early). The Cotswolds has an economy aside from tourism, and you'll feel it here.

Moreton has a tiny, sleepy train station two blocks from High Street, lots of bus connections, and the best **TI** in the region (Mon–Fri 8:45–17:00, Sat 10:00–13:00, closed Sun, good public WC, free *Town Trail* leaflet for self-guided walk, rail and bus schedules, racks of fliers, tel. 01608/650-881). While there is no formal baggage storage in town, the Black Bear Pub (next to TI) lets you leave bags there free if you buy a drink. Parking is easy—anywhere on High Street is fine any time, as long as you want, for free.

Moreton-in-Marsh

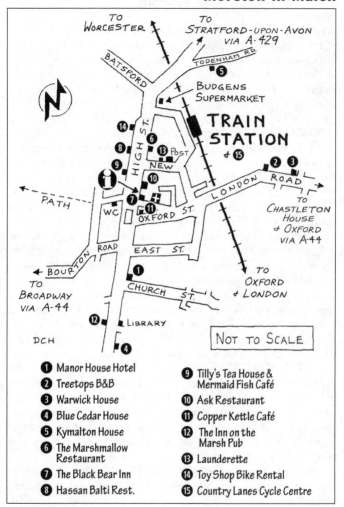

1. Manor House Hotel
2. Treetops B&B
3. Warwick House
4. Blue Cedar House
5. Kymalton House
6. The Marshmallow Restaurant
7. The Black Bear Inn
8. Hassan Balti Rest.
9. Tilly's Tea House & Mermaid Fish Café
10. Ask Restaurant
11. Copper Kettle Café
12. The Inn on the Marsh Pub
13. Launderette
14. Toy Shop Bike Rental
15. Country Lanes Cycle Centre

Helpful Hints

Internet Access: It's free at the TI (same hours as above) and at the library on High Street (Tue and Thu all day, Fri afternoon only, and Sat morning only).

Launderette: The handy **Laundercentre** is a block in front of the train station on New Road (daily 7:30–20:00, £4.50 self-service, or drop off Mon–Fri 9:00–10:30 for £1 extra and same-day service, tel. 01608/650-888).

Bike Rental, Taxis, and Car Rental: See "Getting Around the Cotswolds" (page 213).

SLEEPING

(£1 = about $1.80, country code: 44, area code: 01608)

$$$ Manor House Hotel is Moreton's big old hotel, dating from 1545 but sporting such modern amenities as toilets, electricity, and a swimming pool. Its 38 classy-for-the-Cotswolds rooms and its garden invite relaxation (Sb-£115–155, Db-£135–200, family suite-£170–215, elevator, log fire in winter, attached restaurant, on far end of High Street away from train station, tel. 01608/650-501, fax 01608/651-481, www.cotswold-inns-hotels.co.uk).

$ Treetops B&B is plush, with six spacious, attractive rooms, a sun lounge, and a three-quarter-acre backyard. Liz and Ben (the family dog) will make you feel right at home—if you meet their two-night minimum (large Db-£50, gigantic Db-£52, ground-floor rooms have patios, set far back from the busy road, London Road, tel. & fax 01608/651-036, www.treetopscotswolds.co.uk, treetops1@talk21.com, Liz and Brian Dean). It's an eight-minute walk from town and the railway station (exit station, keep left, go left on bridge over train tracks, look for sign, then long driveway).

$ Warwick House, just down the road from Treetops, is a nondescript house renting three rooms, with a friendly, laid-back atmosphere (Db-£42–44, cash only, each room has a VCR and Cotswolds video, will pick up from train station, access to nearby Fire Service College Leisure Club swimming pool, London Road, tel. 01608/650-773, www.snoozeandsizzle.com).

$ Blue Cedar House has four comfortable rooms and two bungalow apartments with an airy breakfast room full of plants. It's on a busy road but has double-paned windows and a pleasing setting, surrounded by a large garden (S-£25, D/Db-£50, apartment-£70, cash only, non-smoking, 5-min walk from center, Stow Road, tel. 01608/650-299, gandsib@dialstart.net, Sandra and Graham Billinger).

$ Kymalton House has two recently refurbished, bright rooms in a gracious modern house. With a pleasant garden, it's set back off of a busy street just outside the town center (Db-£50, double beds only, cash only, non-smoking, closed Dec–Jan, tel. 01608/650-487, mobile 0781-070-4952, kymalton@uwclub.net, Sylvia and Doug Gould). It's a 10-minute walk from town (walk past Budgens supermarket, turn right on Todenham Road, look for house on the right). They'll happily pick up and drop train travelers at the station.

EATING

A stroll up and down High Street lets you survey your small-town options.

The Marshmallow is relatively upscale but affordable, with a menu that includes traditional English dishes as well as lasagna and salads (£8–11 entrées, 15 fancy teas, Wed–Sat 10:00–21:00, Tue and Sun 10:00–16:00, closed Mon, reservations advised, shady back garden for summer dining, tel. 01608/651-536).

The Black Bear Inn offers traditional English food (£5–8 meals and daily specials, daily 12:00–14:00 & 18:30–21:00; after entering, head to dining room on the left, pub on the right; tel. 01608/652-992).

Hassan Balti, with tasty Bangladeshi food, is a fine value for sit-down or take-out (£7 meals, daily 12:00–14:00 & 18:00–23:30, tel. 01608/650-798).

Tilly's Tea House serves fresh soups, salads, sandwiches, and pastries for lunch in a cheerful spot on High Street across from the TI (£3–5 light meals, daily 9:00–17:00, tel. 01608/650-000).

Ask, a chain restaurant across the street, has decent pastas, pizzas, salads, and a breezy, family-friendly atmosphere (£7 pizzas, daily, take-out available, tel. 01608/651-119).

Copper Kettle is good for a light bite or sandwiches to go (daily 9:00–17:00, on Oxford Street, tel. 01608/650-082).

The Inn on the Marsh pub offers good pub grub; a great selection of ales and wine; a separate, cozy non-smoking dining conservatory; and a cute back garden (daily 12:00–14:00 & 19:00–21:00, 2-min walk from center, directly across street from library on road to Stow, tel. 01608/650-709).

Mermaid Fish is popular for its take-out fish and tasty selection of traditional pies (closed Sun), and the **Budgens** supermarket is indeed super (Mon–Sat 8:00–22:00, Sun 10:00–16:00, far end of High Street). There are picnic tables across the busy street in pleasant Victoria Park.

Near Moreton-in-Marsh

▲**Chastleton House**—Located about five miles southeast of Moreton-in-Marsh, this stately home was actually lived in by

the same family from 1607 until 1991. It offers a rare peek into a Jacobean gentry house. (Jacobean, which comes from the Latin for James, indicates the style from the time of King James I—the early 1600s.) Built, like most Cotswold palaces, with wool money, it gradually declined with the fortunes of its aristocratic family until, according to the last lady of the house, it was "held together by cobwebs." It came to the National Trust on condition that they would maintain its musty Jacobean ambience. Wander on creaky floorboards, many of them original, and chat with volunteer guides stationed in each room. It's an uppity place that doesn't encourage spontaneity. The docents are proudly one of the best croquet teams in the region (the rules of croquet were formalized in this house in 1868). Page through the early 20th-century family photo albums in the room just off the entry. Because only 175 visitors a day are allowed (25 people per half hour), you're wise to call in advance to get a timed entry—but it's not possible on the same day (£6, late March–Oct Wed–Sat 13:00–17:00, closed Sun–Tue and Nov–late March, well-signposted, 5-min hike to house from free parking lot, tel. 01494/755-560, reservations tel. 01494/755-585).

TRANSPORTATION CONNECTIONS

Moreton, the only Cotswolds town with a train station, is also the best base to explore the region by bus (see below).

From Moreton by Train to: London's Paddington Station (one-way-£25, round-trip after 8:15-£27, 10/day, 1.75 hrs; One-Day Travelcard for £26.20 includes round-trip and London tube travel), **Heathrow** (10/day, 2.5 hrs, train to Reading, then RailAir Link shuttle bus to airport), **Bath** (10/day, 1.5 hrs, transfers at Oxford and Didcot Parkway), **Oxford** (10/day, 40 min), **Ironbridge Gorge** (1/hr, 3.5 hrs, with transfers at Worcester Shrub Hill and Birmingham New Street, arrive Telford, then catch bus or cab 7 miles to Ironbridge Gorge). Train info: tel. 08457-484-950.

By Bus to: Blenheim (catch bus to Chipping Norton—2/day, 20 min; then transfer to bus to Woodstock Road—nearly hrly, 50-min trip). Tell the driver you want to stop at Blenheim.

STRATFORD-UPON-AVON

Stratford is Shakespeare's hometown. To see or not to see? Stratford is a must for every big-bus tour in England and probably the single most popular side-trip from London. Sure, it's touristy. But nobody back home would understand if you skipped Shakespeare's house. A walking tour with a play's the thing to bring the Bard to life. And the town's riverside charm, coupled with its hard-working tourist industry, makes it a fun stop.

While you're in the area, explore Warwick, England's finest medieval castle; and stop by Coventry, a blue-collar town with a spirit that Nazi bombs couldn't destroy.

Planning Your Time

Stratford, Warwick, and Coventry are a made-to-order day for drivers connecting the Cotswolds with Ironbridge Gorge (IBG) or North Wales. While connections from the Cotswolds to IBG are tough, Stratford, Warwick, and Coventry are well-served by public transportation.

If you're just passing through Stratford, it's worth a half day, but to see a play, you'll need to spend the night or drive in from the nearby Cotswolds (30 min to the south, see previous chapter).

Warwick is England's single most spectacular castle. It's very touristy, but it's also historic and fun (worth 3 hours of your time). Have lunch in Warwick town. Coventry, the least-important stop on a quick trip, is most interesting as a chance to see a real, struggling, North English industrial city (with some decent sightseeing).

If you're speedy, hit all three sights on a one-day drive-through. If you're more relaxed, see a play and stay in Stratford,

Stratford Area

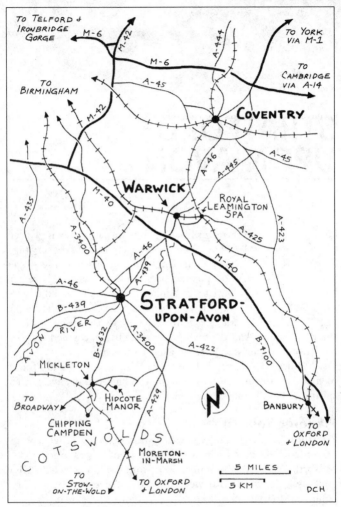

then stop by Warwick and Coventry the following morning en route to your next destination.

ORIENTATION

The old town is compact, with the TI and theater along the riverbank, and Shakespeare's birthplace a few blocks inland; you can walk easily to everything except Anne Hathaway's and Mary Arden's places. The river has an idyllic yet playful feel, with a park along both banks, paddleboats, hungry

The Look of Stratford

There's much more to Stratford than Shakespeare sights. Take time to appreciate the look of the town itself. While the main street goes back to Roman times, the key date for the city was 1196, when the king gave the town "market privileges." Stratford was shaped by its marketplace years. The market's many "departments" were located on logically named streets, whose names still remain: Sheep Street, Corn Street, and so on. Today's street plan—and even the 57' 9" width of the lots—survives from the 12th century. (The modern Woolworths store is the exact same width.)

Starting about 1600, three great fires gutted the town, leaving very few buildings older than that era. Since those great fires, tinderbox thatch roofs were prohibited—the Old Thatch Tavern on Greenhill Street is the only remaining thatch roof in town, pre-dating the law and grandfathered in.

The town's main drag, Bridge Street, is the oldest street in town, but looks the youngest. It was built in the Regency style—a result of a rough little middle row of wattle-and-daub houses being torn down in the 1820s to double the street's width. Today's Bridge Street buildings retain that early 19th-century style—Regency.

Throughout Stratford, you'll see striking black-and-white, half-timbered buildings, as well as half-timbered structures that were partially plastered over and covered up in the 19th century. During Victorian times, the half-timbered style was considered low-class, but in the 20th century—just as tourists came, preferring the ye olde style—timbers came back into vogue, and the plaster was removed on many old buildings. But any black and white you see is likely to be modern paint. The original coloring was "biscuit yellow" and brown.

swans, and an old, crank-powered ferry.

Tourist Information

The TI is as central as can be; it's where the main street hits the river. While the office has been swallowed whole by gimmicky knickknacks and fliers—and corrupted by a sales-pitch fervor—the people here can still be of some help (April–Oct Mon–Sat 9:00–17:30, Sun 10:30–16:30; shorter hours off-season; room-finding service-£3, on Bridgefoot, tel. 0870-160-7930, www.shakespeare-company.co.uk).

Helpful Hints

Internet Access: Get online at **Cyber Junction** (Mon–Fri 10:00–18:00, Sat 10:00–17:30, Sun 10:00–17:00, 28 Greenhill Street, tel. 01789/263-400) or the **library**, on Henley Street just below Shakespeare's Birthplace (daily, tel. 01789/292-209).

Taxis: Try **007 Taxis** (tel. 01789/414-007) or **Platinum Cars** (tel. 01789/264-626). A taxi stand is on Woodbridge, near the intersection with High Street.

Launderette: Sparklean is a 10-minute walk from the city center; it's near the Grove Road and Broad Walk B&Bs (daily 8:00–21:00, self-serve wash-£5, 4-hour service if you drop before 12:00 on weekdays, 74 Bull Street, tel. 01789/269-075).

TOURS

Shakespeare's Life in Stratford Walks—These walks, the brainchild of a brilliant actor and writer named Jonathan Milton, offer an energetic, intellectual, and fascinating two-hour, small-group trek through town. They give you a wonderful insight into Stratford, the acting scene here, and Shakespeare's life. Led by Jonathan or his actor friends, the tours start and end at the tour desk in the lobby of the Royal Shakespeare Theatre (£8, Sat at 10:30, April–Sept also Thu at 10:30, for info call 01789/403-405, thewalkinstratford@ntlworld.com). Jonathan also does private tours (£75 for small groups).

Stratford Town Walks—These entertaining 90-minute walks introduce you to the town and its famous playwright. Tours run year-round, rain or shine. Just show up at the Swan fountain in front of the Royal Shakespeare Theatre and pay the guide (£5, kids-£2, family-£12, Mon–Wed at 11:00, Thu–Sun at 14:00, tel. 01789/292-478, www.stratfordtownwalk.co.uk).

City Sightseeing Bus Tours—The open-top buses constantly make the rounds, allowing visitors to hop on and hop off at all the Shakespeare sights. Given the far-flung nature of two of the Shakespeare sights, and the value of the fun commentary provided, this tour makes the town more manageable. The full circuit takes about an hour, and comes with a steady and informative commentary (£8, buy tickets on bus or as you board, buses leave from the TI 2–3 times an hour from 9:00–17:40; buses basically alternate between tape-recorded commentary and live guides—if you want the best tour, wait for a live guide; tel. 01789/299-866, www.city-sightseeing.com).

The same company runs tours of the **Cotswolds** (£15, late March–early Oct, daily departure at 14:00, buy ticket at and depart from City Sightseeing Tourism Centre on Rother Street, tel. 01789/299-866). Your tour bus drives through 15 villages with brief stops in some of them, including Stanton (15 min), Chipping Campden (20 min), and Stow (30 min). Sitting atop the bus on a sunny day with all that scenery slapping you in the face is hard to beat.

SIGHTS

Shakespearean Sights

Fans of the Bard's work will want to visit at least a few of the following sights. Shakespeare's Exhibition and Birthplace has the best historical introduction to the playwright (as well as a disappointing house where he spent his early years). There are four other Shakespearean properties in and near Stratford, all run by the Shakespeare Birthplace Trust. Each has a garden and helpful docents who love to tell a story. Pilgrims save money by buying combo-tickets: £10 gets you in to the in-town sights (Birthplace, Hall's Croft, and Nash's House); £13 grants you entry for all five sights (Birthplace, Anne Hathaway's Cottage, Mary Arden's House, Hall's Croft, and Nash's House).

The Royal Shakespeare Theatre and the Swan Theatre is not covered under the combo-ticket, and neither is **Shakespeare's grave** (luckily, it's free to view). To see his final resting place, head to the riverside Holy Trinity Church (a 10-min walk past the theater, see its graceful spire as you gaze down the river). The church marks the ninth-century birthplace of the town, which was once a religious settlement.

▲Shakespeare Exhibition and Birthplace—Touring this sight, you'll visit an excellent modern museum before seeing Shakespeare's place of birth. (Shakespeare lived from 1564 to 1616.)

The **Shakespeare exhibition** provides a fine historical background, with actual historic artifacts. Linger in the museum rather than rushing to the old house, since this is the meat of your visit here. It's the best introduction to the life and work of Shakespeare in Stratford. The exhibit has an original 1623 First Folio of Shakespeare's work. Of the 700 printed, about 150 survive. (Most are in America, but three are in Stratford.) Western literature owes much to this folio, which collects 36 of the 37 known Shakespeare's plays (Pericles missed out). It came with an engraving of the only portrait from living memory of Shakespeare, and likely the most accurate depiction of the great playwright.

The **birthplace**, a half-timbered Elizabethan building furnished as it was when young William was growing up, is filled with bits about his life and work. I found the old house disappointing—only the creaky floorboards feel authentic. After the Shakespeares moved out, the building was used as a pub and a butcher's shop. Since its restoration in the 1800s, it feels like millions of visitors have rubbed it clean of anything

Stratford-upon-Avon

1 Arden Park Hotel & Emsley Guest House
2 Parkfield B&B
3 Salamander & Woodstock Guest Houses
4 The Payton Hotel
5 To Hemmingford House Hostel
6 Lambs, Coconut Lagoon, Barnaby's & The Oppo Rests.
7 Russons Restaurant
8 Marks & Spencer Grocery
9 Somerfield Grocery
10 Safeway Grocery
11 Internet Café
12 Launderette
13 City Bus Tours
14 Swan Fountain (Town Walks)
15 Falstaff Experience
16 Cox's Yard
17 Bridgefoot Parking Garage

traditional. While the furnishings seem tacky and modern, they're supposed to be true to 1575, when William was 11. The house becomes interesting only if you talk up the attendants in each room (£6.70, June–Aug Mon–Sat 9:00–17:00, Sun 9:30–17:00; April–May and Sept–Oct daily 10:00–17:00; Nov–March daily 10:00–16:00; these are last entry times, in town center on Henley Street, tel. 01789/204-016, www.shakespeare.org.uk).

While William Shakespeare was born in this house, he spent most of his career in London. It was there that he taught his play-going public about human nature, with plots that entertained both the highest and the lowest minds. His tool was an unrivaled mastery of the English language. He retired—rich and famous—back in Stratford, spending his last five years at a house (now long gone) called New Place.

Little is known about Shakespeare the man. The scope of his brilliant work, his humble beginnings, and the fact that no original Shakespeare manuscripts survives raise a few scholarly eyebrows. While some wonder who penned all these plays, all serious scholars accept his authorship.

▲**Anne Hathaway's Cottage**—Located a mile out of town (in Shottery), this is a picturesque, thatched, 12-room farmhouse where the Bard's wife grew up. William courted Anne here—she

was 26, he was only 18—and his tactics proved successful. (Maybe a little too much, as she was several months pregnant at their wedding.) They lived together for 34 years, until his death at age 52.

Stop in the first room for a fun eight-minute intro talk. (Notice how the place shakes every time a tourist thunks a head on the low beams.)

The Hathaway family lived here for 400 years, until 1912, and much of the family's 92-acre farm remains part of the site. While the house has little to do with Shakespeare, it offers an intimate peek at life in Shakespeare's day. Guides in each room do their best to lecture to the stampeding crowds. The garden comes with a prize-winning "traditional cottage garden," a yew maze (only planted in 2001 so not yet a challenge), a great photo-op statue of the British Isles, and an exhibit called "Dig This! A History of Spades" (£5.20, daily June–Aug 9:00–17:00, April–May and Sept–Oct 9:30–17:00, Nov–March 10:00–16:00, these are last entry times, 1.5 miles from town—a 30-min walk; a stop on the hop-on, hop-off tour bus or a quick taxi ride; well-signposted for drivers entering Stratford from any direction, easy and free parking).

▲▲**Mary Arden's House and Shakespeare Countryside Museum**—Along with the birthplace museum, this is my favorite of the five Shakespearean sights. Famous as the girlhood home of William's mom, this house is in Wilmcote (about 3 miles from town). Built around two historic farmhouses, it's an open-air folk museum depicting 16th-century farm life. The first building, **Palmer's farm** (long mistaken as Mary Arden's home), is furnished as it would have been in Shakespeare's day. It has many more domestic artifacts—and sees far fewer tourists—than the other Shakespeare sites. Without the hordes, the guides in each room have a chance to do better guiding. If you ask a question, they'll offer a fascinating insight. (Ask for a wattle-and-daub primer and a demonstration of the wood joints used in construction.) Mary Arden actually lived in the neighboring **farmhouse**. Dorothy Holmes, who lived here until 1979, left it as a 1920s time warp, and that's just what you'll see today.

The grounds also host a 19th-century farming exhibit, as well as **falconry demonstrations** with lots of mean-footed birds. Their human masters just hang around with nothing better to do than talk and wait for hunger to set the birds to flight (a round trip earns the bird a bit of food; the birds fly when hungry—but don't have the energy if they're *too* hungry). Like Katherine, the wife described as "my falcon" in *The Taming of the Shrew*, these birds are tamed and trained with food as a reward (£6, daily June–Aug 9:30–17:00, April–May and Sept–Oct 10:00–17:00, Nov–March 10:00–16:00, these are last entry times). The only convenient way to get here is by car or the hop-on, hop-off bus tour.

Hall's Croft—This former home of Shakespeare's daughter is in the town center. A fine, old, Jacobean house, it's the fanciest of the group (she married a doctor). You'll find it interesting only if you're into 17th-century medicine (£3.50, daily June–Aug 9:30–17:00, April–May and Sept–Oct 11:00–17:00, Nov–March 11:00–16:00, these are last entry times).

Nash's House—Built beside New Place (the house where Shakespeare retired), this is the least impressive of the Shakespeare-related properties. (Nash was the first husband of Shakespeare's granddaughter.) While Shakespeare's New Place is long gone (notice the foundation in the adjacent garden as you leave), Nash's house has survived. Your visit starts here with a short, guided intro in the parlor. It has the town's only general-history exhibit—fascinating only if you like chips of Roman pottery (£3.50, same hours as Hall's Croft, above).

Royal Shakespeare Theatre and the Swan Theatre—These side-by-side theaters host the Royal Shakespeare Company (see listing below). The original **Royal Shakespeare Theatre,** built to honor the bard in 1879, burnt down in 1926. The big replacement building you see today (facing the riverside park) was erected in 1932. During the design phrase, no actors were consulted; as a result, they built the stodgy Edwardian "picture frame"–style stage, when the more dynamic

"thrust"-style stage—which makes it easier for the audience to become engaged—is the actors' choice. (It would have also been closer to Shakespeare's Globe stage, which juts into the crowd.) The big theater will close for several years, starting in 2007, to be

Stratford Thanks America

Residents of Stratford are thankful for the many contributions Americans have made to their city and its heritage. Along with pumping up the economy day in and day out with tourist visits, Americans paid for half the rebuilding of the Royal Shakespeare Theatre after it burned down in 1926. The Swan Theatre renovation was funded entirely by American aid. Harvard University inherited—you guessed it—the Harvard House, and it maintains the house today. London's much-loved theater, Shakespeare's Globe, was the brainchild (and gift) of an American. And there's even a odd but prominent "American Fountain" overlooking Stratford's market square on Rother Street, which was given in 1887 to celebrate the Golden Jubilee of the rule of Queen Victoria.

gutted and finally given an updated, thrust-style stage.

Adjacent is the smaller, Elizabethan style, **Swan Theater**. This galleried playhouse opened in 1986. It hosts a small **Historic Theatre Exhibition** (£3 with audioguide, included in theater tour ticket below, Mon–Fri 13:30–18:30, Sat 10:30–18:30, Sun 11:30–16:30). There's a free and fun-for-kids dress-up bin filled with child-size costumes in the lobby—it's a huge hit with prospective actors and actresses.

Theater tours take place most days. The 45-minute tour shows you how both theaters work, leading you onto each stage. The tours finish in the Historic Theatre Exhibition (£5, entry to Exhibition included in price, tours leave at 13:30 and 17:00 if there's no matinee; 17:30 on matinee days and Sat; Sun at 12:00, 13:00, 14:00, and 15:00; the schedule is subject to change and groups are limited to 60—it's wise to book in advance, drop by the desk in the Royal Shakespeare Theatre lobby or call 01789/403-405 during regular business hours).

▲▲**Royal Shakespeare Company**—The RSC, undoubtedly the best Shakespeare company on earth, performs year-round in Stratford and in London (see page 113). If you're a Shakespeare fan, see if the RSC schedule fits into your itinerary. Tickets in Stratford range from £5 (standing) to £52 (Mon–Sat at 19:30, matinees vary, sporadic shows Sun; standing tickets available in advance at the Swan theater, and the day of performance only at the Royal Shakespeare Theatre). You'll probably need to buy your tickets ahead of time, although restricted-view and standing-room places are saved to be sold each morning in person at the box office (from 9:30, £5–16), and returned tickets can sometimes be picked up with cash the evening of an otherwise-sold-out show (box office

Stratford, the Birthplace of...Teletubbies

Every three-year-old's favorite TV series, *Teletubbies* was first produced at a secret location somewhere around Stratford. Ragdoll, the local TV production company that made *Teletubbies*, became phenomenally successful, also creating the kids' series *Rosie and Jim*, *Brum*, and *Boohbah*. *Teletubbies*, comprising 365 episodes, is no longer in production, but its creator, Ann Wood, has had quite a ride. Sales of her little stuffed animals went through the roof in Britain, thanks to American televangelist Jerry Falwell. Falwell infamously declared that Tinky Winky, the purse-toting purple tubby with the triangle above his head, was gay; he issued an alert to parents that stated that the tubbies were sinisterly promoting deviant lifestyles among preschoolers. At first, Mrs. Wood—a proper and decent English woman—was crushed to hear about his claim. Then sales skyrocketed, and she went on to become Britain's fifth wealthiest woman, the beneficiary of Falwell's homophobic paranoia. Stratford's Ragdoll shop, long a local fixture, closed in 2005, and plans to move to a bigger location soon (www.ragdoll.co.uk).

window open Mon–Sat 9:30–20:00, ticket hotline open 24/7, tel. 0870-609-1110, www.rsc.org.uk). Because the RSC website is so user-friendly, it makes absolutely no sense pay extra to book tickets through any other source. If you're feeling bold, buy a £5 standing ticket and then slip into an open seat as the lights dim—if there's not something available right away, chances are there will be plenty of seats after intermission.

The year 2006 will be festive, with Stratford hosting a flurry of Shakespeare drama (all 34 or so of his plays will be performed here over the year) before the big theater closes in 2007 for a major renovation. (The Swan will be open as usual, and a nearby and temporary theater will host the RSC during the big theater's construction.)

Non-Shakespearean Sights

Falstaff Experience—While a bit gimmicky, this is about the best non-Shakespeare historical sight in the town center. Filling Shrieve's House Barn with an informative and entertaining exhibit, it sweeps through the town's history from the plague to the English Civil War (daily 10:30–17:30, Sheep Street).

Avon Riverfront—The River Avon is a playground of swans and canal boats. The swans have been the mascots of Stratford since 1623, when, seven years after the Bard's death, a poem in his First Folio nicknamed him "the sweet swan of Avon." Join in the bird-scene fun and buy **swan food** (50p) to feed swans and ducks. Don't feed the Canada geese, which locals disdain (according to them, the geese are vicious and have been messing up the eco-balance since they were imported by a king in 1665). Ask at the ice cream boat for details on feeding the birds.

The **canal boats** saw their workhorse days during the short window of time between the start of the Industrial Revolution and the establishment of the railways. Today, they're mostly pleasure boats. The boats are long and narrow, so two can pass in the slim canals. There are 2,000 miles of canals in England's Midlands, built to connect centers of industry with seaports, and provide vital transportation during the early days of the Industrial Revolution. Stratford was as far inland as you could sail on natural rivers from Bristol; it was the terminus of the man-made Birmingham Canal, built in 1816. Even today, you can motor your canal boat all the way to London from here.

For a little bit of mellow river action, rent a **rowboat** (£5 per couple per hour) or, for more of a challenge, pole yourself around on a Cambridge-style **punt** (canal is pole-able—only 4 or 5 feet deep, same price and more memories/embarrassment if you do the punting; don't pay £10 per hour for a punter). Take a short stop on your lazy tour of the English countryside, and moor your canal boat at Stratford's Canal Basin. Try a sleepy half-hour **river cruises** (£3.50, no commentary), or jump on the only surviving **crank ferry** (c. 1930) in Britain (40p), which shuttles people across the river just beyond the theater.

Cox's Yard, a timber yard until the 1990s, is a rare physical remnant of the days when Stratford was an industrial port. Today, Cox's is a lowbrow food-and-entertainment zone.

SLEEPING

If you want to spend the night after you catch a show, options abound. Ye olde timbered hotels are scattered through the city center. Most B&Bs are on busy streets on the fringes of town. Unless otherwise noted, breakfast is included and the rooms are all non-smoking. Fridays and Saturdays are particularly tight through the season. This town is so reliant upon the theater for its business that some B&Bs have secondary insurance covering their loss if the Royal Shakespeare Company stops performing in Stratford for any reason.

$$ Arden Park Hotel, just around the corner from Shakespeare's birthplace, has nine attractive rooms, a garden, and a comfy lounge with free Internet access (Db-£58–80 depending on room, discount for 2 nights, ground-floor rooms available,

Sleep Code

(£1 = about $1.80, country code: 44, area code: 01789)
S = Single, **D** = Double/Twin, **T** = Triple, **Q** = Quad, **b** = bathroom,
s = shower only. Unless noted otherwise, you can assume
credit cards are accepted.

To help you sort easily through these listings, I've divided
the rooms into three categories based on the price for a standard double room with bath:

$$$ **Higher Priced**—Most rooms £90 or more.
  $$ **Moderately Priced**—Most rooms between £60–90.
   $ **Lower Priced**—Most rooms £60 or less.

6 Arden Street, tel. 01789/262-126, www.ardenparkhotel.co.uk,
enquiries@ardenparkhotel.co.uk).

$$ Woodstock Guest House is a friendly, frilly, pink place
with comfortable rooms (Sb-£30–36, D/Db-£64, family room-
£72–80, 30 Grove Road, tel. 01789/299-881, www.woodstock-house
.co.uk, info@woodstock-house.co.uk).

$ Emsley Guest House, two doors down from the Arden
Park, rents bright and subtle rooms named after different coun-
ties in England in a homey and inviting atmosphere (Sb-£45, Db-
£55–60, Tb-£75, Q-£110, families welcome, 4 Arden Street, tel.
01789/299-557, www.theemsley.co.uk, val@theemsley.co.uk).

$ Parkfield B&B has seven colorful rooms and plenty of local
guidebooks and theater reviews in the lounge. Some rooms have a
shower and a toilet, while the others have private facilities in the
hall, but the price is the same for both (Sb-£30, Db-£50, can book
theater tickets, 3 Broad Walk, tel. & fax 01789/293-313, www
.parkfieldbandb.co.uk, parkfield@btinternet.com, Roger and Jo).

$ Salamander Guest House, run by gregarious Frenchman
Pascal and his wife Anna, rents seven well-priced, simple rooms
on a busy street across from a small garden on the edge of town
(S-£25–30, Db-£55–60, Tb-£80, Qb-£100, 40 Grove Road,
tel. & fax 01789/205-728, www.salamanderguesthouse.co.uk,
p.delin@btinternet.com).

$$ The Payton, tucked away on John Street, has a central
and quiet location, as well as five tight but pleasant rooms (Db-
£66–72, 6 John Street, tel. & fax 01789/266-442, www.payton
.co.uk, info@payton.co.uk).

$ *Hostel:* Hemmingford House, with 132 beds in two- to
10-bed rooms, is a 10-minute bus ride from town (from £21 for
non-members, includes breakfast; take bus #X18, #18, or #77 to
Alveston; tel. 01789/297-093, stratford@yha.org.uk).

EATING

Stratford's numerous eateries vie for your pre- and post-theater business, with special hours and meal deals. (Most offer light two- and three-course menus from 17:30–19:00.) You'll find many hard-working places lined up along Sheep Street and Waterside. Here are several good options:

Russons Restaurant, serving international cuisine with lots of fresh fish, is probably the best place in town. It's cheery and chic with a woody and yellow candlelit ambience. Don't show up without a reservation (£10–15 plates, Tue–Sat 11:30–13:30 & 17:15–21:30, closed Sun–Mon, least central listing at 8 Church Street, tel. 01789/268-822).

The Coconut Lagoon serves tasty, spicy nouveau–South Indian cuisine (pre-theater 2-course special-£10, 3 courses-£13, available only until 19:00, open daily 12:30–14:30 and 17:00–23:00, 21 Sheep Street, tel. 01789/293-546).

Lambs is an intimate place serving meat, fish, and veggie dishes with panache (2-course special-£15, 3 courses-£20, 12 Sheep Street, tel. 01789/292-554).

The Oppo Restaurant, lively and family-friendly, has tight seating, a basic English menu, and a good reputation for value (£10 meals, daily, 13 Sheep Street, tel. 01789/269-980).

Barnaby's is a decent fish-and-chips joint near the theater (eat in or take out—riverside park is just a block away, daily 11:30–19:30, at Sheep Street and Waterside).

Supermarkets: For groceries, you'll find **Marks & Spencer** on Bridge Street (daily), **Somerfield** in the Town Centre mall (daily), and a huge **Safeway** next to the train station (Mon–Sat 8:00–20:00, Sun 10:00–16:00, pharmacy, tel. 01789/267-106).

To picnic, head to the canal and riverfront park between the Royal Shakespeare Theatre and the TI. Choose a bench with views of the river or of vacation houseboats, and munch your fish and chips while tossing a few fries into the river to attract swans. It's a fine way to spend a midsummer night's eve.

TRANSPORTATION CONNECTIONS

From Stratford to: London (4 trains/day, 2.5 hrs, direct to Paddington Station), **Chipping Campden** (9 buses/day, 1 hr, on First Midland Red bus, tel. 01905/763-888), **Warwick** (hrly, 15 min, by train or Stagecoach bus, tel. 01926/422-462), **Coventry** (hrly, 1 hr, tel. 01788/535-555). Train info: tel. 08457-484-950. Most intercity buses stop on Stratford's Bridge Street (a block up from the TI).

By Car: Driving is easy and distances are brief: **Stow** (20 miles), **Warwick** (8 miles), **Coventry** (10 miles).

Near Stratford:
Warwick and Coventry

Warwick

Pleasant Warwick Town—home to England's finest medieval castle—goes about its business almost oblivious to the busloads of tourists passing through. From the castle, a lane leads into the old-town center, a block away, where you'll find the **TI** (daily 9:30–16:30, tel. 01926/492-212), plenty of eateries, and several minor attractions.

SIGHTS

Warwick Castle

Almost *too* groomed and organized, this ▲▲ sight gives its crowds of visitors a decent value for the steep £15 entry fee (includes gardens and nearly all castle attractions).

The cash-poor but enterprising lord hired the folks at Madame Tussaud's to wring maximum tourist dollars out of the castle. The greedy feel of the place is a little annoying, considering the already-steep admission. But—especially for kids—there just isn't a better castle experience in England.

With a lush, green, grassy moat and fairy-tale fortifications, Warwick will entertain you from dungeon to lookout. Standing inside the castle gate, you can see the mound where the original Norman castle of 1068 stood. Under this "motte," the wooden stockade (or "bailey") defined the courtyard in the way the castle walls do today. The castle is a 14th- and 15th-century fortified shell, holding an 18th- and 19th-century royal residence, surrounded by another one of dandy "Capability" Brown's landscape jobs (like at Blenheim Palace).

Within the castle's mighty walls, there's something for every taste. The Great Hall and six lavish staterooms are the sumptuous highlights. You'll also find a Madame Tussaud–mastered re-creation of a royal weekend party—an 1898 game of statue-maker. You can ponder the weapons in the fine and educational armory, then line up to descend into a terrible torture chamber (the line here can be torturous by itself). The "King Maker" exhibit (set in 1471, when the townsfolk are getting ready for battle) is highly promoted, but not quite as good as a Disney ride. From the classic ramparts, the tower is a one-way, no-return, 250-step climb, offering a fun perch from which to fire your imaginary longbow. A recently restored mill and engine house come with an attendant who explains how the castle was electrified in 1894. (The "ghosts alive" experience costs extra.) And all around is a lush, peacock-patrolled, picnic-perfect park, complete with a Victorian rose garden. The castle grounds are often enlivened by a knight in shining armor on a horse that rotates with a merry band of musical jesters.

Cost, Hours, Information: Steep £15 entry fee, daily April–Oct 10:00–18:00, Nov–March 10:00–17:00. The £3 audioguide provides 60 easy-listening minutes of number-coded descriptions of the individual rooms (rent from kiosk 20 yards after turnstile), while the £4 guidebook gives you nearly the same script in souvenir-booklet form. (Either is worthwhile if you want to understand the various rooms.) If you tour without help, pick the brains of the earnest and talkative docents (15-min walk from Warwick train station, tel. 0870-442-2375, recorded info tel. 0870-442-2000, www.warwick-castle.co.uk). Special entertainment and events (great for kids) are scheduled every half hour throughout the day (jousting, giant catapult, longbow demo, sword fights, jester acts, and so on). Pick up the daily events flier (which also lists kiosks that sell snacks) and plan accordingly.

Eating: The castle has three main lunch options. **The Coach House** has cafeteria fare and grungy seating (located just before the turnstiles). **The Undercroft** offers the best onsite cooked food and has a sandwich buffet line (located inside, in basement of palace); you can sit under medieval vaults or escape with your food and picnic outside. The **riverside pavilion** sells sandwiches and fish-and-chips and has fine outdoor seating (in park just before the bridge, behind castle). Literally a hundred yards from the castle turnstiles—through a tiny gate in the wall—is the workaday commercial district of the town of Warwick, with several much more elegant and competitive eateries that serve fine lunches at non-Tussaud prices.

SLEEPING

$$ Forth House rents two big suites in a restored 16th-century house and stable in the center of Warwick. Friendly and classy, it has lavish public spaces and a fine garden (Db-£78, Tb-£90, non-smoking, 3-min walk from the castle to 44 High Street, tel.

01926/401-512, www.forthhouseuk.co.uk, info@forthhouseuk
.co.uk, Elizabeth Draisey).

TRANSPORTATION CONNECTIONS

From Warwick by Train to: London (2/hr, 1.75 hrs), **Stratford** (every 2 hours, 30 min—buses are better, see below). Warwick's little train station is a 15-minute walk (or £2 taxi) from the castle. It has no official baggage check, but you can ask politely. The castle has a baggage-check facility.

By Bus to: Stratford (1/hr, 20 min, bus #X16).

By Car: The main Stratford–Coventry road cuts right through Warwick. Coming from Stratford (8 miles to the south) you'll hit the castle parking lot first (£3; if it's full, lurk until a few cars leave and they'll let you in). The castle lot is expensive, and a 10-minute walk from the actual castle. Consider continuing into the town center (on main road). At the TI (near the big square church spire), grab any street-side parking (free for 2 hours). The castle is a block behind the TI.

Coventry

The Germans bombed Coventry, a ▲ sight, to smithereens in 1940. From that point on, the German phrase for "to really blast the heck out of a place" was "to coventrate" it. But Coventry rose from its ashes, and its message to our world is one of forgiveness and reconciliation and the importance of peace. The symbol of Coventry is the bombed-out hulk of its old **cathedral,** with the huge new one adjoining it. The inspirational complex welcomes visitors. Climb the tower (£1.50, 180 steps, daily 9:00–16:30, tel. 02476/267-070).

Coventry's most famous hometown girl, Lady Godiva, rode bareback through the town in the 11th century to help lower taxes. You'll see her bronze statue a block from the cathedral (near Broadgate). Just beyond that is the **Coventry Transport Museum**—the first, fastest, and most famous cars and motorcycles came from this British "Detroit" (free, daily 10:00–17:00). Other sights include the **Herbert Art Gallery and Museum,** which cover the city's history (free, Mon–Sat 10:00–17:30, Sun 12:00–17:00), and **St. Mary's Guildhall,** with 14th-century tapestries, stained glass, and an ornate ceiling (free, Easter–Sept Sun–Thu 10:00–16:00, closed Fri–Sat, during events, and off-season).

Browse through Coventry, the closest thing to normal, everyday, urban England you'll see. Get a map at the **TI** (Mon–Fri 9:30–17:00, Sat–Sun 10:00–16:30, shorter hours off-season, 4 Priory

Row, tel. 02476/227-264, fax 02476/227-255, www.visitcoventry.co.uk).

TRANSPORTATION CONNECTIONS

Route Tips for Drivers

Stratford to Ironbridge Gorge via Warwick and Coventry: Entering Stratford from the Cotswolds, you cross a bridge and pass the TI. Veer right (following *Through Traffic*, *P*, and *Wark* signs), go around the block—turning right and right and right—entering the multistory Bridgefoot garage (80p/hr, £6/day, you'll find no place easier or cheaper). The TI and City Sightseeing bus stop are a block away. Leaving the garage, circle to the right around the same block but stay on "the Wark" (Warwick Road, A439). Warwick is eight miles away. The castle is just south of town on the right. (For parking advice, see "Transportation Connections—By Car," in Warwick above.)

After touring the castle, carry on through the center of Warwick and follow signs to Coventry (still A439, then A46). If you're stopping in Coventry, follow signs painted on the road into the "city centre" and then to cathedral parking. Grab a place in the high-rise parking lot. Leaving Coventry, follow signs to Nuneaton and M6 North through lots of sprawl, and you're on your way. If you're skirting Coventry, take the M69 (direction: Leicester) and follow M6 as it threads through giant Birmingham. Try to avoid the 14:00–20:00 rush hour (see next chapter for tips). M6 divides into a free M6 and a toll M6 (designed to help drivers cut through the Birmingham traffic chaos). The £3.50 toll is a small price to pay to avoid all that nasty traffic.

When battling through sprawling Birmingham, keep your sights on M6. If you're heading for any points north—North Wales, Ironbridge Gorge (Telford), Liverpool, Blackpool, or the Lakes (Kendal for the South Lake District, Keswick for the North Lake District)—just stay relentlessly on M6 (direction: Northwest). Each destination is clearly signed directly from M6. For Ironbridge Gorge, take M54 to the Telford/Ironbridge exit. Follow the *Ironbridge* signs and do-si-do through a long series of roundabouts until you're there.

IRONBRIDGE GORGE

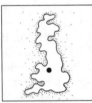

The Industrial Revolution was born in the Severn River Valley. In its glory days, this valley (blessed with abundant deposits of iron ore and coal and a river for transport) gave the world its first iron wheels, steam-powered locomotive, and cast-iron bridge. The museums in Ironbridge Gorge take you back into the days when Britain was racing into the modern age and pulling the rest of the West with her.

Planning Your Time

Without a car, Ironbridge Gorge isn't worth the headache. Drivers can slip it in between the Cotswolds/Stratford/Warwick and North Wales. Speed demons zip in for a midday tour of Blists Hill, look at the bridge, and speed out. For an overnight visit, arrive in the early evening to browse the town and spend the morning and early afternoon touring the sights before driving on to North Wales (10:00–Museum of the Gorge; 11:00–Blists Hill Victorian Town for lunch and sightseeing; 15:30–Drive to North Wales).

With a month in Britain, I'd spend two nights and a leisurely day: 9:30–Iron Bridge and the town; 10:30–Museum of the Gorge; 11:30–Coalbrookdale Museum of Iron; 14:30–Blists Hill, dinner at Coalbrookdale Inn.

ORIENTATION

(area code: 01952)

The town is just a few blocks gathered around the Iron Bridge, which spans the peaceful, tree-lined Severn River. While the smoke-belching bustle is long gone, knowing that this wooded, sleepy river valley was the Silicon Valley of the 19th century makes wandering its brick streets almost a pilgrimage. The actual museum sites are scattered over three miles. The modern cooling towers (for coal, not nuclear energy) that loom ominously over these red-brick remnants seem strangely appropriate.

Tourist Information

The TI is in the tollhouse on the Iron Bridge (Mon–Fri 9:00–17:00, Sat–Sun 10:00–17:00, room-finding service, tel. 01952/884-391). The TI has lots of booklets for sale; hikers like the homegrown *Walks in the Severn Gorge* (11 walks, £3.50). If you're here on the weekend, ask the TI for the schedule of the steam train that runs for fun most Sundays in Ironbridge Gorge.

Getting Around Ironbridge Gorge

On weekends, the Gorge Connect buses link the museum sites (50p per ride regardless of distance, pay each time you board, 1–2/hr, Sat–Sun 9:00–18:00 year-round, a couple mid-morning runs go all the way to the Telford rail station, tel. 01952/200-005).

SIGHTS

In Ironbridge Gorge

▲▲**Iron Bridge**—While England was at war with her American colonies, this first cast-iron bridge was built in 1779 to show off a wonderful new building material. Lacking experience with cast iron, the builders erred on the side of sturdiness and constructed it as if it were made out of wood. Notice that the original construction used traditional timber-jointing techniques rather than rivets. (Any rivets are from later repairs.) The valley's centerpiece is free, open all the time, and thought-provoking. Walk across the bridge to the tollhouse/TI/gift shop/museum (free, daily 10:00–17:00). Read the fee schedule and notice the subtle slam against royalty (England was not immune to the revolutionary sentiment brewing in the colonies at this time). Pedestrians paid half a penny to cross; poor people crossed cheaper by coracle—a crude tublike wood-and-canvas shuttle ferry (you'll see old photos of these upstairs). Cross back to the town and enjoy a pleasant walk downstream along the towpath. Where horses once dragged boats laden with Industrial Age cargo, today locals walk their dogs.

▲▲▲**Ironbridge Gorge Industrial Revolution Museums**—This group of widely scattered sites has varied admission charges (usually £2.25–5.45; Blists Hill is £8.75). The £13.25 Passport ticket (families-£42) gets you into all the sights, which all have the same hours (daily 10:00–17:00, a few Coalbrookdale sights close Nov–March, www.ironbridge.org.uk). While several of the sights

Ironbridge Gorge

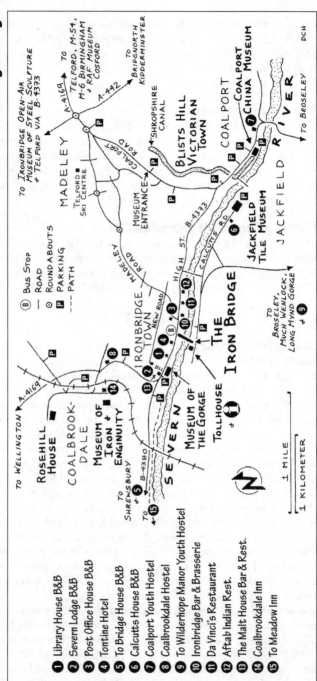

Legend:
- ⓑ Bus Stop
- — Road
- ⊙ Roundabouts
- P Parking
- --- Path

1. Library House B&B
2. Severn Lodge B&B
3. Post Office House B&B
4. Tontine Hotel
5. To Bridge House B&B
6. Calcutts House B&B
7. Coalport Youth Hostel
8. Coalbrookdale Hostel
9. To Wilderhope Manor Youth Hostel
10. Ironbridge Bar & Brasserie
11. Da Vinci's Restaurant
12. Aftab Indian Rest.
13. The Malt House Bar & Rest.
14. Coalbrookdale Inn
15. To Meadow Inn

may not be worth your time, seeing Blists Hill Victorian Town, Museum of the Gorge, and the Coalbrookdale Museum of Iron costs £16.45 without the £13.25 Passport ticket.

Museum of the Gorge: Orient yourself to the valley here in the Severn Warehouse (£2.10, daily 10:00–17:00, 500 yards upstream from the bridge, parking-£1). See the eight-minute introductory movie, check out the exhibit and the model of the gorge in its heyday, and buy a Blists Hill guidebook and Passport ticket. Farther upstream from the museum parking lot is the fine riverside Dale End Park, with picnic areas and a playground.

Blists Hill Victorian Town: Save most of your time and energy for this wonderful town. You'll wander through 50 acres of Victorian industry, factories, and a re-created community from the 1890s, complete with carriage rides, chemists, a candy shop, an ancient dentist's chair, candle makers, a working pub, a green-grocer's shop, a fascinating squatter's cottage, and a snorty, slippery pigsty. Don't miss the explanation of the winding machine at the Blists Hill Mine (demos throughout the day, call for times). Walk along the canal to the "inclined plane." Grab lunch in the Victorian Pub or in the cafeteria near the squatter's cottage and children's old-time rides. The board by the entry lists which exhibits are staffed and lively (with docents in Victorian dress). The £2 Blists Hill guidebook gives a good step-by-step rundown (£8.75, daily 10:00–17:00, tel. 01952/583-003).

Coalbrookdale Museum of Iron: This does a fine job of explaining the original iron-smelting process (£5.45, opposite Darby's furnace—see below). The Coalbrookdale neighborhood is the birthplace of the Industrial Revolution. Abraham Darby's blast furnace sits like a shrine inside a big glass pyramid (free), surrounded by the evocative Industrial Age ruins. It was here that, in 1709, Darby first smelted iron, using coke as fuel. If you're like me, "coke" is a drink, and "smelt" is the past tense of smell...nevertheless, this event kicked off the modern Industrial Age.

All the ingredients of the recipe for big industry were here in abundance—iron ore, top-grade coal, and water for power and shipping. Wander around Abraham Darby's furnace. Before this furnace was built, iron ore was laboriously melted by charcoal. With a huge waterwheel-powered bellows, Darby burned top-grade coal superhot (burning off the impurities to make "coke"). Local iron ore was dumped into the furnace and melted. Impurities floated to the top, while the pure iron sank to the bottom of a clay tub in the bottom of the furnace. Twice a day, the plugs were knocked off, allowing the "slag" to drain away on the top and the molten iron to drain out on the bottom. The low-grade slag was used locally on walls and paths. The high-grade iron trickled into molds formed in the sand below the furnace. It cooled into pig iron (named because the molds look like piglets suckling their mother). The pig-iron "planks" were broken off by sledgehammers and shipped away. The Severn River became one of Europe's busiest, shipping pig iron to distant foundries, where it was remelted and made into cast iron (for projects such as the Iron Bridge), or to forges, where it was worked like toffee into wrought iron.

Enginuity, next door, is a hands-on funfest for kids. Riffing on Ironbridge's engineering roots, this converted 1709 foundry is full of mesmerizing water contraptions, pumps, magnets, and laser games. Build a dam, try your hand at earthquake-proof construction, navigate a water maze, operate a remote-controlled robot, or power a turbine with your own steam (£5.45, family-£16, daily 10:00–17:00).

Rosehill House, just up the hill, is the 18th-century Darby mansion furnished as a Quaker ironmaster's home would have been in 1850 (£3.20, April–Sept daily 10:00–17:00, closed Oct–March). The adjacent Dale House from the 1780s is less interesting.

Coalport China Museum, Jackfield Tile Museum, and Broseley Pipeworks: Housed in their original factories, these showcase the region's porcelain, decorated tiles, and clay tobacco pipes. These industries were developed to pick up the slack when the iron industry shifted away from Severn Valley. Each museum features finely decorated pieces, and the china and tile museums offer low-energy workshops.

Ironbridge Open-Air Museum of Steel Sculpture—This park is a striking tribute to the region's industrial heritage. Stroll the 10-acre grounds and spot works by Roy Kitchin and other sculptors stashed in the forest and perched in rolling grasslands (£2, March–Nov Tue–Sun 10:00–17:00, usually closed Mon but open Mon bank holidays, closed Dec–Feb, 2 miles from Iron Bridge, Moss House, Cherry Tree Hill, Coalbrookdale, Telford, tel. 01952/433-152, www.go2.co.uk/steelsculpture).

Near Ironbridge Gorge

Skiing, Swimming, and Fishing—There's a small, brush-covered ski slope with two Poma lifts at Telford Ski Centre in Madeley, two miles from Ironbridge Gorge; you'll see the signs for it as you drive into Ironbridge Gorge (£9.25/hr including gear, less for kids, unreliably open Mon–Thu 10:00–20:00, Tue until 22:00, Fri 12:00–22:00, Sat 13:00–14:00 & 16:00–18:00, Sun 10:00–16:00 & 18:00–20:00, tel. 01952/586-862). A public swimming pool is next door. The Woodlands Farm, on Beech Road, runs a private fishing business where only barbless hooks are used and locals toss their catch back to hook again (kind of a fish hell).

Royal Air Force Museum Cosford—This Red Baron magnet displays more than 80 aircraft, from warplanes to rockets. Get the background on ejection seats and a primer on the principles of propulsion (free, daily 10:00–18:00, last entry 16:00, Shifnal, Shropshire, on A41 near junction with M54, tel. 01902/376-200, www.rafmuseum.org).

More Sights—If you're looking for reasons to linger in Ironbridge Gorge, these sights are all within a short drive: the medieval town of Shrewsbury, abbey village of Much Wenlock, scenic Long Mynd gorge at Church Stretton, castle at Ludlow, and the steam railway at the river town of Bridgnorth. Shoppers like Chester (en route to North Wales).

SLEEPING

In the Town Center

$$$ **Library House** is *Better Homes and Gardens* elegant. In the town center, a half-block downhill from the bridge, it's classy, friendly, and a fine value. Helpful Chris and George Maddocks run this smoke-free place, and their breakfast won a "healthy heartbeat" award. The complimentary drink upon arrival is a welcome touch (Sb-£55, Db-£65–70, Tb-£85, family room-£80, cash only, video library, free parking, 11 Severn Bank, Ironbridge Gorge, tel. 01952/432-299, fax 01952/433-967, www.libraryhouse .com, info@libraryhouse.com). George will pick you up from the Telford train station if you request it in advance.

$$$ **Severn Lodge B&B** is an elegant, Georgian "captain of industry" house offering three fine, newly refurbished rooms (Sb-£59, Db-£72–81, 2-night minimum stay, cash only, non-smoking, walled garden, easy parking, 200 yards above river, a block above town center on New Road, take Wharfage Steps off main road

---

Sleep Code

(£1 = about $1.80, country code: 44, area code: 09152)
S = Single, **D** = Double/Twin, **T** = Triple, **Q** = Quad, **b** = bathroom, **s** = shower only. You can assume credit cards are accepted unless noted otherwise.

To help you sort easily through these listings, I've divided the rooms into three categories based on the price for a standard double room with bath during high season:

$$$ **Higher Priced**—Most rooms £60 or more.
$$ **Moderately Priced**—Most rooms between £35–60.
$ **Lower Priced**—Most rooms £35 or less.

next to purple gate, tel. 01952/432-147, fax 01952/432-148, www
.severnlodge.com, Julia).

Two lesser places, right in the town center, overlook the
bridge:

$$ Post Office House B&B is literally above the post office,
where the postmaster's wife, Janet Hunter, rents three rooms (Db-
£52–58, discount for 2 nights or more, family rooms available,
cash only, 6 The Square, tel. 01952/433-201, fax 01952/433-582,
hunter@pohouse-ironbridge.fsnet.co.uk).

$$ Tontine Hotel is the town's big, 12-room, musty, smoky,
Industrial Age hotel (S-£25, D-£40, Db-£56, 10 percent dis-
count with this book in 2006, The Square, tel. 01952/432-127, fax
01952/432-094, tontine@netscapeonline.co.uk). Check out the
historic photos in the bar.

Outside of Town

$$$ Bridge House rents four rooms in a 17th-century residence
on the banks of the Severn River, two miles from the town center
on B4380 (Sb-£50, Db-£68, family room-from £92, non-smoking
rooms, Buildwas Road, tel. & fax 01952/432-105).

$$ Calcutts House rents seven rooms in their 18th-century
ironmaster's home and adjacent coach house. Rooms in the main
house are elegant, while the coach house rooms are simpler, but
still bright and tastefully done. Ask the owners how the rooms were
named (main house Db-£65, coach house Db-£40–59 depending on room size, on Calcutts Road, Gorge Connect Jackfield bus
stop is across street, tel. 01952/882-631, enquiries@calcuttshouse
.co.uk).

$ Coalport Youth Hostel, plush for a hostel, fills an old fac-
tory at the China Museum in Coalport (bunk-bed Db-£36, most
beds are in quads). The **Coakbrookdale Hostel,** built in 1859 as
the grand Coalbrookdale Institute, is another fine hostel (a 20-min
walk from the Iron Bridge down A4169 toward Wellington, 4- to
6-bed rooms, cash only). Each hostel charges £14 per bed with
sheets, serves meals, has a self-service laundry, closes from 10:00
to 17:00, requires that you have a hostel membership (available for
£14), and uses the same telephone number and e-mail address (tel.
01952/588-755, ironbridge@yha.org).

$ Wilderhope Manor Youth Hostel, a beautifully remote
and haunted 400-year-old manor house, is one of Europe's best
hostels. On Saturdays, tourists actually pay to see what hostel-
ers sleep in (£15.50, under 18-£12.50, £3 less for members, dinner
served at 19:00, unreliable hours throughout year, reservations recommended, tel. 01694/771-363, wilderhope@yha.org.uk). It's six
miles from Much Wenlock down B4371 toward Church Stretton.

EATING

Ironbridge Bar & Brasserie is an inviting bistro with an imaginative menu and a focus on fish, good wine, and real ale (£16 meals, £6 bar meals, Tue–Sun 18:00–23:00, also Sat–Sun lunch, closed Mon, plenty of indoor/outdoor seating, non-smoking, veggie options, reservations smart, on High Street half a block uphill from Oliver's, tel. 01952/432-716). Its cool wine bar is a fun place for a drink.

Da Vinci's serves good, though pricey, Italian food in a dressy ambience (£16 main courses, Mon–Sat 19:00–22:00, closed Sun, 26 High Street, tel. 01952/432-250).

Aftab is the place for Indian food—eat in or take out (daily 17:30–24:00, 25 High Street, tel. 01952/432-055).

The Malt House, located in an 18th-century beer house, offers an English menu with a European accent. This is a very popular scene with the local twenty-something gang—and consequently smoky (£12 main courses, bar menu at the Jazz Bar, daily 12:00–14:30 & 18:30–21:00, near Museum of the Gorge, 5-min walk from center, The Wharfage, tel. 01952/433-712). The Malt House is *the* vibrant nightspot in town, with live music and a fun crowd generally from Wednesday through Sunday.

For a local scene, excellent ales, and surprisingly good food, try **Coalbrookdale Inn** (lunches 12:00–14:30, dinner from 18:00, last order 20:00, no food Sun night or all day Mon, reservations unnecessary for the bar but a good idea for the fancier restaurant, lively ladies' loo, across street from Coalbrookdale Museum of Iron, 1 mile from Ironbridge Gorge, tel. 01952/433-953, Danny and Dawn Wood). This former "best pub in Britain" has a tradition of offering free samples from a lineup of featured beers. Ask what real ales are available.

Lawrence Welk would prefer eating at the **Meadow Inn,** a local favorite that serves prizewinning pub grub and has lovely riverside outdoor seating if the weather cooperates (£8 meals, daily 12:00–21:30, can get crowded, no reservations; a pleasant 15-min walk from the center, head upstream, at Dale End Park take the path along the river, the inn is just after railway bridge; tel. 01952/433-193).

TRANSPORTATION CONNECTIONS

Ironbridge Gorge is five miles from Telford, which has the nearest train station. To get between Ironbridge Gorge and Telford, take a bus (£1.30, 1–2/hr, 20 min, none on Sun) or taxi (£7.50). Although Telford's train and bus stations are an annoying 15-minute walk apart, you can connect on bus #44 (every 10 min, 50p) or #55 (every 20 min), or with a £2 cab ride. The Telford bus station is part of a large modern mall, an easy place to wait for the hourly bus to Ironbridge Gorge. The Gorge Connect bus service, which runs among Ironbridge Gorge sights on weekends, makes a couple of morning runs between Ironbridge Gorge and the Telford train station. For schedule information on the Gorge Connect and other bus routes, call Telford Travelink at 0870-608-2608. If you need a **taxi** while in Ironbridge Gorge, call 01952/501-050.

By Train from Telford to: Birmingham (2/hr, 40 min), **Conwy** in North Wales (9/day, 3 hrs, 1–2 changes usually include Chester), **Blackpool** (1–2/hr, 3.5 hrs, usually 2 changes), **Keswick/ Lake District** (every 2 hrs, 3.5 hrs to Penrith with 2 changes, then catch a bus to Keswick, hrly except Sun 6/day, 40 min), **Edinburgh** (hrly, 5–6.5 hrs, 1–2 transfers). Train info: tel. 08457-484-950.

By Car to Telford: Driving in from the **Cotswolds** and **Stratford,** take M6 through Birmingham then M54 to the Telford/Ironbridge exit. Follow the brown *Ironbridge* signs through lots of roundabouts to Ironbridge Gorge. The traffic north through Birmingham is miserable from 14:00 to 20:00, especially on Fridays. From **Warwick,** consider the M40, M42, Kidderminster alternative, coming into Ironbridge Gorge on the A442 via Bridgnorth to avoid the Birmingham traffic. Driving from Ironbridge Gorge to North Wales takes two hours to Ruthin or 2.5 hours to Conwy.

NORTH WALES

Wales' top historical, cultural, and natural wonders are found in the north. From towering Mount Snowdon to lush forests to desolate moor country, North Wales is a poem written in landscape. For sightseeing thrills and diversity, North Wales is Britain's most interesting slice of the Celtic crescent. But be careful not to be waylaid by the many gimmicky sights and bogus "best of" lists. The region's economy is poor, and they're wringing every possible pound out of the tourist trade. Sort carefully through your options.

Planning Your Time

On a three-week Britain trip, give North Wales two nights and a day, and it'll give you mighty castles, a giant slate mine, and some of Britain's most beautiful scenery. Many visitors are charmed and find an extra day.

By Public Transportation: Use Conwy as a home base, and skip Ruthin. From Conwy, you can get around Snowdonia and Caernarfon by bus, train, or private driving tour.

By Car: Drivers interested in a medieval banquet should set up in Ruthin and do this loop: 9:00–Drive over Llanberis mountain pass to Caernarfon (with possible short stops in Trefriw Woolen Mills, Betws-y-Coed, Pen Y Gwryd Hotel Pub, and Llanberis); 12:00–Caernarfon Castle. Catch the noon tour and 13:00 movie in Eagle Tower. See the Prince Charles (of Wales) exhibit. Climb to the top for the view. Browse through Caernarfon town and have lunch. 14:30–Drive the scenic road (A4085) to Blaenau Ffestiniog; 15:30–Tour Llechwedd Slate Mine; 17:30–Drive home to Ruthin; 19:00–Arrive home; 19:45–Medieval banquet at castle (if you didn't

Welsh: The Language and Choirs

The Welsh language, Cymraeg, has been a written language since about A.D. 600 and was spoken 300 years before French or German. It remains alive and well. Although English imperialism tried to kill it, today Welsh and those who speak it are protected by law. In northwest Wales, well over half the population is fluent in Welsh. It's either the first or the required second language in the public schools. Tourists hardly notice that the locals chatter away in Welsh and, as they turn to you, switch seamlessly to English. Listen in.

Welsh is a Celtic language (like Irish) and most closely related to the Breton language in western France. The common "ll" is pronounced as if you were ready to make an "l" sound and then blew it out (a bit like the *tl* in "antler"). Like in Scotland, "ch" is a soft, guttural k, pronounced in the back of the throat. The language is phonetic, but comes with a few tricks: the Welsh "dd" sounds like the English "th," f = v, ff = f, w = the "u" in "push," y = i. In a pub, impress your friends (or make some) by toasting the guy who just bought your drink. Say "Yeach-hid dah" (YECH-id dah, "Good health to you") and "Dee olch" ("Thank you") or "Dee olch un vowr" (dee olch un vawr, "Thanks very much"). If the beer's bad, just make something up.

Choirs: Every town has a choir (men's or mixed) that practices weekly. Visitors are usually welcome to observe and very often follow the choir down to the pub afterwards for a good, old-fashioned, beer-lubricated singsong. Choirs practice weekly in the towns of **Ruthin** (mixed choir at Tabernacle Church, Thu 20:00–21:30 except Aug), **Llangollen** (men's choir Fri at 19:30 at Hand Hotel, 21:00 pub singsong afterward, tel. 01978/860-303), **Denbigh** (men's choir Mon at 19:00 except in Aug), **Llandudno** (Sun 19:30–21:00, near Conwy), and **Caernarfon** (Tue 19:45–21:30 at Conservative Club on Castle Street, except Aug). Confirm choir schedules with your B&B hosts or a local TI.

already do it on the night of your arrival).

With a second day, add the train up Mount Snowdon. With more time and a desire to hike, consider using the mountain village of Beddgelert as your base.

If you have no interest in the banquet or a hike, skip Ruthin and shorten your drive time by spending two nights in Conwy.

Getting Around North Wales

By Public Transportation: North Wales (except Ruthin) is well covered by a combination of buses and trains. A main train line zips

North Wales

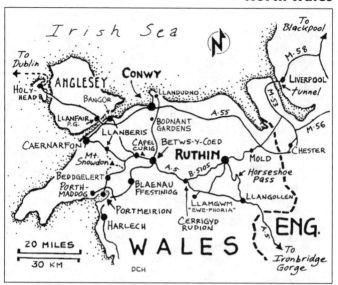

along the north coast from Chester to Holyhead via Llandudno Junction, Conwy, and Bangor (1/hr). From Llandudno Junction, the Conwy Valley line goes scenically south to Betws-y-Coed and Blaenau Ffestiniog (5/day, 1 hr). Without a car, you'll be fine if you use these two train lines, public buses (get the Gwynedd Public Transport Guide at any local TI), and Arriva buses, which circle Snowdonia National Park with the needs of hikers in mind (£5.40 day pass available, buy on bus, tel. 0870-608-2608).

By Private Tour: Mari Roberts does driving tours of the area out of Ruthin, but will happily pick you up in Conwy (£12.50/hr, tel. 01824/702-713, mari@wernfechan.fsnet.co.uk).

Ruthin

Ruthin (RITH-in) is a low-key market town whose charm is in its ordinary Welshness. The people are the sights. Admission is free if you start the conversation. The market square, castle, TI, bus station, and in-town accommodations are all within five blocks of each other. Ruthin is Welsh as can be, makes a handy base for drivers doing North Wales, and serves up a medieval banquet.

Tourist Information: You'll find the TI in the busy crafts center (June–Sept daily 10:00–17:30; Oct–May Mon–Sat 10:00–17:00, Sun 12:00–17:00, tel. 01824/703-992).

Ruthin

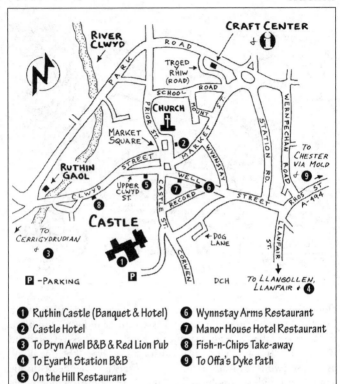

- **1** Ruthin Castle (Banquet & Hotel)
- **2** Castle Hotel
- **3** To Bryn Awel B&B & Red Lion Pub
- **4** To Eyarth Station B&B
- **5** On the Hill Restaurant
- **6** Wynnstay Arms Restaurant
- **7** Manor House Hotel Restaurant
- **8** Fish-n-Chips Take-away
- **9** To Offa's Dyke Path

SIGHTS

▲▲Ruthin Castle Welsh Medieval Banquet—English, Scottish, Irish, and Welsh medieval banquets are all variations on the same touristy theme. This one, while growing more tired and tacky each year, remains fun and more culturally justifiable (if that's necessary) than most. You'll be greeted with a chunk of bread dipped in salt, which, the maiden explains, will "guarantee your safety." Your medieval master of ceremonies then seats you, and the candlelit evening of food, drink, and music rolls gaily on. You'll enjoy harp music, angelic singing, and lots of entertainment, including insults slung at the Irish, Scots, English, and even us brash colonists. With fanfare (and historic

explanation), wenches serve mead, spiced wine, and four hearty traditional courses. Drink from a pewter goblet, wear a bib, and eat with your fingers and a dagger. Food and mead are unlimited—just ask for more (£36, starts at 19:45, 2–5 nights per week year-round, depending upon demand; vegetarian options, non-smoking, call for reservations, easy doorstep parking, down Castle Street from town square, tel. 01824/703-435 or, after hours, the hotel at tel. 01824/702-664). Ask to be seated with other readers of this book to avoid being stuck in a dreary tour group.

Ruthin Gaol—Get a glimpse into crime and punishment in 17th- to early 20th-century Wales in this 100-cell prison. Explore the "dark" and condemned cells, give the dreaded hand-crank a whirl, and learn about the men, women, and children who did time here before the prison closed in 1916 (£3, family-£8, daily 10:00–17:00, Thu until 19:00, Nov–March closed Mon, last entry 60 min before closing, Clwyd Street, tel. 01824/708-281, www.ruthingaol.co.uk).

Walks—For a scenic and interesting one-hour walk, try the Offa's Dyke Path to Moel Famau (the "Jubilee Tower," a 200-year-old war memorial on a peak overlooking stark moorlands). The trailhead is a 10-minute drive east of Ruthin on A-494.

▲▲**Welsh Choir**—The mixed choir performs at the Tabernacle Church on Thursday 20:00–21:30 (except Aug, tel. 01824/703-757).

SLEEPING

In Ruthin

$$$ Ruthin Castle, the ultimate in creaky, faded, Old World elegance for North Wales, is actually not a castle, but a hotel near castle ruins (Sb-£70–80, standard Db-£108–120, less off-season, tel. 01824/702-664, fax 01824/705-978, www.ruthincastle.co.uk). Enjoy lavish public spaces, armor, antlers, ghosts, and your private snooker table (giant billiards, £1/hr). Explore the fascinating grounds, complete with a drowning pool and 40 peacocks. You'll wake up to their cry thinking it's a Looney Tunes damsel in distress.

$$$ The **Castle Hotel,** not to be confused with the Ruthin Castle hotel, is a more modern 19-room hotel on the town square (Sb-£50, Db-£80, family suites-£100, front rooms are larger and overlook the square, non-smoking rooms, St. Peter's Square, tel. 01824/702-479, fax 01824/703-488, enquiries@castlehotel.co.uk).

Near Ruthin

These places, just outside town, are better for drivers.

$$ Bryn Awel, a traditional and charming farmhouse B&B with a paradise garden, is run by Beryl and John Jones in the hamlet of Bontuchel just outside of Ruthin. Beryl, a prizewinning

Sleep Code

(£1 = about $1.80, country code: 44, area code: 01824)
S = Single, **D** = Double/Twin, **T** = Triple, **Q** = Quad, **b** = bathroom,
s = shower only. You can assume credit cards are accepted
unless otherwise noted.

To help you sort easily through these listings, I've divided
the rooms into three categories based on the price for a standard double room with bath:

$$$ **Higher Priced**—Most rooms £65 or more.
 $$ **Moderately Priced**—Most rooms between £45–65.
  $ **Lower Priced**—Most rooms £45 or less.

quilter, is helpful with travel tips and key Welsh words (Db-£50,
£4 less per night for 2 nights or more, cash only, non-smoking,
Bontuchel, tel. 01824/702-481, www.accomodata.co.uk/010797
.htm, beryljjones@msn.com). From Ruthin, take Bala road #494,
then B5105/Cerrigydrudion road. Turn right after the church, at
the *Bontuchel/Cyffylliog* sign. Look for the B&B sign on the right,
1.8 fragrant miles down a narrow road.

$$ Eyarth Station, an old railway station converted to a country guest house, rents six rooms in the scenic Vale of Clwyd about
a mile outside Ruthin (Sb-£40, Db-£56, country supper-£14, non-smoking rooms, closed Nov–Feb, Llanfair D.C., tel. 01824/703-643, www.eyarthstation.co.uk, stay@eyarthstation.com).

For cheap beds, go to the **Llangollen Youth Hostel** (15 miles
from Ruthin in Llangollen, see page 275).

EATING

For pub grub, try **Wynnstay Arms,** the classier **Manor House
Hotel Restaurant** (a tad expensive), or the **Red Lion** pub (a mile
out of town in Cyffylliog). In Ruthin, **On the Hill** serves hearty
£3–6 lunches and £7–10 dinners—mostly made with fresh local
ingredients—to an enthusiastic crowd (Tue–Sat 11:45–14:00
& 17:30–21:00, closed Sun–Mon, 1 Upper Clwyd Street, tel.
01824/707-736). For fish-and-chips, locals paddle over to the bottom of Clwyd Street (take-away only).

TRANSPORTATION CONNECTIONS

From Ruthin to: Llangollen (4 buses/day but never on Sun, 1 hr,
15 miles), **Betws-y-Coed** (3–4 hrs, bus to Rhyl, train to Llandudno
Junction, then train to Betws-y-Coed, 30 miles total), **Conwy**

(3 hrs by bus, with transfer at Rhyl or Llanrwst), **Chester** (5 buses/day, 30 min, or a £20 taxi).

Llangollen

Worth a stop if you have a car, Llangollen is famous for its **International Musical Eisteddfod** (July 4–9 in 2006, tel. 01978/862-000, www.international-eisteddfod.co.uk), a very popular and very crowded festival of folk songs and dance. Men's choir practice is held on Friday nights throughout the year (19:30 at the Hand Hotel, 21:00 pub singsong afterward, tel. 01978/860-303).

In Llangollen, you can walk or ride a horse-drawn boat down the old canal (£4.50, March–Oct, 45 min, 3-mile round trip, tel. 01978/860-702) toward the lovely 13th-century **Cistercian Vale Crucis Abbey** (£2, daily 10:00–17:00) near the even older cross, **Eliseg's Pillar.** The same cruise company offers relaxing and scenic narrow-boat canal trips (£8, 2 hrs).

Llangollen has a handful of other amusements and attractions, including scenic steam-train trips (daily Easter–Dec), the world's largest permanent exhibition of model railways, and the biggest *Doctor Who* exhibition anywhere. (**TI** open daily 9:30–17:30, shorter hours in winter, tel. 01978/860-828.)

Sleeping in Llangollen: **$$ Glasgwm B&B** rents spacious rooms in a Victorian townhouse (Sb-£30, Db-£54, Abbey Road, tel. 01978/861-975, glasgwm@llangollen.co.uk). **$ Llangollen Youth Hostel** is cheap (£15 per bed in 2- to 20-bed rooms, £3 less for members, tel. 01978/860-330, llangollen@yha.org.uk).

Transportation Connections: Llangollen is a 30-minute drive from Ruthin. Llangollen is connected by bus with Ruthin (4/day, none on Sun, 60 min, year-round) and by bus with train stations at Chirk (hrly), Ruabon (hrly), and Wrexham (hrly).

Conwy

This garrison town was built with the Conwy castle in the 1280s to give Edward I an English toehold in Wales (see page 279). What's left today are the best medieval walls in Britain surrounding a humble town and crowned by the bleak and barren hulk of a castle that was awesome in its day. Conwy's charming High Street leads from Lancaster Square (with the bus stop, unmanned train station, and a column honoring the town's founder, Welsh prince Llywelyn the Great) down to a fishy harbor that permitted Edward to safely restock his castle. Since the highway was tunneled under the town, a strolling ambience has returned to Conwy. Beyond the castle, the mighty Telford suspension bridge is a 19th-century slice of English imperialism, built in 1826 to better connect (and control) the route to Ireland.

ORIENTATION

Tourist Information

The TI is near the castle (daily April–May and Oct 9:30–17:00, June–Sept until 18:00, Nov–March until 16:00 and opens at 11:00 on Sun, tel. 01492/592-248). Ask about train or bus schedules for your departure (Conwy doesn't have a staffed train or bus station—only a lonely train platform and bus stop). The TI sells books and maps on the area, such as *Footprints' Walks around Snowdonia* (£3.50, 16 walks with maps). The TI also reserves rooms for a £1 fee and makes theater bookings.

Don't confuse the TI with the tacky "Conwy Visitors Centre"—with its goofy little 80p video show—near the station.

Helpful Hints

Trains: Train schedules are posted outside the unstaffed station. Trains do drop off and pick up in Conwy (if your train is listed with an "x," you'll need to flag it down and hope the conductor is paying attention). The nearest "real" train station is in Llandudno Junction, a mile away, and is a safer bet for more regular trains (as the conductor may not see you at the Conwy stop if you are wearing neutral colors). When you are getting train information, make sure to ask for trains that stop at Llandudno Junction, and not Llandudno proper, which is much farther from Conwy.

Internet Access: Try the library at the bottom of High Street (free, Mon and Thu–Fri 10:00–17:30, Tue 10:00–19:00, Wed and Sat 10:00–13:00, closed Sun, tel. 01492/596-242), Llys Llywelyn B&B (starting at £2, see "Sleeping," page 283), or O.J. Williams bakery on High Street (1 terminal in back room, £2.20/hr, daily 8:30–17:30).

Market: Every Tuesday, a small market hums in the train station's parking lot (year-round, canceled if rainy).

Music: Every Monday night, the gritty Malt Loaf pub hosts the Conwy Folk Music Club (across from train station) from 20:30 on.

Bike Rental: Conwy Outdoor rents bikes via Snowdonia Bicycle Hire for £14 per half day, including helmets (daily 9:00–18:00, packed lunches available, 9 Castle Street, tel. 01492/878-771 or 01492/593-390, www.snowdoniacyclehire.co.uk).

Car Rental: A dozen car-rental agencies in the city of Llandudno (1.5 miles away, beyond the town of Llandudno Junction) offer

Conwy

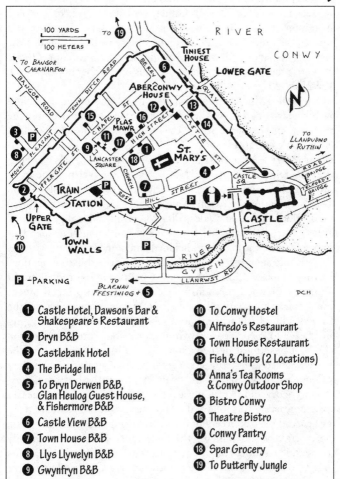

- ❶ Castle Hotel, Dawson's Bar & Shakespeare's Restaurant
- ❷ Bryn B&B
- ❸ Castlebank Hotel
- ❹ The Bridge Inn
- ❺ To Bryn Derwen B&B, Glan Heulog Guest House, & Fishermore B&B
- ❻ Castle View B&B
- ❼ Town House B&B
- ❽ Llys Llywelyn B&B
- ❾ Gwynfryn B&B
- ❿ To Conwy Hostel
- ⓫ Alfredo's Restaurant
- ⓬ Town House Restaurant
- ⓭ Fish & Chips (2 Locations)
- ⓮ Anna's Tea Rooms & Conwy Outdoor Shop
- ⓯ Bistro Conwy
- ⓰ Theatre Bistro
- ⓱ Conwy Pantry
- ⓲ Spar Grocery
- ⓳ To Butterfly Jungle

cars for about £40 per day and can deliver to you in Conwy (get list of car-rental agencies from Conwy TI). The closest is Avis, a 10-minute walk from Conwy (tel. 01492/585-101).

SIGHTS AND ACTIVITIES

▲**Conwy Castle**—Built dramatically on a rock overlooking the sea with eight linebacker towers, this castle has an interesting story to tell. Built in four years, the castle had a water gate that allowed safe entry for English boats in a land of hostile Welsh (£4, or £6.50 Joint Ticket with Plas Mawr, daily April–May and Oct 9:30–17:00,

June–Sept until 18:00, Nov–March until 16:00 and opens at 11:00 on Sun, tel. 01492/592-358). Guides wait inside to take you on a 60-minute, £1 tour. If the booth is empty, look for the group and join it. The guides also do inexpensive city walking tours in the evening; consider enthusiastic Neville Hortop (minimum £10 for the entire tour, price per person depends on number of people, tel. 01492/878-209).

▲**City Wall**—Much of the wall, with its 22 towers and castle and harbor views, can be walked for free. Start at Upper Gate (the highest point) or Berry Street (the lowest), or do the small section at the castle entrance.

▲**Plas Mawr**—A rare Elizabethan house from 1580, this was built after the reign of Henry VIII. It was the first Welsh home to be built within Conwy's walls. (The Tudor family was Welsh—and therefore relations between Wales and England warmed.) Billed as the oldest house in Wales, Plas Mawr offers a delightful look 16th-century domestic life to anyone patient enough to spend an hour following the excellent included audioguide.

Visitors stepping into the house were wowed by the heraldry over the fireplace. This symbol, now repainted in its original bright colors, proclaimed the family's rich lineage and princely stock. The kitchen came with all the circa-1600 conveniences: hay on the floor to add a little warmth and soak up the spillage; a hanging bread cage to keep food away from wandering critters; and a good supply of fresh meat in the pantry. The bedroom of the lady of the house doubled as a sitting room—with a finely carved four-poster bed and a foot warmer by the chair. At night, the bedroom's curtains were drawn to keep in warmth. In the great chamber, hearty evening feasting was followed by boisterous gaming, dancing, and music. And fixed above all of this extravagant entertainment was... more heraldry, pronouncing the important—if unproven—family connections and leaving a powerful impact on impressed guests (£4.50, or £6.50 Joint Ticket with Conwy Castle, April–Aug Tue–Sun 9:30–18:00, closed Mon, shorter hours Sept–Oct, closed Nov–March, tel. 01492/580-167).

St. Mary's Parish Church—Sitting lonely in the center of town, Conwy's church was the centerpiece of a Cistercian abbey that stood here a hundred years before the town. The Cistercians were French monks who built their abbeys in lonely places, "far from the haunts of man." Popular here because they were French and *not* English, the Cistercians taught locals farming and mussel-gathering techniques. Edward moved the monks 12 miles upstream but kept the church for his town. Notice the tombstone of a victim of the Battle of Trafalgar just left of the north transept. On the other side of the church, a tomb containing seven brothers and sisters is marked "We Are Seven." It inspired William Wordsworth to

King Edward's Castles

In the 13th century, the Welsh, under two great princes named Llywelyn, created a united and independent Wales. The English king Edward I fought hard to end this Welsh sovereignty. In 1282, Llywelyn was killed (and went where everyone speaks Welsh). King Edward spent the next 20 years building or rebuilding 17 great castles to consolidate his English foothold in troublesome North Wales. The greatest of these (such as Conwy Castle) were masterpieces of medieval engineering, with round towers (tough to undermine by tunneling), a castle-within-a-castle defense (giving defenders a place to retreat and wreak havoc on the advancing enemy...or just wait for reinforcements), and sea access (safe to stock from England). These were English islands in the middle of angry Wales. Most were built with a fortified grid-plan town attached and were filled with English settlers. (With this blatant abuse of Wales, you have to wonder, where was Greenpeace 700 years ago?) Edward I was arguably England's best monarch. By establishing and consolidating the United Kingdom (adding Wales and Scotland to England), he made his kingdom big enough to compete with the rising European powers.

Castle-lovers will want to tour each of Edward's five greatest castles (see map on page 289). With a car and two days, this makes one of Europe's best castle tours. I'd rate them in this order:

Caernarfon is most entertaining and best presented (page 285).

Conwy is attached to the cutest medieval town and has the best public transport (see page 275).

Harlech is the most dramatic (£3, June–Sept daily 9:30–18:00; April–May and Oct daily 9:30–17:00; Nov–March Mon–Sat 9:30–16:00, Sun 11:00–16:00; tel. 01766/780-552, TI is open Easter–Oct, tel. 01766/780-658).

Beaumaris, surrounded by a swan-filled moat, was the last, largest, and most romantic (£3, June–Sept daily 9:30–18:00; April–May and Oct daily 9:30–17:00; Nov–March Mon–Sat 9:30–16:00, Sun 11:00–16:00; tel. 01248/810-361).

Criccieth (KRICK-ith), built in 1230 by Llywelyn, is also dramatic and remote (£3, same hours as Harlech and Beaumaris, tel. 01766/522-227).

For photos and more information on the castles, as well as information on Welsh historic monuments in general, check www.cadw.wales.gov.uk.

write his poem of the same name. The slate tombstones look new even though many are hundreds of years old. Pure slate weathers better than marble (cemetery always open, church may be staffed June–Aug Mon–Fri 10:00–12:00 & 14:00–16:00).

High Street—Lancaster Square marks the top of Conwy's charming High Street. Its centerpiece is a column honoring the town's founder, the Welsh prince Llywelyn the Great. Find the cute pointed arch built into the medieval wall so the train could get through. Side-trip up York Place (past Alfredo's restaurant) to a wall of slate memorials from the 1937 coronation of King George (his wife, the Queen Consort Elizabeth, is the late Queen Mum). Notice the Welsh lesson here: the counties (shires), months (only *mai* is recognizable), days, numbers, and alphabet with its different letters.

High Street leads down to the harborfront. Wander downhill, enjoying the slice-of-Welsh-life scene: bakery, butcher, newsstand, old timers, and maybe even suds in the fountain. Plas Mawr (on the left), the first Welsh house built within the town walls, dates from the time of Henry VIII (well worth touring, described above). Opposite the Castle Hotel, a lane leads to the Carmel Church. This is a fine example of stark Methodist "statement architecture": stern, with no frills, and typical of these churches built in the early 20th century.

Aberconwy House marks the bottom of High Street. One of the oldest houses in town, it's a museum (not worth touring). Imagine this garrison town filled with half-timbered buildings like this. From here, Barry Street leads left. Originally "burial street," it was a big ditch for mass burials during a 17th-century plague. Continue downhill, crossing under the wall to the harborfront.

▲Harborfront—Still called the King's Quay, the stones date from the 13th century, when the harbor served Edward's castle and town. Conwy was once a busy slate port. Slate, barged downstream to here, was loaded onto big three-masters and shipped off to the Continent. Back when much of Europe was roofed with Welsh slate, Conwy was a boomtown. In 1900, it had 48 pubs. All the mud is new, as the modern bridge caused this part of the river to silt up.

Conwy's harbor is now a laid-back area locals treat like a town square. On summer evenings, the action is on the quay. The scene is mellow, multigenerational, and perfectly Welsh. It's a small town and everyone is here: enjoying the local cuisine—fries, ice cream, and beer—and savoring that great British pastime...torturing little crabs.

Strolling along the harbor from the castle end, you'll find plenty of interest. The harbormaster house fills the former customs building. The lifeboat house welcomes visitors. Each coastal town has a similar house, outfitted with a rescue boat suited to the area—in the shallow waters around Conwy, inflatable boats work best. Mussels, historically a big "crop" for Conwy, are processed "in the months with an r" by the **Mussels Center.** In the other months, it's open to visitors (free). The benches are great for a picnic (two fish-and-chips shops are just around the corner, see "Eating," page 284) or a visit with the noisy gulls. The **Queen Victoria tour boat** departs from here (£4, lazy 30-min cruise, nearly hourly 11:00–17:00 depending on tides, pay on boat, tel. 01492/592-830).

The **Liverpool Arms pub** was built by a captain who ran a ferry service to Liverpool in the 19th century, when the North Wales coast was discovered by English holiday-goers. Today it remains a salty and characteristic hangout. It's easy to miss **The Tiniest House in Britain,** but don't. It's red, 72 inches wide, 122 inches high, and worth 75p to pop in and listen to the short audio-tour. (No WC—but it did have a bedpan.)

From the quay, there's a peaceful half-mile shoreline stroll along the harbor promenade (from tiny house, walk through wall gate and keep going).

Butterfly Jungle—Butterflies flutter in a steamy, lush greenhouse with tropical forest sounds. It's sweet, small, and too humid to linger long (£4, families-£10, ticket valid all day—OK to return, 50p identification chart not necessary because charts posted inside, daily April–Aug 10:00–17:30, Sept–Oct 10:00–15:30, closed Nov–March, follow signs from harbor, nice 5-min walk north, tel. 01492/593-149). If it's not busy, ask the owner why he started a butterfly house.

▲Bodnant Garden—This sumptuous 80-acre display of floral color is six miles south of Conwy. Set in the lush green of Snowdonia, this garden is one of Britain's best. It's famous for its magnolias, rhododendrons, camellias, and floral arch made of bright-yellow laburnum, which blooms late May through June (£5.50, mid-March–Oct daily 10:00–17:00, closed Nov–mid-March, café, best in spring, phone message tells what's blooming, tel. 01492/650-460).

Hill Climb—For lovely views across the bay to Llandudno, take a pleasant walk (40 min one way) along the footpath up Conwy Mount (follow Sychnant Pass Road past the Bryn B&B, look for fields on the right and a sign with a stick-figure of a walker).

SLEEPING

(£1 = about $1.80, country code: 44, area code: 01492)
Conwy has decent budget B&Bs, each located within a few minutes' walk from the bus and train station. There's no launderette in town.

$$$ Castle Hotel in the town center rents 29 elegant rooms where Old World antique furnishings mingle with modern amenities. Owners Peter and Bobbi Lavin are eager to make your stay comfortable (Sb-£70–80, superior Sb-£79–84, Db-£90–110, superior Db-£100–140, posh new suites-£140–300, rates vary with season, 10 percent discount if you show this book when checking in during 2006, non-smoking rooms, High Street, tel. 01492/582-800, fax 01492/582-300, www.castlewales.co.uk, mail@castlewales .co.uk). Award-winning chef Graham Tinsley helps Peter run Shakespeare's Restaurant, a hit with locals and worth the splurge; for a lighter meal, try the hotel bar's bistro (see "Eating," below).

$$$ Castlebank Hotel is a small hotel with nine spacious, newly refurbished rooms and a pleasant lounge and bar (Sb-from £55, Db-from £70, 10 percent discount with this book for 2 or more nights through 2006, family rooms, non-smoking, easy parking, open for evening meals nightly except Tue, just outside town wall at Mount Pleasant, tel. 01492/593-888, www.castlebankhotel .co.uk, bookings@castlebankhotel.co.uk).

$$ Bryn B&B offers four large, clutter-free rooms in a big 19th-century house with the city wall right in the backyard. Owner Alison Archard is proud of her fresh, organic breakfasts and can cater to special diets (Sb-£35, Db-£50, cash only, non-smoking, 1 ground-floor room, parking, immediately outside upper gate of wall, Sychnant Pass Road, tel. 01492/592-449, www.bryn.org.uk).

$$ Fishermore B&B, a 10-minute walk from downtown Conwy, is family-run in a large house with a sprawling yard, sweet garden patio, and three tidy rooms with flowery bedspreads (Db-£47, cash only, closed Oct–Easter, non-smoking rooms, off-road parking available, half-mile south of Conwy on Llanrwst Road, tel. 01492/592-891, www.northwalesbandb.co.uk, dyers@tesco .net, helpful Cath and Peter Dyer).

$$ Bryn Derwen, an eight-minute walk from town, is in a near-mansion atop a hill, set back from a busy road. Its six rooms are bright, white, and cheery (Db-£45, cash only, antlered breakfast room with medieval-type table; exit train station from its furthest and lowest corner, go through gate in city wall to busy road—Woodlands—and turn right, look for sign and climb to hotel; tel. 01492/596-134, www.conwybrynderwen.co.uk, Alan and Wendy).

$$ Glan Heulog Guest House, next door to Bryn Derwen, is also good, with fresh, bright rooms and a pleasant enclosed sun porch. Practice speaking Welsh with your host, Stanley (Sb-£26–30, Db-£42–54, non-smoking, ask about healthy breakfast option, will pick up from train station, tel. 01492/593-845, www .snowdoniabandb.co.uk, info@snowdoniabandb.co.uk, Stanley and Vivien Watson-Jones).

$$ Town House B&B rents six tidy, bright, newly redone rooms—some with views—near the entrance of the castle (S-£30, D-£45, Db-£55, discount with this book in 2006 for 2-night stays, cash only, completely non-smoking, parking, 18 Rosehill Street, tel. 01492/596-454, mobile 0797/465-0609, www.thetownhousebb.co.uk, thetownhousebb@aol.com, friendly Alan and Elaine Naughton).

$$ Gwynfryn B&B rents five newly redone, bright, airy, and clutter-free rooms, each with a DVD player and access to a DVD library. Out back, there's a patio for pleasant breakfasts in good weather (Db-£55–60, cash only, 4 York Place, in alley just off Lancaster Square, near recommended Alfredo's Restaurant, tel. 01492/576-733, www.gwynfrynbandb.co.uk, gwynfrynbb@supanet .com, energetic Monica Leboutillier).

$ Castle View B&B, near the waterfront, rents two cozy, pleasant rooms decorated with warm wood furnishings (D-£36, T-£45, cash only, non-smoking, 3 Berry Street, tel. 01492/596-888, elainepritchard156@hotmail.com, Matthew and Elaine Pritchard).

$$ The Bridge Inn rents five brightly decorated rooms above its pub. While the floor just above the pub is noisy, particularly on weekend nights, the top floor is quieter (Db-from £50 Sun–Thu and from £60 Fri–Sat, discount for 2-night stay, some views, non-smoking, separate entrance from pub, intersection of Rosehill and Castle streets, tel. 01492/573-482).

$ Llys Llywelyn B&B has nine faded rooms, but Alan Hughes' pleasant nature helps compensate (Sb-£28, Db-£45, 10 percent discount with this book in 2006, Internet access in lobby starting at £2, easy parking, ramp from parking lot allows access to 1st-floor rooms, next to Castlebank Hotel—see above, Mount Pleasant, tel. 01492/593-257).

$ The Conwy Hostel, welcoming travelers of any age, has super views from all its rooms (including 4 bunk-bed doubles) and a spacious garden. Each room is equipped with either two or four bunk beds and a shower; toilets are down the hall. The airy dining hall and glorious rooftop deck make you feel like you're in the majestic midst of Wales (Ds-£35–40, bed in Qs-£14 per person, book in advance for doubles, Internet access in lobby, laundry, lockers, dinners, elevator, parking, no lock-out times, 10-min uphill walk from upper gate of Conwy's wall, Larkhill, Sychnant Pass Road, tel. 01492/593-571, fax 01492/593-580, conwy@yha.org.uk).

EATING

For dinner, stroll down High Street, comparing the cute teahouses and smoky pubs. At the top, on Lancaster Square, is **Alfredo's Restaurant,** a family-friendly place serving good and reasonable

Italian food (nightly from 18:00, last orders at 22:00, reservations recommended, tel. 01492/592-381, Christine).

For a splurge, try **Shakespeare's Restaurant** (£20 meals, daily for dinner, also Sun for lunch, reservations smart, at recommended Castle Hotel on High Street, tel. 01492/582-800). For lighter bistro-style meals, try the adjoining hotel bar, **Dawson's** (daily 12:00–21:30).

Town House Restaurant serves modern English cuisine in a romantic candlelit setting (£17 dinners, Mon–Sat 10:00–16:00 & 18:30–21:00, Sun only 10:00–16:00, High Street, reservations wise, tel. 01492/596-436).

Conwy Pantry has cheap, hearty daily lunch specials and homemade sweets (daily 9:00–17:00, 26 High Street, tel. 01492/592-436).

At the bottom of High Street, two fish-and-chips joints—**Galleon's** (daily) and **Fisherman's** (daily, closed Mon off-season)—both brag that they're the best (Fisherman's probably is). Consider taking your fish-and-chips down to the harbor and sharing it with the noisy seagulls.

Locals like **Anna's Tea Rooms,** located upstairs in the Conwy Outdoor Shop (daily 10:00–17:00, near Fisherman's fish-and-chips, 9 Castle Street, tel. 01492/580-908).

The busy **Bistro Conwy,** tucked away on Chapel Street, serves freshly prepared modern and traditional Welsh cuisine in a cozy wood-floor and candlelit setting. The menu (with tasty daily specials) is a delight and the food must be the best in town (£13–16 entrées with vegetables, potato, and salad, Tue–Sat 18:30–21:00, closed Sun–Mon, reservations a must, tel. 01492/596-326).

Theatre Bistro dishes up continental cuisine with an up-to-date twist in a relaxed loft space off High Street (£9–14 meals, daily 12:00–14:30 & 18:00–21:00, closed Wed, tel. 01492/581-942, www.theatrebistro.net).

The smoky **Bridge Inn,** at the intersection of Rosehill and Castle streets, serves decent grub (daily 12:00–14:30 & 18:00–20:00).

For picnic fixings, try the **Spar** grocery (daily 7:00–22:00, top of High Street).

TRANSPORTATION CONNECTIONS

Be proactive whether taking the bus or train; let the driver or conductor know you want to stop at Conwy. Consider getting train times and connections for your onward journey at a bigger station before you get to Conwy. For train information in town, ask at the TI or call 08457-484-950. If you want to depart Conwy by train, flag down the train. For a quick pick of more frequent trains, go to Llandudno Junction (catch a bus, take a £2.50 taxi, or walk a mile).

From Conwy to: Llandudno Junction (1 bus/hr, 5 min; 4 trains/day, 5 min), **Caernarfon** (at least 2 buses/hr, 1.5 hrs), **Trefriw–Betws-y-Coed–Penygwryd–Llanberis** (bus #19, 1/hr in summer).

From Llandudno Junction by Train to: Chester (2/hr, 1 hr), **Birmingham** (2/hr, 2.5 hrs, some with change in Crewe), **London's Euston Station** (1/hr, 3.5 hrs, most with 1 change).

Caernarfon

The small and lively little town of Caernarfon (kah-NAR-von) is famous for its striking castle—the place where the Prince of Wales is "invested." Like Conwy, it was an Edward I garrison town marching out from the castle. It still follows the original medieval grid plan laid within its well-preserved ramparts.

But Caernarfon is mostly a 19th-century town. At that time, the most important thing in town wasn't the castle but the area—now a parking lot—that sprawls below the castle. This was once a booming slate port, shipping tidy bundles of slate from North Wales mining towns to roofs all over Europe.

The statue of local boy David Lloyd George looks over the town square. A member of parliament from 1890 to 1945, he was the most important politician Wales ever sent to London and ultimately became Britain's prime minister. Boy George began his career as a noisy nonconformist liberal advocating Welsh rights. He ended up an eloquent spokesperson for the notion of Great Britain, convincing his slate-mining constituents that only as part of the Union would their slate industry boom.

Caernarfon bustles with shops, cafés, and people. Market-day activities fill its main square on Saturdays year-round; a smaller, sleepy market yawns on Monday from late May to September. The charming grid-plan medieval town is worth a wander.

ORIENTATION

Tourist Information: The TI, across from the castle entrance, has a wonderful free town map/guide (with a good self-guided town walk) and train and bus schedules. They sell hiking books, and book rooms here and elsewhere for a £1 fee (daily April–Oct 9:30–17:00, Nov–March 10:00–13:00 & 14:00–16:30, tel. 01286/672-232).

Arrival in Caernarfon: If you arrive by bus, walk a few steps to Bridge Street, then go left on Bridge Street until you hit the main square (with a post office) and the castle. The TI faces the castle entrance. Public WCs are off the main square, on the road down to the harbor parking lot. Drivers pay £2.50 to park below the castle.

Helpful Hints

Internet Access: Get wired at Dylan Thomas Internet Café (Mon–Sat 9:00–18:00, closed Sun, 4 Bangor Street, across from Turf Square, near bus stop, tel. 01286/678-777).

Launderette: Pete's Laundromat is on Skinner Street (Mon–Sat 9:00–17:30, Sun 11:00–17:30, same-day full-service-£5/load, self-service-£4/load, near bus stop, tel. 01286/678-395).

Bike Rental: Try Cycle Hire on the harbor (£10/half-day, £14/day, long-term rental discounts, tel. 01286/676-804).

Local Guide: Donna "Caernarfon is more than a castle" Goodman leads historic walks almost nightly through the season (£3.50, 1.5 hours), as well as day trips of the area (for private hire-£180/day—book a few days in advance, tel. 01286/677-059 for her schedule, mobile 07946-163-906, info@turnstonetours .co.uk).

SIGHTS

▲▲**Caernarfon Castle**—Edward I built this impressive castle 700 years ago to establish English rule over North Wales. Modeled after the striped and angular walls of ancient Constantinople, the castle—while impressive—was never finished and never really used. From the inner courtyard, you can see the notched walls ready for more walls that were never built. Its fame is due to its physical grandeur and from its association with the Prince of Wales. The English king got the angry Welsh to agree that if he presented them with "a prince, born in Wales, who spoke not a word of English," they would submit to the crown. In time, Edward had a son born in Wales, who spoke not a word of English, Welsh, or any other language—as an infant. In modern times, as another political maneuver, the Prince of Wales has been "invested" (given his title) here. This "tradition" actually dates only from the 20th century, and only two of 21 Princes of Wales have taken part.

In spite of its disappointing history, it's a great castle to tour. An essential part of any visit is the guided tour (50-min tours for £1.50 leave on the hour—and occasionally on the half hour—from the courtyard steps just beyond the ticket booth; if you're late, ask to join one in progress). In the huge Eagle Tower (on the seaward side), see the *Chieftains and Princes* history exhibit (ground floor), watch the 20-minute movie (a broad mix of Welsh legend and history, shown on the hour and half hour, upstairs, comfortable theater seats), and climb the tower for a great view. In the nearby Queen's Tower, you'll find several semi-interesting videos of various British battles, firearms, and military strategies. The northeast tower, at the opposite end of the castle, has an exhibit about the investiture of Prince Charles in 1969.

Cost and Hours: £4.75, June–Sept daily 9:30–18:00, April–May and Oct daily 9:30–17:00, Nov–March Mon–Sat 9:30–16:00, Sun 11:00–16:00, tel. 01286/677-617. Martin de Lewandowicz gives mind-bending tours of the castle (tel. 01286/674-369).

Distractions—A Welsh Highland **steam train** billows through the countryside to Rhyd Ddu and back (£9 round-trip to Waunfawr, 1.5 hrs; £16 round-trip to Rhyd Ddu, 2 hrs; March–Oct daily, 4/day, tel. 01766/516-000, www.festrail .co.uk).

Narrated **harbor cruises** on the *Queen of the Sea* run daily in summer (June–Sept 11:30–18:00 or 19:00, depending on weather, tides, and demand; 40 min, castle views, tel. 01286/672-772).

The **Segontium Roman Fort,** dating from A.D. 77, is the westernmost Roman fort. It was manned for more than 300 years to keep the Welsh and the coast quiet. Little is left but foundations (free, Tue–Sun 12:30–16:30, closed Mon, tel. 01286/675-625).

For **pony riding,** try Snowdonia Riding Stables (£15/1 hr, longer and shorter time available, 3 miles from Caernarfon, off the road to Beddgelert, bus #89 or #95 from Caernarfon, tel. 01286/650-342).

Welsh Choir—If spending a Tuesday night, drop by the local men's choir practice (Tue 19:45–21:30 at Conservative Club on Castle Street, except Aug).

SLEEPING

(£1 = about $1.80, country code: 44, area code: 01286)
$$$ Celtic Royal Hotel rents 110 comfortable rooms with a gym, pool, Jacuzzi, and sauna. Its grand, old-fashioned look comes with modern-day conveniences—but it's still overpriced (Db-£110–136, non-smoking rooms, bar, restaurant; it's a 5-min walk from bus stop: go right on Bridge Street, which turns into Bangor Street; on Bangor Street, tel. 01286/674-477, fax 01286/674-139, www .celtic-royal.co.uk).

$$ Caer Menai B&B rents seven bright, attractive rooms and prepares evening meals as well as breakfast (Db-£52–55, family room-£70–80, ask for harbor view room, cash only, non-smoking, 15 Church Street, tel. 01286/672-612, www.caermenai.co.uk, info @caermenai.co.uk, John and Sandy Price).

$$ Victoria House B&B, next door to the Caer Menai, rents five airy, fresh, large-for-Britain rooms (Db-£50, cash only, non-smoking, 14 Church Street, tel. 01286/678-263, www .thevictoriahouse.co.uk, jan@thevictoriahouse.co.uk, friendly Jan Baker).

$ Totters Hostel is a creative little hostel well run by Bob and Henriette (28 beds in 5 dorm rooms, £13 per bed with sheets, includes continental breakfast, cash only, couples can have their own room when available-£30, open all day, lockers, welcoming game room/lounge, free kitchen, a block from castle at 2 High Street, tel. 01286/672-963, mobile 07979-830-470, www.totters .co.uk, bob@totters.free-online.co.uk).

EATING

You'll find charming cafés and bistros lining "Hole-in-the-Wall Street" (between Castle Square and TI), and plenty of cheap and cheery sandwich shops and tearooms on nearby High Street. **J&C's**, a fish-and-chips joint, is one block from the main square on Pool Street. The most convenient supermarket is **Farm Foods** (Mon–Sat 9:00–18:00, Thu–Fri until 19:00, Sun 10:00–16:00, Pool Street). Kwik Save and a larger Safeway are a five-minute walk from the city center on Bangor Street.

TRANSPORTATION CONNECTIONS

From Caernarfon by Bus to: Conwy (2/hr, hrly on Sun, 1.25 hrs), **Llanberis** (2/hr, 30 min), **Beddgelert** (1/hr, 30 min), **Blaenau Ffestiniog** (1/hr, 1.5 hrs), **Beddgelert–Penygwryd–Llanberis** (bus #95, every 2 hrs, 1.5 hrs, June–Sept only). Buy tickets from the driver.

Snowdonia National Park

This is Britain's second-largest national park, and its centerpiece— the tallest mountain in England and Wales—is Mount Snowdon. Each year, half a million people ascend one of seven different paths to the top of 3,560-foot Snowdon (the small £2 book *The Ascent of Snowdon*, by E. G. Bowland, describes the routes sold by local TIs). Hikes take from five to seven hours. If you're fit and the weather's good, it's an exciting day. Trail info abounds. As you explore, notice the slate roofs—the local specialty.

Snowdonia Area

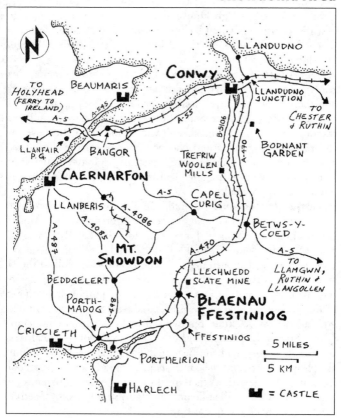

SIGHTS

Betws-y-Coed—The resort center of Snowdonia National Park, Betws-y-Coed (BET-oos-uh-coyd) bursts with tour buses and souvenir shops, but remains picturesque. Its good national park office, TI, and guided walks make a stop worthwhile (daily April–Oct 9:30–17:30, Nov–March 9:30–12:30 & 13:30–16:30, tel. 01690/710-426). Consider a long but not strenuous guided walk in the hills (£3.50, April–early Sept Thu–Sun, check TI for departure place/time, 6- to 8-mile hike, see list of walks going that day or call Robin Hamlett to book with him: Mon–Tue call tel. 0151/488-0052, Wed–Sat 17:00–19:00 call mobile 07790-851-333). Trains run from Llandudno Junction near Conwy through Betws-y-Coed to Blaenau Ffestiniog (6/day).

Nearby: If you drive west out of town on A5, after two miles you'll see the car park for scenic **Swallow Falls,** a pleasant five-minute walk from the road. A half-mile past the falls on the right, you'll see **The Ugly House,** built overnight to take advantage of a 15th-century law that let any quickie building avoid fees and taxes. Buses connect Conwy and Betws-y-Coed (with a change, 1/hr June–Aug, 50 min).

▲**Ewe-Phoria Sheepdog Show**—Despite the goofy name, this really is a fun and fascinating peek into the world of sheep farmers and their frantically loyal, well-trained dogs. Drop in for one of two daily shows (Easter–Sept 11:00 and 13:00). First, you'll see the dogs rounding up the sheep (who seem to roll their eyes at this polished demonstration); then you'll head into the barn to see a sheep show and shearing (£4.50, just off A5 mid-way between Betws-y-Coed and Llangollen in Llamgwm, tel. 01490/460-369, www.ewe-phoria.co.uk).

▲**Trefriw Woolen Mills**—The mill in Trefriw (TREV-roo), five miles north of Betws-y-Coed, is free and surprisingly interesting if the machines are running (June–Sept Mon–Sat 9:30–17:30, closed Sun; Oct–May Mon–Fri 10:00–17:00, closed Sat–Sun; off-season only weaving is demonstrated, tel. 01492/640-462). Follow the 11 stages of wool transformation: warping, weaving, carding, hanking, spanking, spinning, and so on. The hand-spinning house (next to the WC) has a charming spinster and a petting cupboard filled with all the various kinds of raw wool that can be spun into cloth (June–Sept only, Mon–Fri 10:00–17:00). Silkworms are also at work (and on display) here. Be sure to enjoy the fine woolen shop, the pleasant town, and the coffee shop. The grade school next door is rambunctious with Welsh-speaking kids—fun to listen to at recess. The woolen mill at Penmachno (also near Betws-y-Coed) is smaller and much less interesting.

▲**Beddgelert**—This is the quintessential Snowdon village, packing a scenic mountain punch without the tourist crowds (17 miles from Betws-y-Coed). Set on a river in the shadow of Snowdon and her sisters, with a fine variety of hikes from its doorstep and pretty good bus service, Beddgelert (BETH-geh-lert) makes a good stop for those wanting to experience the peace of Snowdonia. The Glaslyn Homemade Ice Cream shop offers surprising quality and selection for this altitude. (TI: April–Oct daily 9:30–17:30; Nov–March Fri–Sun 9:30–16:30—but closes for lunch, closed Mon–Thu, tel. 01766/890-615.)

Locals can recommend walks. You can follow the lane along the river (3 miles round-trip), walk down the river and around the hill (3 hrs, 6 miles, 900-foot gain, via Cwm Bycham), hike along (or around) Llyn Gwynant Lake and four miles back to Beddgelert (ride the bus to the lake), or try the dramatic ridge walks on Moel Hebog (Hawk Hill).

How Beddgelert Got its Name

Prince Llywelyn, who had a dog named Gelert, went hunting one day, leaving his baby son with his dog. When the prince came home, he found the crib overturned and blood everywhere. The prince immediately drew his sword and killed the dog. In that instant, he heard a baby crying from under the crib. He turned the crib over and found the baby. Nearby, a dead wolf lay in the corner. The prince realized that his faithful dog Gelert had killed the preying wolf to protect the baby. He buried Gelert in a grave (*bedd* in Welsh).

Actually, the town is named for a 6th-century saint. Years ago, some clever entrepreneur invented the canine legend and set up a fake grave to attract visitors. To this day, local kids love to spy on gullible tourists mourning at the grave.

Sleeping in Beddgelert: **$$$ Royal Goat Hotel** offers well-worn, chandeliered, woody elegance in a grand hotel built for the rugged 19th-century aristocrat (Sb-£53, Db-£90, 10 percent discount with this book in 2006, tel. 01766/890-224, fax 01766/890-422, www.royalgoathotel.co.uk).

$$ Plas Tan Y Graig Guest House, at the village bridge, is newly refurbished and lovingly maintained (Db-£45–60 depending on room, family room, fine lounge, tea garden, tel. 01766/890-310, fax 01766/890-329, http://plas-tanygraig.co.uk).

$$ Plas Colwyn Guest House is a bigger place nearby (D-£46, Db-£54, bed only-from £17 per person, tel. 01766/890-458, www.plascolwyn.co.uk, info@plascolwyn.co.uk).

$$ Plas Gwyn Guest House, also just over the bridge, rents six rooms in a cozy, cheery, 19th-century town house with a comfy lounge (S-£27, Db-£54, 10 percent discount with this book in 2006, family deals, cash only, non-smoking, tel. 01766/890-215, www.plas-gwyn.com, bandb@beddgelert.fsbusiness.co.uk, friendly Brian Wheatley).

$ Beddgelert Antiques, Tea Rooms, and B&B is juggled by Sheila Johnson Porter in a 300-year-old house that's cramped and creaky, but clean (Db-£46, snug bistro bar, tel. 01766/890-543, beddgelertbistro@hotmail.com).

Sleeping and Eating near Beddgelert: Mountaineers note that this area was used by Sir Edmund Hillary and his men as they practiced for the first ascent of Mount Everest. **$$$ Pen Y Gwryd Hotel Pub,** at the top of the pass north of Beddgelert, is strewn with fascinating memorabilia from Hillary's 1953 climb (D-£60, Db-£72, cash only, saggy beds, smoky, old-time-elegant public rooms, D rooms have museum-piece Victorian tubs and showers, grand 5-course dinners-£20, tel. 01286/870-211, www.pyg.co.uk). With its crampon ambience, it's ideal for well-bred hikers.

Llanberis—A town of 2,000 people with as many tourists on a sunny day, Llanberis is a popular base for Snowdon activities. Along with the station for the Snowdon train, it has a good information center, a few touristy museums, pony trekking, and good bus connections (1 bus/hr to Beddgelert, 45 min). To explore an old slate mine frozen in time, stop by the free Welsh Slate Museum to catch the giant water wheel and the slate-splitting demo (Easter–Oct daily 10:00–17:00, Nov–Easter Sun–Fri 10:00–16:00, closed Sat, last entry 1 hour before closing).

Sleeping in Llanberis: **$$ Dolafon Hotel** is an 1860s Victorian building with seven traditionally furnished rooms (Db-£56–75, non-smoking, garden, High Street, tel. & fax 01286/870-993, www.dolafon.com).

▲▲**Mount Snowdon and the Mountain Railway**—The easiest and most popular ascent of Mount Snowdon is by the Snowdon Mountain Railway, a rack-and-pinion railway from 1896 that climbs 3,500 feet more than 4.5 miles from Llanberis to the summit. On the way up, you'll hear a constant narration on legends, geology, and history. On the way down, there's only engine noise (£20 round-trip, 2.5 hrs, includes 30-min stop at the top, tel. 0870-458-0033, www.snowdonrailway.co.uk).

The first departure is often at 9:00 (and is half-price except in July–Aug). While the schedule flexes with weather and demand, they try to run several trips each day mid-March through October (2/hr in peak season). On sunny summer days, trains fill up (office opens at 9:00, waits are longer in the afternoon, arrive by lunchtime and get a departure appointment time—usually a wait of 1–2 hours, reservations possible a day in advance). Off-season trains often stop short of the summit (due to snow and high winds).

Blaenau Ffestiniog

Blaenau Ffestiniog (BLIGH-nigh FES-tin-yog) is a quintessential Welsh slate-mining town, notable for its slate-mine tour and its old steam train. The town—a dark, poor place—seems to struggle on, oblivious to the tourists who nip in and out. Take a walk. The shops are right out of the 1950s. Long rows of humble "two-up and two-down" houses (4 rooms) feel pretty grim. There are some buses from the town to the slate mines; the road isn't pedestrian friendly.

Tourist Information: Easter–Oct daily 9:30–12:30 & 13:30–17:30, closed Nov–Easter, tel. 01766/830-360.

SIGHTS

In Blaenau Ffestiniog

▲▲Llechwedd Slate-Mine Tour—Slate mining played a block-buster role in Welsh heritage, and this mine on the northern edge of Blaenau Ffestiniog does a fine job of explaining the mining culture of Victorian Wales. The Welsh mined and split most of the slate roofs of Europe. For every ton of usable slate found, 10 tons were mined. The exhibit has three parts: a tiny Victorian mining town (with a miners' pub and a view from "The Top of the Tip," free and worthwhile) and two 30-minute tours (3/hr). Do the

"tramway" tour first—a level train ride with three stops, no walking, and a live guide. It focuses on working life and traditional mining techniques. Plan to stay for the cool slate-splitting demonstration, which occurs only at certain times (often 11:00, 13:00, 15:00, and 16:30). Then descend into the "deep mine" for a tour featuring an audiovisual dramatization of social life and a half-mile of walking. Both tours are different and, considering the cheap combo-ticket, worthwhile (£8.75 for 1 tour, £13 for both tours, daily March–Sept 10:00–18:00, Oct–Feb 10:00–17:00, last tour starts 45 min before closing, tel. 01766/830-306, www.llechwedd -slate-caverns.co.uk).

Dress warmly—I mean it. You'll freeze underground without a sweater. Lines are longer when rain drives in the hikers.

▲Ffestiniog Railway—This 13-mile narrow-gauge train line was built in 1836 for small horse-drawn wagons to transport the slate from the Ffestiniog mines to the port of Porthmadog. In the 1860s, horses gave way to steam trains. Today, hikers and tourists enjoy these tiny titans (£16 round-trip, 1/hr in peak season, 2.5 hours round-trip, first-class observation cars cost £5 extra, during midweek the first trains of the day are £3.50 cheaper, tel. 01766/516-000). This is a novel steam-train experience, but the full-size Llandudno–Blaenau Ffestiniog train is more scenic and works better for hikers.

Near Blaenau Ffestiniog

Portmeirion—Ten miles southwest of Blaenau Ffestiniog, this "Italian Village" was the lifework of a rich local architect who began building it in 1925. Set idyllically on the coast just beyond the poverty of the slate-mine towns, this flower-filled fantasy is extravagant. Surrounded by lush Welsh greenery and a windswept mudflat at low tide, the village is an artistic glob of palazzo arches, fountains, gardens, and promenades filled with cafés, tacky shops, a hotel, and local tourists who always wanted to go to Italy (or who are fans of the cultish British 1960s TV series *The Prisoner*). The architect explains his purpose in a videotaped slide presentation (not worth the £6 admission, daily 9:30–17:30, 2 miles from Porthmadog, tel. 01766/770-000).

TRANSPORTATION CONNECTIONS

North Wales

Two major transfer points out of (or into) North Wales are Crewe and Chester. Figure out your complete connection at www .nationalrail.co.uk.

From Crewe by Train to: London (2/hr, 2 hrs), **Bristol,** near Bath (1/hr, 2.5 hrs), **Cardiff** (1/hr, 2.5 hrs), **Holyhead** (nearly 1/hr, 2 hrs), **Blackpool** (4/day, 2.5 hrs, more frequent with transfer in Preston), **Keswick** in the Lake District (1/hr, 1.75 hrs to Penrith, then catch a bus to Keswick, 1/hr except Sun 6/day, 40 min), **Glasgow** (nearly 1/hr, 3.5 hrs).

From Chester by Train to: London (1/hr, 3.5 hrs), **Liverpool** (2/hr, 50 min), **Birmingham** (1/hr, 2 hrs); points in North Wales including **Conwy** (almost hrly, 1 hr, some with transfer in Llandudno Junction).

Ferry Connections between North Wales and Ireland

Holyhead and Dun Laoghaire: Stena Line sails between Holyhead (North Wales) and Dun Laoghaire near Dublin (3/day, 2 hrs, one-way walk-on fare-£32, extra to use credit card, reserve by phone or online—they book up long in advance on summer weekends, Dun Laoghaire tel. 01/204-7777—dial 00-353-1-204-7777 from Britain, Holyhead tel. 01407/606-606, general reservations number for Stena Line in Britain tel. 08705-707-070, can book online at www.stenaline.com).

Holyhead and Dublin: Irish Ferries sail between Holyhead (North Wales) and Dublin (5/day—2 slow, 3 fast; slow boats 3.25 hrs, one-way walk-on fare-£22–25, price depends on month; fast boats 2 hrs, £28–32, price depends on month, reserve online for best fares; car fares prohibitively expensive, Britain tel. 08705-329-129, Dublin tel. 01/638-3333—dial 00-353-1-638-3333 from Britain, www.irishferries.co.uk).

Sleeping near Holyhead Dock: Both places are a 15-minute uphill walk from the dock. The fine **$ Monravon B&B** has seven non-smoking rooms (Db-£44–50, family deals, Porth-Y-Felin Road, tel. & fax 01407/762-944, www.monravon.co.uk, len@monravon.co.uk). **$ Orotavia B&B** is family-run, with three rooms (S-£20, D-£40–45, 66 Walthew Avenue, tel. 01407/760-259, www.orotavia.co.uk, shirley@orotavia.co.uk, Shirley and Martin Williams).

Route Tips for Drivers

Ironbridge Gorge to Ruthin: Drive for an hour to Wales via A5 through Shrewsbury, crossing into Wales and following A5 to Llangollen. Cross the bridge in Llangollen, turn left, and follow A542 and A525 past the romantic Valle Crucis abbey, over the scenic Horseshoe Pass, and into Ruthin. Driving to Conwy is faster via Wrexham and then A55, but more scenic if you stay on the A5 from Llangollen to Betws-y-Coed and then zip north to Conwy from there.

Ruthin to Caernarfon (56 miles) to Blaenau Ffestiniog (34 miles) to Ruthin (35 miles): This route connects the top sights with the most scenic routes. From Ruthin, take B5105 (steepest road off main square) and follow signs to Cerrigydrudion. Then follow A5 into Betws-y-Coed, with a possible quick detour to the Trefriw Woolen Mills (5 miles north on B5106, well signposted). Climb west on A5 through Capel Curig, then take A4086 over the rugged Pass of Llanberis, under the summit of Mount Snowdon (to the south, behind those clouds), and on to Caernarfon. Park under the castle in the harborside car park (£2.50).

Leaving Caernarfon, take the lovely A4085 southeast through Beddgelert to Penrhyndeudraeth. (Make things even more beautiful by taking the little B4410 road from Garreg through Rhyd.) Then take A487 toward What Maentwrog and A496 to Blaenau Ffestiniog. Go through the dark and depressing mining town of Blaenau Ffestiniog on A470, continue over hills of slate, and turn right into the Llechwedd Slate Mine.

After the mine, continue uphill on A470, snapping photos north through Dolwyddelan (passing a fine old Welsh castle ruin) and back to A5. For a high and desolate detour, return to Ruthin via the curvy A543 road. Go over the stark moors to the Sportsman's Arms Pub (the highest pub in Wales, good food), continue through Denbigh, and then go home.

BLACKPOOL
AND LIVERPOOL

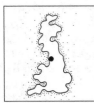

These two bustling cities—wedged between serene North Wales and the even-more-serene Lake District—provide an opportunity to sample the "real" England, both at work (Liverpool) and at play (Blackpool). Scream down roller coasters and eat "candy floss" until you're deliriously queasy at fun-loving Blackpool. In Liverpool, experience industrial England and relive the early mop-top days of some famous Liverpudlians...meet the Beatles.

Blackpool

Blackpool is Britain's fun puddle. It's one of England's most-visited attractions, the private domain of its working class, a faded and sticky mix of Coney Island, Las Vegas, and Woolworths. Juveniles of any age love it. My kids declared it better than Disneyland.

Blackpool grew up with the Industrial Revolution. In the mid-1800s, entire mill towns would close down and take a two-week break here. They came to drink in the fresh air (much needed after a hard year in the mills) and—literally—the seawater. Back then they figured it was healthy.

Blackpool's heyday is past now, as more and more working people can afford the cheap charter flights to sunny Spain. Recently, the resort has become popular for "stag" and "hen" (bachelor and bachelorette) parties—basically a cheap drunk weekend for the twenty-something crowd. Consequently, the late-night ambience can suffer on weekends. Within a couple of years, Blackpool will probably add a few casinos and draw more crowds. No matter what, the town remains an accessible and affordable fun zone for the Flo and Andy Capps of northern England. People come year after year. They stay for a week, and they love it.

Most Americans don't even consider a stop in Blackpool. Many won't like it. It's an ears-pierced-while-you-wait, tipsy-toupee kind of place. Tacky, yes. Lowbrow, OK. But it's as English as can be, and that's what you're here for. An itinerary should feature as many facets of a culture as possible. Blackpool is as English as the queen—and considerably more fun.

Spend the day "muckin' about" the beach promenade of fortune-tellers, fish-and-chips joints, amusement piers, warped mirrors, and Englanders wearing hats with built-in ponytails. A million greedy doors try every trick to get you inside. Huge arcade halls advertise free toilets and broadcast bingo numbers into the streets; the wind machine under a wax Marilyn Monroe blows at a steady gale; and the smell of fries, tobacco, and sugar is everywhere. Milk comes in raspberry or banana in this land where people under incredibly bad wigs look normal. If you're bored in Blackpool, you're just too classy.

Planning Your Time

Ideally, get to Blackpool around lunchtime for a free afternoon and evening of making bubbles in this cultural mud puddle. For full effect, it's best to visit during peak season: June through early November.

Blackpool's Illuminations, when much of the waterfront is decorated with lights, draws crowds in fall, particularly on weekends (Sept 1–Nov 5 in 2006). The early-evening light is great with the sun setting over the sea. Walk out along the peaceful North Pier at twilight.

Blackpool is easy by car or train. Speed demons with a car can treat it as a midday break (it's just off M6 on M55) and continue north. If you have kids, they'll want more time here (hey, it's cheaper than Disneyland). If you're into nightlife, this town delivers. If you're before or beyond kids and not into kitsch and greasy spoons, skip it. If the weather's great and you love nature, the lakes are just a few hours north. A visit to Blackpool does sharpen the wonders of Windermere.

ORIENTATION

(area code: 01253)

Everything clusters along the six-mile beachfront promenade, a tacky, glittering good-time strip mall punctuated by three fun-filled piers reaching out into the sea. The Pleasure Beach rides are near the South Pier. Jutting up near the North Pier is Blackpool's

Blackpool

stubby Eiffel-type tower. The most interesting shops, eateries, and theaters are inland from the North Pier. For a break from glitz, you can hike north along the waterfront path for 20 miles or so.

Tourist Information

There are two TIs near the tower. The main one is on Clifton Street (April–early Nov Mon–Sat 9:00–17:00, closed Sun, £1.50 fee to book shows, tel. 01253/478-222—the same number gives recorded entertainment info after hours, www.blackpooltourism .com). The other TI is on The Promenade (June–early Nov daily 9:30–17:00, closed off-season).

At either TI, get the city map (£1), pick up brochures on the amusement centers, and ask about special shows. The *What's On* booklet listing local events costs £1.75. If you're doing the amusement blitz, buy your tickets at the TI for Sandcastle and the Blackpool Tower to save a few pounds. Both TIs do same-day room bookings for one-night stays for a £3 fee (room-finding service closes at 16:30).

For a history fix, get the TI's *Heritage Trail* booklet, which takes you on an hour's walk through downtown Blackpool. Saying much about little, it's endearing (60p).

Arrival in Blackpool

The main (north) train station is three blocks from the town center (no maps given but one is posted, no ATM in station but many in town). While the station has no luggage lockers, nearby hotels offer the service. If arriving by car, the motorway funnels you down Yeadon Way into a giant parking zone.

Helpful Hints

Markets: At the **Abingdon Market,** vendors sell fruit, bras, jewelry, eggs, and more (Mon–Sat 9:00–17:30, closed Sun, on Abingdon Street next to P.O.). The **Fleetwood Market,**

eight miles north, is huge, with two buildings full of produce, clothes, and crafts spilling out into the street (May–Oct Mon–Tue and Thu–Sat 9:30–16:30, closed Wed and Sun; Nov–April Tue, Fri, and Sat only; catch tram marked *Fleetwood*, 30 min, £2 one-way).

Tipping: The pubs of Blackpool have a unique tradition of "and your own, luv." Say that here and your barmaid will add 20p to your bill and drop it into her tip jar. (Say it anywhere else and they won't know what you mean.)

Internet Access: Try the public library in the big domed building on Queen Street (Mon–Sat 9:00–17:00, Tue and Thu until 19:00, closed Sun, 24 computers, tel. 01253/478-111).

Post Office: The main P.O. is on Abingdon Street, a block inland from the TI (Mon–Sat 9:00–17:30, closed Sun).

Car Rental: In case you decide to tour the Lake District by car, you'll find plenty of rental agencies in Blackpool (closed Sat afternoon and Sun), including **Avis** (292 Waterloo Road, tel. 01253/408-003) and **Budget** (242 Waterloo Road, tel. 01253/691-632).

Getting Around Blackpool

Vintage and zippy bus-like **tram cars** run 13 miles up and down the waterfront, connecting all the sights. This first electric tramway in Europe dates from 1885 (£1.20–2.50 depending on length of trip, £5.25 for all-day pass, pay conductor, trams come every 5 min or so, Nov–May every 10–20 min, runs 6:00–24:00).

A City Sightseeing **hop-on, hop-off bus tour** with a recorded commentary and 16 stops leaves the Blackpool Tower every 15–30 minutes (£5, June–early Nov from 9:30, last departure at 20:00, doesn't run off-season, www.city-sightseeing.com).

Taxis are easy to snare in Blackpool, and three to five people travel cheaper by cab than by tram. Hotels can get a taxi by phone within three minutes (no extra charge).

SIGHTS

▲▲**The Piers**—Blackpool's famous piers were originally built for Victorian landlubbers who wanted to go to sea but were afraid of getting seasick. Each of the three amusement piers has a personality and is a joy to wander. The sedate North Pier is most traditional and refreshingly uncluttered. Dance down its empty planks at twilight to the early English rock on its speakers. Its Carousel Bar at the end is great for families—with a free kids' DJ nightly from 20:30 to 23:00 (parents drink good beer while the kids bunny-hop and boogie). The something-for-everyone Central Pier is lots of fun. Ride its great Ferris wheel for the best view in Blackpool (rich photography at twilight, get the operator to spin you as you bottom out). And check out the masochist running the adjacent Waltzer ride—just watch the miserably ecstatic people spinning. The rollicking South Pier is all rides. From the far end of any pier, you can see the natural-gas drilling platforms lining the horizon.

▲**Blackpool Tower**—This mini-Eiffel Tower is a 100-year-old vertical fun center. You pay £12 to get in (less on weekdays, tickets cheaper at TI every day); after that, the fun is free. Work your way up from the bottom through layer after layer of noisy enter-

tainment: a circus (2–3 acts/day, generally at 15:00 and 19:00), Out of This World, a dinosaur ride, an aquarium, and a wonderful old ballroom with barely live music and golden oldies dancing to golden oldies all day. Enjoy a break at the dance-floor-level pub or on a balcony perch. Kids love this place. With a little marijuana, adults would, too. Ride the glass elevator to the tip of the 500-foot-tall symbol of Blackpool for a smashing view, especially at sunset (Easter–May daily 10:00–18:00, June–early Nov daily 10:00–23:00, early Nov–Easter weekends only 10:00–18:00, top of tower closed when windy, tel. 01253/292-029, www.theblackpooltower .co.uk). If you want to leave and return, request a hand stamp.

▲**Pleasure Beach**—These 42 acres, littered with more than 100 rides (including "the best selection of white-knuckle rides in Europe"), ice-skating, circus and illusion shows, and amusements, attract seven million people a year. The top two rides are The Pepsi Max Big One (one of the world's fastest and highest roller coasters at 235 feet, 85 mph) and Ice Blast (which rockets you straight up before letting you bungee down). Also memorable are the Pasaje del Terror and the Steeple Chase—carousel horses stampeding down a roller-coaster track. The Irn-Bru Revolution speeds you over a steep

drop and upside-down in a loop, then does it again backwards. The Valhalla ride zips you on a Viking boat in watery darkness past scary Nordic things like lutefisk. With two 80-foot drops and lots of hype, first you're scared, then you're soaked, and—finally—you're just glad you survived. Most of the rides are variations on the roller-coaster theme. Pleasure Beach medics advise brittle senior travelers to avoid the old wooden-framed rides, which are much jerkier. Only the admission is free. You can pay individually for rides with your £1 tickets (most are a few tickets each), or get unlimited rides with a £30 armband (armbands a few pounds cheaper if purchased in advance on their Web site, not available from TI; daily March–early Nov, opens at about 10:30 and closes as early as 17:00 or as late as 24:00, depending on season, weather, and demand; tel. 0870-444-5566, www.blackpoolpleasurebeach.co.uk).

Sandcastle—The popular water park, across the street from Pleasure Beach, has a big pool, long slides, and a wave machine (£9, kids-£7.50, minimal discounts after 14:00, TI's all-day tickets cheaper than discounted afternoon price, July–Aug daily 10:00–17:30, last admission 1 hour before closing, shorter hours off-season, tel. 01253/343-602).

▲▲▲People-Watching—Blackpool's top sight is its people. You'll see England here as nowhere else. Grab someone's hand and a big stick of rock (candy), and stroll. Grown men walk around with huge teddy bears looking for places to play "bowlingo," a short-lane version of bowling. Ponder the thought of actually retiring here and spending your last years, day after day, surrounded by Blackpool and wearing a hat with a built-in ponytail. Blackpool puts people in a talkative mood. Ask someone to explain the difference between tea and supper. Back at your hotel, join in the lounge chat sessions.

▲Illuminations—Blackpool was the first town in England to "go electric" in 1879. Now, every fall (Sept 1–Nov 5 in 2006), Blackpool stretches its tourist season by illuminating its six miles of waterfront with countless lights, all blinking and twinkling. The American in me kept saying, "I've seen bigger, and I've seen better," but I filled his mouth with cotton candy and just had some simple fun like everyone else on my specially decorated tram. Look for the animated tableaux on North Shore.

NIGHTLIFE

▲Showtime—Blackpool always has a few razzle-dazzle music, dancing-girl, racy-humor, magic, and tumbling shows. Box offices around town can give you a rundown on what's available (£7–15 tickets). Your hotel has the latest. For something more highbrow, try the Opera House for musicals (tel. 01253/292-029) and the Grand Theatre for drama and ballet (£15–25, tel. 01253/290-190). Both are on Church Street, a couple of blocks behind the tower. For the latest in evening entertainment, see the window display at the tourist office on Clifton Street.

▲▲Funny Girls—Blackpool's current hot bar is in a dazzling location a couple blocks from the train station. Most nights from 20:15 to 23:30, Funny Girls puts on a "glam bam thank you ma'am" burlesque-in-drag show that delights footballers and grannies alike. Cover is only £5 (£7 on weekends, dinner before show-£15, dinner reservations required). Get your drinks at the bar unless the transvestites are dancing on it. The show, while racy, is not raunchy. The music is very loud. The crowd is young, old, straight, gay, very down-to-earth, and fun-loving. Go on a weeknight; Friday and Saturday are too jammed. While the area up front can be a mosh pit, there are more sedate tables in back, where service comes with a vampish smile. You can pay £12 for VIP seats on Sun and Tue–Thu to avoid lines and look down on the show and crowded floor from a mezzanine level (shows Tue–Sun, closed Mon, must be 18 to enter, 5 Dickson Street, to reserve in advance call tel. 01253/624-901).

Other Nightspots—Blackpool's clubs and discos are cheap, with live bands and an interesting crowd (nightly 22:00–2:00). With all the stag and hen parties, the late-night streets can be clotted with rude rowdies.

SLEEPING

Blackpool's 140,000 people provide 120,000 beds in 3,500 mostly dumpy, cheap, nondescript hotels and B&Bs. Remember, the town's in the business of accommodating the people who can't afford to go to Spain. Most have the same design—minimal character, maximum number of springy beds—and charge £15–20 per person. Empty beds abound except from September through early November and summer weekends. It's only really tight on Illuminations weekends (when everyone bumps prices up). I've listed regular high-season prices. With the huge number of hotels in town, prices get really soft in the off-season. There's usually a launderette within a five-minute walk of your hotel; ask your host or hostess.

North of the Tower

These listings are on or near the waterfront in the quiet area they call "the posh end," a mile or two north of Blackpool Tower, with easy parking and easy access to the center by tram.

$$$ I know, staying at the **Hilton Hotel** in Blackpool is like wearing a tux to eat falafel. But if you need a splurge, this is a grand place with lots of views, a pool, sauna, kids' playground, gym, and comfortable rooms (Db-£110–170, "club deal Db" with lots of extras-£20 more, ask if there are any "special rates" being advertised, swinging weekend deals if you call in advance, request room with view for no extra charge, includes breakfast, non-smoking rooms, tram stop: Warley Road, North Promenade, tel. 01253/623-434, fax 01253/627-864, www.hilton.com).

Sleep Code

(£1 = about $1.80, country code: 44, area code: 01253)
S = Single, **D** = Double/Twin, **T** = Triple, **Q** = Quad, **b** = bathroom,
s = shower only. You can assume credit cards are accepted
unless otherwise noted.

To help you sort easily through these listings, I've divided
the rooms into three categories based on the price for a standard double room with bath:

$$$ **Higher Priced**—Most rooms £90 or more.
$$ **Moderately Priced**—Most rooms between £45–90.
$ **Lower Priced**—Most rooms £45 or less.

$$ The **Best Western Carlton Hotel** rents business-class rooms (Sb-from £40, Db-from £65, best rates are online, a long block closer to town from the Hilton, tram stop: Pleasant Street, North Promenade, tel. 01253/628-966, fax 01253/752-587, www.carltonhotelblackpool.co.uk, mail@carltonhotelblackpool.co.uk).

$$ Robin Hood Hotel is a cheery place with a big, welcoming living room and 10 tastefully refurbished, spacious rooms with big beds and sea views (especially rooms 1, 5, and 9). Run by nutritionist and therapist Kathy, it also serves as a diet retreat center (Sb-£22–27, Db-£44–54, proudly non-smoking, various facial and massage treatments available, tram stop: St. Stephen's Avenue and walk 1 block north; 1.5 miles north of tower across from a peaceful stretch of beach, 100 Queens Promenade, North Shore, tel. 01253/351-599, www.robinhoodhotel.co.uk, rhhblackpool@hotmail.com).

$ Beechcliffe Private Hotel is clean, non-smoking, and family-run, with more charm than average and cute but tight rooms (Sb-£20–24, Db-£40–48, cocktail bar, tram stop: Uncle Tom's; turn left from tram stop, then right at Sheraton, and walk a block away from beach; 16 Shaftesbury Avenue, North Shore, tel. 01253/353-075, www.beechcliffehotel.com, info@beechcliffehotel.com, Shaun and Susan).

Near the Train Station

$ Valentine Private Hotel is a handy and friendly 13-room place. Smoking is allowed, but the breakfast room is smoke-free. Owners Denise and Garry are avid collectors; check out their bar and breakfast-room niches (Db-from £36, bunky family deals, 1 kid sleeps free; 2 blocks from station: with back to tracks, exit station far right, go up Springfield 2 blocks to Dickson, 35 Dickson Road; tel. 01253/622-775, Denise and Garry Hinchliffe). The Funny Girls bar is a block away.

Central Blackpool

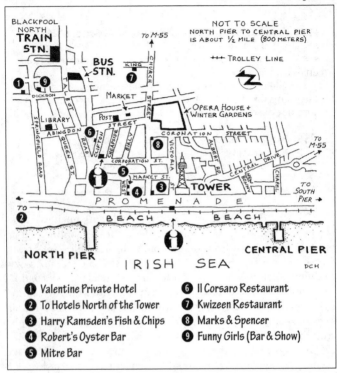

BLACKPOOL
NORTH
TRAIN STN.

TO M-55

NOT TO SCALE
NORTH PIER TO CENTRAL PIER
IS ABOUT ½ MILE (800 METERS)

+++ TROLLEY LINE

BUS STN.

KING

CHURCH STREET

DICKSON

TALBOT

MARKET

POST

STREET

LIBRARY

ABINGDON

SPRINGFIELD ROAD

QUEEN ST.

ROAD

CLIFTON

CHEAPSIDE

BIRLEY

OPERA HOUSE +
WINTER GARDENS

CORONATION STREET

VICTORIA ST.

ALBERT RD.

CENTRAL DRIVE

TO M-55

CORPORATION ST.

MARKET ST.

WEST ST.

TOWER

HENRY BOWN

CHAPEL

TO SOUTH PIER →

P R O M E N A D E

TO

B E A C H   B E A C H

NORTH PIER

CENTRAL PIER

I R I S H   S E A   DCH

1 Valentine Private Hotel
2 To Hotels North of the Tower
3 Harry Ramsden's Fish & Chips
4 Robert's Oyster Bar
5 Mitre Bar
6 Il Corsaro Restaurant
7 Kwizeen Restaurant
8 Marks & Spencer
9 Funny Girls (Bar & Show)

EATING

Your hotel may serve a cheap, early-evening meal. Generally, food in the tower and along the promenade is terrible. The following places are all between Blackpool Tower and the North Pier.

"World Famous" **Harry Ramsden's** is *the* place for mushy peas, good fish-and-chips, and a chance to get goofy with waiters—call the place *Henry* Ramsden's and see what happens (£5–9 meals, order a side of mushy peas, daily 11:30–22:00, off-season until 20:00, 60 The Promenade, tel. 01253/294-386).

Robert's Oyster Bar is a fixture that actually predates the resort—as do some of its employees. Read the plaque on the outside wall. You can take out or eat in—just point to what looks good (daily 10:00–22:00, much shorter in the off-season or during bad weather, at the corner of West Street and The Promenade, 1 block south of North Pier).

The **Mitre Bar** serves light lunches and beers in a truly rare old-time Blackpool ambience. Drop in anytime to survey the fun photos of old Blackpool and for the great people scene (daily

11:00–23:00, around corner from Oyster Bar on West Street, tel. 01253/623-718).

Clifton Street is lined with decent eateries: Indian, Chinese, and Italian. **Il Corsaro** takes its Italian cooking seriously (£8–15, Mon–Sat 18:00–23:00, Sun 19:00–23:00, 36 Clifton Street, tel. 01253/627-440).

For splurges, locals like **Kwizeen,** a bistro that serves good Mediterranean and modern English "kwizeen" in a—refreshing for Blackpool—plain atmosphere (£12 main courses, Mon–Sat from 18:00, closed Sun, 47 King Street, tel. 01253/290-045).

Supermarket: **Marks & Spencer** has a big supermarket in its basement (Mon–Sat 9:00–18:00, Sun 10:30–16:30, near recommended eateries, on Coronation Street and Church Street). Picnic at the beach.

TRANSPORTATION CONNECTIONS

If you're heading to (or from) Blackpool by train, you'll usually need to transfer at **Preston** (3/hr, 30 min). The following trains leave from Blackpool's main (north) station.

From Blackpool to: Keswick/Lake District (hrly trains, allow up to 4 hours total for journey: transfer in Preston—30 minutes away, then 1 hr to Penrith, then catch a bus to Keswick, 1/hr except Sun 6/day, 40 min), **Edinburgh** (8/day, 3.5 hrs, transfer in Preston), **Glasgow** (hrly, 3 hrs, transfer in Preston), **Liverpool** (every 2 hrs, 1.5 hrs, direct), **York** (hrly, 3.25 hrs, direct), **Moreton-in-Marsh** in the Cotswolds (every 2 hrs, 5 hrs, 2 transfers), **Bath** (hrly, 5 hrs, 2 transfers), **Conwy** in North Wales (nearly hrly, 3–4 hrs, 1–2 transfers), **London** (nearly hrly, 4 hrs, usually 2 transfers). Train info: tel. 08457-484-950.

By Bus to: Edinburgh (1/day on Fri, Sat, Mon only; requires change in Glasgow, 5 hrs).

Drivers Entering and Leaving Blackpool: As you approach Blackpool, the motorway takes you to Yeadon Way and a huge city parking lot. Day-trippers need to park here. Leaving, to go anywhere, follow signs to M55, which starts at Blackpool and zips you to the M6 (for points north or south).

Liverpool

Liverpool, a surprisingly friendly and enjoyable city, is a fascinating stop for Beatles fans and those who would like to look urban England straight in the eye. Liverpool is becoming a favorite holiday spot for Brits, who enjoy its lively atmosphere and cultural and historical sites. When you visit, banners, signs, and locals proudly

Liverpool

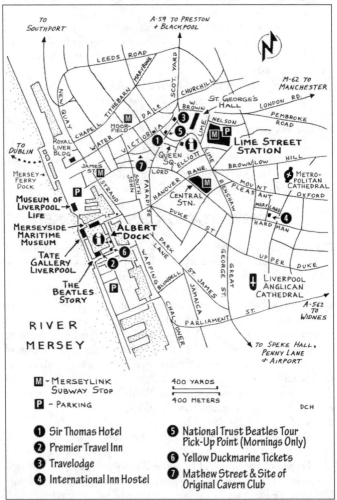

M – MERSEYLINK
SUBWAY STOP

P – PARKING

400 YARDS

400 METERS

DCH

1 Sir Thomas Hotel

2 Premier Travel Inn

3 Travelodge

4 International Inn Hostel

5 National Trust Beatles Tour
Pick-Up Point (Mornings Only)

6 Yellow Duckmarine Tickets

7 Mathew Street & Site of
Original Cavern Club

announce that Liverpool has been named the European Capital of
Culture 2008. Construction and architectural face-lifts abound as
Liverpool preens for this event.

Planning Your Time

Liverpool makes a good half-day stop, though Beatles fans could
easily spend a day and overnight.

Here's an easy half-day plan: From the main Lime Street train
station, take the Metro or bus to Albert Dock. At the dock, choose
among museums, shops, cafés, and The Beatles Story, depending

on your interest. Consider a 50-minute ferry cruise on the river (departs Mersey Ferry dock, a 5-min walk from Albert Dock). On your way back to the train station, stop at Mathew Street if you're a Beatles fan (to see the famous Cavern Club, the new Cavern Club nearby, a statue of the young John Lennon, and the Beatles Shop at #31) and browse the central pedestrian core (Church Street, Williamson Square, and more). You'll have seen the art and the heart of the city.

Note: If you've reserved in advance for a morning departure of the Lennon and McCartney Homes tour, you'll be picked up at the Conservation Centre, a few minutes' walk from the Lime Street train station and 100 yards downhill from the TI.

ORIENTATION

Tourist Information

Liverpool's main TI is a three-minute walk downhill from the train station to Queen Square—just follow the signs (Mon–Sat 9:00–17:30, Tue from 10:00, Sun 10:30–16:30, tel. 0151/708-8854, www.visitliverpool.com). Get a free, small map (also available at station for £1). In summer, guided hour-long city **walking tours** leave from here (£3.50, May–Aug Sun at 14:00, sometimes depart from other locations, call 0151/709-5111). There is a smaller, kiosk-style TI in the midst of most of the sights—on the huge, tidy Albert Dock (same hours as main TI).

Arrival in Liverpool

From the Lime Street station to Albert Dock, it's a 20-minute walk or short ride on a bus (#1, £1 each way, £2 day-ticket), by taxi (£3), or on the Metro (£1, get off at James Street). When returning to the center from Albert Dock, it's best to walk or take the bus (since the Metro makes a long loop before returning to the station). Luggage storage at the station costs an astounding £5 per item (daily 7:00–22:00). For public-transportation information, call Merseytravel (tel. 0151/236-7676 or 0870-608-2608).

TOURS

▲**Lennon and McCartney Homes**—John and Paul's boyhood homes are now both restored circa 1950s and open for visits, but if you want to go inside, you have to take a National Trust Tour. Reservations are recommended (£12, April–Oct Wed–Sun only, 4 tours/day, 2 hrs, photos, mobile phones, and large bags prohibited inside the homes). Morning tours depart from the Conservation Centre in Liverpool (near the TI, on Whitechapel, recorded info tel. 0870-900-0256, booking tel. 0151/708-8574). Afternoon tours leave from Speke Hall, eight miles southeast of Liverpool (booking tel. 0151/427-7231).

It's a worthwhile pilgrimage for the faithful. A minibus shuttles up to 16 people at a time from Albert Dock out to the 'burbs, first to 20 Forthlin Road, the tidy, tiny postwar council house where Paul invited John over to play. There, a guide answers questions; you hear an audioguide with reminiscences from Paul, his family, and friends; and have 40 minutes to wander. Stand in the humble front parlor where Paul and John spent their afternoons bent over their guitars strumming up "I Saw You Standing There" and more. Then wander into the dining room and check out the Beatles tchotchkes on display in the glass cabinet.

Next, the bus takes you to the posher part of town and Mendips, where John moved in with his aunt and uncle in 1945 at age five and lived until he, his wife Cynthia, and son Julian moved to London. After a brief introduction, you're armed with a brochure and set free for 20 minutes to explore the peaceful, spacious 1930s home where John wrote poetry, painted, and learned to play the guitar. Along with photographs of John as a boy, the house features a desk and china cupboard that belonged to his Aunt Mimi, and period furniture designed to recapture the feel of the place during the Beatles' early years.

Beatles Tours—Beatles fans may want to invest a couple of hours taking the **"Magical Mystery" bus tour,** which hits the lads' homes (from the outside), Penny Lane, and so on (£12, 2 hrs, generally departing the Queens Square TI daily at 12:00 and 14:30). The TI has specifics.

For something more extensive, fun, and intimate, consider a four-hour minibus Beatles tour from **Phil Hughes.** It's longer because it includes information on historic Liverpool as well as the Beatles stuff (£12/person, minimum £65/group, includes free beverages and Beatles Story discount, can coordinate times with National Trust tour of Lennon and McCartney homes, 8-seat minibus, tel. & fax 0151/228-4565, mobile 07961-511-223, www.tourliverpool.co.uk).

Jackie Spencer also hits the highlights and does private tours—just say when and where you want to go (5 people in minivan-£140, 4 people in private taxi-£100, 2.5 hrs, will pick you up at hotel or train station, mobile 0799-076-1478, www.liveapool.com, live@pooltours.com).

The "sights" each tour covers are basically houses where the Fab Four grew up (outside only), places they performed, and spots made famous by the lyrics of their hits ("Penny Lane," "Strawberry Fields," the Eleanor Rigby graveyard, and so on). While boring to anyone not into the Beatles, fans will enjoy the commentary and seeing the shelter on the roundabout, the fire station with the clean machine, and the barber who shaves another customer.

Ferry Cruise—Mersey Ferries offers narrated cruises departing from Mersey Dock, an easy five-minute walk from Albert Dock. The cruise makes two brief stops on the other side of the river; you can hop off and catch the next boat back (£5, year-round, Mon–Fri 10:00–15:00, Sat–Sun 10:00–18:00, leaves at top of hour, café, WCs on board, tel. 0151/639-0609, www.merseyferries.co.uk).

Harbor and City Tour—The Yellow Duckmarine runs wacky tours of Liverpool's waterfront, city, and docks by land and by sea in its amphibious tourist assault vehicles. Be prepared to quack (£10, buy tickets at Gower Street bus stop or office on Albert Dock near Beatles Story, departs mid-Feb–Dec daily every 75 min 11:00–16:00 from Albert's Dock, tel. 0151/708-7799, www.theyellowduckmarine.co.uk).

SIGHTS

All of these sights are at Albert Dock.

Albert Dock—Opened in 1852 by Prince Albert and enclosing seven acres of water, Albert Dock is surrounded by five-story brick warehouses. In its day, Liverpool was England's greatest seaport, but at the end of the 19th century, the port wasn't deep enough for the big new ships; trade declined after 1890, and by 1972 it was closed entirely. Like Liverpool itself, the docks have enjoyed a renaissance. Today, they contain the city's main attractions. A half-dozen trendy eateries are lined up here, out of the rain, and padded by lots of shopping mall–type distractions. There's plenty of parking.

▲Merseyside Maritime Museum—This museum tells the story of Liverpool, once the second city of the British Empire. The port prospered in the 18th century as one corner of a commerce triangle with Africa and America. The British shippers profited greatly through exploitation. From Liverpool, they exported manufactured goods to Africa in exchange for enslaved Africans; the slaves were then shipped to the Americas, where they were traded for raw material (cotton, sugar, and tobacco); the goods were then brought back to Britain. While the merchants on all three sides made money, the big profit came home to England. As Britain's economy boomed, so did Liverpool's.

After participation in the slave trade was outlawed in Britain in the early 1800s, Liverpool kept its port busy as a transfer point for emigrants. If your ancestors came from Scandinavia, the

Ukraine, or Ireland, there's a good chance they left Europe from this port. Between 1830 and 1930, nine million emigrants sailed from Liverpool to find their dreams in the New World. Awe-inspiring steamers such as the *Lusitania* called this port home (free, daily 10:00–17:00, tel. 0151/478-4499). The associated **Museum of Liverpool Life** offers a good look at the town's story (also free, same hours, check events board upon arrival, tel. 0151/478-4080).

Tate Gallery Liverpool—This prestigious gallery of modern art is next to the Maritime Museum. It won't entertain you as well as its London sister, the Tate Modern, but if you're into modern art, any Tate's great (free, special exhibits-£5, July–Aug daily 10:00–18:00, Sept–June closed Mon, tel. 0151/702-7400, www.tate.org.uk /liverpool).

▲**The Beatles Story**—It's sad to think the Beatles are stuck in a museum (and Ringo's in reruns of *Shining Time Station*). Still, while overpriced and not very creative, the story's a fascinating one, and even an avid fan will pick up some new information (£8.45, daily 10:00–18:00, until 17:00 in winter, sometimes open until 20:00 Sat July–Aug, last admission 1 hour before closing—but if you arrive later, ask if they'll let you in for a discount, tel. 0151/709-1963, www.beatlesstory.com). The shop has an impressive pile of Beatles buyables.

SLEEPING

(£1 = about $1.80, country code: 44, area code: 0151)
B&Bs are a rarity in urban Liverpool. Your best budget options are the boring, predictable, and central chain hotels.

$$$ Sir Thomas Hotel is a centrally located budget hotel with 39 decent rooms, refurbished in 2005 (Db-£100, up to 2 adults and 2 kids OK, parallel to Mathew Street, 5-min walk from station, 45 Victoria Street, tel. 0151/236-1366, fax 0151/227-1541, www .sirthomashotel.co.uk, reservations@sirthomashotel.co.uk).

$$ Premier Travel Inn, which has comfortable, American-style rooms and a friendly staff, is right on Albert Dock (Db-£53, £56 Fri–Sat, mediocre breakfast costs extra—try good cafés nearby instead, best to book online, located next to Beatles Story in East Britannia Building, Albert Dock, tel. 0870-990-6432, www .premiertravelinn.com).

$$ The Travelodge, a 10-minute downhill walk from the Lime Street train station, is a dependable option (Db-£47 Mon–Fri, £65 Sat–Sun, 2 adults and 2 kids OK, £4 in-room continental breakfast available, 25 Old Haymarket, tel. 0870-085-0950, Internet deals at www.travelodge.co.uk). Exit the train station on Lime Street, turn right on St. John's Lane, go one block, and turn left at the roundabout; it's the giant cement-and-glass building on the corner.

$ International Inn Hostel, run by the daughter of the Beatles' first manager, is located in a former Victorian warehouse and has 100 budget beds (Db-£36–37, bed in 4- to 10-bed room-£15–16, includes sheets, all rooms have bathrooms, free toast and tea/coffee, Internet access in lobby, laundry room-£2/load, games in lobby, TV lounge, video library, café, 4 South Hunter Street; if taking a taxi, tell them it's the Hunter Street near Hardman Street; tel. & fax 0151/709-8135, www.internationalinn.co.uk, info@internationalinn.co.uk).

TRANSPORTATION CONNECTIONS

From Liverpool by Train to: Blackpool (every 2 hrs, 1.5 hrs, more frequent with transfer at Preston), **York** (1/hr, 3 hrs), **Edinburgh** (7/day, 4 hrs, some involve transfer), **Glasgow** (1–2/hr, 4 hrs Mon–Fri, 6–8 hrs Sat–Sun, requires 1–3 transfers), **London** (1/hr, 2.5 hrs), **Crewe** (18/day, 45 min), **Chester** (2/hr, 45 min). Train info: tel. 08457-484-950.

By Ferry to Dublin, Republic of Ireland: SeaCat and Irish Sea Express have ferries for car and foot passengers (4 hrs, daily, Princes Landing Stage, tel. 0870-552-3523, book for both on www .steam-packet.com). Car-only ferries are run by P&O Irish Sea Ferries (7.5 hrs, daily, Liverpool Freeport dock, tel. 0870-242-4777, www.poirishsea.com) and Norse Merchant (8 hrs, Mon–Sat only, Birkenhead Port, tel. 0870-600-4321, www.norsemerchant.com). All ferries require you to check in one to two hours before the sailing time—call to confirm details.

By Ferry to Belfast, Northern Ireland: Norse Merchant Ferries sails most mornings (Tue–Sun) and every evening year-round (9 hrs, £30 one-way day crossing, £40 one-way overnight, cabins-£50 extra, can carry cars, tel. 0870-600-4321, www.norsemerchant .com).

Route Tips for Drivers

Ruthin, North Wales, to Blackpool via Liverpool: From Ruthin, follow signs to the town of Mold, then Queensferry, then Manchester M56, then Liverpool M53, which tunnels under the Mersey River (£1). In Liverpool, follow signs to City Center and Albert Dock, where you'll find a huge car park at the dock. Leaving Liverpool, drive north along the waterfront, following signs to M58 (Preston). Once on M58 (and not before), follow signs to M6, and then M55 into Blackpool.

Ruthin to Blackpool (100 miles): From Ruthin, take A494 through the town of Mold and follow the blue signs to the motorway. M56 zips you to M6, where you'll turn north toward Preston and Lancaster (don't miss your turnoff). A few minutes after Preston, take the not-very-clearly signed next exit (#32, M55) into Blackpool and drive as close as you can to the stubby Eiffel-type tower in the town center. Downtown parking is terrible. If you're just spending the day, head for one of the huge £6/day garages. If you're spending the night, drive to the waterfront and head north. My top accommodations are north on The Promenade (easy parking).

THE LAKE DISTRICT

In the pristine Lake District, Wordsworth's poems still shiver in trees and ripple on ponds. This is a land where nature rules, and man keeps a wide-eyed but low profile. Relax, recharge, take a cruise or a hike, and maybe even write a poem. Renew your poetic license at Wordsworth's famous Dove Cottage.

The Lake District, about 30 miles long and 30 miles wide, is nature's lush, green playground. Explore it by foot, bike, bus, or car. While not impressive in sheer height (Scafell Pike, the tallest peak in England, is only 3,206 feet), there's a walking-stick charm about the way nature and the local culture mix. Locals are fond of claiming that their mountains are older than the Himalayas and were once as tall, but have been worn down by the ages. Walking along a windblown ridge or climbing over a rock fence to look into the eyes of a ragamuffin sheep, even tenderfeet get a chance to feel very outdoorsy.

You'll probably have rain mixed with brilliant bright spells. Drizzly days can be followed by delightful evenings. Pubs offer atmospheric shelter at every turn. As the locals are fond of saying, "There's no such thing as bad weather, only unsuitable clothing."

Plan to spend the majority of your time in the unspoiled North Lake District. In this chapter, I focus on the town of Keswick, the lake called Derwentwater, and the vast, time-passed Newlands Valley. The North Lake District works great by car or by bus (with easy train access via Penrith), and is manna to nature lovers, with good accommodations to boot. The South Lake District—famous primarily for its Wordsworth and Beatrix Potter sights—is closer to London, and gets the promotion, the tour crowds, and the tackiness that comes with them. I strongly recommend that you skip

The Lake District

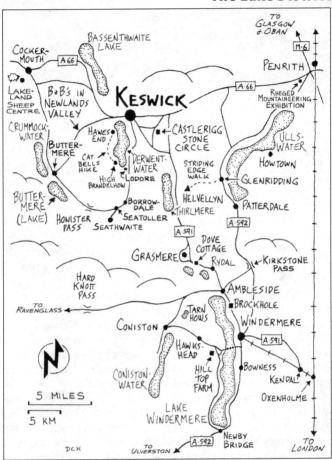

the South Lake District, and enter the region from the north via Penrith. Make your home base in or near Keswick, and side-trip from here into the South Lake District only if you're interested in the Wordsworth and Beatrix Potter sights.

Planning Your Time

On a three-week trip in Britain, I'd spend two days and two nights in the area. Penrith is the nearest train station, just 40 minutes by bus or car from Keswick.

Those without a car will use Keswick as a springboard. Cruise the lake and take one of the many hikes in the Cat Bells area. Non-hikers can hop on a minibus tour.

Here's the most exciting way for drivers (who'd like to visit South Lake District sights en route to the North Lake District) to pack their day of arrival: Get an early start if you're coming from Blackpool or North Wales; leave the motorway at Kendal by 10:30; drive along Windermere and through Ambleside; 11:30–Tour Dove Cottage; 12:30–Backtrack to Ambleside, where a small road leads up and over the dramatic Kirkstone Pass (far more scenic north-bound than southbound, get out and bite the wind) and down to Glenridding on Lake Ullswater. You could catch the 15:00 boat. Hike six miles (3–4 hrs, 15:30–19:00) from Howtown back to Glenridding. Drive to your farmhouse B&B near Keswick, with a stop as the sun sets at Castlerigg Stone Circle.

On your second day, make the circular drive from Keswick through the Newlands Valley, Buttermere, Honister Pass, and Borrowdale, and do the Cat Bells High Ridge Hike. Spend the evening at the same farmhouse B&B.

If great scenery is commonplace in your life, the Lake District can be more soothing (and rainy) than exciting. If you're rushed, you could make this area a one-night stand—or even a quick drive-through.

Getting Around the Lake District

Those based in Keswick without a car manage fine.

By Foot: Hiking information is available everywhere you turn. Consider buying a detailed map (good selection at Keswick TI, or borrow one from your B&B). For easy hikes, the fliers at TIs and B&Bs that describe particular routes are helpful. The Lake District's TIs advise hikers to check the weather before setting out (for an up-to-date weather report, ask at TI or call 0870-055-0575), wear suitable clothing, and bring a map.

By Boat: A circular boat service glides you around Derwentwater, with several hiker-aiding stops along the way (for a cruise/hike option, see the Derwentwater listing, page 320).

By Bus: Keswick has no real bus station; all buses stop at a turnout in front of the Booths Supermarket. Local buses take you quickly and easily (if not always frequently) to all nearby points of interest. The exhaustive *Lakeland Explorer* bus brochure (42 pages, free, at TI or on any bus) explains the schedules. You can purchase one-day passes on the bus (£8.50, for bus and rail info visit www.traveline.org.uk or call 0870-608-2608).

These buses connect Keswick with about everything of interest:

Bus #79, the Borrowdale Rambler, goes topless in the summer, affording a wonderful sightseeing experience in and of itself (hrly, 30 min each way, route: Keswick–Lodore Hotel–Grange Bridge–Rosthwaite–Seatoller at the base of Honister Pass).

Bus #77, the Honister Rambler, makes the gorgeous circle from Keswick around Derwentwater, over Honister Pass, past Buttermere, and through Whinlatter Valley (£5.50, 4/day clockwise, 4/day "anti-clockwise," daily May–Oct, 2-hour circle).

Bus #555/556 connects Keswick with the south (hrly, 30 min to Grasmere and Windermere). From Grasmere, you can hop onto the Lakeland Experience (#599, see below) for more breezy fun.

Bus #599, the open-top Lakeland Experience, runs along the main Windermere corridor, connecting the big tourist attractions in the south (£6 all-day pass, 3/hr daily April–Aug, 50 min each way, route: Grasmere–Rydal Mount–Ambleside–Brockhole–Windermere–Bowness Pier, see "Getting Around the South Lake District—By Bus," page 337).

Bus #208, the Ullswater Connexion, goes from Keswick to Glenridding to meet up with the lake steamers (5/day, only in summer, see "Ullswater," page 336).

Bus #X5 heads from Penrith train station to Keswick (hrly, 30 min).

By Tour: For organized bus tours that run the roads of the Lake District, see below.

By Bike: Several shops rent bikes in Keswick. Keswick Mountain Bikes has the largest selection (£17/day mountain bikes, daily 9:00–17:30, includes helmet, guided bike tours by request, behind Pencil Museum, tel. 017687/75202, www.keswickbikes.co.uk). Keswick Motor Company in the town center also rents bikes (£12 or £15 per day with helmet, see below for details). Keswick Mountain Bikes and the TI sell various cycling maps.

By Car: Nothing is very far from Keswick and Derwentwater. Pick up a good map, get off the big roads, and leave the car, at least occasionally, for some walking. In summer, the Keswick–

Ambleside–Windermere–Bowness corridor (A591) suffers from congestion.

Keswick Motor Company rents cars in Keswick (from £32/day with insurance, Mon–Sat 8:30–17:00, closed Sun, only ages 25–70, must have U.S. license and passport, Lake Road, a block from Moot Hall in town center, tel. 017687/72064).

Parking is tight throughout the region. It's easiest to just park in the pay-and-display lots (gather small coins, machine rarely make change). If you're parking free on the roadside, don't block the vital turnouts. Where there are double yellow lines, you must be beyond them.

The North Lake District

Keswick

As far as touristy Lake District towns go, Keswick (KEZ-ick: pop. 5,000) is far more enjoyable than Windermere, Bowness, or Ambleside. An important mining center for slate, copper, and lead through the Middle Ages, Keswick became a resort in the 19th century. Its fine Victorian buildings recall those Romantic days when city slickers first learned about "communing with nature." Today, the compact town is lined with tearooms, pubs, gift shops, and hiking-gear shops. Lake Derwentwater is a pleasant five-minute walk from the town center.

ORIENTATION

Keswick is an ideal home base, with plenty of good B&Bs (see "Sleeping," page 328), an easy bus connection to the nearest train station at Penrith, and a prime location near the best lake in the area, Derwentwater. In Keswick, everything is within a five-minute walk of everything else: the pedestrian market square, the TI, recommended B&Bs, a grocery store, the municipal pitch-and-putt golf course, the bus stop, a lakeside boat dock, the post office (with Internet access), and a central parking lot. Saturday is market day, but the town square is lively throughout the summer.

Keswick town is a delight for wandering. Its centerpiece,

Moot Hall (meaning meeting hall), was a 16th-century copper warehouse upstairs with an arcade below (closed after World War II). "Keswick" means "cheese market"—a legacy from the time when the town square was the spot to sell cheese. The market square recently went pedestrian-only, and locals are all abuzz about people tripping over the curbs. (The English are thrilled by the ever-present danger of "watch your head," "watch the step," and "mind the gap.")

Tourist Information

The helpful TI is in Moot Hall, right in the middle of the main square (daily Easter–Oct 9:30–17:30, Nov–Easter 9:30–16:30, tel. 017687/72645, www.lake-district.gov.uk). The staff are pros at advising you about hiking routes. They'll also help you figure out public transportation to outlying sights. They also book rooms (you'll leave a 10 percent deposit and pay a higher price for your room; it's cheaper to call B&Bs direct).

The TI sells bus passes, theater tickets, passes for various minibus tours, Keswick Launch tickets (discounted £1), and brochures and maps that outline nearby hikes (50p–£1.50, including a Keswick Town Trail for history buffs, and a very simple and driver-friendly £1.30 *Lap Map* featuring sights, walks, and a mileage chart). The TI bookstore has books and maps for hikers, cyclists, and drivers.

Check the "What's On" boards (inside TI's foyer and on outside wall at post-office end) for information about walks, talks, and entertainment. The daily weather forecast is posted just outside the front door (or call 0870-055-0575). Pop upstairs for a series of short videos about the history of Keswick and the Lake District (free).

Walks with varying levels of difficulty depart from the Keswick TI daily at 10:15. They're led by local guides, leave regardless of the weather, and generally incorporate a bus ride into the outing (£7, Easter–Oct, bring lunch and water, return by 17:00, TI tel. 017687/72645 or 017687/71292, www.keswickrambles.co.uk). TIs throughout the region also offer free walks by the "Voluntary Rangers" (generally from Keswick on Sun and Wed in summer, ask for schedule).

Helpful Hints

Book Ahead for July: Keswick hosts a huge religious convention that packs the town with 4,000 Methodists for three weeks each July. Reserve your room well in advance (but pubs should be wide open).

Internet Access: Located above the post office, **U-Compute** provides Internet access (£3/hr, Mon–Sat 9:00–17:30, Sun 9:30–16:30; 10 terminals and Wi-Fi, corner of Main and Bank streets; tel. 017687/75127). The **library** also has six terminals (50p minimum charge, £2/hr, Mon–Wed and Fri 9:30–19:00, Thu and Sat 9:30–12:30, closed Sun, tel. 017687/72656).

Launderette: It's around the corner from the bus station on Main Street (daily 7:30–19:00, £4.70/load wash and dry, change machine and coin-op flake dispenser; for about £1 extra you get full service, hikers can drop off before 9:00—just leave clothes and a note inside by the office door closest to the front, tel. 017687/75448).

Keswick

P – PARKING

❶ Howe Keld Lakeland Hotel & Parkfield B&B
❷ Berkeley Guest House & Brundholme B&B
❸ Stanger Street B&Bs
❹ Keswick Youth Hostel
❺ Denton House Hostel
❻ The Dog and Gun Pub
❼ Morrel's Restaurant
❽ Pack Horse Inn
❾ The Lakeland Pedlar Vegetarian Rest.
❿ Maysons Whole Food Rest.
⓫ Zenith Restaurant
⓬ Bryson's Bakery & Tea Room
⓭ Library
⓮ Theatre by the Lake
⓯ Keswick Launch Cruises
⓰ Keswick Motor Co. (Bike & Car Rental)
⓱ Cricket Pitch
⓲ Lawn Bowling
⓳ Photo Fun with Sheep

TOURS

Bus tours are great for people with bucks who'd like to wring maximum experience out of their limited time and see the area without lots of hiking or messing with public transport. For a cheaper alternative, take public bus #77 or #79 (see "Getting Around the Lake District—By Bus," above).

Lake District Tours—They offer a variety of mostly half-day tours from Keswick (the general schedule: Mon and Wed—Heart of the Lakes, Tue—North Lakes Explorer, Thu—full day Best of the Lakes, Fri—Ullswater). Their half-day "North Lakes Explorer" tour features the area around Keswick: Borrowdale, Buttermere, and Honister Pass. Guide Graham takes from four to 11 people in his mini-bus, and gives my readers who book direct and pay cash a 10 percent discount (£16/half-day, tours depart 13:00 April–Oct Mon–Fri, none Sat or Sun, book by phone or at 19 Church Street, private tours possible, tel. 017687/80732, www.laketours.co.uk).

Mountain Goat Tours—The region's dominant tour company runs a few minibus tours from Keswick (£20/half-day, £30/day, Easter–Oct if there are sufficient sign-ups, minimum 4 to a maximum of 16 per hearty bus, book in advance with Keswick TI or by calling tel. 015394/45161, www.mountain-goat.com). Note that most of their tours are Windermere-based. Confirm that the tour you're taking is actually a Keswick tour, and you won't be shuttled down to Windermere to catch the tour (adding an hour of needless driving to your day).

Touchstone Tours—Lucy Harrison takes small groups in her minibus for fascinating days out and about. Each tour has a theme (explained at www.touchstonetours.co.uk); the most popular goes to Hadrian's Wall (£55 includes snacks, lunch, a photo disk of the day's events; 10 percent discount with this 2006 book, tours start at 13:00, 2–7 per group, tel. 017687/79599 to book). If you'd like to continue on from Hadrian's Wall, ask to be dropped at a convenient train station.

SIGHTS

In Keswick

▲Derwentwater—One of Cumbria's most photographed and popular lakes, Derwentwater has four islands, good circular boat service, plenty of trails, and the pleasant town of Keswick at its north end. The roadside views aren't much, so hike or cruise. You can walk around the lake (fine trail, floods in heavy rains, 9

miles, 4 hrs) or cruise it (1 hour). I suggest a hike/sail combo. The Lodore Walk (page 323) and Cat Bells High Ridge Hike (page 325) start from Derwentwater docks.

▲**Pencil Museum**—Graphite was first discovered centuries ago in Keswick. A hunk of the stuff proved great for marking sheep in the 15th century. In 1832, the first crude Keswick pencil factory opened, and the rest is history (which is what you'll learn about here). While you can't actually tour the 150-year-old factory where the famous Derwent pencils are made, you can enjoy the smell of thousands of pencils getting sharpened for the first time. The adjacent, charming, and kid-friendly museum is a good way to pass a rainy hour. Take a look at the "war pencils" made for WWII bomber crews (and filled with tiny maps and compasses) and relax for 10 minutes watching *The Humble Pencil* video in the theater (£3, daily July–Aug 9:30–17:30, Sept–June 9:30–16:00, 3-min walk from the town center, signposted off Main Street, tel. 017687/73626, www.pencils.co.uk).

Fitz Park—An inviting, grassy park stretches alongside Keswick's tree-lined, duck-filled River Greta. There's plenty of room for kids to burn off energy. Consider an after-dinner stroll on the footpath. You may catch men in white (or frisky schoolboys in uniform) playing a game of cricket. There's the serious bowls green (where you're welcome to watch the experts play), and the public one where tourists are welcome to give lawn bowling a go (£2.50). You can try tennis on a grass court (£5/hr with rackets) or enjoy the putting green (£2).

Near Keswick

▲▲**Castlerigg Stone Circle**—For some reason, 70 percent of England's stone circles are here in Cumbria. This one's the best.

These 38 stones—90 feet across and 3,000 years old—are mysteriously laid out on a line between the two tallest peaks on the horizon. They serve as a celestial calendar for ritual celebrations. Imagine the Woodstock-like ambience here, as ancient people filled this clearing in spring to celebrate fertility, and in fall to confront their fear of death. Festival dates were dictated by how the sun rose and set in relation to the stones. The more that modern academics study this circle, the more meaning they find in the placement of the stones. The two front stones face due north, towards a cut in the mountains. The rare-for-stone-circles "sanctuary" lines up with its center stone to mark where the sun rises on May Day. (Party!) For maximum goose pimples (as they say here), show up at sunset (free, open all the time, 3 miles east of Keswick—follow brown signs, 3 min off A66, easy parking).

▲**Lakeland Sheep and Wool Centre**—If you have a car, this is worth a stop to watch working sheepdogs in action. Catch a dem-

onstration, see the twenty or so different breeds of sheep in Britain, and learn why each is bred. (Kneading the wool of the Merino sheep, you'll understand why it's so popular for sweaters.) You'll also see the quintessential sheepdog—the border col-

lie—at work. At the end, you can pet whatever is still on stage: dogs, cows, sheep, and sometimes a goose...if you can catch one. While the Visitors Centre and shop is free, it's not really worth the trip unless you catch a sheep show (£4 for demo; March–Oct Sun–Thu at 10:30, 12:00, 14:00, and 15:30; no shows Fri–Sat or Dec–Feb, 13 miles east of Keswick on the A66 road A5086 roundabout in Cockermouth, tel. 01900-822-673, www.sheep -woolcentre.co.uk).

Rheged Centre and National Mountaineering Exhibition— This strange shopping and exhibition center, just off a highway roundabout (near Penrith, on A66 a mile west of the Keswick exit #40 off M6), is a good rainy-day option for anyone into moun- tain climbing—or adventures on Mount Everest. While it's mostly a modern shopping mall (showcasing and selling the best of Cumbria), it has a mountaineering exhibition with fascinat- ing artifacts (such as the evolution of high-tech boots—and the amputated, frost-bitten toes of a climber who could have used better ones). Don't miss the 15-minute video recounting the his- tory of climbing Mount Everest, and the British conquest of the peak in 1953 (plays any time, on demand). The second attraction is an IMAX theater showing four special movies throughout the day, including the 60-minute *Rheged: The Lost Kingdom*, which tells the story of the region's original Celtic inhabitants (£6 for the Mountaineering Exhibition, £6 more for any movie, combo deals, daily 10:00–17:30, call ahead to check movie times, the #X4 and #X5 Keswick–Penrith buses stop right here, tel. 017688/68000, www.rheged.com).

ACTIVITIES

In Keswick

▲**Golf**—A lush nine-hole pitch-and-putt golf course separates the town from the lake and offers a classy, cheap, and convenient chance to golf near the birthplace of the sport (£2.80 for 9 holes, £1.40 for putting, £1.60 for 18 tame holes of "obstacle golf," Easter–Oct daily 9:30–20:00 or dusk, closed Nov–Easter, tel. 017687/73445).

Swimming—While the Leisure Center doesn't have a serious adult pool, it does have an indoor pool kids love, with a huge water slide and wave machine (pool: £4, kids-£3, Mon–Fri 9:00–16:00, Sat–Sun 10:00–17:00, shorter hours off-season, longer during school break, no towels or suits for rent, lockers-50p deposit, a 10-min walk from town center, follow Station Road past Fitz Park and veer left, tel. 017687/72760).

Boating—Keswick Launch runs boats from mid-March to October (2/hr—alternating clockwise and "anti-clockwise"—daily 10:00–19:00, shoulder season until 16:30; in winter 5/day on weekends only, at end of Lake Road, tel. 017687/72263, www.keswick-launch.co.uk). Boats make seven stops on each 60-minute round-trip. The boat trip costs £6 per circle (£5 if you book through TI), with free stopovers, or £1.10 per segment. Stand on the pier Gilligan-style, or the boat may not stop. Keswick Launch also rents **rowboats** for two (£5/30 min, £8/hr).

Keswick Launch's **evening cruise** is a delightful little trip that comes with a glass of wine and a mid-lake stop for a short commentary (60-min, 19:30 every evening late May through mid-September weather permitting, £7, families for £15). You're welcome to bring a picnic dinner and munch scenically as you cruise.

HIKES AND DRIVES

Near Keswick

Lodore Walk—The best hour-long lakeside walk is the 1.5-mile path between the docks at High Brandelhow and Hawes End. Continue on foot along the lake back into Keswick or—better yet—go on to Lodore.

Lodore is a good stop for two reasons: Lodore Falls is a 10-minute walk from the dock (behind Lodore Hotel), and Shepherds Crag (a rockface overlooking Lodore) was made famous by pioneer rock climbers. (Their descendants hang from little ridges on its face today.) This is serious climbing (with several fatalities a year).

For a great lunch or tea and cakes, drop into the much-loved High Lodore Farm Café, where sheep farmer Martin is busy making hikers and day-trippers happy (daily 9:00–19:00; from the

Derwentwater and the Newlands Valley

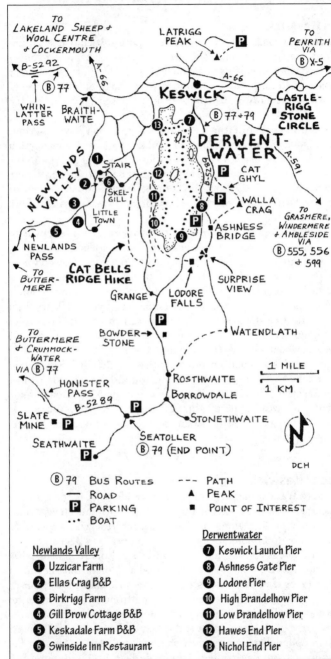

TO LAKELAND SHEEP & WOOL CENTRE & COCKERMOUTH

LATRIGG PEAK

TO PENRITH VIA (B) X-5

B-5292

(B) 77

WHIN-LATTER PASS

BRAITH-WAITE

KESWICK

(B) 77 & 79

CASTLE-RIGG STONE CIRCLE

A-66

A-591

DERWENT-WATER

NEWLANDS VALLEY

STAIR

SKEL-GILL

LITTLE TOWN

B-5289

CAT GHYL

WALLA CRAG

TO GRASMERE, WINDERMERE & AMBLESIDE VIA (B) 555, 556 & 599

ASHNESS BRIDGE

NEWLANDS PASS

TO BUTTER-MERE

CAT BELLS RIDGE HIKE

GRANGE

LODORE FALLS

SURPRISE VIEW

TO BUTTERMERE & CRUMMOCK-WATER VIA (B) 77

BOWDER STONE

WATENDLATH

HONISTER PASS

B-5289

ROSTHWAITE

BORROWDALE

STONETHWAITE

1 MILE

1 KM

SLATE MINE

SEATHWAITE

SEATOLLER (B) 79 (END POINT)

N

DCH

(B) 79   BUS ROUTES
———   ROAD
P   PARKING
···   BOAT

- - -   PATH
▲   PEAK
■   POINT OF INTEREST

Newlands Valley
1 Uzzicar Farm
2 Ellas Crag B&B
3 Birkrigg Farm
4 Gill Brow Cottage B&B
5 Keskadale Farm B&B
6 Swinside Inn Restaurant

Derwentwater
7 Keswick Launch Pier
8 Ashness Gate Pier
9 Lodore Pier
10 High Brandelhow Pier
11 Low Brandelhow Pier
12 Hawes End Pier
13 Nichol End Pier

dock, walk up the road, turn right over bridge uphill to café; tel. 017687/77221).

▲▲Buttermere Hike—The ideal little lake with a lovely, circular four-mile stroll offers nonstop, no-sweat Lake District beauty. If you're not a hiker (but kind of wish you were), take this walk. If you're very short on time, at least stop here and get your shoes dirty.

Buttermere is connected with Borrowdale and Derwentwater by a great road that runs over the rugged Honister Pass (described below, under "Scenic Circle Drive South of Keswick"). From May through October, bus #77 makes a round-trip loop between Keswick and Buttermere over Honister Pass ("Getting Around the Lake District—By Bus," page 315). The two-pub hamlet of Buttermere has a pay-and-display parking lot, but many drivers park free along the side of the road. You're welcome to leave your car at the Fish Hotel if you eat in their pub (recommended). There's also a pay parking lot at the Honister Pass end of the lake (at Gatesgarth Farm, £3). The Syke Farm (in the hamlet of Buttermere) is popular for its homemade ice cream.

▲▲Cat Bells High Ridge Hike—For a great (and fairly easy) "king of the mountain" feeling, sweeping views, and a close-up look at the weather blowing over the ridge, hike about two hours from Hawes End up along the ridge to Cat Bells (1,480 feet) and down to High Brandelhow. From there, you can catch the boat or take the easy path along the shore of Derwentwater to your Hawes End starting point. (Extending the hike to Lodore takes you to a waterfall, rock climbers, a fine café, and another boat dock for a convenient return to Keswick—described above.) Cat Bells is probably the most dramatic family walk in the area (but wear sturdy shoes, bring a raincoat, and watch your footing). From Keswick, the lake, or your farmhouse B&B, you can see silhouetted stick figures hiking along this ridge. Drivers can park free at Hawes End. The Keswick TI sells a *Skiddaw and Cat Bells* brochure about the hike (60p).

Cat Bells is just the first of a series of peaks all connected by a fine ridge trail. Hardier hikers continue up to nine miles along this same ridge, enjoying valley and lake views as they arc around the Newlands Valley toward (and even down to) Buttermere. After High Spy, you can descend an easy path into Newlands Valley. An ultimate very full day-plan would be to bus to Buttermere, climb Robinson, and follow the ridge around to Cat Bells and back to Keswick.

▲▲**More Hikes**—The area is riddled with wonderful hikes. B&Bs all have fine advice, but consider these as well:

From downtown Keswick, you can walk the seven-mile **Latrigg** trail, which includes the Castlerigg Stone Circle (pick up 60p map/guide from TI, for more on the stone circle, see page 321). For a very short hike and the easiest mountain-climbing sensation around, drive to the Underscar parking lot just north of Keswick, and hike 20 minutes to the top of the 1,200 foot high hill for a commanding view of the town and lake.

From the parking lot at Newlands Pass, at the top of Newlands Valley, an easy one-mile walk to **Knottrigg** from Newlands Pass probably offers more TPCB (thrills per calorie burned) than any walk in the region.

From your Keswick B&B, a fine 2-hour walk to **Walla Crag** offers a great fell (mountain) walking and ridge-walk experience without the necessity of a bus or car. Start by strolling along the lake to Great Wood parking lot, and head up Cat Ghyl (where fell runners practice) to Walla Crag. You'll be treated to great panoramic views over Derwentwater and surrounding peaks. You can do a shorter version of this walk from the parking lot at Ashness Bridge.

▲▲**Car Hiking from Keswick**—Distances are short, roads are narrow and have turnouts, and views are rewarding. Get a good map and ask your B&B host for advice. Two miles south of Keswick on the lakeside Borrowdale Valley Road (B5289), take the small road left (signposted *Ashness Bridge, Watendlath*) for a half mile to the Ashness Packhorse Bridge (a quintessential Lake District scene, parking lot just above on right). A half mile farther (parking lot on left) and you're startled by the "surprise view" of Derwentwater (great for a lakes photo op). Continuing from here, the road gets extremely narrow en route to the hamlet of Watendlath, which has a tiny lake and lazy farm animals. Return down to Borrowdale Valley Road and back to Keswick, or farther south to scenic Borrowdale and over the dramatic Honister Pass to Buttermere.

▲▲**Scenic Circle Drive South of Keswick**—This hour-long drive, which includes Newlands Valley, Buttermere, Honister Pass, and Borrowdale, is demanding. But it's also filled with the best scenery you'll find in the North Lake District. From Keswick, head west on the Cockermouth Road (A66). Take the second Newlands Valley exit (through Braithwaite), and follow signs up the majestic **Newlands Valley**. If the place had a lake, it

would be packed with tourists. But it doesn't—and it isn't.

The valley is studded with 500-year-old farms that have been in the same family for centuries. Shearing day is reason to rush home from school. Sons get school out of the way A.S.A.P., and follow their dads into the family business. Neighbor girls marry those sons and move in. Grandparents retire to the cottage next door. With the price of wool depressed, most of the wives supplement the family income by running B&Bs (virtually every farm in the valley rents rooms—see recommendations on page 333). The road has one lane, with turnouts for passing. From Newlands Pass summit, notice the glacial-shaped wilds, once forested, now not. There's an easy hike from your car to a little waterfall (or a thrilling one to Knottrigg, described above).

After Newlands Pass, descend to **Buttermere** (scenic lake, tiny hamlet, see recommended hike, above, and pub), turn left and climb over the rugged **Honister Pass**, strewn with glacial debris, remnants from the old slate mines, and curious shaggy Swaledale sheep (looking more like goats with their curly horns). The valleys you'll see are a textbook example of the kind that were carved out by glaciers. Look high on the hillsides for "hanging valleys"—small

Buttermere Hike

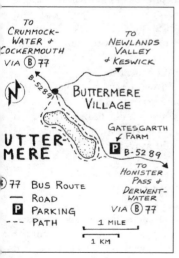

glacial-shaped scoops cut off by the huge flow of the biggest glacier, which swept down the main valley. An **old slate mine** at the summit of Honister Pass has reopened for tours (£9.50, 90 min; departures at 10:30, 12:30, and 15:30; tel. 017687/77230 to book, worthwhile slate-filled shop).

After stark and lonely Honister Pass, drop into sweet and homey **Borrowdale,** with a few lonely hamlets and fine hikes from Seathwaite (get specifics from your B&B or the TI on walks here). Circling back to Keswick past Borrowdale, you pass a number of popular local attractions (the house-sized Bowder Stone—signposted, a few minutes walk off the main road), the postcard-pretty Ashness Bridge and "surprise view" (described above, turn-out signposted), and the rock climbers above Lodore. After that, you're home. A short detour before returning to Keswick takes you to the Castlerigg Stone Circle (see sight listing above).

NIGHTLIFE

▲▲**Theatre by the Lake**—Keswickians brag they enjoy "London theatre quality at Keswick prices." Their theater offers events year-round and a wonderful rotation of four to six plays through the summer (a different play each night, with music concerts on Sun). There are two stages: the main one seats 400, and the smaller "studio" theater seats 70 (and features more risqué plays, with rough language and nudity, £10–12). Attending a play here is a fine opportunity to do something completely local (£10–18, discounts for old and young, 20:00 shows in summer, 19:30 in winter, book ahead July–Aug, parking at the pay-and-display lot adjacent is free after 19:00, tel. 017687/74411, www.theatrebythelake.com).

▲▲**Evenings in Keswick**—For a small and remote town, Keswick has lots of great things to do in the evening. Remember, at this latitude it's light until 22:00 in the midsummer. You can **golf** (fine course, pitch-and-putt, goofy golf, or just enjoy the putting green, see page 323), or **walk** among the grazing sheep as the sun gets ready to set (between the lake and the golf course, access from just above the beach, great photo ops on a balmy eve).

To socialize with locals, head to a pub for one of their special evenings: There's **folk music** at the Queens Hotel pub (£2, 20:30 Tue), and **quiz night** at the Pack Horse Pub (21:30 Wed) and Dog and Gun (21:30 Thu, £1, proceeds go to Keswick's Mountain Rescue team). At a quiz night, tourists are more than welcome. Drop in, say you want to join a team, and you're in. If you like trivia, it's a great way to get to know people here.

Other options: Join Bob, the Town Crier, when he does his routine many summer Tuesday evenings (see TI for details). Catch a **show** at the Alhambra Cinema, a good, old-fashioned English theater. An **evening lake cruise** is perfect for an extremely scenic and relaxing picnic dinner (19:30 May–Sept, see page 323 for details).

SLEEPING

The Lake District abounds with attractive B&Bs, guest houses, and hostels. It needs them all when summer hordes threaten the serenity of this Romantic mecca. Book well in advance if you plan to visit during Keswick's annual convention in July.

Outside of summer, you should have no trouble finding a room. But to get a particular place (especially on Sat), call ahead. If you're using public transportation, you should stay in Keswick. For drivers, this town is your best chance for a remote farmhouse experience. Lakeland hostels offer £15 beds and come with an interesting crowd.

Sleep Code

(£1 = about $1.80, country code: 44, area code: 017687)
S = Single, **D** = Double/Twin, **T** = Triple, **Q** = Quad, **b** = bathroom,
s = shower only. You can assume credit cards are accepted
unless otherwise noted, and all B&B stays include breakfast.

To help you sort easily through these listings, I've divided
the rooms into three categories based on the price for a double room with bath:

$$$ **Higher Priced**—Most rooms £60 or more.
 $$ **Moderately Priced**—Most rooms between £30–60.
  $ **Lower Priced**—Most rooms £30 or less.

In Keswick, I've featured two streets, each within three blocks
of the bus station and town square. "The Heads" is a classier area
lined with proud Victorian houses, close to the lake and new theater, overlooking a golf course. Stanger Street, a bit humbler but
also quiet and handy, has smaller homes.

My Keswick listings are strictly non-smoking. Many charge
extra for a one-night stay. Most have a two-night minimum on
weekends and don't welcome children under 12 (unless extremely
well-behaved). Owners are enthusiastic about getting you on the
right walking trail, offering plenty of advice. These accommodations have inviting lounges with libraries of books on the region
and loaner maps. Take advantage of plush lounges, and make your
humble B&B room suddenly a suite.

This is still the countryside—expect huge breakfasts (with big
selections including vegetarian options), no phones in the rooms,
and shower systems that often need to be switched on to get hot
water. Parking is pretty easy (either in congested little private lots
or on the street).

The Heads

$$$ **Howe Keld Lakeland Hotel,** while the most formal of the
accommodations I list in Keswick, is still warm, welcoming, and
family-run, with 15 fine rooms and a wide variety of breakfast
selections (Sb-£33, Db-£66, these prices are for 2-night stays,
more for 1-night stays, prefers cash, 2 ground-floor rooms, fam-
ily deals, 5 The Heads, tel. & fax 017687/72417, www.howekeld
.co.uk, david@howekeld.co.uk, run with care by David and Valerie
Fisher).

$$ **Berkeley Guest House,** a big slate mansion enthusiastically run by Barbara Crompton, has a pleasant lounge, narrow
hallways, and carefully appointed, comfortable rooms. The chirpy,

skylight-bright £42 bathless double in the attic is a fine value if you don't mind the stairs (D-£42, Db-£58 with this book, family deals, great family room, cash only, The Heads, tel. 017687/74222, www.berkeley-keswick.com, berkeley@tesco.net).

$$ Parkfield B&B, thoughtfully run and decorated by John and Susan Berry, is another big Victorian house—bright and pastel with fine views (Db-£60 with this book through 2006, 2-night minimum stay, 8 rooms, 1 on the ground floor, no kids under 16, plenty of fruit at breakfast, The Heads, tel. 017687/72328, www.parkfieldkeswick.co.uk, enquiries@parkfieldkeswick.co.uk).

$$ Brundholme B&B, next door to the Berkeley, is run by friendly Barbara and Paul Motler. It has three bright and comfy rooms (2 with grand views), old carpets, and a welcoming atmosphere (Db-£50–52, cash only, The Heads, tel. 017687/73305, www.brundholme.co.uk, barbara@brundholme.co.uk).

Stanger Street

The street, quiet but just a block from Keswick's town center, is lined with B&Bs. Each of these places is small, family-run, and accepts cash only. They are all good, with little to differentiate between them.

$$ Dunsford Guest House is an old Victorian slate townhouse where they rent four color-coordinated rooms at a good price. Stained glass and wooden pews give the blue-and-cream breakfast room a country-chapel feel (Db-£54, prices promised in 2006 with this book, no kids under 16, 16 Stanger Street, tel. 017687/75059, www.dunsford.net, enquiries@dunsford.net, Richard and Linda).

$$ Badgers Wood B&B, at the top of the street, has six bright, pastel, stocking-feet-comfortable view rooms, each named after a different tree (Sb-£28, Db-£56, minimum 2 nights, 30 Stanger Street, tel. 017687/72621, www.badgers-wood.co.uk, enquiries@badgers-wood.co.uk, Andrew and Anne).

$$ Ellergill Guest House has three spick-and-span rooms, one with a super view (D-£52, Db-£54 with this 2006 book, 2-night minimum, 22 Stanger Street, tel. 017687/73347, www.ellergill.co.uk, stay@ellergill.co.uk, run by Keith Taylor, a lively one-man show).

$$ Fell House B&B, with six charming rooms, is run by Barbara Hossack, who sets out cakes in the afternoon (S-£25, D-£46, Db-£56, parking, 28 Stanger Street, tel. & fax 017687/72669, www.fellhouse.co.uk, info@fellhouse.co.uk).

$$ Abacourt House, with a daisy-fresh breakfast room, has five pleasant doubles (Db-£56, no children, 26 Stanger Street, tel. 017687/72967, www.abacourt.co.uk, abacourt@btinternet.com, Judith and David Lewis).

$$ Pinewood House rents three earth-toned, fresh, and cheery rooms. Guests enjoy a lovely lounge with views and a small library (Db-£54 with this book in 2006, 19 Stanger Street, tel. 017687/75767, www.keswick-bedandbreakfast.com, peter@keswick-bedandbreakfast.com, Peter and Annette Lawes).

Hostels in and near Keswick

The Lake District's inexpensive hostels, usually located in great old buildings, are handy sources of information and social fun. The Lake District's free hostel booking service (Easter–Oct daily 9:30–17:00, tel. 015394/31117) will tell you which of the area's 30 hostels have available beds, and can even book a place on your credit card (no more than 7 days in advance). Since most hostels don't answer their phones during the day and many are full, this can be a helpful service, but don't consider this service the final word. (Since the service takes a commission from the hostels, hostels may have a space when they tell this service that they're full.) Non-members pay about £3 extra a night, or buy a £14 membership. These first two hostels are former hotels, offering Internet access, laundry machines, and three cheap meals daily:

$ Keswick Youth Hostel, with 90 beds in a converted old mill overlooking the river, has a great riverside balcony and plenty of handy facilities (£12.50 beds for members, £15.50 for non-members, mostly 3–4-bed rooms, 23:30 curfew, center of town just off Station Road before river, tel. 017687/72484, keswick@yha.org.uk).

$ Derwentwater Hostel, two miles south of Keswick, has 88 beds (£12 beds in 4–22-bed rooms, family rooms-£25–43, 23:00 curfew, follow B5289 from Keswick, look for sign 100 yards after Ashness exit, tel. 017687/77246, derwentwater@yha.org.uk).

$ Denton House is Keswick's other hostel. This one is independent (not YHA), spartan, and grimly institutional, but provides good basic bunk beds in barracks for £12 with a kitchen (£12 beds in 4–10 bed dorm rooms, no lockers, on Penrith Road between the fire station and railway bridge at the east edge of town, tel. 017687/75351, www.vividevents.co.uk).

West of Keswick, in the Newlands Valley

If you have a car, drive 10 minutes past Keswick down the majestic Newlands Valley (described above under "Scenic Circle Drive South of Keswick"). The valley is studded with 500-year-old farms that have been in the same family for centuries, but now rent rooms to supplement the family income. The rooms are a bit plainer than in town. Traditionally, farmhouses lacked central heating, and while they are now heated, you can still request a hot-water bottle to warm up your bed.

Getting to the Newlands Valley: Leave Keswick heading west on the Cockermouth Road (A66). Take the second Newlands Valley exit through Braithwaite, and follow signs through Newlands Valley (drive toward Buttermere). All five recommended B&Bs are on this road: Uzzicar Farm (under the shale field, which local boys love hiking up to glissade down), Ellas Crag B&B, then (just after a curious—and haunted—purple house), Birkrigg Farm B&B, Gill Brow Cottage B&B, and finally—the last house before the stark summit—Keskadale Farm B&B (about 4 miles before Buttermere). The road has one lane, with turnouts for passing. Each place offers easy parking, grand views, and perfect tranquility. These are listed in the geographical order, the first being a five-minute drive from Keswick and the last being at the top of the valley (about a 15-min drive from Keswick).

$$ Uzzicar Farm is a big rustic place with a comfy B&B zone in the middle where youthful Lyn Edmondson rents three fine rooms in her very old and low-ceilinged farmhouse (£26 per person in S, D, or Db; 10 percent discount with this 2006 book, family deals, cash only, tel. 017687/78200, http://uzzicar.bravehost.com, lynne@uzzicar.wanadoo.co.uk).

$$ Ellas Crag B&B, with four rooms, is more of a comfortable stone house than a farm. This homey place offers a good mix of modern and traditional decor (Db-£54, bigger Db-£58, cash only, 2-night minimum, non-smoking, packed lunches available, laundry-£5, Newlands Valley, tel. 017687/78217, www.ellascrag.co.uk, ellascrag@talk21.com, Jane and Ed Ma and their small children).

$$ Birkrigg Farm is a fine and grand-motherly farmhouse B&B. Mrs. Margaret Beaty offers visitors a comfy lounge, evening tea (good for socializing with her other guests), a classy breakfast, and a view of the surrounding territory. Take your toast and last cup of tea out to the front-yard bench (£21 per person in S, D, T, or Q; 2-night minimum, discounts for kids, cash only, 1 shower, 1 tub, and 3 toilets for 4 rooms; closed Dec–March, Newlands Pass Road, tel. 017687/78278).

$$ Gill Brow Cottage B&B is a rough, working farmhouse where Anne Wilson and her delightful 12-year-old daughter Laura rent two simple but fine rooms (D-£46, Db-£50, 10 percent discount with this 2006 book and 2-night stay, tel. 017687/78270, www.gillbrow-keswick.co.uk, wilson_gillbrow@hotmail.com).

$$ Keskadale Farm B&B is another good farmhouse experience, with ponderosa hospitality. One of the valley's oldest, the house is made from 500-year-old ship beams. This working farm has lots of curly-horned sheep and three rooms to rent. While her boys are now old enough to help dad in the fields, Margaret Harryman runs the B&B (Db-£54, £2 extra for one night, cash only, non-smoking, closed Dec–Feb, tel. 017687/78544, fax 017687/78150, www.keskadalefarm.co.uk, keskadale.b.b@kencomp.net).

Southwest of Keswick, in Buttermere

$$$ The **Bridge Hotel,** just beyond Newlands Valley at Buttermere, offers 21 rooms and a classic, Old World, country-side-hotel experience (Db-£120 for B&B, Db-£150 with a fancy dinner, non-smoking rooms, tel. 017687/70252, fax 017687/70215, www.bridge-hotel.com, enquiries@bridge-hotel.com). There are no shops within 10 miles—only peace and quiet a stone's throw from one of the region's most beautiful lakes.

$ The **Buttermere King George VI Memorial Hostel,** a quarter-mile south of Buttermere village on Honister Pass Road, has good food, 70 beds, family rooms, and a royal setting (£15/bed in 4- to 6-bed rooms, includes breakfast, inexpensive lunches and dinners, office open 7:00–10:00 & 17:00–23:00, 23:00 curfew, tel. 0870-770-5736, buttermere@yha.org.uk).

South of Keswick, near Borrowdale

$$ **Seatoller Farm B&B** is a rustic old building in a five-building hamlet where Christine Simpson rents three rooms (Db-£52, tel. 017687/77232, csimpson@ktdinternet.com). Honister's Yew Tree pub is just across the street (with a museum of old-time photos decorating its walls, daily lunch and dinner Thu–Sun).

$ **Borrowdale Hostel,** in secluded in Borrowdale Valley just south of Rosthwaite, is a well-run place surrounded by many ways of immerse yourself in nature (88 beds, £12 beds, Internet access in lobby, laundry machines, 23:00 curfew, 3 cheap meals daily, tel. 0870-770-5706, borrowdale@yha.org.uk).

EATING

Keswick has a huge variety of restaurants catering to its many visitors. Most restaurants stop serving by 21:00. Here's a selection of favorites:

Morrel's Restaurant is the Keswick favorite for a splurge—simple yet elegant, serving famously good and creative modern English cuisine (£15–20 meals, daily 17:30–21:00, reservations recommended, don't expect a fast dinner, all meals cooked to order, 34 Lake Road, tel. 017687/72666).

Zenith Restaurant, with fine traditional English cuisine, is above a mod wine bar in a renovated old garage. It's Morrel's major competition for gourmet lakeland cooking (£15 meals, 12:00–13:45, 18:00–21:00, closed Mon, 21 Station Street, tel. 017687/80430).

Pack Horse Inn offers a great pub atmosphere, low exposed-beam ceilings, a fireplace, and what most locals consider the best pub food in town (£9 meals, daily 12:00–14:30 & 18:00–21:30, smoky but better upstairs, find alley off of Market Street leading to Pack Horse courtyard, tel. 017687/71389).

The Dog and Gun serves good pub food, but mind your head—low ceilings and wooden beams (£7 meals, daily 12:00–23:00, meals until 21:00, goulash, no chips and proud of it, can get smoky, 2 Lake Road, tel. 017687/73463, warmly run by Ede family).

The Lakeland Pedlar Vegetarian Restaurant, a wholesome, pleasant café (with a bike shop upstairs), serves freshly baked vegan and vegetarian fare, including soups, organic bread, and daily specials. Their interior is cute. Outside tables face a big parking lot (£6.50 meals, Sun–Thu 9:00–17:00, Fri–Sat 9:00–21:00, Hendersons Yard, find the narrow walkway off Market Street between the pink Johnson's sweet shop and Ye Olde Golden Lion Inn, tel. 017687/74492).

Bryson's Bakery and Tea Room has an enticing ground-floor bakery, with sandwiches and light lunches. The upstairs is a popular tea room. Order lunch to go from the bakery, or eat either sitting on stools or at a couple of sidewalk tables for a few pence more (Mon–Sat 8:30–17:30, Sun 9:30–17:00, 42 Main Street, tel. 017687/72257). Consider their Farmhouse Tea, which is like a London High Tea, but for a quarter the price and made with local products; it comes on a three-tiered platter: sandwiches, scones, and little cakes with tea for £7 (perfectly splitable).

Maysons Whole Food Restaurant, with Californian ambience, is fast and easy, with a buffet line of curry, Cajun, and vegetarian options. It's nothing fancy: You point, and they dish up and microwave (£7, June–Oct daily 10:00–20:45, lunch only off-season, family-friendly, also take-out—great for evening cruise picnic, 33 Lake Road, tel. 017687/74104).

Keswick Tea Room, in a big shopping center at the bus station, is popular with locals and features cheap and cheery regional specialties (Mon–Sat 8:30–18:00, Sun 10:00–17:00).

Picnicking: The fine **supermarket** faces the bus station (Mon–Sat 9:00–20:00, Sun 10:00–16:00, The Headslands). **Bryson's Bakery** (see above) does good sandwiches to go. **The Keswickian** serves up old fashioned fish-and-chips to go (daily 11:00–23:30, on the main square). Just around the corner, **The Cornish Pasty** offers an enticing variety of fresh meat pies to go until they're sold out (£2.30 pies, daily 9:30–17:00, across from the Dog and Gun Pub on Borrowdale Road).

Newlands Valley

The farmhouse B&Bs of Newlands Valley don't serve dinner, so their guests have three options: Go into Keswick, walk to the **Swinside Inn** (daily 18:30–20:45, reservations required, tel. 017687/78253), or take the lovely 10-minute drive to Buttermere for your evening meal at the **Fish Hotel Pub**, which has fine indoor and outdoor seating, but takes no reservations (£7 meals, daily 12:00–14:00 & 18:00–21:00, family-friendly, good fish and daily specials with fresh vegetables). The neighboring **Bridge Hotel Pub** is a bit cozier, but less popular (£6–7 meals, daily 12:00–21:30).

TRANSPORTATION CONNECTIONS

The nearest train station to Keswick is in Penrith. Penrith's small train station has a ticket window (Mon–Sat 5:30–21:00, Sun 11:30–21:00) but no lockers. For train and bus info, check at a local TI, visit www.traveline.org.uk, or call 08457-484-950 (for train), or either tel. 0870-608-2608 or 01604/676-060 (for buses). Most routes run less frequently on Sundays.

From Keswick by Bus to: See "Getting Around the Lake District—By Bus," page 315.

From Penrith by Bus to: Keswick (1/hr 7:15–22:30, only 6 on Sun, 40 min, £3.80, pay driver, Stagecoach buses #X4, #X5, and #X50), **Ullswater** and **Glenridding** (6/day, 1 hr, direction: Patterdale). The Penrith bus stop is in the train station's parking lot (bus schedules posted inside and outside station).

From Penrith by Train to: Oban (1/hr to Glasgow, 2 hrs; then to Oban, 2/day, 3 hrs), **Edinburgh** (6/day, 2 hrs), **Glasgow** (hrly, 2 hrs to Penrith), **Blackpool** (1/hr to Preston, 1 hr; then to Blackpool, 3/hr, 30 min), **Liverpool** (1/day, 2.5 hrs), **Birmingham**'s New Street Station (2/hr, 2 hrs), **London**'s Euston Station (1/hr, 4 hrs).

Route Tips for Drivers

Coming from (or Going to) the West: Only 1,300 feet above sea level, Hard Knott Pass is a thriller, with a narrow, winding, steeply graded road. Just over the pass are the scant but evocative remains of the Hard Knott Roman fortress. There are great views but miserable rainstorms, and it can be very slow and frustrating when the one-lane road with turnouts is clogged by traffic. Avoid it on summer weekends.

North Wales or Blackpool to the Lake District: The direct, easy way to Keswick is to leave M6 at Penrith and take the A66 highway for 16 miles to Keswick. For the scenic sightseeing drive through the south lakes to Keswick, exit M6 on A590/A591 through the towns of Kendal and Windermere to reach Brockhole National Park Visitors Centre. From Brockhole, the A road to

Keswick is fastest, but the high road—the tiny road over Kirkstone Pass to Glenridding and lovely Ullswater—is much more dramatic. See above for sightseeing details.

For the drive north to **Oban,** see page 490 of the Oban chapter.

Ullswater

▲▲**Ullswater Hike and Boat Ride**—Long, narrow Ullswater— which some consider the loveliest lake in the area—offers eight miles of diverse and grand Lake District scenery. While you can drive it or cruise it, I'd ride the boat from the south tip halfway up (to Howtown—which is nothing more than a dock) and hike back. Boats leave **Glenridding** regularly for Howtown (4–9/day depend- ing on the season, £5 one-way, £7

round-trip, daily 9:45–16:45, less off-season, 35-min ride; safe pay- and-display parking lot costs £2/2 hrs, £4/12 hrs; café, free time- table shows walking route, tel. 017684/82229 for schedule, www .ullswater-steamers.co.uk). From Howtown, spend three to four hours hiking and dawdling along the well-marked path by the lake south to Patterdale, and then along the road back to Glenridding. This is a serious seven-mile walk with good views, varied terrain, and a few bridges and farms along the way. For a shorter hike from Howtown Pier, consider a three-mile loop around Hallin Fell.

Several **steamer trips** chug daily up and down Ullswater. A bad-weather plan is to ride the covered boat up and down the lake (to the furthest point—Pooley Bridge, £10 round-trip, 2 hrs) or to Howtown and back (£7 round-trip, 1 hr). Bus access from Keswick to Glenridding is only practical in the summer (bus #208, late July–Aug only, 5/day, 40 min).

Helvellyn—Often considered the best high-mountain hike in the Lake District, this breathtaking round-trip route from Glenridding includes the spectacular Striding Edge—about a half mile along the ridge. Be careful; do this six-hour hike only in good weather since the wind can be fierce. Get advice from the Glenridding TI (summer daily 9:30–17:30; winter Fri–Sun 9:30–15:30, maybe closed Mon–Thu; tel. 017684/82414). While there are shorter routes, the Glenridding ascent is best. The Keswick TI has a help- ful *Helvellyn from Glenridding* leaflet on the hike (60p).

The South Lake District

The South Lake District has a cheesiness similar to other popular British resort destinations, such as Blackpool. Here, piles of low-end vacationers eat ice cream and get candy floss caught in their hair. The area around Windermere is worth a drive-through if you're a fan of Wordsworth or Beatrix Potter; otherwise, spend the majority of your Lake District time (and book your accommodations) up north.

Getting Around the South Lake District

By Car: This is your best option to see the small towns and sights clustered in the South Lake District; consider combining your drive with the bus trip mentioned below.

If you're coming to or leaving the South Lake District from the west, you could take the Hard Knott Pass for a scenic introduction to the area (see page 335).

By Bus: As mentioned at the beginning of the chapter, the topless (open-top) bus #599 stops at Bowness Pier (lake cruises), Windermere (train station), Brockhole (national park center), Ambleside, Rydal Mount, and Grasmere (Dove Cottage). It's a fine way to lace together this gauntlet of sights in the congested Lake Windermere neighborhood. Consider leaving your car at Grasmere and enjoying the breezy and extremely scenic ride, hopping off and on as you like (all-day pass-£6, family-£12, buy from the driver, daily April–Aug, 3/hr, 50 min each way).

SIGHTS

Wordsworth Sights

William Wordsworth was one of the first writers to reject fast-paced city life. During England's Industrial Age, hearts were muzzled and brains ruled. Science was in, machines were taming nature, and factory hours were taming humans. In reaction to these brainy ideals, a rare few—dubbed Romantics—began to embrace untamed nature and undomesticated emotions.

Nobody back then climbed a mountain just because it's there, but Wordsworth did. He'd "wander lonely as a cloud" through the countryside, finding inspiration in "plain living and high thinking." He soon attracted a circle of like-minded creative friends.

The emotional highs the Romantics felt weren't all natural. Wordsworth's poet friends Samuel Taylor Coleridge and Thomas de Quincey got stoned on opium and wrote about it, combining their generation's standard painkiller drug with their tree-hugging passions. Today, opium is out of vogue, but the Romantic

Wordsworth at Dove Cottage

William Wordsworth (1770–1850) was a Lake District homeboy. Born in Cockermouth (in a house open to the public), he was schooled in Hawkshead. In adulthood, he married a local girl, settled down in Grasmere and Ambleside, and was buried in Grasmere's St. Oswald's churchyard.

But the 30-year-old man who moved into Dove Cottage in 1779 was not the carefree lad who'd roamed the District's lakes and fields. At Cambridge University, he'd been a C student, graduating with no job skills and no interest in a "nine-to-five" career. Instead, he and a buddy hiked through Europe, where Wordsworth had an epiphany of the "sublime" atop Switzerland's Alps. He lived a year in France, watching the Revolution rage. It stirred his soul. He fell in love with a Frenchwoman who bore his daughter, Caroline. But lack of money forced him to return to England, and the outbreak of war with France kept them apart.

Pining away in London, William hung out in the pubs and coffee houses with fellow radicals, where he met fellow poet Samuel Taylor Coleridge. They inspired each other to write, they edited each other's work, and they jointly published a groundbreaking book of poetry.

In 1799, his head buzzing with words and ideas, William and his sister (and soulmate) Dorothy moved into the white-washed, slate-tiled former inn now known as Dove Cottage. He came into a small inheritance, and dedicated himself to poetry full time. In 1802, with the war over, William returned to France to finally meet his daughter. (He wrote of the rich experience: "It is a beauteous evening, calm and free.../Dear child! Dear Girl! that walkest with me here,/If thou appear untouched by solemn thought,/Thy nature is not therefore less divine.")

Having achieved closure, Wordsworth returned home to marry a former kindergarten classmate, Mary. She moved into Dove Cottage, along with an initially jealous Dorothy. Three of their five children were born here, and the Cottage was also home to Mary's sister, the family dog Pepper (a gift from Sir Walter Scott; see Pepper's portrait), and frequent house-guests who bedded down in the pantry: Scott, Coleridge, and Thomas de Quincey, the Timothy Leary of opium.

After nearly nine years here, Wordsworth's family and social status were outgrowing the humble cottage. They moved first to a house in Grasmere before settling down in Rydal Hall. Wordsworth was changing. After the Dove years, he would write less, settle into a regular government job, quarrel with Coleridge, drift to the right politically, and endure criticism from old friends who branded him a sellout. Still, his poetry—most of it written at Dove—became increasingly famous, and he died honored as England's Poet Laureate.

movement thrives as visitors continue to inundate the region.

▲▲**Dove Cottage and Wordsworth Museum**—The poet whose appreciation of nature and a back-to-basics lifestyle put this area on the map spent his most productive years (1799–1808) in this well-preserved stone cottage on the edge of Grasmere. After functioning as the Dove and Olive Bow pub for nearly 200 years, it was bought by his family. This is where he got married, had kids, and wrote much of his best poetry. The furniture, still owned by the Wordsworth family, was his, and the place comes with some amazing artifacts, including the poet's passport and suitcase (he packed light). Today, Dove Cottage is *the* obligatory sight for any Wordsworth admirer. Even if you're not a fan, Wordsworth's "plain living and high thinking," his appreciation of nature, his Romanticism, and the ways his friends unleashed their creative talents with such abandon are appealing. The 30-minute cottage **tour** (departures on the hour and half hour) and adjoining **museum**—with lots of actual manuscripts handwritten by Wordsworth and his illustrious friends—are each excellent. In dry weather, the garden where the poet was much inspired is worth a wander. (Visit before leaving the cottage, pick up the description at the back door.) Allow at least an hour for this two-part attraction (£6, daily mid-Feb–mid-Jan 9:30–17:30, last entry at 17:00, closed mid-Jan–mid-Feb, tel. 015394/35544, www.wordsworth.org.uk). Parking is free and easy on the Dove Cottage lot facing the main road (A591).

Poetry Readings: On Tuesday evenings in summer, the Wordsworth Trust puts on poetry readings, where national poets read their own works. They're hoping to continue the poetry tradition of the Lake District. Readings are held at Prince of Wales Hotel (18:30 Tue, 2 45-min sessions followed by an optional dinner, £6 at the door or £5 pre-booked, across the big road from Dove Cottage, tel. 015394/35544).

Rydal Mount—Wordsworth's final, higher-class home, with a lovely garden and view, lacks the charm of Dove Cottage. He lived

here 37 years. His family repurchased it in 1969 (after a 100-year gap), and his great-great-granddaughter still calls it home on occasion. Located just down the road from Dove Cottage, it's worthwhile only for Wordsworth fans (£4.50, March–Oct daily 9:30–17:00; Nov–Feb Wed–Mon 10:00–16:00, closed Tue; 1.5 miles north of Ambleside, well-signed, free and easy parking, tel. 015394/33002). If you're visiting Dove Cottage and Rydal Mount, a discount coupon saves you 75p.

Wordsworth's Poetry at Dove

At Dove Cottage, Wordsworth was immersed in the beauty of nature and the simple joy of his young, growing family. It was here that he reflected on both his idyllic childhood and his troubled 20s. The following are select lines from two well-known poems from this fertile time.

Ode: Intimations of Immortality

There was a time when meadow, grove, and stream,
The earth, and every common sight, to me did seem
Apparelled in celestial light, the glory and the
    freshness of a dream.
It is not now as it hath been of yore; turn wheresoe'er
    I may, by night or day,
The things which I have seen I now can see no more.
Now while the birds thus sing a joyous song...
To me alone there came a thought of grief...
Whither is fled the visionary gleam?
Where is it now, the glory and the dream?
Our birth is but a sleep and a forgetting:
The Soul...cometh from afar...
Trailing clouds of glory do we come
From God, who is our home.

I Wandered Lonely as a Cloud

I wandered lonely as a cloud
That floats on high o'er vales and hills,
When all at once I saw a crowd,
A host, of golden daffodils;
Beside the lake, beneath the trees,
Fluttering and dancing in the breeze...
For oft, when on my couch I lie
In vacant or in pensive mood,
They flash upon that inward eye
Which is the bliss of solitude;
And then my heart with pleasure fills,
And dances with the daffodils.

Beatrix Potter Sights

Of the many Beatrix Potter commercial ventures in the Lake District, there are two serious Beatrix Potter sights: her farm (Hill Top Farm) and her husband's former office, which is now an art gallery filled with her sketches and paintings (Beatrix Potter Gallery). Both sights are in or near Hawkshead, a 10-minute drive south of Ambleside. If you're coming over from Windermere, catch the cute little 18-car ferry (£2.50, 10-min trip, runs constantly). Note that these sights both are closed on Thursday and Friday.

Beatrix Potter
(1866–1943)

As a girl growing up in London, Beatrix Potter vacationed in the Lake District, where she became inspired to write her popular children's books. Unable to get a publisher, she self-published the first two editions of *The Tale of Peter Rabbit* in 1901 and 1902. When she finally landed a publisher, sales of her books were phenomenal. With the money she made, she bought Hill Top Farm, a 17th-century cottage; she fixed it up, living there from 1905 until she married in 1913. Potter was more than a children's book writer; she was a fine artist, an avid gardener, and a successful farmer. She married a lawyer and put her knack for business to use, amassing a 4,000-acre estate. An early conservationist, she used the garden-cradled cottage as a place to study nature. She willed it—along with the rest of her vast estate—to the National Trust, which she enthusiastically supported.

Hill Top Farm—A hit with Beatrix Potter fans, this farm was left just as it was when she died in 1943. While there's no information here (you'll need to buy the £3 guidebook for details on what you see), the dark and intimate cottage, swallowed up in the inspirational and rough nature around it, provides an enjoyable if quick experience (£5, April–Oct Sat–Wed 10:30–16:30, closed Thu–Fri and Nov–March, last entry 30 min before closing, in Near Sawrey village, 2 miles south of Hawkshead, tel. 015394/36269). Park and buy your ticket 150 yards down the road, and walk back to tour the place.

▲▲Beatrix Potter Gallery—Located in the cute but extremely touristy town of Hawkshead (see below), this gallery fills her husband's former law office with the wonderful and intimate drawings and watercolors that Potter did to illustrate her books. The best of the Potter sights, the gallery has plenty of explanation about her life and work. You'll find surprisingly interesting art even for non-Potter fans. Of about 700 works in the gallery's possession, a rotation of about 40 are shown at any one time (£3.50, tiny discount with Hill Top Farm, April–Oct Sat–Wed 10:30–16:30, closed Thu–Fri and Nov–March, Main Street, use the pay-and-display lot by the TI and walk 200 yards to the town center, tel. 015394/36355).

Hawkshead—The town of Hawkshead is engulfed in Potter tourism, and the extreme quaintness of it all is off-putting. If you must linger, use the pay-and-display lot. Just across from the parking lot is the interesting Hawkshead Grammar School, founded in 1585, where William Wordsworth studied from 1779 to 1787. It shows off old school benches and desks that were whittled with penknife graffiti (£1, daily 10:00–17:00).

The World of Beatrix Potter—This tour, a hit with children, is a gimmicky exhibit with all the history of a Disney ride. The 45-minute experience features a five-minute video trip into the world of Mrs. Tiggywinkle and company, a series of Lake District tableaux starring the same imaginary gang, and an all-about-Beatrix section, with an eight-minute video biography (£5, daily Easter–Sept 10:00–17:30, Oct–Easter 10:00–16:30, closed Jan, in Bowness near Windermere town, tel. 015394/88444, www.hop-skip-jump.com).

On Lake Windermere

▲**Brockhole National Park Visitors Centre**—This center, engulfed in a nicely groomed lakeside park, offers a free 15-minute life-in-the-Lake District slide show (played upon request), an information desk, organized walks, exhibits, a bookshop (excellent selection of maps and guidebooks), a fine cafeteria, gardens, nature walks, and a large parking lot. Check the events board as you enter (free entry but steep £3.50 to park—coins only or buy ticket at the Visitors Centre 100 yards away, April–Oct daily 10:00–17:00, less shoulder season, closed Nov–March, tel. 015394/46601, www.lake-district.gov.uk). It's in a stately old lakeside mansion between Ambleside and the town of Windermere on A591. For a joyride around famous Windermere, catch the Brockhole cruise (40-min circle, 2/hr, £6, scant narration).

In Ambleside

Hayes Garden World—This extensive gardening center, a popular weekend excursion for locals, offers garden supplies, a bookstore, playground, and gorgeous grounds. Gardeners could wander this place all afternoon. Upstairs is a fine cafeteria-style restaurant (Mon–Sat 9:00–18:00, Sun 11:00–17:00, at south end of Ambleside on main drag, see Garden Centre signs, tel. 015394/33434, www.hayesgardenworld.co.uk).

YORK

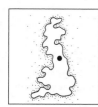

Historic York is loaded with world-class sights. Marvel at the York Minster, England's finest Gothic church. Ramble the Shambles, York's wonderfully preserved medieval quarter. Enjoy a walking tour led by an old Yorker. Hop a train at Europe's greatest railway museum, travel to the 1800s in the York Castle Museum, and head back a thousand years to Viking York at the Jorvik exhibit.

York has a rich history. In A.D. 71, it was Eboracum, a Roman provincial capital—the northernmost city in the Empire. Constantine was actually proclaimed emperor here in A.D. 306. In the fifth century, as Rome was toppling, a Roman emperor sent a letter telling England it was on its own, and York became Eoforwic, the capital of the Anglo-Saxon kingdom of Northumbria. A church was built here in 627, and the town became an early Christian center of learning. The Vikings later took the town, and from the ninth through the 11th centuries, it was a Danish trading center called Jorvik. The invading and conquering Normans destroyed then rebuilt the city, fortifying it with a castle and the walls you see today. Medieval York, with 9,000 inhabitants, grew rich on the wool trade and became England's second city. Henry VIII used the city's fine Minster as his Anglican Church's northern capital. The Archbishop of York is second only to the Archbishop of Canterbury in the Anglican Church. In the Industrial Age, York was the railway hub of North England. When it was built, York's train station was the world's largest. Today York's leading industry is tourism.

Planning Your Time

York rivals Edinburgh as the best sightseeing city in Britain after London. On even a 10-day trip through Britain, it deserves two nights and a day. For the best 36 hours, follow this plan: Catch the 18:45 city walking tour on the evening of your arrival (evening tours offered mid-June through Aug). The next morning, be at the Castle Museum at 9:30 when it opens—it's worth a good two hours. Then browse and sightsee through the day. Train buffs love the National Railway Museum, and scholars give the Yorkshire Museum high ratings. Tour the Minster at 16:00 before catching the 17:30 evensong service (16:00 on Sun). Finish your day with an early evening stroll along the wall and perhaps through the abbey gardens. This schedule assumes you're there in the summer (evening orientation walk) and that there's an evensong on. Confirm your plans with the TI.

ORIENTATION

(area code: 01904)

The sightseer's York is small. Virtually everything is within a few minutes' walk: sights, train station, TI, and B&Bs. The longest walk a visitor might take (from a B&B across the old town to the Castle Museum) is 15 minutes.

Bootham Bar, a gate in the medieval town wall, is the hub of your York visit. (In York, a "bar" is a gate and a "gate" is a street. Go ahead, blame the Vikings.) At Bootham Bar and on Exhibition Square facing it, you'll find the TI; the starting points for most walking tours and bus tours; handy access to the medieval town wall; and Bootham Street, which leads to the recommended B&Bs. When finding your way, navigate by sighting the tower of the Minster or the strategically placed green signposts pointing out all places of interest to tourists.

Tourist Information

The TI at Bootham Bar sells a £1 *York Map and Guide*. Ask for the free monthly *What's On* guide and the *York MiniGuide*, which includes a map and some discounts (April–Oct Mon–Sat 9:00–18:00, Sun 10:00–17:00, likely 10:00–16:00 off-season, WCs next door, tel. 01904/621-756). The TI books rooms for a £4 fee (and takes 10 percent from your host). The train-station TI is smaller but provides all the same information and services (same hours as main TI).

York Day Pass: The TI sells a pass that covers most York sights (but not Jorvik or the Castle Museum), major sights in the region, and the city hop-on, hop-off bus tour. If you take the bus tour and are a busy sightseer, it can save money (£19/1 day, £25/2 days, £32/3 days).

Arrival in York

The train station, which stores luggage for day-trippers (£4, Mon–Sat 8:00–20:30, Sun 9:00–20:30, platform 1), is a five-minute **walk** from town. From the station, turn left down Station Road and follow the crowd toward the Gothic towers of the Minster. After the bridge, a block before the Minster, signs to the TI send you left on St. Leonard's Place. Recommended B&Bs are a five-minute walk from there. (For a shortcut to B&B area from the train station, walk 1 block toward the Minster, cut through parks to riverside, cross railway bridge/pedestrian walkway, cross parking lot for B&Bs on St. Mary's Street, or duck through pedestrian walkway under tracks to B&Bs on Sycamore and Queen Anne's Road.)

Taxis zip new arrivals to their B&B for £3–4. (To summon one, call 01904/623-332 or 01904/638-833; cabbies don't start the meter until you get in.)

Helpful Hints

Study Ahead: York has a great Web site: www.visityork.org.

Festivals: The Viking Festival features *lur* horn-blowing, warrior drills, and re-created battles (Feb 18–26). The Late Music Festival is March 10–29...if it starts on time. The Early Music Festival (medieval minstrels, Renaissance dance, and so on) zings its strings from July 6–15 (www.ncem.co.uk/yemf.shtml). And the York Festival of Food and Drink takes a bite out of the end of September (Sept 22–Oct 1 www.yorkfestivaloffoodanddrink .com). Book a room well in advance during festival times and weekends any time of year.

Internet Access: Get online at the creaky, hip, and funky **Evil Eye Café** (daily 10:00–23:00, 10 terminals, 42 Stonegate) or **Gateway Internet Exchange** (Mon–Sat 11:00–18:00, closed Sun, in the basement of the City Screens Cinema on Coney Street, tel. 01904/646-446).

Laundry: Near the Bootham B&Bs, **Regency Dry Cleaning** is expensive (£4/kilogram—about 2 lbs, Mon–Fri 8:30–18:00, Sat 9:00–17:00, closed Sun, drop off by 9:30 for same-day service, 75 Bootham, at intersection with Queen Anne's Road, tel. 01904/613-311). The next-nearest place is **Washeteria Launderette,** a long 15-minute walk away (self-service or drop-off, 124 Haxby Road, tel. 01904/623-379).

Bike Rental: Trotters, just outside Monk Bar, rents bikes and has free cycling maps (£12/day, tandem-£30/day, includes helmets, Mon–Sat 9:00–17:30, Sun 10:00–16:00, tel. 01904/622-868). **Europcar** at the train station also rents bikes (£10/day, platform 1, tel. 01904/656-161).

The riverside path is pleasant.

Car Rental: If you're nearing the end of your trip, consider dropping your car upon arrival in York. The money saved by turning it in early nearly pays for the train ticket that whisks you effortlessly to Edinburgh or London. In York, you'll find: **Avis** (Mon–Sat, closed Sat afternoon and Sun, 3 Layerthorpe, tel. 01904/610-460); **Hertz** (April–Sept daily, Sat–Sun until 13:00, at train station, tel. 01904/612-586); **Sixt** (Mon–Sat, closed Sun, inconveniently 3 miles out of town at Clifton Moor Industrial Estate, tel. 01904/479-715); **Budget** (daily, Sat and Sun only 9:00–11:00, a mile past recommended B&Bs at Clifton 82, tel. 01904/644-919); and **Europcar** (Mon–Fri 8:00–18:00, Sat–Sun until 13:00, train station platform 1, tel. 01904/656-161, central reservations tel. 0870-607-5000). Beware, car-rental agencies close Saturday afternoon and some close all day Sunday—when drop-offs are OK, but picking up is impossible.

TOURS

▲▲▲**Walking Tours**—Charming local volunteer guides give energetic, entertaining, and free two-hour walks through York (daily at 10:15 all year, plus 14:15 April–Oct, plus 18:45 mid-June–Aug, from Exhibition Square across from TI). These tours often go long because the guides love to teach and tell stories. You're welcome to cut out early—but say so or they'll worry, thinking they lost you.

There are many other commercial York walking tours. YorkWalk Tours, for example, has reliable guides and many themes from which to choose, such as Roman York, City Walls, or Snickelways—small alleys (£5, tel. 01904/622-303, www .yorkwalk.co.uk, TI has schedule). The ghost tours, all offered after nightfall, are more fun than informative. Haunted Walk relies a bit more on storytelling and history than on masks and surprises (£3, April–Nov nightly at 20:00, 90 min, just show up, depart from Exhibition Square, across street from TI, end in the Shambles, tel. 01904/621-003).

▲**Hop-on, Hop-off Bus Tours**—With one £8 ticket, you can jump on or off your choice of the two tours circling York. The tours generally follow the same route. The main difference is that the Guide Friday York Tour is longer and has live guides (green bus, 60-min loop, with a few extra stops, including York Racecourse and Rowntree Park), and the City Sightseeing tour has recorded narration (red bus, 45 min). Both tours cover secondary York sights that the city walking tours skip—the mundane perimeter of town (pay driver cash, can also buy from TI with credit card, departures every 10 min or more from 9:00 until about 17:00, less

York

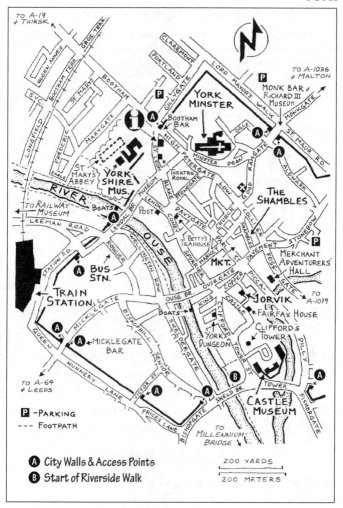

frequent off-season, Guide Friday tours don't run Nov–March, tel. 01904/655-585). While you can hop on and off all day, the tours are of no real value from a transportation-to-the-sights point of view because York is so compact. I'd catch either tour at the Bootham Bar TI and ride it for an orientation all the way around or get off at the Railway Museum, skipping the last five minutes.

Boat Cruise—The York Boat does a lazy 60-minute lap along the River Ouse (£6.50, Feb–Nov daily from 10:30 on, every 30 min from April–Oct, narrated cruise, leaves from Lendal Bridge and King's Staith landing) and also offers themed evening

England's Anglican Church

The Anglican Church came into existence in 1534 when Henry VIII declared that he, and not Pope Clement VII, was the head of England's Catholics. The Pope had refused to allow Henry to divorce his wife to marry his mistress Anne Boleyn (which Henry did anyway, resulting in the birth of the future Elizabeth I). Still, Henry regarded himself as a faithful Catholic—just not a *Roman* Catholic—and made relatively few changes in how and what Anglicans worshipped.

Henry's son Edward VI instituted many of the changes that Reformation Protestants were bringing about in continental Europe (emphasis on preaching, people in the pews actually reading the Bible, clergy being allowed to marry, and a more "Protestant" liturgy in English from the revised Book of Common Prayer, 1549). The next monarch, Edward's sister Mary I, returned England to the Roman Catholic Church (1553), earning the nickname of "Bloody Mary" for her brutal suppression of Protestant elements. When Elizabeth I succeeded Mary (1558), she soon broke from Rome again. Today, many regard the Anglican Church as a compromise between the Catholic and Protestant traditions.

Is York's Minster the leading Anglican church in England? Yes and no (but mostly no). After a long feud, the archbishops of Canterbury and York agreed that York's bishop would have the title "Primate of England" and Canterbury's would be the "Primate of All England," directing Anglicans on the national level.

cruises—ghost, dinner, floodlit, and so on (boat rentals possible, tel. 01904/628-324, www.yorkboat.com).

SELF-GUIDED WALK

Wall Walk from the Minster

Start your time in York at its spectacular Minster (see sight listing below). After visiting the Minster, consider taking this stroll up along a segment of York's wall.

• *Head just across from the Minster to the...*

Roman Column: Erected in 1971, this column commemorates the 1,900th anniversary of the Roman founding of Eboracum (later called York). Across the street is a statue of the emperor Constantine, who was in York when his father died. The troops declared him emperor, and six years later, he went to Rome and claimed his throne. In 312, Constantine legalized Christianity, and in 314, York got its first bishop. Today's Minster stands upon the remains of a Roman fort.

Study the Minster. You're looking at the glory of Gothic. The main tower was intended to hold a towering spire—too much. Even without all that extra weight, the church stands today only with the help of big, modern braces holding the foundation together.

• *Hike past the west portal of the Minster and down the street to...*

Bootham Bar: This is one of four gates on York's medieval walls (free, open until dusk). The 12th-century walls are three miles long. Norman kings built the walls to assert control over North England. This was a center for Romans, Normans, and Henry VIII (16th century). In the 19th century, York was a center of industry (and hub of the railway system).

• *Now climb up on...*

The Wall: Hike along the top of the wall behind the Minster to the first corner. Notice the pivots in the crenellations (square notches at the top of a medieval wall), which once held wooden hatches that provided cover for archers. At the corner, you can see the moat outside and a fine view of the Minster, with its truncated main tower and the pointy rooftop of its chapter house. The roofing—traditionally lead—melts during a fire and cascades to the ground.

Continue on to the next gate, **Monk Bar.** Keep an eye on the 12th-century guards, with their stones raised and primed to protect the town. Descend the wall at Monk Bar and step past the portcullis and outside the city's protective wall. Lean against the last bollard and gaze up at the tower, imagining 10 archers behind the arrow slits.

Walking back into town from here, you'll find a number of good eateries on Goodramgate (see "Eating," page 363). At the first corner, College Street leads right to the east end of the Minster along St. Williams College (1461) and the home of bishops and priests.

SIGHTS

York Minster

The pride of York, and worth ▲▲▲, this largest Gothic church north of the Alps (540 feet long, 200 feet tall) brilliantly shows that the High Middle Ages were far from dark. The word "minster" means a place from which people go out to minister or spread the word of God. As it's the seat of a bishop, it's also a cathedral. While Henry VIII destroyed the great abbeys, this was

York at a Glance

▲▲▲**Minster** York's pride and joy, and one of England's finest churches, with stunning stained-glass windows, textbook Decorated Gothic design, and glorious evensong services. **Hours:** Open for worship daily from 7:00 and for sightseeing Mon–Sat from 9:30, Sun from 12:30; flexible closing time (roughly May–Oct at 18:30, earlier off-season); shorter hours for tower and undercroft; evensong services Mon–Sat 17:30, Sun 16:00, sometimes no services mid-July–Aug.

▲▲▲**Castle Museum** Excellent, far-ranging collection includes replicas of century-old streets and everyday objects from Victorian times to the present. **Hours:** Daily 9:30–17:00.

▲▲**National Railway Museum** Train buff's nirvana, tracing the history of all manner of rail-bound transport. **Hours:** Daily 10:00–18:00.

▲▲**Yorkshire Museum** Sophisticated archaeology museum with York's best Viking exhibit, plus Roman, Saxon, Norman, and Gothic artifacts. **Hours:** Daily 10:00–17:00.

▲**The Shambles** Atmospheric old butcher's quarter, with colorful, tipsy medieval buildings. **Hours:** Always open.

▲**Jorvik** Cheesy, crowded, but not-quite-Disney-quality exhibit/ride exploring Viking lifestyles and artifacts. **Hours:** Daily April–Sept 10:00–17:00, Oct–March until 16:00.

▲**Fairfax House** Glimpse into an 18th-century Georgian house, with enjoyably chatty docents. **Hours:** Mon–Thu and Sat 11:00–17:00, Sun 13:30–17:00, Fri by tour only at 11:00 and 14:00.

not part of a monastery and therefore left standing. It seats 2,000 comfortably; on Christmas and Easter, more than 4,000 worshipers pack the place. Today, more than 250 employees and 300 volunteers work to preserve its heritage and welcome the half-million visitors each year.

Cost, Hours, Tours: The cathedral opens daily for worship at 7:00 and for sightseeing Mon–Sat from 9:30 and Sunday from 12:30, when they begin charging £5 admission. The closing time flexes with the season (roughly May–Oct at 18:30, earlier off-season—call for details, tel. 01904/557-216). The tower (£3) and undercroft (£3.50, or £7 combo-ticket includes undercroft and cathedral entry, saves you £1.50) have shorter hours, typically opening a half hour later and closing a half hour earlier than the Minster.

When you enter, go directly to the welcome desk, pick up the worthwhile *Welcome to the York Minster* flier, and ask when the next free guided 60-minute **tour** departs (2/hr, 9:30–14:00, they go even with just 1 or 2 people; you can join one in progress, or if none is scheduled, request a departure). The helpful Minster guides, wearing blue armbands, are happy to answer your questions.

Evensong and Church Bells: To experience the cathedral in musical and spiritual action, attend an evensong (Mon–Sat 17:30, Sun 16:00, 45 min). When the choir is off on school break (mid-July–Aug), visiting choirs usually fill in (confirm at church or TI). Arrive 10 minutes early and wait just outside the choir in the center of the church. You'll be ushered in and can sit in one of the big wooden stalls. If you're a fan of church bells, you'll experience ding-dong ecstasy on Sunday morning (about 10:00) and the Tuesday-evening practice (19:30–21:30). Stand in front of the church's west portal and imagine the gang pulling on a dozen ropes (halfway up the right tower—you can actually see the ropes through a little window).

◑ Self-Guided Tour: Upon entering, head left, to the back (west end) of the church. Stand in front of the grand **west door** (used only on Sundays) on the *Deo Gratias 627–1927* plaque—a place of worship for 1,300 years, thanks to God. On the door, the list of bishops goes unbroken back to the 600s. The statue of Peter with the key and Bible is a reminder that the church is dedicated to St. Peter, and the key to Heaven is found through the word of God. While the Minster sits on the remains of a Romanesque church (c. 1100), today's church was begun in 1220 and took 250 years to complete. King Edward I and II used it as a base, actually holding parliament here in the Chapter House (rather than in London) while fighting Scotland.

Looking down the church, your first impression might be the spaciousness and brightness of the nave (built 1280–1350). The nave—from the middle period of Gothic, called "Decorated Gothic"—is one of the widest Gothic naves in Europe. Rather than risk a stone roof, builders spanned the space with wood. Colorful shields on the arcades are the coats of arms of nobles who helped Edward I fight the Scots. The coats of arms in the clerestory (upper-level) glass represent the nobles who helped Edward II in the same fight. There's more medieval glass in this building than in the rest of England combined. This precious glass survived World War II—hidden in stately homes throughout Yorkshire.

Walk to the very center of the church, under the **central tower.** Look up. Look down. Read about how gifts and skill saved this tower from collapse. (The first tower collapsed in 1407.) While the tower is 60 yards tall, it was intended to be much taller. Use the neck-saving mirror to marvel at it.

From here, you can survey many impressive features of the church:

In the **north transept,** the grisaille windows—dubbed the "Five Sisters"—are dedicated to women of the empire who died in all wars. Made in 1250 (before colored glass was produced in England), these contain more than 100,000 pieces of glass.

The **south transept** features the tourists' entry, where stairs lead down to the undercroft. The new "bosses" (carved medallions decorating the point where the ribs meet on the ceiling) are a reminder that the roof of this wing of the church was destroyed by fire in 1984. Some believe the fire was God's angry response to a new bishop, David Jenkins, who questioned the literal truth of Jesus' miracles. Others blame an electricity box hit by lightning. Regardless, the entire country came to York's aid. Blue Peter (England's top kids' show) conducted a competition among their young viewers to design new bosses. Out of 30,000 entries, there were six winners (the blue ones—e.g., man on the moon, feed the children, save the whales).

Look back at the west end to marvel at the **Great West Window,** especially the stone tracery. While its nickname is the "Heart of York," it represents the sacred heart of Christ and reminds people of his love for the world.

Find the **dragon** on the right of the nave (two-thirds of the way up). While no one is sure of its purpose, it pivots and has a hole through its neck—so it was likely a mechanism designed to raise a lid on a baptismal font.

The **choir screen** is an ornate wall of carvings separating the nave from the choir. It's lined with all the English kings from William I (the Conqueror) to Henry VI (during whose reign it was carved, 1461). Numbers indicate the years each reigned. To say "it's slathered in gold leaf" sounds impressive, but the gold's very thin... a nugget the size of a sugar cube is pounded into a sheet the size of a driveway.

Step into the **choir,** where Mass is held daily. All the carving was redone after an 1829 fire, but its tradition of glorious evensong services (sung by choristers from the Minster School) goes all the way back to the eighth century.

The astronomical clock in the **north transept** commemorates the 18,000 airmen who died in World War II flying from bases here in northern England. The Book of Remembrance contains all those names.

A corridor that functions as a small church museum leads to the Gothic, octagonal **chapter room**—the traditional meeting place of the governing body (or chapter) of the Minster. It's remarkable (almost frightening) for its breadth without an interior support. The fanciful carvings decorating the canopies above the stalls date from 1280 (80 percent are originals) and are some of the Minster's finest. Above the doorway, the Virgin holds baby Jesus while standing on the devilish serpent. Grates still send hot air up robes of attendees on cold winter mornings. A model of the wooden construction illustrates the impressive 1285 engineering.

The **east end** is square, lacking a semicircular apse, typical of England's Perpendicular Gothic style (15th century). The window, the size of a tennis court, is a carefully designed ensemble of biblical symbolism with God the Father presiding over ranks of saints and angels on the top; nine rows of 117 panels telling Bible stories in the middle; and a row of bishops and kings on the bottom. A chart (on the right, with a tiny, more helpful chart within—locate panels with color-coded numbers) highlights the core Old Testament scenes in this hard-to-read masterpiece. Enjoy the art close up on the chart, then step back and find the real thing. Because of its immense size, there's an extra layer of supportive stonework, making parts of it wide enough to walk along. In fact, for special occasions, the choir sings from the walkway halfway up the window. Monuments (almost no graves) were once strewn throughout the church, but in the Victorian age, they were gathered into the east end, where you see them today.

Tower and Undercroft: There are two extra sights to consider, both accessed from the south transept. You can scale the 275-step **tower** for the panoramic view (£3). The **undercroft** consists of the crypt, treasury, and foundations (£3.50 including audioguide, or £7 combo-ticket for Minster and crypt but not tower). The crypt is an actual bit of the Romanesque church, featuring 12th-century Romanesque art, excavated in modern times. The foundations give you a chance to climb down—archaeologically and physically— through the centuries to see the roots of the much smaller, but still huge, Norman (Romanesque) church from 1100 that stood on this spot and, below that, the Roman excavations. As you wander, ponder the fact that Constantine was proclaimed Roman emperor here in A.D. 306. Peek also at the modern concrete save-the-church foundations.

More Sights

▲**The Shambles**—This is the most colorful old street in the half-timbered, traffic-free core of town. Walk to the midway point, at the intersection with Little Shambles. Ye olde downtown York feels made for window-shopping, street musicians, and people-watching. This 100-yard-long street was once the "street of the butchers" (the name is derived from *shammell*—a butcher's cutting block). In the 16th century, it was busy with red meat. On the hooks under the eaves once hung rabbit, pheasant, beef, lamb, and pigs' heads. Fresh slabs were displayed on the fat sills. People lived above—as they did even in Roman times. The soil here wasn't great for building. Notice how things settled in the absence of a good soil engineer.

Little Shambles leads to the frumpy Newgate Market (popular for cheap produce and clothing), created in the 1960s with the

demolition of a bunch of lanes as colorful as the Shambles. Return to the Shambles a little farther along, through a covered lane (or "snickelway"). Study the 16th-century oak carpentry—mortar and tenon joints with wooden plugs rather than nails.

For a cheap lunch, consider the cute, tiny **St. Crux Parish Hall.** This medieval church is now used by a medley of charities selling tea, homemade cakes, and light meals. They each book the church for a day, often a year in advance. Chat up the volunteers (Mon–Sat 10:00–16:00, closed Sun, at bottom end of the Shambles, at intersection with Pavement).

▲▲▲**Castle Museum**—Truly one of Europe's top museums, this is a Victorian home show, the closest thing to a time-tunnel experience England has to offer. Even a speedy museumgoer will want a couple hours here. Stroll down the museum's two recreated streets: **Kirkgate,** from the Victorian era, and **Half Moon Court**, from the Edwardian (early 20th-century) period. These streets are a collection of old shops shown exactly as they were a century or so ago. The post office, where you could buy nearly anything along with your stamps, doubled as the general store. Double-parked just outside the post office is the Rolls-Royce of Roma (Gypsy) caravans (which was restored to its 19th-century splendor by local Roma). The candy shop is stocked with old-time sweets still remembered by local grannies. In the watch-repair shop, it seems like the watchmaker just stepped out for a cup of tea.

The "From Cradle to Grave" clothing exhibit and fine costume collection are also impressive. The one-way plan assures you'll see everything: a working water mill, prison cells with related exhibits, the domestic side of World War II, Victorian toys, and a century of swimsuit fashions. The museum's £3 guidebook isn't necessary, but it makes a fine souvenir. The museum proudly offers no audioguides, as its living guides in each room are enthusiastic about talking—engage them (£6.50, daily 9:30–17:00, gift shop, parking, cafeteria midway through museum, tel. 01904/650-333, www.yorkcastlemuseum.org.uk; at the bottom of the hop-on, hop-off bus route; museum can call you a taxi—worthwhile if you're hurrying to the National Railway Museum).

Clifford's Tower—Located across from the Castle Museum, this ruin is all that's left of York's 13th-century castle, the site of a 1190 massacre of local Jews (read about this at base of hill). If you climb inside, there are fine city views from the top of the ramparts (not worth the £2.80, daily April–Sept 10:00–18:00, Oct–March until 16:00).

▲Jorvik—Take the "Pirates of the Caribbean," sail them north and back 1,000 years, and you get Jorvik—more a ride than a museum. Innovative 10 years ago, the commercial success of Jorvik (YOR-vik) inspired copycat ride/museums all over England. You'll ride a little Disney-type train car for 20 minutes through the re-created Viking street of Coppergate. It's the year 975, and you're in the village of Jorvik. Next, your little train takes you through the actual excavation site that inspired the reconstructed village. Everything is true to the dig—even the faces of the models are derived by computer from skulls dug up here. Finally you'll browse through a small gallery of Viking shoes, combs, locks, and other intimate glimpses of that redheaded culture. The exhibit on bone archaeology is fascinating (£7.45, daily April–Sept 10:00–17:00, Oct–March until 16:00, tel. 01904/643-211, www.vikingjorvik.com).

Midday lines can be an hour long in the peak of summer. Avoid the line by going very early or very late in the day, or by pre-booking (call 01904/543-403, you're given a time slot, £1 booking fee). Some love this attraction, while others call it a gimmicky rip-off. If you're looking for a grown-up museum, the Viking exhibit at the Yorkshire Museum is far better. If you're thinking Disneyland with a splash of history, Jorvik's fun. To me, Jorvik is a commercial venture designed for kids, with nearly as much square footage devoted to its shop as to the museum.

▲▲National Railway Museum—If you like model railways, this is train-car heaven. The thunderous museum shows 200 illustrious years of British railroad history. Fanning out from a grand round-house is an array of historic cars and engines, including Queen Victoria's lavish royal car and the very first "stagecoaches on rails," with its crude steam engine from 1830. A working steam engine is sliced open, showing cylinders, driving wheels, and smoke box in action. You'll trace the evolution of steam-powered transportation to the era of the aerodynamic Mallard, famous as the first train to travel at a startling two miles per minute (a marvel back in 1938). There's much more, including exhibits on dining cars, post cars, sleeping cars, train posters, and videos. At the Works section, you can see live train switchboards. And don't miss the English Channel Tunnel video (showing the first handshake at breakthrough). Purple-shirted "explainers" are everywhere, eager to talk trains. This biggest and best railroad museum anywhere is interesting even to people who think "Pullman" means "don't push" (free, £3 audioguide with 60 bits of railroad lore is worthwhile for train buffs, daily 10:00–18:00, snack bar sells Thomas the Tank Engine lunch sacks, tel. 01904/621-261, www.nrm.org.uk). A cute little "street train" shuttles you between the Minster and the Railway Museum (£1.50 each way, Easter–Oct, leaves Railway Museum every 30 min from 12:00 to 17:00 at the top and bottom of the hour; leaves the town—from Duncombe Place, 100 yards in front of the Minster—every 30 min, :15 and :45 min after the hour).

▲▲**Yorkshire Museum**—Located in a lush, picnic-perfect park next to the stately ruins of St. Mary's Abbey, Yorkshire Museum is the city's forgotten, serious "archaeology of York" museum. While the hordes line up at Jorvik, the best Viking artifacts are here—with no crowds and a better historical context.

Your museum stroll starts in ancient times. The Roman collection includes slice-of-life exhibits from Roman gods and goddesses and the skull of a man killed by a sword blow to the head. (The latter makes it graphically clear that the struggle between Romans and barbarians was a violent one.) A fine eighth-century Anglo-Saxon helmet shows a bit of barbarian refinement; you'll notice that the Vikings wore some pretty decent shoes, and actually combed their hair.

The Middleham Jewel, an exquisitely etched 15th-century pendant, is considered the finest piece of Gothic jewelry in Britain. The noble lady who wore this on a necklace believed that it helped her worship and protected her from illness. The back of the pendant, which rested near her heart, shows the nativity. The front shows the Holy Trinity crowned by a sapphire (which people believed put their prayers at the top of God's to-do list).

The 20-minute video about the creation of the abbey plays continuously, and is worth a look (£4, daily 10:00–17:00, tel. 01904/687-687, www.yorkshiremuseum.org.uk). Before leaving, enjoy the evocative ruins of the abbey in the park (destroyed by Henry VIII in 16th century).

▲**Fairfax House**—This well-furnished building is perfectly Georgian inside, with docents happy to talk with you. It's compact and bursting with insights into aristocratic life in 18th-century England. Pianists may be allowed to actually pluck the harpsichord (£4.50, Mon–Thu and Sat 11:00–17:00, Sun 13:30–17:00, Fri by tour only at 11:00 and 14:00—the tours are worthwhile, on Castlegate, near Jorvik, tel. 01904/655-543).

Theatre Royal—A full variety of dramas, comedies, and works by Shakespeare is put on to entertain the locals in either the main theater or the little 100-seat theater-in-the-round (£8–20, almost nightly at 19:30, closed much of Aug, tickets easy to get, on St. Leonard's Place next to TI and a 5-min walk from recommended B&Bs, booking tel. 01904/623-568, www.yorktheatreroyal.co.uk). Those under 25 get tickets for only £3.50.

Traditional Tea—York is famous for its elegant teahouses. Drop into one around 16:00 for tea and cakes. Ladies love **Betty's Teahouse,** where you pay £6 for a Yorkshire Cream Tea (tea and scones with clotted Yorkshire cream and strawberry jam) or £11 for a full traditional English afternoon tea (tea, delicate sandwiches, scones, and sweets). Your table is so full of doily niceties that the food is served on a little three-tray tower. While you'll pay a little extra here (and the food's nothing special), the ambience and people-watching are hard to beat (daily 9:00–21:00, piano music nightly 18:00–21:00, non-smoking, St. Helen's Square; fine view of street scene from a window seat on the main floor, downstairs near WC is a mirror signed by WWII bomber pilots—read the story). If there's a line, it moves quickly (except at dinner time). Wait for a seat by the windows on the ground level rather than sit in the much bigger basement.

Riverside Walk—The New Walk is a mile-long, tree-lined, riverside lane created in the 1730s as a promenade for York's dandy class to stroll, see, and be seen. With the creation of York's Millennium Bridge, it's now possible to take this walk, cross over, and return to York passing through Rowntree Park (a great Edwardian park with lawn bowling for the public, plus family fun including a playground and adventure rides for kids). This hour-long walk is a great way to enjoy a dose of countryside from York. It's clearly described in the TI's *New Walk* flier (50p). You start from the riverside under Skeldergate Bridge (near the Castle Museum), walk away from town for a mile until you hit a modern bridge, cross the river, and walk home.

Honorable Mentions

York has a number of other sights and activities (described in TI material) that, while interesting, pale in comparison to the biggies.

Hall of the Merchant Adventurers—Claiming to be the finest medieval guildhall in Europe (from 1361), it's basically a vast half-timbered building with marvelous exposed beams and 15 minutes' worth of interesting displays about life and commerce back in the days when York was England's second city (£2.50, Mon–Sat 9:00–17:00, Sun 12:00–16:00, shorter hours off-season, below the

Shambles off Piccadilly, tel. 01904/654-818).

Richard III Museum—This is interesting only for Richard III enthusiasts (£2, daily March–Aug 9:00–20:00, Sept–Oct 9:30–17:00, Nov–Feb until 16:00, Monk Bar, tel. 01904/634-191).

York Dungeon—It's gimmicky, but if you insist on papier-mâché gore, it's better than the London Dungeon (£11, daily 10:00–17:00, less off-season, 12 Clifford Street, tel. 01904/632-599).

Lawn Bowling Green—Visitors are welcome to watch the action—best in the evenings—at the green on Sycamore Place; you can buy a pint of beer (near recommended B&Bs, tell them which B&B you're staying at). Another green is in front of the Coach House Hotel Pub on Marygate.

Near York

Eden Camp—Once an internment camp for German and Italian POWs during World War II, this is now a theme museum on Britain's war experience. Various barracks detail the rise of Hitler and the fury of the Blitz (with the sound of bombs, the acrid smell of burning, and quotes such as, "Hitler will send no warning—so always carry your gas mask"). This award-winning museum energetically conveys the spirit of a country Hitler couldn't conquer. Don't miss hut #10, which details the actual purpose of the camp—a prison for captured Nazis during World War II. Consider the relative delight of being in the care of the gentlemanly English rather than in a Nazi camp. It's no wonder the Germans settled right in.

Cost, Hours, Information: £4, daily 10:00–17:00, closed late-Dec–mid-Jan, mess-kitchen cafeteria, tel. 01653/697-777, www.edencamp.co.uk.

Getting There: It's in Malton, 18 miles northeast of York. From York, catch the Coastliner bus at the York Railway Station (leaves from front of station, on station side of road). Buses are marked with the destination "Whitby" or "Pickering" and are numbered #840, #842, or #X40, depending on the time of day (£4 round-trip, Mon–Sat 11/day, fewer on Sun, 50 min). From York, drivers take A169 toward Scarborough, then follow signs to the camp.

SHOPPING

With its medieval lanes lined with classy as well as tacky little shops, York is a hit with shoppers. I find the **antique malls** interesting. Three places within a few blocks of each other are filled with stalls and cases owned by antique dealers from the countryside. The malls sell the dealers' bygones on commission. Serious shoppers do better heading for the countryside, but York's shops are a fun browse: The Antiques Centre York (daily 9:00–18:00, 41 Stonegate, tel. 01904/635-888), the antique mall at 2 Lendal (Mon–Sat 10:00–17:00, closed Sun, tel. 01904/641-582), and the Red House Antiques Centre (daily 9:30–17:30, as late as 19:00 in summer, a block from Minster at Duncombe Place, tel. 01904/637-000).

SLEEPING

I've listed peak-season, book-direct prices. Don't use the TI. Outside of July and August, some prices go soft. B&Bs will sometimes turn away one-night bookings, particularly for peak-season Saturdays. (York is worth 2 nights anyway.) Remember to book ahead during festival times (Feb, March, mid-June, mid-July, and late Sept—see "Helpful Hints," page 345) and weekends year-round.

B&Bs and Small Hotels near Bootham

These recommendations are in the handiest B&B neighborhood, a quiet residential area just outside the old-town wall's Bootham gate, along the road called Bootham. All are within a five-minute walk of the Minster and TI and a 10-minute walk or taxi ride (£3–4) from the station. If driving, head for the cathedral and follow the medieval wall to the gate called Bootham Bar. The street called Bootham leads away from Bootham Bar.

These B&Bs are all small, non-smoking, and family-run. They come with plenty of steep stairs but no traffic noise. For a good selection, call well in advance. B&B owners will generally hold a room with a phone call and work hard to help their guests sightsee and eat smartly. Most have permits for street parking.

$$$ The Hazelwood, my most hotelesque listing in this neighborhood, is plush, and more formal than a B&B. This spacious house has 14 beautifully decorated rooms with modern furnishings and lots of thoughtful touches (Db-£80/90/100 depending on room size, 2 ground-floor rooms, laundry service-£5; parking, a fridge, ice, and great travel library in the pleasant basement lounge; 24 Portland Street, tel. 01904/626-548, fax 01904/628-032, www.thehazelwoodyork.com, reservations@thehazelwoodyork.com, Ian and Carolyn).

$$ 23 St. Mary's is extravagantly decorated. Chris and Julie Simpson have done everything just right and offer nine spacious and comfy rooms, a classy lounge, and all the doily touches (Sb-£36–45, Db-£70–90 depending on season and size, DVD library and some rooms with DVD players, 23 St. Mary's, tel. 01904/622-738, fax 01904/628-802, www.23stmarys.co.uk, stmarys23@hotmail.com).

$$ Crook Lodge B&B has seven charming, tight rooms (Db-£64–72, 10 percent less with this 2006 book if you mention

---

Sleep Code

(£1 = about $1.80, country code: 44, area code: 01904)
S = Single, **D** = Double/Twin, **T** = Triple, **Q** = Quad, **b** = bathroom,
s = shower only. You can assume credit cards are accepted
unless otherwise noted.

To help you sort easily through these listings, I've divided
the rooms into three categories based on the price for a standard double room with bath (during high season):

$$$ **Higher Priced**—Most rooms £90 or more.
 $$ **Moderately Priced**—Most rooms between £60–90.
  $ **Lower Priced**—Most rooms £60 or less.

---

while booking, less on weekdays, parking, quiet, 26 St. Mary's,
tel. 01904/655-614, fax 01904/625-915, www.crooklodge.co.uk,
crooklodge@hotmail.com, Brian and Louise Aiken).

$$ The Coach House Hotel is a labyrinthine, well-located,
17th-century coach house, facing a bowling green and the abbey
walls. It offers 12 freshly redone rooms, some with views of the
Minster, and a comfy lounge (Sb-£38, Db-£76–80, free parking,
20 Marygate, Bootham, tel. 01904/652-780, fax 01904/679-943,
www.coachhousehotel-york.com, info@coachhousehotel-york
.com, gracious Dawn and Paul Fielding and terrier Macy).

$$ Arnot House, run by a hardworking daughter-and-mother
team, is homey and lushly decorated with early-1900s memora-
bilia. The four well-furnished rooms have little libraries and VCRs
(Db-£64–68, 2-night minimum stay, video library, 17 Grosvenor
Terrace, tel. 01904/641-966, www.arnothouseyork.co.uk, kim
.robbins@virgin.net, Kim and Ann Robbins).

$$ Abbeyfields Guest House has eight bright rooms and
a quiet lounge. This doily-free place, which lacks the usual clut-
ter, has been designed with care (Sb-£41, Db-£68, cash only, 19
Bootham Terrace, tel. 01904/636-471, www.abbeyfields.co.uk,
guest@abbeyfields.co.uk, Richard and Gwen Martin).

$$ Hedley House Hotel has 16 simple, clean rooms on the
same quiet street as the Abbeyfields (Sb-£45–70, Db-£70–90, less
off-season, family rooms, daily breakfast specials, 3-course evening meals for £15, parking, outside hot tub if you're willing to
brave the weather, 3 Bootham Terrace, tel. 01904/637-404, www
.hedleyhouse.com, greg@hedleyhouse.com, Greg Harrand and
Cairn terrier Oscar).

$ Airden House, the most central of my Bootham-area list-
ings, is clean and simple, with eight spacious rooms and a cozy
TV lounge (D-£48, Db-£56–60, 10 percent discount with 2-night

York Hotels and Restaurants

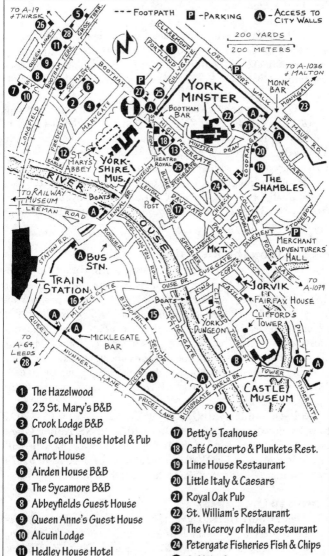

1. The Hazelwood
2. 23 St. Mary's B&B
3. Crook Lodge B&B
4. The Coach House Hotel & Pub
5. Arnot House
6. Airden House B&B
7. The Sycamore B&B
8. Abbeyfields Guest House
9. Queen Anne's Guest House
10. Alcuin Lodge
11. Hedley House Hotel
12. Riverside Walk B&B & Abbey Guest House
13. Dean Court Hotel
14. Travelodge
15. York Youth Hotel
16. York Backpackers Hostel
17. Betty's Teahouse
18. Café Concerto & Plunkets Rest.
19. Lime House Restaurant
20. Little Italy & Caesars
21. Royal Oak Pub
22. St. William's Restaurant
23. The Viceroy of India Restaurant
24. Petergate Fisheries Fish & Chips
25. Café No. 8
26. Grange Hotel Brasserie
27. Jackson's Grocery Store
28. Launderettes (2)
29. Evil Eye Internet Café
30. To Millenium Bridge

minimum and this book in 2006, 1 St. Mary's, tel. 01904/638-915, www.airdenhouse.co.uk, info@airdenhouse.co.uk, Mark and Emma Turner).

$ The Sycamore is a fine value, with six homey rooms at the end of a dead-end street opposite a fun-to-watch bowling green (D-£46, Db-£50–60, family room-£60–70, ask about discounts, cash only, 19 Sycamore Place off Bootham Terrace, tel. 01904/624-712, www.thesycamore.co.uk, Elizabeth).

$ Queen Anne's Guest House has seven clean, cheery rooms (April–Sept: D-£44, Db-£48; Oct–March: D-£36, Db-£40; prices good through 2006 with this book, family room, lounge, 24 Queen Anne's Road, tel. 01904/629-389, www.queen-annes-guesthouse .co.uk, queen.annes@btopenworld.com, John and Linda).

$ Alcuin Lodge has five fine rooms and solid-wood furnishings (1 small top-floor D-£45–50, Db-£50–60, 15 Sycamore Place, tel. 01904/632-222, www.alcuinlodge.com, info@alcuinlodge .com, Pete and Izzy).

B&Bs Along the Riverside

Hillery Summers runs two simple, well-worn workers' cottages fronting the River Ouse midway between the train station and the Minster. Each comes with small rooms, steep stairs, narrow hallways, a delightful front garden, and no traffic noise. Both face a pleasant pedestrian path; front rooms overlook the river, while back rooms watch a sprawling car park (see prices below, 10 percent discount with this book in 2006, 2.5 percent extra to pay with credit card, Internet access in lobby, laundry, free parking, fax 01904/671-743, www.bedandbreakfastyork.co.uk, abbey@rsummers.cix .co.uk).

$$ Riverside Walk B&B has 12 rooms (Db-£54–70, 8 Earlsborough Terrace, tel. 01904/620-769). **$$ Abbey Guest House,** with four rooms, is a bit cheaper since you have to walk next door to Riverside Walk for breakfast (D-£52, Db-£62–70, free parking, 14 Earlsborough Terrace, tel. 01904/627-782).

Hotels in the Center

$$$ Dean Court Hotel, facing the Minster, is a big, stately Best Western hotel with classy lounges and 37 comfortable rooms (small Db-£125, standard Db-£150, superior Db-£175, spacious deluxe Db-£190, some non-smoking rooms, tearoom, restaurant, elevator to most rooms, Duncombe Place, tel. 01904/625-082, fax 01904/620-305, www.deancourt-york.co.uk).

$$ Travelodge offers 90 identical, affordable rooms near the Castle Museum (Db-£65, kids' bed free, some non-smoking rooms, 90 Piccadilly, central reservations tel. 0870-085-0950, www.travelodge.co.uk, Internet deals as low as £26).

$ York Youth Hotel is a well-run hostel, with a kitchen, launderette, game room, and 120 beds (S-£25, bunk-bed D-£38, beds in 4- to 6-bed dorms-£16, beds in larger dorms-£12, less for multi-night stays, family rates, same-sex or coed possible, no breakfast, 10-min walk from station at 11 Bishophill Senior Road, tel. 01904/625-904, fax 01904/612-494, www.yorkyouthhotel.com, info@yorkyouthhotel.com).

$ York Backpackers Hostel offers cheap beds a few minutes' walk from the train station. The jovial staff welcomes backpackers and budget travelers of any age, with 24-hour access, no lockouts, and a guests-only bar in the basement, complete with support beams made of reclaimed ship timbers (£13–14 beds in 18- to 20-bed dorms, 88 Mickelgate, tel. 01904/627-720, www.yorkbackpackers .co.uk, mail@yorkbackpackers.co.uk).

EATING

York is bursting with inviting eateries. Picnic and light-meals-to-go options abound, and it's easy to find a churchyard, bench, or riverside perch upon which to munch cheaply. Perhaps the best picnic spot in town on a sunny day is under the evocative 12th-century ruins of St. Mary's Abbey in the Museum Gardens (near Bootham Bar).

There's a pub serving grub on every street. The best traditional chippie left in the center is **Petergate Fisheries** (good, cheap take-away fish-and-chips, daily 11:00–18:00, 95 Low Petergate).

Near the Minster

Café Concerto, a casual bistro with a fun menu, has an understandably loyal following (soup, sandwich, and salad meals-£8; fancier dinners-£15; daily 10:00–22:00, non-smoking, smart to reserve for dinner, facing the Minster, 21 High Petergate, tel. 01904/610-478).

Plunkets Restaurant is a bit oxymoronic—serving Tex-Mex cuisine among B&W glamour photos with dark, hardwood, candlelit English ambience—but the food is fine (daily 12:00–23:00, £7 early-bird special—main course and a beer or wine until 18:00, no reservations and often a line on weekends, 9 High Petergate, tel. 01904/637-722).

St. Williams Restaurant is just behind the great east window of the Minster in a wonderful half-timbered, 15th-century building (read the history on the menu). This is where the priests use their meal card. It serves quick and tasty lunches and elegant candlelit dinners (English and Mediterranean dishes, £8 lunches 12:00–14:30, 3-course £15 specials 17:30–18:45, £15 plates, daily April–Sept, closed Sun–Mon Oct–March, College Street, tel. 01904/634-830).

Outside seating with a Minster view is fine when balmy.

Betty's Teahouse, a favorite among local ladies, is popular for its traditional English afternoon tea (which works as a meal—£11 for tea, delicate sandwiches, scones, and sweets; for details, see page 357).

On and near Goodramgate, in the Old Town Center

Royal Oak Pub, a traditional, mellow old English pub, serves £6 meals throughout the day with hand-pulled ale. They happily swap out the peas and potatoes for more interesting vegetables—just ask (meals daily 11:00–20:00, 3 cozy rooms—one non-smoking, hearty meat dishes, homemade desserts, Goodramgate, a block inside Monk Bar, tel. 01904/653-856).

Lime House Restaurant is a small, modern, candlelit place serving international dishes and always a good vegetarian plate. They offer a free glass of house wine to anyone with this book in 2006 (lunch plates-£7, dinner plates-£12–15, 10 percent off orders before 19:15, Tue–Sat 12:00–14:00 & 18:00–21:30, closed Sun–Mon, 55 Goodramgate, tel. 01904/632-734).

Two popular Italian places along Goodramgate offer pizzas and pastas for £7: **Little Italy** is a little more intimate (Tue–Sun 17:00–23:00, closed Mon, #12, tel. 01904/623-539), while **Caesars** is bright and boisterous (daily 12:00–14:30 & 17:30–24:00, #27, tel. 01904/670-914).

The Viceroy of India, just outside Monk Bar (and therefore outside the tourist zone), serves great Indian food at good prices to locals in the know. If you've yet to eat Indian on your trip, do it here (£8 plates, Mon–Sat 17:30–24:00, Sun 12:00–24:00, friendly staff, out Monk Bar to 26 Monkgate, tel. 01904/622-370, Mahmood welcomes you).

Near Bootham Bar and Your B&B

Café No. 8 is a local favorite and your best bistro choice on Gillygate, serving modern European comfort food, veggie options, and a shady little garden out back if the weather's good. Chef Pragnell lets what's fresh in the market shape his menu (£5–7 lunches, £12 dinners, daily 10:00–22:00, 8 Gillygate, tel. 01904/653-074).

The Coach House serves good-quality fresh food, with veggie options and homemade sweets, in a cozy atmosphere (£8–11, nightly 18:30–21:00, attached to a classic old guesthouse, 20 Marygate, tel. 01904/652-780).

The **Grange Hotel Brasserie,** a couple of blocks from the B&Bs, is classier than a pub and serves a smattering of traditional European dishes. Eat downstairs rather than in the pricey main-floor restaurant (£9–13 main dishes, Mon–Fri 12:00–14:00 & 18:00–22:00, Sat 12:00–22:30, Sun 19:00–22:00, 1 Clifton, tel. 01904/644-744).

Jackson's grocery store is open daily 7:00–23:00 (near B&Bs, 50 yards outside Bootham Bar, on Bootham).

TRANSPORTATION CONNECTIONS

From York by Train to: Durham (1–3/hr, 45–60 min), **Edinburgh** (2/hr, 2.5 hrs), **Glasgow** (10/day, 3.5 hrs), **London** (2/hr, 2 hrs), **Bath** (hrly, 5 hrs, change in Bristol), **Cambridge** (nearly hrly, 2.5 hrs, change in Peterborough), **Birmingham** (2/hr, 2.5 hrs), **Keswick** (with transfers to Penrith then bus, 4.5 hrs). Train info: tel. 08457-484-950.

Connections with London's Airports: Heathrow (hrly, allow 2.5–3 hrs, from airport take Heathrow Express train to London's Paddington Station, tube to King's Cross, train to York—2/hr, 2 hrs), **Gatwick** (from Gatwick catch low-profile Thameslink train to King's Cross–Thameslink station in London; from there, walk 100 yards to King's Cross Station, train to York—2/hr, 2 hrs).

Buses: The **York Bus Information Centre** is at 20 Hudson Street, near the train station (Mon–Fri 8:30–17:00, closed Sat–Sun, tel. 01904/551-400, phone answered Mon–Sat 8:00–20:00, Sun 8:00–14:00).

Route Tips for Drivers

As you near York (and your B&B), you'll hit the A1237 ring road. Follow this to the A19/Thirsk roundabout (next to river on northeast side of town). From the roundabout, follow signs for York City, traveling through Clifton into Bootham. All recommended B&Bs are four or five blocks before you hit the medieval city gate (see neighborhood map, page 361). If you're approaching York from the south, take M1 until it becomes A1M, turn on A64 and follow it for 10 miles until you reach York's ring road (A1237), which allows you to avoid driving through the city center. If you have more time, the A1 is a slower and more scenic route into York.

North York Moors

In the lonesome North York Moors, you can wander through the stark beauty of its time-passed villages, bored sheep, and powerful landscapes. Park your car and take a hike across the moors on any small road. You'll come upon tidy villages and maybe even old Roman roads.

North York Moors

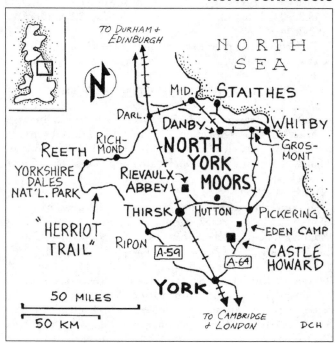

The **Moors Visitors Centre** provides the best orientation for exploring the moors. It's a grand old lodge that offers exhibits, shows, nature walks, an information desk with plenty of books and maps, brass rubbing, a cheery cafeteria, and brochures on several good walks that start right there (free entry but £1.50 parking fee, April–Oct daily 10:00–17:00, March daily 11:00–16:00, Nov–Feb weekends only 11:00–16:00, located three-fourths of a mile from Danby in Esk Valley in northern park of park, tel. 01439/772-737, www.moors.uk.net).

If you're driving, get a map. Without wheels, you have three choices: Take a bus/steam-train combination (described below). Choose one of several guided bus tours from York, focusing on Herriot or Brontë country, moors, Lake District, or Holy Island (different tour every day, offered by various companies for roughly £10/half-day or £16/day). Or hire a private guide, such as John Smith, a licensed guide and driver who can take up to three people on one of his Yorkshire Tours; you can choose from a tour of Herriot Country, a Castle Howard/steam train/Whitby combination, or a tour tailored to your interests (£17/hr, admissions extra, tel. 01904/636-653, mobile 07850-260-511).

▲**North Yorkshire Moors Railway**—This 18-mile, one-hour steam-engine ride between Pickering and Grosmont (GROW-mont) goes nearly hourly through some of the best parts of the moors. Even with the small and dirty windows (wipe off the outside of yours before you roll), and the track mostly in a scenic gully, it's a good ride. You can stop along the way for a walk in the moors and catch the next train (£12 round-trip, April–Oct, first train departs Pickering about 10:15, last train departs Grosmont about 16:45, allow 3.5 hrs round-trip due to scheduling, tel. 01751/472-508 or 01751/473-799). It's not possible to leave luggage at any stop on the steam-train line—pack light if you decide to hike.

Pickering—With its rural-life museum, castle, and Monday market (produce, knickknacks), this town is worth a stop. You could catch an early York–Pickering bus (Mon–Sat 1/hr, only one bus on Sun, 65 min, leaves from train station), see Pickering, and carry on to Grosmont on the North Yorkshire Moors Railway (see above). Grosmont is on a regular train line with limited connections to Whitby (see next page) and points north and south (TI tel. 01751/473-791).

▲**Hutton-le-Hole**—This postcard-pretty town is home of the fine Ryedale Folk Museum, illustrating farm life in the moors through reconstructed and furnished 18th-century local buildings (£4.50, mid-March–Oct daily 10:00–17:30, last entry at 16:30, closed off-season, tel. 01751/417-367).

Castle Howard—Especially popular since the filming of *Brideshead Revisited* 25 years ago, this fine, palatial 300-year-old home is about half as interesting as Blenheim Palace in the Cotswolds (£9.50, daily 11:00–17:00, last entry 1 hour before closing, closed early Nov–mid-Feb, 1 bus/day from York, 40 min, tel. 01653/648-333).

Rievaulx Abbey—Rievaulx (ree-VOH) is a highlight of the North York Moors and beautifully situated, but if you've seen other fine old abbeys, this is a rerun (£4.50, April–Sept daily 10:00–18:00; Oct–March Thu–Mon 10:00–16:00, closed Tue-Wed; tel. 01439/798-228).

World of James Herriot—Devotees of the *All Creatures* books and television series can visit the folksy veterinarian's digs in Thirsk. Built in the original surgery room of the late author/vet Alf Wight, this museum recreates the 1940s Skeldale House featured in the novels and explores the development of veterinary science. Try out the interactive exhibit on horse dentistry and find out if you're strong enough to calve a cow (£5, daily April–Oct 10:00–18:00, Nov–March 11:00–16:00, last admission 1 hour before closing, 23 Kirkgate, tel. 01845-524-234, www.worldofjamesherriot.org).

Herriot fans will find the Yorkshire Dales more interesting than the neighboring moors. Local booklets at the TI lay out the

All Creatures Great and Small pilgrimage route for drivers, or you could consider a tour from York (leaflets at TI).

Near York:
Whitby and Staithes

These towns are seaside escapes worth a stop for the seagulls, surf, and Captain Cook lore. Whitby is accessible by train, but Staithes makes sense only with a car.

Whitby

An important port since the 12th century, Whitby is now a fun coastal resort town with a busy harbor and steep and salty old streets. It's a carousel of Coney Island–type amusements over-seen by the stately ruins of its seventh-century abbey. The **TI** is on the harbor next to the train and bus stations (daily May–Sept 9:30–18:00, Oct–April 10:00–16:30, often closed for lunch, tel. 01947/602-674).

If driving, upon arrival park across from the TI at the pay-and-display supermarket lot near the train and bus station. Wander the harbor out along Pier Road and Fish Quay past all the carnival distractions. The **Magpie Restaurant** is famous for its fish-and-chips (generally a line of hungry pilgrims waiting to get in). The small Dracula exhibit is a reminder that some of that story was set here.

As you return to your car, cross the bridge, where you'll find a warren of touristy lanes filled with hard candy, knickknack shops, and the small **Captain Cook Memorial Museum,** offering an interesting look at the famous hometown sailor and his exotic voyages (£3, March–Oct daily 9:45–17:00, closed Nov–Feb, down Grape Lane in the old town just over the bridge). Two of Captain Cook's boats (*Resolution* and *Endeavour*) were built in the Whitby shipyards.

Sleeping in Whitby: Whitby has plenty of accommodations. August is the only tight month. **$$ Dolphin Hotel,** in the old-town center at the bridge overlooking the harbor, is a colorful old pub with five salty rooms upstairs (Db-£60, pub closes at 23:30, 3 blocks from train station, Bridge Street, tel. 01947/602-197). **$ Crescent Lodge B&B** is a good choice (7 rooms, Db-£55, 27

Crescent Avenue, tel. 01947/820-073, arthurcrescentlodge@telco4u .com, Elizabeth and Arthur Mittens). The **$ hostel** is next to the abbey above the town (£11/bed, 58 beds in 8 rooms, office closed 10:00–17:00, tel. 01947/602-878).

Staithes

A ragamuffin village where the boy who became Captain James Cook got his first taste of the sea, Staithes (just north of Whitby)

is a salty tumble of cottages bunny-hopping down a ravine into a tiny harbor. While tranquil today, in 1816 it was home to 70 boats and the busiest fishing station in North England. Ten years ago, the town supported 20 fishing boats—today, only three. But fishermen (who pronounce their town "steers") still outnumber tourists in undiscovered Staithes. The town has changed little since Captain Cook's days. Little is done to woo tourism here. Lots of flies and seagulls seem to have picked the barren cliffs raw. There's nothing to do but drop by the lifeboat house (a big deal in England; page through the history book, read the not-quite-stirring accounts of the boats being called to duty, and drop a coin in the box), stroll the beach, and nurse a harborside beer or ice cream. An easy drive north of Whitby, Staithes is worthwhile by car, but probably not by bus (hourly Whitby–Staithes buses, 30 min; 10-min walk from bus stop into town). Parking is tough—generally, you can drive in only to unload. Service trucks clog the windy main (and only) lane much of the day. There's a pay-and-display lot at the top of the town (when paying the night before, time spills over past 9:00 the next morning).

Sleeping in Staithes: There are no fancy rooms. It's a cash-only town with no ATMs. Each of these two places is cramped, with tangled floor plans that make you feel like a stowaway. **$$ Endeavour Restaurant B&B,** tidy and small, is the only place in town that offers parking (Db-£65–80, serves great food—see below, 1 High Street, tel. 01947/840-825, www.endeavour-restaurant .co.uk, Brian Kay and Charlotte Willoughby). **$$ Harborside Guest House,** newly refurbished, is the only place actually on the harbor. It provides two seaview rooms and the sound of waves to lull you to sleep (Db-£70–75, cash only, tel. 01947/841-296).

Eating in Staithes: The **Endeavour Restaurant,** oddly classy for this town, offers excellent £25 dinners (Tue–Sat 18:45–21:30, closed Sun–Mon, seafood, vegetarian options, reservations wise, tel. 01947/840-825). Two pubs serve dinner (generally 19:00–21:00): the **Black Lion** and the **Royal George.** For a scenic brew, stop by the **Cod and Lobster,** overlooking the harbor, with outdoor benches and a cozy living room warmed by a coal fire. Drop in to see its old-time Staithes photos. For fish-and-chips or a coffee on the harbor, try the friendly **Sea Drift Sweet Shop** or **Harborside Guest House.**

TRANSPORTATION CONNECTIONS

Buses connect **Whitby** and **York** (4–6/day depending on season, 2 hrs, tel. 01653/692-556). Trains connect **Durham** with **Middlesbrough** (5/day, 50 min, more frequent with transfer in Darlington); the **Middlesbrough–Whitby** train (4/day, 90 min) stops at **Grosmont** (where you can catch the Moors steam train) and **Danby** (near the Moors Visitors Centre—see page 366).

DURHAM
and NORTHEAST ENGLAND

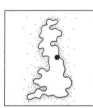

Some of England's best history is harbored in the northeast. Hadrian's Wall reminds us that Britain was an important Roman colony 2,000 years ago. After a Roman ramble, you can make a pilgrimage to Holy Island, where Christianity gained its first toehold in Britain. At Durham, marvel at England's greatest Norman church and enjoy an evensong service. At the Beamish Open-Air Museum, travel back in time to the year 1913.

Planning Your Time

For train travelers, Durham is the most convenient overnight stop in this region. If you like Roman ruins, visit Hadrian's Wall en route between Edinburgh and Durham (doable with transfers, easiest mid-May–mid-Sept). The Beamish Open-Air Museum is an easy day trip from Durham (hrly bus, 25 min).

By car, it's easy. On a one-month driving trip, connect Edinburgh and Durham with this string of sights—Holy Island, Bamburgh Castle, Hadrian's Wall, and Beamish Open-Air Museum. Spend a night near Hadrian's Wall and a night in Durham.

For drivers or train travelers with 36 hours between Edinburgh and York, leave Edinburgh early, hike a bit of Hadrian's Wall and tour Housesteads Roman Fort, and get to Durham in time to tour the cathedral and enjoy the evensong service (Tue–Sat 17:15, Sun 15:30). Sleep in Durham. Visit Beamish (15 min north of Durham by car) the next morning. Drivers can then tour the North York Moors, arriving in York by late afternoon.

Durham

Without its cathedral, it would hardly be noticed. But this magnificently situated cathedral is hard to miss (even if you're zooming by on the train). Durham sits, seemingly happy to go nowhere, along its river and below its castle and famous cathedral. It has a medieval, cobbled atmosphere and a scraggly peasant's indoor market just off the main square. While Durham is the home to England's third-oldest university, the town feels working-class, surrounded by recently closed coal mines and filled with tattooed and pierced people in search of job security and a good karaoke bar. Yet Durham has a youthful vibrancy and a small-town warmth that shines—especially on sunny days, when most everyone is licking an ice-cream cone.

ORIENTATION

(area code: 0191)
As it has for a thousand years, tidy little Durham clusters everything safely under its castle, within the protective hairpin bend of the River Wear. The longest walk you'd make would be a 20-minute jaunt from the train station to the cathedral.

Tourist Information
The TI books rooms and local theater tickets, and provides train times (Mon–Sat 9:30–17:30, Sun 11:00–16:00, WC, café, 1 block north of Market Place, past St. Nicholas Church, in Gala Theatre building, tel. 0191/384-3720, www.durhamtourism.co.uk).

Arrival in Durham
From the train station, follow the road downhill and take the second pedestrian turnoff (within sight of railway bridge), which leads almost immediately over a bridge above busy Alexander Crescent road. Then take North Road into town or to the first couple of B&Bs (take Alexander Crescent to the other B&Bs). Day-trippers can store luggage at the station (£1.50, daily 7:00–20:00, ask at platform 1, bags may be searched by security). Drivers simply surrender to the wonderful Prince Bishop's parking lot (at the roundabout at the base of the old town). It's perfectly safe and inexpensive, and an elevator deposits you right in the heart of Durham (a short block from Market Place).

Helpful Hints
Internet Access: The library, across from the TI, has about 40
   terminals and free Internet access (Mon–Fri 9:30–19:00, Sat

---

The History of Durham

Durham's location, tucked inside a tight bend in the river, was ideal to easily fortify. But it was never settled until the arrival of St. Cuthbert's body in A.D. 995, buried in Durham Cathedral. Shortly after that, a small church (to hold the relic) and fortification were built upon the site of today's castle and church. The castle was a classic "motte-and-bailey" design (with the "motte," or mound, providing a lookout tower for the stockade encircling the protected area, or "bailey"). Around 1100, the Prince Bishop's bailey was filled with villagers—and he wanted everyone out. This was *his* place! He provided a wider protective wall and had the town resettle below, around today's Market Place. But this displaced the cows of the townsfolk, so the Prince Bishop constructed a fine stone bridge (today's Framwellgate) connecting the new town to land he established as grazing land over the river. The bridge had a defensive gate, with a wall circling the peninsula and the river serving as a moat.

9:00–17:00, closed Sun, need to show ID, tel. 0191/386-4003).
Tours: The TI offers 60-minute city walking tours on summer weekends (£3.50, June–Sept Sat–Sun, schedule varies often—confirm with TI). David Butler, the town historian, gives excellent private tours (reasonable prices, tel. 0191/386-1500, dhent@dhent.fsnet.co.uk).

Getting Around Durham

While all listed hotels, eateries, and sights are easily walkable in Durham, taxis are available to zip tired tourists to their B&Bs or back to the station (£3, wait on Market Place or on west side of Framwellgate Bridge).

SELF-GUIDED WALK

Welcome to Durham

• *Begin at Framwellgate Bridge (which connects the train station with the center).*

Framwellgate Bridge was a wonder when it was built in the 12th century—much longer than the river is wide and higher than seemingly necessary. It was well-designed to connect stretches of solid high ground and avoid steep descents to the marshy river. Note how elegantly today's Silver Street (which leads toward town) slopes into the Framwellgate Bridge. (Imagine that as late as 1970s, this people-friendly lane was congested with traffic and buses.)

Durham

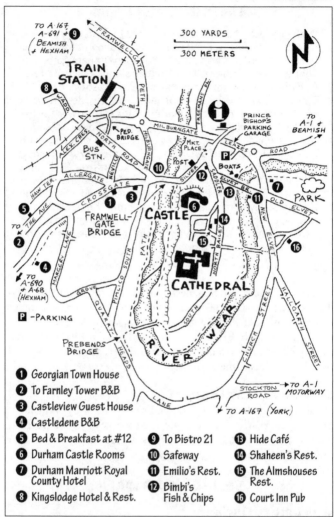

TO A-167
A-691 &
BEAMISH
(& HEXHAM)

TO A-1 &
BEAMISH

FRAMWELLGATE PETH

TRAIN STATION

WADD

MILBURNGATE

PRINCE BISHOPS PARKING GARAGE

TO A-1 &
BEAMISH

300 YARDS
300 METERS

N

ALEX. CRES.

NORTH ROAD

PED. BRIDGE

MILBURNGATE

MKT. PLACE

LEAZES ROAD

BUS STN.

NEVILLE

CROSSGATE

ALLERGATE

POST

SILVER

BOATS

ELVET BR.

OLD ELVET

PARK

HAW TER.

THE AVE.

FRAMWELLGATE BRIDGE

CASTLE

SADDLER

NEW ELVET

MARGERY LANE

TO A-690
& A-68
(HEXHAM)

PILGRIM SOUTH PATH

GROVE

QUARRY HEADS

CATHEDRAL

NORTH BAILEY

CHURCH STREET

HALLGARTH STREET

P –Parking

PREBENDS BRIDGE

RIVER WEAR

LANE

STOCKTON ROAD

TO A-1 MOTORWAY

TO A-167 (YORK)

1 Georgian Town House
2 To Farnley Tower B&B
3 Castleview Guest House
4 Castledene B&B
5 Bed & Breakfast at #12
6 Durham Castle Rooms
7 Durham Marriott Royal County Hotel
8 Kingslodge Hotel & Rest.

9 To Bistro 21
10 Safeway
11 Emilio's Rest.
12 Bimbi's Fish & Chips

13 Hide Café
14 Shaheen's Rest.
15 The Almshouses Rest.
16 Court Inn Pub

• *Follow Silver Street to the town's main square.*

Durham's **Market Place** retains the same platting the Prince Bishop gave it when he moved villagers here in about 1100. Each plot of land was the same width (about 8 yards). Find today's distinctly narrow buildings (Thomas Cook, Whittard, and the optician shop)—they still fit the 800-year-old plan. The rest of the buildings fronting the square are multiples of that first shop width. Plots were long and skinny, maximizing the number of shops that could have a piece of the Market Place action.

Examine the square's **statues.** Coal has long been the basis of this region's economy. The statue of Neptune was part of an ill-fated attempt by a coal baron to bribe the townsfolk into embracing a canal project that would make the shipment of his coal more efficient. The statue of the fancy guy on the horse is Marcus of Londonderry. A general in Wellington's army, he was an Irish aristocrat who married a local coal heiress. A clever and aggressive businessman, he managed to create a vast business empire controlling every link in the coal business chain—mines, railroads, boats, harbors, and so on.

In the 1850s throughout England, towns were moving their markets off squares and into Industrial Age iron-and-glass market halls. Durham was no exception, and today its **indoor market** (which faces Market Place) is a funky 19th-century delight to explore.

Do you enjoy the sparse traffic in Durham's old town? It was the first city in England to institute a "congestion fee." Look where traffic enters the old town on the downhill side of the square. The bollard is up, blocking traffic Monday through Friday from 10:00–16:00. Anyone can drive in...but it costs £5 to get out. This has cut downtown traffic by more than 50 percent. Locals brag that London (which now has a similar congestion fee) was inspired by their success.

• *Head up to the cathedral along Saddler Street, on the left, you'll see a bridge.*

A 12th-century construction, **Elvet Bridge** led to a town market over the river. Like Framwellgate, it was very long (17 arches) to avoid river muck and steep inclines. Even today, Elvet Bridge leads to an unusually wide road—a reminder that it was once swollen to accommodate the market action. Shops lined the right-hand side of Elvet Bridge in the 12th century as they do today. An alley separated the bridge from the buildings on the left. When the bridge was widened, it met the upper stories of the buildings on the left, which became "street level."

The Scots were on the rampage in the 14th century. After their victory at Bannockburn in 1314, they pushed further south, and actually burned part of Durham. With this new threat, Durham's **city walls** were built. Since people settled within the walls, the population density soared. Soon open lanes were covered by residences, becoming tunnels (called "vennels"). A classic vennel leads to Saddlers Yard, a fine little 16th-century courtyard (immediately opposite Elvet Bridge). While these are cute today, centuries ago these were Dickensian nightmares...the filthiest of hovels.

• *Continue up Saddler Street. Between the two "Georgian Window" signs, go through the purple door to see a bit of the medieval wall incorporated into the brickwork of a newer building, and a turret from an earlier wall. Back on Saddler Street, you can see the ghost of the old wall. (It's exactly the width of the building now housing the Salvation Army.) Veer right as you continue uphill, until you reach the Palace Green.*

At the **Palace Green,** you're now within the original defenses of 12th-century Durham. The original 11th-century Saxon town was right here, filling this green between the castle and an earlier church. With the threat presented by the Vikings, it's no wonder people found comfort in a spot like this.

The **castle** still stands—like it has for a thousand years—on its motte (man-made mound). The castle is now part of Durham University. Like Oxford and Cambridge, Durham U. is a collection of colleges scattered throughout the town. And, like Oxford and Cambridge, the town has a youthful liveliness because of its university. Look into the old courtyard from the castle gate. It traces the very first and smallest bailey. As future bishops expanded the castle, they left their coat of arms as a way of "signing" the wing they built. Because the Norman kings appointed the Prince Bishops here to rule this part of their realm, Durham was the seat of power for much of northern England. The bishops had their own army and even minted their own coins.

• *This walk ends at Durham's stunning **cathedral**, described below.*

SIGHTS

Durham's Cathedral

Built to house the much-venerated bones of St. Cuthbert from Lindisfarne, Durham's cathedral, a ▲▲▲ sight, offers the best look at Norman architecture in England. (Norman is British for Romanesque.) The cathedral is free, but a £4 donation is requested (Mon–Sat 9:30–18:15, Sun 12:30–17:00, June–Aug until 20:00, open at 7:30 for worship and prayer, tel. 0191/386-4266, www .durhamcathedral.co.uk). For various fees, you can also climb the tower, ogle the treasury, and tour the Monk's Dormitory. Try to fit in an evensong service (see below). No photos or videos are allowed. A bookshop, cafeteria, and WC are tucked away in the cloisters.

Evensong: For a thousand years, this cradle of English Christianity has been praising God. To really experience the cathedral, go for an evensong service. Arrive early and ask to be seated in the choir. It's a spiritual Oz, as 40 boys sing psalms—a red-and-white-robed pillow of praise, raised up by the powerful pipe organ. If you're lucky and the service went well, the organist runs a spiritual musical victory lap as the congregation breaks up (Tue–Sat 17:15, Sun at 15:30, 1 hr, normally not sung on Mon; when choir is off on school break during mid-July–Aug, visiting choirs nearly always fill in; tel. 0191/386-2367).

Harry Potter's Hogwarts— A Gothic Mishmash

Hogwarts, Harry's prestigious wizarding prep school, is a movie creation. But it's made from a number of locations that showcase some of Britain's premier Gothic architecture. You'll see towers from Durham, ramparts from Alnwick, classrooms from Lacock, and hallways from Gloucester. (You won't see the castle-on-a-rock-by-a-lake exterior shown in the films—those are sets.)

Harry first learns to fly a broomstick on the green grass of Hogwarts school grounds, filmed inside the walls of **Alnwick** (AWN-ick) **Castle,** located at the northeast tip of England. Harry soars after Draco, flying above and around the old castle's ramparts and towers. (In film #2, this is also where the Weasleys' flying car crashes into the Whomping Willow.)

Oliver Wood, Gryffindor's Quidditch captain, chooses Harry for the team in a scene shot in the halls of the 13th-century **Lacock Abbey**, northeast of Bath. Harry attends Professor Snape's class in one of the Abbey's bare, peeling-plaster rooms—appropriate to Snape's temperament.

In the first film, Harry walks with his white owl, Hedwig, through a snowy cloister courtyard located in **Durham Cathedral**. The bird soars up and over the church's twin 13th-century towers.

The mysterious side of Hogwarts is often set in the elaborate, fan-vaulted corridors of the **Gloucester Cathedral cloisters**, 50 miles north of Bath. When Harry and Ron set out to save Hermione, they look down a long, dark Gloucester hallway and spot a 20-foot troll at the far end. And it's here that the walls whisper ominously to Harry, and letters in blood warn: "Enemies of the heir, beware."

For more Harry Potter sights, also see the sidebars for London (page 88) and in Scotland (page 475).

◑ **Self-Guided Tour:** From the cathedral green, notice how this fortress of God stands boldly opposite the Norman keep of Durham's fortress of man.

The **exterior** of this awe-inspiring cathedral—if you look closely—has a serious skin problem. In the 1770s, as the stone was crumbling, they crudely peeled it back a few inches. The scrape marks give the cathedral a bad complexion to this day. For proof of this odd "restoration," study the masonry 10 yards to the right of the door. The L-shaped stones in the corner would normally never be found in a church like this—they only became L-shaped when the surface was cut back.

At the cathedral **door,** the big, bronze, lion-faced knocker

Durham's Cathedral

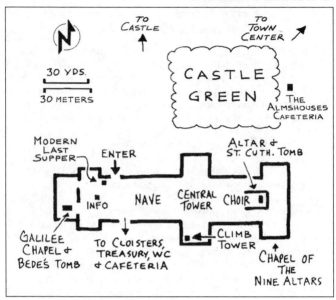

(a replica of the 12th-century original—now in the treasury) was used by criminals seeking sanctuary (read the explanation).

Immediately inside, at the **information desk,** church attendants are standing by to happily answer questions. Ideally, follow a church tour (£3.50 donation, mid-July–Aug Mon–Fri at 11:00 and 14:30, Sat at 18:15, Sun at 18:00, if one's in session you're welcome to join, call to confirm schedule, tel. 0191/386-4266). The pamphlet, *A Short Guide to Durham Cathedral,* is informative but dull.

Notice the **modern window** with the novel depiction of the Last Supper (above and to the left of the entry door). It was given to the church by a local department store in 1984. The shapes of the apostles represent worlds and persons of every kind, from the shadowy Judas to the brightness of Jesus. This window is a good reminder that the cathedral remains a living part of the community.

Near the info desk, the **black marble strip** on the floor was as close to the altar as women were allowed in the days when this was a Benedictine church (until 1540). Sit down (ignoring the black line) and let the fine proportions of England's best Norman—and arguably Europe's best Romanesque—nave stir you. Any frilly woodwork and stonework were added in later centuries.

The architecture of the **nave** is particularly harmonious because it was built in a mere 40 years (1093–1133). The round arches and zigzag carved decorations are textbook Norman. The church was also proto-Gothic, built by well-traveled French masons and architects who knew the latest innovations from Europe. Its stone and ribbed roof, pointed arches, and flying buttresses were revolutionary in England. Notice the clean lines and simplicity. It's not as cluttered as other churches for several reasons: Out of respect for St. Cuthbert, for centuries no one else was buried here. During Reformation times, sumptuous Catholic decor was cleaned out. And subsequent fires and wars destroyed what Protestants didn't.

Enter the **Galilee Chapel** (late Norman, from 1175) in the back of the nave. The paintings of St. Cuthbert and St. Oswald (7th-century king of Northumbria) on the side walls of the side altar niche are rare examples of Romanesque (Norman) paintings. Facing this altar, look above to your right to see more faint paintings on the upper walls above the columns. Near the center of the chapel, the upraised tomb topped with a black slab contains the remains of the Venerable Bede, an eighth-century Christian scholar who wrote the first history of England. The Latin reads: *In this tomb are the bones of the Venerable Bede.*

Back in the main church, stroll down the nave to the **center,** under the highest bell tower in Europe (218 feet). Gaze up. The ropes turn wheels upon which bells are mounted. If you're stirred by the cheery ringing of church bells, tune into the cathedral on Sunday (9:30–10:00 & 14:30–15:00) or Thursday (19:30 practice) when the resounding notes tumble merrily through the entire town.

Continuing east (all medieval churches faced east), you enter the **choir.** Monks worshipped many times a day, and the choir in the center of the church provided a cozy place to gather in this vast, dark, and chilly building. Here in the heart of the cathedral, Mass has been said daily for 900 years. The fancy wooden chairs are from the 17th century. Behind the altar is the delicately carved stone Neville Screen from 1380 (made of Normandy stone in London, shipped to Newcastle by sea, then brought here by wagon). Until the Reformation, the niches contained statues of 107 saints. Exit the choir from the far right side (south). Look for the stained-glass window (to your right) commemorating the church's 1,000th anniversary in 1995. The colorful scenes depict England's history, from coal miners to cows to computers.

Step down behind the high altar into the east end of the church, which contains the 13th-century **Chapel of the Nine Altars.** Built later then the rest of the church, this is Gothic—taller, lighter, and relatively more extravagant than the Norman nave.

Climb a few steps to the **tomb of St. Cuthbert.** An inspirational leader of the early Christian Church in north England, St. Cuthbert lived in the Lindisfarne monastery on Holy Island (100 miles north of Durham). He died in 687. Eleven years later, his body was exhumed and found to be miraculously preserved. This stoked the popularity of his shrine, and pilgrims came in growing numbers. When Vikings raided Lindisfarne in 875, the monks fled with his body (and the famous illuminated *Lindisfarne Gospels,* now in the British Library in London). In 995, after 120 years of roaming, the monks settled in Durham on an easy-to-defend tight bend in the River Wear. This cathedral was built over Cuthbert's tomb.

Throughout the Middle Ages, a shrine stood here and was visited by countless pilgrims. In 1539, during the Reformation—whose proponents advocated focusing on God rather than saints—the shrine was destroyed. But pilgrims still come.

Other Cathedral Sights: The entry to the **tower** is in the south transept; the view from the tower will cost you 325 steps and £2.50 (Mon–Sat 10:00–16:00, closed Sun and during bad weather). The following sights are within the cloisters: The **treasury,** filled with medieval bits and holy pieces (including Cuthbert's coffin, vestments, and cross), fleshes out this otherwise stark building. The actual relics from St. Cuthbert's tomb are at the far end (treasury well worth the £2.50 admission, Mon–Sat 10:00–16:30, Sun 14:00–16:30). The **Monks' Dormitory,** now a library with an original 14th-century timber roof filled with Anglo-Saxon stones, is worth its £1 admission (Mon–Sat 10:00–15:30, Sun 12:30–15:15). The unexceptional **AV show** in the unexceptional undercroft tells about St. Cuthbert (not worth £1, Mon–Sat 10:00–15:00, no showings Sun, off-season also no showings Fri).

Near the treasury, you'll find the **WCs, bookshop** (in the old kitchen), and fine **cafeteria** (June–mid-Oct Mon–Sat 10:00–17:00, Sun 10:30–17:00; closes at 16:30 mid-Oct–May, lunch served 12:00–14:00, non-smoking).

Near Durham

Beamish Open-Air Museum—This huge museum, which re-creates the years 1825 and 1913 in northeast England, takes at least three hours to explore. Vintage trams and cool circa-1910 double-decker buses shuttle visitors to the four stations: Colliery Village, The Town, Pockerly Manor/Waggonway, and Home Farm. Tram routes are more plentiful than bus routes, but attendants on both are helpful and knowledgeable. Signs on the trams advertise a variety of 19th-century products, from "Borax, for washing everything" to "Murton's Reliable Travelling Trunks."

This isn't a wax museum. If you touch the exhibits, they may smack you. Attendants at each stop happily explain everything. In fact, the place is only really interesting if you talk to the attendants.

Start with the **Colliery Village** (company town around a coal mine), with a school, a church, miners' homes, and a fascinating—if claustrophobic—20-minute tour into the Mahogany drift mine. Your guide will tell you about beams collapsing, gas exploding, and flooding; after that cheerful speech, you'll don a hard hat as you're led into the mine.

The Town is a bustling street featuring a 1913 candy shop (the chocolate room in back is worth a stop for chocolate fans), a dentist's office, a garage, a working pub (fun for a smoky beer), Barclays Bank, and a hardware store featuring a variety of "toilet sets" (not what you think). For lunch, try the modern, smoke-free cafeteria (Dainty Dinah's Tea Room, upstairs). If the weather is good, picnic in the grassy pavilion next to the tram stop.

Pockerley Manor and the Waggonway has an 1820s manor house whose attendants have plenty to explain. Enjoy the lovely view from the gardens behind the manor, then enter through the kitchen, where they bake bread several times a week. Ask for a sample if you have a taste for tough rye. Adjacent is the re-created first-ever passenger train from 1825, which takes modern-day visitors for a spin on 1825 tracks—a hit with railway buffs.

Home Farm is the least interesting section.

Cost and Hours: £15, April–Oct daily 10:00–17:00; from Nov–March only The Town is open, Tue–Thu and Sat–Sun 10:00–16:00, closed Mon and Fri; check events schedule as you enter, last tickets sold 2 hours before closing, tel. 0191/370-4000, www .beamish.org.uk.

Getting There: The museum is five minutes off the A1/M1 motorway (one exit north of Durham at Chester-le-Street, well signposted). To get to Beamish from Durham, catch the #720 bus from the bus station (marked *Stanley via Beamish*, 1/hr, 25 min, £3 round-trip, stops 50 yards from museum gate in front of the Shepherd and Shepherdess pub).

ACTIVITIES

Riverside Walk—For a 20-minute woodsy escape, walk Durham's riverside path from busy Framwellgate Bridge to sleepy Prebends Bridge.

Boat Cruise and Rental—For a relaxing 60-minute narrated cruise of the river that nearly surrounds Durham, hop on the *Prince Bishop* (£4.50, for schedule call 0191/386-9525, check at TI, or go down to dock at Brown's Boat House at Elvet Bridge, just east of old town). Sailings vary based on weather and tides. For some exercise with the same scenery, you can rent a rowboat at the same pier (£3/hr per person, £5 deposit, Easter–Sept daily 10:00–18:00, last boat rental 1 hour before dusk, tel. 0191/386-3779).

SLEEPING

B&Bs

$$$ Georgian Town House, near Framwellgate Bridge, has a cheery bossa-nova ambience with two rooms, a breezy garden, plush sitting room, and a new pancake café and tearoom next door (Db-£80, first night discount with this book in 2006, cash only, non-smoking, breakfast in conservatory, tubs lack showers, 10 Crossgate, tel. & fax 0191/386-8070, Charlotte and Lucy Weil).

$$$ Farnley Tower, a luxurious B&B, has 13 spacious rooms with all the comforts. The hotel is on a quiet street at the top of a hill, a 10-minute uphill hike from the town center (1 Sb-£55, Db-£80, superior Db-£90, some rooms have views, family rooms available, paying with credit card costs 2 percent extra, phones in rooms, easy parking, inviting yard, The Avenue, tel. 0191/375-0011, fax 0191/383-9694, www.farnley-tower.co.uk, enquiries@farnley -tower.co.uk, Raj and Roopal Naik).

$$ Castleview Guest House rents six airy, comfortable rooms in a classy, well-located house (Sb-£50, Db-£70, cash only, prices promised with book through 2006, 4 Crossgate, tel. 0191/386-8852, www.castle-view.co.uk, castle_view@hotmail.com, Mike and Anne Williams).

$ Castledene B&B is tidy, simple, and friendly. Lorna and Brian fill their home with a welcoming warmth (S-£25, twin D-£40, cash only; if you're walking: at intersection of Crossgate and Margery Lane, go up stairway to pedestrian-only walkway—running parallel to Crossgate Path—on and on to the last house; 37 Nevilledale Terrace; drivers go a few yards past Crossgate intersection and turn right on Summerville, tel. & fax 0191/384-8386).

$ The low-key **Bed & Breakfast at #12** has two simple rooms on a quiet dead-end street (small S-£21, D-£42, cash only, no sign

---

Sleep Code

(£1 = about $1.80, country code: 44, area code: 0191)
S = Single, **D** = Double/Twin, **T** = Triple, **Q** = Quad, **b** = bathroom, **s** = shower only. You can assume credit cards are accepted unless otherwise noted.

To help you sort easily through these listings, I've divided the rooms into three categories based on the price for a standard double room with bath (during high season):

$$$ Higher Priced—Most rooms £80 or more.
$$ Moderately Priced—Most rooms between £50–80.
$ Lower Priced—Most rooms £50 or less.

on door, 12 The Avenue, tel. 0191/384-1020, jan.hanim@aol.com, Jan Metcalfe).

$ Student Housing—Open to Anyone: Durham Castle, a student residence actually on the castle grounds facing the cathedral, rents 100 singles and 30 doubles during the summer break (July–Sept only, £27/person, £37 with private facilities, can reserve long in advance, elegant breakfast hall, parking-£2 on cathedral green, University College, The Castle, Palace Green, tel. 0191/334-4106, fax 0191/374-7470, castle.reception1@durham.ac.uk, Julie Marshall). Request a room in the classy old main building, or you may get one of the few bomb shelter–style modern dorm rooms.

Hotels

$$$ Durham Marriott Royal County Hotel, a four-star hotel, scatters its 150 posh rooms among several buildings sprawling along the river near the city center. The Leisure Club has a pool, sauna, Jacuzzi, and fitness equipment (Db-£145, £30 less on weekends, breakfast extra, 2 restaurants, bar, parking, Old Elvet, tel. 0191/386-6821, fax 0191/386-0704, www.marriotthotels.co.uk).

$$$ Kingslodge Hotel & Restaurant, a renovated lodge with charming terraces, an attached restaurant, and a champagne and oyster bar, is a cushy option convenient to the train station (Sb-£85, Db-£105, includes breakfast, parking, Waddington Street, Flass Vale, tel. 0191/370-9977).

EATING

Durham is a university town with plenty of lively, inexpensive eateries. Stroll down North Road, across Framwellgate Bridge, through Market Place, and up Saddler Street, and consider these places.

Emilio's, just over Elvet Bridge on the other side of town, is perhaps the most popular Italian place in Durham, with £7 pizzas and pastas in an inviting setting (daily until 22:30, even cheaper at 17:30 during happy hour, 96 Elvet Bridge, tel. 0191/384-0096).

Bimbi's, on Market Place, is a standby for fish-and-chips (daily 9:30–18:30, much later on weekends).

Saddler Street, leading from Market Place up to the cathedral, is lined with eateries. The hip **Hide Café,** with youthful, jazz-filled ambience, serves the best modern continental cuisine in the old town (£8–10 meals, gourmet evening plates-£15, good fish, daily 9:30–21:30, reservations smart, 39 Saddler Street, tel. 0191/384-1999).

Shaheen's is the place for good Indian cuisine (£5–9 meals, Tue–Sun 18:00–23:30, closed Mon, 48 Saddler Street, just past turnoff to cathedral, tel. 0191/386-0960).

The Almshouses, on the cathedral green, serves tasty, light meals in a cheap cafeteria setting (£6 plates, daily June–Sept 9:00–20:00, Oct–May 9:00–17:00, tel. 0191/386-1054).

Court Inn, on the outskirts of town, is a local favorite for traditional pub grub (£7–10 bar meals, daily 11:00–22:30, 5-min walk east of old town over Elvet Bridge, Court Lane, tel. 0191/384-7350).

Drivers looking for a nontouristy splurge can eat modern French/Mediterranean fare and good seafood at **Bistro 21** (£25 meals, Mon–Sat 12:00–14:00 & 19:00–22:00, closed Sun, Aykley Heads, 3 miles north of town, tel. 0191/384-4354).

Supermarkets: Of Durham's two supermarkets, **Safeway** has longer hours and is closer to the recommended B&Bs (Mon–Fri 8:30–20:00, Sat 8:30–18:00, Sun 11:00–17:00, in Millburngate Shopping Center, west end of Framwellgate Bridge). In the old town, try **Marks & Spencer,** just off the main square (Mon–Sat 9:00–18:00, Sun 11:00–17:00, on Silver Street; across from P.O., which has same hours as M&S). You can **picnic** on the benches and grass outside the cathedral entrance (but not on the Palace Green, unless the park police have gone home).

TRANSPORTATION CONNECTIONS

From Durham by Train to: Edinburgh (nearly hrly, 2 hrs, less frequent in winter), **Glasgow** (2/hr, 3 hrs, may require change in Edinburgh), **York** (1–3/hr, 45-60 min), **London** (hrly, 3 hrs), **Hadrian's Wall** (take train to Newcastle—1–4/hr, 15 min, then a train/bus combination to Hadrian's Wall, see "Hadrian's Wall," below), **Bristol** (near Bath, 9/day, 5 hrs). From September to May, only about half of the London–Edinburgh trains stop in little Durham, and frequency drops to about six trains daily in winter (but you don't need to wait; from Durham, catch a train to busier Newcastle—1–4/hr, 15 min—where all the trains stop). Train info: tel. 08457-484-950.

Hadrian's Wall

This is one of England's most thought-provoking sights. In about A.D. 130, during the reign of Emperor Hadrian, the Romans built this great stone wall. Its actual purpose is still debated. While Rome ruled Britain for 400 years, it never quite ruled its people. The wall may have been used for any number of reasons: to define the northern edge of the empire, to protect Roman Britain from invading Scottish clans (or at least cut down on pesky border raids), to monitor the movement of people, or to simply give an otherwise

Durham and Northeast England

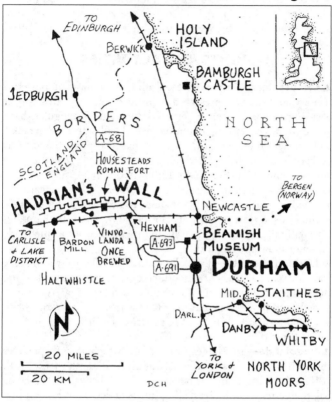

bored army something to do. (Emperors understood that nothing's more dangerous than a bored army.) Stretching 75 miles coast to coast across the narrowest stretch of northern England, it was built and defended by nearly 20,000 troops. The wall was flanked by ditches, and a military road lies on the south side. At every mile of the wall, a castle guards a gate, and two turrets stand between each castle. The mile castles are numbered. (Eighty of them cover the 75 miles, because a Roman mile was slightly shorter than our mile.)

Today, several chunks of the wall, ruined forts, and museums thrill history buffs. About a dozen Roman sites cling along the wall's route; the best are Housesteads Roman Fort and Vindolanda. Housesteads shows you where the Romans lived; Vindolanda's museum shows you how they lived (tel. 01434/322-002, www.hadrians-wall.org). The Hadrian's Wall National Trail follows the wall's route from coast to coast (for details, see www.nationaltrail.co.uk/HadriansWall).

SIGHTS AND ACTIVITIES

▲▲**Housesteads Roman Fort**—With its tiny museum, powerful scenery, and the best-preserved segment of the wall, this is your best single stop. All Roman forts were the same rectangular shape and design, containing a commander's headquarters, barracks, and latrines (lower end); this fort even has a hospital. The fort was built right up to the wall, which is on the far side (£3.60 for site and museum, May–Sept daily 10:00–18:00, Oct–April closes at 16:00 or dusk, parking-£2, tel. 01434/344-363). At the car park are WCs, a snack bar, and a gift shop. You can leave your baggage at the gift shop, but confirm its closing hours. From the car park, it's a half mile, mostly uphill walk to the entrance of the minuscule museum and sprawling fort.

▲▲**Hiking the Wall**—From Housesteads, hike west along the wall speaking Latin. For a good, craggy, three-mile walk along the wall, hike between Housesteads and Steel Rigg. You'll pass a castle sitting in a nick in a crag (castle #39, called Castle Nick). There's a car park near Steel Rigg (take the little road up from Twice Brewed Pub).

▲**Vindolanda**—This larger Roman fort (which actually predates the wall by 40 years) and museum are just south of the wall. Although Housesteads has better ruins and the wall, Vindolanda has the better museum, revealing intimate details of Roman life. It's an active dig—April through September, you'll see the work in progress. Eight forts were built on this spot. The Romans, by carefully sealing the foundations from each successive fort, left modern-day archaeologists seven yards of remarkably well-preserved artifacts to excavate: keys, coins, brooches, scales, pottery, glass, tools, leather shoes, bits of cloth, and even a wig. Impressive examples of early Roman writing were recently discovered here. While the actual letters—written on thin pieces of wood—are in London's British Museum, see the interesting video here and read the translations, including the first known example of a woman writing to a woman (an invitation to a birthday party). These varied letters, about parties held, money owed, and sympathy shared, bring Romans to life in a way that stones alone can't.

Cost, Hours, Location: £4.50, £6.50 combo-ticket includes Roman Army Museum (see below), daily 10:00–17:00 or 18:00 depending on the season, closed mid-Nov–early Feb, can leave baggage at entrance, tel. 01434/344-277. From the parking lot, you'll pay at the entrance, then walk 500 yards of grassy parkland decorated by the foundation stones of the Roman fort and a full-size replica chunk of the wall. At the far side of the site are the museum, gift shop, and cafeteria.

The **Roman Army Museum,** a few miles farther west at Greenhead, is redundant if you've seen Vindolanda (£3.50, or buy combo-ticket, see above, same hours, tel. 016977/47485).

SLEEPING AND EATING

(£1 = about $1.80, country code: 44)

Between Haltwhistle and Hexham
(area code: 01434)

$$ Montcoffer, a restored country home in Bardon Mill, is decorated with statues, old enameled advertising signs, and other artifacts collected by owner John McGrellis and his wife Dehlia, whose textile art is displayed in and around your room (Sb-£50, Db-£70, £10 less for 2 nights, includes hearty breakfasts, 2 miles from Vindolanda, Bardon Mill, tel. 01434/344-138, fax 01434/344-730, www.montcoffer.co.uk, john-dehlia@talk21.com).

$$ High Reins offers three rooms in a stone house built by a shipping tycoon in the 1920s (Db-£53–55, cash only, non-smoking, ground-floor bedrooms, lounge, 1 mile west of train station on the western outskirts of Hexham, Leazes Lane, tel. 01434/603-590, www.highreins.co.uk, walton45@hotmail.com, Jan Walton).

$$ Twice Brewed Pub and Hotel, two miles west of Housesteads, rents rooms and serves decent pub grub nightly to a local darts-and-pool crowd (D-£40, Db-£60, Internet access next to reception desk, tel. 01434/344-534).

$ Crow's Nest B&B offers three rooms in a remodeled farmhouse a quarter-mile from the wall (D-£45, cash only, on B6318 road 500 yards from Once Brewed TI, Bardon Mill, tel. 01434/344-348, Claire Watson). The nearby **Mile Castle Pub** cooks up all sorts of exotic game and offers the best dinner around, according to hungry national park rangers (daily 12:00–20:30, tel. 01434/321-372).

$ West Wharmley Farm rents two rooms in a friendly farmhouse about seven miles from the wall near Hexham (Sb-£30, Db-£50, cash only, family deals, non-smoking, lounge, off A69 between Hexham and Haydon Bridge, follow signs, tel. 01434/674-227, Ros Johnson).

$ Once Brewed Youth Hostel is a comfortable place near the Twice Brewed Pub (£12/bed with sheets, £2 extra for non-members, 4–8 beds/room, breakfast-£4, cheap lunches and dinners, Military Road, Bardon Mill, tel. 01434/344-360, fax 01434/344-045, oncebrewed@yha.org.uk).

In Haltwhistle
(area code: 01434)

$$ Ashcroft Guest House, a former vicarage, is 400 yards from the Haltwhistle train station. The family-run B&B has seven rooms, pleasant gardens, and views from the comfy lounge (Sb-£30, Db-£60, four-poster Db-£68, non-smoking, 1.5 miles from the wall, Lanty's Lonnen, tel. 01434/320-213, fax 01434/321-641, www.ashcroftguesthouse.co.uk, ashcroft.1@btconnect.com, Geoff and Christine).

$ Doors Cottage B&B rents a couple of rooms just across the street from a section of the Roman wall and five miles from Housesteads Roman Fort (S-£22–25, D-£44–50, includes good breakfast, non-smoking, Shield Hill, Haltwhistle, tel. 01434/322-556, doors-cottage@supanet.com). Your proprietress owns a dress shop on main street; if you don't find her at the B&B during the day, call her phone number, which forwards to her shop.

Near Carlisle
(area code: 01228)

$$ Bessiestown Farm B&B, located northwest of the Hadrian sights, is convenient for drivers connecting the Lake District and Scotland. It's a quiet and soothing stop in the middle of sheep pastures (Sb-£39, Db-£65, family room-£75, discounts for 3-night stays, non-smoking; in Catlowdy, midway between Gretna Green and Hadrian's Wall just north of Carlisle; tel. 01228/577-219, fax 01228/577-019, www.bessiestown.co.uk, info@bessiestown.co.uk).

TRANSPORTATION CONNECTIONS

By Car: Take B6318; it parallels the wall and passes several viewpoints, minor sights, and "severe dips." (If there's a certified nerd or bozo in the car, these road signs add a lot to a photo portrait. I've had my picture taken here.) Buy a good map locally to help you explore this interesting area more easily and thoroughly.

By Train and Bus: A train/bus combination (which operates with greatest frequency mid-May–mid-Sept) delivers you to the wall. Newcastle and Carlisle are the gateways to the train route that parallels the wall (Mon–Sat 8:30–16:30 every 30 min to Hexham, every hour to Haltwhistle, Sun hrly 9:00–18:30; from Newcastle, it's 30 min to Hexham, 20 more min to Haltwhistle). But the train only gets you near the wall. During peak season (mid-May–mid-Sept), take Hadrian's Wall bus #122AD to get to the Wall and all the Roman sights. Purists can take this bus for the entire length of the wall (1/day in each direction, 4 hours if you make the entire journey in one trip). This bus stops in Newcastle at 9:15. It also runs with regularity from Carlisle (6 buses/day), which has frequent train service from both the north and the south. If you're heading from Newcastle and miss the morning bus, get off the train at either Hexham or Haltwhistle to catch it (6 buses/day in each direction, late May–late Sept; Hexham–Housesteads 30 min, Housesteads–Vindolanda 10 min, Vindolanda–Haltwhistle 20 min). For those spending the night, this bus also stops at the Once Brewed Youth Hostel, which is less than a five-minute walk from the Crow's Nest B&B and the Twice Brewed Pub and Hotel.

At Newcastle's train station, pick up a Hadrian's Wall bus schedule at the TI (Mon–Fri 9:30–17:00, Sat 9:00–17:00, closed Sun, or call for schedule, tel. 0191/232-7021; luggage storage at station). If you're coming into Carlisle, you can get the same schedule at the information racks next to the entrance. You can also call Haltwhistle's helpful TI for schedule information (Easter–Oct Mon–Sat 9:30–13:00 & 14:00–17:30, Sun 13:00–17:00; Nov–Easter Mon–Tue and Thu–Sat 9:30–12:00 & 13:00–15:30, closed Wed and Sun, tel. 01434/322-002, www.hadrians-wall.org).

To visit Housesteads off-season (late Sept–late May), take a train to Haltwhistle and catch a taxi (taxi services: Haltwhistle tel. 01434/322-556, Sprouls tel. 01434/321-064, Turnbulls tel. 01434/320-105, one-way-£8; arrange for return pickup or have museum staff call a taxi; many taxis are contracted to pick up school kids between 15:00–16:00, confirm their availability if you need a cab during this time). If you're staying on the wall, your B&B host can arrange a taxi.

Holy Island and Bamburgh Castle

This area is only worthwhile for those with a car.

▲**Holy Island**—Twelve hundred years ago, this "Holy Island" was Christianity's toehold on England. It was the home of St.

Cuthbert. We know it today for the *Lindisfarne Gospels,* decorated by monks in the seventh century with some of the finest art from Europe's "Dark Ages" (now in the British Museum). It's a pleasant visit—a quiet town with a striking castle (not worth touring) and an evocative priory. The Priory Exhibit is a tiny but instructive museum adjacent to the ruined abbey (£3.60, daily 9:30–17:00, tel. 01289/389-200). You can wander the abbey grounds and graveyard and pop into the church without paying. Holy Island is reached by a two-mile causeway that's cut off daily by high tides. Tidal charts are posted, warning you when this holy place becomes Holy Island—and you become stranded. For TI and tide information, call the **Berwick TI** at tel. 01289/330-733 (May–Sept Mon–Sat 10:00–17:00, Sun 11:00–15:00, off-season 10:00–16:00). Park at the pay-and-display lot and walk five minutes into the village.

Sleeping: For a peaceful overnight in the center, try **$ Castle Reigh B&B** (S-£25, D-£44, Db-£50, cash only, tel. 01289/389-218, Mrs. Patterson).

▲▲**Bamburgh Castle**—About 10 miles south of Holy Island, this grand castle dominates the Northumbrian countryside and overlooks Britain's loveliest beach. The place was bought and passionately refurbished by Lord Armstrong, a Ted Turner–like industrialist and engineer in the 1890s. Its interior, lined with well-described history, feels lived in because it still is—with Armstrong family portraits and aristocratic-yet-homey knickknacks hanging everywhere. Take advantage of the talkative guides posted throughout the castle. The included **Armstrong Museum** features the inventions of the industrialist family that has owned the castle through modern times (£5.50, daily 11:00–17:00, last entry 16:30, closed Nov–March, tel. 01668/214-515, www.bamburghcastle .com). Rolling dunes crisscrossed by walking paths lead to a vast sandy beach and lots of families on holiday.

EDINBURGH

Edinburgh is the historical and cultural capital of Scotland. Once a medieval powerhouse sitting on a lava flow, it sprouted into Europe's first great grid-planned modern city. Today, the colorful home of Robert Louis Stevenson, Sir Walter Scott, and Robert Burns is Scotland's showpiece and one of Europe's most entertaining cities. Historic, monumental, fun, and well-organized, it's a tourist's delight—especially in August, when the Edinburgh Festival takes over the town.

Promenade down the Royal Mile through Old Town. Historic buildings pack the Royal Mile between the grand castle (on the top) and the Palace of Holyroodhouse (on the bottom). Medieval skyscrapers stand shoulder to shoulder, hiding peaceful courtyards connected to High Street by narrow lanes or even tunnels. This colorful jumble is the tourist's Edinburgh.

Edinburgh (ED'n-burah) was once the most crowded city in Europe—famed for its skyscrapers and filth. The rich and poor virtually lived atop one another. In the Age of Enlightenment, a magnificent Georgian city (today's New Town) was laid out to the north, giving Edinburgh's upper class a respectable place to promenade. Georgian Edinburgh—like the city of Bath—shines with broad boulevards, straight streets, square squares, circular circuses, and elegant mansions decked out in colonnades, pediments, and sphinxes in the proud neoclassical style of 200 years ago.

While the Georgian city celebrated the union of Scotland and England (with streets and squares named after English kings and emblems), "devolution" is the latest trend. For the past several centuries, Scotland was ruled from London, and parliament had not met in Edinburgh since 1707. In a 1998 election, the Scots voted to

Greater Edinburgh

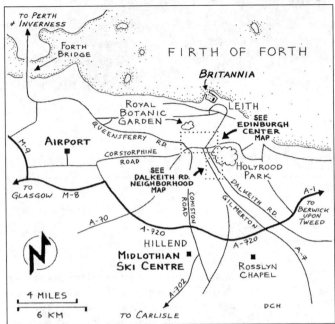

gain more autonomy and bring their parliament home. In 2000, Edinburgh resumed its position as home to the Scottish Parliament (although London still calls the strategic shots). A strikingly modern new parliament building, which opened in 2004, is one more jewel in Edinburgh's crown.

Planning Your Time

While the major sights can be seen in a day, on a three-week tour of Britain, I'd give Edinburgh two days and three nights.

Day 1: Tour the castle. Then consider either catching an 11:00 walking tour (leaves from Mercat Cross on the Royal Mile) or one of the city bus tours (from a block below the castle at The Hub/ Tolbooth church) for a 60-minute loop, returning to the castle. Wander down the Royal Mile, having lunch, going to museums, and shopping. (Note that another walking tour leaves at 14:00 from Mercat Cross in August.) Finish your sightseeing day with a tour of the Palace of Holyroodhouse, at the bottom of the Mile.

Day 2: Tour the Museum of Scotland. After lunch, stroll through the Princes Street Gardens and the National Gallery of Scotland. Then tour the good ship *Britannia*.

Evenings: Options include various "haunted Edinburgh" walks, literary pub crawls, live music in pubs, or a touristy bagpipe-music evening. Sadly, traditional folk shows are just about extinct, surviving only in excruciatingly schmaltzy variety shows put on for tour-bus groups. Perhaps the most authentic local evening out is just settling down in a pub to sample the whisky and local beers while meeting the natives and attempting to understand their Scottish accents.

ORIENTATION

(area code: 0131)

The center of Edinburgh holds the Princes Street Gardens park and Waverley Bridge, where you'll find the TI, Princes Mall, train station, bus info office (starting point for most city bus tours), National Gallery, and a covered dance-and-music pavilion. Weather blows in and out—bring your sweater. Locals say the bad weather is one of the disadvantages of living so close to England.

Tourist Information

The crowded TI is as central as can be atop the Princes Mall and train station (July–Aug Mon–Sat 9:00–20:00, Sun 10:00–20:00; May–June and Sept Mon–Sat 9:00–19:00, Sun 10:00–19:00; April–Oct Mon–Wed 9:00–17:00, Thu–Sat until 18:00, Sun 10:00–17:00; ATM outside entrance, tel. 0845-225-5121). The staff is knowledgeable and eager to help, but much of their information—including their assessment of museums and even which car-rental companies "exist"—is skewed by tourism payola.

Buy a map, either the £1 version—if it's in stock—or the excellent £4 Collins Illustrated Edinburgh map (which comes with opinionated commentary and locates virtually every major shop and sight). If you're interested in late-night music, ask for the free monthly entertainment *Gig Guide*. The *Essential Guide to Edinburgh* (£1), while not truly essential, lists additional sights and services. The TI also sells the mediocre Edinburgh Pass, which provides unlimited bus travel (includes the airport) and entry to dozens of B-list sights (£26/1 day, £34/2 days, £40/3 days, doesn't include Edinburgh Castle, www.edinburghpass.org).

Book your room direct, using my listings, without the TI's help (as the TI takes 10 percent plus a £3 booking fee, and B&Bs charge more for rooms booked through the TI). Browse the racks—tucked away in hallway at back of TI—for brochures on the various Scottish folk shows, walking tours, and regional bus tours.

Connect@edinburgh, a small Internet café, is beyond the brochure racks (see "Helpful Hints," page 394). The best monthly entertainment listing, *The List*, sells for £2.20 at newsstands.

Arrival in Edinburgh

By Train: Arriving by train at Waverley Station puts you in the city center and below the TI. High-security luggage storage is near platform 1 (£5/24 hrs, daily 7:00–23:00). Taxis queue almost track-side. The ramp they come and go on leads to Waverley Bridge. If there's a long line for taxis, it's faster to hike the ramp and hail one on the street. From the station, *Way Out to Princes Street* signs lead up to the TI and the city bus stop (for bus directions from here to my recommended B&Bs, see page 425). For picnic supplies, there's a Marks & Spencer Simply Food near platform 1.

By Bus: Both Scottish Citylink and National Express buses use the **bus station** (which has luggage lockers) two blocks north of the train station on St. Andrew Square in the New Town.

By Plane: Edinburgh's slingshot-of-an-airport is 10 miles northwest of the center and well-connected by taxi (£15, 30 min to the center) and shuttle bus (LRT Airlink bus #100 to Waverley Bridge, £3.30, or £5 with all-day Airsaver city-bus pass, 6/hr, 30 min, roughly 5:00–24:00). Flight info: tel. 0870-040-0007; bmi british midland: tel. 0870-607-0555 (www.flybmi.com); British Airways: tel. 0870-850-9850 (www.ba.com).

Helpful Hints

Sunday Activities: Many minor sights close on Sunday, but the major sights are open. Sunday is a good day for a Royal Mile walking tour or a city bus tour (which go faster in light Sunday traffic). Arthur's Seat is lively with locals on weekends (see "Arthur's Seat Hike," page 419).

Internet Access: Get online at **easyInternetcafé** (daily 7:00–21:00, 400 terminals, a block from National Gallery at 58 Rose Street); **Connect@edinburgh** (in the TI, Mon–Sat 9:00–19:00, Sun 10:00–19:00, shorter hours off-season); or **Elephant House Café** (4 stations, 24 George IV Bridge, off top of Royal Mile, see page 430).

Laundry: Sun Dial launderette is located near the Dalkeith B&Bs (Mon–Fri 8:00–19:00, Sat 9:00–16:00, Sun 10:00–15:00, self-service or drop-off; along the bus route to the city center at 13 South Clerk Street, opposite Queens Hall; tel. 0131/667-0549).

Car Rental: Except for Budget, these places have offices in the town center and at the airport: **Avis** (5 West Park Place, tel. 0131/337-6363, airport tel. 0131/344-3900), **Europcar** (24 East London Street, tel. 0131/557-3456, airport tel. 0131/333-2588), **Hertz** (10 Picardy Place, tel. 0131/556-8311, airport tel. 0131/333-1019), and **Budget** (airport only, tel. 0131/333-1926). If you're going to rent a car, pick it up on your way out of Edinburgh, since you won't need it in town.

Local Guide: Ken Hanley wears his kilt as if pants don't exist, and loves sharing his passion for Edinburgh and Scotland. A licensed Blue Badge guide, Ken comes equipped with a car and all the great stories (£60/half-day, £100/day, extra if he uses his car, tel. 0131/666-1944, mobile 07710-342-044, www .small-world-tours.co.uk, k.hanley@blueyonder.co.uk).

Getting Around Edinburgh

Nearly all of Edinburgh's sights are within walking distance of each other.

City **buses** are handy (about 80p/ride, buy tickets on bus, LRT transit office at Old Town end of Waverley Bridge has schedules and route maps, tel. 0131/555-6363). Tell the driver where you're going, have change handy (buses require exact change—you lose any excess), take your ticket as you board, and ping the bell as you near your stop. Double-deckers come with fine views upstairs. Two companies handle the city routes: LRT (or Lothian) does most of it, and First does the rest. (To get from the city center to the recommended B&Bs on Dalkeith Road, you can catch LRT buses #14, #30, and #33, or First bus #86; for details, see page 425.) Day passes sold by each company are valid only on their buses (£2.50, or £2 after 9:30 weekdays and all day weekends, buy from driver). Buses run from about 6:00 to 23:00.

The 1,300 **taxis** cruising Edinburgh's streets are easy to flag down (a ride between downtown and B&B district costs about £5). As they can turn on a dime, hail them in either direction.

TOURS

In Edinburgh

Royal Mile Walking Tours—**Mercat Tours** offers 90-minute guided walks of the Mile—more entertaining than historic (£7.50, daily at 11:00, from Mercat Cross on the Royal Mile, tel. 0131/557-6464). The guides, who enjoy making a short story long, ignore the big sights and take you behind the scenes with piles of barely historic gossip, bully-pulpit Scottish pride, and fun but forgettable trivia. They also offer a variety of other tours.

In August only, the **Voluntary Guides Association** leads free two-hour tours of Edinburgh (generally departing daily at about 10:00 and 14:00, check at TI or call for a schedule, tel. 0131/664-7180 or 0131/669-8263).

Edinburgh Bus Tours—Four different 60-minute, hop-on, hop-off bus tours, all operated by LRT, circle the town center and stop along one route at the biggies: Waverley Bridge, the castle, Royal Mile, Georgian New Town, and Princes Street. You can hop on and off at any stop with one ticket all day (pick-ups about

every 10–15 min). To compare your options, talk to the guides and drivers at the Waverley Bridge starting point. (Why four different tours, all owned by the same big company? It has to do with local anti-monopoly laws.)

The ride comes with informative narration. Two of the tours have live guides: **Mac Tours' City Tour** (live Mon–Fri with "vintage buses") and **Edinburgh Tour** (always live). Avoid the **City Sightseeing Tours**, which have a recorded narration (better for non-English speakers). The tours have virtually the same route, cost, and frequency, except the **Majestic Tour**, whose regular route is longer and includes a stop at the *Britannia* and the Royal Botanic Garden (£8.50, tickets give 10 percent discount off castle admission, valid 24 hours, buy on bus, tel. 0131/220-0770, Web site for all 4 companies—www.edinburghtour.com). Buses run daily year-round; in peak season, they leave Waverley Bridge daily between around 9:15 and 19:00 (mid-June–early Sept; hours shrink off-season). On sunny days they go topless (the buses), but they also suffer from traffic noise and exhaust fumes.

Busy sightseers might want to get the **Royal Edinburgh Ticket** (for £32.50), which covers two days unlimited travel on all four tour buses, as well as admission to Edinburgh Castle (normally costs £9.80), the Palace of Holyroodhouse (£8.50), and the *Britannia* (£9). If you plan to visit all these sights and to use a tour bus both days, the ticket will save you a few pounds (and, in the summer, help you bypass any lines). You can buy these tickets from the staff at the pick-up point on Waverley Bridge. If your main interest is seeing the *Britannia*, you'll save money taking a regular bus instead (see page 418).

From Edinburgh

Many companies run day trips to regional sights. Study the brochures at the TI's rack.

Heart of Scotland Tours offers various itineraries, but the best are the experience- and information-packed day trips of the Highlands and Loch Ness (£32, £3 discount with this book in 2006, departures Wed and Sat–Sun, 8:00–20:00, leaves from 25 Waterloo Place near Waverley Station, fewer tours off-season, reserve at least a day ahead by phone or online, tel. 0131/558-8855, www.heartofscotlandtours.co.uk, run by Nick Roche). The tour gives those with limited time a chance to experience the wonders of Scotland's wild and legend-soaked Highlands in a long

Edinburgh

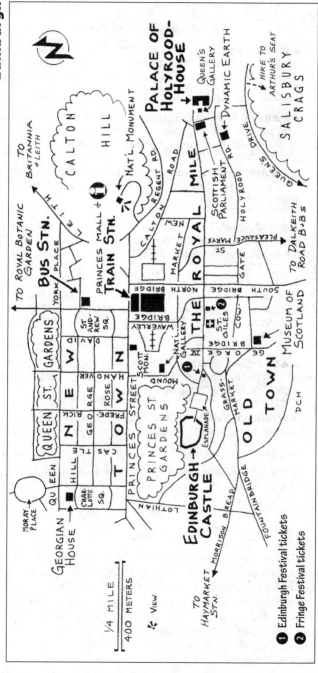

Edinburgh at a Glance

▲▲▲**Edinburgh Castle** Iconic 11th-century hilltop fort and royal residence complete with Crown Jewels, Romanesque chapel, memorial, and fine military museum. **Hours:** Daily April–Oct 9:30–18:00, Nov–March 9:30–17:00.

▲▲▲**Royal Mile** Historic road—good for walking—stretching from the castle to the palace, lined with museums, pubs, and shops. **Hours:** Always open, but best during business hours.

▲▲▲**Museum of Scotland** Intriguing, well-displayed artifacts from prehistoric times to the 20th century. **Hours:** Mon–Sat 10:00–17:00, Tue until 20:00, Sun 12:00–17:00.

▲▲**Gladstone's Land** 16th-century Royal Mile merchant's residence. **Hours:** April–Oct Mon–Sat 10:00–17:00, Sun 14:00–17:00, July–Aug daily until 19:00, closed Nov–March.

▲▲**St. Giles Cathedral** Preaching grounds of Calvinist John Knox, with spectacular organ, neo-Gothic chapel, and distinctive crown spire. **Hours:** May–Sept Mon–Fri 9:00–19:00, Sat 9:00–17:00, Sun 13:00–17:00; Oct–April Mon–Sat 9:00–17:00, Sun 13:00–17:00.

▲▲**Georgian House** Intimate peek at upper-crust life in the late 1700s. **Hours:** Daily April–Oct 10:00–17:00, March and Nov 11:00–15:00, closed Dec–Feb.

▲▲**National Gallery of Scotland** Choice sampling of European masters and Scotland's finest. **Hours:** Daily 10:00–17:00, Thu until 19:00.

▲**Writers' Museum at Lady Stair's House** Tribute to Scottish literary triumvirate: Robert Burns, Sir Walter Scott, and Robert Louis Stevenson. **Hours:** Mon–Sat 10:00–17:00, closed Sun.

day (14- or 24-seat bus, talkative driver, good sound system). This Highlands joyride keeps a tight schedule, punctuated by several 30- to 90-minute stops. You'll see the vast and brutal Rannoch Moor; Glencoe, still evocative with memories of the clan massacre; views of Britain's highest mountain, Ben Nevis; Fort Augustus on Loch Ness (at the 90-min stop here, you can take the optional £6 boat ride or, if not into Nessie, enjoy free time in town); a scenic walk in the woods; and a 45-minute tea or pub break in the fine little village of Dunkeld. You'll learn a bit about Edinburgh to

▲**Museum of Childhood** Five stories of historic fun. **Hours:** Mon–Sat 10:00–17:00, closed Sun except July–Aug.

▲**John Knox House** Reputed 16th-century digs of the great reformer. **Hours:** Mon–Sat 10:00–18:00, closed Sun.

▲**People's Story** Proletarian life from the 18th to 20th centuries. **Hours:** Mon–Sat 10:00–17:00, closed Sun.

▲**Museum of Edinburgh** Historic mementos, from the original National Covenant scribed on animal skin to early golf balls. **Hours:** Mon–Sat 10:00–17:00, closed Sun.

▲**Scottish Parliament Building** Controversial new headquarters for the recently-returned Parliament. **Hours:** Mon and Fri 10:00–18:00, Tue–Thu 9:00–19:00, Sat–Sun 10:00–16:00, shorter hours off-season and when Parliament is in recess.

▲**Palace of Holyroodhouse** The queen's splendid home-away-from-home, with lavish rooms, 12th-century abbey, and gallery with rotating exhibits. **Hours:** Daily May–Oct 9:30–18:00, Nov–April 9:30–16:30.

▲**Georgian New Town** Elegant 1776 subdivision spiced with trendy shops, bars, and eateries. **Hours:** Always open.

▲**Sir Walter Scott Monument** Climbable tribute to the famed novelist. **Hours:** April–Sept Mon–Sat 9:00–18:00, Sun 10:00–18:00, Oct–March daily 10:00–15:00.

▲*Britannia* The royal yacht with a history of distinguished passengers, a 15-minute trip out of town. **Hours:** Daily March–Oct 9:30–16:30, Nov–Feb 10:00–15:30.

boot as you drive in and out.

Haggis Backpackers runs cheap tours on 22- to 35-seat buses with a very Scottish driver/guide. Their day trips (£23) include a distillery visit and the northern Highlands, or Loch Lomond and the southern Highlands. Their overnight trips are designed for young backpackers, but they welcome travelers of any age who want a quick look at the bonny countryside (£85/3 days, £150/6 days, hostels £12–14/night extra; office hours: Mon–Sat 9:00–18:00, summer Sun 13:00–18:00; 60 High Street, at Blackfriars Street, tel.

0131/557-9393, www.radicaltravel.com). They also offer an eight-day Island Adventure, visiting the Hebrides and the Orkney Islands.

Glasgow, Scotland's biggest city, is a happening cultural center and a mecca for those interested in architecture (particularly the Art Nouveau designs of Charles Rennie Mackintosh). Only 45 minutes away by train from Edinburgh (4/hr, £9 round-trip), it makes an interesting day trip (see Glasgow chapter on page 438).

SIGHTS

Edinburgh Castle

The fortified birthplace of the city 1,300 years ago, this imposing symbol of Edinburgh—worth ▲▲▲—sits proudly on a rock high

above the city. While the castle has been both a fort and a royal residence since the 11th century, most of the buildings today are from its more recent use as a military garrison. This fascinating and multifaceted sight deserves several hours of your time.

Cost, Hours, Services: £9.80, daily April–Oct 9:30–18:00, Nov–March 9:30–17:00, last entrance 45 min before closing, tel. 0131/225-9846. The clean WC at the entry annually wins "British Loo of the Year" awards (marvel at the plaques near men's room; the one-way mirrors peeking into the women's sink area are now shut-

tered—thanks in part to readers of this book complaining). The Red Coat Cafeteria and Jacobite Room is a handy cafeteria in the castle (see "Eating," page 430).

Getting There: While regular city buses drop you far below (at the top of the Royal Mile, near the Camera Obscura), taxis take you right to the esplanade, in front of the gate. A new castle bus does a circuit through central Edinburgh, beginning at George Street (near train station) and leaving you at the castle's esplanade (£1, July–Aug only, daily 10:00–8:00, 4/hr in peak times, driver also sells £10 Fast Track Ticket for castle allowing you to bypass the line, though at 50p extra it's only worth considering in Aug, Edinburgh's busiest time).

Entry Gate: Start with the wonderfully droll 20-minute guided introduction tour (free with admission, 2–4/hr, departs from entry, see clock for next departure; few tours run off-season). The audioguide is excellent, with four hours of quick-dial digital descriptions of the sights, including the National War Museum of Scotland (£3, pay at ticket office, pick up at entry gate before meeting the live guide).

William Wallace
(c. 1276–1305)

In 1286, Scotland's king died without an heir, plunging the prosperous country into a generation of chaos. As Scottish nobles bickered over a successor, the English king Edward I —nicknamed "Longshanks" because of his height—invaded and assumed power (1296). He placed a figurehead on the throne, forced Scottish nobles to sign a pledge of allegiance to England (the "Ragman's Roll"), and carried off the 336-pound, highly symbolic Stone of Scone to London, where it would remain for the next seven centuries.

A year later, the Scots rose against Edward, led by William Wallace (nicknamed "Braveheart"). A mix of history and legend portrays Wallace as the son of a poor-but-knightly family that refused to sign the Ragman's Roll. Exceptionally tall and strong, he learned Latin and French from two uncles who were priests. In his teenage years, his father and older brother were killed by the English. Later, he killed an English sheriff to avenge the death of his wife, Marion. Wallace's rage inspired his fellow Scots to revolt.

In the summer of 1297, Wallace and his guerrillas scored a series of stunning victories over the English. On September 11, a large, well-equipped English army of 10,000 soldiers and 300 horsemen began crossing Stirling Bridge. Half the army had made it across when Wallace's men attacked. In the chaos, the bridge collapsed, splitting the English ranks in two, and the ragtag Scots drove the confused English into the river. The Battle of Stirling Bridge was a rout, and Wallace was knighted and appointed Guardian of Scotland.

All through the winter, King Edward chased Wallace, continually frustrated by the Scots' hit-and-run tactics. Finally, at the Battle of Falkirk (April 1, 1298), they drew Wallace's men out onto the open battlefield. The English with their horses and archers easily routed the spear-carrying Scots. Wallace resigned in disgrace and went on the lam, while his successors negotiated truces with the English, finally surrendering unconditionally in 1304. Wallace alone held out.

In 1305, he was tracked down and taken to London, convicted of treason, and mocked with a crown of oak leaves as "King of Scotland." On August 23, they stripped him naked and dragged him to the execution site. There he was strangled to near death, castrated, and dismembered. His head was stuck on a stick atop London Bridge, while his body parts were sent on tour around the realm to spook future rebels. But Wallace's martyrdom only served to inspire his countrymen, and the torch of independence was picked up by Robert the Bruce (see sidebar on page 404).

The castle has five essential stops: Crown Jewels, Royal Palace, Scottish National War Memorial, St. Margaret's Chapel (with a city view), and the excellent National War Museum of Scotland. The first four are at the highest and most secure point—on or near the castle square, where your introductory guided tour ends (and the sights described below begin). Consider the National War Museum of Scotland (50 yards below the cafeteria and big shop) a separate sight and worth a serious look.

1. Crown Jewels: There are two ways to see the jewels. You can go in directly from the courtyard, but there's often a line. To avoid the line, enter the building around to the left (next to WC), where you'll get to the jewels via the "Honors of Scotland" exhibition—a kid-friendly series of displays (which often moves at a very slow shuffle) telling the story of the Crown Jewels and how they survived the harrowing centuries.

Scotland's **Crown Jewels,** though not as impressive as England's, are older and at least as treasured by the locals. While Oliver Cromwell destroyed England's jewels, the Scots managed to hide theirs. Longtime symbols of Scottish nationalism, they were made in Edinburgh—in 1540 for a 1543 coronation—out of Scottish diamonds, gems, and gold...some say the personal gold of King Robert the Bruce melted down (see Robert the Bruce sidebar, page 404). They were last used to crown Charles II in 1651. When the Act of Union was forced upon the Scots in 1707—dissolving Scotland's parliament into England's to create the United Kingdom—part of the deal was that the Scots could keep their jewels locked up in Edinburgh. The jewels remained hidden for more than 100 years. In 1818, Sir Walter Scott and a royal commission rediscovered them intact. In 1999, for the first time in nearly three centuries, the crown of Scotland was brought from the castle for the opening of the Scottish Parliament (see photos on the wall where the "Honors of Scotland" exhibit meets the Crown Jewels room; a smiling Queen Elizabeth II presides over the historic occasion).

The **Stone of Scone** (a.k.a. the "Stone of Destiny") sits plain and strong next to the jewels. This big gray chunk of rock is the coronation stone of Scotland's ancient kings (9th century). Swiped by the English, it sat under the coronation chair at Westminster Abbey from 1296 until 1996. Queen Elizabeth finally agreed to let the stone go home—on one condition: that it be returned to Westminster Abbey in London for all future coronations. With major fanfare, Scotland's treasured Stone of Scone returned to Edinburgh on Saint Andrew's Day, November 30, 1996. Talk to the guard for more details.

2. The Royal Palace: Scottish royalty lived here only when safety or protocol required (preferring the Palace of Holyroodhouse

British, Scottish, and English

Of course, Scotland and England are tied together in a union no one seriously challenges. But history is clearly seen through two very different filters.

If you tour a British-oriented sight, such as the National War Museum of Scotland, you'll find things told in a "happy union" way. The official line: In 1707, it was clear to England and Scotland that it was in their mutual interest to dissolve the Scottish government and fold it into Britain, ruled from London. But talk to a cabbie or your B&B host, and you may get a different spin. In a clever move by England to deflate the military power of its little sister, Scottish Highlanders were sent to fight and die for Britain—in disproportionately higher numbers than their English counterparts. Poignant propaganda posters in the National War Museum of Scotland show a happy lad with the message: "Hey, look! Willie's off to Singapore with the Queen's own Highlanders."

The deep-seated rift shows itself in sports, too. While the English may refer to a British team in international competition as "English," the Scots are careful to call it "British." If a Scottish athlete does well, the English call him "British." If he screws up...he's a clumsy Scot.

at the bottom of the Royal Mile). The Royal Palace, facing castle square under the flagpole, has two historic yet unimpressive rooms (through door marked "1566") and the Great Hall (separate entrance from opposite side of square; see below). Enter the **Mary, Queen of Scots room,** where in 1566 the queen gave birth to James VI of Scotland, who later became King James I of England. The Presence Chamber leads into **Laich Hall** (Lower Hall), the dining room of the royal family.

The **Great Hall** was the castle's ceremonial meeting place in the 16th and 17th centuries. In later times, it was a barracks and a hospital. While most of what you see is Victorian, two medieval elements survive: the fine hammer-beam roof and the big iron-barred peephole (above fireplace on right). This allowed the king to spy on his subjects as they partied.

3. The Scottish National War Memorial: This commemorates the 149,000 Scottish soldiers lost in World War I, the 58,000 lost in World War II, and the 750 (and counting) lost in British battles since. Each bay is dedicated to a particular Scottish regiment. The main shrine, featuring a green Italian-marble memorial that contains the original WWI rolls of honor, sits—almost religiously—on an exposed chunk of the castle rock. Above you, the archangel Michael is busy slaying the dragon. The bronze frieze

Robert the Bruce
(1274–1305)

William Wallace's story (see sidebar on page 401) paints the Scottish fight for independence in black and white terms—the oppressive English versus the plucky Scots. But Scotland had to overcome its own divisiveness, and none was more divided than Robert the Bruce. As Earl of Carrick, he was born with both blood ties to England and a longstanding family claim to the Scottish throne.

When England's King Edward I ("Longshanks") conquered Scotland in 1296, the Bruce family welcomed it, hoping Edward would defeat their rivals and put Bruce's father on the throne. They dutifully signed the "Ragman's Roll" of allegiance...but Edward chose someone else as king.

Twentysomething Robert the Bruce (the "the" comes from his original family name of "de Bruce") then joined William Wallace's revolt against the English. Legend has it that it was he who knighted Wallace after the victory at Stirling Bridge. When Wallace fell from favor, Bruce became co-Guardian of Scotland (caretaker ruler in the absence of a king) and continued fighting the English. But when Edward's armies again got the upper hand in 1302, Robert—along with Scotland's other nobles—diplomatically surrendered and again pledged loyalty.

In 1306, Robert the Bruce murdered his chief rival and boldly claimed to be King of Scotland. Few nobles supported him. Edward crushed the revolt and kidnapped Bruce's wife, the Church excommunicated him, and Bruce went into hiding on a distant North Sea island. He was now the king of nothing. Legend says he gained inspiration by watching a spider patiently build its web.

The following year, Bruce returned to Scotland and weaved alliances with both nobles and the Church, slowly gaining acceptance as Scotland's king by a populace chafing under English rule. On June 24, 1314, he decisively defeated the English (now led by Edward's weak son) at the Battle of Bannockburn. After a generation of turmoil (1286–1314), England was finally driven from Scotland, and the country was united under Robert I, King of Scotland.

As king, Robert the Bruce's priority was to stabilize the monarchy and establish clear lines of succession. His descendants would rule Scotland for the next 400 years, and even today, Bruce blood runs through the veins of Queen Elizabeth II, Prince Charles, and Prince William.

accurately shows the attire of various wings of Scotland's military. The stained glass starts with Cain and Abel on the left and finishes with a celebration of peace on the right. To appreciate how important this place is, consider that one out of every three adult Scottish men died in World War I.

4. St. Margaret's Chapel: The oldest building in Edinburgh is dedicated to Queen Margaret, who died here in 1093 and was sainted in 1250. Built in 1130 in the Romanesque style of the Norman invaders, it's wonderfully simple, with classic Norman zigzags decorating the round arch that separates the tiny nave from the sacristy. Used as a powder magazine for 400 years, very little survives. You'll see an 11th-century gospel book of St. Margaret's and small windows featuring St. Margaret, St. Columba (who brought Christianity to Scotland via Iona, see sidebar on page 471), and William Wallace (the brave-hearted defender of Scotland, see sidebar on page 401). The place is popular for weddings—and, since it seats only 20, it's particularly popular with brides' fathers.

Mons Meg, in front of the church, is a huge and once-upon-a-time frightening 15th-century siege cannon that fired 330-pound stones nearly two miles. It was a gift from the Belgians, who shared a common enemy in England, and were eager to arm Scotland.

Belly up to the banister (outside the chapel below the cannon) to enjoy the grand view. Below you are the guns—which fire the one o'clock salute—and a sweet little line of doggie tombstones, marking the soldiers' pet cemetery. Beyond stretches the Georgian New Town (read the informative plaque).

Crowds gather for the 13:00 gun blast, a tradition that gives ships in the bay something to set their navigational devices by. (The frugal Scots don't fire it at high noon, as that would cost 11 extra rounds a day.)

5. The National War Museum of Scotland: This museum thoughtfully covers four centuries of Scottish military history. Instead of the usual musty, dusty displays of endless armor, this museum has an interesting mix of short films, uniforms, weapons, medals, mementos, and eloquent excerpts from soldiers' letters. A pleasant surprise just when you thought your castle visit was about over, this rivals any military museum you'll see in Europe.

Here, you'll learn the story of how the fierce and courageous Scottish warrior changed from being a symbol of resistance against Britain to being a champion of that same empire. Along the way, these military men received many decorations for valor, and did more than their share of dying in battle. But even when fighting for—rather than against—England, Scottish regiments promoted the romantic, kilted-warrior image.

Queen Victoria fueled this ideal throughout the 19th century. (She was infatuated with the Scottish Highlands and the culture's untamed and rustic mystique.) Highland soldiers, especially officers, went to great personal expense to sport all their elaborate regalia, and the kilted men fought best to the tune of their beloved bagpipes. For centuries, the stirring drone of bagpipes has accompanied Highland soldieries into battle—inspiring them, raising their spirits, and announcing to the enemy that they were about to meet a fierce and mighty foe.

This museum shows the human side of war, as well as how clever government-sponsored ad campaigns kept the lads enlisting. Two centuries of recruiting posters make the same pitch that still works today: a hefty signing bonus, steady pay, and job security with the promise of a manly and adventurous life—all spiked with a mix of pride and patriotism.

Leaving the castle, turn around and look back at the gate. There stand King Robert the Bruce (on the left, 1274–1329) and Sir William Wallace (Braveheart—on the right, 1270–1305). Wallace—now famous, thanks to Mel Gibson—fought long and hard against English domination before being executed in London. Bruce beat the English at Bannockburn in 1314. Bruce and Wallace still defend the spirit of Scotland. The Latin inscription above the gate between them reads, more or less, "What you do to us...we will do to you."

Along the Royal Mile

The Royal Mile—worth ▲▲▲—is one of Europe's most interesting historic walks. Consisting of a series of four different streets—Castlehill, Lawnmarket, High Street, and Canongate (each with its own set of street numbers), the Royal Mile is actually 200 yards longer than a mile. And every inch is packed with shops, cafés, and lanes leading to tiny squares.

Start at the top and amble down to the palace. These sights are listed in walking order. Bus #35 runs along the Mile, handy for going up after you've hit bottom. Entertaining 90-minute guided walks bring the legends and lore of the Royal Mile alive (described under "Tours," above).

As you walk, remember that originally there were two settlements here, divided by a wall: Edinburgh lined the ridge from the castle at the top. The lower end, Canongate, was outside the wall until 1856. By poking down the many side alleys, you'll find a few surviving rough edges of an

Royal Mile

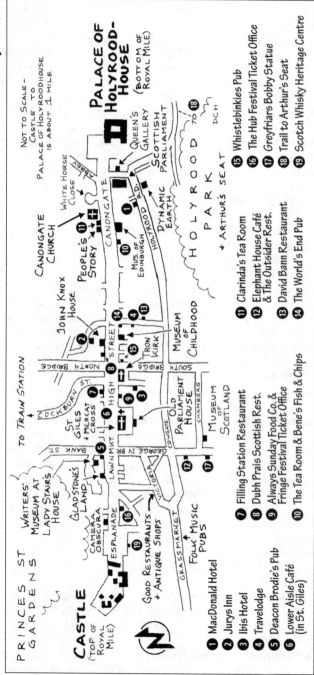

Not to Scale –
Castle to
Palace of Holyroodhouse
is about 1 mile.

CANONGATE CHURCH

WHITE HORSE CLOSE

PEOPLE'S STORY

CANONGATE

JOHN KNOX HOUSE

MUS. OF EDINBURGH

HOLYROOD RD.

DYNAMIC EARTH

PALACE OF HOLYROODHOUSE
(bottom of Royal Mile)

QUEEN'S GALLERY

SCOTTISH PARLIAMENT

HOLYROOD PARK
+ ARTHUR'S SEAT

TO TRAIN STATION

NORTH BRIDGE

SOUTH BRIDGE

HIGH STREET

TRON KIRK

MUSEUM OF CHILDHOOD

COCKBURN ST.

ST. GILES + MERCAT CROSS

OLD PARLIAMENT HOUSE

COWGATE

CHAMBERS

MUSEUM OF SCOTLAND

BANK ST.

GEORGE IV BRIDGE

GLADSTONE'S LAND

LAWN MKT.

VICTORIA

GRASSMARKET

FOLK MUSIC PUBS

PRINCES ST. GARDENS

WRITERS' MUSEUM AT LADY STAIRS HOUSE

CAMERA OBSCURA

ESPLANADE

CASTLE
(top of Royal Mile)

GOOD RESTAURANTS + ANTIQUE SHOPS

1 MacDonald Hotel
2 Jurys Inn
3 Ibis Hotel
4 Travelodge
5 Deacon Brodie's Pub
6 Lower Aisle Café (in St. Giles)
7 Filling Station Restaurant
8 Dubh Prais Scottish Rest.
9 Always Sunday Food Co. & Fringe Festival Ticket Office
10 The Tea Room & Bene's Fish & Chips
11 Clarinda's Tea Room
12 Elephant House Café & The Outsider Rest.
13 David Bann Restaurant
14 The World's End Pub
15 Whistlebinkies Pub
16 The Hub Festival Ticket Office
17 Greyfriars Bobby Statue
18 Trail to Arthur's Seat
19 Scotch Whisky Heritage Centre

Old Town well on its way to becoming a touristic mall. See it now. In a few years it'll be all tartans and shortbread, with tourists slaloming through the postcard racks on bagpipe skateboards.

Royal Mile Terminology: A "close" is a tiny alley between two buildings (originally with a door that closed it at night). A close usually leads to a "court," or courtyard. A "land" is a tenement block of apartments. A "pend" is an arched gateway. A "wynd" is a narrow, winding lane. And "gate" is from an old Scandinavian word for street.

Castle Esplanade—At the top of the Royal Mile, the big parking lot leading up to the castle was created as a military parade ground in 1816. It's often cluttered with bleachers for the Military Tattoo—a spectacular massing of the bands, filling the square nightly for most of August (see "Edinburgh Festival," page 421). At the bottom, on the left (where the square hits the road), a plaque above the tiny witch's fountain memorializes 300 women who were accused of witchcraft and burned here. Scotland burned more witches per capita than any other country—17,000 between 1479 and 1722. The plaque shows two witches: one good and one bad.

Camera Obscura—A big deal when it was built in 1853, this observatory topped with a mirror reflected images onto a disc before the wide eyes of people who had never seen a photograph or captured image. Today, you can climb 100 steps for an entertaining 15-minute demonstration (3/hr). At the top, enjoy the best view anywhere of the Royal Mile. Then work your way down through three floors of illusions, holograms, and early photos. This is a big hit with kids (£6.50, daily July–Aug 9:30–19:30, April–June and Sept–Oct 9:30–18:00, Nov–March 10:00–17:00, tel. 0131/226-3709).

Scotch Whisky Heritage Centre (a.k.a. "Malt Disney")—This touristy ambush is designed only to distill £8.50 out of your pocket. You kick things off with a wee dram followed by a video history, a short talk, and a little whisky-keg train-car ride before finding yourself in the shop 50 minutes later. Those in a hurry are offered the unadvertised quickie—a sample and a whisky-keg ride for £3.50. People do seem to enjoy it, but that might have something to do with the sample—which now comes at the start rather than the end of the experience (daily 10:00–17:00, tel. 0131/220-0441). Serious connoisseurs of the Scottish firewater will want to pop into Cadenhead's Whisky Shop at the bottom of the Royal Mile (described below).

The Hub (Tolbooth Church)—This neo-Gothic church (1844), with the tallest spire in the city, is now The Hub, Edinburgh's Festival Ticket and Information Centre (for ticket information, see page 421).

▲▲Gladstone's Land—This typical 16th- to 17th-century merchant's house comes complete with an almost-lived-in furnished interior and guides in each room who love to talk (£5, April–Oct Mon–Sat 10:00–17:00, Sun 14:00–17:00, July–Aug daily until 19:00, last entry 30 min before closing, closed Nov–March). For a good Royal Mile photo, lean out the upper-floor window (or simply climb the curved stairway outside the museum to the left of the entrance). Notice the snoozing pig outside the front door. Just like every house has a vacuum cleaner today, in the good old days a snorting rubbish collector was a standard feature of any well-equipped house.

▲**Writers' Museum at Lady Stair's House**—This aristocrat's house, built in 1622, is filled with well-described manuscripts and knickknacks of Scotland's three greatest literary figures: Robert Burns, Sir Walter Scott, and Robert Louis Stevenson. Edinburgh's high society would gather in homes like this in the 1780s to hear the great poet Burns read his work. Burns' work is meant to be read aloud rather than in silence. In the Burns room, you can hear his poetry—worth a few minutes for anyone, and essential for fans (free, Mon–Sat 10:00–17:00, closed Sun).

Wander around the courtyard here. Edinburgh was a wonder in the 17th and 18th centuries. Tourists came here to see its skyscrapers, which towered 10 stories and higher. No city in Europe was so densely populated—or polluted—as "Auld Reekie."

Deacon Brodie's Pub—Read the "Doctor Jekyll and Mister Hyde" story of this pub's notorious namesake on the wall facing Bank Street. Then, to see his spooky split personality, check out both sides of the hanging signpost.

Heart of Midlothian—Near the street in front of the cathedral, a heart-shaped outline in the brickwork marks the spot of a gallows and a prison (now long gone). Traditionally, locals stand on the rim of the heart and spit into it. Hitting the middle brings good luck. Go ahead...do as the locals do.

▲▲**St. Giles Cathedral**—This is Scotland's most important church. Its ornate spire—the Scottish crown steeple from 1495—is a proud part of Edinburgh's skyline. As the church functions as a kind of Westminster Abbey of Scotland, the interior is fascinating (May–Sept Mon–Fri 9:00–19:00, Sat 9:00–17:00, Sun 13:00–17:00; Oct–April Mon–Sat 9:00–17:00, Sun 13:00–17:00; ask about concerts—some are free, usually Thu at 13:10; café and WC downstairs, see "Eating," page 430; tel. 0131/225-9442). Cathedral guides are strolling around waiting for you to engage them in conversation. You'll be glad you did.

Scotland's Literary Greats: Burns, Stevenson, Scott

Edinburgh was home to Scotland's three greatest literary figures: Robert Burns, Robert Louis Stevenson, and Sir Walter Scott.

Robert Burns (1759–1796) was Scotland's bard. A poor farmer tuned into the social inequities of the late 1700s, he was an ardent supporter of the French Revolution. Even though Robby, as he's lovingly called even today, dared to speak up for the common man and attack social rank, he was a favorite of Edinburgh's high society, who'd gather in fine homes to hear the national poet recite.

One hundred years later, **Robert Louis Stevenson** (1850–1894) also stirred the Scottish soul with his pen. An avid traveler who always packed his notepad, Stevenson created settings that are vivid and filled with wonder. Traveling through Scotland, Europe, and around the world, he distilled his adventures into Romantic classics, including *Kidnapped* and *Treasure Island* (as well as *The Strange Case of Dr. Jekyll and Mr. Hyde*). Stevenson, who spent his last years in the South Pacific, wrote, "Youth is the time to travel—both in mind and in body—to try the manners of different nations." He said "I travel not to go anywhere...but to simply go." Travel was his inspiration and his success.

Sir Walter Scott (1771–1832) wrote the *Waverly* novels, including *Ivanhoe* and *Rob Roy*. He's considered the father of the Romantic historical novel. Through his writing, he generated a worldwide interest in Scotland and re-awakened his fellow countrymen's pride in their inheritance. An avid patriot, he wrote "Every Scottish man has a pedigree. It is a national prerogative, as unalienable as his pride and his poverty." Scott is so revered in Edinburgh that his towering neo-Gothic monument dominates the city center (see page 418). With his favorite hound by his side, Sir Walter Scott overlooks the city that he inspired and that inspired him.

The best way to learn about and experience these literary greats is to visit the Writers' Museum at Lady Stair's House (see page 409) and take Edinburgh's Literary Pub Tour (see page 422).

Stepping inside, find **John Knox's statue.** Look into his eyes for 10 seconds from 10 inches away, and think of the Reformation struggles of the 16th century. Knox, the great reformer and founder of austere Scottish Presbyterianism, first preached here in 1559. His insistence that every person should be able to read the word of God gave Scotland an educational system 300 years ahead of the rest of Europe. Thanks partly to Knox, it was Scottish minds that led the way in math, science, medicine, and engineering. Voltaire called Scotland "the intellectual capital of Europe."

Knox preached Calvinism. Consider that the Dutch and the Scots both embraced this creed of hard work, frugality, and strict ethics. This helps explain why Scots are so different from the English (and why the Dutch and the Scots—both famous for their thriftiness and industriousness—are so much alike).

The oldest parts of the cathedral—the **four massive central pillars**—date from 1120. After the English burned the cathedral in 1385, it was rebuilt bigger and better than ever, and in 1495, its famous crown spire was completed. During the Reformation—when Knox preached here (1559–1572)—the place was simplified and whitewashed. Before this, with the emphasis on holy services provided by priests, there were lots of little niches. With the new focus on sermons rather than rituals, the grand pulpit took center stage. The **organ** (1992, Austrian-built, one of Europe's finest) comes with a glass panel in the back for peeking into the mechanism. Knox had the church's fancy medieval glass replaced with clear glass, and 19th-century Victorians had Knox's glass replaced with the brilliantly colored glass you see today.

The **modern window** filling the west wall celebrates Scotland's favorite poet, Robert Burns. It was made in 1985 by an Icelandic artist (Leifur Breidfjord). The green of the lower level symbolizes the natural world—God's creation. The middle zone with the circle shows the brotherhood of man; Burns was a great internationalist. The top is a rosy red sunburst of creativity, reminding Scots of Burns' famous line, "My love is like a red, red rose"—part of a song near and dear to every Scottish heart. Why honor this "live fast and die young" Romantic here? This is Scotland's top church, and even this prodigal son has a place...a big place.

To the right of the Burns window is a fine pre-Raphaelite window. Like most in the church, it's a memorial to an important patron (in this case, John Marshall). From here stretches a great swath of war memorials.

The neo-Gothic **Chapel of the Knights of the Thistle** (in the far right corner, from 1911), with its intricate wood-carving, was built in two years entirely with Scottish materials and labor. It is the private chapel of the Knights of the Thistle, the only Scottish chivalric order, and it's used about once a year to inaugurate new members. Scotland recognizes its leading citizens by bestowing upon them a membership. The queen presides over the ritual from her fancy stall, marked by her Scottish coat of arms—a heraldic zoo of symbolism. Are there bagpipes in heaven? Find the tooting angel above the door to the right.

John Knox is buried out back—with appropriate austerity—under the parking lot, at spot 23. The statue among the cars shows King Charles II riding to a toga party back in 1685. Near parking spot 15, enter the...

Old Parliament House—Step in to see the grand hall with its fine 1639 hammer-beam ceiling and stained glass. This hall housed the Scottish Parliament until the Act of Union in 1707 (explained in the history exhibition under the big stained-glass depiction of the initiation of the first Scottish High Court in 1532). It now holds the law courts and is busy with wigged and robed lawyers hard at work in the old library (peek through the door) or pacing the hall deep in discussion. The friendly doorman is helpful (free, public welcome Mon–Fri 9:00–17:00, best action midmornings Tue–Fri, open-to-the-public trials 10:00–16:00—doorman has day's docket, enter behind St. Giles Cathedral).

Mercat Cross—This chunky pedestal, on the downhill side of St. Giles, holds a slender column topped with a white unicorn. Royal proclamations have been read here since the 14th century. The tradition survives. In 1952, three days (traditionally the time it took for a horse to speed here from London) after the actual event, a town crier heralded the news that England had a new queen. Today, Mercat Cross is the meeting point of various walking tours—both historic and ghostly. A few doors downhill is the...

Police Information Center—This center provides a pleasant police presence (say that 3 times) and a little local law-and-order history to boot (free, daily May–Aug 10:00–21:30, less off-season). Pick up *For the Record*, the police brag mag ("Thirteen murders in the last year...and all of them solved!"). Ask the officer on duty about the grave-robber William Burke's skin and creative poetic justice, Edinburgh-style.

Cockburn Street—This street was cut through High Street's dense wall of medieval skyscrapers in the 1860s to give easy access to the Georgian New Town and the train station. Notice how the sliced buildings were thoughtfully capped with facades in a faux-16th-century Scottish baronial style. In the Middle Ages, only tiny lanes (like the Fleshmarket Lane just uphill from Cockburn Street) interrupted the long line of Royal Mile buildings.

Tron Kirk—This fine old building across from Cockburn Street, used as a sales base for a local walking-tour company, sits over an old excavation site. It houses a free Old Town history display (daily 10:00–17:00). (Perhaps even more important, just above Tron Kirk is a Starbucks with fine streetside tables and a spacious upstairs lounge.) Continue downhill 100 yards to the...

▲**Museum of Childhood**—This five-story playground of historical toys and games is rich in nostalgia and history (free, Mon–Sat 10:00–17:00, closed Sun except July–Aug). Just downhill is a fragrant fudge shop offering delicious free samples.

▲**John Knox House**—Intriguing for Reformation buffs, this fine 16th-century house offers a well-explained look at the life of the great reformer (£3, Mon–Sat 10:00–18:00, closed Sun, 43 High Street, tel. 0131/556-9579). While some contend Knox never actually lived here, preservationists called it "his house" to save it from the wrecking ball in 1850. The museum has been undergoing periodic renovation and may be closed sporadically.

The World's End—For centuries, a wall halfway down the Royal Mile marked the end of Edinburgh and the beginning of Canongate, a community associated with Holyrood Abbey. Today, where the Mile hits St. Mary's and Jeffrey Streets, High Street becomes Canongate. Just below John Knox House (at #43), notice the hanging sign showing the old gate. At the intersection, find the brass bricks that trace the gate (demolished in 1764). Look down St. Mary's Street to see a surviving bit of that old wall. Then, entering Canongate, you leave what was Edinburgh and head for...

Cadenhead's Whisky Shop—The shop is not a tourist sight. It's a firm, founded in 1842, that prides itself on bottling good malt whisky from kegs straight from the best distilleries, without all the compromises that come with profitable mass production (coloring with sugar to fit the expected look, watering down to lessen the alcohol tax, and so on). Those drinking from Cadenhead-bottled whiskies will enjoy the distilleries' pure product as the owners of the distilleries themselves do, not as the sorry public does. If you want to learn about whisky—and perhaps pick up a bottle—they love to talk (Mon–Sat 10:30–17:30, closed Sun, 172 Canongate, tel. 0131/556-5864).

▲**People's Story**—This interesting exhibition traces the conditions of the working class through the 18th, 19th, and 20th centuries (free, Mon–Sat 10:00–17:00, closed Sun, tel. 0131/529-4057). Curiously, while this museum is dedicated to the proletariat, immediately around the back (embedded in the wall of the museum) is the tomb of Adam Smith—the author of *Wealth of Nations* and the father of modern free-market capitalism (1723–1790).

▲**Museum of Edinburgh**—Another old house full of old stuff, this one is worth a look for its early Edinburgh history and handy ground-floor WC. Don't miss the original copy of the National Covenant (written in 1638 on an animal skin), sketches of pre-Georgian Edinburgh (which show a lake, later filled in to become Princes Street Gardens when the New Town was built), and early golf balls. "Balls," said the queen, "If I had two, I'd be king." The king laughed. He had to. (Free, Mon–Sat 10:00–17:00, closed Sun, tel. 0131/529-4143.)

White Horse Close—Step into this 17th-century courtyard (bottom of Canongate, on the left, a block before the Palace of Holyroodhouse). It was from here that the Edinburgh stagecoach left for London. Eight days later, the horse-drawn carriage pulled into its destination: Scotland Yard. Across the street is the new...

▲**Scottish Parliament Building**—Scotland's parliament originated in 1293, was dissolved by England in 1707, and returned in 2000. Their extravagant, and therefore controversial, new digs opened in 2004. The Catalan architect Enric Miralles mixed wild angles, lots of light, bold windows, and local stone into a startling complex that would, as he envisioned, "arise from the sloping base of Arthur's Seat and arrive into the city almost surging out of the rock." For a conversation starter, ask a local what he or she thinks about the place.

For a peek at the new building and a lesson in how the Scottish Parliament works, drop in and find the visitors' desk (free, April–Oct Mon and Fri 10:00–18:00, Tue–Thu 9:00–19:00 or 10:00–18:00 if Parliament is in recess, Sat–Sun 10:00–16:00; Nov–March Mon and Fri–Sun 10:00–16:00, Tue–Thu 9:00–19:00 or 10:00–18:00 if Parliament is in recess; last entry 45 min before closing). You can sign up to witness the Scottish Parliament's debates (usually Wed 14:30–17:30, Thu 9:30–12:30 & 14:30–17:30, tel. 0131/348-5200). Guided tours are sometimes available (£3.50, sporadic, call for times and details or check www.scottish.parliament.uk).

Queen's Gallery—The museum features rotating exhibits of drawings from the royal collection. For more than five centuries, the royal family has amassed a wealth of art treasures. While the queen keeps most in her many private palaces, she shares an impressive load of it here, with exhibits changing about every six months. Though it's just two rooms, it can be exquisite, and generally comes with a well-done audioguide (£5, £11 combo-ticket includes Palace of Holyroodhouse, daily 9:30–18:00, Nov–April until 16:30, on the palace grounds, to the right of the palace entrance).

▲**Palace of Holyroodhouse**—Since the 14th century, this palace has marked the end of the Royal Mile. The queen spends a week in the Palace each summer. The abbey—part of a 12th-century Augustinian monastery—originally stood in its place. It was named for a piece of the cross brought here as a relic by Queen (and later Saint) Margaret. As Scotland's royalty preferred living at Holyroodhouse to the blustery castle on the rock, the palace evolved over time.

Consider touring the interior (£8.50, £11 combo-ticket

includes Queen's Gallery, palace guidebook-£4.50, daily May–Oct 9:30–18:00, Nov–April 9:30–16:30, last entry 45 min before closing, tel. 0131/556-5100, www.royal.gov.uk; palace closed when the queen is at home—generally for a week around July 1—and whenever a prince or someone else important drops in). The building, rich in history and decor, is filled with elegantly furnished rooms and a few darker, older rooms with glass cases of historic bits and Scottish pieces that locals find fascinating. Bring the palace to life with the included one-hour audioguide. You'll learn which of the kings featured in the 110 portraits lining the Great Gallery are real and which are fictional, what touches were added to the bedchambers to flatter King Charles II, and why the exiled Comte d'Artois took refuge in the palace. You'll also hear a goofy reenactment of the moment when conspirators—dispatched by Mary, Queen of Scots' jealous second husband—stormed into the queen's chambers and stabbed her male secretary.

After exiting, you're free to stroll through the ruined abbey and the queen's gardens. Hikers: Note that the wonderful trail up Arthur's Seat starts just across the street from the gardens.

Dynamic Earth—This immense exhibit tells the story of our planet, filling several underground floors under a vast Gore-Tex tent. It's pitched, appropriately, at the base of the Salisbury Crags. The exhibit is designed for younger kids and does the same thing an American science exhibit would do—but with a charming Scottish accent. Standing in a time tunnel, you watch time rewind from Churchill to dinosaurs to the big bang. After several short films on stars, tectonic plates, and ice caps, you're free to wander past salty pools, a re-created rain forest, and various TV screens. End your visit with a 12-minute video finale (£9, family deals, daily 10:00–17:00, last ticket sold 70 min before closing, on Holyrood Road, between the palace and mountain, tel. 0131/550-7800). Dynamic Earth is a stop on the hop-on-hop-off bus route.

▲▲▲Museum of Scotland—This huge museum has amassed more historic artifacts than everything I've seen in Scotland combined. It's all wonderfully displayed with fine descriptions offering a best-anywhere hike through the history of Scotland. Start in the basement and work your way through the story: prehistoric, Roman, Viking, the "birth of Scotland," Edinburgh's witch-burning craze, clan massacres, all the way to life in the 20th century. Free audioguides offer a pleasant description of various rooms and exhibits, and even provide mood music for your wanderings.

The **Kingdom of the Scots** exhibit shows evidence of a vibrant early nation. While cut off from Europe by hostilities with England, Scotland connected with the rest of Europe due to trade, the church, and their Renaissance monarch, Mary, Queen of Scots. Throughout Scotland's long, underdog struggle with

England, its people found inspiration from romantic (and almost legendary) Scottish leaders, including Mary. Educated and raised in France during the Renaissance, Mary brought refinement to the Scottish throne. After she was imprisoned and then executed by the English, her countrymen rallied each other by invoking her memory. Pendants and coins with her portrait stoked the irrepressible Scottish spirit. Near Mary's tomb are tiny cameos, pieces of jewelry, and coins with her image.

The industry exhibit explains how (eventually) the Scots were tamed, and the union with England brought stability and investment. Powered by the Scottish work ethic and the new opportunities that came from the Industrial Revolution, the country came into relative prosperity. Education and medicine thrived. Cast iron and foundries were huge, this became one of the most industrialized places in Europe. With the dawn of the modern age came leisure time, the concept of "healthful sports," and golf—a Scottish invention. The first golf balls, which date from about 1820, were leather stuffed with feathers (free, Mon–Sat 10:00–17:00, Tue until 20:00, Sun 12:00–17:00; free 30-min intro tours generally at 10:30, 12:30, and 15:30; 2 long blocks south of Royal Mile from St. Giles Cathedral, Chambers Street, off George IV Bridge, tel. 0131/247-4422, www.nms.ac.uk).

The **Royal Museum,** next door, fills a fine iron-and-glass Industrial Age building (built to house the museum in 1851) with all the natural sciences as it "presents the world to Scotland." It's great for school kids, but of no special interest to foreign visitors (free, same hours as Museum of Scotland).

Greyfriars Bobby—The underwhelming yet famous statue of Greyfriars Bobby (Edinburgh's favorite dog—a terrier immortalized by Disney who stood by his master's grave for 14 years) is across the street from the Museum of Scotland. Every business nearby is named for the pooch that put the fidelity into Fido.

Bonny Wee Sights in the New Town

Cross Waverley Bridge and walk through the Georgian New Town. According to the 1776 plan, it was three streets (Princes, George, and Queen) flanked by two squares (St. Andrew and Charlotte), woven together by alleys (Thistle and Rose). George Street—20 feet wider than the others (so a four-horse carriage could make a U-turn)—was the main drag. And, while Princes Street has gone down-market, George Street still maintains its old grace. The entire elegantly planned New Town—laid out when George was king—celebrated the hard-to-sell notion that Scotland was an integral part of the United Kingdom. The streets and squares are named after the British royalty (Hanover was the royal family surname). Even Thistle and Rose streets are emblems of the

Scottish Words

While **scotch** is the peaty drink the bartender serves you, the bartender himself is a **Scot**. Here are some other Scottish words that may come in handy during your time in Edinburgh:

aye	yes	**inch, innis**	island
ben	mountain	**inver**	river, mouth
bonny	beautiful	**kyle**	strait
cairn	pile of stones	**loch**	lake
cellotape	Scotch tape	**neeps**	turnips
creag	rock, cliff	**tattie**	potato
haggis	rich assortment of oats and sheep organs stuffed into a chunk of sheep intestine, liberally seasoned, boiled, and eaten mostly by tourists. Usually served with "neeps and tatties." Tastier than it sounds.		

two happily paired nations. Rose Street, mostly pedestrian-only, is famous for its rowdy pubs. Where it hits St. Andrew Square, Rose Street is flanked by the venerable Jenners department store and a Sainsbury's supermarket. Sprinkled with popular restaurants and bars, the stately New Town is turning trendy.

▲▲**Georgian House**—This refurbished Georgian house, set on Edinburgh's finest Georgian square, is a trip back to 1796. A volunteer guide in each of the five rooms shares stories and trivia—from the kitchen in the basement to the fully stocked medicine cabinet in the bedroom. Start your visit with two interesting videos that cover architecture and Georgian lifestyles (40 min total, shown in basement, £5 entry, daily April–Oct 10:00–17:00, March and Nov 11:00–15:00, closed Dec–Feb, 7 Charlotte Square, tel. 0131/226-3318). A walk down George Street after your visit here can be fun for the imagination.

▲▲**National Gallery of Scotland**—The elegant neoclassical building has a delightfully small but impressive collection of European masterpieces, from Raphael, Titian, and Peter Paul Rubens to Thomas Gainsborough, Claude Monet, and Vincent van Gogh. And it offers the best look you'll get at Scottish paintings (free, daily 10:00–17:00, Thu until 19:00, tel. 0131/624-6200). The Royal Scottish Academy, next door, hosts temporary art exhibits. After your National Gallery visit, if the sun's out, enjoy a wander through Princes Street Gardens. At the garden level (underneath the gallery), the newly built Weston Link building has a fine café (same hours as the gallery).

Princes Street Gardens—The grassy park, a former lakebed, separates Edinburgh's New and Old Towns and offers a wonderful escape from the city. Once the private domain of the local wealthy, it was opened to the public in about 1870—not as a democratic gesture, but because it was thought that allowing the public into the park would increase sales for the Princes Street department stores. Join the local office workers for a picnic lunch break. There are also cheap concerts (£2, Mon and Tue at 19:30 in June–July, at Ross Bandstand), plus the oldest floral clock in the world.

The big lake, Nord Loch, was drained in about 1800 as part of the Georgian expansion of Edinburgh. Before that, the lake was the town's sewer, water reservoir, and handy place for drowning witches. Much was written about the town's infamous stink (a.k.a. the "flowers of Edinburgh"), and the town's nickname, "Auld Reekie," referred to both the smoke of its industry and the stench of its squalor.

While the Loch is now long gone, memories of the countless women drowned as witches remain. With their thumbs tied to their ankles, they'd be lashed to dunking stools. Those who survived the ordeal were considered "aided by the devil" and burned as witches. If they died, they were innocent and given a good Christian burial. Until 1720, Edinburgh was Europe's witch-burning mecca—as little a sign as a birthmark could condemn you.

▲**Sir Walter Scott Monument**—Built in 1840, this elaborate neo-Gothic monument honors the great author, one of Edinburgh's many illustrious sons. Scott, who died in 1832, is considered the father of the Romantic historical novel. The 200-foot monument shelters a marble statue of Scott and his favorite dog, Maida; this deerhound was one of the 30 canines this dog lover had during his lifetime. They're surrounded by busts of 16 great Scottish poets and 64 characters from his books. Climbing 287 steps earns you a fine city view (£3, April–Sept Mon–Sat 9:00–18:00, Sun 10:00–18:00; Oct–March daily 10:00–15:00, tel. 0131/529-4098).

Near Edinburgh

▲**Britannia**—This much-revered vessel, which carted around Britain's royal family for more than 40 years and 900 voyages before being retired in 1997, is permanently moored at the Ocean Terminal Shopping Mall in Edinburgh's Port of Leith. It's open to the public and worth the 15-minute bus or taxi ride from the center. Explore the museum, filled with engrossing royal-family-afloat history. Then, armed with your included audioguide, you're welcome aboard.

This was the last in a line of royal yachts that stretches back to 1660. With all its royal functions, the ship required a crew of more than 200. The captain's bridge feels like it's preserved from the day it was launched in 1953. Queen Elizabeth II, who enjoyed the ship for 40 years, said, "This is the only place I can truly relax." This sunny lounge just off the back Veranda Deck was the Queen's favorite, with teak from Burma (now Myanmar, in Southeast Asia) and the same phone system she was used to in Buckingham Palace.

The back deck was the favorite place for outdoor entertainment. Ronald Reagan, Boris Yeltsin, Bill Clinton, and Nelson Mandela all sipped champagne here with the queen. When she wasn't entertaining, the queen liked it quiet. The crew wore sneakers, communicated in hand signals, and (at least near the queen's quarters) had to be finished with all their work by 8:00.

The dining room, decorated with gifts given by the ship's many noteworthy guests, enabled the queen to entertain a good-size crowd. The silver pantry was just down the hall. The drawing room, while rather simple, is perfect for casual relaxing among royals. Princess Diana played the piano, which is bolted to the deck. Royal family photos evoke the fine times the Windsors enjoyed on the *Britannia* (£9, daily March–Oct 9:30–16:30, Nov–Feb 10:00–15:30, last entry 90 min before closing, tel. 0131/555-5566, www.royalyachtbritannia.co.uk). To get here from Edinburgh, catch LRT bus #22, #34, or #35 at Waverley Bridge (£2.50 round-trip). If you're doing a city bus tour, consider the Majestic Tour, which includes transportation to the *Britannia* (see page 396).

Rosslyn Chapel—Founded in 1446 by the Knights Templar, this church has become famous recently for its role in final scenes of *The Da Vinci Code* (£6, Mon–Sat 9:30–18:00, Sun 12:00–16:45, located in Roslin Village, www.rosslynchapel.org.uk). To get to the chapel by bus, take LRT bus #15A (not #15) or First service #62 (no Sun service for either). By car, take A701 to Penicuik/Peebles, and follow signs for Roslin; once you're in the village, there are signs for the chapel.

Royal Botanic Garden—Britain's second-oldest botanical garden (after Oxford) was established in 1670 for medicinal herbs, and is now one of Europe's best (gardens free, conservatory admission-£3.50, daily March and Oct 10:00–18:00, April–Sept 10:00–19:00, Nov–Feb 10:00–15:30, 90-min "rain forest to desert" tours April–Sept daily at 11:00 and 14:00 for £2.50, a mile north of center at Inverleith Row, Majestic Tour stops here—see page 396, tel. 0131/552-7171, www.rbge.org.uk).

ACTIVITIES

▲▲**Arthur's Seat Hike**—A 45-minute hike up the 822-foot volcanic mountain (surrounded by a fine park overlooking Edinburgh) starts from the Palace of Holyroodhouse and rewards you with a commanding view. You can run up like they did in *Chariots of*

Fire, or just stroll. At the summit you'll enjoy commanding views of the town and surroundings. On May Day, be on the summit at dawn and wash your face in the morning dew to commemorate the Celtic holiday Beltaine, which was the celebration of spring. (It's also supposedly very good for your complexion.)

From the parking lot below the Palace of Holyroodhouse, two trails go up. Take the wide path on the left (easier grade, through the abbey ruins and "Hunter's Bog"). After making the summit, you can return along the other path (to the right, with the steps), which skirts the base of the cliffs.

Those staying at my recommended B&Bs can enjoy a pre-breakfast or late-evening hike starting from the other side (in June, the sun comes up early, and it stays light until nearly midnight). From the Commonwealth Pool, take Holyrood Park Road, turn right (on Queen's Drive), and continue to a small parking lot. From here, it's a 20-minute hike.

Drivers can drive up most of the way from behind (follow the one-way street from palace, park by little lake and hike up).

Brush Skiing—If you'd rather be skiing, the Midlothian Ski Centre in Hillend has a hill on the edge of town with a chairlift, two slopes, a jump slope, and rentable skis, boots, and poles. While you're actually skiing over what seems like a million toothbrushes, it feels like snow skiing on a slushy day. Beware: Local doctors are used to treating an ailment called "Hillend Thumb"—thumbs dislocated when people fall here and get tangled in the brush (£7.80/first hr, then £3.20/hr, includes gear, Mon–Fri 9:30–21:00, Sat–Sun 9:30–19:00, closed last 2 weeks of June, LRT bus #4 from Princes Street—garden side, tel. 0131/445-4433, ski.midlothian.gov.uk). It closes if it snows.

▲Royal Commonwealth Games Swimming Pool—The immense pool is open to the public, with a well-equipped fitness center (£6.30, includes swim), sauna (£7.50), and a coffee shop overlooking the pool (pool admission only-£3.90, Mon–Fri 6:00–21:30, Sat 6:00–7:45 & 10:00–16:30, Sun 10:00–16:30, closed 9:00–10:00 every Wed, no towels or suit rentals, tel. 0131/667-7211).

More Hikes—You can hike along the river (called Water of Leith) through Edinburgh. Locals favor the stretch between Roseburn and Dean Village, but the 1.5-mile walk from Dean Village to the Royal Botanic Garden is also good. This and other hikes are described in the TI's *Walks in and around Edinburgh* (ask for the free 1-page flier, not their £2 guide to walks).

Shopping—The streets to browse are Princes Street (the elegant old Jenners department store is nearby on Rose Street, at St. Andrew Square), Victoria Street (antiques galore), Nicolson Street (south of the Royal Mile for a line of interesting second-hand stores), and the Royal Mile (touristy but competitively priced).

Shops are usually open from 9:00 to 17:30 (later on Thu, some closed Sun).

Edinburgh Festival

One of Europe's great cultural events, Edinburgh's annual festival turns the city into a carnival of the arts. There are enough music, dance, drama, and multicultural events to make even the most jaded traveler drool with excitement. Every day is jammed with formal and spontaneous fun. A riot of festivals—official, fringe, book, film, and jazz and blues—rage simultaneously for about three weeks each August, with the Military Tattoo starting a week earlier (the best overall Web site is www.edinburghfestivals.co.uk). Many city sights run on extended hours, and those along the Royal Mile that normally close on Sunday open in the afternoon. It's a glorious time to be in Edinburgh.

The **official festival** (Aug 13–Sept 3 in 2006) is the original, more formal, and most likely to get booked up. Major events sell out well in advance. The ticket office is at **The Hub,** located in the former Tolbooth Church, near the top of the Royal Mile (tickets-£4–55, booking from mid-April, office open Mon–Sat 10:00–17:00 or longer, in Aug until 19:30 plus Sun 10:00–19:30, tel. 0131/473-2000, fax 0131/473-2003). You can also book online at www.eif .co.uk.

The less-formal **Fringe Festival** features "on the edge" comedy and theater (Aug 6–28 in 2006, ticket/info office just below St. Giles Cathedral on the Royal Mile, 180 High Street, tel. 0131/226-0026, bookings tel. 0131/226-0000, can book online from late June on, www.edfringe.com). Tickets are usually available at the door, but popular shows can sell out.

The **Military Tattoo** is a massing of the bands, drums, and bagpipes with groups from all over what was the British Empire. Displaying military finesse with a stirring lone-piper finale, this grand spectacle fills the castle esplanade nightly except Sunday, normally from a week before the festival starts until a week before it finishes (Aug 4–26 in 2006, Mon–Fri at 21:00, Sat at 19:30 and 22:30, £9–30, booking starts in Dec, Fri–Sat shows sell out first, all seats generally sold out 2 months ahead, some scattered same-day tickets may be available; office open Mon–Fri 10:00–17:00, during Tattoo open until show time and Sat 10:00–22:30 and Sun 12:00–17:00; 32 Market Street, behind Waverley train station, tel. 0131/225-1188 or 0870-755-5118, www.edinburgh-tattoo.co.uk). If nothing else, it is a really big show.

If you do manage to hit Edinburgh during the festival, book a room far in advance and extend your stay by a day or two. Once you know your dates, reserve tickets to any show that you really want to see. Call and order your ticket with your credit-card number (see The Hub contact info, above). Pick up your ticket at the office the day of the show. Several publications—including the festival's official schedule, the *Edinburgh Festivals Guide Daily, The List,* the *Fringe Program,* and the *Daily Diary*—list and evaluate festival events.

Other summer festivals: jazz and blues (tel. 0131/553-4000, www.edinburghjazzfestival.co.uk), film (tel. 0131/229-2550, www.edfilmfest.org.uk), and books (tel. 0131/624-5050, www.edbookfest.co.uk).

NIGHTLIFE

▲**Ghost Walks**—These walks are an entertaining and cheap night out (offered nightly, usually around 19:00 and 21:00, easy socializing for solo travelers). The theatrical and creatively staged **Witchery Tours,** the most established outfit, offers two different walks: "Ghosts and Gore" and "Murder and Mystery" (£7.50, 90 min, leave from top of Royal Mile near castle esplanade, reservations required, tel. 0131/225-6745, www.witcherytours.com).

Auld Reekie Tours offers a scary array of walks daily and nightly (£6–9, 90 min, leaves from front steps of Tron Kirk, pick up brochure or visit www.auldreekietours.co.uk). Auld Reekie is into the paranormal, witch covens, and pagan temples, taking groups into the "vaults" under the old bridges "where it was so dark, so crowded, and so squalid that the people there knew each other not by how they looked, but by how they sounded, felt, and smelt. If you had a candle, you weren't poor enough to live in the vaults. Then the great fire came. They crowded in, thinking that a brick refuge like this wouldn't burn...and they all roasted. To this day, creepy things happen in the haunted vaults of Edinburgh." If you want more, there's plenty of it (complete with screaming Gothic "jumpers").

▲▲**Literary Pub Tour**—This two-hour walk is interesting even if you think Sir Walter Scott was an arctic explorer. You'll follow the witty dialogue of two actors as they debate whether the great literature of Scotland was high art or the creative recreation of fun-loving louts fueled by a love of whisky. You'll wander from the Grassmarket, over the Old Town to the New Town, with stops in three pubs as your guides share their takes on Scotland's literary greats. The tour meets at the Beehive Pub on Grassmarket (£8, book online and save £1, May–Sept nightly at 19:30, March–April and Oct Thu–Sun, Nov–March Fri only, call 0800-169-7410 to confirm, www.edinburghliterarypubtour.co.uk).

Scottish Folk Evenings—These £35–40 dinner shows, generally for tour groups intent on photographing old cultural clichés, are held in huge halls of expensive hotels. (Prices are bloated to include

20 percent commissions.) Your "traditional" meal is followed by a full slate of swirling kilts, blaring bagpipes, and Scottish folk dancing with an "old-time music hall" emcee. If you like Lawrence Welk, you're in for a treat. But for most travelers, these are painfully cheesy variety shows. You can sometimes see the show without dinner for about two-thirds the price. The TI has fliers on all the latest venues.

Prestonfield House offers its kitschy Scottish folk evening—a plaid fantasy of smiling performers accompanied by electric keyboards—with or without dinner Sunday to Friday. For £30.50, you get the show with two drinks and a wad of haggis (20:00–22:00); £43 buys you the same, plus a four-course meal and wine (be there at 18:45). It's in the stables of "the handsomest house in Edinburgh," which now houses the recommended Rhubarb Restaurant (Priestfield Road, a 10-min walk from Dalkeith Road B&Bs, tel. 0131/225-7800, www.scottishshow.com).

Theater—Even outside of festival time, Edinburgh is a fine place for lively and affordable theater. Pick up *The List* for a complete rundown of what's on (£2.20 at newsstands).

▲**Live Music in Pubs**—Edinburgh used to be a good place for traditional folk music, but in the last few years, pub owners—out of economic necessity—are catering to college-age customers more interested in beer-drinking. Pubs that were regular venues for folk music have gone pop. Rather than list places likely to change their format in a few months, I'll simply recommend the monthly *Gig Guide* (free at TI, accommodations, and various pubs, www.gigguide.co.uk). This simple little sheet lists 8 or 10 places each night that have live music. Listings are divided by genre (pop, rock, world, and folk). Generally, several bars feature live folk music every night.

Pubs in the Old Town: The **Grassmarket** neighborhood (below the castle) is sloppy with live music and rowdy people spilling out of the pubs and into what was (once upon a time) a busy market square. It's fun to just wander through this area late at night and check out the scene at pubs such as Finnegans Wake, Biddy Mulligan, and White Hart Inn. By the music and crowds you'll know where to go...and where not to. Have a beer and follow your ear. On the Royal Mile, **Whistlebinkies** is famous for live music (South Bridge, tel. 0131/557-5114, www.whistlebinkies.com).

Pubs near Dalkeith Road B&Bs: Three fine and classic pubs (without a lot of noisy machines and rowdy twentysomethings) cluster within 100 yards of each other around the intersection of Duncan Street and Causewayside, near the Dalkeith Road B&B neighborhood (see "Sleeping," below). **Leslie's Pub,** sitting between a working-class and an upper-class neighborhood, has two sides. Originally the gang would go in on the right to gather around the great hardwood bar, glittering with a century of *Cheers* ambience. Meanwhile, the more delicate folks would slip in on the left, with its discreet doors, plush snugs, and ornate ordering windows. Since 1896, this Victorian classic has been appreciated for both its "real ales" and a huge selection of whiskies—the menu is six pages of fine Scotch. (Leslie's is a block downhill from the others at 49 Ratcliffe Terrace.) The **Old Bell Pub,** with a nostalgic sports-bar vibe, serves only drinks after 19:00 (see "Scottish Grub and Pubs," page 424). **Swany's Pub,** perhaps a little less welcoming then the others, is a quintessential smoky hangout for the working-class boys of the neighborhood—with some fun characters to get to know. **Bierex,** a much younger and noisier scene a few blocks away, is a favorite among young people for its cheap drinks (132 Causewayside, see "Scottish Grub and Pubs," page 424).

SLEEPING

The advent of big, cheap hotels has made life tough for B&Bs. Still, book ahead, especially in August, when the annual festival fills Edinburgh. Conventions, school holidays, and weekends can make finding a room tough at almost any time of year. For the best prices, book directly rather than through the TI, which charges a higher room fee and levies a £3 booking fee. "Standard" rooms, with toilets and showers a tissue-toss away, save you £10 a night.

B&Bs Off Dalkeith Road

These B&Bs—south of town near the Royal Commonwealth Pool, just off Dalkeith Road—are all top-end, sporting three or four stars. While pricey, they come with uniformly friendly hosts and great cooked breakfasts, and are a good value for people with enough money. At these not-quite interchangeable places, character is provided by the personality quirks of the hosts.

All listings are non-smoking, on quiet streets, and within a two-minute walk of a bus stop (see "Getting There," below). While you won't find phones in the rooms, several offer Internet access. Most can provide triples or even quads for families.

Prices listed are for most of peak season; if there's a range, prices slide up with summer demand. *Note: Everyone charges at least 10 percent more than these prices in August (when B&Bs are unlikely to accept bookings for 1-night stays).* Conversely, in winter, when there's no demand, prices get really soft. These prices are for cash; expect a 3 to 5 percent fee for using your credit card.

Near the B&Bs, you'll find plenty of good eateries (see "Eating," page 430); several good, classic pubs (see "Nightlife," above); and easy, free parking. If you bring in "take out" food, your host would probably prefer you eat it in the breakfast room rather

Sleep Code

(£1 = about $1.80, country code: 44, area code: 0131)
S = Single, **D** = Double/Twin, **T** = Triple, **Q** = Quad, **b** = bathroom,
s = shower only. You can assume credit cards are accepted
unless otherwise noted.

To help you sort easily through these listings, I've divided
the rooms into three categories based on the price for a standard double room with bath (during high season):

$$$ **Higher Priced**—Most rooms £90 or more.
$$ **Moderately Priced**—Most rooms between £50–90.
$ **Lower Priced**—Most rooms £50 or less.

than muck up your room—ask. The nearest launderette is Sun Dial
(see page 394).

Getting There: This comfortable, safe neighborhood is a 10-
minute bus ride from the Royal Mile. From the train station, TI,
or Sir Walter Scott Monument, cross Princes Street and wait at
the bus stop next to the Disney shop opposite the TI. Buses also
stop on the east side of the station (80p, use exact change—no
change given if you pay more; catch LRT buses #14, #30, and #33,
or First bus #86; tell driver your destination is "Dalkeith Road,"
ride 10 min to first or second stop—depending on B&B—after
the pool, ping the bell, and hop out). These buses also stop at the
corner of North Bridge and High Street on the Royal Mile. Buses
run from 6:00 (9:00 on Sun) to 23:00. Taxi fare between the train
station or Royal Mile and the B&Bs is about £5. Taxis are easy to
hail on Dalkeith Road if it isn't raining.

Listings: The quality of all these B&Bs is more than adequate.
Prices are a bit steep, but the cheaper places are often just as good
as the more expensive ones. Consider the lower-priced B&Bs, and
note that among the moderately priced (**$$**) places, I've listed the
cheaper options first.

$$ Airdenair Guest House, offering views and homemade
sweets made by Jill's parents, has five attractive rooms on the sec-
ond floor with a lofty above-it-all feeling (Sb-£25–35, Db-£52,
Db in July and Aug-£65, Tb-£75–90, 29 Kilmaurs Road, tel.
0131/668-2336, www.airdenair.com, jill@airdenair.com, Jill and
Doug McLennan).

$$ Kenvie Guest House, expertly run by Dorothy Vidler,
comes with six pleasant rooms and lots of personal touches (1 small
twin-£46, D-£48, Db-£56, these prices with cash and this book
in 2006, family deals, 16 Kilmaurs Road, tel. 0131/668-1964, fax
0131/668-1926, www.kenvie.co.uk, dorothy@kenvie.co.uk).

Dalkeith Road Neighborhood

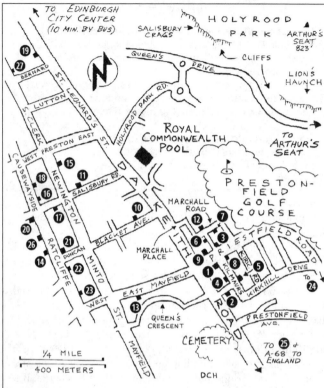

1. Dunedin Guest House
2. Turret & Amar Agua Guest Houses & Aonach Mór B&B
3. Dorstan House
4. Kenvie Guest House
5. Airdenair Guest House
6. Hotel Ceilidh-Donia & Rest.
7. Colquhoun Guest House
8. Priestville Guest House
9. Ard-Na-Said B&B
10. Belford Guest House
11. The Salisbury Hotel
12. Millfield B&B
13. Cherrytree Villa Guest House
14. Pataka Indian Restaurant

15. Wild Elephant Thai & Chinatown Restaurants
16. Sambuca Italian Restaurant
17. Fenwicks Restaurant
18. La Bon Vie Brasserie
19. Blonde Restaurant
20. Bierex Pub
21. New Bell & Old Bell Pubs
22. Swany's Pub
23. Leslie's Pub
24. To Prestonfield House & Rhubarb Restaurant
25. To Sainsbury's Supermarket
26. Tesco Express Supermarket
27. Launderette

$$ Aonach Mór has seven pleasant, lovingly maintained rooms. Leaf through the 19th-century books in your room or dawdle in the welcoming garden outside (S-£28–40, Db-£60–90, deluxe Db-£70–120, these prices and free stiff complimentary welcome drink promised with this book in 2006, family rooms, Internet access, 14 Kilmaurs Terrace, tel. 0131/667-8694, www .aonachmor.com, info@aonachmor.com, Ross and Kathleen Birnie).

$$ Colquhoun Guest House, in another elegant building, has seven fine rooms, several on the ground floor (S-£25–30, D-£46, Db-£58, family room, cash only, 5 Marchhall Road, tel. & fax 0131/667-8481, grace@colquhounhouse.freeserve.co.uk, Grace McAinsh).

$$ Priestville Guest House is homey, with six rooms, VCRs, and a free video library (D-£44–56, Db-£48–64, free Internet access with this book in 2006, 10 Priestfield Road, tel. & fax 0131/667-2435, www.priestville.com, bookings@priestville.com, Trina and Colin Warwick and their dog Torrie).

$$ Dunedin Guest House (dun-EE-din) is a fine value: bright, plush, and elegantly Scottish, with seven huge rooms (S-£30–40, Db-£65–70, family rooms for up to 5, 8 Priestfield Road, tel. 0131/668-1949, fax 0131/668-3636, www.dunedinguesthouse .co.uk, reservations@dunedinguesthouse.co.uk, David and Irene Wright).

$$ Turret Guest House has eight teddy-on-the-beddy cozy rooms, with a vast bay-windowed family room (S-£25–37, D-£50–56, Db-£60–76, £2/person discount with this book and cash in 2006, Internet access, 8 Kilmaurs Terrace, tel. 0131/667-6704, fax 0131/668-1368, www.turretguesthouse.co.uk, contact@turretguesthouse.co.uk, Jimmy and Fiona Mackie).

$$ Amar Agua Guest House is an inviting Victorian home away from home—complete with a friendly Dalmatian and Japanese garden. It's given a little extra sparkle by its energetic young proprietors, Dawn-Ann and Tony Costa (7 rooms, S-£27–40, Db-£60–80, free Internet access, 10 Kilmaurs Terrace, tel. 0131/667-6775, fax 0131/667-7687, www.amaragua.co.uk, rickstevesguest@amaragua.co.uk).

$$ Ard-Na-Said B&B is an elegant 1875 Victorian house with a comfy lounge and six classy rooms (Db-£60–70, 4-poster bed £10 more, family room, 5 Priestfield Road, tel. 0131/667-8754, www.ardnasaid.co.uk, jim@ardnasaid.co.uk, Jim and Olive Lyons).

$$ Cherrytree Villa Guest House is a good value; it's simple and clean with lots of stairs and a unique breakfast room where you can chat with Denise while she cooks your breakfast (S-£22–26, Db-£48–56, less off-season, 9 East Mayfield, tel. 0131/258-0009, www.cherrytreevilla.com, cherrytreevilla@blueyonder.co.uk, Keith and Denise).

$$ Hotel Ceilidh-Donia rents 16 cheery, tricked-out rooms with a pleasant back deck, a bar, a DVD lending library, and the only restaurant in the immediate area (Sb-£50–60, Db-£80–100, less off-season, ask for discount with this book in 2006, free Internet access for guests and diners, laundry service, 14 Marchhall Crescent, tel. 0131/667-2743, www.hotelceilidh-donia.co.uk, reservations @hotelceilidh-donia.co.uk; Max, Annette, and Alan).

$$ Dorstan House is more hotelesque and formal—with a few extra comforts—but still friendly and relaxed. Several of its 14 thoughtfully decorated rooms are on the ground floor (S-£20–40, Sb-£30–50, Ds-£40–70, Db-£40–80, family rooms, laundry service, 7 Priestfield Road, tel. 0131/667-6721, fax 0131/668-4644, www.dorstan-hotel.demon.co.uk, reservations@dorstan-hotel .demon.co.uk, Richard and Maki Stott).

$$ The Salisbury, more like a hotel than its neighbors, fills a classy old Georgian building with eight rooms, a large lounge, and a dumbwaiter in the breakfast room (Sb-£30–35, Db-£52, Db in July and Aug-£60, these prices promised with this book in 2006 for a 2-night minimum stay and payment in cash, 45 Salisbury Road, tel. & fax 0131/667-1264, www.salisburyguesthouse.co.uk, brenda-wright @btconnect.com, Brenda Wright).

$ Belford Guest House is a tidy, homey place offering seven good rooms and a warm welcome (D-£40, Db-£50, family deals, 5 percent off with cash, 13 Blacket Avenue, tel. 0131/667-2422, fax 0131/667-7508, www.belfordguesthouse.com, tom@belfordguesthouse.com, Tom Borthwick).

$ Millfield B&B, run graciously by Liz Broomfield, is thoughtfully furnished with antique class, a rare sit-and-chat ambience, and a comfy TV lounge. Since the showers are down the hall, you'll get spacious rooms and great prices (S-£23–25, D-£44–46, T-£60–64, cash only, reconfirm reservation by phone, 12 Marchhall Road, tel. & fax 0131/667-4428). Decipher the breakfast prayer by Robert Burns. Then try the "Taste of Scotland" breakfast option. See how many stone (14 pounds) you weigh in the elegant throne room.

Big, Modern Hotels

The last three of these listings are cheap as hotels go and offer more comfort than character. The first one's a splurge. In each case I'd skip the institutional breakfast and eat out.

$$$ MacDonald Hotel, my only fancy listing, is an opulent four-star splurge with 156 rooms up the street from the new parliament building. With its classy marble-and-wood decor, fitness center, and pool, it's hard to leave. On a gray winter day in Edinburgh, this could be worth it. Prices can vary wildly (Db-£110, includes breakfast, near bottom of Royal Mile, across from Dynamic Earth, Holyrood Road, tel. 0131/550-4500, fax 0131/550-4545, www .macdonaldhotels.co.uk).

$$$ Jurys Inn, a cookie-cutter place with 186 dependably comfortable rooms, is capably run and well-located a short walk from the station (Sb, Db, and Tb-all £104 Fri–Sat, £83 Sun–Thu, much cheaper off-season, breakfast-£9, 2 kids sleep free, non-smoking rooms, some views, pub/restaurant, on quiet street just off Royal Mile, 43 Jeffrey Street, tel. 0131/200-3300, fax 0131/200-0400, www.jurys.com).

$$ Ibis Hotel, mid–Royal Mile behind Tron Kirk, is well-run and perfectly located. It has 98 soulless but clean and comfy rooms drenched in prefab American charm (Db in June–Sept-£70, discounted in off-season, lousy continental breakfast-£5, non-smoking rooms, elevator, Internet access in lobby, 6 Hunter Square, tel. 0131/240-7000, fax 0131/240-7007, www.ibishotels .com, h2039@accor.com).

$$ Travelodge has 193 no-nonsense rooms all decorated in dark blue and a great location. All rooms are the same, and suitable for two adults with two kids or three adults. While sleepable, it has a cheap feel with a quickly revolving staff (Sb, Db, and Tb-all £70, cheaper off-season, breakfast-£7, 33 St. Mary's Street, a block off Royal Mile, tel. 08700-850-950, www.travelodge.co.uk). Travelodge offers a swinging £26-per-room deal for a limited number of midweek bookings on their Web site.

Hostels

Edinburgh's cheap hostels are well-run and open to all, but they're scruffy and don't include breakfast. They do offer Internet access, laundry facilities, and £12–14 (unless otherwise noted) bunk beds in eight- to 16-bed single-sex dorms (about a £9–12 savings per person over B&Bs).

These three sister hostels are popular crash pads for young backpackers—youthful, hip, and beautifully located in the noisy center (www.scotlands-top-hostels.com): **High Street Hostel** (laundry-£2.50, kitchen, 8 Blackfriars Street, just off High Street/Royal Mile, tel. 0131/557-3984); **Royal Mile Backpackers** (105 High Street, tel. 0131/557-6120); and **Castle Rock Hostel** (just below the castle and above the pubs, 15 Johnston Terrace, tel. 0131/225-9666).

Brodies 2 Backpacker Hostel, spartan, clean, and beautifully located in the middle of the Royal Mile, rents 70 cheap beds in four- to eight-bed dorms (£15–20 per bed, less off-season, lockers, kitchen, free Internet access, laundry, 93 High Street, tel. 0131/556-2223, www.brodieshostels.co.uk). Older travelers feel more comfortable here than in the above hostels.

For more regulations and less color, try the two IYHF hostels: **Bruntsfield Hostel** (6–12 beds/room, near golf course, 7 Bruntsfield Crescent; buses #11, #15, #16, and #17 from Princes Street; tel. 0131/447-2994) and **Edinburgh Hostel** (4–10 beds/room, 5-min walk from Haymarket station, 18 Eglinton Crescent, tel. 0131/337-1120).

EATING

Along the Royal Mile

Historic pubs and doily cafés with reasonable, unremarkable meals abound. While the eateries along this most-crowded stretch of the city are invariably touristy, the scene is fun and competition makes a well-chosen place a good value. Here are some handy, affordable options for a good bite to eat (listed in downhill order; for locations, see map on page 433).

The Red Coat Café and Jacobite Room is a big, bright, efficient cafeteria in the heart of the castle (£6 quick, healthy meals). Punctuating the two parts of your castle visit (the castle itself and the impressive National War Museum of Scotland) with a break here is smart.

The Hub, a classy place in the old Tolbooth Church at the top of the Mile, serves gourmet sandwiches and fine desserts. While it's a bit pricey, the food is delightfully presented, the service is smart, and you're supporting the Edinburgh Festival (which owns the restaurant, and also has its booking office here). Sit in the bright-yellow Gothic interior or outside, with a wonderful Royal Mile perch (£6 sandwiches, inexpensive lunch menu is stowed at 17:30, £15 dinners from 18:00, open Mon–Sat 9:30–22:00, Sun 9:30–18:00, Castlehill, tel. 0131/473-2067).

The Elephant House, two blocks out of the touristy zone, is where locals browse newspapers in the stay-a-while back room, listen to soft rock, and sip coffee or munch a light meal. The friendly staff explains their enticing buffet line most of the day, then switches to table service after 18:00 (vegetarian-friendly, daily 8:00–22:00, 4 computers with cheap and fast Internet access, 2 blocks south of Royal Mile near Museum of Scotland at 21 George IV Bridge, tel. 0131/220-5355). It's easy to imagine J. K. Rowling annoying waiters with her baby pram while spending long afternoons gathering ideas for her Harry Potter saga in cafés like this.

The Outsider, also without a hint of Royal Mile tourism, is a sleek spot serving modern Mediterranean and Southeast Asian cuisine (good fish and stir-fry) in a minimalist maxi-chic setting. Cobble together a fun meal of £8–10 plates from their creative and trendy menu. As you'll be competing with local yuppies, reserve for dinner (daily 12:00–23:00, ground floor is non-smoking, 30 yards up from Elephant House at 15 George IV Bridge, tel. 0131/226-3131).

Deacon Brodie's Tavern is a sloppy pub serving soup, sandwiches, and snacks on the ground floor and basic £9 pub meals upstairs in the restaurant. While painfully touristy, it's dead center on the Mile with a fun history (daily 12:00–22:00, kids are welcome upstairs, tel. 0131/225-6531).

St. Giles Cathedral Lower Aisle, hiding under the landmark church, is *the* place for paupers to munch prayerfully. Stairs on the back side of the church lead into the basement, where you'll find simple, light lunches from 11:45 and coffee with cakes all day (Mon–Fri 9:00–16:30, Sun 10:00–13:30, closed Sat).

Always Sunday Food Company is a tiny place with a wonderful formula. It's a flexible fantasy of Scottish and Mediterranean hot dishes, fresh salads, smoked salmon, sharp cheese, homemade desserts, and so on. You're invited to mix and match at their user-friendly, create-a-lunch buffet line. They use healthy ingredients and are hip to any diet concerns. Sit inside or people-watch from Royal Mile tables outside (£6 lunches, daily 8:00–18:00, 30 yards below St. Giles Cathedral at 170 High Street, tel. 0131/622-0667).

The Filling Station, a big, noisy eatery decorated with old car parts, has an American-type menu and rocks at night. Behind its youthful bar stretches a family-friendly dining hall where you'll get pizza, pasta, and burgers for £7–10, as well as breakfast (daily 9:00–11:15 & 12:00–23:30, 235 High Street, near North Bridge, tel. 0131/226-2488).

Dubh Prais Scottish Restaurant is a dressy eight-table place filling a cellar 10 steps and a world away from the High Street bustle. The owner-chef, James McWilliams, proudly serves Scottish "fayre" at its very best (including gourmet haggis). The daily specials are not printed, to guard against "zombie waiters." They like to get to know you a bit by explaining things (£8.50 2-course lunches Tue–Fri 12:00–14:00, £27 dinners Tue–Sat 18:30–22:30, closed Sun–Mon, reservations smart at night, opposite Radisson SAS Hotel at 123 High Street, tel. 0131/557-5732).

The World's End Pub, a colorful old place, dishes up hearty £6 meals from a creative menu in a fun, dark, and noisy space (daily 11:00–21:00, 4 High Street, tel. 0131/556-3628).

The Tea Room is a fragile hole-in-the-wall serving light lunches, scones, and fine tea in yellow elegance (daily 10:30–16:30, next to Museum of Edinburgh at 158 Canongate). Next door, **Bene's** fries up good, greasy fish-and-chips to go (munch in graveyard across street).

David Bann is a worthwhile pit stop for vegetarians in need of a break from the morning fry. Upscale (there's a cocktail bar) and organic, they serve polenta, tartlets, soups, and light meals (£5 starters, £7.50 lunches, £10 dinners, vegan options, daily 11:00–midnight, 56–58 St. Mary's Street, tel. 0131/556-5888).

Clarinda's Tea Room, near the bottom of the Royal Mile, is charming and girlish—a fine and tasty place to relax after touring the Mile or the Palace of Holyroodhouse (quiche, salad, and soup lunches for £5, Mon–Sat 9:00–16:45, Sun 10:00–16:45, 69 Canongate, tel. 0131/557-1888). It's great for tea and cake anytime.

In the New Town

While most of your sightseeing will be along the Royal Mile, it's important that your Edinburgh experience stretches beyond this happy tourist gauntlet. Just a few minutes away, in the Georgian town, you'll find a bustling world of office workers, students, and pensioners doing their thing. At midday that includes eating. Simply hiking over to one of these places will give you a good helping of Edinburgh today. All these places are within a few minutes' walk of the TI and main Waverley Bridge tour bus depot.

Café Royal is a movie producer's dream pub—the perfect *fin de siècle* setting for a coffee, beer, or light meal. (In fact, parts of *Chariots of Fire* were filmed here.) Drop in, if only to admire the 1880 tiles featuring famous inventors (daily 12:00–14:00 & 19:00–late, 2 blocks from Princes Mall on West Register Street, tel. 0131/556-1884). There are two eateries here: the pub (basic £6 meals) and the dressier restaurant, specializing in fish and game (2-course lunch with wine for £15, £20 plates, reserve for dinner as it's quite small and understandably popular).

The Dome Restaurant, in what was a fancy bank, serves decent meals around a classy bar and under the elegant 19th-century skylight dome. With soft jazz and dressy, white-tablecloth ambience, it feels a world apart (£13 plates until 17:00, £18 dinners until 22:00, daily 12:00–22:00, modern international cuisine, open for a drink anytime under the dome or in the adjacent Art Deco bar, 14 George Street, tel. 0131/624-8624, reserve for dinner). Notice the facade of this former bank building—the various ways to make money fill the pediment with all the nobility of classical gods.

The St. Andrew's Church Undercroft, in the basement of a fine old church, is the cheapest place in town for lunch (£2 sandwich and soup, Mon–Fri 12:00–14:00, closed Sat–Sun, on George Street, just off St. Andrew Square). Your tiny bill helps support the good work of the Church of Scotland.

Henderson's Salad Table and Wine Bar has fed a generation of New Town vegetarians hearty cuisine and salads (3-course lunch for £8.25, Mon–Sat 7:30–22:45, closed Sun, non-smoking, strictly vegetarian, pleasant live music nightly, always jazz on weekends, between Queen and George streets at

Edinburgh's New Town

¼ MILE — 400 METERS

TO ROYAL BOTANIC GARDEN & BRITANNIA

MORAY PL.

QUEEN — QUEEN ST. GARDENS — YORK PLACE

HILL ST.

GEORGIAN HOUSE

CHARLOTTE SQ.

CASTLE ST. — GEORGE ST. — ROSE ST. — FREDERICK ST. — HANOVER ST. — DAVID ST.

❺ ❻ ❸ ❷ ❼ ❽

ST. ANDREW SQ.

BUS STN.

❹

PRINCES MALL, TRAIN STN., ❶

PRINCES ST.

LOTHIAN RD.

PRINCES ST. GARDENS

SCOTT MON.

MOUND

NAT'L. GALLERY

WAVERLEY BRIDGE

❶ Princes Mall Food Court
❷ The Dome Restaurant
❸ St. Andrew's Undercroft Café
❹ Café Royal
❺ Henderson's Salad Table & Wine Bar
❻ Ristorante la Lanterna
❼ Sainsbury's Supermarket
❽ easyInternetcafé

94 Hanover Street, tel. 0131/225-2131). Henderson's two different seating areas use the same self-serve cafeteria line. For the same healthy food with more elegant seating and table service, eat at the attached **Henderson's Bistro.**

Ristorante la Lanterna is packed with local office workers who enjoy good southern Italian cuisine with friendly service (£5 pastas, £12 plates, pricier at dinner, no pizza, Mon–Sat 12:00–14:30 & 17:30–22:30, closed Sun, dinner reservations wise, 2 blocks off Princes Street, 83 Hanover Street, tel. 0131/226-3090, attentive Antonietta oversees the action).

Princes Mall Food Court, below the TI and above the station, is a circus of sticky fast-food joints littered with paper plates and shoppers (Mon–Sat 8:30–18:00, Thu until 19:00, Sun 11:00–17:00). If you'd prefer pubs, browse nearby Rose Street.

Supermarket: The glorious **Sainsbury's** supermarket, with a tasty assortment of take-away food and specialty coffees, is just one block from the Sir Walter Scott Monument and the lovely picnic-perfect Princes Street Gardens (Mon–Sat 7:00–22:00, Sun 9:00–20:00, on corner of Rose Street, on St. Andrew Square, across the street from Jenners, the classy department store).

Dalkeith Road Area, near Your B&B

All these places are within a 10-minute walk of my recommended B&Bs. Most are on or near the intersection of Newington and East Preston Streets. For locations, see map on page 426.

The nearest supermarket is the new **Tesco Express;** it's small-ish, but has plenty of fresh produce and picnic supplies (daily 6:00–23:00, 158 Causewayside). **Sainsbury's** is a 10-minute walk or a quick bus ride down Dalkeith Road away from town in the Cameron Toll shopping complex (Mon–Sat 7:30–22:00, Sun 8:00–19:00, tel. 0131/666-5200).

Scottish/French Restaurants

These classy little eight-table places feature "Auld Alliance" cuisine—Scottish cooking with a French flair (seasoned with a joint historic disdain for England). They offer small menus with three or four items per course for two- or three-course meals (about £10 for a 2-course lunch, £20 for a 3-course dinner). For a cozy drink after dinner, visit the recommended pubs in the area (see "Nightlife," page 422).

Fenwicks is cozy and reliable, with tasty Scottish and continental food and no French fries. It's pricey, but this little linoleum, brown, and woody bistro is considered a good value by locals (main course-£13–16, 3-course £20 *menu*, daily 12:00–14:00 & 18:00–late, 15 Salisbury Place, tel. 0131/667-4265).

La Bon Vie Brasserie is candlelit chic with an enticing menu. This upmarket place serves modern Scottish/French cuisine (early special: a *plat du jour* with coffee-£5 until 19:00, later the 4-course gourmet *menu* is £20, you can B.Y.O. wine for £2 cork fee; daily 12:00–14:00 & 18:00–22:00, 49 Causewayside, tel. 0131/667-1110).

Blonde Restaurant, with a more eclectic and European menu, is less expensive, bigger, and more crowded than the others, with no set-price dinners. It's a bit out of the way, but a hit with locals (about £14 for 2 courses, good vegetarian options, Tue–Sun 12:00–14:30 & 18:00–22:00, open for dinner only on Mon, 75 St. Leonard's Street, tel. 0131/668-2917).

Hotel Ceilidh-Donia serves well-prepared fish, meat, and vegetarian dishes in a flagstone-floored, high-ceilinged space with a small, friendly adjoining pub. The decor is likeably kitschy with attitude, and the garden seating is a delight (£10 plates with good vegetables, dinner from 18:00, closed Sun, free Internet access for customers, 14 Marchhall Crescent, tel. 0131/667-2743). This is the only place in the immediate neighborhood of the recommended B&Bs.

Scottish Grub and Pubs

The New Bell serves up filling modern Scottish fare from steak and salmon to haggis in a Victorian living room setting above the lovable Old Bell Pub. Along with wonderfully presented meals, you'll enjoy white tablecloths, oriental carpets on hardwood floors, and a relaxing spaciousness under open beams (2-course £11 special until 18:45, £13 plates 17:30–22:00, open daily, always a veggie option, 233 Causewayside, tel. 0131/668-2868).

The Old Bell Pub, with an old-time sports-bar ambience—fishing, golf, horses—serves simpler £7 pub meals from the same fine kitchen on the ground floor. This is a classic snug pub, littered with evocative knickknacks. It comes with fine sidewalk seating and a mixed-age crowd (nightly, last meal order at 19:00, then drinks only, 233 Causewayside, tel. 0131/668-2868).

Bierex, a youthful pub, is the neighborhood favorite for modern dishes, camaraderie, and cheap booze. It's a spacious, bright, mahogany-and-leather place popular for its long and varied happy hours (£6 plates, daily 10:00–24:00, food served 10:00–21:00, Fri–Sat until 20:00, 132 Causewayside, tel. 0131/667-2335).

Rhubarb Restaurant is the hottest thing in Old World elegance. It's in "Edinburgh's most handsome house"—a riot of antiques, velvet, tassels, and fringes. The plush rhubarb color theme reminds visitors that this was the place where rhubarb was first grown in Britain. It's a 10-minute walk past the other recommended eateries behind Arthur's Seat, in a huge estate with big, shaggy Highland cows enjoying their salads *al fresco*. While most spend a wad here (plates about £20), smart budget travelers time their visit to take advantage of the great off-hours two-course meal for £17 (served 12:00–15:00, 18:00–19:00, and 22:00–23:00; reserve in advance and dress up if you can, in Prestonfield House, Priestfield Road, tel. 0131/225-1333, www.rhubarb-restaurant .com). For details on the Scottish folk evening offered here, see "Nightlife," page 422.

The noisy **Poolside Café** at the huge Commonwealth Pool on Dalkeith Road has sandwiches, soup, and salads for hungry swimmers and budget travelers alike (Mon–Fri 10:00–18:00, Sat–Sun 10:00–17:00, pass the entry without paying).

Ethnic Options

Pataka Indian Restaurant is a tight little 10-table "Indian bistro" with attentive service and great food. With big portions and small prices, it's understandably popular with locals (£8 dishes, daily 12:00–14:00 & 17:30–23:30, also offers take-away, 190 Causewayside, tel. 0131/668-1167).

Wild Elephant Thai Restaurant is a small, hardworking eatery that locals consider the best around for Thai (main dishes £6–10, £10 3-course meal until 20:00, open daily 17:00–23:00, also does take-away, 21 Newington Road, tel. 0131/662-8822).

Chinatown is an energetic little place that packs a lot of happy eating into its one small dining room (£6–9 meals, Tue–Fri 12:00–14:00 & 17:30–23:00, Sat–Sun 17:30–23:30, closed Mon, reservations smart on weekend nights, take-away food 25 percent cheaper, 13 Newington Road, tel. 0131/662-0555).

Sambuca Italian Restaurant dishes up good pizza and pasta in a lively bistro where the only decor is the food and the only music is the sound of contented eaters (£8–10 dishes, Mon–Sat 12:00–14:30 & 17:00–late, Sun 17:00–10:00, 103 Causewayside, tel. 0131/667-3307).

TRANSPORTATION CONNECTIONS

From Edinburgh by Train to: Glasgow (4/hr, 45 min, £7 one-way, £9 round-trip), **Inverness** (8/day, 3.5 hrs, more with change in Perth), **Oban** (3/day, 4.5 hrs, change in Glasgow), **York** (2/hr, 2.5 hrs), **London** (hrly, 4.5 hrs), **Durham** (nearly hrly, 2 hrs, less frequent in winter), **Newcastle** (hrly, 1.5 hrs), **Keswick/Lake District** (south past Carlisle to Penrith, then catch bus to Keswick, 6/day, fewer Sun, 3 hrs including bus transfer in Penrith), **Birmingham** (6/day, 4.5 hrs), **Crewe** (6/day, 3.5 hrs), **Bristol/near Bath** (hrly, 6–7 hrs), **Blackpool** (8/day, 3.5 hrs, transfer in Preston). Train info: tel. 08457-484-950, www.thetrainline.com.

By Bus to: Oban (4/day, 4 hrs, not on Sun), **Fort William** (1/day, 4 hrs), **Inverness** (hrly, 4 hrs), **Blackpool** (Fri, Sat, Mon only, requires change in Glasgow, 5 hrs), **York** (1/day at 9:45, 5 hrs). For bus info, call Scottish Citylink (tel. 08705-505-050, www.citylink.co.uk) or National Express (tel. 08705-808-080). You can get info and tickets at the bus desk inside the Princes Mall TI.

Route Tips for Drivers

Arriving in Edinburgh from the North: Rather than drive through downtown Edinburgh to the recommended B&Bs, circle the city on the A720 City Bypass road. Approaching Edinburgh on the M9, take the M8 (direction: Glasgow) and quickly get onto the A720 City Bypass (direction: Edinburgh South). After four miles you'll hit a roundabout. Ignore signs directing you into Edinburgh North and stay on A720 for 10 more miles to the next and last roundabout, named Sheriffhall. Exit the roundabout on the first left (A7 Edinburgh). From here it's four miles to the B&B neighborhood (see "Arriving from the South," below, and B&B neighborhood map, page 426).

Arriving from the South: Coming into town on A68 from the south, take the A7 Edinburgh exit off the roundabout. A7 becomes Dalkeith Road. If you see the huge swimming pool, you've gone a couple of blocks too far (avoid this by referring to B&B neighborhood map).

Leaving Edinburgh, Heading South: It's 100 miles from Edinburgh to Hadrian's Wall; to Durham it's another 50 miles. From Edinburgh, Dalkeith Road leads south and eventually becomes A68 (handy Cameron Toll supermarket with cheap gas is on the left as you leave Edinburgh Town, 10 min south of Edinburgh; gas and parking behind store). A68 takes you to Hadrian's Wall in two hours. You'll pass Jedburgh and its abbey after one hour. (For one last shot of Scotland shopping, there's a coach tour's delight just before Jedburgh, with kilt makers, woolens, and a sheepskin shop.) Across from Jedburgh's lovely abbey is a free parking lot, a good visitors center, and public toilets (20p to pee). The England/Scotland border is a fun, quick stop (great view, ice cream, and tea caravan). Just after the turn for Colwell, turn right onto A6079 and roller-coaster four miles down to Low Brunton. Then turn right onto B6318, and stay on it by turning left at Chollerford, following the Roman wall westward. (For information on Hadrian's Wall, see page 384.)

GLASGOW

Glasgow, though bigger than Edinburgh, lives forever in the shadow of its more popular neighbor. Once a decrepit former port city, Glasgow—astride the River Clyde—has climbed out of its recession in recent years. Today, it's both a workaday Scottish city and a cosmopolitan destination with an energetic nightlife scene. You'll be hard-pressed to find a single souvenir shop in Glasgow—and that's just how the locals like it.

Edinburgh, a short train-trip away, may have the royal aura, but Glasgow has soul. As my cab driver said: "The people of Glasgow have a better time at a funeral than the people of Edinburgh have at a wedding." In Glasgow, there's no upper-crust history, and no one puts on airs. Locals, for example, call sanded and polished concrete, "Glasgow marble." In this newly revitalized city, visitors are a novelty, and locals do their best to introduce you to the fun-loving, laid-back Glaswegian (rhymes with Norwegian) way of life.

Planning Your Time

The Glasgow you'll see today is vibrant and urban, full of Victorian architecture with modern twists. On a three-week tour of Britain, give Glasgow a day.

Day 1: Even if you're only in Glasgow for an afternoon, see Charles Rennie Mackintosh's visionary architecture (included in walking tour below), especially the Glasgow School of Art. For a full day, start the walking tour at the Lighthouse in the morning, break for lunch on or near Sauchiehall Street, and be in line for the Glasgow School of Art in the early afternoon. Energetic sightseers can hit the Kelvingrove Gallery before it closes.

Day 2: With more time, consider using the West End neighborhood as your home base (10 min from downtown by car, 20 min by bus). If you haven't seen it already, stop by the Kelvingrove Gallery (also in the West End) in the morning, and consider making the trip out to the Burrell Collection. Tack on the sights in the East End if time allows.

Evenings: Glasgow comes to life at night, when the downtown core turns up the volume, and bars and cafés of the West End and Merchant City dim the lights (for recommendations, see "Nightlife," page 451).

Day Trip from Edinburgh: For a full day, grab breakfast in Edinburgh, and catch the 9:30 train to Glasgow (morning trains every 15 min, you can buy tickets ahead of time at www .firstscotrail.com); it will arrive at the Queen Street Train Station at roughly 10:20. Call to arrange tickets to tour the Glasgow School of Art (best times: 13:30, 14:00, or 14:30—which leave you time for lunch beforehand). Take the walking tour (skip the Lighthouse if it's Tue or Sun, since it opens later). Hit the Tenement House before it closes (at 17:00). For dinner, try one of the recommended downtown restaurants, or—if you're not in a rush—take a cab from the Tenement House (already on the west side of town) to the West End; have dinner at atmospheric Òran Mòr or at one of the Ashton Lane eateries. Return to the Queen Street Station and catch the 21:00 train back to Edinburgh (evening trains every 30 min). Cab it back to your Edinburgh B&B.

ORIENTATION

(area code: 0141)
While greater Glasgow is a sprawling city of 2.1 million people, the tourist's Glasgow has three main parts: the West End (mellow nightlife and B&B–like hotels), the city center, and the cluster of sights near the cathedral, in the east. Glasgow, a major shopping destination, has two main drags, both as crowded with stores as any American mall: Sauchiehall (pronounced "Sockyhall," running west to east) and Buchanan Street (running north to south). Many of Glasgow's major sights—including art museums and some of architect Charles Rennie Mackintosh's projects—are well outside the downtown core.

Tourist Information

The TI is opposite Queen Street Station in the southwest corner of George Square (at #11, Mon–Sat 9:00–20:00, Sun 10:00–18:00, tel. 0141/204-4400, www.seeglasgow.com). Direct buses to the West End stop right in front of the TI (see "Getting to the West End," page 454). Pick up a copy of the free Glasgow tourist map at the TI, since it's better than any that you can buy.

The TI also sells the Mackintosh Trail Ticket, good for die-hard fans of Mackintosh architecture. It's a do-it-yourself ticket that provides entry and public transportation to get to the "Charles Rennie Mac" sights outside the city limits (£12; includes a map, public transit, and entry to all Mackintosh sights in Glasgow).

Arrival in Glasgow

Glasgow, a major Scottish transportation hub, has two train stations and **Buchanan Street Bus Station** (Killermont Street, 2 blocks behind Queen Street Train Station). Glasgow's **Central Train Station** is on Gordon Street at the intersection with Renfield/Union Street; the left-luggage station is between tracks 9 and 10 (£5 per piece). The **Queen Street Train Station** is handier for reaching the TI: Take the North Hanover Street exit and head across George Square to #11. Trains from Edinburgh arrive at the Queen Street Train Station. Both train stations have pay WCs (20p). A seven-minute walk or a handy shuttle bus (#398) connects all three stations (50p, pay driver, or free if connecting between train stations—show train ticket to driver; Mon–Sat 7:00–22:00, Sun 10:00–22:00, every 10 min). The only convenient subway stop in downtown is at the Buchanan Street Station (for more on the subway, see below).

Helpful Hints

Sightseeing: Glasgow's city-owned museums are free to enter (for online info, see www.glasgowmuseums.com).

Safety: The city center, which is packed with ambitious career types during the day, can feel deserted at night. Avoid the area near the River Clyde entirely (hookers and thugs), and confine yourself to the streets north of Argyle Street if you're in the downtown quarter. The West End and Merchant City (east of the train stations) bustle with crowded restaurants well into the evening, and feel well-populated in the wee hours.

If you pick up a football (soccer) jersey or scarf as a souvenir, don't wear it in Glasgow; local passions run high, and most drunken brawls in town are between supporters of Glasgow's two rival soccer teams: Celtic (green and white) and Rangers (blue, red, and white).

Internet Access: Try the **Hub,** conveniently located a couple of blocks from Central Station, where owner Kevin and his helpful staff will bring you a coffee, tea, or pastry as you surf (£1.80/hr, Mon–Thu 7:30–22:00, Fri–Sat 7:30–21:00, Sun

10:00–21:00, 8 Renfield Street, tel. 0141/222-2227). A big **easyInternet** outlet is between Central and Queen Street stations, at 57–61 St. Vincent Street (£2/hr, Mon–Fri 7:00–22:00, Sat–Sun 8:00–21:00).

Supermarkets: For good ready-to-eat picnic fare, stop by the small **Marks & Spencer Simply Food** in the Central Station (daily 7:00–23:00, tel. 0141/248-6728). A second, larger **Marks & Spencer** is on the corner of Bothwell and Wellington streets (Mon–Fri 7:30–19:00, Sat 9:00–18:00, closed Sun, 50 Bothwell Street, tel. 0141/248-2526), and **Sainsbury's** supermarket is directly across the street (Mon–Fri 7:00–21:00, Sat 7:00–20:00, Sun 11:00–19:00, 53 Bothwell Street, tel. 0141/248-6362). You'll also find supermarkets dotted along Sauchiehall Street.

Sunday Travel: Although Glasgow is a Grand Central-type transit hub, bus and train schedules slow down dramatically on Sundays—most routes have only half the departure times they normally have during the week. (Edinburgh, only 50 min away, is still easily accessible.) If you plan to leave Glasgow for a remote destination on Sunday, check the schedules carefully when you arrive. All trains also run less often in the off-season; if you want to get to the Highlands by bus on Sunday in winter, forget it.

Local Guide: Joan Dobbie, a native Glaswegian and registered Scottish Tourist Guide, will give you the insider's take on Glasgow's sights (£68/half-day, tel. 1355/236-749, mobile 7773-555-151, joan.leo@lineone.net).

Getting Around Glasgow

Buses run in a near-constant loop from Sauchiehall Street to the Central Station, and most are operated by private companies (predominantly First Glasgow), not a city-wide service. Buses run every few minutes down Glasgow's main thoroughfares (such as Sauchiehall Street) to the downtown core (train stations). If you're waiting at a stop and bus comes along, ask the driver if he's headed to Central Station; chances are he'll say yes. (For information on buses to the West End, see "Getting to the West End," page 454.)

Taxis are cheap, plentiful, and come with the nicest and chattiest cabbies—all speaking in the cryptic local accent—that you're likely to meet. Just smile and nod. Most taxi rides in the downtown area will cost about £3; from the West End, a one-way trip is about £5. Use taxis and public transport to connect Glasgow's more remote sights; splurge for a taxi (for safety) any time you're traveling late at night.

Glasgow's orange-line **subway**—nicknamed "clockwork orange"—runs in two concentric circles around the edge of the city center; the full route takes 24 minutes. The central downtown stop—at Buchanan Street station—is good for those arriving by bus. Because most other stops lie outside the city center, for tourists, it's not as useful as buses, taxis, or walking. To reach the West End, the Hillhead stop is best (£1 single journey, £1.90 Discovery Ticket lets you travel all day after 9:30, subway open Mon–Sat 6:30–23:30, but Sun only 11:00–18:00, www.spt.co.uk/subway).

TOURS

Glasgow Bus Tours—A hop-on, hop-off tourist bus connects Glasgow's far-flung historic sights in a 75-minute loop (£8.50, daily 9:30–17:00; stops in front of Central Station, George Square, and major hotels; tel. 0141/204-0444, www.citysightseeingglasgow .co.uk). If there's a particular sight you want to see, confirm that it's on the route.

SELF-GUIDED WALK

Get to Know Glasgow

While Glasgow is not a romantic city, it has earthy charm, and it's a major destination for architecture buffs. The trick to sightseeing in Glasgow is to always look up—above the chain restaurants and mall stores, you'll see a wealth of Victorian facades, complete with ornate friezes and 3-D sculptures.

Many of its downtown buildings are unremarkable, but its best sights are time capsules from the end of the 1800s. During this time, when the rest of Great Britain was in enthralled by Victorianism, Glasgow set its own course, mostly because of the artistic bravado of Charles Rennie Mackintosh and his friends, nicknamed the "Glasgow Four." This tour takes three to four hours, including one hour at the Glasgow School of Art—Mackintosh's masterpiece; it's best to phone ahead to reserve your tour time (see page 440).

• *Begin at the Central Station. Exit the train station north (Gordon Street), and turn right. You'll come to Mitchell Street. Make a right onto Mitchell, and look up to see a multi-story brick water tower on the left side of the street, with a rounded cap up top. Turn down a small alley (Mitchell Lane) just in front of the tower, and within about 25 yards, you'll see the entrance to...*

The Lighthouse: This museum of architecture and design is really made of two parts: a water tower designed by Charles Rennie Mackintosh in the early 1900s, and a new, modern glass-and-metal museum built alongside

Glasgow Walk

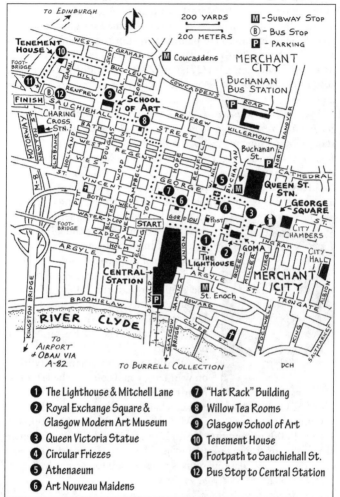

200 YARDS
200 METERS

Ⓜ - SUBWAY STOP
Ⓑ - BUS STOP
Ⓟ - PARKING

Ⓜ Cowcaddens

MERCHANT CITY

TENEMENT HOUSE
FOOTBRIDGE
FINISH
CHARING CROSS STN.
SCHOOL OF ART
BUCHANAN BUS STATION

WEST GRAHAM
GARN
HILL
BUCCLEUCH
RENFREW
COWCADDENS
KILLERMONT
ROAD
SAUCHIEHALL
BATH
ST.
RENFREW
STREET
Buchanan St.
WEST REGENT
Queen St. Stn.
WEST GEORGE
GEORGE
CATHEDRAL
NORTH HANOVER
QUEEN SQUARE
GEORGE SQUARE
CITY CHAMBERS
WEST NILE
BUCHANAN
WEST CAMPBELL
HOPE
RENFIELD
UNION
QUEEN
VIRGINIA
INGRAM
CITY HALL
VINCENT
BOTHWELL
WATERLOO
FOOTBRIDGE
GORDON
POST
GOMA
THE LIGHTHOUSE
ARGYLE
MERCHANT CITY
CADOGAN
HOLM
ARGYLE ST.
JAMAICA
START
CENTRAL STATION
ⓅBROOMIELAW
St. Enoch Ⓜ
HOWARD
CLYDE
STOCKWELL
KING
TRONGATE
ALBION
SALTMARKET
KINGSTON BRIDGE
RIVER CLYDE
GLASGOW BRIDGE
TO AIRPORT & OBAN VIA A-82
TO BURRELL COLLECTION
DCH

❶ The Lighthouse & Mitchell Lane
❷ Royal Exchange Square & Glasgow Modern Art Museum
❸ Queen Victoria Statue
❹ Circular Friezes
❺ Athenaeum
❻ Art Nouveau Maidens
❼ "Hat Rack" Building
❽ Willow Tea Rooms
❾ Glasgow School of Art
❿ Tenement House
⓫ Footpath to Sauchiehall St.
⓬ Bus Stop to Central Station

the water tower. The Lighthouse is mostly filled with design exhibitions and lonely floors of conference rooms, but it's worth paying the entrance fee if you're in the mood to get a sweeping view of the city. Before you head up, be sure to request the free *View from the Top* pamphlet, which indicates the buildings you'll see in the panorama.

You have two options for scaling the heights: take the elevator to the sixth (view) floor; or (better) head to the third floor and climb the 130 spiral steps inside the water tower itself—at the top, you'll be able to walk out onto a wrap-around balcony with

360-degree views. On the third floor of the Lighthouse, you'll find information about Mackintosh, with architecture plans and scale models, but better artifacts come later at the Glasgow School of Art. Linger only if you're planning to skip the school (£3, Mon and Wed–Sat 10:30–17:00, Tue 11:00–17:00, Sun 12:00–17:00, 11 Mitchell Lane, tel. 0141/221-6362, www.thelighthouse.co.uk). A café called Doocot is on the fifth floor (same hours as the museum).

• *From the Lighthouse, make a right and then an immediate left onto Buchanan, a pedestrian shopping street. Along with Sauchiehall, this street is Glasgow's outdoor mall. (We'll leave it quickly.) From Buchanan, make the first right onto Royal Exchange, and pass through the arch. You emerge onto the...*

Royal Exchange Square: From here, Merchant City lies to the east. This square holds two interesting buildings. The one

on your left, with its Ancient Greece–inspired design, looks as though it could be a bank. Instead, it was a **private mansion** of one of the tobacco lords, the über-rich businessmen who reigned here from the 1750s through the 1800s, stomping through the city with gold-tipped canes. During the port's heyday, these entrepreneurs made Glasgow Europe's sixth biggest city.

Walking past the mansion (with it on your left), you'll come to the **Glasgow Modern Art Museum**, nicknamed GoMA. GoMA has an unusual charter: It displays only the work of living artists (free entry, Mon–Wed and Sat 10:00–17:00, Thu 10:00–20:00, Fri and Sun 11:00–17:00, tel. 0141/287-3050). Notice the funky, mirrored mosaic in the otherwise classical facade—an example of how Glasgow refuses to take itself too seriously.

• *With GoMA behind you, make a left onto Queen Street. Within a block, you'll be in the southwest corner of...*

George Square: Here, at the heart of the city, you'll find the TI (just to your right as you come to the square, stop in to grab a map if you'll be exploring Glasgow beyond this tour), the Queen Street station, the Glasgow City Chambers (big neoclassical building to the east, not worth visiting), and many statues of Glasgow's favorite sons—a Scottish Hall of Fame. Notice statues of James Watt (inventor of the steam engine),

Robert Burns (poet), and Sir Walter Scott (poet and novelist). As you head north along the edge of the square, you'll see an idealized, surprisingly skinny **Queen Victoria statue** riding a horse. But you won't see a statue of King George III, for whom the square is named. The stubborn Scots are still angry at George for losing the colonies (a.k.a. us), and they never commissioned a statue of him.

• *Make a left on West George Street, and within a block you'll see a small church. Walk to the left of it, and look up at the **three circular friezes** on the second floor of the former Stock Exchange, built in 1875. These idealized heads, which were cleaned and restored five years ago, represent the industries that made Glasgow prosperous during its heyday: mining, engineering, and building.*

Walk around the back of the church, and look to the other side of the street, to the...

Athenaeum: Now a law office, this was founded in 1847 as a school and city library during Glasgow's golden age. (Charles Dickens gave the building's inaugural address.) Like Edinburgh, Glasgow was at the forefront of the 17th-century Scottish Enlightenment, a celebration of education and intellectualism. The Scots were known for their extremely practical brand of humanism; all members of society, including the merchant and working classes, were expected to be well-educated. (Tobacco lords, for example, often knew Latin and Greek.) On the second-story facade, find the symbolic **statue of a reader** sharing books with young children, an embodiment of this ideal.

• *At the next street, make a left onto West Nile, and one block later, turn right onto St. Vincent Street. On the left-hand side of the street, at #115 (on the second floor), you'll see **sculptures of Art Nouveau maidens**. Their elongated, melancholy faces and downcast eyes seem to reflect Glasgow's difficult recent past, decades of economic decline and urban decay. (They mirror similar faces in Art Nouveau paintings in the Glasgow School of Art, particularly in the artwork of Margaret MacDonald, Charles Rennie Mackintosh's wife and artistic partner— see sidebar on page 447.)*

One block down on the right at #144, come to the building locals nicknamed the...

"Hat Rack" Building: Look up at the very top, and you'll see pointy spikes. Glasgow had roaring iron forges back in the day, and elaborate ironwork—like the kind that crowns this building—throughout the city. Much of it is reconstructed, since the decorative pieces were melted down during the height of World War II, when iron was in short supply. Above the left doorway as you face the building, notice the stained-glass ship in turbulent seas, another fitting icon for the city that's seen more than its share of ups and downs.

• *Continue down the block and make a right on Wellington; you'll come to the crest of the hill, where the two- and three-story buildings have a pleasing, uniform look. These sandstone structures were the homes of Glasgow's upper middle class, the factory managers who worked for the city's barons (such as the titan who owned the mansion on Royal Exchange Square). In the strict Victorian class structure, the people who lived here were distinctly higher on the social scale than the kind of people who lived in the tenements (which we'll see at the end of this tour).*

Make a left on Bath Street, and a right onto West Campbell Street. It opens onto Sauchiehall, Glasgow's main commercial street. Make a left, and half a block later at #217, you'll see a black-and-white Art Nouveau building with the sign reading...

Willow Tea Rooms: Charles Rennie Mackintosh made his living from design commissions, including multiple tea rooms for

businesswoman Kate Cranston. The Willow Tea Rooms—rated ▲—are the most intact, but others (on Ingram and Argyle streets) are in the process of being restored. (You might also see fake "Mockintosh" tea rooms sprinkled throughout the city—ignore them.) A well-known control freak, Mackintosh designed

everything here—down to the furniture, lighting, and cutlery.

In the design of these tea rooms, there was a meeting of the (very modern) minds. Cranston wanted a place for women to be able to gather while unescorted, in a time when traveling solo could give a woman a less-than-desirable reputation. An ardent women's rights supporter, Cranston requested that the rooms be bathed in white, the suffragists' signature color.

Enter the Willow Tea Rooms and make your way past the tacky jewelry and trinket store than now inhabits the bottom floor. On the open mezzanine level, you'll find 20 crowded tables run like a diner from a corner kitchen, serving bland meals to middle-class people, just as it was originally intended to do. If you plan to have a spot of tea and a pastry here (as they did in 1903—the year it opened), request to sit upstairs, in the almost-hidden Room de Luxe. Head up the stairs (following signs for the toilet) to see the peaceful tea room space. While some parts of the Room de Luxe are reproductions (such as the chairs and the doors, which were too fragile to survive), the rest is just as it was in Mackintosh's day (Mon–Sat 9:30–17:00, Sun 11:00–16:15, last orders 30 min before closing, 217 Sauchiehall Street, tel. 0141/332-0521, www .willowtearooms.co.uk).

Charles Rennie Mackintosh
(1868–1928)

During his lifetime, Charles Rennie Mackintosh brought an exuberant Art Nouveau influence to the architecture of his hometown. His designs challenged the city planners of the otherwise practical, working-class port city to create beauty in the buildings they commissioned. A radical thinker, he freely shared credit with his artist wife, Margaret MacDonald.

When Mackintosh was a young student at the Glasgow School of Art, the Industrial Age dominated life here. Fires of the factories belched black soot into the city as they burned coal and forged steel. As the Romantics did before them, Mackintosh and his circle of artist friends drew their solace and inspiration from nature; they went on to create some of the original Art Nouveau buildings, paintings, drawings, and furniture.

As a student traveling abroad in Italy, Mackintosh ignored the famous Renaissance paintings inside the museum walls and set up his easel to paint the exteriors of churches and buildings instead. He rejected the architectural traditions of ancient Greece and Rome. In Venice and Ravenna, he fell under the spell of Byzantine design, and in Siena, he saw a unified medieval city design he would try to import with a Scottish flavor and palette to his own home town.

His first commission came in 1893, to design an extension to the Glasgow Herald building, and more work soon followed, including the Glasgow School of Art and the Willow Tea Rooms 10 years later. Mackintosh envisioned a world without artistic borders, where an Islamic flourish could find its way onto a workaday building in a Scottish city. Inspired by the great buildings of the past and by his Art Nouveau peers, he in turn influenced others, such as painter Gustav Klimt and Bauhaus founder Walter Gropius. A century after Scotland's greatest architect set pencil to paper, his hometown is at last celebrating his unique vision.

• *From here, it's a 10-minute walk mostly uphill to the only must-see Mackintosh sight within the town center. Walk a block and a half west on Sauchiehall, and make a right onto Dalhousie Street; the big brown building on the left at the top of the hill is the Glasgow School of Art.*

If you have time to kill before your tour starts, you can get a drink or a snack at the government-subsidized student cafeteria (listed below) or, if you have at least an hour, head to the Tenement Museum (listed on page 449, closed mornings and Nov–Feb), a preserved home from the early 1900s—right when Mackintosh was doing his most important work. Otherwise, queue up for your spot in a student-guided tour at the...

Glasgow School of Art: A pinnacle of artistic and architectural achievement, the Glasgow School of Art—a working art school and a ▲▲ sight—represented a unique opportunity for Mackintosh. Like Antoni Gaudí in Barcelona, Mackintosh had a chance to design a massive project entirely to his own liking, down to every last detail. These details—from a fireplace that looks like a kimono to windows that soar for multiple stories—are the beauty of the Glasgow School of Art.

Mackintosh loved the hands-on ideology of the Arts and Crafts movement, but he was also a practical Scot. Study the outside of the building. Those protruding wrought-iron brackets that hover outside the multi-paned windows were a new invention during the time of the Industrial Revolution; they reinforce the windows, allowing the big, fragile glass windows to flood natural light into the school. He brought all the most recent technologies to this work, and added them to his artistic palate. Eventually, he merged clean, modernist lines, Asian influences, and Art Nouveau flourishes.

Walk up the stairs into the main vestibule and buy or pick up your tickets if you ordered ahead. (Does it smell like oil paint? Are there canvases lining the upstairs halls?) When the building was first opened, it was modern and minimalist. Today, you'll see elements like the lobby's tile mosaics—added in the 100 years since the building was opened to students—that show the artistic greats, including mustached Mackintosh (who hovers over the gift shop). These mosaics, like the classical sculptures you'll see littering the hallways, were the antithesis of Mackintosh's ideal. He wanted every corner of the school to be well-lit, uncluttered, and usable for young artists. (During the years before this building was part of the school—when Mackintosh and his friends studied here in cramped quarters—he came to appreciate the need for good studio space.)

A determined iconoclast, he did his best to blow raspberries at authority. He made the professors' quarters—which are on the school's top floor, and should be flooded with light—the most dark and depressing. (Students call the hall "the dungeon.") A resolute pagan in a very Protestant city, he romanticized the ideals of nature, and included an abstract icon of a spiral-within-a-circle rose design on many of his works. (Get a preview by heading to the bathroom and checking out the swinging doors.)

The mandatory guided tour will walk you through his most important rooms. You'll be able to linger a few minutes in the major rooms, such as the forest-like library and the furniture gallery (original tables and chairs from the Willow Tea Rooms). Walking through the GSA, it's hard to remember that all of this work was the Art Nouveau original, and that Frank Lloyd Wright, the Art Deco Chrysler Building, and everything that resembles it came well after "Charles Rennie Mack's" time.

Because the Glasgow School of Art is still a working school, you must reserve a ticket before you go. In the summer, tours are frequent; on the off-season, they're twice a day. Call before you start this self-guided city walk or take your chances on lucking into a tour—they sometimes add a second guide if crowds are heavy (April–Sept tours at 10:30, 11:00, 11:30, 13:30, 14:00, 14:30; Oct–March Mon–Sat 11:00 and 14:00, closed Sun; fewer tours May and June, when the student guides have finals; tip the starving students a pound or two if you get a good spiel; call the GSA Shop at 0141/353-4526 or e-mail shop@gsa.ac.uk to confirm times and reserve a guided tour ticket; www.gsa.ac.uk).

Once you're done, consider heading across the street to the student café called **Where the Monkey Sleeps** for a cheap, subsidized lunch (available to the general public, choice of two hot meals a day for £3, soups for £2, and sandwiches for £3). Nothing is ever more than £3.50. It's your chance to mingle with the city's next generation of artists, and hear more of that lilting Glaswegian accent (Sept–June Mon–Fri 8:00–18:00, closed Sat–Sun, same hours outside of the school year but with fewer foods to choose from, entrance is on the left as you face the multi-colored windows, 167 Renfrew Street, tel. 0141/353-4728). The excellent CCA café is also nearby, down on Sauchiehall Street (see listing under Eating, below).

• *If you're in the mood for a wee bit of urban "hillwalking" (a popular Scottish pastime), head north from the Glasgow School of Art on Scott Street. Huff and puff your way over the crest of the hill, and make a left onto Buccleuch Street. The last house on the left is the...*

Tenement House: Packrats of the world, unite! A strange quirk of fate—a 10-year hospitalization of a woman who never redecorated—created this perfectly preserved middle-class residence (worth ▲). The Scottish Trust bought this otherwise ordinary row home, located in a residential neighborhood, because of the peculiar tendencies of Miss Toward. For decades, she kept her home essentially unchanged. The kitchen calendar is still set for 1935, and an intact "feet shampoo" packet lies on the bathroom shelf. It's a time-warp experience.

In Glasgow, tenements like these were typical for every class except the richest. With the city's economic decline, tenements went the way of the dodo bird as the city's population shrank. Today, the house is staffed by caring volunteers; ask them to demonstrate how to make the bed in the kitchen or why the rooms still smell like natural gas. As you look through the rooms stuffed with lace and Victorian oddities—such as the ceramic dogs on the living room's fireplace mantle—consider how different they are from Mackintosh's stark, minimalist designs from the same period (March–Oct daily 13:00–17:00, closed Nov–Feb, 145 Buccleuch Street at the top of Garnethill, tel. 0141/333-0183, info available on National Trust of Scotland's Web site—www.nts.org.uk).

• *To return to the Central Station, leave the Tenement House, make a left when you return to the street, and another left down the hill. Look for the leafy footpath that slopes downhill and take it, following along the highway. After about three minutes, you'll come out of the other side of the small park. Go straight ahead one more block (ignoring the pedestrian bridge, on your right) until you arrive back at the far end of Sauchiehall Street. Make a left, walking to the first bus shelter, and take the #16, #18, or #57 back to the Central Station (£0.85, every 10 min, other buses go the station—ask the driver if another bus pulls up while you're waiting). Taxis zip by on Sauchiehall; a ride to the station will cost you about £3.*

SIGHTS

Away from the Center

▲**Kelvingrove Gallery**—Set to reopen in June 2006, this museum has a fine collection of Dutch and Flemish paintings, as well as works by local Scottish artists. With the renovation, the Kelvingrove seems designated to be Glasgow's one-stop art emporium, and important works from other museums (such as Salvador Dali's *Christ of St. John of the Cross*, which was in St. Mungo's) have been moved to Kelvingrove to consolidate the collection (free, Mon–Thu and Sat 10:00–17:00, Fri and Sun 11:00–17:00, Argyle Street, subway to Kelvinhall stop—5-min walk from station; buses #62, #9, and #16 all stop nearby; tel. 0141/287-2699).

▲**Burrell Collection**—This eclectic art collection of a wealthy local shipping magnate is one of Glasgow's top destinations, but it's three miles outside the city center. If you'd like to visit, plan to make an afternoon of it, and leave time to walk around the surrounding park, where Highland cattle graze. The diverse contents of this museum includes sculptures (from Roman to Rodin), stained glass, tapestries, furniture, Asian and Islamic works, and halls of paintings—starring Cézanne, Renoir, Degas, and

a Rembrandt self-portrait (free, Mon–Thu and Sat 10:00–17:00, Fri–Sun 11:00–17:00, Pollok Country Park, 2060 Pollokshaws Road). To get here from Central Station, take bus #45, #47, or #57 to Pollokshaws Road, or take a train to the Pollokshaws West train station; the entrance is a 10-minute walk from either the bus stop or the station (£2.35 for all-day ticket, exact change required). By car, take the M8 to exit at junction 22 onto M77 Ayr; exit junction 1 on M77 and follow signs.

Sights East of the Center

To reach these sights from the TI on George Square, head up North Hanover Street, turn right on Cathedral Street, and walk about 10 minutes. All sights are free.

▲**Provand's Lordship**—With low beams and medieval interior decoration, this creaky home (complete with a few pieces of furniture from the 17th and 18th centuries) shows the *Lifestyles of the Rich and Famous*...circa 1471 (Mon–Thu and Fri 10:00–17:00, Fri and Sun 11:00–17:00, across the street from St. Mungo Museum at 3 Castle Street, tel. 0141/552-8819).

Glasgow Cathedral—This blackened, Gothic-to-the-extreme cathedral is a rare example of an intact pre-Reformation Scottish cathedral. Dip down into the Blackfriars chapel, and look up to see the "ceiling bosses"—colorful carved demons, dragons, and skulls (April–Sept Mon–Sat 9:30–18:00, Sun 13:00–17:00, Oct–March 9:30–16:00, Sun 13:00–16:00, tel. 0141/552-6891, www.glasgowcathedral.org.uk).

St. Mungo Museum of Religious Life and Art—The museum, next to the cathedral, aims to promote religious understanding. Dull but well-meaning, it does its best to provide an overview of religion's big themes (Mon–Thu and Fri 10:00–17:00, Fri and Sun 11:00–17:00, cheap café in basement, 2 Castle Street, tel. 0141/553-2557).

Necropolis—Built to resemble Paris' Père Lachaise cemetery, Glasgow's huge burial hill has a similar wistful, ramshackle appeal, along with an occasional deer. Its gravestones that seem poised to slide down the hill (open erratic hours at the caretaker's whim, mostly 10:00–16:00 year-round, if main black gates are closed, walk around to the side and see if you can get in and out through a side alleyway).

NIGHTLIFE

Glasgow is a young city, and its nightlife scene is renowned. Walking through the city center, you'll pass one or two clubs/bars on every block. For the latest, pick up a copy of *The List* (£2.20, sold at newsstands).

The city's most popular new nightclub is probably **Òran Mòr**, a converted church that hosts everything from rock concerts to traditional Scottish music nights. Built in 1862, it now holds a bar, a restaurant, and a nightclub in its auditorium, formerly the church's nave, now painted with funky murals (fancy restaurant has £30–60 fixed-price menus, casual bar has £8.50 daily lunch special and £4 sandwiches, daily 12:00–2:00 in the morning, small outdoor beer garden during the day in summer, top of Byres Road at 731–735 Great Western Road, tel. 0141/357-6200, www.oran-mor.co.uk).

For a more traditional night on the town, consider visiting the **Pot Still**, a malt whisky bar from 1835 that boasts a formidable selection of 300 choices. You'll see locals of all ages sitting in its leathery interior, watching football (soccer) and discussing their drinks. They have whisky aged in sherry casks, whisky preferred by wine drinkers, and whisky from every region of Scotland. Give them a little background on your beverage tastes, and they'll narrow down a good choice for you from their long list (whisky runs from £1.40 to £240 a glass, average price £4–5, Sun–Thu 11:00–23:00, Fri–Sat 11:00–24:00, 154 Hope Street, tel. 0141/333-0980, www.thepotstill.co.uk).

SLEEPING

You have two choices for Glasgow: stay in the city center, or hang out with the locals in the less-convenient (but sweet and neighborly) West End.

In the Center

$$ Old Schoolhouse B&B, located a block from the Glasgow School of Art, has 22 stylish rooms in a renovated neoclassical schoolhouse (Sb-£26–30, Db-£52–60, includes breakfast,

---

Sleep Code

(£1 = about $1.80, country code: 44, area code: 0131)
S = Single, **D** = Double/Twin, **T** = Triple, **Q** = Quad, **b** = bathroom, **s** = shower only. You can assume credit cards are accepted unless otherwise noted.

To help you sort easily through these listings, I've divided the rooms into three categories based on the price for a standard double room with bath (during high season):

$$$ **Higher Priced**—Most rooms £90 or more.
$$ **Moderately Priced**—Most rooms between £50–90.
$ **Lower Priced**—Most rooms £50 or less.

Glasgow Hotels and Restaurants

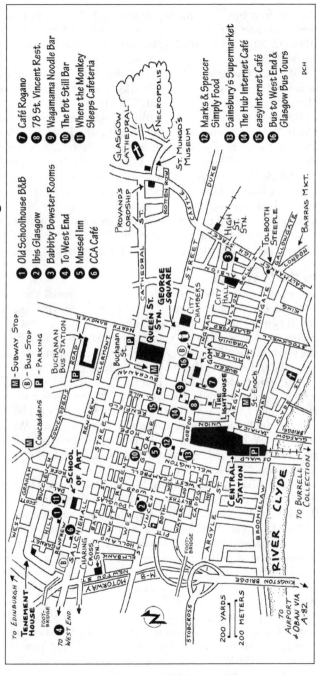

1 Old Schoolhouse B&B
2 Ibis Glasgow
3 Babbity Bowster Rooms
4 To West End
5 Mussel Inn
6 CCA Café

7 Café Rogano
8 78 St. Vincent Rest.
9 Wagamama Noodle Bar
10 The Pot Still Bar
11 Where the Monkey Sleeps Cafeteria

12 Marks & Spencer Simply Food
13 Sainsbury's Supermarket
14 The Hub Internet Café
15 easyInternet Café
16 Bus to West End & Glasgow Bus Tours

194 Renfrew Street, at the top of a steep hill—best to take £3 taxi if arriving at train station, easier walk from bus station, tel. 0141/332-7600, fax 0141/332-8684, oschoolh@hotmail.com, Ken McMillan).

$$ Ibis Glasgow, the modern hotel chain, has 140 reliably comfortable rooms about seven blocks from either train station (Db-£45–55, attached restaurant, 220 West Regent Street, tel. 0141/225-6000, fax 0141/225-6010, www.ibishotel.com). From Central Station, go north on Hope Street and take a left on West Regent. From the Queen Street Station, take Bath Street west, then turn left on Douglas to reach West Regent.

$$ Babbity Bowster, which has a traditional Scottish pub (run by a French chef) and a restaurant on its bottom two floors, has six basic rooms up top. It's located in the trendy Merchant City, with clubs and restaurants within easy walking distance (Sb-£40, Db-£55, no elevator, lots of stairs, 5-min walk from Central Station, 16–18 Blackfriars Street, tel. 0141/552-5055).

In the West End

These B&B–style hotels are in the pleasant, residential West End, a 10-minute taxi ride or an easy 20-minute bus ride from the center. They are within one block of the Botanic Gardens (now under renovation), Byers Street (a neighborhood commercial lane), and the Òran Mòr (see "Nightlife," above). They're also just a five-minute walk to the street of eateries, Ashton Lane (see below).

Getting to the West End: From the Central Station, the West End is a £5 taxi ride. The bus stop for the #20 or #66 is directly in front of the TI, in the southwest corner of George Square (£1.20, runs every 10 min). The bus heads north, and then takes Great Western Road west. When you see the castle-like University on your left, look for Botanic Hotel and others on the left, and get off at the Botanic Gardens stop. The first two hotels are on Alfred Terrace, which lies above the buildings that line Great Western Road; the last is directly across the street from them, along a line of other not-as-good B&Bs. The subway also runs to the West End; the most convenient stops are Hillhead (for hotels) and Kelvinhall (see subway info page 441).

$$ Botanic Hotel has 16 bright, cheerful rooms in an elegant, high-ceilinged building that has the comfort of a neighborhood B&B (S-£28, Sb-£35, Db-£52, Tb-£70, Qb-£80, includes breakfast, 1 Alfred Terrace, tel. 0141/337-7007, fax 0141/337-7070, botanichotel@hotmail.co.uk).

$$ The Heritage Hotel, next door to the Botanic, has the same friendly vibe. Its 27 rooms have a woody, Scandinavian feel (Sb-£35, Db-£55, Tb-75, includes breakfast, 4 Alfred Terrace, tel. & fax 0141/339-6955, www.smoothhound.co.uk/hotels/heritageh, bookings@heritagehotel.fsbusiness.co.uk).

$$ Kelvin Hotel is slightly more run-down than the first two, but it has the same great location, and 21 clean, basic rooms (S-£28, Sb-£45, D-£48, Db-£58, Qb-£92, includes breakfast, 15 Buckingham Terrace, tel. 0141/339-7143, fax 0141/339-5215, www .kelvinhotel.com, enquiries@kelvinhotel.com).

EATING

In the Center

Mussel Inn offers light, good-value fish dinners and seafood plates in an airy, informal environment. The restaurant is a cooperative, owned and run by shellfish farmers, and their £10 "kilo pot" of Scottish mussels is popular with locals and big enough to share (£5 salads, £6 small grilled platters, Mon–Fri 12:00–14:30 & 17:30–22:00, Sat 12:00–22:00, Sun 17:00–22:00, 157 Hope Street, between St. Vincent and West George streets, tel. 0141/572-1405).

CCA Café, located in the first floor of the Glasgow's edgy contemporary art museum, has delicious designer food at art-student prices. An 18th-century facade, discovered when the site was excavated to build the museum, stands tall over the courtyard restaurant (£5 salads, £6.50 main courses, same prices for lunch or dinner, Tue–Fri 9:00–23:00, Sat 9:00–24:00, closed Sun–Mon, 350 Sauchiehall Street, tel. 0141/332-7959).

Café Rogano is a Glasgow institution, with essentially the same Art Deco interior that it had when it opened in 1935. Eating upstairs, in the fancier restaurant, is like dining on the officers' deck of the *Titanic;* the bistro downstairs, while still dressy and elegant, has a 1930s-Hollywood glamour (upstairs—£5 lunch sandwiches, £20 fish dinners; bistro—£11 meals, daily 11:00–24:00, 11 Exchange Place—just before giant archway from Buchanan Street, reservations smart on weekends, tel. 0141/248-4055).

78 St. Vincent, offering modern British cuisine made with Scottish produce, has elegant tables and booths in a high-windowed former bank. Their rotating gourmet menu is heavy on the meat and fish dishes, with beef from nearby towns and salmon and cod caught off west coast of Scotland (2-course lunch special £12.50, 3-course-£15.50, dinner-£18, Mon–Sat 8:30–15:00 & 17:00–22:00, Sun 10:00–15:00 & 17:00–22:00, 78 St. Vincent Street, tel. 0141/248-7878).

Wagamama is part of a huge UK chain that serves delicious noodles at a reasonable price (£7–8 dishes, Mon–Sat 12:00–23:00, Sun 12:30–22:30, 97–103 West George Street, tel. 0141/229-1468).

Dozens of restaurants line the main commercial areas of town: Sauchiehall Street, Buchanan Street, and the Merchant City area. Most are very similar, with trendy interiors, euro disco-pop soundtracks, and dinner for about £15–20 per person.

In the West End

A collection of fine and fun eateries line Ashton Lane, a small street just off bustling Byers Road. Once a student haven, Ashton Lane has become *the* neighborhood hangout in the West End. Comparison-shop the menus along Ashton and Cresswell Lane (just to the north), and you'll find vegetarian options, Belgian beers, hot curry, and even Scottish food.

Ubiquitous Chip, which was first to settle in the lane, has a downstairs gourmet restaurant with a fern-bar feel (2-course lunch-£23, 2-course dinner-£33), a more casual upstairs pub (£6–7 main dishes), and a "wee pub" for drinks and light snacks around the side (Mon–Sat 12:00–23:00, Sun 12:30–23:00, 12 Ashton Lane, tel. 0141/334-5007).

The Loft, a few doors down from the Chip, is cavernous and cool, with photos of Hollywood stars blown up to the size of movie screens. It has appropriate decor, since the restaurant is part of a movie complex. The Loft, and the smaller bar downstairs (called "The Lane") attract a young, hip crowd—offering a nice break from Glasgow's tatties (potatoes), neeps (turnips), and tartan (pizza-£8, plates-£9, Mon–Fri 12:00–22:00, Sat–Sun 10:00–22:00, reservations smart on weekends, in the Grosvenor Theatre on Ashton Lane, tel. 0141/341-1234).

Café Andaluz, at the north end of Creswell Lane, offers tapas and sangria behind lacy wooden screens, as the waitstaff clicks past on the cool tiles (tapas-£3–4, combo-plates-£15, Sun–Thu 12:00–23:00, Fri–Sat 12:00–24:00, 2 Cresswell Lane, tel. 0141/339-1111).

TRANSPORTATION CONNECTIONS

Traveline Scotland has a journey planner that's linked to all of Scotland's train and bus schedule info. Go online (www.traveline.org.uk); call them at 0870-608-2608; or use the individual train and bus Web sites listed below.

From Glasgow's Central Station by Train to: Keswick in the Lake District (hrly, 2 hrs to Penrith, then catch a bus to Keswick, hrly except Sun 6/day, 40 min), **Stranraer** and ferry to Belfast (4/day direct, 7/day with change in Ayr, 2.5 hrs), **Troon** and ferry to Belfast (2/hr, 40 min), **Preston** (hrly, 3 hrs, easy 30-min connection to Blackpool), **Liverpool** (1–2/hrs, 4hrs Mon–Fri, 6–8 hrs Sat–Sun, requires 1–3 transfers), **Durham** (2/hrs, 3hrs, may require change in Edinburgh), **York** (10/day, 3.5 hrs), **London** (hrly, 6 hrs, check schedules to both Euston and King's Cross stations). Train info: tel. 0845-748-4950 or www.firstscotrail.com.

From Glasgow's Queen Street Station by Train to: Oban (Mon–Sat 6/day, 3/day Sun, 3 hrs), **Inverness** (3/day, 3.5 hrs, more frequent with change in Perth), **Edinburgh** (4/hr, 50 min). Train info: tel. 0845-748-4950 or www.firstscotrail.com.

From Glasgow by Bus to: Oban (3/day, 3 hrs), **Inverness** (hrly, 4–4.5 hrs, some transfer in Perth), **Pitlochry** (8/day, 2 hrs, transfer in Perth), **Edinburgh** (3/hr, 70 min). Bus info: tel. 0141/332-9644 or www.citylink.co.uk.

From Glasgow by Car: The M8, which cuts a long slice through downtown Glasgow, is the easiest way in and out of the city. Ask your hotel for directions to and from the M8, and connect with highways in all directions from there.

Glasgow International Airport: Located eight miles west of the city, this small airport has currency-exchange desks, an information center, and ATMs. Left luggage is open daily 6:00 to 22:45 (£4.50/item up to 4 hours, £10/item for 24 hours). Taxis connect downtown to the airport for about £17. Bus #905 runs to central Glasgow (daily 6:00–24:00, 3–6/hr, £3.30/one-way, £5/round-trip, 25-min trip to city center, pick up at bays 1 and 2 at the airport, stops at Queen Street and Buchanan stations). More info at tel. 0870-040-0008 or at www.glasgowairport.com.

Prestwick Airport: A hub for Ryanair (as well as the U.S. military, which refuels planes here), this airport is about 30 miles southwest of the city center. A train connects the airport and the Central Station (Mon–Sat 2/hr, Sun 1/hr, 44 min). Buses run to and from Buchanan Street Station—ask at the airport TI or check www.travelinescotland.com to confirm your travel times for all carriers (£4–6, 1–3/hr, 50 min, daily 7:00–22:00). For more information about Prestwick airport, visit www.gpia.co.uk or call 0871-223-0700 ext 1006.

OBAN, ISLANDS, AND HIGHLANDS

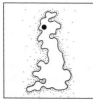

Filled with more natural and historical mystique than people, the Highlands are where Scottish dreams are set. Legends of Bonnie Prince Charlie swirl around crumbling castles as pipers in kilts swirl around tourists. The harbor of Oban is a fruit crate of Scottish traditions, and the wind-bitten Hebrides Islands are just a hop, skip, and jump away.

The Highlands are cut in two by the impressive Caledonian Canal, with Oban at one end and Inverness at the other (see color map at the start of this book). The major sights cluster along the scenic 120-mile stretch between these two towns. Oban is a fine home base for western Scotland, and Inverness makes a good overnight stop on your way through eastern Scotland.

Planning Your Time

While Ireland has more charm and Wales has better sights, this area provides your best look at rural Scottish culture. There are a lot of miles, but they're scenic, the roads are good, and the traffic is light. In two days you can get a feel for the area with the car hike described below. To do the islands, you'll need more time. Iona is worthwhile but adds a day to your trip. Generally, the region is hungry for the tourist dollar, and everything overtly Scottish is designed to woo the tourist. You'll need more than this quick visit to get away from that.

The charm of the Highlands deserves more time and a trip farther north (ideally to the Isle of Skye, see page 484). But with a car and two days to connect the Lake District and Edinburgh, this blitz tour is more interesting than two more days in England.

Day 1: 9:00–Leave Lake District (see Castlerigg Stone Circle if you haven't yet); 12:00–Rest stop on Loch Lomond, then joyride on; 13:00–Lunch in Inveraray; 16:00–Arrive in Oban, tour whisky distillery, and drop by the TI; 20:00–Have dinner with music at McTavish's Kitchens or dinner with class at The Studio.

Day 2: 9:00–Leave Oban; 10:00–Visit Glencoe museum and the valley's Visitors Centre; 12:00–Drive to Fort William and follow Caledonian Canal to Inverness, stopping at Fort Augustus to see the locks and at Loch Ness to search for monsters; 16:00–Visit the Culloden Battlefield (closes earlier off-season) near Inverness; 17:00–Drive south; 20:00–Set up in Edinburgh.

With an extra day, spend a second night in Oban and tour Iona, or sleep in Inverness or Pitlochry, both fun and entertaining towns. With even more time, visit the Isle of Skye.

Oban

Oban (pronounced OH-bin) is called the "gateway to the isles." This busy little ferry-and-train terminal has no important sights.

It's a low-key resort, with a winding promenade lined by gravel beaches, ice-cream stands, and fish-and-chip take-away shops. When the rain clears, you'll see sun-starved Scots sitting in benches along The Esplanade, leaning back to catch some rays. Wind, boats, gulls, layers of islands, and the promise of a wide-open Atlantic beyond give Oban a rugged charm.

ORIENTATION

(area code: 01631)
Oban's business action, just a couple of streets deep, stretches along the harbor and its promenade. Everything is close together, and the town seems eager to please its many visitors. There's live, touristy music nightly in several bars and restaurants; wool and tweed are perpetually on sale (tourist shops open until 20:00 in summer and on Sun); and posters announce a variety of day tours to Scotland's wild and rabbit-strewn western islands.

Tourist Information
The TI, located in a former church, sells bus tickets and has brochures and information on everything from bike rental to golf courses to horseback riding to rainy-day activities, as well as a fine

Oban

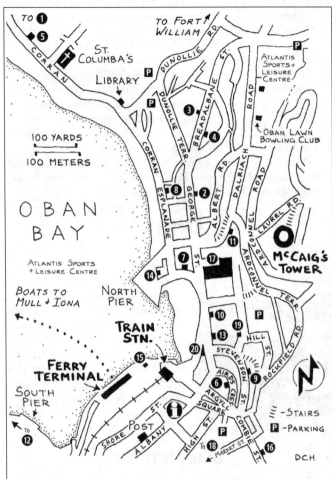

1. To Glenburnie & Barriemore Hotels & Kilchrenan House B&B
2. Rowan Tree Hotel
3. Tanglin B&B, Strathlachlan, Raniven, Gramarvin & Sandvilla Guest Houses
4. Oban Backpackers
5. IYHF Hostel
6. Jeremy Inglis' Hostel
7. Oban Inn Restaurant
8. Coasters Restaurant
9. The Lorne Pub
10. McTavish's Kitchens
11. The Studio Restaurant
12. To Manor House Hotel Rest.
13. The Kitchen Garden Deli & Café
14. Ee'usk Restaurant
15. Shellfish Shack
16. Cafe 41 Bistro
17. Whisky Distillery
18. To Supermarket & Bike Rental
19. Launderette
20. Bowman's Tours & West Coast Motors (Left Luggage)

bookshop (mid-June–Aug Mon–Sat 9:00–20:00, Sun 9:00–19:00; Sept–mid-June Mon–Sat 9:00–18:00, Sun 10:00–17:00; coin-operated Internet access, £3 room-reservation fee, no WC, on Argyll Square, just off harbor a block from train station, tel. 01631/563-122, www.visitscottishheartlands.org). Wander through their exhibit on the area and pick up a few phones to hear hardy locals talk about their life on the wild, west edge of Scotland. Check the TI's "What's On" board for the latest on Oban's small-town evening scene (free live entertainment nightly at the Great Western Hotel, Scottish Night every Wed or Thu, call for details, tel. 01631/563-101).

Helpful Hints

Internet Access: Your cheapest bet is the library at The Esplanade and Dunollie Road, but you need to book a time slot in advance (free, daily 10:00–13:00 & 14:00–17:00, closed Sun, Tue, and Sat afternoon, tel. 01631/571-444). The only other option in town is the TI (see above).

Laundry: Oban Quality Laundry is a block from the TI, where Stevenson and Tweedle streets intersect (Mon–Sat 9:00–5:30, closed Sun, drop-off service, tel. 01631/565-866). Oban Backpackers and the IYHF hostels have laundry service for guests.

Bike Rental: Try Oban Cycles (£8/half-day, £12.50/day, Mon–Fri 9:00–17:30, Sat 9:00–17:00, closed Sun but rentals can be arranged in advance, across from Tesco supermarket on Lochside Street, tel. 01631/566-996, www.obancycles.com, info@obancycles.com). Look for a pathway to Tesco one block past the TI, on the right—from this parking lot, the bike-rental shop is on the left. Oban Backpackers also rents bikes (£6/half-day, £12/day, see listing in "Sleeping," below).

Left Luggage: The lockers are off-limits in the train station, but if you're desperate, West Coast Motors (next to Bowman's Tours) has a left-luggage service with highway-robbery rates (£1/hour per piece, unsecured in main office, daily 9:00–13:00 & 14:00–17:00—but *Back in 20 Minutes* sign often in window, so allow for plenty of time to pick up bags).

TOURS

Oban and Beyond

Highland Horror—Oban has joined the "haunted towns" bandwagon, and offers a walking tour in late summer that includes the eerie sound of bagpipes and a dram of malt whisky (£6, Aug–Sept Fri–Tue at 19:30, 60 min, meets in front of TI at Argyll Square, info tel. 01631/570-638).

Nearby Islands—For the best day trip from Oban, tour the islands of Iona and Mull (offered daily May–Oct, fully described on page 468)—or consider staying overnight on remote and beautiful Iona (see page 470 for more details). Oban's tour companies offer an array of tours. You can spend an entire day on Mull. Those more interested in nature than church history will enjoy trips to the wildly scenic Isle of Staffa with Fingal's Cave. Trips to Treshnish Island brim with puffins, seals, and other sea critters.

Intro to Ancient Scotland—Once a week (usually Mon in summer, Fri in winter), Oban Backpackers offers an all-day tour that includes monuments, cairns, a castle, and the Isle of Seil (£18, departs 9:00 from hostel on Breadalbane Street, returns 18:30, call to confirm, tel. 01631/562-107).

SIGHTS AND ACTIVITIES

In Oban

▲**West Highland Malt Scotch Whisky Distillery Tours**—The 200-year-old Oban Whisky Distillery produces more than 14,500 liters a week. They offer serious and fragrant 45-minute, £4 tours explaining the process from start to finish, with a free, smooth sample and a discount coupon for the shop. The exhibition that precedes the tour gives a quick, whisky-centric history of Scotland. This is the handiest whisky tour you'll see, just a block off the harbor and better than anything in Edinburgh (July–Sept Mon–Fri 9:30–19:30, Sat 9:30–17:00, Sun 12:00–17:00; April–June and Oct Mon–Sat 9:30–17:00, closed Sun; March and Nov Mon–Fri 10:00–17:00, closed Sat–Sun; Feb Mon–Fri 12:30–16:00, closed Sat–Sun; closed all of Dec–Jan; last tour always 1 hour before closing—tel. 01631/572-004). In high season, these tours (which are limited to 15 people every 15 min) fill up quickly. Call or stop by early in the day to reserve your time slot.

McCaig's Tower—The unfinished "colosseum" on the hill overlooking town was an employ-the-workers-and-build-me-a-fine-memorial project undertaken by an early Oban tycoon in 1900. While the structure itself is nothing to see close-up, a 10-minute hike through a Victorian residential neighborhood gets you to a peaceful garden and a mediocre view.

Atlantis Sports and Leisure Centre—The industrial-type sports center is a good place to get some exercise on a rainy day or let the kids run wild for a few hours. There's an indoor swimming pool with a big water slide, a rock-climbing wall, tennis courts, and a small kids' playground (center open Mon–Fri 7:00–22:00, Sat–Sun 8:30–21:00, July–Aug closes Sat–Sun at 18:00; pool hours vary by season, call or check online; pool entry: adults-£3, kids-£2, no rental towels or suits, lockers-20p, on the north end of Dalriach

Road, tel. 01631/566-800, www.atlantisleisure.co.uk). The center's outdoor playground is free and open all the time.

Oban Lawn Bowling Club—The club has welcomed visitors since 1869. This elegant green is the scene of a wonderfully British spectacle of old men tiptoeing wishfully after their balls. It's fun to watch, and—if there's no match and the weather's dry—for £3 each, anyone can rent shoes and balls and actually play (daily 10:00–16:00 & 17:00 or "however long the weather lasts," just south of sports center on Dalriach Road).

Near Oban

Kerrera—Two miles south of Oban, this stark but very green island offers a quick, easy opportunity to get that romantic island experience (ferry-£3 round-trip, 50p for bikes, 5-min trip, Mon–Sat 15 ferries/day, Sun 14/day, 6/day in winter, at Gallanach's dock, tel. 01631/563-665, if no answer contact Oban TI for info—see above). If you want to overnight here, your only option is the Bunkhouse, a converted 18th-century stable that has beds in dorm-like compartments (sleeps 7, £10 per person, £50 for whole bunkhouse, open year-round, free parking, tel. 01631/570-223, good ferry info on www.kerrerabunkhouse.co.uk, info@kerrerabunkhouse.co.uk, Andy and Jo). They also run a teahouse (summers only).

Isle of Seil—Enjoy a drive, a walk, some solitude, and the sea. Drive 12 miles south of Oban on A816 to B844 to the Isle of Seil, connected to the mainland by a bridge. Just over the bridge on the Isle of Seil is a pub called Tigh-an-Truish ("House of Trousers"). After a 1745 English law forbade the wearing of kilts on the mainland, Highlanders used this pub to change from kilts to trousers before crossing the bridge. The pub serves great meals to those in kilts or pants (food served daily July–Aug 12:30–21:00, Easter–Oct 12:30–17:00 & 18:00–21:00, Nov–Easter 12:20–14:00 & 17:00–21:00; bar open until 23:00, darts anytime, good seafood dishes, tel. 01852/300-242). Five miles across the island, on a tiny second island and facing the open Atlantic, is Easdale, a historic, touristy, windy little slate-mining town—with a slate-town museum and incredibly tacky egomaniac's "Highland Arts" shop (shuttle ferry goes the 300 yards).

SLEEPING

The B&Bs in Oban offer a better value than the hotels.

Hotels

$$$ Glenburnie Hotel, a stately Victorian home on Oban's waterfront, has an elegant breakfast room overlooking the bay. Its spacious and comfortable rooms are furnished like plush living

Sleep Code

(£1 = about $1.80, country code: 44, area code: 01631)
S = Single, **D** = Double/Twin, **T** = Triple, **Q** = Quad, **b** = bathroom, **s** = shower only. Unless otherwise noted, you can assume credit cards are accepted at hotels and hostels—but not B&Bs—and breakfast is included.

To help you sort easily through these listings, I've divided the rooms into three categories based on the price for a standard double room with bath (during high season):

$$$ **Higher Priced**—Most rooms £65 or more.
 $$ **Moderately Priced**—Most rooms between £30–65.
  $ **Lower Priced**—Most rooms £30 or less.

rooms (Sb-£30–45, Db-£60–90, good breakfast and views, non-smoking, parking, closed mid-Nov–mid-March, The Esplanade, tel. & fax 01631/562-089, www.glenburnie.co.uk, graeme.strachan @btinternet.com, Graeme and Allyson).

$$$ Barriemore Hotel is the last place on Oban's grand waterfront esplanade. It has a dark, woody, equestrian feel and 13 large, well-appointed rooms (Sb-£50–55, Db-£60–84, fine views, non-smoking, The Esplanade, tel. 01631/566-356, fax 01631/571-084, www.barriemore-hotel.co.uk, reception@barriemore-hotel .co.uk, Nic and Sarah Jones).

$$$ Kilchrenan House, the turreted former retreat of a textile magnate, has 10 tastefully renovated, large rooms, most with bay views (Sb-£32–45, Db-£64–90, lower prices for off-season and 2-night stays, try for room 5, non-smoking, closed Dec–Jan, a few houses past church on The Esplanade, tel. 01631/562-663, fax 01631/570-021, www.kilchrenanhouse.co.uk, info @kilchrenanhouse.co.uk, Alison and Kenny).

$$$ Rowan Tree Hotel is a group-friendly place with a tacky lobby, 24 basic, cleanser-clean rooms, and a central locale right on Oban's main drag (Sb-£62, Db-£84, cheaper for walk-ins, easy parking, George Street, tel. 01631/562-954, fax 01631/565-071).

Guest Houses and B&Bs

The following guest houses are well located on a quiet, flowery street two blocks off the harbor, three blocks from the center, and a 12-minute walk from the train station. By car, as you enter town, turn left after King's Knoll Hotel and take your first right onto Breadalbane Street. Each has parking from an alley behind the buildings. Note that these B&Bs don't accept credit cards.

$$ Tanglin B&B is a winner. Liz and Jim Montgomery offer five bright, non-smoking, homey rooms with an easygoing atmosphere (S-£22, D-£40, Db-£44, flexible rates and family deals, non-smoking, 3 Strathaven Terrace, Breadalbane Street, tel. 01631/563-247, jimtanglin@aol.com).

$$ Strathlachlan Guest House, next door, offers a fine value and the Scottish hospitality of Rena Anderson. Each of the four rooms has a private adjacent bathroom, and they share a TV lounge (S-£18, D-£36, family deals, non-smoking, 2 Breadalbane Street, tel. 01631/563-861).

$$ Raniven Guest House, with six tastefully decorated rooms, is friendly and a great value (Db-£50, non-smoking, 1 Strathlachlan Terrace, tel. 01631/562-713, Jessie Turnbull).

$$ Gramarvin Guest House has five comfy, quiet rooms (Sb-£23–28, Db-£45–50, family deals, non-smoking, Breadalbane Street, tel. 01631/564-622, www.gramarvin.co.uk, mary @gramarvin.com, Mary).

$$ Sandvilla Guest House, a lesser value, rents five rooms cheerier than the owner, Scott (Db-£45–52, 4 Breadalbane Street, tel. 01631/562-803, www.holidayoban.co.uk, sandvilla @holidayoban.co.uk).

Hostels

Oban offers plenty of cheap dorm beds. Your choice: fun, orderly, or spacey.

$ Oban Backpackers is the most central, laid-back, and fun, with a wonderful sprawling public living room and 48 beds (£12–13/bed in July–Aug, £12 off-season when open, 6–12 bunks per room, closed Nov–Feb, no breakfast, Internet terminal and £2.50 laundry service for guests only, tours leave from hostel 1/week—see above, bike rentals—£6/half-day, £12/day, 10-min walk from station, on Breadalbane Street, tel. 01631/562-107, www.scotlands -top-hostels.com, oban@scotlands-top-hostels.com).

$ The orderly **IYHF hostel,** on the scenic waterfront Esplanade, is in a grand building with 130 beds and smashing views of the harbor and islands (£13 per bed in 4- to 10-bed rooms, 11 Db-£30—not available June–Aug, cheaper for youths under 18, breakfast-£2.30, great facilities and public rooms, Internet access, 1 laundry machine, tel. 01631/562-025, oban@syha.org.uk).

$ Jeremy Inglis' Hostel, run like a low-rent B&B, is two blocks from the TI and train station. It's the least expensive and feels more like a commune than a youth hostel (£8.50/bed, cash only, breakfast comes with Jeremy's homemade jam, 12 beds, 21 Airds Crescent, tel. 01631/565-065).

EATING

Oban has plenty of fun options. The downtown is full of cheap eateries and pubs serving decent grub: Consider the harborfront **Oban Inn,** the oldest building in town with a hole-in-the-wall downstairs bar and a quiet lounge upstairs (£6 meals, Mon–Sat 12:00–22:00, Sun 12:30–midnight, stained-glass coats-of-arms and comfy booth seating, 1 Stafford Street, tel. 01631/562-484). **Coasters** has good views (£5–9, daily 12:00–23:00, on Corran Esplanade, 1 block past William Street heading away from station, tel. 01631/566-881). Just off the main drag is **The Lorne,** a lively, friendly, high-ceilinged pub popular with locals (£7–12, food served Sun–Fri 12:00–14:30 & 17:00–21:00, Sat 12:00–14:30 & 17:00–20:30 only—in order to get ready for live bands, Stevenson Street, tel. 01631/570-020).

At **McTavish's Kitchens,** you can gum haggis while taking in a sappy folk show at a reasonable price. This huge, cafeteria-style eating hall (with a retirement-home feel) is an Oban institution, featuring live but tired folk music and dancing. This is your basic tourist trap filled with English vacationers. The food is inexpensive and edible (£6 for haggis, neeps, and tatties; £14–20 for a super Scottish multicourse *menu*). The piping, dancing, and singing starts nightly at 20:00 May through September (mostly a fiddle and 2 accordions, with precious little dancing and bagpiping, tel. 01631/563-064). The show costs £4.50 without a meal, £2.50 with dinner, or is free with dinner if you have a coupon from your B&B. No reservations are required. Non-smokers get the best harbor views. Smokers sit closest to the stage.

Ee'usk (a phonetic rendering of *iasg*, Scots Gaelic for "fish") is a stylish, family-run place on the waterfront. It has tall tables, a casual-chic atmosphere, sweeping views, and fish dishes that are favored by both locals and tourists (£9–17 meals, daily 12:00–15:00 & 18:00–21:30, North Pier, tel. 01631/565-666). Reservations are smart every day in summer and weekends in off-season; if you want to wait for a table, they have a loft bar with comfy sofas.

The Studio is a small, tightly packed restaurant with '70s decor, featuring serious, first-class Scottish cooking (£13 for a full Scottish meal until 18:30, £15 for 3-course meal after 18:30, or a pricey à la carte menu, April–Oct nightly 18:00–22:00, closed Nov–March, reservations recommended, uphill at intersection of Craigard Road and Albert Road, tel. 01631/562-030). It has fine steaks, trout, and a prawn-and-clam chowder that hits the spot on a stormy day.

The well-polished **Manor House Hotel** offers *nouveau* cuisine and a genteel dining experience—pricey but worthwhile for a waterfront splurge (£33 5-course meal, nightly 18:45–21:00, reservations wise in summer, a short drive or £2–3 taxi ride south of town on the waterfront, Gallanach Road, tel. 01631/562-087).

The Kitchen Garden is fine for soup, salad, or sandwiches. It's a deli and gourmet-foods store with a charming café upstairs (£5–7 dishes, Mon–Sat 8:30–17:30, Sun 11:00–17:30, closed Sun Jan–March, 14 George Street, tel. 01631/566-332).

Cafe 41 Bistro is a relaxed BYOB option with an emphasis on Scottish and French cuisine (£11–16 entrées, Sun and Wed–Thu 18:30–20:45, Fri–Sat until 21:30, closed Mon–Tue, 10-min walk from town center at 41 Combie Street, tel. 01631/564-117).

The **Shellfish** shack at the ferry dock is the best spot to pick up a seafood appetizer (often free salmon samples, inexpensive coffee, meal-size salmon sandwiches; picnic tables nearby, open until the boat unloads from Mull in the late afternoon—a pleasant way to cap off your day trip to the islands).

Supermarket: **Tesco** is a five-minute walk from the TI (Mon–Sat 8:00–22:00, Sun 9:00–20:00, WC in front by registers, inexpensive cafeteria, look for entrance to large parking lot a block past TI on right-hand side, Lochside Road).

TRANSPORTATION CONNECTIONS

Oban

Trains link Oban to the nearest transportation hub in **Glasgow** (3/day, 3 hrs). Oban's small train station has no lockers (ticket window open Mon–Sat 7:15–18:10, Sun 11:00–18:00, free WC). Train info: tel. 08457-484-950, www.gner.co.uk.

Ferries fan out from Oban to the **southern Hebrides** (see information on the islands of Iona and Mull, below). Caledonian MacBrayne Ferry info: tel. 01631/566-688, www.calmac.co.uk.

Buses operated by Scottish Citylink (www.citylink.co.uk) run between Oban, Glencoe, and Inverness, but not on Sunday.

From Oban by Bus to: Glencoe (1/day, allow 8.5 hrs due to 6.5-hr layover in Tyndrum, £13 one-way), **Inverness** (3/day July–Aug, 2/day Sept–June, 4 hrs, transfer in Fort William, £13 one-way). **Fort William,** a transfer point on the Oban–Inverness route, is a bleak town with a grocery store and no real station (see Harry Potter connection on page 475). Pay the driver cash or buy tickets in advance by calling Citylink at tel. 08705-505-050; or, even easier, drop by the TI. Buses arrive and depart in front of the Caledonian Hotel, across from the train station.

Oban, Islands, and Highlands

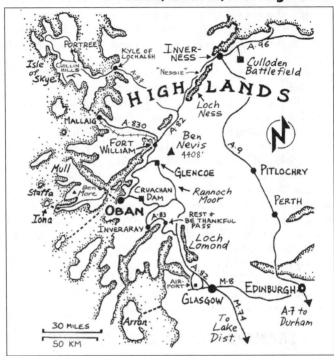

Islands: Mull and Iona

For the best one-day look at the dramatic and historic Hebrides (HEB-rid-eez) Islands, take the Iona/Mull tour from Oban.

Here's the game plan: You'll take a ferry from Oban to Mull (40 min), ride a Bowman's bus across Mull (75 min), then board a quick ferry from Mull to Iona. The total round-trip travel time is 5.5 hours and all of it is incredibly scenic. Buy your set of six tickets—one for each leg—at the Bowman's office in Oban (£30, £2 discount with this book in 2006 for Iona/Mull tour, no tours Nov–March, book one day ahead in July–Sept, bus tickets can sell out during busy summer weekends, office open daily 8:00–18:00,

1 Queens Park Place, a block from train station, tel. 01631/566-809 or 01631/563-221, www.bowmanstours.co.uk).

You'll leave in the morning from the Oban pier on the huge

Oban–Mull ferry run by Caledonia MacBrayne (boats depart Sun–Fri at 10:00, Sat at 9:30, returning daily at 17:45—but confirm schedule). The best seats on the ferry—with the biggest windows—are in the sofa lounge on the uppermost deck on the back end of the boat. (Follow signs for toilets, and look for big staircase to the top floor; this floor also has its own small snack bar with £3 sandwiches and £4 box lunches.) On board, if it's a clear day, ask a local or a crew member to point out Ben Nevis, the tallest mountain in Great Britain. The ferry has a fine cafeteria and a bookshop (though guidebooks are cheaper in Oban). Five minutes before landing on Mull, you'll see the striking Duart Castle on the left.

Upon arrival in Mull, you'll find your tour company's bus for the entertaining and informative bus ride across the Isle of Mull. All drivers spend the entire ride chattering away about life on Mull. They are hardworking local boys who make historical trivia fascinating—or at least fun. Your destination is Mull's westernmost ferry terminal (Fionnphort), where you'll board a small, rockier ferry for the brief ride to Iona. Unless you stay overnight (see below), you'll have only about two hours to roam freely around the island, before taking the ferry–bus–ferry ride in reverse back to Oban.

Mull

The **Isle of Mull,** the third-largest in Scotland, has 300 scenic miles of coastline and castles and a 3,169-foot-high mountain. Called Ben More ("big hill" in Gaelic), it was once much bigger. The last active volcano in northern Europe, it was 10,000 feet tall—the entire island of Mull—before it blew. It's calmer now, and similarly, Mull has a notably laid-back population. My bus driver reported there are no deaths from stress and only a few from boredom.

With steep, fog-covered hillsides topped by cairns (ancient stone circles, sometimes indicating graves), Mull has a gloomy, otherworldly charm. Bring plenty of rain protection and wear layers in case the sun peeks through the clouds. As my driver said, Mull is a place of cold, wet, windy winters and mild, wet, windy summers.

On the far side of Mull, the caravan of tour buses unloads at a tiny ferry town. The ferry takes about 200 walk-ons. Confirm clearly with the bus driver when to catch the boat off Iona for your return, then hustle off the bus (listening to your driver for the return time) and to the dock to avoid the 30-minute delay if you don't make the first trip over. There's a small ferry-passenger building/meager snack bar (and a pay WC). After the 10-minute ride, you wash ashore on sleepy Iona. The ferry mobs that crowded your steps seem to disappear into Iona's back lanes.

Mull has a taxi service that can get you around Mull or Iona (tel. 01681/700-507 or mobile 0788-777-4550, www.mullionataxi.com).

Iona

The tiny island of **Iona,** just three miles by 1.5 miles, is famous as the birthplace of Christianity in Scotland. You'll have about

two hours here on your own before you retrace your steps; you'll dock back in Oban by about 17:45. While the day is spectacular when it's sunny, it's worthwhile in any weather.

A pristine light and a thoughtful peace pervade the stark, car-free island and its tiny community. While the present abbey, nunnery, and graveyard go back to the 13th century, much of what you'll see was rebuilt in the 19th century. It's free to see the ruins and the graveyard, but the abbey itself has a small fee (£3.50 entry, daily April–Sept 9:30–18:30, Oct–March 9:30–16:30, tel. 01681/700-512). It's worth the cost just to sit in the stillness of its lovely, peaceful interior courtyard. But with buoyant clouds bouncing playfully off of distant bluffs, sparkling white sand crescents, and lone tourists camped thoughtfully atop huge rocks just looking out to sea, it's a place perfect for meditation. Climb a peak—nothing's higher than 300 feet above the sea.

The village, Baile Mor, has shops, a restaurant/pub, enough beds, a meager heritage center, and no bank. The Finlay Ross Shop rents bikes (near ferry dock, £4.50/4 hrs, £8/day, tel. 01681/700-357). Iona's official Web site (www.isle-of-iona.com) has good information about the island, as well as an in-depth map.

Staying Overnight in Iona: For a chance to really experience peaceful, idyllic Iona, consider spending a night or two. Scots bring their kids and stay on this tiny island for a week. If you want to overnight in Iona, don't buy your tickets at Bowman's in Oban because they require a same-day return. Instead, buy each leg of the ferry–bus–ferry (and return) trip separately. Get your Oban–Mull ferry ticket in the Oban ferry office (see above, one-way for walk-on passengers-£4, round-trip-£7). Once you arrive in Mull (Craignure), follow the crowds to the Bowman buses and buy a ticket directly from the driver (£9 round-trip). Once you arrive at the ferry terminal (Fionnphort), walk into the

History of Iona

St. Columba, an Irish scholar, soldier, priest, and founder of monasteries, got into a small war over the possession of an illegally copied psalm book. Victorious but sickened by the

bloodshed, Columba left Ireland, vowing never to return. According to legend, the first bit of land out of sight of his homeland was Iona. He stopped here in 563 and established the abbey.

Columba's monastic community flourished, and Iona became the center of Celtic Christianity. Iona missionaries spread the gospel through Scotland and North England, while scholarly monks established Iona as a center of art and learning. The *Book of Kells*—perhaps the finest piece of art from "Dark Ages" Europe—was probably made on Iona in the eighth century. The island was so important that it was the legendary burial place for ancient Scottish and even Scandinavian kings (including Shakespeare's Macbeth).

Slowly the importance of Iona ebbed. Vikings massacred 68 monks in 806. Fearing more raids, the monks evacuated most of Iona's treasures (including the *Book of Kells,* which is now in Dublin) to Ireland. Much later, with the Reformation, the abbey was abandoned, and most of its finely carved crosses were destroyed. In the 17th century, locals used the abbey only as a handy quarry for other building projects.

Iona's population peaked at about 500 in the 1830s. In the 1840s, a potato famine hit. In the 1850s, a third of the islanders emigrated to Canada or Australia. By 1900, the population was down to 210, and today it's only around 100.

But in our generation, a new religious community has given the abbey new life. The Iona community is an ecumenical gathering of men and women who seek new ways of living the Gospel in today's world, with a focus on worship, peace and justice issues, and reconciliation.

small trailer ferry office to buy single-journey tickets to Iona.

SLEEPING AND EATING

On Iona
(£1 = about $1.80, country code: 44, area code: 01681)
$$$ **Argyll Hotel,** built in 1867, sits proudly overlooking the waterfront, with 15 rooms and pleasingly creaky hallways lined with

bookshelves (S-£61–65, Sb-£74–78, Db-£104–150 depending on season, extra bed for kids-£15, includes breakfast and dinner, Internet access in lobby, closed Dec–Jan, tel. 01681/700-334, fax 01681/700-510, www.argyllhoteliona.co.uk, reception@argyllhoteliona.co.uk, Daniel and Claire). Its restaurant, open to the public, has an elegant, white-linen dining room and serves £20 dinners.

$$$ St. Columba Hotel, situated in the middle of a peaceful garden with picnic tables, has 27 pleasant rooms and spacious, lodge-like common spaces (Sb-£67–77, Db-£62–71, prices higher for sea view but windows are small, includes breakfast and dinner, cheaper in winter, extra bed for kids-£15, located next door to abbey on road up from dock, open Easter–Nov only, tel. 01681/700-304, fax 01681/700-688, www.stcolumba-hotel.co.uk, info@stcolumba-hotel.co.uk). Their fine 14-table restaurant, open to the public, overlooks the water (£10 lunches, £17 dinners, daily 11:00–16:00 & 18:30–20:00).

$$ Iona Cottage B&B, compact and comfortable, has four rooms with a woody, seabrushed feel in one of the oldest houses on Iona (S-£30, D-£60, located 50 feet directly up from ferry dock, includes breakfast, book ahead for Aug, tel. 01681/700-579).

$$ Finlay B&B, a last resort, rents 11 no-charm rooms in front of the ferry dock (S-from £29, Sb-£31, D-£50, Db-£56, Qb-£78, reception at Finlay Ross Shop, tel. 01681/700-357, fax 01681/700-562, finlayross@ukgateway.net).

The Highlands: From Oban to Inverness

Discover Glencoe's dark secrets in the Weeping Glen, where Britain's highest peak, Ben Nevis, keeps its head in the clouds. Explore the locks and lochs of the Caledonian Canal while the Loch Ness monster plays hide-and-seek. Hear the music of the Highlands in Inverness and the echo of muskets in Culloden, where the English put down Bonnie Prince Charlie and conquered the clans of the Highlands.

Getting Around the Highlands

In the Highlands, a car will provide you with the most options and the greatest flexibility (car-rental info at Oban TI, see page 459). Two buses a day (3 in early summer) connect the towns from Oban to Inverness (4 hours); but always confirm schedules at TI, especially if you're sight-hopping.

Glencoe

This valley is the essence of the wild, powerful, and stark beauty of the Highlands (and, I think, excuses the hurried tourist from needing to go north of Inverness). Along with its scenery, Glencoe offers a good dose of bloody clan history.

Glencoe town is just a line of houses. One is a tiny, thatched, early-18th-century croft house jammed with local history. The huggable **Glencoe and North Lorn Folk Museum**, staffed by enthusiastic volunteers, is filled with humble exhibits gleaned from the town's old closets and attics (which come to life when explained by a local). When one house was being rethatched, its owner found a cache of 200-year-old swords and pistols hidden there from the British Redcoats after the disastrous battle of Culloden (£2, Mon–Sat 10:00–17:30, closed Sun, tel. 01855/811-314).

A mile into the dramatic valley on the A82, you'll find the **Glencoe Visitors Centre.** Built as a traditional *clachan*, or settlement, the Centre offers an exhibit on the surrounding landscape and local history. Take a touch-screen climb up a virtual mountain, or watch one of three videos: one on mountaineering, a more-interesting-than-it-sounds geology video, and 14 minutes on the 1692 massacre when the Redcoats killed sleeping MacDonalds and the valley earned the nickname "The Weeping Glen" (£4.50, April–Aug daily 9:30–17:30; Sept–Oct daily 10:00–17:00; Nov–Feb Thu–Sun 10:00–16:00; March daily 10:00–16:00; café, WC, shop, tel. 01855/811-307). The nearest **TI** is in Ballachulish (bus timetables, room-booking service for a fee, café, shop, all-Scotland info tel. 01855/811-296).

Walks: For a steep one-mile hike, climb the Devil's Staircase (trail leaves from A82, 8 miles east of Glencoe). For a three-hour hike, ask at the Visitors Centre about the Lost Valley of the MacDonalds (trail leaves from A82, 3 miles east of Glencoe). For an easy walk from Glencoe, head to the mansion on the hill (over the bridge, turn left, fine loch views). Above Glencoe is a mansion built by Canadian Pacific Railway magnate Lord Strathcona for his wife, a Canadian Indian. She was homesick for the Rockies, so he had the grounds landscaped to represent the lakes, trees, and mountains of her home country. It didn't work, and they eventually returned to British Columbia. The house originally had 365 windows to allow a different view each day.

Glencoe's Burial Island and Island of Discussion: In the loch just outside Glencoe, notice the burial island—where the souls of those who "take the low road" are piped home. (Ask a local about "You take the high road, and I'll take the low road.") The next island was the Island of Discussion—where those in dispute went until they found agreement.

SLEEPING AND EATING

(£1 = about $1.80, country code: 44, area code: 01855)

Many find Glencoe more interesting than Oban for an overnight stop. Try the **$$ Mack-Leven House B&B** (Db-£40, family deals, smoke-free rooms, homey lounge, conservatory, cash only, Lorn Drive, Glencoe, tel. 01855/811-215, Mackintosh family) or **$$ Tulachgorm B&B** (D-from £34, cash only, soft prices off-season, non-smoking, on the main street in the village, tel. 01855/811-391, Ann Blake speaks English and Gaelic).

Nearby hotels and pubs serve food. Ask your B&B host for a recommendation. For evening fun, take a walk or ask your B&B host where to find music and dancing.

MORE SIGHTS IN THE HIGHLANDS

Ben Nevis

From Fort William, take a peek at Britain's highest peak, Ben Nevis (more than 4,400 feet). Thousands walk to its summit each year. On a clear day you can admire it from a distance. Scotland's only mountain cable cars can take you to a not-very-lofty 2,150-foot perch for a closer look (£8, July–Aug daily 9:30–18:00, Thu–Fri until 21:00, otherwise daily 10:00–17:00, 15-min ride, signposted on A82, tel. 01397/705-825).

Caledonian Canal

Three lochs and a series of canals cut Scotland in two. Oich, Lochy, and Ness were connected in the early 1800s by the great British engineer Thomas Telford. Traveling between Fort William and Inverness (60 miles), you'll follow Telford's work—20 miles of canals and locks between 40 miles of lakes, raising ships from sea level to 51 feet (Ness), to 93 feet (Lochy), and to 106 feet (Oich).

While "Neptune's Staircase," a series of locks near Fort William, is cleverly named, the best lock stop is Fort Augustus, where the canal hits Loch Ness. In Fort Augustus, the Caledonian Canal Heritage Centre, three locks above the main road, gives a good rundown on Telford's work (free). Stroll to the top of the locks past several shops and eateries for a fine view.

Sleeping in Fort William: **$$ Glenmorven Guest House** is a friendly family-run place with views of Loch Linnhe (Db-£38–46, discounts for 2 or more nights, includes breakfast, Union Road, Fort William, tel. 01397/703-236, www.glenmorven.co.uk).

Harry Potter—The Hogwarts Express

The magical steam train that transports Harry Potter to the wizard school of Hogwarts—cutting through spectacular countryside—is an actual train line in western Scotland. The **West Highland Railway Line** runs 42 miles from Fort William to Mallaig (£26/2nd class, £39/1st class, leaves at 10:20 and returns at 16:00, www.steamtrain.info). Along the way, the train passes by some of the scenery shown in the film, including Ben Nevis (Scotland's highest peak, 4,400 feet) and the lakes and rugged countryside of Glen Nevis. Steal Falls, the waterfall at the base of the mountain, is the locale for Harry's battle with a dragon for the Triwizard Tournament in *Harry Potter and the Goblet of Fire*.

At **Glenfinnan Viaduct**, the Hogwarts Express steams across 416 yards of raised track over 21 supporting arches. In film #2, Harry and Ron miss the train and fly to Hogwarts in a car that zooms around and through some of the viaduct's 100-foot-high arches. In film #3, the train stalls atop the viaduct, as Dementors stalk the train and torture Harry.

Other scenes filmed in the Highlands include a craggy, desolate hillside with Hagrid's stone hut in **Glencoe.** They find Hagrid skipping stones across the water at **Loch Eilt.**

The end of the line for the Hogwarts Express is not real-life Mallaig, but fictional Hogsmeade Station, filmed at **Goathland Station** in northeast England. With humble grey stone buildings lining the platform, the station provides a backdrop as Harry and the other students meet Hagrid to catch a boat across the lake to Hogwarts.

For more Harry Potter sights, see the sidebars in London (page 88) and Durham (page 377).

Loch Ness

I'll admit it: I had my zoom lens out and my eyes on the water. The local tourist industry thrives on the legend of the Loch Ness Monster. It's a thrilling thought, and there have been several seemingly reliable "sightings" (monks, police officers, and sonar images). The loch, 24 miles long, less than a mile wide, and the third deepest in Europe, is deepest near the Urquhart Castle. Most monster sightings are in this area.

The Nessie commercialization is so tacky that there are two "official" Loch Ness Exhibition Centres within 100 yards of each other. Each has a tour-bus parking lot and more square footage devoted to their kitschy shop than to the exhibit. The exhibitions, while fascinating, are overpriced. The one in the big stone mansion (closest to Inverness), headed by a marine biologist who has spent more than 15 years researching lake ecology and scientific

Bonnie Prince Charlie
(1720–1788)

The Battle of Culloden (April 16, 1746) marks the end of the Scottish Highland clans and the start of years of repression of Scottish culture by the English. At the center was the charismatic, enigmatic Bonnie Prince Charlie.

Charles Edward Stuart, from his first breath, was raised with a single purpose—to restore his family to the British throne. His grandfather was King James II, deposed in 1688 by Parliament for his tyranny and pro-Catholic bias. In 1744, young Charlie crossed the Channel from exile in France to seize the throne for his father. He landed on the west coast of Scotland and rallied support for the "Jacobite" cause (from the Latin for "James"). Though Charles was not Scottish, many Scots joined the Stuart family's rebellion out of resentment for English domination.

Bagpipes droned, and "Bonnie" (handsome) Charlie led an army of 2,000 tartan-wearing, Gaelic-speaking Highlanders across Scotland, seizing Edinburgh. Now 6,000 strong, they marched south toward London, and King George II made plans to flee the country. But the anticipated support for the Jacobites failed to materialize (both in England and from the French), and Charles reluctantly retreated to the Scottish Highlands, with the English on his heels.

They faced off at Culloden moor on flat, barren terrain that was unsuited to the Highlanders' guerrilla tactics. Scots

phenomena, is better. With a 30-minute series of video bits and special effects, this exhibit explains the geological and historical environment that bred the monster story and the various searches (£6, daily July–Aug 9:00–20:00, June and Sept 9:00–18:00, April–May and Oct 9:30–17:00, Nov–March 10:00–16:00, last admission 30 min before closing, tel. 01456/450-573, www.loch-ness-scotland.com). The other (closest to Oban) is a high school–quality photo report followed by the 30-minute *We Believe in the Loch Ness Monster* movie, which features credible-sounding locals explaining what they saw and a review of modern Nessie searches (£5, daily April–June 9:00–18:00, July–Aug 9:00–21:00, Sept–March 9:00–17:00, tel. 01456/450-342).

The nearby **Urquhart Castle** ruins are gloriously situated with a view of virtually the entire lake. Although its Visitors Centre has a museum with castle artifacts, the castle itself is an overpriced empty shell swarming with tourists (£6, daily 9:30–18:30, sometimes later in summer, last entry 45 min before closing, tel. 01456/450-551).

brandishing broadswords and spears were mowed down by English cannons and horsemen. In less than an hour, the English routed Charles' army, but that was just the start. They spent the next weeks methodically hunting down ringleaders and sympathizers, ruthlessly killing, imprisoning, and banishing thousands.

Charles fled with a £30,000 price on his head. He escaped to the Isle of Skye, hidden by a woman named **Flora MacDonald** (her statue is outside the Inverness Castle), who dressed him in women's clothes and passed him off as her maid. Legends persist that Charles and Flora had a romantic fling during their week together on the run. Flora was arrested and thrown in the Tower of London before being released and treated like a celebrity.

Charles escaped to France. He spent the rest of his life wandering Europe trying to drum up support to retake the throne. He drifted into short-lived romantic affairs and alcohol, and died in obscurity in Rome.

The Battle of Culloden was the end of 60 years of Jacobite rebellions, the last battle fought on British soil, and the last stand of the Highlanders. From then on, clan chiefs were deposed; kilts, tartans, and bagpipes became illegal paraphernalia; and farmers were cleared off their ancestral land, replaced by more-profitable sheep. Scottish culture would never recover from the events of the year called "the '46."

Culloden Battlefield

Scottish troops under Bonnie Prince Charlie were defeated here by the English in 1746. This last land battle fought on British soil spelled the end of Jacobite resistance and the fall of the clans. Wandering the battlefield, you feel that something terrible occurred here. Locals still bring flowers and speak of "the '46" as if it just happened.

The excellent Visitors Centre shows a stirring 16-minute audiovisual program (2/hr). Wander through a furnished old cottage and the battlegrounds (£5, daily June–Aug 9:00–18:00, April–May and Sept–Oct 9:00–17:30, Nov–Dec and Feb–March 11:00–16:00, closed Jan, June–Aug look for period actors and £4 guided tours—4/day, good tearoom, tel. 01463/790-607, www.nts .org.uk). If you're there after hours, you can still walk through any time for free.

Inverness

The only sizable town in the north of Scotland, with 42,000 people, Inverness is pleasantly located on the River Ness at the base of a castle (not worth a look) and has a free little museum (worth a look, Mon–Sat 9:00–17:00, closed Sun, across the street from the castle, cheap café). Check out the bustling pedestrian downtown or stroll the picnic-friendly riverside paths, where after dark, couples hold hands and stroll along the water (several footbridges).

ORIENTATION

Tourist Information

At the centrally located TI, run by Visit Scotland, you can pick up activity and day-trip brochures and *What's On* for the latest showings in theater, music, and film (Mon–Sat 9:00–18:00, Sun 9:30–16:00, shorter hours off-season, Internet access-£1/20 min, £2.50/hr, free WCs behind TI, Castle Wynd, tel. 01463/234-353, www.highlandfreedom.com or www.visitscotland.com).

Helpful Hints

Laundry: New City Launderette is a block down is just across the Ness Bridge crossing (self-service-£8, same-day full-service-£10–12, drop off by 15:00, Internet access-£2.50/hr, Mon–Fri 8:00–20:00, Sat 8:00–18:00, Sun 10:00–16:00, 17 Young Street, tel. 01463/242-507).

Internet Access: Mailboxes Etc., next door to the station, has pricey Internet access (£5/hr) and can mail your packages home (Mon–Fri 8:30–18:00, Sat 9:00–16:00, closed Sun, tel. 01463/234-700). The library behind the bus station offers free Internet access, but you have to reserve a time slot in advance (Mon and Fri 9:00–19:30, Tue and Thu 9:00–18:30, Wed 10:00–17:00, Sat 9:00–17:00, closed Sun). The launderette listed above also has Internet access.

Biggest Non-Sight: The Inverness Castle has nice views from its front lawn, but the castle itself isn't worth visiting. The statue outside is of Flora MacDonald, who helped Bonnie Prince Charlie escape from the English (see page 477). The castle is used as a courthouse, and when trials are in session, loutish-looking men hang out here, waiting for their bewigged barristers to arrive.

TOURS

In Inverness
Bus Tour—**City Sightseeing** runs 45-minute hop-on, hop-off tours of Inverness (£6, June–Sept every 45 min from TI, recorded narration, 14 stops).

Walking Tour—Walking tours are offered twice a day except Sunday in summer (£6, July–Aug Mon–Sat 11:00 and 14:00, 75 min, meet at TI).

From Inverness
While thin on sights of its own, Inverness is a great home base for day trips. The biggest attraction is Loch Ness, a 20-minute drive southwest. All tours depart from and sell tickets at the TI.

Discover Loch Ness—For a bit of history and geology mixed in with your Loch Ness lore, consider Discover Loch Ness, with excursions that include Urquhart Castle, a cruise on the lake, and admission to the better Loch Ness exhibit (£25/half-day, £39/day, economy stand-by tickets sometimes available for £10; all depart at 9:30, live guides, reserve ahead at TI, tel. 0800-731-5564 or 01456/450-168, www.discoverlochness.com).

Jacobite Tours—Their tours come in a variety of options, from a one-hour basic boat ride to a six-hour extravaganza. Its 3.5-hour "Sensation" tour is their most popular, and includes a guided bus tour with live narration, a cruise of Loch Ness with recorded commentary, and an hour each at the Urquhart Castle and the better Loch Ness exhibit (£19.50, includes admissions to both sights, departs from TI—buy your tickets there, tel. 01463/233-999, www.jacobite.co.uk). They also run bus-and-boat "Passion" tours in various combinations priced from £8.50 to £29.50. If you'd like to see the Culloden Battlefield, their "Culloden" tour heads to that iconic sight, as well as to the Clava Cairns (£12.50, 2.25 hours, leaves from TI).

Puffin Express—They offer daylong "Over the Sea to Skye" tours. The tour goes along Loch Ness and gives you a few hours on Skye; unfortunately, it goes only as far as the Sleat peninsula at the island's southern end (£28, includes entry to Armadale Castle Gardens, departs from in front of Inverness TI at 9:15, returns at 19:45; convoluted schedule runs Sun, Wed, and Fri April–mid-Oct; also Mon May–mid-Oct, Tue June–Sept, Thu June–Sept, Sat June–Sept; reservations recommended, tel. 01463/717-181, www .puffinexpress.co.uk). For more on the Isle of Skye, see page 484.

More Options—Several other companies host daily excursions to Culloden Battlefield, whisky distilleries, Cawdor Castle, and the nearby bay for dolphin-watching (ask at TI).

Inverness

1 Craigside Lodge B&B
2 Ardconnel House & Crown Guest House
3 Melness Guest House
4 Ryeford B&B
5 Bazpackers Backpackers Hotel & Inverness Student Hotel
6 Number 27 Rest.
7 Café 1
8 La Tortilla Asesina Rest.
9 Nico's Rest.
10 Redcliff Hotel Restaurant
11 Girvans Rest.
12 Rajah Indian Rest.
13 Hootananny Café/Bar
14 The Mustard Seed Rest.
15 Leakey's Bookshop/Café
16 Scottish Showtime Experience (in Ramada)
17 Safeway
18 Library
19 Launderette
20 Mailboxes Etc. (Internet Access)
21 River Walking Paths

SIGHTS

Folk Show—The **Scottish Showtime Experience** evening is a fun-loving, hardworking, Lawrence Welk-ish show giving you all the clichés in a clap-along two-hour package. I prefer it to the big hotel spectacles in Edinburgh (usually June–Sept Mon–Fri at 20:30, no meals, £14, get £2 off if booked through TI, £1.50 off at Ramada reception desk, in Ramada Hotel at 33 Church Street, tel. 0800-015-8001 or 01463/235-181).

SLEEPING

(£1 = about $1.80, country code: 44, area code: 01463)

These B&Bs are popular; book ahead for July and August, and be aware that some require a two-night minimum during busy times. These rooms are all a 10-minute walk from the train station and town center. To get to the B&Bs, either catch a taxi (£4) or walk: From the station, go left on Academy Street. At the first stoplight (the second if you're coming from the bus station), veer right onto Inglis Street in the pedestrian zone. Go up the Market Brae steps. At the top, turn right onto Ardconnel Street toward the B&Bs and hostels (except Ryeford).

$$ Craigside Lodge B&B is a treat. Its five spacious, cheery rooms share a cozy lounge with a great city view (Sb-£25, Db-£50, non-smoking, some street noise, just above Castle Street at 4 Gordon Terrace, tel. 01463/231-576, fax 01463/713-409, craigsidelodge@amserve.net).

$$ Melness Guest House has two lovely rooms, a comfy lounge, and a matching pair of West Highland Terriers (Db-£58, less off-season, 2-night minimum in summer, completely non-smoking, 8 Old Edinburgh Road, tel. 01463/ 220-963, www.melnessie.co.uk, joy@melnessie.co.uk, Joy Joyce).

$$ Ryeford B&B has six flowery rooms with plenty of teddy bears (Sb-£25, Db-£50, Tb-£75, family deals, vegetarian breakfast available, back room has fine garden view, above Market Brae steps, go left on Ardconnel Terrace to #21, tel. 01463/242-871, ryeford@btinternet.com, Joan and brusque George Anderson).

$$ Crown Guest House has six clean, bright rooms and a cheery blue-and-yellow breakfast room (S-£30, Sb-£30, Db-£50, family room-£70–80, 19 Ardconnel Street, tel. 01463/231-135, www.crownhotel-inverness.co.uk, gordon@crownhotel-inverness .co.uk, friendly and hardworking Gordon and Catriona—pronounced Katrina—Barbour).

$$ Ardconnel House has six tasteful, spacious, and comfy rooms with lots of extra touches (Sb-£35, Db-£60, £70 family room, 2-night discount, family deals but no kids under 10, non-smoking, 21 Ardconnel Street, tel. & fax 01463/240-455, www .ardconnel-inverness.co.uk, ardconnel@gmail.com; if you have a reservation, John and Elizabeth can pick you up at the train or bus station).

Hostels on Culduthel Road

For inexpensive dorm beds near the center and the recommended Castle Street restaurants, consider these friendly, side-by-side hostels (a 12-min walk from the train station). Both offer Internet access and laundry service.

Tattoos and the Painted People

In Inverness, as in other Scottish cities such as Glasgow and Edinburgh, hip pubs are filled with tattooed kids. In parts of Scotland, however, tattoos aren't a recent phenomenon...this form of body art has been around longer than the buildings and sights. Some of the area's earliest known settlers of the Highlands were called the Picts, named the "Painted People," by their enemy, the Romans. The Picts, who conquered the northeast corner of Scotland (including Inverness), were believed to have ruled from the first century A.D. to approximately the ninth century, when they united with the Scots and were lost to written history.

Picts were known for their elaborate, full-body tattoos. The local plant they used for their ink, called *woad*, had built-in healing properties, helping to coagulate blood (a property particularly handy in battle). The elaborate, tattooed designs also led to their other fighting technique: going to war naked. The Picts saw their tattoos as a kind of "psychological armor," a combination of symbols and magical signs that would protect them more than any metal could. Imagine a Scottish hillside teeming with screaming, head-to-toe dyed-blue warriors, most with elaborate tattooed designs—and all of them buck naked. In *Braveheart*, Mel Gibson included the blue fighting colors (looking more like football-fan face-paint than mystical tattoos), but left the naked truth about the Picts off the big screen.

$ Bazpackers Backpackers Hotel, a stone's throw from the castle, has a pleasant common room and 28 beds (beds-£12, D-£26–30, non-smoking, linen provided, 4 Culduthel Road, tel. 01463/717-663).

$ Inverness Student Hotel has 57 beds and a cozy, inviting, laid-back lounge with a bay window overlooking the River Ness. They accommodate groups doing the hop-on, hop-off bus circuit, but travelers of any age are welcome (£12–13 beds in 6- to 10-bed rooms, breakfast-£1.90, 8 Culduthel Road, tel. 01463/236-556, www.scotlands-top-hostels.com, inverness@scotlands-top-hostels.com).

EATING

You'll find a lot of traditional Highland fare—game, fish, lamb, and beef. Reservations are smart at most of these places, especially on summer weekends.

Several inviting eateries line Castle Street near the recommended B&Bs. **Number 27,** a local favorite, is the Scottish version of T.G.I. Friday's, with something for everyone—salads, burgers, seafood, and more (£5–12 entrées, Sun–Fri 12:00–14:45 & 17:00–21:45, Sat 12:00–21:30, until 21:00 off-season, generous portions, noisy adjacent bar up front, quieter restaurant in back, 27 Castle Street, tel. 01463/241-999). The trendy **Café 1,** on the same street, serves up local meaty dishes with an elegant bistro flair (£8–15 entrées, lunch and early-bird dinner specials 18:00–19:90, open Mon–Sat 12:00–14:00 & 18:00–21:30, closed Sun, 75 Castle Street, tel. 01463/226-200). The nearby **La Tortilla Asesina** has lively Spanish tapas such as spicy king prawns (the house specialty). It's an appealing late-night dining option (cold and hot tapas-£3–4, a few make a meal, Mon–Thu 12:00–23:00, Fri–Sat until midnight, 99 Castle Street, tel. 01463/709-809).

For good seafood, consider **Nico's,** a buttoned-down, wood-beamed, candlelit restaurant a few minutes' walk beyond Castle Street (£10–25 entrées, daily 12:00–14:30 & 17:00–22:00, reservations required, part of Glen Mhor Hotel on Ness Bank, 100 yards from Castle Street, tel. 01463/234-308).

The **Redcliff Hotel** restaurant is convenient—on the B&B street—for decent dinners in a bright, leafy sunroom (dinner-£10–15, daily 17:00–21:30, 1 Gordon Terrace, tel. 01463/232-767); the adjacent bar serves £4–6 pub grub (daily 12:00–14:00 & 17:00–21:30).

For sandwiches and tempting pastries, stop in the easygoing **Girvans** at the end of the pedestrian zone nearest the train station (£4–7 meals, Mon–Sat 9:00–21:00, Sun opens at 10:00, shorter hours off-season, 2 Stephens Brae, tel. 01463/711-900).

Rajah Indian Restaurant provides a tasty break from meat and potatoes with vegetarian options served in a classy red-velvet and white-linen atmosphere (£7–13 meals, 10 percent discount for take-out, Mon–Sat 12:00–23:00, Sun 15:00–23:00, just off Church Street at 2 Post Office Avenue, tel. 01463/237-190).

Hootananny serves simple food and features live local music every evening; it's got a great, join-in-the-fun vibe at night (£8–10 entrées, music begins at 21:30, traditional music every night, 67 Church Street, tel. 01463/233-651, www.hootananny.com). Upstairs is the Mad Hatter's nightclub, complete with a "chill-out room."

The Mustard Seed is a favorite with locals, serving contemporary Scottish food with a gourmet twist and a view of the river in a bright, lively atmosphere. Ask for a seat on the balcony if the weather cooperates (£5–12 meals, non-smoking, daily 12:00–22:00, on the corner of Bank and Fraser Streets, 16 Fraser Street, tel. 01463/220-220).

Leakey's Bookshop and Café, located in a 1649 converted church, has the best lunch deal in town. Browse through stacks of old books and vintage maps, warm up by the wood-burning stove, and climb the spiral staircase to the loft for hearty home-made soups, sandwiches, and sweets (£2–4 lunches, Mon–Sat 10:30–16:30, bookstore stays open until 17:30, in Greyfriar's Hall on Church Street, tel. 01463/239-947, Charles Leakey).

Supermarket: For groceries, a mega **Safeway** is next to the bus station (WC, pharmacy, Mon–Sat 8:30–20:00, Sun 9:00–18:00). From the bus station, follow signs in the west corner of the plaza to cut through the parking garage to the supermarket.

TRANSPORTATION CONNECTIONS

From Inverness by Train to: Pitlochry (9/day, 1.5 hrs), **Edinburgh** (8/day, 3.5 hrs, more with change in Perth), **Glasgow** (3/day, 3.5 hrs, more frequent with change in Perth). ScotRail does a great sleeper service to **London** (£150 first class or £119 standard class for a private compartment with breakfast, not available Sat night, www.scotrail.co.uk). Consider dropping your car in Inverness and riding to London by train. Train info: tel. 08457-484-950.

By Bus to: Oban (3/day July–mid-Aug, 2/day Sept–June, 4 hrs, Mon–Sat only, £13 one-way, transfer in Fort William), **Glencoe** (2/day July–Aug, 1/day off-season, 3.5 hrs, can have long layover, Mon–Sat only, £12 one-way, transfer in Fort William), **Portree/Isle of Skye** (2/day, 3.25–4 hrs, change at Invergarry or Uig). The buses are run by Scottish Citylink; for schedules, see www.citylink.co.uk. Pay the driver cash or buy tickets in advance by calling Citylink at tel. 08705-505-050 or stopping by the Inverness bus station (Mon–Sat 8:30–17:30, Sun 9:00–17:30, extra for credit cards, daily luggage storage-£3/bag, 2 blocks from train station on Margaret Street, tel. 01463/233-371).

Isle of Skye

The rugged Isle of Skye has a reputation for tourist throngs and unpredictable weather ("Skye" means "cloud" in Old Norse)—but it offers some of Scotland's best scenery, and it rarely fails to charm visitors. Narrow, twisty roads wind you around Skye in the shadows of craggy, black, bald mountains. Skye seems to have a lot more sheep than people; 200 years ago, many human residents were forced to move off the island to make room for more livestock during the Highland Clearances.

Skye has some of the most ardently Gaelic Scots in Scotland. The island's Sleat peninsula is home to a rustic but important Gaelic college. Half of all island residents speak Gaelic (which they pronounce "gallic"), rather than English, as their first language.

You may just meet one of the very few Gaelic-speaking teenagers on the planet.

Getting Around the Isle of Skye

Even if you're doing the rest of your trip by public transportation, a car rental is cheap and worthwhile to bypass the frustrating public-transportation options (public buses connect the island's major towns, but service is skimpy on weekends and in the winter). Instead of renting a car elsewhere to drive to the island, rent on Skye to save on gas and bridge tolls. Try **MacCrea's Garage,** located in Portree (10-min walk from downtown Portree, call one week in advance in summer, tel. 01478/612-554) or ask at Portree TI (see below).

SIGHTS

The island's capital and main population center is **Portree** (accommodations listed below), with a **TI** that can find you a room and give you ideas on how to spend your time here (June–Aug Mon–Sat 9:00–18:00, Sun 10:00–16:00; Easter–May Mon–Sat 9:00–17:00, Sun 10:00–16:00; Nov–Easter and Sept–Oct Mon–Fri 9:00–17:00, Sat 10:00–16:00, closed Sun; just south of Bridge Street, tel. 01478/612-137). If you need to get out of the rain, Portree's **Aros Centre** offers a multimedia show about the island's history (£4, daily 9:00–18:00, open later July–Aug, last entry 30 min before closing, a mile south of town center on Viewfield Road, tel. 01478/613-649, www.aros.co.uk).

Cuillin Hills—These dramatic hills along the southeast coast of the island are its biggest attraction. The road to the seaside village of Glenbrittle gets you close to the most scenic stretch of this volcanic range.

Trotternish Peninsula—This striking peninsula north of Portree is packed with bizarre geological formations. There's good hiking around the spiky Old Man of Storr, and farther north you'll find Lealt Falls, Kilt Rock, the village of Staffin, and, at the island's northern tip, the ruins of Duntulm Castle.

Castle and Lighthouse—To the west, near the village of Glendale, you'll discover fewer crowds, the Romantic renovation of **Dunvegan Castle** (£7, daily mid-March–Oct 10:00–17:00, Nov–mid-March 11:00–16:00, also hosts chamber music concerts, tel. 01470/521-206, www.dunvegancastle.com), and a hardy but scenic hike to the **lighthouse** at Neist Point (half-mile footpath begins at end of Glendale-to-Waterstein road; rooms and good food available—see Three Chimneys listing in Colbost, below).

Talisker Distillery—Consider a tour of this distillery in Carbost (£5, July–Sept Mon–Sat 9:30–16:30, closed Sun; April–June and

Oct Mon–Fri 9:30–16:30, closed Sat–Sun; Nov–March Mon–Fri 14:00–16:30, closed Sat–Sun; tel. 01478/614-308; good restaurant in town, listed below).

SLEEPING AND EATING

(£1 = about $1.80, country code: 44, area code: 01478)
In Portree: There's not much to see here, but it's a convenient home base. Consider the 20-room **$$$ Rosedale Hotel,** with a fine attached restaurant with a stunning harbor view (Sb-£40–55, Db-£70–130, Beaumont Crescent, tel. 01478/613-131, fax 01478/612-531, www.rosedalehotelskye.co.uk, rosedalehotelsky@aol.com).

In Waternish: Try the four-room **$$ Stein Inn,** built in 1790 and proudly claiming to be "the oldest inn on Skye" (small Db-£52, larger Db-£72, all with sea views, includes breakfast, tel. 01470/592-362, www.steininn.co.uk, angus.teresa@steininn .co.uk).

In Glendale: For a scenic but remote setting on the northwestern fringe of the island, rent a room or a cottage at the **$$ Neist Point Lighthouse** (Db-£40, 2-bedroom cottage-£475/week, 3-bedroom cottage-£525/week, all rates less off-season; tel. & fax 01470/511-200, www.skye-lighthouse.com, info@skye-lighthouse .com).

In Colbost: Consider splurging at **Three Chimneys Restaurant** (£42 for 3 courses, £48 for 4 courses, dinner nightly from 18:30, lunch March–Oct Mon–Sat 12:30–14:00, no lunch Sun, reservations recommended, call ahead to be sure they're open in winter, near Dunvegan Castle, tel. 01470/511-258, www .threechimneys.co.uk); they also rent six swanky, pricey suites next door (Db-£240).

TRANSPORTATION CONNECTIONS

By Bus: Scottish CityLink buses are the best way to reach the Isle of Skye by public transportation (www.citylink.co.uk). Buses between Inverness and Portree run twice daily in both directions (3.25 hrs). There is no train station on the Isle of Skye; the closest one is across the Skye Bridge in Kyle of Lochalsh.

By Car: The mainland town Kyle of Lochalsh is connected to the island town of Kyleakin by the controversial Skye Bridge—Europe's most expensive toll bridge (£5 per car each way—but the defiant local SKAT group refuses to pay; for the scoop, see www .skat.org.uk). Though the new bridge severely damaged B&B business in the towns it connects, it has been a boon for Skye tourism—making a quick visit to the island possible without having to wait on a ferry.

The island can also be reached from the mainland via a pair of car ferry crossings: Mallaig to Armadale (mid-July–Aug, operated by Caledonian MacBrayne, www.calmac.co.uk) and Glenelg to Kylerhea (mid-April–Oct, sometimes no service on Sun, Skye Ferry, www.skyeferry.co.uk).

Pitlochry

This likable tourist town, famous for its whisky, makes an enjoyable overnight stop. Navigate easily by following the black directional signs to Pitlochry's handful of sights. The town also has plenty of forest walks (brochures at TI) and a salmon ladder that climbs alongside its lazy river (free viewing area—best in May, 10-min walk from town).

Tourist Information

The helpful TI provides train schedules and sells good maps for walks and scenic drives (Mon–Sat 9:30–18:00, Sun 9:30–16:00; in Aug Mon–Sat 9:00–19:00, Sun 9:00–18:00; no luggage storage—but if you ask politely, they might keep it for you; exit from station and follow small road to the right with trains behind you, turn right on Atholl Road, and walk 5 min to TI on left; tel. 01796/472-215).

Helpful Hints

Bike Rental: Escape Route Bikes, located across the street and a block from the TI (away from town), rents mountain bikes for adults and kids (£10/4 hours, £18/24 hours, price includes helmets and lock if you ask, open Mon–Sat 9:00–17:30, Sun 10:00–17:00, fewer hours in winter, 3 Athol Road, tel. 01796/473-859).

SELF-GUIDED WALK

Pitlochry Whisky Walk

If you were a Hobbit in a previous life, consider spending an afternoon walking from downtown Pitlochry to both distilleries (listed below). The entire loop trip takes two to three hours, depending on how long you linger in the distilleries (at least 45 min–1 hour of walking each way). It's a good way to see some green rolling hills, especially if you've only experienced urban Scotland. The walk is largely uphill on the way to the Edradour Distillery; wear good shoes, bring a rain jacket just in case, and be happy that you'll stroll easily downhill *after* you've had your whisky sample.

At the TI, pick up the *Pitlochry Walks* brochure (50p). You'll be taking the **Edradour Walk** (with the yellow hiker icons; on the map, it's a series of yellow dots). Leave the TI and head left along busy A924. While the walk can be done either direction, I'll describe it counterclockwise.

Within 10 minutes, you'll come to Bell's Blair Athol Distillery. If you're a whisky buff, stop in here. Otherwise, hold out for the much more atmospheric Edradour. After passing a few B&Bs and suburban homes, you'll see a sign (marked *Edradour Walk*) on the left side of the road, leading you up and off the highway. You'll come to a clearing, and as the road gets steeper, you'll see signs directing you 50 yards off the main path to see the "Black Spout"—a wonderful waterfall well worth the extra trip.

At the top of the hill, you'll come to a clearing, where a narrow path leads along a field. Low rolling hills surround you in all directions. It seems like there's not another person around for miles, with just thistles to keep you company. It's an easy 20 minutes to the distillery from here.

Stop into the Edradour Distillery (described below). After the tour, leave the distillery heading right, following the paved road (Old North Road). In about five minutes, there's a sign that seems to point right into the field. Take the small footpath that runs along the left side of the road. (If you see the driveway with stone lions on both sides, you've gone a few steps too far.) You'll walk parallel to the route you took getting to the distillery, then you'll head back into the forest. Cross the footbridge and make a left (as the map indicates), staying on the wide road. You'll pass a B&B, and you'll hear traffic noises as you emerge out of the forest. The trail leads back to the highway, with the TI only a few blocks ahead on the right.

SIGHTS

Distillery Tours—The cute **Edradour Scotch Distillery,** the smallest in Scotland, takes pride in making its whisky with a

minimum of machinery. Small white-and-red buildings are nestled in an impossibly green Scottish hillside. Wander through the buildings and take the free one-hour guided tour. They offer a 10-minute audiovisual show, and, of course, a free sample dram. Unlike the bigger distilleries, they allow you to take photos of the equipment (Mon–Sat 9:30–17:00, Sun 12:00–17:00, tel. 01796/472-095). Most come to the distillery by car, but you can also get there by a peaceful hiking trail that you'll have all to yourself (see above).

The big, ivy-covered **Bell's Blair Athol Distillery** gives £4 hour-long tours with a wee taste at the end (2/hr, Easter–Sept Mon–Sat 9:30–17:00, June–Sept also Sun 12:00–17:00; Oct–Easter Mon–Fri 11:00–16:00, closed Sat–Sun; last tour starts at one hour before closing, half-mile from town, tel. 01796/482-003).

Pitlochry Power Station—The station, adjacent to the salmon ladder, offers a mildly entertaining exhibit about hydroelectric power in the region (£3, April–Oct Mon–Fri 10:30–17:30, closed Sat–Sun, July–Aug also open weekends, closed Nov–March, tel. 01796/473-152).

Theater—From May through October, the Pitlochry Festival Theatre presents a different play every night and concerts on some Sundays (both £17.50–21.50, purchase tickets at TI or theater, tel. 01796/484-626). Some productions are staged outside, in the Scottish Plant Collector's Garden adjacent to the theater (the garden is also available for visits Mon–Sat 10:00–17:00, Sun 11:00–17:00).

SLEEPING AND EATING

(£1 = about $1.80, country code: 44, area code: 01796)

Sleeping: **$$** Try **Craigroyston House,** a quaint, large Victorian country house with eight non-smoking, Laura Ashley–style bedrooms run by charming Gretta and Douglas Maxwell (Db-£50–65, family room, cash only, behind the TI—small gate at back of parking lot—and next to the church at 2 Lower Oakfield, tel. & fax 01796/472-053, www.craigroyston.co.uk, reservations @craigroyston.co.uk). Gretta can find you another B&B if her place is full.

$ The fine **hostel** is on Knockard Road (£12 bunks, Internet access, above main street, office open 7:30–10:30 & 14:00–23:00, tel. 01796/472-308, fax 01796/473-729, pitlochry@syha.org.uk).

Eating: Try **Victoria's** restaurant and coffee shop, located midway between the train station and the TI, for good grilled or cold sandwiches (£5, daily 10:00–21:30, patio seating, at corner of city garden at 45 Atholl Road, tel. 01796/472-670).

TRANSPORTATION CONNECTIONS

The train station is open daily 8:00–18:00 (maybe less in winter).

From Pitlochry by Train to: Inverness (9/day, 1.5 hrs), **Edinburgh** (6/day, 2 hrs), **Glasgow** (8/day, 2 hrs, transfer in Perth). Train info: tel. 08457-484-950.

Route Tips for Drivers

Lake District to Oban (220 miles): From Keswick, take A66 for 18 miles to M6 and speed nonstop north (via Penrith and Carlisle), crossing Hadrian's Wall into Scotland. The road becomes M74 south of Glasgow. To slip quickly through Glasgow, leave M74 at Junction 4 onto M73, following signs to M8/Glasgow. Leave M73 at Junction 2, exiting onto M8. Stay on M8 west through Glasgow, exit on Junction 30, cross Erskine Bridge (60p), and turn left on A82, following signs to Crianlarich and Loch Lomond. (For a scenic drive through Glasgow, take exit 17 off M8 and stay on A82 toward Dumbarton.) You'll soon be driving along scenic Loch Lomond. The first picnic turnout has the best lake views, benches, a park, and a playground. Halfway up the loch, at Tarbet, take the "tourist route" left onto A83, driving along Loch Long toward Inveraray via Rest-and-Be-Thankful Pass. (This colorful name comes from the 1880s, when second- and third-class coach passengers got out and pushed the coach and first-class passengers up the hill.) Stop in Inveraray, a lovely castle town on Loch Fyne. Park near the pier. (TI open daily April–Oct 9:00–17:00, July–Aug until 18:00, Nov–March 10:00–15:00, tel. 01499/302-063.) The town jail, now a museum, is a "19th-century living prison" (£6, daily 9:30–18:00, last entry 17:00, shorter hours off-season, tel. 01499/302-381). Leaving Inveraray, drive through a gate (at the Woolen Mill) to A819, through Glen Aray, and along Loch Awe. A85 takes you into Oban.

Oban to Glencoe (45 miles) to Loch Ness (75 miles) to Inverness (20 miles) to Edinburgh (150 miles): Barring traffic, you'll make great time on good, mostly two-lane roads. Be careful, but if you're timid about passing, diesel fumes and large trucks might be your memory of this drive. From Oban, follow the coastal A828 toward Fort William. After about 20 miles, you'll see the photogenic Castle Staulker marooned on a lonely island. At Loch Leven and Ballachulish Village, leave A828, taking A82 into Glencoe. Drive through the village up the valley (Glencoe) for 10 minutes for a grand view and a chance to hear a bagpiper in the wind—Highland buskers. If you play the recorder (and no other tourists are there), ask to finger a tune while the piper does the hard work.

At the top of the valley, you hit the vast Rannoch Moor—500 square and desolate miles with barely enough decent land to graze a sheep. Then make a U-turn and return through Glencoe. Continue north on A82, over the bridge, and past Fort William toward Loch Ness. Follow the Caledonian Canal on A82 for 60 miles, stop at Loch Ness, and then continue on A82 to Inverness.

Leaving Inverness, follow signs to A9 (south toward Perth). Just as you leave Inverness, detour four miles east off A9 on B9006 to the Culloden Battlefield Visitors Centre. Back on A9, it's a wonderfully speedy, scenic highway (A9, M90, A90) all the way to Edinburgh (Inverness–Edinburgh, minimum 3 hrs).

For a scenic shortcut, head north only as far as Glencoe and then cut to Edinburgh via Rannoch Moor and Tyndrum. For directions to B&Bs, see the Edinburgh chapter (page 436).

BRITISH HISTORY AND CULTURE

Britain was created by force and held together by force. It's really a nation of the 19th century. Its traditional industry, buildings, and the popularity of the notion of "Great" Britain are a product of the wealth derived from the empire that was at its peak through the Victorian era...the 19th century. Generally, the nice and bad stories are not true and the boring ones are. To best understand the many fascinating guides you'll encounter in your travels, have a basic handle on the sweeping story of this land.

What's So Great about Britain?

Regardless of the revolution we had 200 years ago, many American travelers feel that they "go home" to Britain. This most popular tourist destination has a strange influence and power over us. The more you know of Britain's roots, the better you'll get in touch with your own.

Geographically, the isle of Britain is small (about the size of Uganda or Idaho)—600 miles long and 300 miles at its widest point. Its highest mountain is 4,400 feet, a foothill by our standards. The population is a fifth that of the United States. At its peak in the mid-1800s, Britain owned one-fifth of the world and accounted for more than half of the planet's industrial output. Today, the empire is down to the isle of Britain itself and a few token and troublesome chunks, such as the Falklands, Gibraltar, and Northern Ireland.

Economically, Great Britain's industrial production is about 5 percent of the world's total. For the first time in history, Ireland has a higher per-capita income than Britain. Still, the economy is booming, and inflation, unemployment, and interest rates are all low.

Culturally, Britain is still a world leader. Her heritage, her culture, and her people cannot be measured in traditional units of power. London is a major exporter of actors, movies, and theater, of rock and classical music, and of writers, painters, and sculptors.

Ethnically, the British Isles are a mix of the descendants of the early Celtic natives (like Scots and Gaels, in Scotland, Ireland, and Wales) and descendants of the invading Anglo-Saxons who took southeast England in the Dark Ages. Cynics call the United Kingdom an English empire ruled by London, whose dominant Anglo-Saxon English (49 million) far outnumber their Celtic brothers and sisters (8 million).

Politically, Britain is ruled by the House of Commons, with some guidance from the mostly figurehead Queen and House of Lords. Just as the United States Congress is dominated by Democrats and Republicans, Britain's Parliament is dominated by two parties: Labour and Conservative ("Tories"). (George W. Bush would fit the Conservative Party and Bill Clinton the Labour Party like political gloves.)

The prime minister is the chief executive. He's not elected directly by voters; rather, he assumes power as the head of the party that wins a majority in parliamentary elections.

In the 1980s and early 1990s, Conservatives under prime ministers Margaret Thatcher and John Major were in charge. As proponents of traditional, Victorian values—community, family, hard work, thrift, and trickle-down economics—they took a Reaganesque approach to Britain's serious social and economic problems.

In 1997, a huge Labour victory brought Tony Blair to the prime ministership. Labour began shoring up a social-service system (health care, education, the minimum wage) undercut by years of Conservative rule. Blair's Labour Party is "New Labour"—akin to Clinton's "New Democrats"—meaning they're fiscally conservative but attentive to the needs of the people. Conservative Party fears of old-fashioned, big-spending, bleeding-heart, union-style liberalism have proved unfounded. The liberal Parliament is more open to integration with Europe.

Tony Blair—relatively young, family-oriented, personable, easy-going, and forever flashing his toothy grin—has been a respected and well-liked PM, but his popularity took a dive after he propelled the country into a war with Iraq that has had no real end. However, after his party's victory in May 2005's general election, Blair is now serving a third consecutive term as prime minister. The London bombings in July 2005 further united the country behind him and his ratings have recently climbed.

Basic British History for the Traveler

When Julius Caesar landed on the misty and mysterious isle of Britain in 55 B.C., England entered the history books. The

Get It Right

Americans tend to use "England," "Britain," and "U.K." interchangeably, but they're not quite the same:

- **England** is the country occupying the southeast part of the island.
- **Britain** is the name of the island.
- **Great Britain** is the political union of the island's three countries, England, Scotland, and Wales.
- The **United Kingdom** adds a fourth country, Northern Ireland.
- The **British Isles** (not a political entity) also includes the independent Republic of Ireland.
- The **British Commonwealth** is a loose association of possessions and former colonies (including Canada, Australia, and India) that profess at least symbolic loyalty to the Crown.

You can call the modern nation either the United Kingdom ("the U.K.") or just simply "Britain."

primitive Celtic tribes he conquered were themselves invaders, who had earlier conquered the even more mysterious people who built Stonehenge. The Romans built towns and roads and established their capital at Londinium. The Celtic natives in Scotland and Wales—consisting of Gaels, Picts, and Scots—were not subdued so easily. The Romans built Hadrian's Wall near the Scottish border as protection against their troublesome northern neighbors. Even today, the Celtic language and influence are strongest in these far reaches of Britain.

As Rome fell, so fell Roman Britain, a victim of invaders and internal troubles. Barbarian tribes from Germany and Denmark, called Angles and Saxons, swept through the southern part of the island, establishing Angle-land. These were the days of the real King Arthur, possibly a Christianized Roman general who fought valiantly, but in vain, against invading barbarians. The island was plunged into 500 years of Dark Ages—wars, plagues, and poverty—lit only by the dim candle of a few learned Christian monks and missionaries trying to convert the barbarians. The sightseer sees little from this Anglo-Saxon period.

Modern England began with yet another invasion. William the Conqueror and his Norman troops crossed the English Channel from France in 1066. William crowned himself king in Westminster Abbey (where all subsequent coronations would take place) and began building the Tower of London. French-speaking Norman kings ruled the country for two centuries. Then followed two centuries of civil wars, with various noble families vying for

Royal Lineage

802–1066	Saxon and Danish kings
1066–1154	Norman invasion (William the Conqueror), Norman kings
1154–1399	Plantagenet
1399–1461	Lancaster
1462–1485	York
1485–1603	Tudor (Henry VIII, Elizabeth I)
1603–1649	Stuart (civil war and beheading of Charles I)
1649–1653	Commonwealth, no royal head of state
1653–1659	Protectorate, with Cromwell as Lord Protector
1660–1714	Restoration of Stuart monarchy
1714–1901	Hanover (four Georges, Victoria)
1901–1910	Edward VII
1910–present	Windsor (George V, Edward VIII, George VI, Elizabeth II)

the crown. In one of the most bitter feuds, the York and Lancaster families fought the Wars of the Roses, so-called because of the white and red flowers the combatants chose as their symbols. Battles, intrigues, kings, nobles, and ladies imprisoned and executed in the Tower—it's a wonder the country survived its rulers.

England was finally united by the "third-party" Tudor family. Henry VIII, a Tudor, was England's Renaissance king. He was handsome, athletic, highly sexed, a poet, a scholar, and a musician. He was also arrogant, cruel, gluttonous, and paranoid. He went through six wives in 40 years, divorcing, imprisoning, or beheading them when they no longer suited his needs.

Henry also "divorced" England from the Catholic Church, establishing the Protestant Church of England (the Anglican Church) and setting in motion years of religious squabbles. He also "dissolved" the monasteries (about 1540), left just the shells of many formerly glorious abbeys dotting the countryside, and pocketed their land and wealth for the crown.

Henry's daughter, Queen Elizabeth I, who reigned for 45 years, made England a great trading and naval power (defeating the Spanish Armada) and presided over the Elizabethan era of great writers (such as William Shakespeare) and scientists (such as Francis Bacon).

The longstanding quarrel between England's divine-right

kings and Parliament's nobles finally erupted into a civil war (1643). Parliament forces under the Protestant Puritan farmer Oliver Cromwell defeated—and beheaded—King Charles I. This civil war left its mark on much of what you'll see in Britain. Eventually, Parliament invited Charles' son to take the throne. This "restoration of the monarchy" was accompanied by a great colonial expansion and the rebuilding of London (including Christopher Wren's St. Paul's Cathedral), which had been devastated by the Great Fire of 1666.

Britain grew as a naval superpower, colonizing and trading with all parts of the globe. Admiral Horatio Nelson's victory over Napoleon's fleet at the Battle of Trafalgar secured her naval superiority ("Britannia rules the waves"), and 10 years later, the Duke of Wellington stomped Napoleon on land at Waterloo. Nelson and Wellington—both buried in London's St. Paul's Cathedral—are memorialized by many arches, columns, and squares throughout England.

Economically, Britain led the world into the Industrial Age with her mills, factories, coal mines, and trains. By the time of Queen Victoria's reign (1837–1901), Britain was at its zenith of power, with a colonial empire that covered one-fifth of the world.

The 20th century was not kind to Britain. Two world wars devastated the population. The Nazi blitzkrieg reduced much of London to rubble. The colonial empire has dwindled to almost nothing, and Britain is no longer an economic superpower. The "Irish Troubles" are constant, as the Catholic inhabitants of British-ruled Northern Ireland fight for the independence their southern neighbors won decades ago. The war over the Falkland Islands in 1982 showed how little of the British Empire is left—and how determined the British are to hang on to what remains.

But the tradition (if not the substance) of greatness continues, presided over by Queen Elizabeth II, her husband Prince Philip, and Prince Charles. With economic problems, the marital turmoil of Charles and the late Princess Diana, and a relentless popular press, the royal family has had a tough time. But the queen has stayed above it all, and most British people still jump at an opportunity to see royalty. With the death of Princess Diana and the historic outpouring of grief, it's clear that the concept of royalty was still alive and well as Britain entered the third millennium.

Queen Elizabeth marked her 50th year on the throne in 2002 at age 76. While many wonder who will succeed her, the case is fairly straightforward: The queen sees her job as a lifelong position, and legally, Charles (who wants to be king) cannot be skipped over for his son William. Given the longevity in the family (the queen's mum, born in August of 1900, made it to 101 before she died in 2002), Charles is in for a long wait.

Architecture in Britain

From Stonehenge to Big Ben, travelers are storming castle walls, climbing spiral staircases, and snapping the pictures of 5,000 years of architecture. Let's sort it out.

The oldest ruins—mysterious and prehistoric—date from before Roman times back to 3000 B.C. The earliest sites, such as Stonehenge and Avebury, were built during the Stone and Bronze ages. The remains from these periods are made of huge stones or mounds of earth, even man-made hills, and were created as celestial calendars and for worship or burial. Britain is crisscrossed with lines of these mysterious sights (ley lines). Iron Age people (600 B.C.–A.D. 50) left desolate stone forts. The Romans thrived in Britain from A.D. 50 to 400, building cities, walls, and roads. Evidence of Roman greatness can be seen in lavish villas with ornate mosaic floors, temples uncovered beneath great English churches, and Roman stones in medieval city walls. Roman roads sliced across the island in straight lines. Today, unusually straight rural roads are very likely laid directly on these ancient roads.

As Rome crumbled in the fifth century, so did Roman Britain. Little architecture survives from Dark Ages England, the Saxon period from 500 to 1000. Architecturally, the light was switched on with the Norman conquest in 1066. As William earned his title "the Conqueror," his French architects built churches and castles in the European Romanesque style.

English Romanesque is called Norman (1066–1200). Norman churches had round arches, thick walls, and small windows; Durham Cathedral and the Chapel of St. John in the Tower of London are typical examples. The Tower of London, with its square keep, small windows, and spiral stone stairways, is a typical Norman castle. You'll see plenty of Norman castles—all built to secure the conquest of these invaders from Normandy.

Gothic architecture (1200–1600) replaced the heavy Norman style with light, vertical buildings, pointed arches, soaring spires, and bigger windows. English Gothic is divided into three stages. Early English (1200–1300) features tall, simple spires; beautifully carved capitals; and elaborate chapter houses (such as the Wells Cathedral). Decorated Gothic (1300–1400) gets fancier, with more elaborate tracery, bigger windows, and ornately carved pinnacles, as you'll see at Westminster Abbey. Finally, the Perpendicular style (1400–1600, also called "rectilinear") returns to square towers and emphasizes straight, uninterrupted vertical lines from ceiling to floor, with vast windows and exuberant decoration, including fan-vaulted ceilings (King's College Chapel at Cambridge). Through this evolution, the structural ribs (arches meeting at the top of the ceilings) became more and more decorative and fanciful (the most fancy being the star vaulting and fan vaulting of the Perpendicular style).

As you tour the great medieval churches of Britain, remember that nearly everything is symbolic. For instance, on the tombs, if the figure has crossed legs, he was a Crusader. If his feet rest on a dog, he died at home, but if the legs rest on a lion, he died in battle. Local guides and books help us modern pilgrims understand at least a little of what we see.

Wales is particularly rich in English castles, which were needed to subdue the stubborn Welsh. Edward I built a ring of powerful castles in Wales, including Conwy and Caernarfon.

Gothic houses were a simple mix of woven strips of thin wood, rubble, and plaster called wattle and daub. The famous black-and-white Tudor, or half-timbered, look came simply from filling in heavy oak frames with wattle and daub.

The Tudor period (1485–1560) was a time of relative peace (the Wars of the Roses were finally over), prosperity, and renaissance. Henry VIII broke with the Catholic Church and "dissolved" (destroyed) the monasteries, leaving scores of Britain's greatest churches as gutted shells. These hauntingly beautiful abbey ruins (Glastonbury, Whitby, and Tintern) surrounded by lush lawns are now pleasant city parks.

Although few churches were built during the Tudor period, this was a time of house and mansion construction. Heating a home was becoming popular and affordable, and Tudor buildings featured small square windows and many chimneys. In towns, where land was scarce, many Tudor houses grew up and out, getting wider with each overhanging floor.

The Elizabethan and Jacobean periods (1560–1620) were followed by the English Renaissance style (1620–1720). English architects mixed Gothic and classical styles, then Baroque and classical styles. Although the ornate Baroque never really grabbed Britain, the classical style of the Italian architect Andrea Palladio did. Inigo Jones (1573–1652), Christopher Wren (1632–1723), and those they inspired plastered Britain with enough columns, domes, and symmetry to please a Caesar. The Great Fire of London (1666) cleared the way for an ambitious young Wren to put his mark on London forever with a grand rebuilding scheme, including the great St. Paul's Cathedral and more than 50 other churches.

The celebrants of the Boston Tea Party remember Britain's Georgian period (1720–1840) for its lousy German kings. Georgian architecture was rich and showed off by being very classical. Grand ornamental doorways, fine cast-ironwork on balconies and railings, Chippendale furniture, and white-on-blue Wedgwood ceramics graced rich homes everywhere. John Wood Jr. and Sr. led the way, giving the trendsetting city of Bath its crescents and circles of aristocratic Georgian row houses. "Georgian" is English for "neoclassical."

The Industrial Revolution shaped the Victorian period (1840–1890) with glass, steel, and iron. Britain had a huge new erector set (so did France's Mr. Eiffel). This was also a Romantic period, reviving the "more Christian" Gothic style. London's Houses of Parliament are neo-Gothic—just 100 years old but looking 700, except for the telltale modern precision and craftsmanship. Whereas Gothic was stone or concrete, neo-Gothic was often red brick. These were Britain's glory days, and there was more building in this period than in all previous ages combined.

The architecture of modern times obeys the formula "form follows function"—it worries more about your needs than your eyes. Britain treasures its heritage and takes great pains to build tastefully in historic districts and to preserve its many "listed" buildings. With a booming tourist trade, these quaint reminders of its past—and ours—are becoming a valuable part of the British economy.

British TV

British television is so good—and so British—that it deserves a mention as a sightseeing treat. After a hard day of castle climbing, watch the telly over tea in the living room of your village B&B.

There are currently five free channels that any television can receive. BBC-1 and BBC-2 are government regulated and commercial free. Broadcasting of these two channels (and of the five BBC radio stations) is funded by a mandatory £125-per-year-per-household television and radio license (hmmm, 60 cents per day to escape commercials and public-broadcasting pledge drives). Channels 3, 4, and 5 are privately owned, are a little more lowbrow, and have commercials—but those commercials are often clever and sophisticated, providing a fun look at British life. In addition, about 60 percent of households now receive digital cable or satellite television, which offer dozens of specialty channels, similar to those available in North America.

Britain is about to leap into the Digital Age ahead of the rest of the TV-watching world. Beginning in 2007, a few areas will receive only a digital signal, which will require a digitally-equipped set. More regions will gradually follow, and by 2012 the old analog signals will be switched off and only digital signals will be broadcast. Ultimately every house will enjoy literally hundreds of high-definition channels with no need for cable or satellites.

Whereas California "accents" fill our airwaves 24 hours a day, homogenizing the way our country speaks, Britain protects and promotes its regional accents by its choice of TV and radio announcers. See if you can tell where each is from (or ask a local for help).

Commercial-free British TV, while looser than it used to be, is still careful about what it airs and when. But after the 21:00 "watershed" hour, when children are expected to be in bed, some nudity and profanity is allowed and may cause you to spill your tea.

American programs (such as *Desperate Housewives, Lost, Oprah,* and trash-talk shows) are very popular. The visiting viewer should be sure to tune the TV to a few typical British shows, including a dose of British situation- and political-comedy fun and the top-notch BBC evening news. Quiz shows are taken very seriously here (where *Who Wants to Be a Millionaire?* and *The Weakest Link* originated). Michael Parkinson is the Johnny Carson of Britain for late-night talk. For a tear-filled, slice-of-life taste of British soaps dealing in all the controversial issues, see the popular *Emmerdale, Coronation Street,* or *EastEnders.*

APPENDIX

Let's Talk Telephones

Here's a primer on making direct phone calls. For information specific to Britain, see "Telephones" in the Introduction.

Making Calls within a European Country: About half of all European countries—including Britain—use area codes; the other half uses a direct-dial system without area codes.

In countries that use area codes (such as Austria, Britain, Finland, Germany, Ireland, the Netherlands, and Sweden), you dial the local number when calling within a city, and you add the area code if calling long distance within the country.

To make calls within a country that uses a direct-dial system (Belgium, the Czech Republic, Denmark, France, Italy, Portugal, Norway, Spain, and Switzerland), you dial the same number whether you're calling across the country or across the street.

Making International Calls: You always start with the international access code (011 if you're calling from America or Canada, or 00 from virtually anywhere in Europe), then dial the country code of the country you're calling (see chart below).

What you dial next depends on the phone system of the country you're calling. If the country uses area codes, drop the initial zero of the area code, then dial the rest of the number.

Countries that use direct-dial systems (no area codes) vary in how they're accessed internationally by phone. For instance, if you're making an international call to the Czech Republic, Denmark, Italy, Norway, Portugal, or Spain, simply dial the international access code, country code, and phone number. But if you're calling Belgium, France, or Switzerland, drop the initial zero of the phone number. Example: To call a Paris hotel (tel. 01 47 05 49 15) from London, dial 00, 33 (France's country code), then 1 47 05 49 15 (phone number without the initial zero).

European Calling Chart

Just smile and dial, using this key:
AC = Area Code, LN = Local Number.

European Country	Calling long distance within ...	Calling from the U.S.A./ Canada to ...	Calling from a European country to ...
Austria	AC + LN	011 + 43 + AC (without the initial zero) + LN	00 + 43 + AC (without the initial zero) + LN
Belgium	LN	011 + 32 + LN (without initial zero)	00 + 32 + LN (without initial zero)
Britain	AC + LN	011 + 44 + AC (without initial zero) + LN	00 + 44 + AC (without initial zero) + LN
Croatia	AC + LN	011 + 385 + AC (without initial zero) + LN	00 + 385 + AC (without initial zero) + LN
Czech Republic	LN	011 + 420 + LN	00 + 420 + LN
Denmark	LN	011 + 45 + LN	00 + 45 + LN
Finland	AC + LN	011 + 358 + AC (without initial zero) + LN	00 + 358 + AC (without initial zero) + LN
France	LN	011 + 33 + LN (without initial zero)	00 + 33 + LN (without initial zero)
Germany	AC + LN	011 + 49 + AC (without initial zero) + LN	00 + 49 + AC (without initial zero) + LN
Greece	LN	011 + 30 + LN	00 + 30 + LN
Hungary	06 + AC + LN	011 + 36 + AC + LN	00 + 36 + AC + LN
Ireland	AC + LN	011 + 353 + AC (without initial zero) + LN	00 + 353 + AC (without initial zero) + LN
Italy	LN	011 + 39 + LN	00 + 39 + LN

European Country	Calling long distance within ...	Calling from the U.S.A./ Canada to ...	Calling from a European country to ...
Netherlands	AC + LN	011 + 31 + AC (without initial zero) + LN	00 + 31 + AC (without initial zero) + LN
Norway	LN	011 + 47 + LN	00 + 47 + LN
Poland	AC + LN	011 + 48 + AC (without initial zero) + LN	00 + 48 + AC (without initial zero) + LN
Portugal	LN	011 + 351 + LN	00 + 351 + LN
Slovakia	AC + LN	011 + 421 + AC (without initial zero) + LN	00 + 421 + AC (without initial zero) + LN
Slovenia	AC + LN	011 + 386 + AC (without initial zero) + LN	00 + 386 + AC (without initial zero) + LN
Spain	LN	011 + 34 + LN	00 + 34 + LN
Sweden	AC + LN	011 + 46 + AC (without initial zero) + LN	00 + 46 + AC (without initial zero) + LN
Switzerland	LN	011 + 41 + LN (without initial zero)	00 + 41 + LN (without initial zero)
Turkey	AC (if no initial zero is included, add one) + LN	011 + 90 + AC (without initial zero) + LN	00 + 90 + AC (without initial zero) + LN

The instructions above apply whether you're calling a fixed phone or mobile phone.

The international access codes (the first numbers you dial when making an international call) are 011 if you're calling from the U.S.A./Canada, or 00 if you're calling from anywhere in Europe.

To call the U.S.A. or Canada from Europe, dial 00, then 1 (the country code for the U.S.A. and Canada), then the area code and number. In short, 00 + 1 + AC + LN = Hi, Mom!

Country Codes

After you've dialed the international access code (00 if you're calling from Europe, 011 if calling from the United States or Canada), dial the code of the country you're calling.

Austria—43	Italy—39
Belgium—32	Morocco—212
Britain—44	Netherlands—31
Canada—1	Norway—47
Croatia—385	Poland—48
Czech Rep.—420	Portugal—351
Denmark—45	Slovakia—421
Estonia—372	Slovenia—386
Finland—358	Spain—34
France—33	Sweden—46
Germany—49	Switzerland—41
Gibraltar—350	Turkey—90
Greece—30	U.S.A.—1
Ireland—353	

Telephone Directory

Understand the various prefixes: 09 numbers are telephone sex-type expensive. The prefixes 0845 (4p/min, 2p evenings and weekends) and 0870 (8p/min, 4p evenings and weekends) are local calls nationwide. And 0800 numbers are toll-free. If you have questions about a prefix, call 100 for free help.

Useful Numbers in Britain

Emergency (police and ambulance): tel. 999
Operator Assistance: tel. 100
Directory Assistance: tel. 192 (20p from phone booth, otherwise expensive)
International Info: tel. 153 (20p from phone booth, £1.50 otherwise)
International Assistance: tel. 155
United States Embassy (in London): 24 Grosvenor Square, Tube: Bond Street, tel. 020/7499-9000, www.usembassy.org.uk
Eurostar (Chunnel Info): tel. 08705-186-186 (www.eurostar.com)
Trains to all points in Europe: tel. 08705-848-848 (www.raileurope.com)
Train information for trips within England: tel. 0845-748-4950

London Airports

For online information on the first three airports, check www.baa .co.uk
Heathrow (flight info): tel. 0870-000-0123

Gatwick (general info): tel. 0870-000-2468 for all airlines, except British Airways—tel. 0870-551-1155 (flights) or tel. 0870-850-9850 (booking)
Stansted (general info): tel. 0870-000-0303
Luton (general info): tel. 01582/405-100 (www.london-luton.com)
London City: tel. 020/7646-0088 (www.londoncityairport.com)

Airlines
Aer Lingus: tel. 0845-084-4444 (www.aerlingus.ie)
Air Canada: tel. 0870-524-7226 (www.aircanada.ca)
Alitalia: reservations tel. 0870-544-8259, Heathrow tel. 020/8745-5812 (www.alitalia.it)
American: tel. 0845-789-0890 (www.aa.com)
British Airways: reservations tel. 0870-850-9850, flight info tel. 0870-551-1155 (www.britishairways.com), cool voice-activated system
bmi british midland: reservations tel. 0870-607-0555, info tel. 020/8745-7321 (www.flybmi.com)
Continental Airlines: tel. 0845-607-6760 (www.continental.com)
easyJet (cheap fares): tel. 0871-750-0100 (www.easyjet.com)
KLM Royal Dutch Airlines: tel. 0870-507-4074 (www.klm.com)
Lufthansa: tel. 0870-837-7747 (www.lufthansa.co.uk)
Ryanair (cheap fares): tel. 0871-246-0000 (www.ryanair.com)
Scandinavian Airlines (SAS): tel. 0870-607-27727 (www.scandinavian.net)
United Airlines: tel. 0845-844-4777, tel. 07626/915-500 (www.ual.com)
US Airways: tel. 0845-600-3300 (www.usairways.com)
Virgin Express: tel. 020/7744-0004 (www.virgin-express.com)

London Heathrow Car-Rental Agencies
Avis: tel. 0870-0100-287
Budget: tel. 0870-156-5656
Europcar: tel. 0870-607-5000 or 020/8897-0811
Hertz: tel. 0870-599-6699 or 020/8897-2072
National: tel. 0870-600-6666 or 020/8750-2800

Festivals and Public Holidays
Great Britain (including banks and some sights) closes down on these holidays: January 1 (New Year's Day, Britain), January 2 (New Year's Holiday, Scotland), Good Friday (April 14 in 2006), Easter Sunday and Monday (April 16 and 17), May 1 (May Day, Britain), May 29 (Spring Bank Holiday, Britain), August 28 (Late Summer Bank Holiday, Britain), November 1 (All Saints' Day, Britain), and December 24, 25, and 26.

For specifics and a more comprehensive list of festivals, contact the Visit Britain office in the United States (see page 8) and

visit www.whatsonwhen.com, www.travelbritain.org, or www
.londontouristboard.com.

Here's a partial list of events:

Feb 18–26	Jorvik Viking Festival (costumed warriors, battles), York
March 4–12	Literature Festival (www.bathlitfest.org.uk), Bath
March 10–29	Late Music Festival, York
early to mid-May	Annual Spring Flower Show (displays, food, music, dancers), Bath
mid-May	Jazz Festival, Keswick
May 19–June 4	International Music Festival (www.bathmusicfest.org.uk), Bath
late May	Chelsea Flower Show (www.rhs.org.uk/chelsea), London
May 26–June 11	Fringe Festival (alternative music, dance, theater; www.bathfringe.co.uk), Bath
June 3–4	Beer Festival (music, shows, www.keswickbeerfestival.co.uk), Keswick
mid-June	Mersey River Festival (maritime festival, www.merseyriverfestival.co.uk), Liverpool
mid-June	Trooping the Color (military bands & pageantry), London
June 20–24	Royal Ascot Horse Race (www.ascot.co.uk), Ascot (near Windsor)
mid- to late June	Royal Highland Show (Scottish county fair, www.royalhighlandshow.org), Edinburgh
June 26–July 9	Wimbledon Tennis Championship (www.wimbledon.org), London
early to mid-July	Greenwich and Docklands Arts Festival (www.festival.org), Greenwich
July 4–9	International Eisteddfod (folk songs, dances, www.international-eisteddfod.co.uk), Llangollen
July 6–15	Early Music Festival (www.ncem.co.uk/yemf.shtml), York
late July	Folk Festival (acoustic music, food, www.cam-folkfest.co.uk), Cambridge
late July	Merseyside International Street Festival (music, dance, theater, www.brouhaha.uk.com), Liverpool
Aug 4–26	Military Tattoo (massing of bands, www.edinburgh-tattoo.co.uk), Edinburgh
Aug 6–28	Fringe Festival (offbeat theater and

2006

JANUARY

S	M	T	W	T	F	S
1	2	3	4	5	6	7
8	9	10	11	12	13	14
15	16	17	18	19	20	21
22	23	24	25	26	27	28
29	30	31				

FEBRUARY

S	M	T	W	T	F	S
			1	2	3	4
5	6	7	8	9	10	11
12	13	14	15	16	17	18
19	20	21	22	23	24	25
26	27	28				

MARCH

S	M	T	W	T	F	S
			1	2	3	4
5	6	7	8	9	10	11
12	13	14	15	16	17	18
19	20	21	22	23	24	25
26	27	28	29	30	31	

APRIL

S	M	T	W	T	F	S
						1
2	3	4	5	6	7	8
9	10	11	12	13	14	15
16	17	18	19	20	21	22
23/30	24	25	26	27	28	29

MAY

S	M	T	W	T	F	S
	1	2	3	4	5	6
7	8	9	10	11	12	13
14	15	16	17	18	19	20
21	22	23	24	25	26	27
28	29	30	31			

JUNE

S	M	T	W	T	F	S
				1	2	3
4	5	6	7	8	9	10
11	12	13	14	15	16	17
18	19	20	21	22	23	24
25	26	27	28	29	30	

JULY

S	M	T	W	T	F	S
						1
2	3	4	5	6	7	8
9	10	11	12	13	14	15
16	17	18	19	20	21	22
23/30	24/31	25	26	27	28	29

AUGUST

S	M	T	W	T	F	S
		1	2	3	4	5
6	7	8	9	10	11	12
13	14	15	16	17	18	19
20	21	22	23	24	25	26
27	28	29	30	31		

SEPTEMBER

S	M	T	W	T	F	S
					1	2
3	4	5	6	7	8	9
10	11	12	13	14	15	16
17	18	19	20	21	22	23
24	25	26	27	28	29	30

OCTOBER

S	M	T	W	T	F	S
1	2	3	4	5	6	7
8	9	10	11	12	13	14
15	16	17	18	19	20	21
22	23	24	25	26	27	28
29	30	31				

NOVEMBER

S	M	T	W	T	F	S
			1	2	3	4
5	6	7	8	9	10	11
12	13	14	15	16	17	18
19	20	21	22	23	24	25
26	27	28	29	30		

DECEMBER

S	M	T	W	T	F	S
					1	2
3	4	5	6	7	8	9
10	11	12	13	14	15	16
17	18	19	20	21	22	23
24/31	25	26	27	28	29	30

	comedy, www.edfringe.com), Edinburgh
Aug 13–Sept 3	Edinburgh Festival (music, dance, shows, www.eif.co.uk), Edinburgh
late Aug	Notting Hill Carnival (costumes, Caribbean music), London
Sept 1–Nov 5	Illuminations (waterfront light festival), Blackpool
Sept 22–Oct 1	Festival of Food and Drink (www .yorkfestivaloffoodanddrink.com), York
mid- to late Sept	Jane Austen Festival (www .janeaustenfestival.co.uk), Bath
late Nov to early Dec	St. Nicholas Fayre (markets, music, entertainment, www.yuletideyork.com), York
Nov 5	Guy Fawkes Day (fireworks, effigy burning of traitor "Guy Fawkes"), Britain

| early Dec | Victorian Fayre (music, dance, carolers), Keswick |
| Dec 31–Jan 2 | Hogmanay (music, street theater, carnival, www.hogmanay.net), Scotland |

Climate

The first line is average low temperature, the second line is average high, and the third line is the number of days with no rain.

	J	F	M	A	M	J	J	A	S	O	N	D
LONDON												
	36°	36°	38°	42°	47°	53°	56°	56°	52°	46°	42°	38°
	43°	44°	50°	56°	62°	69°	71°	71°	65°	58°	50°	45°
	16	15	20	18	19	19	19	20	17	18	15	16
CARDIFF (South Wales)												
	35°	35°	38°	41°	46°	51°	54°	55°	51°	46°	41°	37°
	45°	45°	50°	56°	61°	68°	69°	69°	64°	58°	51°	46°
	13	14	18	17	18	17	17	16	14	15	13	13
YORK												
	33°	34°	36°	40°	44°	50°	54°	53°	50°	44°	39°	36°
	43°	44°	49°	55°	61°	67°	70°	69°	64°	57°	49°	45°
	14	13	18	17	18	16	16	17	16	16	13	14
EDINBURGH												
	34°	34°	36°	39°	43°	49°	52°	52°	49°	44°	39°	36°
	42°	43°	46°	51°	56°	62°	65°	64°	60°	54°	48°	44°
	14	13	16	16	17	15	14	15	14	14	13	13

Metric Conversion (approximate)

1 inch = 25 millimeters	32° F = 0° C
1 foot = 0.3 meter	82° F = about 28° C
1 yard = 0.9 meter	1 ounce = 28 grams
1 mile = 1.6 kilometers	1 kilogram = 2.2 pounds
1 centimeter = 0.4 inch	1 quart = 0.95 liter
1 meter = 39.4 inches	1 square yard = 0.8 square meter
1 kilometer = .62 mile	1 acre = 0.4 hectare

Weights and Measures

1 British pint = 1.2 U.S. pints
1 imperial gallon = 1.2 U.S. gallons or about 4.5 liters
1 stone = 14 pounds (a 168-pound person weighs 12 stone)
28 degrees Celsius = 82 degrees Fahrenheit
Shoe sizes = about .5 to 1.5 sizes smaller than in the United States

Numbers and Stumblers

- The British write a couple of their numbers differently than we do. 1 = ⁄ and 4 = ⁴. Learn the difference or miss your train.
- Throughout Europe, dates appear as day/month/year, so Christmas is 25/12/06.
- When pointing, use your whole hand, palm down.
- When counting with fingers, start with your thumb. If you hold up your first finger to request one item, you'll probably get two.
- What Americans call the second floor of a building is the first floor in Europe.
- Europeans keep the left "lane" open for passing on escalators and moving sidewalks. Keep to the right.
- And please...don't call your waist pack a "fanny pack."

Converting Temperatures: Fahrenheit and Celsius

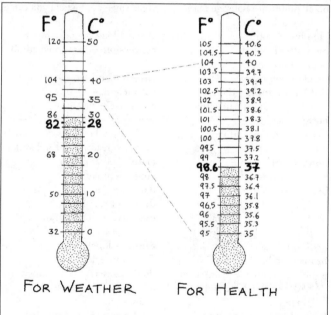

Europe takes its temperature using the Celsius scale, while we opt for Fahrenheit. For weather, remember that 28° C is 82° F—perfect. For health, 37° C is just right.

British–Yankee Vocabulary

advert—advertisement

afters—dessert

anticlockwise—counterclock-wise

aubergine—eggplant

banger—sausage

bangers and mash—sausage and mashed potatoes

bank holiday—legal holiday

bap—hamburger-type bun

bespoke—custom-made

billion—a thousand of our billions (a million million)

biro—ballpoint pen

biscuit—cookie

black pudding—sausage made from dried blood

bloody—damn

blow off—fart

bobby—policeman ("copper" is more common)

Bob's your uncle—there you go (with a shrug), naturally

boffin—nerd

bolshy—argumentative

bomb—success

bonnet—car hood

boot—car trunk

braces—suspenders

bridge roll—hot dog bun

bridle way—path for walkers, bikers, and horse riders

brilliant—cool

brolly—umbrella

bubble and squeak—cold meat fried with cabbage and potatoes

bum—bottom or "backside"

candy floss—cotton candy

caravan—trailer

car boot sale—temporary flea market with car trunk displays (a good place to buy back your stolen goods)

car park—parking lot

casualty—emergency room

cat's eyes—road reflectors

ceilidh (KAY-lee)—informal evening of song and folk fun (Scottish and Irish)

cheap and cheerful—budget but adequate

cheap and nasty—cheap and bad quality

cheers—good-bye or thanks

chemist—pharmacist

chicory—endive

chips—French fries

chock-a-block—jam-packed

chuffed—pleased

cider—alcoholic apple cider

clearway—road where you can't stop

coach—long-distance bus

concession—discounted admission

cos—romaine lettuce

cotton buds—Q-tips

courgette—zucchini

craic (pronounced "crack")—fun, good conversation (Irish and spreading to England)

crisps—potato chips

cuppa—cup of tea

dear—expensive

dicey—iffy, risky

digestives—round graham cookies

dinner—lunch or dinner

diversion—detour

donkey's years—ages, long time

draughts—checkers

draw—marijuana

dual carriageway—divided highway (four lanes)

dummy—baby pacifier

elvers—baby eels

elevenses—mid-morning snack

face flannel—washcloth

fag—cigarette

fagged—exhausted

faggot—meatball

fanny—vagina
fell—hill or high plain
first floor—second floor
flutter—a bet
football—soccer
force—waterfall (Lake District)
fortnight—two weeks
fringe—hair bangs
Frogs—French people
fruit machine—slot machine
full Monty—whole shebang; everything
gallery—balcony
gammon—ham
gangway—aisle
gaol—jail (same pronunciation)
gateau (or gateaux)—cake
give way—yield
glen—narrow valley
goods wagon—freight truck
grammar school—high school
half eight—8:30 (not 7:30)
heath—open treeless land
holiday—vacation
homely—likable or cozy
hoover—vacuum
ice lolly—Popsicle
interval—intermission
ironmonger—hardware store
jacket potato—baked potato
jelly—Jell-O
Joe Bloggs—John Doe
jumble—sale, rummage sale
jumper—sweater
just a tick—just a second
keep your pecker up—be brave
kipper—smoked herring
knackered—exhausted (Cockney: cream crackered)
knickers—ladies' panties
knocking shop—brothel
knock up—wake up or visit
ladybird—ladybug
lady fingers—flat, spongy cookie; also okra
left luggage—baggage check
lemon squash—lemonade
let—rent

listed—protected historic building
loo—toilet or bathroom
lorry—truck
mac—mackintosh raincoat
mangetout—snow peas
mate—buddy (boy or girl)
mean—stingy
mews—courtyard stables, often used as cottages
mobile—(MOH-bile) mobile phone
moggie—cat
naff—dorky
napkin—sanitary pad
nappy—diaper
natter—talk and talk
neep—Scottish for turnip
nought—zero
noughts & crosses—tic-tac-toe
off license—store selling take-away liquor
on offer—on sale
pants—underwear, briefs
pasty (PASS-tee)—crusted savory (usually meat) pie
pavement—sidewalk
pear-shaped—messed up, gone wrong
petrol—gas
pillar box—postbox
pissed (rude), paralytic, bevvied, wellied, popped up, trollied, ratted, rat-arsed, pissed as a newt—drunk
pitch—playing field
plaster—Band-Aid
publican—pub manager
public convenience—toilets
public school—private "prep" school (Eton)
pudding—dessert in general
pull, to—to attract romantic attention
punter—customer
put a sock in it—shut up
queue—line
queue up—line up

quid—pound (money, worth about $1.80)
randy—horny
rasher—slice of bacon
redundant, made—fired
Remembrance Day—Veterans' Day
return ticket—round trip
ring up—call (telephone)
roundabout—traffic circle
rubber—eraser
sausage roll—sausage wrapped in a flaky pastry
Scotch egg—hard-boiled egg wrapped in sausage meat
self-catering—apartment with kitchen
sellotape—Scotch tape
serviette—napkin
shag—intercourse
silencer—car muffler
single ticket—one-way ticket
skip—dumpster
sleeping policeman—speed bumps
smalls—underwear
snogging—kissing, cuddling
solicitor—lawyer
spanner—wrench
spend a penny—urinate
starkers—buck naked
starters—appetizers
state school—public school
sticking plaster—Band-Aid
sticky tape—Scotch tape
stone—14 pounds (weight)
stroppy—bad-tempered
subway—underground pedestrian passageway
sultanas—golden raisins
surgical spirit—rubbing alcohol
suspenders—garters
suss out—figure out
swede—rutabaga
ta—thank you
take the mickey—tease
tatty—worn out or tacky
taxi rank—taxi stand
telly—TV

theatre—live stage
tick—a check mark
tight as a fish's bum—cheapskate (water-tight)
tights—panty hose
tin—can
tip—public dump
tipper lorry—dump truck
to let—for rent
toffee-nosed—stuck up, snobby
top hole—first rate
top up—refill a drink
torch—flashlight
towel, press-on—panty liner
towpath—the path along a river
trousers—pants
Tube—subway
twee—quaint, cute
twitcher—bird watcher
Underground—subway
vegetable marrow—summer squash
verge—grassy edge of road
verger—church official
way out—exit
wee—urinate
Wellingtons, wellies—rubber boots
whacked—exhausted
whinge (rhymes with hinge)—whine
witter on—gab and gab
yob—hooligan
zebra crossing—crosswalk
zed—the letter "z"

Making Your Hotel Reservation

Most hotel managers know basic "hotel English." Faxing or e-mailing are the preferred methods for reserving a room. They're more accurate than telephoning and much faster than writing a letter. Use this handy form for your fax or find it online at www.ricksteves.com/reservation. Photocopy and fax away.

One-Page Fax

To: _____ @ _____
　　　　　　　　　　 hotel 　　　　　　　　　　　　　　　 *fax*

From: _____ @ _____
　　　　　　　　　 name 　　　　　　　　　　　　　　　　 *fax*

Today's date: _____ / _____ / _____
　　　　　　　　　 day 　 *month* 　 *year*

Dear Hotel _____ ,
Please make this reservation for me:

Name: _____

Total # of people: _____ # of rooms: _____ # of nights: _____

Arriving: _____ / _____ / _____　My time of arrival (24-hr clock): _____
　　　　　 day 　 *month* 　 *year* 　　　(I will telephone if I will be late)

Departing: _____ / _____ / _____
　　　　　　 day 　 *month* 　 *year*

Room(s): Single _____ Double _____ Twin _____ Triple _____ Quad _____

With: Toilet _____ Shower _____ Bath _____ Sink only _____

Special needs: View _____ Quiet _____ Cheapest _____ Ground Floor _____

Please fax, mail, or e-mail confirmation of my reservation, along with the type of room reserved and the price. Please also inform me of your cancellation policy. After I hear from you, I will quickly send my credit-card information as a deposit to hold the room. Thank you.

_____
Signature

_____
Name

_____
Address

_____
City 　　　　　　　　　　**State** 　　　**Zip Code** 　**Country**

_____
E-mail Address

INDEX

CREDITS

Contributor

Gene Openshaw
Gene is the co-author of eight Rick Steves books. For this book, he wrote material on Europe's art, history, and contemporary culture. When not traveling, Gene enjoys composing music, recovering from his 1973 trip to Europe with Rick, and living everyday life with his wife and daughter.

Researchers

Darbi Macy
Darbi Macy, who has worked for Rick Steves for five years, spends summers in Britain and Ireland researching guidebooks, guiding tours, learning to speak Irish, and eating banoffee pie. When not in Europe, Darbi works in the HR department of Rick Steves' Europe Through the Back Door.

Jennifer Hauseman
Jennifer Hauseman, an editor and researcher for Rick Steves, originally hails from the East Coast but has since become an honorary Seattleite. For this book, Jen researched Scotland, zipping through the Highlands by bus, tromping down Iona's gravel lanes, and dodging taxis while writing the Glasgow chapter.

Images

Front color matter: Village of Stanton — Nik Wheeler

Front color matter: Bagpipe player in Loch Ness — Randy Wells

London: Houses of Parliament — Rick Steves

Greenwich, Windsor, and Cambridge: Windsor's Changing of the Guard — Lauren Mills

Bath: Pulteney Bridge — Lauren Mills

Near Bath: Avebury Stone Circle — David C. Hoerlein

The Cotswolds: Typical Cotswold Scene — Dominic Bonuccelli

Start your trip at
www.ricksteves.com

Rick Steves' website is packed with over 3,000 pages of timely travel information. It's also your gateway to getting FREE monthly travel news from Rick—and more!

Free Monthly European Travel News

Fresh articles on Europe's most interesting destinations and happenings. Rick will even send you an e-mail every month (often direct from Europe) with his latest discoveries!

Timely Travel Tips

Rick Steves' best money-and-stress-saving tips on trip planning, packing, transportation, hotels, health, safety, finances, hurdling the language barrier…and more.

Travelers' Graffiti Wall

Candid advice and opinions from thousands of travelers on everything listed above, plus whatever topics are hot at the moment (discount flights, packing tips, scams…you name it).

Rick's Annual Guide to European Railpasses

The clearest, most comprehensive guide to the confusing array of railpass options out there, and how to choo-choose the railpass that best fits your itinerary and budget. Then you can order your railpass (and get a bunch of great freebies) online from us!

Great Gear at the Rick Steves Travel Store

Enjoy bargains on Rick's guidebooks, planning maps and TV series DVDs—and on his custom-designed carry-on bags, wheeled bags, day bags and light-packing accessories.

Rick Steves Tours

Every year more than 6,000 lucky travelers explore Europe on a Rick Steves tour. Learn more about our 30 different one-to-three-week itineraries, read uncensored feedback from our tour alums, and sign up for your dream trip online!

Rick on Radio and TV

Read the scripts and run clips from public television's "Rick Steves' Europe" and public radio's "Travel with Rick Steves."

Respect for Your Privacy

Ordering online from us is secure. When you buy something from us, join a tour, or subscribe to Rick's free monthly travel news e-mails, we promise to never share your name, information, or e-mail address with anyone else. You won't be spammed!

Have fun raising your Travel I.Q. at
www.ricksteves.com

Travel smart...carry on!

The latest generation of Rick Steves' carry-on travel bags is easily the best—benefiting from two decades of on-the-road attention to what really matters: maximum quality and strength; practical, flexible features; and no unnecessary frills. You won't find a better value anywhere!

Convertible, expandable, and carry-on-size:
Rick Steves' Back Door Bag $99

This is the same bag that Rick Steves lives out of for three months every summer. It's made of rugged water-resistant 1000 denier Cordura nylon, and best of all, it converts easily from a smart-looking suitcase to a handy backpack with comfortably-curved shoulder straps and a padded waistbelt.

This roomy, versatile 9" x 21" x 14" bag has a large 2600 cubic-inch main compartment, plus three outside pockets (small, medium and huge) that are perfect for often-used items. And the cinch-tight compression straps will keep your load compact and close to your back—not sagging like a sack of potatoes.

Wishing you had even more room to bring home souvenirs? Pull open the full-perimeter expando-zipper and its capacity jumps from 2600 to 3000 cubic inches. When you want to use it as a suitcase or check it as luggage (required when "expanded"), the straps and belt hide away in a zippered compartment in the back.

Attention travelers under 5'4" tall: This bag also comes in an inch-shorter version, for a compact-friendlier fit between the waistbelt and shoulder straps.

Convenient, expandable, and carry-on-size:
Rick Steves' Wheeled Bag $129

At 9" x 21" x 14" our sturdy Rick Steves' Wheeled Bag is rucksack-soft in front, but the rest is lined with a hard ABS-lexan shell to give maximum protection to your belongings. We've spared no expense on moving parts, splurging on an extra-long button-release handle and big, tough inline skate wheels for easy rolling on rough surfaces.

Wishing you had even more room to bring home souvenirs? Pull open the full-perimeter expando-zipper and its capacity jumps from 2600 to 3000 cubic inches.

Rick Steves' Wheeled Bag has exactly the same three-outside-pocket configuration as our Back Door Bag, plus a handy "add-a-bag" strap and full lining.

Our Back Door Bags and Wheeled Bags come in black, navy, blue spruce, evergreen and merlot.

For great deals on a wide selection of travel goodies, begin your next trip at the Rick Steves Travel Store!

Visit the Rick Steves Travel Store at
www.ricksteves.com

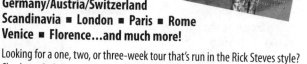

Rick Steves

More *Savvy*. More *Surprising*. More *Fun*.

COUNTRY GUIDES 2006

England
France
Germany & Austria
Great Britain
Ireland
Italy
Portugal
Scandinavia
Spain
Switzerland

CITY GUIDES 2006

Amsterdam, Bruges & Brussels
Florence & Tuscany
London
Paris
Prague & The Czech Republic
Provence & The French Riviera
Rome
Venice

BEST OF GUIDES

Best of Eastern Europe
Best of Europe

As the #1 authority on European travel, Rick gives you inside information on what to visit, where to stay, and how to get there—economically and hassle-free.

www.ricksteves.com

PHRASE BOOKS & DICTIONARIES

French
French, Italian & German
German
Italian
Portuguese
Spanish

MORE EUROPE FROM RICK STEVES

Easy Access Europe
Europe 101
Europe Through the Back Door
Postcards from Europe

RICK STEVES' EUROPE DVDs

All 43 Shows 2000-2005
Britain
Eastern Europe
France & Benelux
Germany, The Swiss Alps & Travel Skills
Ireland
Italy
Spain & Portugal

PLANNING MAPS

Britain & Ireland
Europe
France
Germany, Austria & Switzerland
Italy
Spain & Portugal

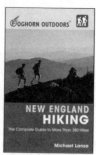
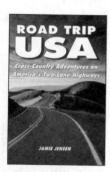

For a complete list of Rick Steves' guidebooks, see page 9.

Thanks to my wife, Anne, for making home my favorite travel destination. Thanks also to Roy and Jodi Nicholls for their research help, to our readers for their input, and to friends listed in this book who put the "Great" in Britain.

AVALON
publishing group incorporated

Avalon Travel Publishing
1400 65th Street, Suite 250
Emeryville, CA 94608
Avalon Travel Publishing is an Imprint of Avalon Publishing Group, Inc.

Printed in the U.S.A. by Worzalla
First printing January 2006
Distributed by Publishers Group West, Berkeley, California

ISBN (10) 1-56691-725-5
ISBN (13) 978-1-56691-725-4
ISSN 1090-6843

For the latest on Rick's lectures, guidebooks, tours, public radio show, and public television series, contact Europe Through the Back Door, Box 2009, Edmonds, WA 98020, 425/771-8303, fax 425/771-0833, www.ricksteves.com, rick@ricksteves.com.

Europe Through the Back Door Managing Editor: Risa Laib
ETBD Editors: Jennifer Hauseman, Kevin Yip, Lauren Mills
Avalon Travel Publishing Series Manager & Editor: Patrick Collins
Avalon Travel Publishing Project Editor: Madhu Prasher
Research Assistance: Darbi Macy, Jennifer Hauseman (wrote Glasgow chapter)
Copy Editor: Matthew Reed Baker
Production and Layout: Patrick David Barber, Holly McGuire
Interior Design: Jane Musser, Laura Mazer, Amber Pirker
Cover Design: Kari Gim, Laura Mazer
Maps and Graphics: David C. Hoerlein, Laura VanDeventer, Lauren Mills, Mike Morgenfeld
Indexer: Stephen Callahan
Front matter color photos: p. i, Village of Stanton © Nik Wheeler; p. viii, Bagpipe player in Loch Ness © Randy Wells
Front Cover Photos: front image, Bodnut Gardens, North Wales © Rick Steves; back image: Guard at Buckingham Palace © Richard I'Anson/Lonely Planet Images
Additional Photography: Rick Steves, Gene Openshaw, Bruce VanDeventer, Lauren Mills, David C. Hoerlein, Jennifer Hauseman